GLOBAL CHANGE AND EAST ASIAN POLICY INITIATIVES

SHAHID YUSUF

M. ANJUM ALTAF

AND

KAORU NABESHIMA

Editors

THE WORLD BANK
Washington, D.C.

A copublication of
the World Bank and
Oxford University Press

© 2004 The International Bank for Reconstruction and Development / The World Bank
1818 H Street, NW
Washington, DC 20433
Telephone: 202-473-1000
Internet: www.worldbank.org
E-mail: feedback@worldbank.org

1   2   3   4   07   06   05   04

A copublication of the World Bank and Oxford University Press.
Oxford University Press
198 Madison Avenue
New York, NY 10016

The findings, interpretations, and conclusions expressed herein are those of the author(s) and do not necessarily reflect the views of the Board of Executive Directors of the World Bank or the governments they represent.

The World Bank does not guarantee the accuracy of the data included in this work. The boundaries, colors, denominations, and other information shown on any map in this work do not imply any judgment on the part of the World Bank concerning the legal status of any territory or the endorsement or acceptance of such boundaries.

ISBN 0-8213-5620-8

Library of Congress Cataloging-in-Publication Data
Global change and East Asian policy initiatives / edited by Shahid Yusuf, M. Anjum Altaf,
   Kaoru Nabeshima.
      p. cm.
      "A copublication of the World Bank and Oxford University Press."
      Includes bibliographical references and index.
      ISBN 0-8213-5620-8
      1. East Asia—Economic policy. 2. East Asia—Foreign economic relations.
   3. International trade—East Asia. 4. International finance—East Asia.
   5. Globalization—Economic aspects. I. Yusuf, Shahid, 1949– II. Altaf, M. Anjum, 1950–
   III. Nabeshima, Kaoru.

HC460.5.G66 2004
337.5—dc22   2004042228

CONTENTS

     Law   293
     Dwight H. Perkins

8   Governance and the Internet   337
     Richard Rose

9   Education for Growth: Deepening or Widening?   365
     Howard Pack

10   Venture Capital Industries   391
     Martin Kenney, Kyonghee Han, and Shoko Tanaka

     Index   429

     About the Editors   451

Figures

Tables

PREFACE

This is the fourth volume in a series of publications from a study cosponsored by the government of Japan and the World Bank to examine the sources of economic growth in East Asia. The study was initiated in 1999 with the objective of identifying the most promising path to development in light of global and regional changes.

The first volume, *Can East Asia Compete?*, was published in 2002. It provides a compact overview of the relevant strategic issues and future policy directions. *Innovative East Asia*, the second volume, was published in 2003. It analyzes each of the main issues and consequent policy choices, drawing comprehensively on recent empirical research and the findings of firm surveys conducted for the study. Its principal message is that sustained economic growth in East Asia will rest on retaining the strengths of the past (stability, openness, investment, and human capital development); on overcoming the sources of current weaknesses in the financial, corporate, judicial, and social sectors; and on implementing the changes required by the evolving economic environment, particularly with respect to technology development. The third volume, *Global Production Networking and Technological Change in East Asia*, is the first of two volumes of papers commissioned for the East Asia study. It presents detailed information, analysis, and case studies showing that economies in East Asia need to adapt to the changing character of global production networks and to nurture and develop technological capabilities if they are to sustain their growth prospects.

This volume, *Global Change and East Asian Policy Initiatives*, includes a set of papers that examine some of the key institutional weaknesses identified in *Innovative East Asia*. Contributors to this volume explore in depth topics ranging from regional issues arising from monetary and financial cooperation, trade, and harmonization to national issues of public expenditure, corporate and public governance, the legal system, tertiary education, and finance. They also offer a wide array of policy options of value to East Asian economies. Some, if not all, of these issues are relevant to every country in East Asia. Both volumes complement *Innovative East Asia* and are addressed to researchers, students, and policymakers.

The financial backing of the government of Japan through its Policy and Human Resources Development Fund provided vital support for this project, as did senior public officials who gave generously of their time. We are deeply grateful to Haruhiko Kuroda, Naoko Ishii, Masahiro Kawai, Kiyoshi Kodera, Rintaro Tamaki, Junichi Maruyama, and Takatoshi Ito. The staff of the World Bank's Tokyo office facilitated the reviews and seminars, and we greatly appreciate the assistance provided by Yukio Yoshimura, Shuzo Nakamura, Mika Iwasaki, Tomoko Hirai, and Hitomi Sasaki. We owe special thanks to K. Migara De Silva for his enthusiastic and tireless support in organizing the seminars in Tokyo and participating in them.

The papers in this volume were presented at seminars and workshops in Cambridge, Massachusetts; Tokyo; and Washington, D.C. The comments received helped the authors revise their drafts. We would like to thank all those who participated in the seminars, along with the many reviewers of the entire manuscript and, in particular, Esra Bennathan.

At the World Bank, the Development Research Group has provided us a conducive environment for this study since its inception. In addition, we are grateful for the support provided by the East Asia and Pacific region. We are especially indebted to Jemal-ud-din Kassum and Homi Kharas for their guidance and strong encouragement.

The study team was ably supported by the research skills of Soumya Chattopadhyay, Farhan Hameed, and Yifan Hu. The manuscript was prepared by Paulina M. Flewitt, Marc Sanford Shotten, and Rebecca Sugui; and we thank Patricia Katayama, Ilma Kramer, and Janet Sasser of the Office of the Publisher for their expert management of the editorial and print production of the volume.

CONTRIBUTORS

M. Anjum Altaf is a senior economist in the East Asia Urban Development Sector Unit, World Bank, Washington, D.C.

Carles Boix is an associate professor in the Department of Political Science, University of Chicago.

Bijit Bora is a counselor in the Economic Research and Statistics Division of the World Trade Organization, Geneva.

Paul Crampton is the head of the Outreach Unit, Competition Division, Organisation for Economic Co-operation and Development, Paris.

Barry Eichengreen is the George C. Pardee and Helen N. Pardee Professor of Economics and Political Science, University of California, Berkeley.

John Gilbert is an assistant professor in the Department of Economics, Utah State University.

Kyonghee Han is a visiting scholar in the Department of Human and Community Development, University of California, Davis.

Martin Kenney is a professor in the Department of Human and Community Development, University of California, Davis.

Peter Lloyd is an emeritus professor in the Department of Economics, Faculty of Economics and Commerce, University of Melbourne, Australia.

Howard Pack is a professor of economics and professor of business and public policy at the Wharton School, University of Pennsylvania.

Dwight H. Perkins is the Harold Hitchings Burbank Professor of Political Economy and director of the Harvard Asia Center, Harvard University.

Richard Rose is the founder-director of the Centre for the Study of Public Policy, University of Strathclyde, Glasgow, Scotland.

Eisuke Sakakibara is the director of the Global Security Research Center, Keio University, Tokyo.

Robert Scollay is the director of the New Zealand APEC Study Centre and a senior lecturer in the Economics Department, University of Auckland.

Shoko Tanaka is a consultant in the Department of Human and Community Development, University of California, Davis.

Kerrin Vautier is a senior lecturer in the Department of Commercial Law and International Business, University of Auckland, New Zealand.

Sharon Yamakawa is a research associate at the Global Security Research Center, Keio University, Tokyo.

Shahid Yusuf is a research manager in the Development Economics Research Group, World Bank, Washington, D.C.

ABBREVIATIONS AND ACRONYMS

ACFTA	ASEAN-China Free Trade Agreement
ADB	Asian Development Bank
AFI	Asian Financial Institute
AFTA	ASEAN Free Trade Area
AIA	ASEAN Investment Area
ANZCERTA	Australia–New Zealand Closer Economic Relations Trade Agreement
APEC	Asia-Pacific Economic Cooperation
APVCA	Asian Pacific Venture Capital Alliance
ASEAN	Association of Southeast Asian Nations
ASEM	Asia-Europe Meeting
B2B	Business-to-business
BIS	Bank for International Settlements
BVCA	British Venture Capital Association
CAP	Collective Action Plan
CER	Closer Economic Relations trade agreement
CGE	Computable general equilibrium
CMI	Chiang Mai Initiative (chapter 2)
CRFTA	Cross-regional free trade areas
DG IV	Directorate-General IV
ECU	European currency units
EMEAP	Executives' Meeting of East Asia–Pacific Central Banks
EMS	European Monetary System
EMU	European Monetary Union
EPZ	Export processing zone

EU	European Union
EV	Equivalent variation
EVCA	European Venture Capital Association
EVSL	Early Voluntary Sector Liberalization
FDI	Foreign direct investment
FECL	Federal Economic Competition Law (Mexico)
FTA	Free trade agreement
FTAA	Free trade area of the Americas
FTSE	Financial Times Stock Exchange (Index)
GAO	U.S. General Accounting Office
GDP	Gross domestic product
GDPPC	Gross domestic product per capita
GTAP	Global Trade Analysis Project
HPAE	High-performing Asian economy
IAP	Individual Action Plan
ICT	Information and communications technology
IMF	International Monetary Fund
IPAP	Investment Promotion Action Plan
IPO	Initial public offering
IT	Information technology
ITU	International Telecommunications Union
JAFCO	Japan Associated Finance Company
JBIC	Japan Bank for International Cooperation
JSEPA	Japan-Singapore New-Age Economic Partnership Agreement
KDIC	Korean Development Investment Corporation
KED	Kyoto Enterprise Development
KOSDAQ	Korean Securities Dealers Automated Quotation
KTAC	Korean Technology Advancement Corporation
KTB	Korea Technology and Banking
KTDC	Korea Technology Development Corporation
MERCOSUR	Southern Cone Common Market (Mercado Común del Sur)
MFN	Most-favored nation
MITI	Ministry of International Trade and Industry (Japan)
MNC	Multinational corporation
MOF	Ministry of Finance
MOTHERS	Market for High-Growth and Emerging Stocks
MTI	Ministry of Trade and Industry (Republic of Korea)
NAFTA	North American Free Trade Agreement

NASDAQ	National Association of Securities Dealers Automated Quotation
NGO	Nongovernmental organization
NIE	Newly industrializing economy
NTEFC	New technology enterprise financial companies
NTEFS	New Technology Enterprise Financial Support (Act)
NVCA	National Venture Capital Association
ODA	Official development assistance
OECD	Organisation for Economic Co-operation and Development
OTC	Over-the-counter
PC	Personal computer
PECC	Pacific Economic Cooperation Council
PPP	Purchasing power parity
PTA	Preferential trading agreement
R&D	Research and development
RPN	Regional production network
RTA	Regional trading agreement
SBIC	Small business investment corporation
SCU	Surveillance Coordinating Unit
SEACEN	South East Asian Central Banks
SEANZA	Southeast Asia, New Zealand, and Australia (Group)
SESDAQ	Singapore Dealing and Automated Quotation
SMEs	Small and medium-size enterprises
SMESS	Small and Medium-Size Enterprise Start-up Support (Act)
TFP	Total factor productivity
TIF	Technopreneurship Investment Fund
TII	Trade intensity index
TNI	Transnationality index
UN	United Nations
UNCTAD	United Nations Conference on Trade and Development
VC	Venture capital
WTO	World Trade Organization

CHAPTER 1

WHAT GLOBALIZATION MEANS FOR EAST ASIA

M. Anjum Altaf and Shahid Yusuf

The recent economic performance of East Asia draws a large share of its dynamism and some of its occasional turbulence from the march of globalization. The growth of trade has provided the region's liberalizing economies with the pull of market opportunities for an ever-widening range of manufactures. It has also intensified competition, thereby forcing exporters—as well as producers for the domestic market, which are now exposed to the threat from imports—to raise productivity (Lawrence and Weinstein 2001). To the gains from trade must be added the benefits from the transfer of knowledge and technologies arising from tightening global integration, a process that is also associated with a steady expansion of foreign direct investment (FDI) flowing mainly from the industrial countries to the emerging economies. Along with trade, FDI is an important vehicle for technology transfer, and together with an increasing supply of human capital, it has been a force supporting industrial upgrading.[1] FDI has been vital for the export-led development of Singapore, China, Malaysia, Hong Kong (China), and Taiwan (China), and it has played a significant role in exposing those economies to the international circulation of knowledge.

Although researchers still debate the benefits of openness, the extent to which East Asian countries have lowered import barriers, and the growth impetus derived from trade, the weight of research spanning the past three decades suggests that trade-mediated global and regional integration has

---

1. Hsiao and Shen (2003) establish that FDI leads to growth, which then attracts more FDI and so on in a virtuous spiral. According to Hermes and Lensink (2003), the effects of FDI are magnified by an efficient financial system. And Miller and Upadhyay (2000) show that openness and human capital together contribute to the growth of total factor productivity.

supported growth and investment.[2] Similarly, the empirical evidence generally points to productivity-enhancing technology transfer, perhaps more through vertical transmission mechanisms rather than through horizontal spillovers (Nabeshima 2004). Furthermore, for many countries, FDI is a source of industrial funding and in some cases—as in China—offsets distortions in the domestic capital market (Huang 2003).

There is a less positive side to globalization. The integration of trade and the increase in flows of portfolio capital have subjected East Asia to considerable buffeting. In 1997–98, the region was left reeling from exchange rate and financial crises. The suddenness of these crises and their quick spread across markets and countries were rooted in the scale and volatility of capital flows. East Asian economies are also undergoing rapid shifts in the competitiveness of major exports, changes in international production networking, and significant reconfiguration in the geographical composition of production systems that have provided the foundation for the region's growth. These changes have been coupled with demands for social safety nets, which are generated by the increasing openness of East Asian economies and are supported by the emergence of political institutions giving people greater voice (World Bank 2000b). Sustaining dynamism in East Asia requires policy initiatives to contain the risks from shocks and to manage the ongoing shifts and changes in ways that enhance both the competitiveness of firms and the stability of the economies.

Research published over the past few years has exhaustively analyzed the causes and the nature of the 1997–98 crisis. Taking the crisis as a point of departure, researchers have also begun examining changes in the financial sector, in corporate governance, and in innovation capability; the shifts in comparative advantage that have resulted from the integration of China into the global economy; and the working of global value chains triggered by the evolving strategies of multinational corporations (Hanson, Mataloni, and Slaughter 2001; Lardy 2002; Yusuf and Evenett 2002; Yusuf, Altaf, and Nabeshima 2004; Yusuf with others 2003; World Bank 1998, 2000a). Most East Asian economies have registered broadly positive performances during 2000–03, and several have grown vigorously over this period. Future development, however, will depend on the quality and timeliness of policy actions. This volume provides an assessment of the

2. See, for instance, Baldwin (2003) and Srinivasan and Bhagwati (1999) for a review of the evidence linking growth with openness, Wacziarg and Welch (2003) for a recent and positive reading of the empirical evidence, and Rodríguez and Rodrik (2000) for an earlier and trenchant critique reiterated by Lee, Ricci, and Rigobon (forthcoming). A wide-ranging assessment of East Asian development through the mid-1990s can be found in Leipziger (1997).

prospects of the middle- and higher-income countries in the region and an exposition of specific policy responses that could enable those countries to capitalize more fully on regional and global integration while containing the risks of economic, political, and technological turbulence. The volume covers a number of themes, with each author having a specific thematic focus. In this sense, the range of the volume is wider than that of a typical conference proceedings; however, it has a thematic hinge, which is globalization and the associated competitive pressures.

The multiplying links between East Asian countries are increasing the need for coordinated policy measures and for steps toward a harmonization of market institutions. The former can support cooperation and coordination with the aim of minimizing the risk of crises spreading from one country to its neighbors, facilitating trade, and maximizing the economies of scope. The latter can address domestic concerns relating to governance, corporate restructuring, the transition to innovative economies, and social protection against volatility in the future.

The East Asian crisis drew urgent attention to a number of areas where regionwide initiatives were needed. These areas are the focus of the first four papers. In chapter 2, Barry Eichengreen deals with the legacy issue of monetary and financial links, which are at the heart of the crisis of 1997–98. He proposes cooperative mechanisms for increased stability. Then, in chapter 3, Eisuke Sakakibara and Sharon Yamakawa examine the nature of cooperation needed to promote trade and FDI, while in chapter 4, John Gilbert, Robert Scollay, and Bijit Bora chart the welfare implications of the emerging alternatives for regional cooperation. Finally, in chapter 5, Peter Lloyd, Kerrin Vautier, and Paul Crampton highlight the importance of harmonizing competition policy across the region if the benefits of cooperative policies are to be fully realized.

The second set of papers addresses domestic policies and institutional development to complement what is done at the regional level. This set of papers is devoted to situation assessments and policy initiatives needed within individual countries. As Bordo and others (2001) and Eichengreen and Bordo (2002) have noted, global integration has exposed countries to more frequent shocks since 1973 and to the greater likelihood of twin crises—in banking and currency. This observation is, in turn, leading some groups to demand a widening of efforts by the state to provide income security (Rodrik 1997). In addition, it has underscored the importance of corporate and governance reforms that reduce the likelihood of crises. In this context, Carles Boix assesses in chapter 6 the status of public spending on social welfare and predicts a need to protect vulnerable groups. Dwight H. Perkins and Richard Rose address the issues of corporate and political governance, respectively, in chapters 7 and 8, while Howard Pack assesses in chapter 9 the demands that would be placed on higher education to support reforms in governance and accountability. Although such institutional changes can serve to promote stability, perhaps of even greater significance for the future welfare of East Asian nations is the flexibility and resilience that can derive from measures augmenting efficiency and innovation capability.[3] As discussed at length in Yusuf with others (2003) and further underlined by Pack in this volume, higher education is a key to desirable outcomes. Finally, in chapter 10, Martin Kenney, Kyonghee Han, and Shoko Tanaka survey the availability in East Asia of venture capital, which is a vital ingredient in the success of innovative economies.

In the balance of this chapter, we will first present a framework within which to view externally driven changes affecting East Asia and to highlight the cross-cutting themes that run through the chapters. We will then provide an overview of the principal messages of and the links between the themes explored. Finally, we suggest future directions of research on some of the topics covered in this volume.

POLICY AND INSTITUTIONAL RESPONSES TO GLOBALIZATION

Economic integration is affecting the East Asian region at two levels. The first level is integration with other parts of the world, starting primarily with the industrial countries but extending increasingly to developing countries. The second is integration within the region, as proximity and rapid income growth induce trade as well as flows of capital and labor. This process is inexorable. As Basu (2003, p. 898) observes, "Globalization is a bit like gravity. We may discuss whether it is good or bad, but the question of not having it does not seriously arise. We have to live with it . . . [and] a world like the one we have today but without globalization is difficult to imagine." It is in everyone's collective self-interest to make globalization work better.

Until the late 1990s, much of the focus of globalization was on charting the trends in trade and in capital flows and on the factors affecting those flows, mainly trade barriers and regulations affecting capital mobility. The East Asian crisis of 1997–98 forced policymakers and researchers to begin rethinking the easy certainty about the benevolence of globalization and to focus on managing the volatility of factor movements and on minimizing

---

3. On the attempts by Taiwan (China) and the Republic of Korea to build economies capable of innovation, see Amsden and Chu (2003) and Keller and Pauly (2003).

the disruption from inevitable shocks. The crisis also greatly sharpened concerns about the sharing of the gains from globalization within and among countries.

A mapping of trade and factor flows and an analysis of their determinants continue. These efforts are helping us better understand the mechanics of integration. However, at the same time a literature is emerging that is beginning to sketch policies for an integrating world. This literature delineates institutions that will determine the quality of globalization and suggests why—and how—an integration of certain institutions is essential for a globalization that all nations can profitably embrace. This volume offers a unified perspective on this new thinking that brings out the interlacing of trends, policies, and institutions. How globalization unfolds and the nature of its developmental consequences will depend on the crafting of policies and institutions. Moreover, East Asia, which is the fastest-growing and most rapidly integrating region in the world, provides a lens into the defining and plaiting of policies and institutions in four areas:

1. Trade and growth
2. Crisis avoidance and management
3. Safety nets
4. Market institutions.

Trade and Growth

Arguably, flourishing trade has been the defining characteristic of development in East Asia. It is also the principal vehicle for East Asia's close links with the global economy and, more recently, for the tightening regional integration. Starting with policies aimed primarily at promoting exports, East Asian economies gradually liberalized imports in conjunction with the various General Agreement on Tariffs and Trade rounds. Although countries continue to implement the commitments made as a part of the Uruguay Round, in the past few years interest in regional and bilateral trading agreements has surged. This interest was partially initiated and is now increasingly sustained by the enormous expansion of intraregional trade.[4] In the process, a host of regional institutions have emerged. These institutions sustain trade policies that are strengthening the ties among countries around the Pacific Rim. Whether the trade policies will constitute

---

4. For example, Japan and Singapore have signed a free trade agreement, and so have China and Thailand. Furthermore, China and the Association of Southeast Asian Nations have signed an early harvest agreement ("East Asia: ASEAN+3" 2004). See also Urata and Kiyota (2003) for an account of these agreements and estimates of their effects.

"building blocks" for another stage of globalization is still being debated, but there can be no denying their integrating effects in East Asia, both directly through trade channels and indirectly through the stimulus such institutions have provided to FDI and policy coordination in other areas.

Crisis Avoidance and Management

Whether the East Asian crisis proved contagious primarily because of trading links among East Asian countries, because of capital flows, or even because the countries shared the same neighborhood, the fact is that the crisis highlighted the shared interests of East Asian economies in preventing shocks and containing turbulence. The result has been much greater attention to policies affecting the size and composition of external debt, the scale of reserves, and exchange rates. The leading East Asian economies have all successfully cut down their external obligations—particularly their short-term debts—and have vastly enlarged their reserves. Several have also adopted more flexible exchange rate policies, although the currencies of China and Hong Kong, China, remain pegged to the U.S. dollar. In addition, East Asian countries are also seeking institutional guarantees that will buttress national policies. Exchange swaps, albeit on a limited scale, are a step in this direction, but there is interest in formal arrangements for coordinating macroeconomic policies and in surveillance arrangements to monitor compliance. The possibility of creating an Asian Monetary Fund was discussed in the immediate aftermath of the crisis, and although it is no longer under active consideration, the sense of interdependence now apparent in the region means that such institutional pegs for achieving greater stability are beginning to figure on the agenda of policymakers.

Safety Nets

Globalization and the shifts in comparative advantage have sensitized workers to the threat of unemployment. Although the crisis of 1997–98 resulted in an unemployment spike that dissipated within a couple of years, with greater openness certain industries or regions within countries can experience a secular decline that leads to persistent unemployment. Industries in China and Japan are having to cope with such a decline, and governments are forced to face the social and political costs of structural unemployment. In the future, this problem is likely to be compounded in some East Asian countries by a bulge of retirees from an aging labor force. Thus, for East Asian countries, the need for a social security system adequate for the changing circumstances is rising in urgency. Singapore already has a system in place, as do Japan and the Republic of Korea, but such structures are less well developed in the other countries. Although macroeconomic policies offer some protection, East Asian economies will need to augment the safety nets for the more vulnerable segments of society. For many of these countries, this effort must go hand in hand with fiscal initiatives to mobilize the resources needed to finance a solid social security system. By and large, the level of fiscal effort in the middle- and lower-income countries is modest relative to that in the Organisation for Economic Co-operation and Development (OECD) nations. This situation provides room for maneuver, but it also calls for fiscal reforms that are politically contentious, difficult to implement, and possibly deleterious for competitiveness. However, with globalization, the pressure to reshape and strengthen the tax system to augment revenue elasticity, to respond to actions of trading partners, and to take account of e-business, for example, cannot be avoided.[5]

Market Institutions

The pursuit of stability and security under globalization must be complemented by institutions that will maximize the economic benefits. Many of these institutions affect economic performance through their influence on market functioning and on the degree of competition. From a growth perspective, five types of institutions are of special significance. They are institutions

1. That determine the efficacy of the legal system in protecting economic rights
2. That affect the quality of corporate governance and the degree to which it protects the rights of minority shareholders
3. That underpin the financial system (in particular, capital market institutions that mediate access to finance, supply of risk capital, and availability of a variety of financial instruments)
4. That control the flow and volume of information, thereby influencing transaction costs and accountability (most recently by way of the Internet)
5. That define the ground rules for market interaction, such as competition and investment policies and rules for mergers and acquisitions.

With globalization, each of these types of institutions has taken on a heightened significance, because these institutions are the arbiters of competitiveness. If some countries are using information technology (IT)

---

5. The complexities of tax harmonization in the face of trade integration and agglomeration effects are modeled by Baldwin and Krugman (2000).

more creatively to reduce transaction costs, others must follow suit. Weak legal systems and distorted financial markets are a brake on growth and discourage FDI. Moreover, as the region integrates, instituting competition policies, standards, and codes and harmonizing these measures with the institutions of regional partners can be advantageous in the long term.

Sustained attention to policies and institutions will be necessary for integration to yield widely shared gains and to contribute to growth in the region. A round of globalization in the early twentieth century foundered in part because the leading economic powers failed to take the needed policy and institutional steps. How East Asia proceeds will be only one factor influencing the course of globalization, but given the rising importance of the region, its weight can only increase, which is why the policies and institutions described by the contributors to this volume deserve a close reading.

REGIONAL POLICY INITIATIVES

Monetary and Financial Cooperation

The most striking manifestation of the 1997–98 crisis was the monetary and financial instability and the contagion that threatened to engulf the entire region. This vulnerability and a heightened realization of interdependency triggered regionwide initiatives to create a zone of stability for the future. This resolve provides the starting point for Barry Eichengreen's analysis of regional policy alternatives in chapter 2, "Hanging Together?: On Monetary and Financial Cooperation." He argues that more could be achieved collectively than individually but asks whether regional institutions can play an effective role and reinforce the contribution of multilateral institutions in an age of seamless globalization.

Eichengreen comes out categorically against any attempt to establish a system of collectively pegged exchange rates. He argues that they would not be able to withstand the pressures exerted by high capital mobility and more democratic politics. Industrial development now requires raising productivity and pursuing innovation and not holding down wage costs. Furthermore, monetary and exchange rate policies do not act directly on productivity as they do on wages. Eichengreen believes, as others have also noted, that the case for financial cooperation to strengthen the supervision of banking systems is stronger than the case for monetary cooperation to stabilize intra-Asian exchange rates.

In keeping with that argument, Eichengreen recommends cooperation on initiatives to upgrade prudential supervision and regulation and on fostering financial transparency and creditor rights. For this purpose, setting up an Asian Financial Institute (AFI) could be a way of establishing standards,[6] identifying policies, coordinating initiatives, monitoring compliance, and enforcing agreements. In Eichengreen's view, the Association of Southeast Asian Nations (ASEAN), plus China, Japan, and Korea (+3), would be the most appropriate entity to pursue such an initiative.

The AFI would need to fit into the global framework by ensuring that the strategies it promotes do not conflict with those being promulgated at the global level. As a regional body, the AFI would have the flexibility to vary the mix of financial standards to suit the local context: the mix could be different (for example, looser restrictions on portfolio concentrations could be offset by tighter restrictions on capital requirements), but the overall effect need not be any less stringent than that mandated by global standards. This method is one way a regional agreement could add value to existing global agreements.

Trade and Foreign Direct Investment

Trade and FDI have played a major role in the development of emerging economies in East Asia and other parts of the world. Hence, it is natural to ask if regional cooperation could promote them further as contributors to regional prosperity. Given the ongoing reconfiguration of global production systems mentioned earlier, the barriers to cross-border flows have also assumed greater importance, because these barriers can interfere with a country's participation in such networks and can discourage FDI.

In chapter 3, "Trade and Foreign Direct Investment: A Role for Regionalism," Eisuke Sakakibara and Sharon Yamakawa state the consensus view that trade promotes FDI, which, in turn, leads to more trade. However, they argue that, in an emerging global production system, the old way of analyzing the links may no longer be the most useful. The main question today is where do firms choose to locate in order to organize production and access resources as profitably as possible for national, regional, or global markets? The location determines where they invest, where they trade from, and where FDI is directed. Sakakibara and Yamakawa contribute to the evidence showing how China is influencing the region's trade and FDI patterns while multinational corporations (MNCs) from both inside and outside the region shift operations to tap China's markets and to benefit from production cost advantages. Not only have companies

---

6. This point is picked up by Lloyd, Vautier, and Crampton in chapter 5.

such as Seagate, Intel, Dell, and Flextronics relocated their operations in China, but numerous firms from Taiwan (China), such as Quanta; from Thailand, such as Charoen Pokphand; and from Korea, such as Samsung, have set up production facilities to service China's burgeoning demands.

In this dynamic context, Sakakibara and Yamakawa present two approaches to promote trade and FDI in East Asia: regional agreements and regional production networks (RPNs). First, they survey existing regional agreements and note the transition from separate trade and FDI agreements to combined agreements. This trend is reflected in emerging free trade agreements (FTAs), such as the proposed ASEAN-China and ASEAN-Japan FTAs. It could indicate that policymakers are recognizing that MNCs are moving away from the old model, which starts with exporting and proceeds to FDI, to a more integrated one that is built around international production networks and involves the consolidation of production facilities in a few locations and the building of a base of suppliers geographically oriented to efficiently serve the needs of those facilities.

Sakakibara and Yamakawa acknowledge that larger trade groupings might be more welfare enhancing, but they support bilateral agreements as a move toward broader multilateral agreements. This thinking is in line with a major strand in the literature which views FTAs as stepping stones (see Frankel 1997).[7] Sakakibara and Yamakawa conclude that trade and FDI would benefit from including both developing and industrial countries in the agreements, choosing partners with care, and aiming for comprehensive agreements that allow coordination of trade and FDI policies.

Sakakibara and Yamakawa's second proposal is more radical. They argue for the establishment of regional production networks along the lines of global production networks. The authors show that the number of East Asian MNCs from the emerging economies is increasing, but such MNCs are considerably smaller than those of industrial countries and do not have as extensive a geographical reach. Thus, except in a few cases such as Samsung and Hyundai, it is difficult for them to benefit from markets in industrial countries.

Limited RPNs emerged in East Asia when Japanese firms began investing in Southeast Asia, especially following the appreciation of the yen after the Plaza Accord in 1985 (Hatch and Yamamura 1996). The most obvious example is the network of automobile assemblers and their suppliers, which has allowed the industry to grow in the region beyond the confines imposed by limited national markets. Regional production sharing can bring

---

7. On the nature and possibility of dynamic gains in the ASEAN Free Trade Area, see Fukase and Winters (2003).

similar benefits in other industries as well, where producing the entire product at the national level is still common. It would allow specialization at the firm level, while permitting firms to participate in a wider regional market, which might be easier to accomplish than trying to compete in the global market from the outset.

Sakakibara and Yamakawa acknowledge the difficulties in establishing RPNs simply because, for large MNCs, there is a broader set of choices globally than regionally. However, they feel that the East Asian regional economy is now sufficiently large and diverse to allow the comparative advantages of individual countries to be brought together so as to maximize the advantages of the region as a whole.

Cultivating a regional environment appealing to MNCs would take considerable cooperation in policymaking.[8] Policies obstructing cross-border production would need to be eliminated or modified, and standardization of products and customs regulations would help reduce costs and facilitate the flow of goods.[9] The task of creating an environment conducive to networked production by firms is clearly more complex than the mere removal of trade barriers. Political will would be needed to accept possible declines in the importance of certain industries in individual countries as a consequence of leveraging regional comparative advantage. Sakakibara and Yamakawa see a regional approach as a stage between a national and a global approach, which is consonant with their perspective on regional FTAs as stepping stones to multilateral agreements.

Choices among Regional Trading Agreements

It is quite clear that all regional trading agreements cannot be equally effective and that there is need for a systematic evaluation of the various alternatives. In chapter 4, "New Regional Trading Developments in the Asia-Pacific Region: Implications for East Asia," John Gilbert, Robert Scollay, and Bijit Bora complement the chapter by Sakakibara and Yamakawa. They provide a quantitative assessment of the net benefits of the various possible regional preferential trading agreements (PTAs). Gilbert, Scollay, and Bora reiterate that, since 1999, there has been a strong trend in East Asia favoring the formation of PTAs. This trend was stimulated by the crisis and by the experience of the European Union, as

---

8. It could form one item on the agenda of the AFI recommended by Eichengreen in chapter 2.

9. This observation, too, links to the recommendations made by Lloyd, Vautier, and Crampton in chapter 5.

well as by trends in the Americas.[10] In contrast, in the mid-1990s, the Asia-Pacific Economic Cooperation (APEC), with its nonpreferential approach, was considered the main instrument for regional integration. The willingness of large northeast Asian economies to enter PTAs is considered a major break from the past. It reflects a marked shift in long-term perceptions of mutual gains from trade and currency unions, as well as a move by the United States toward a dual-track approach assigning equal importance to free trade and to PTAs.

Using computable general equilibrium model simulations, Gilbert, Scollay, and Bora assess the welfare effects of various regional trading agreements, ranging from bilateral PTAs to an East Asian trading bloc. The purpose of the simulations is to determine whether the new agreements are likely to be building blocks or stumbling blocks in long-term moves to achieve free trade in the Asia-Pacific region.[11]

The results indicate that bilateral PTAs within East Asia will have minimal regionwide welfare effects and possible negative effects for excluded economies. Their proliferation could also complicate the regional trading environment. Economic integration would be better served by PTAs including larger groupings of East Asian economies such as the proposed ASEAN+3 PTA, which seems to be the most favorable alternative. However, if the decision between ASEAN+3 PTA and a China-Japan-Korea PTA were based on welfare effects alone, these three countries would be indifferent.

Trade liberalization within the APEC framework yields better welfare outcomes than East Asian PTAs, including the ASEAN+3 PTA, because the gains for China and Japan are more significant under the APEC framework and outweigh the slightly reduced gains of Southeast Asian economies. Within APEC, two alternatives have been evaluated on the basis of preferential or nondiscriminatory most-favored-nation (MFN) liberalization. Preferential liberalization offers larger welfare gains, but MFN liberalization avoids the negative welfare effects on non-APEC economies and could, therefore, be considered more in line with a multilateral trading system.

Overall, the simulations using the welfare criterion identify three dominant alternatives: ASEAN+3 PTA, APEC MFN liberalization, and

---

10. These trends reflect the acceleration in the formation of PTAs since 1995. Between 1995 and 2001, the World Trade Organization was notified of the formation of more than a hundred PTAs.

11. PTAs are more likely to be building blocks "insofar as they impel or consolidate policy reforms within the members; are open to outsiders; tackle the issues that are too complex for multilateral negotiations; influence negotiations towards free trade; and give non-members unconditional MFN status" ("Regional Trade Agreements" 2002).

APEC preferential liberalization. Gilbert, Scollay, and Bora note that confidence in the ability to achieve APEC MFN liberalization is currently low, but they consider it to have some advantages over the other two options and see it as a potential building block toward an open multilateral trading system. Whether the other PTAs will turn out to be building or stumbling blocks cannot be predicted with equal confidence.

Harmonizing Competition Policies

Regional integration requires agreements on standards and the removal of obstructions to cross-border production and trade, as indicated by Eichengreen in chapter 2 and by Sakakibara and Yamakawa in chapter 3. One aspect of this discussion is taken up by Peter Lloyd, Kerrin Vautier, and Paul Crampton in chapter 5, "Harmonizing Competition Policies." They define *deep integration* as the harmonization of policies that are "beyond the border" and contrast it with *shallow integration*, which is restricted to traditional trade protection measures at the border. Regulatory policies are good candidates for deep integration.[12]

Lloyd, Vautier, and Crampton focus on harmonizing competition law and its benefits, because although many East Asian countries do not have national competition laws, they are increasingly competing in each others' markets, and intercountry trade in goods and FDI are set to increase rapidly under the liberalization schemes identified in previous chapters. The importance of cross-border aspects of competition policies and law can only become more acute over time.[13]

Proceeding from the theoretical benefits of competition and from limited evidence from measures that were taken in the European Community, Lloyd, Vautier, and Crampton focus on competition-promoting policies, of which antitrust law is a subset. The essential principle that they stress is that of competitive neutrality (that is, a level playing field for all businesses to compete on equal terms). Harmonization of competition law is defined to include the development of national laws in countries that have none, the selection of core standards in all countries, and the convergence of standards for the elements in the core where benefits can be shown to result from such convergence. Harmonization does not necessarily mean uniformity of standards.

---

12. Regulatory policies are also important at the sector level, and later chapters deal with their relevance for finance, telecommunications, and venture capital. Policy convergence at the sectoral level would also be beneficial for the regional economies.

13. For a discussion of competition policies, particularly in small open economies, see Gal (2003).

The chapter draws on global experience in harmonizing competition policies and recommends steps that could be taken by East Asian economies. The experiences of the European Community (and later the European Union), MERCOSUR (the Southern Cone Common Market or Mercado Común del Sur), and the Andean Community show that it is possible to arrive at competition policies with a regional coverage without preexisting national laws in all countries and to derive decent returns from the enforcement of these laws (Yusuf and Evenett 2002). The sequencing may indeed be an advantage that allows easier standardization or convergence of important laws.

NATIONAL AND SECTORAL POLICY RESPONSES

In parallel with regional initiatives, there are policy issues that need to be addressed within each country. These policy issues range from strengthening social safety nets, to improving corporate and political governance, to promoting economic efficiency and innovation. These areas have become more urgent in a global economy, which is more open, more competitive, more volatile, and more demanding in terms of transparency and accountability. The remaining chapters in the volume deal with the national or sectoral aspects of policy reform.

Social Protection

The advantages of embeddedness in the global economy and closer links with neighboring countries are accompanied by greater exposure to external shocks, more rapid transmission of disturbances, less control over policy instruments, and, consequently, greater volatility of household incomes. For this reason alone, East Asian countries need to devote attention to the extent and robustness of social safety nets for the future. The priority is raised in the context of a growing political voice of middle-class voters and of aging populations. In chapter 6, "The Public Sector," Carles Boix assesses the state of public sector spending in East Asia from this perspective.

The principal finding is that East Asian economies have a public sector that is small both in absolute terms and in relative terms, given their level of development. The average East Asian public sector (excluding that in Japan) is about half the average OECD public sector and about a third smaller controlling for per capita income levels. In addition, welfare spending remains fairly modest in most of the countries: until the late 1990s, compared with an average OECD allocation of more than 20 percent of gross domestic product to transfers and subsidies, the spending was about 8 percent in Korea and less than 5 percent in the Southeast Asian economies.

According to historical patterns, East Asian countries are likely to see a significant increase in the size of the public sector simply because, in higher-income countries, public spending has tended to grow with moderniza-tion. However, the growth of transfers is linked with the increase in democratization, and so far redistributive pressures remain fairly muted in East Asia compared with European countries, for example.

Boix posits a formal model based on a global dataset to test these hypotheses. His results confirm that the public sector grows as a result of economic modernization, regardless of the political regime, because of increased expenditures on public goods and investments. But increases in transfers and other welfare benefits depend strongly on the extent of democratization.

The model is used to generate a broad estimate of trends in public ex-penditures in East Asia looking forward to 2015. Total public outlay shows an upward trend, which is driven by an aging population and economic modernization, with the high-income countries (Japan and Korea) show-ing a stronger spending pressure compared with the other countries.[14]

The increasing size of the public sector and of welfare expenditures is politically unavoidable, and for most countries in the region, it could be fi-nancially supported despite fiscal deficits, which are currently squeezing social spending in some countries, and contingent liabilities, which could constrain future spending in others. On the basis of the small size of the public sector in relative terms, Boix considers that the scope for growth exists and that there is likely to be political support for such an expansion if East Asia follows the OECD pattern. East Asian governments have gen-erally proved quite adept at dealing with economic shocks, and there is no reason to think that any demand for higher levels of public spending, were it to arise, could not be managed through fiscal actions tailored to the cir-cumstances of individual countries.

Corporate and Political Governance

The role of the state in industrial policy and issues of corporate governance became much discussed topics following the East Asian crisis. *Crony capital-ism* became a popular term to describe a major problem in the region, and corporate reform was a key item on the reform agenda. The recent string of corporate scandals in the United States has weakened the credibility of the conventional reform proposals being introduced in East Asia and has

---

14. The model does not predict well for Singapore.

given some pause for thought. In chapter 7, "Corporate Governance, Industrial Policy, and the Rule of Law," Dwight H. Perkins makes use of the opportunity to examine the issue in greater depth and in its historical context.

Perkins points out that Western corporate financial practice rests on a system in which governments make rules that structure and regulate markets but are not directly involved in the functioning of markets. Nor are governments involved when the rules are violated; legal systems or independent regulators perform the necessary functions. The concerns of corporate governance are to protect investors from predatory managers and to ensure a fair return on investment, without which capital markets, which depend on minority shareholders, would be underdeveloped. In East Asia, during the early years of catch-up development, governments had a defensible activist role in industrial policy. Most firms were financed either by family or by state capital, and judicial systems were quite weak. Thus, expecting a Western style of corporate governance was not realistic.

This situation has been changing as East Asian countries have developed and have become more integrated into the global economy. But the situation has not changed fast enough, because the focus of competition policy has been on how to create internationally competitive firms, not on how to curb domestic market power. This focus, too, would need to change in the future, but given the close ties established over years between governments and large enterprises, both public and private, it is not simple to initiate the process. Who exactly should change the system, and how should it be done? Perkins concludes that reforming the economic system might entail a parallel reform of the political system and its financing, which is a much more complex undertaking.

Perkins's main message is that East Asian economies in the emerging global order would need to rely less on government intervention and more on the market, but that the latter will not deliver without judicial or regulatory bodies strong enough to enforce the rules that govern markets. A set of institutions is needed that can independently, efficiently, and fairly enforce the rules of a market system. The informal institutions that have served East Asia in the past would prove increasingly inadequate for economies wanting to integrate fully into a complex global economy. Although democracy is not a panacea, strengthening the institutions of democracy and giving greater freedom and independence to the press[15] might provide the only secular force consistently moving the system in the desired direction.

---

15. See Dyck and Zingales (2002) on the influence of the media and corporate governance. On the effects of an independent media on voter turnout and political competition, see Besley and Burgess (2002).

Democratization is also a factor in mediating the impact on political governance of disruptive technologies like the Internet. Like Perkins, Richard Rose is not sanguine about the prospects for rapid political change driven by advances in information and communications technology (ICT) and the potential of e-governance. In chapter 8, "Governance and the Internet," Rose argues that the effects of the Internet on political governance depend on the existing state of openness, accountability, and bureaucratic preparedness for the effective use of IT and the rule of law within a country.

In the framework Rose presents, the Internet's effects will vary with the extent to which political accountability and rule-based administration exist within a country. Where both are low, governments will see the Internet's promotion of openness and information flow as a threat and will aim to suppress its spread. Where both are high, the Internet will deliver gains in efficiency and convenience, but the political implications will be marginal.

The more interesting cases are those in which one of the two attributes is high and the other is low. Where rule-based administration is high, but political accountability is low, Rose speculates that the determinant of changes would be the rising expectations of citizens from their governments. The Internet would have a marginal role to play, if any. In the other case, institutions of political accountability provide dissatisfied citizens the avenues to challenge inefficiencies and violations of rules. In such a situation, the Internet could be an effective tool for bureaucratic reform. However, in all cases, the direct link from IT advances to improvements in political governance is weak.

Economic prosperity and political democratization could reasonably be expected to increase the demand for better governance, greater rule of law, and more efficient delivery of services. But servicing this demand would not follow automatically. In chapter 9, "Education for Growth: Deepening or Widening?," Howard Pack makes the point that people with very specific skills and training would be required for the purpose. Pack argues that the emphasis on manufacturing and export markets has led to a neglect of skills needed for the functioning of economies, which are becoming too complex to allow the neglect to continue. The focus on increasing the efficiency of banks, on improving the quality of governance and transparency, and on instituting competition policies and the rule of law has implications in terms of a derived demand for specialized skills needed by providers of producer services. These skills have been underproduced until recently in almost all of the emerging economies because the emphasis has been on the manufacturing sectors.

Pack makes the case for increasing the supply of accountants, auditors, risk specialists, underwriters, actuaries, lawyers, and regulators. As the number of smaller firms increases, more management and executive skills will also be needed. And flexible labor markets will require skills in industrial relations and in the design of portable pension systems. Increasing numbers of start-up firms will call for skills in venture capital provision and in bankruptcy and intellectual property law. The main message is that the fascination with manufacturing technology and the temptation to continue following a successful strategy whose objective is the export of standardized industrial products should not obscure the somewhat mundane need for a host of softer skills that are essential for the functioning of economies that are becoming integrated into the global market system.

Promoting Efficiency and Innovation

The commoditization of many manufactured products and the emergence of China as a lower-cost producer have forced the realization that manufacturing firms in the middle-income countries of East Asia have to both become more productive and move up the value chain by relying on products based on proprietary technology (see Yusuf with others 2003). Such a transition requires investment in productivity-enhancing technologies and the coming together of an innovation system that comprises not just technical innovation but also a variety of institutions and services. These range from institutions required to increase the pool of innovative workers and finance innovative start-ups to services required to protect and market proprietary products. The two remaining chapters address these aspects of efficiency and innovation in East Asian countries.

Education is an obvious starting point. However, Howard Pack cautions against a one-size-fits-all policy. A large country such as China and a more advanced one such as Korea can invest in institutions of higher education of a quality needed to become a steady source of innovative research. Others may find it more cost-effective in the short run to rely, at least partially, on advanced training abroad for basic research, while promoting local schools and research entities to work with industry to generate knowledge for applied research. Whether it is tertiary-level training or research, returns to investment will be maximized through international collaboration that allows East Asian countries to draw on knowledge and expertise from elsewhere in the region as well as from the industrial nations.

The need for East Asian economies to become more technologically innovative is generally accepted. How to get there remains the critical issue. The intense research on the causes of innovation during the recent

dot-com bubble in the United States suggested a close association between innovation and start-up firms in the high-tech sectors. But this
model is not necessarily the only one, and the choice of model has implications for supporting policies and institutions.

The model associated with dynamic start-ups is a highly decentralized
one, which is based on large investments in numerous high-quality
research universities, continuous public funding of basic research, public
funding for cutting-edge defense-related research and applications, an
intensely competitive market economy, and an effective structure of intellectual property rights protection. Such a system can be established only
over a long period of time. Promising ideas for commercial spin-offs from
public and defense-oriented research are brought to market for funding
by entrepreneurs, and venture capitalists provide the seed funding to
nurture them through the development phase. Thus, private venture
capital is a critical component of this system.

Many East Asian economies do not have the elements of such an innovation system in place, nor could one be created instantly even if the funding were available. The alternative to the "wide and shallow" model is
the "narrow and deep" one in which the state jumpstarts the innovative
process in strategically chosen sectors of the economy and through large
firms chosen for the purpose. The examples of Samsung, Hyundai, and
Daewoo in Korea and of Taiwan Semiconductor Manufacturing Company
and UMC in Taiwan (China) come to mind (Amsden and Chu 2003;
Mathews and Cho 2000). The latter model, often the only feasible one at
the outset, is much more risky and can fail more often than it succeeds (for
example, Indonesia's gamble on the aircraft industry or Malaysia's investment in the automobile industry). But there have been notable successes
in Japan and Korea. Private venture capital is of much less importance in
this model. The most helpful outcome is if such an initiative becomes the
nucleus for the evolution of a wide and shallow system through accumulation over time.[16]

Martin Kenney, Kyonghee Han, and Shoko Tanaka have the wide
and shallow model in mind in chapter 10, "Venture Capital Industries."
In that chapter, they assess the status of venture capital in the region. It
is not surprising that they conclude, "If one adopts a Silicon Valley
definition of *venture capital* [VC], then probably only Taiwan, China,
would qualify." Kenney, Han, and Tanaka note important differences

---

16. Taiwan, China, could be considered an intermediate case in which the state invested in the
research infrastructure and the timing coincided with the availability of venture capital from the
Taiwanese diaspora in Silicon Valley.

between VC in the United States and VC in most East Asian countries. In the United States, there are a large number of nonprofit institutional funding sources but no direct government investment. In contrast, East Asian countries rely more on funding from industrial corporations and direct government investment.

The objectives of VC are also different in East Asia. Both in Japan and Korea, VC subsidiaries were first formed by financial institutions, not to seek capital gains through start-up investments, but to develop long-term banking relationships with the firms they funded. This situation began to change only after the Internet boom in the United States, but it slowed down again after the collapse of the boom in 2001. In Korea, the objective at the outset was the establishment of a funding body by the government to assist the transfer of research from state institutes to small and medium-size enterprises, quite different from the U.S. model.

Kenney, Han, and Tanaka elaborate on the essential features of VC in four country groups that share similarities within East Asia: (a) Japan and Korea; (b) Hong Kong (China) and Singapore; (c) China; and (d) the remaining countries (Indonesia, Malaysia, the Philippines, Thailand, and Vietnam). The key requirement for U.S.-style VC to emerge is to have a large enough number of deals to make the VC industry a viable proposition (that is, a competitive market with many more small firms). Allowing pension funds to invest a percentage of their assets in start-ups would provide a boost to the VC industry, but such a change would need to be phased in carefully to prevent a glut of capital and a consequent drop in returns.

Establishing a private VC industry also requires the same reforms in corporate governance as noted by Perkins, without which venture capitalists would feel at a disadvantage in interactions with the owners of the firms. Effective bankruptcy laws and credible and securely regulated exit options in the form of secondary stock markets for launching initial public offerings are also needed for U.S.-style VC to take root in East Asia. The recent economic downturn has posed a major challenge for the VC industry in East Asia, but it also provides the breathing room to reappraise policies, including those related to second stock market boards, and to make the policy changes necessary for the industry to play its part when growth rebounds.

CONCLUSION AND RESEARCH DIRECTIONS

The elements of a future growth agenda for East Asia are gradually falling into place. High on the list are regional measures to minimize shocks and turbulence, to facilitate trade, and to take advantage of the evolving global production networks. The domestic agendas are dominated by reforms in corporate and political governance, by the transition to efficient and innovative economies, and by movement toward social protection in keeping with the greater volatility of the global economy, of which East Asia is an increasingly integral part. In each of those areas, the chapters in this volume offer suggestions that will contribute to the informed discussion that is needed on the issues.

Policies and institutions that are driving growth and integration in East Asia are central to all of the chapters in this volume. The authors draw on the available literature to provide a careful description and rigorous assessment. However, as is typical with topics as complex as the ones covered, many questions remain to be addressed by future research. Here we briefly touch some of the issues that deserve the attention of scholars and policymakers over the medium term.

We are well aware that exchange rate policy and the liberalization of the capital account have been intensively studied. But a lack of clarity regarding the future directions for East Asian countries with respect to exchange rate policies remains in the face of continuing economic integration and fluctuation in the parities of key currencies. There is a similar lack of clarity about the sequencing of capital account liberalization, especially when delaying liberalization can perversely lead to a slowing of financial reform. Policymakers need more precise guidelines in both these areas, not just a range of options.

China's integration into the regional economy and its accession to the World Trade Organization have spurred trade with other East Asian countries and have raised hopes that exports of services to China will also rise. However, it is important to determine whether other East Asian countries can anticipate rising exports as more of the component and machinery production shifts to China. Moreover, how easy will it be for China to implement the liberalization of trade in services if trade reform in the rest of East Asia is slow? We still have only the haziest idea as to how other countries in the region might reshape their industrial sectors to accommodate China's growth and competitiveness across a broad array of products.

This concern takes us to issues regarding industrial organization governance and competition policy in a more integrated world. With the Japanese and Korean forms of industrial organizations viewed with skepticism, and with those of the United States and Europe also seen as flawed, should East Asia be experimenting with hybrid forms of organization and governance? And, if so, what kind of competition policy would be appropriate, and should there be a push to harmonize among countries?

In this volume, we discuss how IT can, in the context of organizational and procedural changes, lead to greater governmental transparency and lower transaction costs for business. However, no one has yet attempted a rigorous and in-depth comparison of IT use in Korea and Singapore to show how it has affected political competition, individual rights, accountability, and transaction costs. In the absence of such work, it is difficult to show how IT use can improve governance.

Finally, in view of East Asia's need to upgrade products and enhance innovation, it is vital to ascertain the combination of financial technology and institutions that would enlarge the research contribution of universities to business without detracting from their teaching functions. With many countries worrying about the apparent shortage of skills, what is the merit, if any, of the human resources planning practiced by Singapore? If East Asia needs a different mix of skills—and needs it soon—how can this mix be achieved? And if it is to be achieved through market processes, could these be accelerated?

REFERENCES

Amsden, Alice H., and Wan-wen Chu. 2003. *Beyond Late Development*. Cambridge, Mass.: MIT Press.

Baldwin, Richard, and Paul Krugman. 2000. "Agglomeration, Integration, and Tax Harmonization." Discussion Paper 2630 (November). Centre for Economic Policy Research, London.

Baldwin, Robert E. 2003. "Openness and Growth: What's the Empirical Relationship?" NBER Working Paper 9578. National Bureau of Economic Research, Cambridge, Mass.

Basu, Kaushik. 2003. "Globalization and the Politics of International Finance: The Stiglitz Verdict." *Journal of Economic Literature* 41(3):885–99.

Besley, Timothy, and Robin Burgess. 2002. "The Political Economy of Government Responsiveness: Theory and Evidence from India." *Quarterly Journal of Economics* 117(4):1415–50.

Bordo, Michael D., Barry Eichengreen, Daniela Klingebiel, and Maria Soledad Martinez-Peria. 2001. "Financial Crises: Lessons from the Last 120 Years." *Economic Policy* (16):53–82.

Dyck, Alexander, and Luigi Zingales. 2002. "The Corporate Governance Role of the Media." NBER Working Paper 9309. National Bureau of Economic Research, Cambridge, Mass.

"East Asia: ASEAN+3." 2004. *Oxford Analytica*, January 8.

Eichengreen, Barry, and Michael D. Bordo. 2002. "Crises Now and Then: What Lessons from the Last Era of Financial Globalization?" NBER Working Paper 8716. National Bureau of Economic Research, Cambridge, Mass.

Frankel, Jeffrey A. 1997. *Regional Trading Blocs*. Washington, D.C.: Institute for International Economics.

Fukase, Emiko, and L. Alan Winters. 2003. "Possible Dynamic Effects of AFTA for the New Member Countries." *World Economy* 26(6):829–51.

Gal, Michal. 2003. *Competition Policy for Small Market Economies*. Cambridge, Mass.: Harvard University Press.

Hanson, Gordon J., Raymond J. Mataloni Jr., and Matthew J. Slaughter. 2001. "Expansion Strategies of U.S. Multinational Firms." U.S. Bureau of Economic Analysis, Washington, D.C. Processed.

Hatch, Walter, and Kozo Yamamura. 1996. *Asia in Japan's Embrace: Building a Regional Production Alliance*. Ithaca, N.Y.: Cornell University Press.

Hermes, Niels, and Robert Lensink. 2003. "Foreign Direct Investment, Financial Development, and Economic Growth." *Journal of Development Studies* 40(1): 142–63.

Hsiao, Cheng, and Yan Shen. 2003. "Foreign Direct Investment and Economic Growth: The Importance of Institutions and Urbanization." *Economic Development and Cultural Change* 51(4):883–96.

Huang, Yasheng. 2003. *Selling China: Foreign Direct Investment during the Reform Era*. New York: Cambridge University Press.

Keller, William W., and Louis W. Pauly. 2003. "Crisis and Adaptation in Taiwan and South Korea." In William W. Keller and Richard J. Samuels, eds., *Crisis and Innovation in Asian Technology*. Cambridge, U.K.: Cambridge University Press.

Lardy, Nicholas R. 2002. *Integrating China into the Global Economy*. Washington, D.C.: Brookings Institution Press.

Lawrence, Robert Z., and David E. Weinstein. 2001. "Trade and Growth: Import-Led or Export-Led Evidence from Japan and Korea." In Joseph E. Stiglitz and Shahid Yusuf, eds., *Rethinking the East Asian Miracle*. New York: Oxford University Press.

Lee, Ha Yan, Lucca Antonio Ricci, and Roberto Rigobon. Forthcoming. "Once Again, Is Openness Good for Growth?" *Journal of Development Economics*.

Leipziger, Danny M. 1997. *Lesson from East Asia*. Ann Arbor: University of Michigan Press.

Mathews, John A., and Dong-Sung Cho. 2000. *Tiger Technology*. Cambridge, U.K.: Cambridge University Press.

Miller, Stephen, and Mukti P. Upadhyay. 2000. "The Effects of Openness, Trade Orientation, and Human Capital on Total Factor Productivity." *Journal of Development Economics* 63:399–423.

Nabeshima, Kaoru. 2004. "The Technology Transfer in East Asia: A Survey." In Shahid Yusuf, M. Anjum Altaf, and Kaoru Nabeshima, eds., *Global Production Networking and Technological Change in East Asia*. New York: Oxford University Press.

"Regional Trade Agreements." 2002. *Oxford Analytica*, July 23.

Rodríguez, Francisco, and Dani Rodrik. 2000. "Trade Policy and Economic Growth: A Skeptic's Guide to the Cross-National Evidence." In Ben Bernanke and Kenneth Rogoff, eds., *NBER Macroeconomics Annual 2000*. Cambridge, Mass.: MIT Press.

Rodrik, Dani. 1997. *Has Globalization Gone Too Far?* Washington, D.C.: Institute for International Economics.

Srinivasan, T. N., and Jagdish Bhagwati. 1999. "Outward-Orientation and Development: Are Revisionists Right?" Discussion Paper 806 (September). Economic Growth Center, New Haven, Conn.

Urata, Shujiro, and Kozo Kiyota. 2003. "The Impacts of an East Asia FTA on Foreign Trade in East Asia." NBER Working Paper 10173. National Bureau of Economic Research, Cambridge, Mass.

Wacziarg, Romain, and Karen Horn Welch. 2003. "Trade Liberalization and Growth: New Evidence." NBER Working Paper 10152. National Bureau of Economic Research, Cambridge, Mass.

World Bank. 1998. *East Asia: Road to Recovery*. Washington, D.C.: World Bank.

———. 2000a. *East Asia: Recovery and Beyond*. Washington, D.C.: World Bank.

———. 2000b. *World Development Report: Entering the 21st Century*. New York: Oxford University Press.

Yusuf, Shahid, and Simon J. Evenett. 2002. *Can East Asia Compete? Innovation for Global Markets*. New York: Oxford University Press.

Yusuf, Shahid, M. Anjum Altaf, and Kaoru Nabeshima, eds. 2004. *Global Production Networking and Technological Change in East Asia*. New York: Oxford University Press.

Yusuf, Shahid, with M. Anjum Altaf, Barry Eichengreen, Sudarshan Gooptu, Kaoru Nabeshima, Charles Kenny, Dwight H. Perkins, and Marc Shotten. 2003. *Innovative East Asia: The Future of Growth*. New York: Oxford University Press.

CHAPTER 2

HANGING TOGETHER? ON MONETARY AND FINANCIAL COOPERATION

Barry Eichengreen

I
n Asia, the idea of wider monetary cooperation has been in the air since
the crisis of 1997–98. The spread of financial instability after the devaluation of the Thai baht highlighted the extent to which one country's
monetary problems could have destabilizing repercussions for other
countries. The perception was that the currency problems of 1997–98 had
been precipitated by the large positions of highly leveraged institutions in
New York and compounded by the less-than-generous assistance of multilateral financial institutions in Washington, D.C. More than a few observers concluded that Asian governments should take steps to create a
zone of monetary stability that would be better insulated from these
factors beyond their control.

The response has been schemes of varying scope and ambition. Least
ambitious are plans to build on already extant arrangements like the Asia-
Pacific Economic Cooperation (APEC) Finance Ministers' Process
(a venue for sharing information and pursuing cooperative programs), the
Executives Meeting of East Asia and Pacific Central Banks (which is designed to encourage regional surveillance), and the Six Markets Group or
G-4+2 (a venue for the exchange of views on monetary and financial issues among the vice ministers of finance and deputy central bank governors of the regional financial centers).[1] The hope is that elaborating these

The author would like to thank Shahid Yusuf, Randall Henning, John Williamson, and
Yeongseop Rhee for helpful comments and Calvin Ho for research assistance. In addition to the
World Bank, the author is grateful to the Ford Foundation, the Hong Kong Institute for Monetary Research, and the Institute for European Studies of the University of California, Berkeley,
for support for this project.

1. The United States has also been invited to attend recent meetings of the Six Markets Group.

arrangements will allow Asian countries to achieve more collectively than they could achieve individually.

A second set of proposals recommends the creation of a common basket peg for exchange rates, perhaps as a way station on the road to the creation of a single Asian currency (Dieter 2000). Several motivations are apparent here. First is the role of currency pegs in the Asian miracle. Their historical role as an anchor for wage and price expectations and as a facilitator of export growth creates understandable skepticism about the compatibility of floating rates with the Asian development model. Second is the role of yen–U.S. dollar fluctuations in setting the stage for the crisis. And third is the tendency, evident in 1997–98, for currency depreciation in one Asian country to spread instability to its neighbors. Observations like these provide the motivation for proposals for a system of collective currency pegs to the yen (Kwan 2001), the U.S. dollar (McKinnon 2001), or a basket of major currencies (Williamson 1999). These proposals have been given prominence by a discussion paper prepared by French and Japanese officials for the Third Asia-Europe Finance Ministers' Meeting in Kobe, Japan, in January 2001 (see Japan 2001).

Similarly, there continues to be discussion of an Asian Monetary Fund to provide crisis countries with financial assistance subject to more appropriate conditions. This idea was first floated by the Japanese government at a meeting in Bangkok in September 1997. It was then torpedoed by opposition from the U.S. government and the International Monetary Fund (IMF), which feared that a regional fund would undermine the effectiveness of IMF conditionality, and by the less-than-enthusiastic reaction of China, which worried that the arrangement would unduly enhance Japanese influence in the region.[2]

The next major initiative emanated from the Association of Southeast Asian Nations (ASEAN) or, more precisely, from ASEAN+3 (ASEAN plus China, Japan, and the Republic of Korea).[3] This agreement is the

---

2. See Bergsten (2000c). This experience prompted the formation of the Manila Framework Group by APEC finance ministers at a meeting in November 1997. Because the Manila Framework Group (a 14-country subset of APEC members) includes not only the crisis countries and Japan but also Australia, New Zealand, and the United States, its makeup can be seen as an attempt to strengthen surveillance on a regional basis but in a manner consistent with existing IMF–World Bank arrangements. In any event, the discussions of the Manila Framework Group produced few concrete results.

3. The members of ASEAN are Brunei Darussalam, Cambodia, Indonesia, the Lao People's Democratic Republic, Malaysia, Myanmar, the Philippines, Singapore, Thailand, and Vietnam.

Chiang Mai Initiative (CMI) of central bank swap arrangements.[4] Drawings through this arrangement, other than small swaps for limited periods, can be used only to supplement existing IMF arrangements and are subject to the latter's conditionality. The CMI is thus embedded in the IMF system. This new willingness of Asian policymakers to link their regional initiative to global financial arrangements has helped mollify opposition in Beijing and Washington, D.C.

What these initiatives bode for the future is unclear. Is it realistic to attempt to build self-standing institutions of Asian monetary cooperation? Or is this effort infeasible in today's world of seamless globalization? Must regional initiatives instead be embedded in the global system of multilateral institutions and arrangements, much as Asia's economy and financial markets are embedded in the global economy and global financial system? Is it possible for Asia to square this circle as Europe has done, by creating regional economic and monetary institutions that are both autonomous and linked to their global counterparts?

This chapter addresses these issues and their implications. The first section, "Postcrisis Trends," summarizes the development of currency- and financial-market conditions since the crisis. It documents the tensions in foreign exchange markets—on the one hand, the de jure transition toward greater exchange rate flexibility and, on the other hand, the de facto tendency to manage exchange rates and limit their fluctuation—and the sharp differences in the response across countries. It also documents a pronounced decline in cross-border bank lending and persistent obstacles to securities-market development. These observations underscore the desirability of a cooperative response to the region's monetary and financial problems.

The second section, "Currency Options," considers possibilities for a cooperative monetary response, reaching generally negative conclusions. It argues that although pegged exchange rates played an important role in the development model pursued by East Asian countries in the second half

---

4. The Chiang Mai Initiative is a descendant of the Asian Swap Arrangement, the facility established in 1977 by the five original ASEAN members and extended to the five other ASEAN members at the Brunei Darussalam ASEAN Finance Ministers' Meeting in March 2000. That arrangement was then transformed, in May 2000, into the Chiang Mai Initiative, encompassing not only the 10 ASEAN countries but also Japan, China, and the Republic of Korea. After the agreement was publicly announced at the ASEAN meeting in Chiang Mai, Thailand, it was finalized in December 2000. Dedicated support lines under the Chiang Mai Initiative are US$1 billion. The previous members are to contribute US$150 million each, while the new ASEAN members will each contribute US$50 million. Countries will be eligible to borrow up to twice their maximum contribution. Swaps can be drawn for up to 6 months, with one 6-month extension possible (Henning 2002).

of the twentieth century, they will be less essential to the development model of the twenty-first. Moreover, Asian policymakers have no solution for the fragility of currency pegs in a world of high capital mobility and democratic politics.[5] I conclude that not even a vastly expanded system of swap arrangements growing out of the Chiang Mai Initiative will enable Asian countries to sustain a system of collective pegs. At worst, the attempt to establish one could be a costly mistake. At best, it will constitute a diversion from the key task at hand.

That task is to strengthen financial institutions and to promote the development of financial markets. Creating a zone of financial stability means (a) cooperatively pursuing initiatives to upgrade prudential supervision and regulation and (b) fostering transparency and creditor rights. The third section of this chapter, "Financial Options," evaluates possibilities for enhancing financial cooperation in this light. I argue that Asian policymakers should establish an Asian Financial Institute (AFI) with the power to set standards for financial market regulation, to identify policies for promoting financial market development, to coordinate national initiatives along these lines, to monitor the compliance of countries with its recommendations, and to apply the appropriate diplomatic and, perhaps, pecuniary sanctions to violators. ASEAN+3 is the logical entity to pursue this initiative.

The concluding section poses several additional questions about the feasibility of this form of Asian monetary and financial cooperation.

POSTCRISIS TRENDS

External developments have contributed little to the development of financial markets and the stabilization of financial conditions since the outbreak of the crisis. Capital flows to emerging markets and to Asia in particular have declined markedly since 1997.[6] The change in the net cross-border loans of Bank for International Settlements (BIS) member reporting banks to Asia-Pacific developing countries moved into negative territory in the third quarter of 1997 and then fell to significant negative levels, on the order of negative US$30 billion of net new commitments

---

5. In this context, I devote special attention to the experience of Singapore, which is frequently mentioned as a country that has succeeded in pegging its exchange rate while at the same time maintaining open capital markets. I show that its success in doing so reflects special circumstances not present in other Asian countries.

6. This and the next paragraph draw on annual reports of the Bank for International Settlements (BIS 2001, 2002).

per quarter. The total net claims of BIS reporting banks on Asia-Pacific developing countries fell by more than 25 percent from their peak in calendar year 1997.[7] Net cross-border bank lending to the region turned positive late in 2001 for the first time since mid-1997 but still remained at relatively low levels compared with the peak years of the 1990s.

This decline in cross-border bank lending has not been offset by the growth of securities markets. Hedge funds and proprietary trading desks curtailed their involvement in developing-country debt and equities after the crisis, thereby diminishing the liquidity of these markets. Emerging market equity issuance fell off sharply from an earlier average of US$16 billion per year (over the 4 years preceding the crisis) to only US$8 billion in 1998 and showed little tendency to recover subsequently (reflecting uncertain economic prospects and the collapse of technology equity prices) apart from a spurt in 1999 (reflecting large privatization transactions). Equity-related flows recovered in the early months of 2002, but whether this momentum will be sustained is yet to be seen.

Net issuance by developing countries of international debt securities (a category that includes international money market instruments, bonds, and notes), which had been running at US$20 billion a quarter (roughly one-third of which had been attributable to Asia and Pacific issuers), fell almost as sharply as bank credits. By the fourth quarter of 1997, net issuance of debt securities had declined to very low levels. Since then, it has remained at those low levels (with the exception of abortive recoveries in the second quarter of 1998 and the fourth quarter of 1999).[8] Asian borrowers have come to the market to refinance maturing international bonds, but they have secured little new financing.[9] Much of that refinancing has been at maturities shorter than maturing obligations, reflecting the limited liquidity of primary markets. Paralleling developments in equity markets, the liquidity of debt markets has declined, reflecting financial sector consolidation and the withdrawal of risk capital used in market-making activities.

Associated with these changes in quantities have been changes in prices. Spreads on emerging market debt securities have become increasingly decoupled from spreads on issues of comparably rated borrowers in the

---

7. Meanwhile, total net claims stagnated, neither rising nor falling significantly, in the case of emerging Europe and Latin America.

8. Negligible in this context means less than US$1 billion. In many of the subsequent quarters, net issuance was negative.

9. The vast majority of the new financing extended to emerging market borrowers in this period went to only four countries, all outside the Asia-Pacific region—Argentina, Brazil, Mexico, and Turkey.

industrial countries.[10] A gap has been growing between spreads on investment grade credits (Hungary, Korea, Malaysia, Mexico, and Poland, for example) and subinvestment grade credits (most other emerging markets). Launch spreads have risen significantly compared with launch spreads in the precrisis period.

Exchange rate volatility rose sharply after the crisis. Most of the countries of the region—aside from China, Hong Kong (China), and Malaysia—moved from fixed or tightly managed exchange rates to freer floating rates, according to the official IMF categorization. Some authors (for example, Kawai and Akiyama 2001; McKinnon 2001) argue that, official labels notwithstanding, rates remain tightly managed and are as stable now as before the crisis. Tables 2.1–2.4 shed some light on this issue.[11] Table 2.1 shows that the exchange rates of six of the Asian countries considered (Indonesia, Korea, Malaysia, the Philippines, Singapore, and Thailand) were unusually stable before the crisis, whether measured by the range of average monthly percentage exchange rate changes or by their standard deviations. Since the crisis, exchange rate variability against the U.S. dollar has increased sharply in many of these countries, the principal exceptions being Hong Kong (China), Malaysia, and Taiwan (China). (In constructing this and subsequent tables, I have omitted the crisis period itself, defined as the second half of 1997 and calendar year 1998.) The picture, in other words, may be more complex than suggested by McKinnon.

Table 2.2 measures whether intervention in foreign exchange markets has risen or declined, displaying the mean absolute monthly percentage change in international reserves and the standard deviation of monthly reserve percentage changes. The relatively high precrisis figures for the Asian countries, compared with those of the United States and Japan, confirm that their exchange rates were tightly managed. After the crisis, reserve volatility, as measured by the standard deviation, fell in Korea, the Philippines, Taiwan (China), and Thailand, while rising in Malaysia and Singapore.[12] Clearly, Malaysia has continued to intervene heavily to peg its currency while Singapore has intervened to maintain its band. These data paint a more mixed picture of intervention in the other countries.

Countries can also resist market pressures by adjusting interest rates. Table 2.3, therefore, reports the range, mean absolute change, and standard

---

10. This decoupling resulted as much from the crisis of August 1998 in the Russian Federation as from the Asian crisis that preceded it. Both events reduced the correlation between the two sets of spreads, although the Russian crisis arguably had a greater effect. In any case, the earlier correlation has shown little tendency to reassert itself.

11. Here, I extend work by Hernandez and Montiel (2001).

12. By this measure, reserve volatility has remained unchanged in Indonesia while falling slightly in Hong Kong, China.

Table 2.1 Monthly Nominal Exchange Rate Volatility

Currency or Country	Period	Range of Mean Absolute Change	Standard Deviation
US$/deutschemark	Precrisis	0.093	0.025
	Postcrisis	0.122	0.027
US$/yen	Precrisis	0.136	0.029
	Postcrisis	0.098	0.025
Chile	Precrisis	0.048	0.011
	Postcrisis	0.169	0.029
Mexico	Precrisis	0.166	0.034
	Postcrisis	0.069	0.018
Indonesia	Precrisis	0.019	0.003
	Postcrisis	0.300	0.066
Korea, Rep. of	Precrisis	0.043	0.011
	Postcrisis	0.113	0.023
Malaysia	Precrisis	0.049	0.009
	Postcrisis	0.000	0.000
Philippines	Precrisis	0.016	0.003
	Postcrisis	0.104	0.020
Thailand	Precrisis	0.015	0.004
	Postcrisis	0.073	0.017
Australia	Precrisis	0.066	0.017
	Postcrisis	0.135	0.028
Hong Kong, China	Precrisis	0.003	0.001
	Postcrisis	0.001	0.000
New Zealand	Precrisis	0.045	0.012
	Postcrisis	0.141	0.030
Singapore	Precrisis	0.021	0.006
	Postcrisis	0.067	0.012
Taiwan, China	Precrisis	0.056	0.011
	Postcrisis	0.059	0.013

Note: Precrisis period is July 1995 to June 1997. Postcrisis period is January 1999 to November 2001, except in Germany (where it ends July 2001) and Mexico (where it ends October 2001). All exchange rates except the first two are against the U.S. dollar.

Source: Author's calculations.

deviation of monthly interest rates (money market rates where possible). Consistent with the results for reserves, monthly interest rate volatility has fallen in Korea and Thailand. This decline indicates a commitment to greater exchange rate flexibility. Monthly interest rate volatility has risen in Hong Kong, China, reflecting the Hong Kong Monetary Authority's commitment to its peg. Not surprisingly, interest rate volatility has also risen in Indonesia, again pointing to continued and generally unsuccessful

Table 2.2 Monthly Reserve Volatility

Country	Period	Mean Absolute Change	Standard Deviation
Germany	Precrisis	0.011	0.013
	Postcrisis	0.032	0.045
Japan	Precrisis	0.015	0.024
	Postcrisis	0.019	0.027
Chile	Precrisis	0.022	0.029
	Postcrisis	0.018	0.027
Mexico	Precrisis	0.066	0.098
	Postcrisis	0.024	0.034
Indonesia	Precrisis	0.021	0.028
	Postcrisis	0.021	0.029
Korea, Rep. of	Precrisis	0.033	0.041
	Postcrisis	0.022	0.019
Malaysia	Precrisis	0.021	0.027
	Postcrisis	0.030	0.038
Philippines	Precrisis	0.043	0.050
	Postcrisis	0.024	0.039
Thailand	Precrisis	0.018	0.029
	Postcrisis	0.014	0.020
Australia	Precrisis	0.052	0.085
	Postcrisis	0.055	0.085
Hong Kong, China	Precrisis	0.006	0.028
	Postcrisis	0.011	0.014
New Zealand	Precrisis	0.059	0.083
	Postcrisis	0.051	0.064
Singapore	Precrisis	0.010	0.008
	Postcrisis	0.014	0.017
Taiwan, China	Precrisis	0.011	0.019
	Postcrisis	0.014	0.015

Note: Precrisis period is July 1995 to June 1997. Postcrisis period is January 1999 to November 2001, except for Germany, Hong Kong (China), Malaysia, Mexico, New Zealand, the Philippines, and Singapore (where it ends October 2001). All exchange rates are against the U.S. dollar.
Source: Author's calculations.

efforts to limit exchange rate fluctuations in a more volatile environment. It has fallen in Malaysia, presumably reflecting the insulation provided by capital controls.[13]

---

13. Malaysia is a different case; there, interest rate volatility fell noticeably after the crisis, reflecting the imposition of capital controls.

Table 2.3 Monthly Interest Rate Volatility

Country	Period	Range	Mean Absolute Change	Standard Deviation
Germany	Precrisis	0.135	0.021	0.031
	Postcrisis	0.289	0.044	0.060
Japan	Precrisis	0.420	0.058	0.099
	Postcrisis	8.000	0.403	1.246
Chile	Precrisis	0.223	0.033	0.047
	Postcrisis	1.350	0.099	0.197
Mexico	Precrisis	0.520	0.116	0.135
	Postcrisis	0.353	0.074	0.086
Indonesia	Precrisis	0.400	0.070	0.098
	Postcrisis	1.351	0.115	0.211
Korea, Rep. of	Precrisis	0.341	0.068	0.089
	Postcrisis	0.158	0.023	0.036
Malaysia	Precrisis	0.680	0.067	0.115
	Postcrisis	0.390	0.036	0.068
Philippines	Precrisis	0.291	0.046	0.068
	Postcrisis	0.818	0.056	0.127
Thailand	Precrisis	0.845	0.214	0.243
	Postcrisis	0.616	0.150	0.181
Australia	Precrisis	0.072	0.013	0.022
	Postcrisis	0.185	0.020	0.034
Hong Kong, China	Precrisis	0.325	0.065	0.084
	Postcrisis	0.895	0.119	0.176
New Zealand	Precrisis	0.171	0.038	0.047
	Postcrisis	0.289	0.030	0.052
Singapore	Precrisis	0.527	0.101	0.130
	Postcrisis	1.153	0.129	0.197
Taiwan, China	Precrisis	0.157	0.026	0.036
	Postcrisis	0.217	0.040	0.053

Note: Precrisis period is July 1995 to June 1997. Postcrisis period is January 1999 to November 2001, except for Australia, Indonesia, and Singapore (where it ends October 2001); Chile (where it ends July 2001); and Japan, Korea, and Malaysia (where it ends September 2001). Note that Japan's postcrisis range is 8 because the interest rate in July 2000 is 0.02 and in August 2000 is 0.16. (There is a 700 percent change.)

Source: Author's calculations.

Table 2.4 summarizes the preceding information, presenting the ratio of exchange rate volatility to interest rate volatility and the ratio of exchange rate volatility to reserve volatility. Rising ratios indicate freer floating—a sign that shocks to currency markets are being absorbed to a greater extent by the exchange rate and to a lesser extent by monetary policy adjustments

Table 2.4 Volatility Ratios

Country	Period	Exchange Rate Changes Relative to Interest Rate Changes	Exchange Rate Changes Relative to Reserve Changes
Germany	Precrisis	0.820	1.938
	Postcrisis	0.453	0.600
Japan	Precrisis	0.297	1.216
	Postcrisis	0.020	0.943
Chile	Precrisis	0.230	0.374
	Postcrisis	0.148	1.096
Mexico	Precrisis	0.248	0.341
	Postcrisis	0.206	0.522
Indonesia	Precrisis	0.118	0.118
	Postcrisis	2.265	2.265
Korea, Rep. of	Precrisis	0.122	0.266
	Postcrisis	0.633	1.176
Malaysia	Precrisis	0.081	0.339
	Postcrisis	0.000	0.000
Philippines	Precrisis	0.049	0.066
	Postcrisis	0.158	0.512
Thailand	Precrisis	0.016	0.132
	Postcrisis	0.096	0.866
Australia	Precrisis	0.728	0.198
	Postcrisis	0.842	0.335
Hong Kong, China	Precrisis	0.009	0.027
	Postcrisis	0.003	0.035
New Zealand	Precrisis	0.260	0.146
	Postcrisis	0.574	0.463
Singapore	Precrisis	0.050	0.851
	Postcrisis	0.063	0.717
Taiwan, China	Precrisis	0.317	0.587
	Postcrisis	0.242	0.851

Note: Precrisis period is July 1995 to June 1997. Postcrisis period is January 1999 to July 2001, except in a few cases, where the period ends earlier because of limited data availability (for details, see preceding tables).
Source: Author's calculations.

and intervention.[14] They confirm the existence in Hong Kong (China) and Malaysia of a continued commitment to pegging in the face of an

---

14. These measures, thus, at least partly address the concern that changes in the components, presented in tables 2.1–2.3, reflect shocks rather than policies.

increasingly volatile macroeconomic and financial environment. Singapore and Taiwan (China) present a mixed picture; in each case, one indicator but not the other suggests freer floating since the crisis. But for Indonesia, Korea, the Philippines, and Thailand, the evidence indicates that governments and central banks have moved to a regime where exchange rates are allowed to move more freely in response to shocks. This finding does not mean that their governments have adopted a policy of benign neglect of the exchange rate; in particular, the countries continue to resist pressure for their exchange rates to appreciate for fear of what this appreciation will do to the competitiveness of their exports. This kind of resistance is clearly evident in the massive accumulation of foreign exchange reserves by the countries of the region. But notwithstanding these tendencies, the data considered here still clearly suggest that the exchange rates of these countries are now noticeably more flexible than before the crisis.

CURRENCY OPTIONS

Various observers have argued that Asia should explore collective solutions to its monetary problems. In this section, I present their arguments and critique their proposals.

The Problem

The openness of Asian economies, not only to trade but also to capital flows, creates a presumption that exchange rate volatility and risk may be even more disruptive to growth there than in other times and places. The implication is that Asia may suffer more damaging consequences from exchange rate instability than other less trade- and investment-oriented parts of the world. Recent empirical work has lent support to the argument that stable exchange rates encourage trade.[15] Asian history is also invoked in this connection. Thus, McKinnon has argued that Japan's policy of pegging the yen to the U.S. dollar from the late 1940s until the early 1970s contributed to the country's emergence as an export powerhouse.[16] Sachs (1985) has ascribed the East Asian economic miracle (in part) to the commitment of Asian governments to peg their exchange rates at competitive

---

15. See, for example, Eichengreen and Irwin (1995). The work of Frankel and Rose (2002) is frequently cited in this connection, but their evidence is based mainly on the trade-promoting effects of a common currency, not of stable exchange rates.

16. See, for example, McKinnon, Ohno, and Shirono (1997).

levels, thereby providing a nominal anchor for wages, the stability of which, in turn, ensured the profitability of exports and stimulated the early growth of low-wage manufacturing. More recently, similar arguments have been made about the importance of China's U.S. dollar peg for the rapid growth of that country's exports, which have been so critical for its economic success. The implication is that exchange rate stability was and is integral to the East Asian miracle. Without it, export-led growth would have been more difficult. The rapid expansion of labor-intensive manufacturing would not have occurred. No Asian country, it is sometimes said, has successfully developed on the basis of a floating rate.

Without necessarily disputing this interpretation of Asia's post–World War II economic history, one must point out that it is still not clear that these arguments will have the same force in the future as in the past. Abundant cheap labor is no longer essential to industrial development in middle- and high-income Asian countries; the key, rather, is rising productivity.[17] And labor productivity, as opposed to the level of nominal wages, is not something on which monetary and exchange rate policies operate directly. Moreover, the high levels of investment that were encouraged historically by stable real exchange rates and a high profits share in national income have lost their luster in the wake of the Asian crisis.

To be sure, there are other reasons why competitive real exchange rates and stable nominal exchange rates are conducive to growth. Realistic real rates are important for commercially open Asian economies that continue to rely on export markets. Stable nominal rates encourage inward foreign investment and outsourcing from Japan, which, in turn, foster technology transfer and productivity growth.[18] The argument has been made that the instability against the yen of Asian currencies, which were effectively pegged to the U.S. dollar until recently, damaged the growth prospects of the East Asian economies in the mid-1990s and set the stage for the subsequent crisis.

At the same time, systematic analyses suggest that the exchange rate regime has come to play a less important role over time. Moreno (2001)

---

17. However, in China and in other late developers, abundant cheap labor clearly continues to play a role.

18. More generally, whether fixed or flexible exchange rates are more conducive to direct foreign investment is ambiguous, both theoretically and empirically. In industries where firms produce the same products in a variety of markets, exchange rate flexibility presumably makes foreign investment more attractive because exchange rate variations are one more source of risk against which producers can hedge by diversifying production internationally. But when foreign firms and subsidiaries produce components rather than final products, currency fluctuations can aggravate cost fluctuations rather than provide insulation from them. This second case—the outsourcing variant—is presumably the one that is more applicable to Asia.

shows that although growth may appear to be faster (even recently) in Asian countries that peg their exchange rates, this pattern is an artifact of survivor bias.[19] The growth effects of stable rates, properly measured, are actually smaller in East Asia than elsewhere. Crosby and Otto (2001) similarly conclude that the connection between growth and real exchange rates is more complex and contingent now than in the past.

Related to this discussion is the argument that the newly industrializing economies of East Asia (not including Japan) must be concerned with the stability of exchange rates vis-à-vis one another and not just with respect to the G-3 currencies (the U.S. dollar, the yen, and the euro). These concerns were pointed out by the Asian crisis, when currency instability in Thailand and Indonesia quickly infected the entire region. Why intraregional currency fluctuations had such devastating effects is unclear, however, making for uncertainty about whether similar fluctuations in the future would necessarily have similar effects. Although frequent reference is made to the competitive devaluation channel (through which the initial devaluations undermined the actual and prospective export competitiveness of other countries in the region), the fact is that trade among the crisis countries was not large.[20] More important were two other effects. First, because the countries of the region all exported into the same North American, Japanese, and European markets, depreciation by one could erode the market shares of the others. Although some sign of this effect is apparent, most of the evidence (for example, Harrigan 2000) suggests that it was small because exports from the crisis countries stagnated in the short run as financial distress led to declining output (rather than their exports rising sharply as this market-share-erosion argument requires).

More important, surely, was what Goldstein (1998) refers to as the wake-up call: that the outbreak of financial instability—signaled by the collapse of the exchange rate—in a country where market participants naively believed that no such thing was possible awakened investors to the possibility of similar problems elsewhere. Once the devaluation of the baht revealed that something was rotten in the Kingdom of Thailand, investors suddenly became aware that all was not well in the neighboring East Asian countries. Currency instability thus served as the starting gun for capital flight by panicked investors.

---

19. It can also be interpreted in terms of reverse causation; that is, countries that grow quickly for independent reasons find it less costly to subordinate their macroeconomic policies to the imperatives of maintaining a stable rate.

20. Admittedly, trade is growing over time (Kwan 2001), which may give this argument more force in the future than it had in the past.

The conviction that currency devaluation was the principal channel for the contagious spread of the 1997–98 crisis and that exchange rate fluctuations, if allowed to persist, could again have equally devastating effects has prompted calls for the reestablishment of fixed parities, for agreement on the nature and composition of these pegs, and for an expanded system of currency swaps and even an international lender of last resort to provide emergency financing to countries that might otherwise be forced to abandon their pegs. Rose (1998) was perhaps the first to invoke the evidence that contagion spreads primarily within regions in his support of the idea of an Asian Monetary Fund to pool the reserves of the participating countries and to support those whose pegs were threatened by market pressures. Bergsten (2000c) has similarly argued that one rationale for monetary cooperation in Asia is that contagion is heavily regional.[21]

The Solution

These arguments have led various observers to propose that Asian economies should resurrect their currency pegs and that governments should agree on the currencies to which to peg to limit intraregional fluctuations. Ito, Ogawa, and Sasaki (1998), as well as Williamson (1999) and a team of French and Japanese officials (Japan 2001), have advanced variants of the argument that East Asian governments should agree on a system of collective basket pegs with weights on the U.S. dollar, the yen, and the euro. Pegging to a basket will avoid disruptions to export competitiveness because of G-3 exchange rate fluctuations, and agreement on the weights will limit intraregional currency swings. Asia's recent history, these authors insist, demonstrates that floating rates are volatile and damaging to the real economy. A policy of benign neglect of the exchange rate, they observe, is not feasible for countries with fragile financial systems, high levels of liability dollarization, and heavy trade dependence. Thus, a number of emerging markets that are officially classified by the IMF as having moved to independent floating (and, more generally, as having adopted

---

21. Actually, this rationale is an argument for regional surveillance and peer pressure to prevent the development of policy inconsistencies, not for an Asian fund to provide support for currencies jeopardized by inconsistent policies. To be sure, the observation that contagion has a regional component points to the possibility that a number of Asian countries could come under pressure from the currency markets simultaneously. But if they did, reserve pooling would be of little help because the countries in question would need to draw on their reserves at the same time. Indeed, having the relatively strong ones lend their reserves to their weaker neighbors might actually weaken confidence in the countries with stronger currencies. In fact, these are precisely the concerns that have been raised by Standard & Poor's, among others, in the context of the Chiang Mai Initiative.

policies of greater exchange rate flexibility) continue to strictly limit the fluctuation of their currencies; they evince "fear of floating," in the widely adopted terminology of Calvo and Reinhart (2000). They display high ratios of international reserve variability and interest rate volatility to exchange rate variability, as if they habitually intervene in domestic and international money markets to limit currency movements.[22] As we saw above, some—but by no means all—Asian countries fall into this camp.

But purporting to float while really continuing to peg (or even strictly limiting the currency's fluctuation) does not enhance credibility when the authorities have no stated commitment to the regime. To the extent that an inconsistency between the de jure and de facto regimes is evident, credibility will be damaged rather than enhanced.[23]

The alternatives are (a) an operating strategy for monetary policy that articulates an explicit role for intervention in foreign exchange markets but not a target for the exchange rate—inflation targeting being one such strategy (see below)—and (b) a hard peg (under which the de jure and de facto regimes are the same). A hard peg is likely to be most attractive to very small, very open economies, of which the region has several. The experience of Hong Kong, China, demonstrates that this kind of arrangement can be compatible with openness, financial and otherwise. But a hard peg like the dollar-based currency board of Hong Kong, China, also has costs insofar as it will subject the economies of the region, with geographically diversified trade, to the vagaries of dollar-yen fluctuations.[24] Moreover, maintaining confidence in a currency board requires strict fiscal discipline and a high degree of wage and price flexibility because adjusting the exchange rate is no longer a way to achieve changes in relative prices. The success of the currency board requires an unquestionable commitment to the imperative of currency stability and an absence of political pressure on the authorities to use their policy instruments to pursue other goals.

---

22. Hausmann, Panizza, and Stein (2000) show that, of countries officially classified as having floating exchange rate systems or very wide bands, those with high levels of liability dollarization have the greatest tendency to limit exchange rate variability (in other words, they have the highest ratios of reserve volatility and interest rate volatility to exchange rate volatility). In addition, weaker evidence shows that countries with the highest rate of pass-through from exchange rates to domestic prices resist exchange rate movements.

23. If the authorities make a point of denying that they are ready to intervene whenever the rate moves by a certain amount, then they will create less *bias in the band* (in other words, stabilizing speculation by market participants when the edge of the range of permissible fluctuations is reached).

24. An Argentine-style currency board with weights on more than one anchor currency is a possibility, although Argentina's early experience with the arrangement is not exactly a sterling advertisement of its merits.

Of course, these prerequisites for currency stability are ones that Argentina, another currency board country of the 1990s, lacked. Its crisis demonstrated in the most graphic way that a currency board is neither a foolproof bulwark against speculative pressure nor a guarantee of exchange rate stability.[25] Hong Kong, China, is different: it trades heavily with the United States and with China, another country that pegs to the U.S. dollar, so fluctuations in the rates between the reserve currency and the currencies of other major trading partners are less of a problem.[26] Hong Kong, China, is endowed with unusually elastic supplies of labor from the mainland and relatively flexible wages and prices. Its unique political system gives the authorities unusual insulation from political pressure to subordinate currency stability to other goals. But in virtually all of these respects, Hong Kong, China, is atypical. The implication is that what works there is less likely to work in other economies in the region.

The shortcomings of a currency board are what attract some observers to the alternative of a common currency band. Williamson (1998) describes the most fully developed of these proposals. Williamson would have countries each declare a fluctuation band with a width of not less than plus-or-minus 5 percent or more than plus-or-minus 15 percent. Although exchange rates would be allowed to float within the band, the authorities would intervene to keep them from straying further. The knowledge that they stand ready to do so would create *bias in the band* (stabilizing speculation, also known as the *honeymoon effect*). But to avoid having to defend indefensible positions, Williamson advises governments to adjust the band whenever a significant change in the equilibrium rate takes place. These realignments should occur before speculative pressure builds up in anticipation of them. So that speculative attacks and costly reserve losses are avoided, jump changes in the exchange rate should be avoided; the new and old bands should overlap, allowing the current rate to be contained in the interior of both. One presumption is that the authorities will intervene to prevent the rate from straying beyond the band; however, if they decide that market pressures are overwhelming, then they can allow the rate to go outside the band. This strategy should avoid forcing the authorities to commit their scarce reserves to a battle with international markets that they cannot win. If those market pressures are not justified by fundamentals, then the rate will, in any case, move back into the band once the speculative flurry has passed.

---

25. One can now find many reviews of the Argentine tragedy. See, for example, Eichengreen (2002, chapter 4).

26. If and when China moves to a more flexible exchange rate against the U.S. dollar, the dilemma of Hong Kong, China, will become more difficult.

This scheme has attractions. The commitment to intervene should encourage stabilizing market behavior, while the soft margins and allowance for them to realign relieve the authorities of the need to engage in a futile battle with the markets. The common weights in the national currency baskets will limit intraregional currency fluctuations. And the knowledge that governments have negotiated an international agreement obliging each of them to behave in this way should enhance the credibility of their commitment to do so and, therefore, the extent of stabilizing speculation.

But Williamson's blueprint also has problems, which are indicative of the limitations of all of the associated proposals. First, he suggests that the weights on the U.S. dollar, the yen, and the euro should be proportional to Asia's trade with the United States, Japan, and Europe.[27] This approach privileges the destination of merchandise exports relative to the currency denomination of those exports, which is not obviously warranted on economic grounds.[28] It privileges trade relative to financial flows, which is not obviously warranted, given that the Asian economies are buffeted as much by financial flows as by trade flows.[29]

A second problem is the reluctance of governments and central banks to adjust the exchange rate when its equilibrium level has changed. To induce stabilizing market behavior, they must reassure the markets that they attach priority to the preservation of the peg. This reassurance, in turn, means that their credibility is tarnished when they renege on that promise and change the rate, which deters them from adjusting the latter

---

27. Actually, Williamson refers to Asian countries' effective exchange rate, but I interpret his meaning in this way.

28. McKinnon (2001) emphasizes this observation. Even if one ignores the preceding point, the fact remains that the appropriate trade weights differ across countries because of differences in the destination of their exports. This dynamic means that either governments will have to compromise on the appropriate country-specific weights, or they will have to sacrifice the objective of eliminating intraregional currency fluctuations. McKinnon (2001) suggests that this problem can be solved if East Asian countries—including Japan—peg to the U.S. dollar instead of a basket. But for many observers, the idea that the yen-dollar rate could be repegged and that Japan would effectively turn over monetary policymaking authority to the U.S. Federal Reserve is highly improbable. The alternative of having other Asian countries peg to the yen solves neither of the problems raised here unless one assumes, after Kwan (2001), that other Asian countries will rapidly reorient their trade and financing so that the vast majority of trade and financing is conducted with Japan. More precisely, Kwan proposes that Asian countries first peg their currencies to a basket. The weight assigned to the yen would then be increased gradually as Japan took steps to deregulate, to upgrade the Tokyo market as an international financial center to make it attractive to nonresidents, and to open its markets to Asian products, thereby deepening the interdependence between Japan and these countries.

29. Although, in principle, agreement is widespread that optimal currency pegs should reflect the sources of financing and the direction of trade, in practice, no agreement has been reached on the model or the weights.

before significant market pressures build up. Moreover, if the authorities reassure the markets that they are prepared to effectively minimize the extent of exchange risk, they will encourage capital to flow in beyond the point where its social return equals its social cost and, thus, set the stage for serious financial difficulties when the peg collapses (Dooley 1997; McKinnon and Pill 1999; Wilson 2000). The authors of collective band proposals assume that these problems can be solved (a) if governments somehow recognize the merits of early exchange rate adjustments (which would solve the "exit problem") and (b) if they commit to restoring depreciated rates to their previous level after each episode of financial pressures (which would limit the financial distress because of unexpected depreciations). This reasoning, however, simply assumes convenient answers to difficult political questions.

A third problem with Williamson's blueprint is that it creates a tradeoff between the credibility and flexibility of the band. If the authorities regularly shift the band before the rate reaches the margins to prevent the buildup of speculative pressure, then the monitoring-band regime will, in practice, differ little from floating. In particular, if, on the one hand, the authorities regularly adjust the margins before they are reached, then there will be no reason for bias in the band. If, on the other hand, they attempt to keep the rate from violating the edges of the band when the latter are approached, then they will have to butt heads with currency speculators. This confrontation will provide a harsh reminder that their foreign reserves are limited, as is their capacity to put the economy through the wringer of high interest rates. This scenario limits the likelihood that they will emerge victorious from this contest with the markets.

A network of credit lines and swaps that pools the reserves of the participating countries is an obvious response to this problem. The European Monetary System (EMS) provides a precedent, and the recently negotiated Chiang Mai Initiative provides the requisite mechanism. Currency speculators attempting to force an unwarranted devaluation would then have to contend with the reserves not only of the targeted country but also of its partners in the regional currency stabilization agreement.[30]

The problems with this solution are well known. Above all is the question of whether strong-currency countries would really be willing to

---

30. Although the collective reserves of the countries participating in the Chiang Mai Initiative are very large, they have committed only a share of these reserves under the swap lines of the initiative. In addition, the lines available to the individual participating countries are only a fraction of the collective swap lines, and in some cases, these lines amount to less than a few billion U.S. dollars, a drop in the bucket relative to the liquidity of international financial markets. See also the section on "Financial Options."

commit a significant fraction of their reserves to supporting weak partner currencies. In Europe, the commitment to collective currency pegs was strong and credible because intra-European trade is so extensive. Intra-Asian trade remains less important by comparison, as Williamson (1999) acknowledges. Moreover, even in Europe, the strong-currency country Germany obtained an opt-out from the provision of the EMS Articles of Agreement that obliged it to intervene without limit in support of its EMS partners, reflecting fears of the costs of unlimited interventions and what unlimited support might imply for its creditworthiness. A noteworthy point in this context is that participants in the Asian Swap Arrangement, the precursor of the Chiang Mai Initiative, can also opt out of that arrangement.[31] Asia's situation is, if anything, even more difficult than Europe's. Throughout its existence, the EMS was supported either by capital controls (before 1992) or by a fixed timetable for completing the transition to monetary union (after 1992). Capital controls limited speculative pressures and, thus, the need for intervention, whereas the commitment to complete the transition to monetary union by 1999, thereby anchoring exchange rate expectations, induced stabilizing speculation more powerful than that which can be provided by a simple commitment to pegged rates.

Above all, the EMS was buttressed by the set of interlocking political, economic, and financial commitments that make up what we now call the European Union. Europe had already established a customs union when the EMS was established. The European project was undergirded by a commitment to political integration, which was driven by the continent's two largest economies, France and Germany. Against this background, one had good reason to believe that member states would be prepared to support the currencies of their EMS partners.

Clearly, the same preconditions are not present in Asia. ASEAN is still struggling to establish a free trade area.[32] Its capital markets are already relatively open. Little appetite for political integration is apparent. There is

---

31. Opting out under "exceptional financial circumstances" was permitted from the inception of the Asian Swap Arrangement, and in 1992, the right to opt out became effectively unlimited (Henning 2002).

32. Some members remain reluctant to subordinate their industrial policies to the goal of regional free trade. In part, this reluctance to put free trade above other goals is indicative of the fact that the benefits of regional free trade are less than compelling as long as the free trade area does not encompass the three large economies of China, Japan, and Korea, not to mention Australia and New Zealand. Reflecting this realization, in November 2000, the leaders of the 10 ASEAN nations commissioned a study of the feasibility of linking their economies with those of China, Japan, and Korea.

no Beijing-Tokyo axis analogous to the axis between Paris and Bonn to push the process forward. As a result, Asia lacks the nexus of contracts that makes for credible currency commitments. If, as Xie and Yam (1999) suggest, Japan were to eventually move away from basing its security arrangements on the United States and create an Asian security system, then this problem would be solved, but at best, this possibility is a long-term prospect. These considerations suggest that a system of collective currency pegs would be fragile. Those with a preference for more graphic metaphors (and clichés) might call it an "engine of crisis" (or a "recipe for disaster").

But doesn't Asia's history suggest otherwise? In particular, hasn't Singapore succeeded in operating a currency band that successfully limits the fluctuation of its currency despite a commitment to open capital markets (Rajan and Siregar 2000)?[33] It has operated an undisclosed ("quiet") band system since 1975. It has limited the fluctuation of the Singapore dollar against a basket of currencies to within a narrow band.[34] One potential explanation for this success is that Singapore has come closest to adopting Williamson's recommendations for how to run an intermediate regime. It operates a "basket, band, and crawl" regime, creating a presumption that the authorities will normally intervene to keep the exchange rate from straying far from the band. At the same time, however, the authorities keep open the option of letting the rate take the strain by going outside the band if they decide that market pressures are overwhelming. The band is wide, which allows the rate to fluctuate in response to cyclical conditions. Singapore has avoided the mistake of targeting a single currency; in 2000–01, for example, it did not have to follow the U.S. dollar up against the euro and the yen. It has adjusted its band periodically in response to changing domestic and international conditions. The implication is that other countries can match this success if they adopt the same formula.

Others would put the emphasis not on the design of the currency band but on other characteristics of the economy. Singapore has been able to credibly commit to adjusting its monetary policy instruments to limit exchange rate fluctuations because it has had an impeccably strong banking and financial system. It has not had a large stock of nonperforming, short-term debts in the corporate sector. It has run fiscal and current account surpluses every year since 1989. It holds large reserves, equivalent to

---

33. Other counterexamples to the hypothesis such as China and Malaysia could be cited. But both countries have been aided in their efforts to peg their currencies by limits on capital inflows and outflows, something that is unlikely to be regarded as feasible and desirable elsewhere in the region.

34. On this history, see Monetary Authority of Singapore (2000). Patterson, Chong, and Eschweiler (2001) estimate that the width of the band is about 2 percent. The U.S. dollar, they estimate, has a weight in the basket of 52 percent, although the weight attached to other Asian currencies has been rising with time.

6–9 months of its imports. Because of its combination of strong growth and flexible labor markets (achieved through a system of variable bonuses), monetary policy adjustments designed to stabilize the exchange rate have not put undue strain on the economy. Because of Singapore's political stability, the commitment to hit those exchange rate targets has political support and, therefore, credibility.

How many other countries can satisfy these prerequisites for the credibility and viability of a monitoring band? Few countries have equally strong banking and financial systems. Few have equally able bank supervisors. Few have equally flexible economies. Few have comparable records of political stability. This review suggests that the answer to the preceding question is "not many."[35]

Then what alternatives remain? Monetary union, which would eliminate intra-Asian exchange rate instability by eliminating intra-Asian exchange rates, remains in the realm of social science fiction.[36] Although capital controls would greatly simplify the defense of a regional system of currency pegs, the region has little appetite for the reimposition of controls, China and Malaysia to the contrary notwithstanding.[37] Rather, governments see the liberalization of financial markets and the internationalization of banking systems as the best ways to solve their financial problems. These reasons all support the thinking that controls may become more difficult to operate in the future.[38]

---

35. This answer points to the question of whether Singapore itself can realistically expect to satisfy the demanding prerequisites for operating this regime in the future. The country may face an even more volatile economic environment in the future than in the past. Its politics may grow more contested. Authors such as Patterson, Chong, and Eschweiler (2001) have already suggested that these trends may force Singapore to move to a more flexible rate.

36. Of note, the Chinese appear reluctant to move to deep integration. As the Chinese Minister of Finance Xiang Huaicheng (Xiang 2001) recently put it, "Given diversified background in history, culture, and level of economic development, the East Asian countries must pursue regional cooperation in a gradual and orderly manner, taking into account their unique characteristics."

37. In particular, assessments of the effects of Malaysia's controls conflict. Kaplan and Rodrik (2001) and Edison and Reinhart (2001) conclude that the controls were effective in insulating the economy from the Asian financial crisis. Others (for example, Spencer 2001) are more critical on the grounds that the controls allowed the authorities to ease regulations on lending to "nonproductive" sectors, to weaken the definition of nonperforming loans, and to reduce capital requirements, which hardly encouraged them to put their financial problems behind them. Moreover, the controls prevented capital inflows that were needed to recapitalize the banking system.

38. Not only financial liberalization but also changes in financial technology (computerized trading, the proliferation of derivative financial instruments) will make capital controls more difficult to operate in the future. To be effective, these kinds of controls will have to be encompassing and draconian. And such measures are not something that residents, jealous of their financial freedom and increasingly able to make that preference known through the medium of democratic politics, are likely to tolerate.

Having ruled out all other options *ad seriatum,* the conclusion is that most Asian countries will move toward freer floating currencies.[39] But floating is not an operating strategy for monetary policy; rather, as one economist has put it, it is the absence of an operating strategy. What, then, should be put in its place? Although there are many possible alternatives to an exchange rate–based monetary policy operating strategy, the obvious one is inflation targeting. Inflation targeting is an operating strategy with four elements: (a) an institutionalized commitment to price stability as the primary goal of monetary policy; (b) mechanisms rendering the central bank accountable for attaining its monetary policy goals; (c) the public announcement of targets for inflation; and (d) a policy of communicating to the public and the markets the rationale for the decisions made by the central bank. Institutionalizing the commitment to price stability lends credibility to that objective and gives the central bank the independence needed to pursue it. Mechanisms for accountability make this pursuit politically acceptable, and they impose costs on central banks that are incompetent or opportunistic. Announcing a target for inflation and articulating the basis for the central bank's decisions allow these mechanisms to operate.[40]

What is the role of the exchange rate in inflation targeting? Exchange rate movements convey information about future inflation and unemployment. Thus, a central bank concerned about minimizing deviations in inflation and unemployment from their targets will respond by adjusting policy when the exchange rate moves. But it will not follow a rigid rule for altering policy when the exchange rate moves to the edge of a preannounced band. How it will respond to exchange rate movements will depend on why the exchange rate moved and what that movement implies for future output and inflation. Briefly, an inflation-targeting central bank will respond differently to exchange rate fluctuations depending on the source and nature of the shock that causes the exchange rate to move. Thus, inflation targeting does not involve benign neglect of the exchange rate, although it involves no longer organizing the country's entire operating strategy for monetary policy around a target level or range for the rate.

---

39. This view is similarly the argument of Corden (2002) and Goldstein (2002), who provide their own lists of particulars for how regimes such as these should be run.

40. The regime I am describing is flexible inflation targeting, not strict inflation targeting. Strict inflation targeting is when only inflation enters the central bank's objective function; flexible inflation targeting is when there is also a positive weight on other variables, for example, output. Under flexible inflation targeting, the central bank does not attempt to immediately return the actual inflation rate to its target under all circumstances, because doing so would create undue volatility in interest rates and output. Rather, it eliminates discrepancies between actual and target inflation gradually over time because it is adverse to sharp fluctuations in output.

What is the role of international cooperation in the operation of this regime? Agreeing on a common inflation target would be a small step in the direction of a common monetary standard (although it is no guarantee of exchange rate stability).[41] The availability of foreign credits and swaps could enhance the credibility of open-economy inflation targeting. When inflation rises temporarily but output falls, the central bank may be reluctant to raise interest rates to defend its inflation target at the cost of aggravating the recession. The availability of foreign credits may resolve this dilemma by financing foreign exchange market intervention that strengthens the exchange rate, thus supporting pursuit of the inflation target without requiring higher interest rates that are counterproductive from the point of view of the full employment target. In reality, the effectiveness of sterilized foreign exchange market intervention is limited in most emerging markets, where the bond markets in which intervention takes place are underdeveloped.

This last observation points to the main respect in which international cooperation can advance the operation of this monetary regime. Asian countries can cooperate in the development of the relevant financial markets. This cooperation not only will facilitate sterilized intervention but also will limit the disruptions caused by the active use of interest rates and the greater flexibility of exchange rates implied by inflation targeting. If countries develop long-term bond markets, the maturity mismatches and short-term exposures that cause financial distress when the interest rate changes will no longer be such a problem. If countries strengthen the management and supervision of domestic banks, the currency mismatches that cause exchange rate changes to provoke widespread bank failures will be less disruptive. In other words, financial stability and development are needed for the successful operation of any monetary regime. Hence, I turn to the implications of this observation.

FINANCIAL OPTIONS

Asian prospects would be enhanced if governments eschewed these efforts to stabilize exchange rates per se and, instead, concentrated on steps to promote financial stability and financial development in the region.

---

41. It is not a guarantee (a) because exchange rates, being asset prices, are more volatile than commodity prices; (b) because different economies will experience different shocks, leading the authorities to accept different amounts of inflation and, hence, different exchange rate movements; and (c) because different central banks will attach different weights to the various arguments in their objective functions.

The Problem

The 1997–98 crisis underscored the importance of buttressing financial stability and promoting financial development. Arguably, problems in the finance company sector were what rendered the Thai crisis so disruptive, and the run on Indonesia's banks was what transformed the depreciation of the rupiah into a full-blown financial panic. Had banks been better supervised and had financial markets been better regulated, the fallout from these currency adjustments would have been less. The output losses from involuntary exchange rate adjustments are smaller when depreciation is not accompanied by major financial sector problems.[42] In the presence of stronger banks and better-regulated financial markets, it follows that the effects of currency adjustments that eliminate misalignments are more likely to be positive.

Similarly, the underdevelopment of the bond markets that are the closest substitutes for bank-generated credit can be blamed for the exaggerated importance of bank financing that turned out to be the gap in the region's financial armor (Goldstein 1998). Securities markets are less conducive than banks to connected lending (securities exchanges being more anonymous) and to the use of finance as an instrument of industrial policy (securities markets being more decentralized and, therefore, difficult to guide). Thus, the development of decentralized, competitive, anonymous financial markets—especially the bond markets that are the most direct substitutes for bank financing—will strengthen market discipline and discourage governments from using financing to further nonfinancial ends, a practice that is incompatible with financial opening and liberalization.

In addition, banks tend to be too big and well connected to be allowed to fail, thus creating a moral hazard of which investors are acutely aware. In the first half of the 1990s, this awareness encouraged indiscriminate bank-to-bank lending that financed the accumulation in banking systems of dubious real estate loans (as in the case of Thailand) and industrial commitments (as in the case of Korea). Much of this foreign financing was short term, reflecting the absence of liquid markets in long-term debt instruments and the artificial incentives of the Basle Capital Accord for short-term, bank-to-bank lending.[43] Consequently, when a shock to

---

42. See, for example, Gupta, Mishra, and Sahay (2000) and Bordo and others (2001). Output losses are two to three times as large when currency crises are allowed to become twin crises (Kaminsky and Reinhart 1999).

43. The latter reflected the assumption of the framers of the accord, which proved erroneous, that short-term loans were less risky because they were more liquid, hence justifying the application of lower capital charges.

confidence caused this capital flow to reverse direction, the stability of entire national banking systems was placed at risk.

Had this money instead been mediated by the bond market, the result would have been different. In response to the shock to confidence, the prices of these assets and liabilities, and not merely their quantities, could have adjusted. Modest adjustments on several margins are easier to accommodate than major adjustments on one. Although the fall in bond and equity prices would not have been painless, it might not have produced as profound a threat to the stability of banking systems and financial markets generally as did the liquidation of bank-to-bank loans.

To contain these threats to stability, prosperity, and growth, Asian countries must secure financial stability and must promote the development of securities markets. A large literature points to the measures needed to achieve these ends.[44] Buttressing financial stability involves applying market discipline to financial institutions and strengthening prudential supervision. Intensifying market discipline, in turn, means removing implicit guarantees and opening banking to foreign competition. Moreover, upgrading prudential supervision means establishing independent supervisory and regulatory agencies; giving them dedicated budgets; ensuring that their employees are adequately trained and compensated; and empowering them to intervene when problems are detected, including, if necessary, giving them the power to reorganize or liquidate distressed intermediaries. Little controversy arises about the ingredients of this recipe, although the best way of blending those ingredients remains a matter of some controversy.

Similarly, how to effectively promote the development of deep and liquid financial markets is well understood in principle. Doing so presupposes the creation of a framework that fosters transparency and strengthens creditor rights. Mandating the prompt and effective dissemination of financial information by those issuing debt securities—something that can be done by adopting securities-market regulations requiring disclosure—will attenuate information asymmetries. In turn, this approach will limit the adverse selection and moral hazard that might otherwise stunt the growth of markets in these assets. But information in the absence of contract enforcement is not enough. In addition, effective creditor rights (in the form of restrictions on going into reorganization, laws mandating that secured creditors be paid first in the event of reorganization, and rules for whether management can stay in place after a reorganization) are needed to contain principal-agent problems that would otherwise discourage the

---

44. For a recent synthesis, see Caprio and Honohan (2001).

development of deep and liquid bond and equity markets (LaPorta and others 1998). Again, although controversy arises about how to best implement these measures, little disagreement is expressed about their desirability.

In the present context, two questions follow. First, does international cooperation have a role to play in advancing these policies? And, second, is there a role for cooperation at the regional level, particularly in Asia?

The arguments for international cooperation are familiar (see, for example, Wyplosz 1999). To the extent that financial crises spill across borders, financial stability has the character of an international public good. Governments will underinvest in providing this stability in the absence of international cooperation. Regulators will be reluctant to hold their banks to expensive capital and liquidity requirements in the absence of international cooperation, because those banks would then lose market share to more laxly regulated foreign competitors able to provide the same services for less. Regulators will be reluctant to require strict disclosure of financial information as a prerequisite for listing an issuer's securities on the local exchange, because the latter will then stand to lose business to exchanges with less stringent requirements. The Basle Capital Accord can be seen as an international response to the first of these problems, and the international standards of the International Organization of Securities Commissions, promulgated in cooperation with the IMF and the Financial Stability Forum, can be seen as an international response to the second.

Because the spread of financial instability and competition for market share do not respect regional borders, it is not obvious that such cooperation should be organized at the regional as opposed to the global level. If the externality is global, the response should be global. Additional rationales are thus needed to justify cooperation at the regional level. Two suggest themselves. First, the transactions costs that must be surmounted to arrange a cooperative response may be lower at the regional level because the number of participating governments is smaller and the countries involved are more cohesive (reflecting similar historical experiences, long-standing diplomatic relationships, or preexisting nonfinancial agreements). Thus, Fratianni and Pattison (2000) attribute the success of the BIS to the fact that, historically, it has been made up of a small number of members at similar stages of development.

Second, regional governments may share common problems, which encourages agreement. Asian countries all share, to one extent or another, problems of security-market underdevelopment, inadequate financial transparency, and bank-dominated financial markets, in turn reflecting the close historical connections between government and finance and the tendency for governments to use financial markets as an instrument of industrial policy.[45] To the extent that Asian governments are aware of these common problems, a regional arrangement is the obvious basis for organizing training programs and technical assistance as well as for promulgating internationally agreed standards for supervision and regulation.

The Solution

Recent initiatives suggest that Asian governments have come to recognize the urgency of addressing these issues. In 2002, three APEC teams began studying issues in capital market development. One of these groups is explicitly charged with framing recommendations for securitization and credit enhancement to improve the risk quality of Asian bonds. ASEAN+3 has formed six working groups to study various aspects of regional financial markets, including securitization, regional credit-rating agencies, regional clearing and settlement systems, and regional credit guarantee agencies. In an effort to jumpstart regional bond markets, the Executives' Meeting of East Asia–Pacific Central Banks (EMEAP) has set up an Asian Bond Fund, with contributions from the foreign reserves of each member bank, to invest US$1 billion in dollar-denominated bonds issued by qualified Asian issuers.[46] To further stimulate regional debt markets, the Korean government has tabled a securitization and guarantee scheme designed to stimulate a supply of high-grade credits to better match existing demand, and officials have given active consideration to proposals for the issuance of debt securities denominated in a basket of Asian currencies.[47]

In a companion paper (Eichengreen 2003), I suggest that these initiatives could be usefully complemented by the creation of an Asian Financial Institute, or AFI.[48] The preceding initiatives identify, in particular, inadequate scale and the inadequate supply of investment grade credits as the main obstacles to bond market development, and they seek to address these problems and encourage the creation of a pan-Asian bond market by focusing on currency and credit risk. In contrast, the AFI as I conceive it

---

45. Given the profound differences between the structure of the economies of either China and Korea or Singapore and Vietnam, this argument clearly should not be pushed too far.

46. Presumably, investments in the local-currency-denominated bonds of qualified Asian issuers will follow at some stage. At the time of writing, a second fund of up to US$1.5 billion for investment in Asian currency risk is under discussion.

47. On the Korean proposal for securitization and credit guarantee, see Oh and Park (2003), and on the Asian currency basket bond idea, see Ito (2003) and Olarn, Supapol, and Sangsubhan (2003).

48. More details on the proposal can be found in Eichengreen (2003).

would promote cooperation in addressing the problems of weak market infrastructure that have stymied financial market development at the national level. It would provide technical assistance to national agencies seeking to strengthen prudential supervision and regulation. It would run training programs for bank inspectors, securities and exchange commissioners, and accountants, enlisting students from all of its members, exploiting economies of scale and scope, and encouraging the efficient pooling of knowledge and expertise. It could be a venue for the negotiation (a) of common agreements on capital and liquidity requirements and regulatory processes intended to promote the stability of banking systems and (b) of standards for information disclosure, securities listing, and corporate governance designed to promote the development of regional financial markets. If one believes, with the present author, that the main obstacle to financial market development in Asia is not inadequate scale or an inadequate supply of investment grade credits but, rather, the underdevelopment of the relevant market and regulatory infrastructure, then a regional institute that applies peer pressure and lends expertise for the development of that infrastructure has a role to play.

To be sure, efforts to apply peer pressure and to provide expertise for the development of stronger financial infrastructure are also under way at the global level. For example, a host of relevant standards and codes are already being promulgated by, among others, the Basle Committee of Banking Supervisors (in the case of capital adequacy for international banks); the Financial Stability Forum (in the case of prudential supervision and regulation); the IMF (in the case of data dissemination, transparency, and codes of conduct for monetary and fiscal policies); and the Organisation for Economic Co-operation and Development (in the case of corporate governance). But having the AFI organize negotiations on the design of a distinct set of regional financial standards appropriate to Asia's circumstances would address concerns that global standard-setting initiatives are not sensitive to the special features of the Asian model.

What might this distinct set of Asian financial standards, sensitive to the economic structure, history, and traditions of the region, look like? How might Asian financial standards differ from the analogous global standards? For example, Asian standards might have fewer and looser restrictions on portfolio concentrations. In many Asian countries, industrial development involves a prominent role for large conglomerates and industrial groups, which draw their external financing from a small number of closely allied banks. This development model implies that portfolio concentrations that are relatively large by international standards may be a necessary corollary of economic development. But allowing claims on individual borrowers to constitute a larger share of individual bank portfolios in turn implies greater financial risk and the need for capital requirements higher than those required by the Basle Committee.

I have chosen this example to illustrate that a distinctive Asian approach to prudential supervision and regulation need not be more lax than that mandated by global financial standards. Looser restrictions in one area, portfolio concentrations, could be offset by tighter restrictions in another, capital requirements. With the appropriate combination of measures, there is no reason why the Asian approach would necessarily be incompatible with the relevant global standards. Clearly, a regional approach to coordinating prudential supervision and regulation would serve no purpose if it amounts simply to setting looser standards than those promulgated globally. The argument for a distinctive Asian approach is not that Asia can afford worse financial regulation than the rest of the world, but that it may wish to attain the same standards of safety, stability, and efficiency in different ways. Thus, a regional approach to financial standard setting must be consistent with its global analog while still possibly differing in its particulars in ways that speak to Asia's special needs.

How would the AFI advance this Asian approach? First, it would take input from the national regulators and other authorities of the participating countries. Those same national authorities would be responsible in the first instance for implementing and monitoring compliance with those standards. In addition, however, the AFI would monitor the compliance of its members and would discipline violators with public announcements and perhaps, ultimately, financial penalties.

In addition, the AFI could provide central banking services. It could serve as a mechanism for coordinating monetary, fiscal, financial, and regulatory policies to promote the development of financial markets in the region while discouraging governments from pursuing strategies that promised to grow their financial markets at the expense of the markets of their neighbors. And under exceptional circumstances, it might provide emergency assistance, in the form of credits and swaps, to countries with financial difficulties that threaten to undermine financial stability and development in the affected country and its neighbors.[49]

In fact, this recommendation is not the first time that such an entity has been proposed. In 1995, Bernie Fraser, then the governor of the Reserve Bank of Australia, suggested establishing an Asian version of the BIS to carry out some of these functions.[50] The institution Fraser envisaged would have been responsible for exchanging information with respect to

---

49. However, one could also imagine establishing an AFI that did not possess a lending capacity.
50. His initiative can be understood as a response to the instability that followed the Mexico crisis of December 1994. It lost steam when the BIS responded preemptively by expanding into Asia.

international financial and monetary policies and for developing contingency plans for dealing with financial crises. It was also expected to offer a venue for sharing information and experience with respect to supervision and surveillance of financial systems and to provide central banking services to member central banks. Still, Fraser's vision was more modest than that described here. In particular, the promulgation and enforcement of standards, regulations, and policies for promoting financial stability and development, which would be among the key functions of the AFI, were not among the responsibilities of the Asian BIS enumerated by Fraser.

More recently, Bergsten (2000a, 2000b) proposed creating an APEC Financial Institute. He advocated the creation of an institution to provide training to bankers, auditors and accountants, lawyers and credit raters, and supervisors and regulators throughout the region.[51] But although Bergsten's motivation is similar, the responsibilities of the institution he envisages would again be more limited than those of the AFI proposed here. Bergsten's institute would provide training, not lending. It would not coordinate regulatory functions. It would not promulgate and monitor compliance with standards. The contrast is not surprising: APEC's heterogeneous membership (including Australia, Canada, New Zealand, and the United States, among others) is not obviously compatible with standard-setting, monitoring, and lending functions expressly tailored to Asia's needs.

ASEAN+3 is a logical organizational basis for the AFI envisaged here. ASEAN+3 is an organization of Asian countries. It already is in the business of providing technical assistance: at the Fourth ASEAN Finance Ministers' Meeting (in March 2000), ASEAN+3 finance ministry and central bank deputies agreed to establish a network of research and training institutions. Since 1998, the association has conducted regional surveillance exercises in the context of the ASEAN Surveillance Process, the purpose of which is to further cooperation in the formulation of monetary, fiscal, and financial policies through information exchange, peer review, and recommendations for action at the regional and national levels. That surveillance process is informed by all members providing the ASEAN Surveillance Coordinating Unit (SCU), which is based in the ASEAN Secretariat in Jakarta, with the same data provided to the IMF in conjunction with its article IV consultations and program negotiations. Although financial assistance (under the provisions of the Chiang Mai Initiative) may be provided in response to the conclusions of this regional surveillance exercise,

---

51. These are realistic ambitions, Bergsten argues, because the new Asian regionalism is proceeding more rapidly on finance than on trade, which is the opposite of the European model. This sequencing is logical, it can be argued, because the Asian crisis was a financial crisis.

this assistance is contingent, as noted elsewhere in this chapter, on the recipient government meeting the conditions set down by the IMF. Thus, folding the Chiang Mai Initiative and the ASEAN Surveillance Process into the AFI would help ensure that the activities of the new AFI were co-ordinated and compatible with those of the Bretton Woods institutions.

Creating an AFI on the platform of ASEAN+3 and housing within it the subscriptions and swap lines of the Chiang Mai Initiative would have the corollary benefit of removing ambiguity about the purposes of the initiative. Those purposes would be clearly defined as furthering the goals of the AFI (namely, fostering financial stability and development, not stabilizing exchange rates). Whether fixed or flexible exchange rates were more conducive to financial stability and development would then be recognized as a separate question.

Might not some other regional grouping provide a better basis for this initiative? The APEC Finance Ministers' Process is not suitable because it involves a larger and even more heterogeneous group of countries, and its concrete achievements have been limited so far to the creation of training programs and seminars on topics such as financial regulation, risk management, and credit analysis. The same is true of the Manila Framework Group, which does not even possess a permanent secretariat, a permanent staff, or dedicated funding. Although EMEAP has among its objectives regional surveillance, the exchange of information, and the promotion of financial market development, its meeting schedule is irregular, and those meetings have lacked coherence and continuity.[52] Firm surveillance, peer pressure, and constructive criticism feature no more prominently in its discussions than in those of ASEAN. The SEANZA (Southeast Asia, New Zealand, and Australia) Group of central banks has many of the same limitations from this point of view.[53]

---

52. EMEAP was organized in the early 1990s with leadership from Japan and Australia. Its members are the Southeast Asian and Australasian members of SEANZA: Australia, China, Hong Kong (China), Indonesia, Japan, Korea, Malaysia, New Zealand, the Philippines, Singapore, and Thailand. There are annual meetings of EMEAP central bank governors, semi-annual meetings of the deputy governors, and working groups concerned with banking supervision, financial markets, and payments and settlement systems.

53. SEANZA grew out of a 1956 meeting of central bank governors from the Asia-Pacific region. The governors agreed that the central banks of the region should pool their resources to provide training courses for promising central bank staff members (the first of which was held in 1957). An offshoot, SEACEN (South East Asian Central Banks), was then established in the 1980s as a training and research organization. The SEANZA Forum of Banking Supervisors was established in 1984 as an additional subsidiary of the main SEANZA Group. The forum was intended to allow for the exchange of information on issues and problems of common interest. More recently, special-purpose regulatory agencies have joined the central banks in this forum. However, the inclusion of a number of smaller Asia-Pacific countries makes it unwieldy for regional cooperation.

An alternative to building an AFI on the foundation of the ASEAN Surveillance Process and the Chiang Mai Initiative is to expand the responsibilities of the Asian Development Bank (ADB). The ADB is already in the business of providing advice on, among other issues, policies for promoting financial development. It already provides technical assistance to governments participating in the ASEAN Surveillance Process and publishes an *Asian Development Outlook* that resembles the *World Economic Outlook* and is integral to the IMF surveillance process. In the same manner that the IMF and the World Bank have organized financial stability reviews, might it not be logical for Asian countries to encourage the ADB to carry out similar functions?

The ADB has not demonstrated the capacity to efficiently carry out an expanded set of functions. In addition, the United States, the larger European countries, a number of Central Asian republics, and some of the micro states of the Pacific are members of the ADB, which would complicate using it as a platform for Asian coordination.[54] The ADB's charter explicitly states that it shall give preference to the smaller countries of the region, a mandate that is not obviously consistent with these other functions.

Alternatively, might not the AFI be established by an entirely new grouping of Asian countries, separate from ASEAN, APEC, SEANZA, EMEAP, and the others? This group could be made up of countries committed to financial openness (leaving out any that prefer to opt for capital controls) and to market-based banking systems (leaving out those that are reluctant to privatize state banks) as well as those at comparable levels of financial development (leaving out the poorest countries with the least developed financial systems). Asian countries that were initially left out could opt in once they met these preconditions. The greater homogeneity of economic structures would allow the development of more detailed standards for prudential supervision and more effective policies for financial development. But limiting initial participation in this way would do less to apply effective peer pressure to those countries that were furthest from best practice to upgrade their arrangements. It would do less to address the special needs of the poorest countries and to create a zone of financial stability encompassing all of Asia.

Moreover, creating yet another regional grouping would only compound the alphabet soup problem—the proliferation of overlapping arrangements that robs regional initiatives in Asia of their coherence.

---

54. The United States is not only a member but also the largest shareholder, along with Japan.

Although folding the AFI into an existing institution does not solve this problem, resisting the temptation to create yet another self-standing grouping can at least prevent making it worse. It will prevent adding another regional surveillance round, for example, to existing ASEAN and APEC surveillance exercises. In addition, there are reasons to think that folding the AFI into an existing regional organization such as ASEAN would enhance the effectiveness of the new institution because the commitments made by AFI members would then become intertwined with the other commitments of ASEAN members.

Alternatively, might these duties not be better discharged by a global institution like the Bank for International Settlements, which has extensive experience relevant to cooperative agreements on the supervision of financial institutions and the regulation of financial markets? The BIS has recently taken on some new Asian members, thus indicating that it recognizes the existence of this market niche. But many Asian policymakers will regard this response as inadequate for the same reasons that they see the IMF as failing to fully meet regional needs. The BIS is dominated by the large Western economies. Its decisions are unlikely to be tailored to the imperatives of the Asian model. Because it is a club of high-income countries, its standards and services are not well suited to the needs of the Lao People's Democratic Republic, Myanmar, the Philippines, or Vietnam. It is in the business of coordinating the supervision of well-developed banking systems and the regulation of well-developed financial markets, not of designing policies to advance the development of those markets where they do not exist.

CONCLUSIONS

This chapter has considered the case for more extensive economic policy cooperation in Asia. It has attempted to push the debate forward by drawing a distinction between monetary cooperation and financial cooperation and by arguing that the case for financial cooperation to strengthen the supervision of banking systems and the development of financial markets is stronger than the case for monetary cooperation to stabilize intra-Asian exchange rates. Exchange rate fluctuations in and of themselves are not the principal threat to financial stability. A clearer and more pressing danger is the inadequate supervision of banking systems and the chronic underdevelopment of equity and, especially, bond markets. On the one hand, cooperation to stabilize exchange rates would be a diversion at best and a costly mistake at worst. On the other hand, cooperation in strengthening banking systems and in promoting the development of bond markets would go a long way toward creating a zone of economic and financial stability.

This perspective has led me to propose the creation of an Asian Financial Institute on the platform of ASEAN+3. The AFI would develop guidelines for the prudential supervision of banking systems and for policies of financial development—guidelines and policies that would be consonant with the Asian model. Its regional surveillance would monitor the compliance of members with those standards and policy guidelines. It would pressure governments that failed to meet its standards and comply with its guidelines. It would provide technical assistance for countries that found it difficult to meet these standards on their own. And in the event of financial difficulties that threatened to derail financial development in a country and destabilize its neighbors, it could provide emergency swaps and credits through the Chiang Mai Initiative.

The case for an AFI on the platform of ASEAN+3 presupposes positive answers to a series of difficult questions. First is the question of what would permit cooperation in developing and monitoring a distinct set of Asian financial standards from leading to overly permissive supervision and regulation. One could imagine a result in which the AFI simply gave aid and comfort to those working to defer rather than to force adjustment.[55] It would be particularly important to address this danger were the Chiang Mai Initiative's swap lines folded into the AFI and used to assist countries experiencing temporary financial difficulties. In part, this problem can be contained by making clear that the development of a separate set of regional guidelines for prudential supervision and regulation does not relieve the participating countries from their obligations to global standards but only helps them meet those obligations in different ways that are better attuned to their particular circumstances. In other words, the Asian financial standards promulgated by the AFI would be counterproductive if they were simply looser than the analogous global standards. But they could serve a useful role if they gave member countries guidance on how to most efficiently meet those standards in ways consistent with their economic and financial structures. In addition, the fact that the vast majority of the credits available to participating countries under the initiative can be drawn only when a country has an agreement with the IMF provides some reassurance that this financing would not be used simply to avoid adjustment.[56]

---

55. This issue is obviously related to the question, raised in the preceding discussion, of whether ASEAN's relatively ineffectual surveillance process can be strengthened.

56. This point suggests further the desirability of not changing this arrangement, as has been suggested by some of the participating governments (see below).

This brings us to the question of whether and how the AFI could fit into the global framework. The mandate of the AFI must make clear that any financial standards it promulgates and financial development strategies it promotes should not conflict with those promulgated and promoted at the global level. The AFI would have to be seen by its members as helping them meet those standards in a fashion consistent with their own special circumstances, not as helping members evade those standards. Coordination is needed not only on targets but also on assessments of compliance. Unlike the Manila Framework Group, where the presence of the IMF as technical secretariat encourages the compatibility of regional surveillance activities with those of the IMF, the ASEAN Surveillance Process includes no comparable arrangement. ASEAN possesses its own Surveillance Coordinating Unit, as noted above. But the understanding that members will provide the SCU with the same information they provide the IMF in conjunction with article IV surveillance and program negotiations is no guarantee that the IMF and the SCU will draw the same conclusions. The two institutions might offer inconsistent, incompatible assessments of performance and recommendations for action, undermining the credibility of one another's advice. This possibility suggests a need to build bridges between the SCU and the IMF and to involve the latter in the AFI's surveillance exercises.[57]

A final question—raised in the earlier discussion but worth repeating— is whether separate regional standards and strategies for prudential supervision and financial development would have significant value added. Is there really a case for distinct Asian financial standards and development strategies, or would efforts such as these at the regional level simply duplicate initiatives and strategies already under development globally? In this chapter, I have suggested some respects in which prudential regulation and financial development strategies might be tailored to Asia's tastes and needs. But are these and other differences between the "Asian way" and ongoing global efforts in these areas substantial enough to justify a major investment in building new institutions of Asian financial cooperation? This question is the one to which advocates of broader Asian financial cooperation must provide a detailed and convincing answer before the ambitious efforts at regional cooperation that they envisage deserve to go ahead.

---

57. The same issues arise in connection with the capital-adequacy standards of the Basle Committee of Banking Supervisors, the broader standard-setting agenda spearheaded by the IMF, and the financial development advice and activities of the World Bank. In each case, the danger is that the AFI's initiatives could be inconsistent with those of its global counterparts, undermining the credibility of all involved. It is essential, therefore, to build in mechanisms for the exchange of views between the AFI and these global bodies.

REFERENCES

Bergsten, C. Fred. 2000a. "Why APEC Needs Revitalizing." *Asia Inc.* 9(6):30–31.

———. 2000b. "A Shanghai Asia Pacific Financial Institute." Institute for International Economics, Washington, D.C. Processed.

———. 2000c. "Towards a Tripartite World." *The Economist*, July 15, pp. 23–26.

BIS (Bank for International Settlements). 2001. *71st Annual Report.* Basel.

———. 2002. *72nd Annual Report.* Basel.

Bordo, Michael, Barry Eichengreen, Daniela Klingebiel, and Maria Soledad Martinez-Peria. 2001. "Is the Crisis Problem Growing More Severe?" *Economic Policy* 32:51–82.

Calvo, Guillermo, and Carmen Reinhart. 2000. "Fear of Floating." NBER Working Paper 7993. National Bureau of Economic Research, Cambridge, Mass.

Caprio, Gerald, and Patrick Honohan. 2001. *Finance for Development.* Washington, D.C.: World Bank.

Corden, W. Max. 2002. *Too Sensational: On the Choice of Exchange Rate Regimes.* Cambridge, Mass.: MIT Press.

Crosby, Mark, and Glenn Otto. 2001. "Growth and the Real Exchange Rate: Evidence from Eleven Countries." Hong Kong Institute for Monetary Research Working Paper 8/2001 (August), Hong Kong Institute for Monetary Research, Hong Kong, China.

Dieter, Heribert. 2000. "Monetary Regionalism: Regional Integration without Financial Crises." CSGR Working Paper 52/00 (May). Centre for the Study of Globalisation and Regionalisation, University of Warwick, Warwick, U.K.

Dooley, Michael. 1997. "A Model of Crises in Emerging Markets." NBER Working Paper 6300 (December). National Bureau of Economic Research, Cambridge, Mass.

Edison, Hali, and Carmen Reinhart. 2001. "Stopping Hot Money." *Journal of Development Economics* 66(2):533–53.

Eichengreen, Barry. 2002. *Financial Crises and What to Do about Them.* Oxford, U.K.: Oxford University Press.

———. 2003. "What to Do with the Chiang Mai Initiative." *Asian Economic Papers* 2:1–49.

Eichengreen, Barry, and Douglas Irwin. 1995. "Trade Blocs, Currency Blocs, and the Reorientation of Trade in the 1930s." *Journal of International Economics* 38(1–2):1–24.

Frankel, Jeffrey, and Andrew Rose. 2002. "An Estimate of the Effect of Currency Unions on Trade and Growth." *Quarterly Journal of Economics* 117(2):437–66.

Fratianni, Michele, and John Pattison. 2000. "An Assessment of the Bank for International Settlements." In International Financial Institution Advisory Commission, *Expert Papers.* Washington, D.C.: Government Printing Office.

Goldstein, Morris. 1998. *The Asian Financial Crisis.* Washington, D.C.: Institute for International Economics.

———. 2002. *Managed Floating Plus.* Washington, D.C.: Institute for International Economics.

Gupta, Poonam, Deepak Mishra, and Ratna Sahay. 2000. "Output Response during Currency Crises." International Monetary Fund, Washington, D.C. Processed.

Harrigan, James. 2000. "The Impact of the Asia Crisis on U.S. Industry: An Almost-Free Lunch?" *Economic Policy Review* (Federal Reserve Bank of New York) 6(3):71–81.

Hausmann, Ricardo, Ugo Panizza, and Ernesto Stein. 2000. "Why Do Countries Float the Way They Float?" IDB Working Paper 418 (May). Inter-American Development Bank, Washington, D.C.

Henning, C. Randall. 2002. *East Asian Financial Cooperation.* Washington, D.C.: Institute for International Economics.

Hernandez, Leonardo, and Peter J. Montiel. 2001. "Post-Crisis Exchange Rate Policy in Five Asian Countries: Filling in the 'Hollow Middle'?" International Monetary Fund, Washington, D.C. Processed.

Ito, Takatoshi. 2003. "Promoting Asian Currency Basket (ABC) Bonds." Paper presented to the Voluntary Working Group Meeting of the Asian Bond Market Initiative, Tokyo, June 17.

Ito, Takatoshi, Eiji Ogawa, and Yuri Sasaki. 1998. "How Did the Dollar Peg Fail in Asia?" *Journal of the Japanese and International Economies* 12(4):256–304.

Japan. 2001. "Exchange Rate Regimes for Emerging Market Economies." Paper jointly prepared by French and Japanese staff members for the ASEM Finance Ministers' Meeting, Kobe, Japan. Available on-line at http://www.mof.go.jp/english/asem/aseme03i2.htm.

Kaminsky, Graciela, and Carmen Reinhart. 1999. "The Twin Crises: The Causes of Banking and Balance of Payments Problems." *American Economic Review* 89(3): 473–500.

Kaplan, Ethan, and Dani Rodrik. 2001. "Did the Malaysian Capital Controls Work?" NBER Working Paper 8142 (February). National Bureau of Economic Research, Cambridge, Mass.

Kawai, Masahiro, and Shigeru Akiyama. 2001. "The Currency Crisis and Exchange Rate Arrangements in Emerging East Asia." World Bank, Washington, D.C. Processed.

Kwan, C. H. 2001. *Yen Bloc: Toward Economic Integration in Asia.* Brookings Institution: Washington, D.C.

LaPorta, Rafael, Florencio Lopez-de-Silanes, Andrei Schleifer, and Robert Vishny. 1998. "Law and Finance." *Journal of Political Economy* 106:1133–55.

McKinnon, Ronald. 2001. "After the Crisis, the East Asian Dollar Standard Resurrected: An Interpretation of High-Frequency Exchange Rate Pegging." In Joseph E. Stiglitz and Shahid Yusuf, eds., *Rethinking the East Asian Miracle.* New York: Oxford University Press.

McKinnon, Ronald, and Huw Pill. 1999. "Exchange Rate Regimes for Emerging Markets: Moral Hazard and International Overborrowing." *Oxford Review of Economic Policy* 14:19–38.

McKinnon, Ronald, Kenichi Ohno, and Kazuko Shirono. 1997. "The Syndrome of the Ever-Higher Yen, 1971–95: American Mercantile Pressure on Japanese Monetary Policy." SIEPR Policy Paper 487. Stanford University, Stanford, Calif.

Monetary Authority of Singapore. 2000. "A Survey of Singapore's Monetary History." Occasional Paper 18 (January). Economic Department, Monetary Authority of Singapore. Processed.

Moreno, Ramon. 2001. "Pegging and Macroeconomic Performance in East Asia." *ASEAN Economic Bulletin* 18:48–62.

Oh, Gyutaeg, and Jae-Ha Park. 2003. "Fostering an Asian Bond Market Using Securitization and Credit Guarantee." Paper presented at the ASEAN+3 Informal Session of

Finance Ministers and Central Bank Deputies on Fostering Asian Bond Markets, Tokyo, February.

Olarn, Chaipravat, Bhasu B. Supapol, and Kanit Sangsubhan. 2003. "Regional Self-Help and Support Mechanisms: Beyond the CMI." Paper submitted to the ASEAN Secretariat, Kuala Lumpur.

Patterson, Rebecca, Hui Chin Chong, and Bernhard Eschweiler. 2001. "The Singapore Dollar Basket Unpacked." *Asian Markets Outlook and Strategy* (e-mail newsletter, J. P. Morgan, Singapore), August 2, pp. 3–6.

Rajan, Ramkishen S., and Reza Siregar. 2000. "The Vanishing Intermediate Regime and the Tale of Two Cities: Hong Kong versus Singapore." Policy Discussion Paper 0031 (July). Centre for International Economic Studies, Adelaide University, Australia.

Rose, Andrew K. 1998. "Limiting Currency Crises and Contagion: Is There a Case for an Asian Monetary Fund?" University of California, Berkeley. Processed.

Sachs, Jeffrey D. 1985. "External Debt and Macroeconomic Performance in Latin America and Asia." *Brookings Papers on Economic Activity* 2:525–74.

Spencer, Michael. 2001. "Malaysia's Return to Normalcy." *Asia Economics Weekly* (Deutsche Bank, Hong Kong), January 29, pp. 2–4.

Williamson, John. 1998. "Crawling Bands or Monitoring Bands: How to Manage Exchange Rates in a World of Capital Mobility." *International Finance* 1:59–80.

———. 1999. "The Case for a Common Basket Peg for East Asian Currencies." In Stefan Collignon, Jean Pisani-Ferry, and Yung Chul Park, eds., *Exchange Rate Policies in Emerging Asian Countries.* London: Routledge.

Wilson, Dominic. 2000. "Managing Capital Flows in East Asia." In Peter Drysdale, ed., *Reform and Recovery in East Asia.* London: Routledge.

Wyplosz, Charles. 1999. "International Financial Instability." In Inge Kaul, Isabelle Grunberg, and Marc A. Stern, eds., *Global Public Goods.* New York: Oxford University Press.

Xiang, Huaicheng. 2001. "Speech on Regional Cooperation." Paper presented at the ASEM Finance Ministers' Meeting, Kobe, Japan, January 14. Available on-line at http://www.mof.go.jp/english/asem/aseme03i3.htm.

Xie, Andy, and Denise Yam. 1999. "East Asia: Is Asian Monetary Union Possible?" *Global Economic Forum* (Morgan Stanley Dean Witter), February 11. Available on-line at http://www.ms.com.

CHAPTER 3

TRADE AND FOREIGN DIRECT INVESTMENT: A ROLE FOR REGIONALISM

Eisuke Sakakibara and Sharon Yamakawa

The case for preferring financial cooperation to monetary cooperation in East Asia has been argued in chapter 2. Other dimensions of regional cooperation, especially related to trade, have also been instrumental in the development of economies worldwide. Although cooperation in many of these dimensions has not occurred as rapidly or as deeply in East Asia as in other regions, the cooperation that has occurred has nonetheless played a significant role in the political stability and economic growth of the region.

At different times in history, there have been a variety of motivating factors for cooperation in East Asia. The first of these factors was political, culminating in the formation of the Association of Southeast Asian Nations (ASEAN) in the 1960s. Progress in European and North American integration in the early 1990s acted as a catalyst for ASEAN's formation of the ASEAN Free Trade Area (AFTA). The financial crisis of 1997–98 provided the impetus for the financial cooperation that led to the implementation of the Chiang Mai Initiative. Japan's decade-long economic stagnation has also been a factor, in that it has affected the patterns of trade, investment, and official development assistance (ODA) in the region.

A new motivating factor is now emerging, and that is China. Most countries in the region see cooperation with China as preferable to competition with the growing economic giant, and this view could lead to even higher levels of cooperation in all areas—political, economic, and financial and monetary.

We would like to acknowledge the support of others in the preparation of this paper. In particular, we would like to thank Shuichi Shimakura and Eri Moriai for data support and Catherine Sasanuma and Shunichi Sueyoshi for their contributions to the research on regional institutions.

Many East Asians desire a regional identity, and this desire is motivating both the drive for a zone of stability referred to by Eichengreen in chapter 2 and the drive for a stronger voice in dealings with the industrial countries of the West as globalization marches inexorably forward. Many in the region prefer to be less dependent on the West, particularly on the United States, and see regionalism as a way to achieve more self-reliance. In addition, East Asia recognizes the benefits in trade, foreign direct investment (FDI), and financing that the European Union (EU) has derived from its deep integration. Although the process of integration would undoubtedly differ in East Asia, the region naturally desires a similar outcome.

Trade and FDI have played major roles in the development of the region. The phenomenal growth of the 1980s and the early 1990s has been attributed to East Asia's liberalization in trade and FDI. These two areas interact in a mutually promoting way. The importance of this link has grown with the increased integration of international production networks. Together, the trade-FDI link and integration of production networks create a synergy that facilitates the efficient functioning of the entire system. Furthermore, the potential for growth is enhanced when there is coordination in the formulation of trade and FDI policies.

In this chapter, we will examine trade and FDI in East Asia from the perspective of regionalism. The goal is to determine what role, if any, regional cooperation can play in the promotion of trade and FDI as contributors to regional prosperity. We will see that there are both global and intraregional elements in East Asia's trade and FDI, and that both of these elements are important to the continued development of the region. Given that situation and the trend in the region to seek regional solutions to common issues, we will suggest two regionally focused approaches to the promotion of trade and FDI: regional agreements and regional production networks.

The organization of this chapter is as follows. First, we present a brief review of trade and FDI links and their effect on growth and development. Then we assess the degree of openness in East Asia's trade and FDI at present. Next we review the trade and FDI patterns of the region, focusing on their intraregional and global aspects. Finally, we examine roles for regionalism in the promotion of trade and FDI in East Asia and make some concluding remarks.

TRADE AND FOREIGN DIRECT INVESTMENT LINKS

In recent years, the link between trade and FDI has generated intense interest in the international community. The link has been discussed at length in major reports produced by international organizations such as the United Nations Conference on Trade and Development (UNCTAD), the World Trade Organization (WTO), and the Organisation for Economic Co-operation and Development (OECD), as well as in other studies.[1] The common debate on this issue centers on whether trade leads to FDI or vice versa and whether trade and FDI are substitutes or complements. In fact, the interrelationship between the two is quite complex, varying by product, by economic sector, and across countries. In other words, the interrelationship depends on the type of FDI and the location and developmental level of the countries concerned.

For example, in the case of natural resources (resource-seeking FDI), trade often leads to FDI, which in turn supports (or creates) trade. If this type of FDI exploits the same competitive advantages as the firms in the host economy do, it will most likely reinforce the existing export patterns of that economy. If this type of FDI exploits different resources than firms in the host economy do, it can change export patterns. In manufacturing (export-oriented manufacturing FDI), existing advantages can be reinforced (for example, when low-cost labor is used to make clothing for export) or changed (for example, through the introduction of new technologies, skills, brand names, and networks).[2] Thus, it appears that trade leads to FDI (eventually), and then FDI leads to more trade (UNCTAD 1996, chapter 3; 1999, section II; 2001, p. 58).

However, the evolution of international production networks suggests that this conclusion is no longer accurate. The issue is no longer one of whether trade leads to FDI or FDI leads to trade, or whether FDI substitutes for or complements trade or the other way around. According to UNCTAD,

> Rather, it is: how do firms access resources—wherever they are located—in the interest of organizing production as profitably as possible for the national, regional or global markets they wish to serve? In other words, the

---

1. See UNCTAD's *World Investment Report* series and other reports; the WTO Working Group on the Relationship between Trade and Investment Web site at <http://www.wto.org/wto/english/tratop_e/invest_e/invest_e.htm>; and OECD (2002). Also, see Brainard (1997), Feenstra and Hanson (1996), Fukasaku and Kimura (2002), Goldberg and Klein (1997), Hanson (2001), Kleinert (2000), Markusen and Venables (1998), and Urata (2001), among others. Some of these are reviewed in OECD (2002).

2. Japan represents a good case of how outward FDI can change the structure of both exports and imports of both host and home countries through international production. Over the course of about 10 years (through 1999), "reverse imports" (imports from Japanese parent firms' affiliates abroad) as a share of total imports have risen from 4 to 15 percent, and these imports are increasing faster than the exports of the parent firms. Also, the composition of Japan's imports is changing: the share of machinery and equipment imports—mostly electrical and electronics machinery—has risen from 17 to 31 percent over the same 10 years (UNCTAD 2002c, p. 46).

issue becomes: where do firms locate their value-added activities? In these circumstances, the decision where to locate is a decision where to invest and from where to trade. And it becomes an FDI decision, if a foreign location is chosen. It follows that, increasingly, what matters are the factors that make particular locations advantageous for particular activities, for both domestic and foreign investors. (UNCTAD 1996, p. xxiv)

Trade and FDI are becoming more tightly linked in today's international production system, and they function together as the machinery that enables the system to operate. And, increasingly, multinational corporations (MNCs) are the facilitators of this process. The growth in size and operation of MNCs has been phenomenal. According to UNCTAD (2003b, pp. 3, 222–23), in 2002 the 866,119 foreign affiliates of the 63,834 MNCs worldwide accounted for one-tenth of world gross domestic product (GDP) and one-third of world exports, and they employed more than 53 million people, more than double the number in 1990.[3] The coverage of MNCs has broadened to include the whole range of manufactured exports, from low- to high-technology goods as well as services. Because MNCs have integrated international and regional production strategies, they can locate production largely wherever they choose. Different activities can be located in different countries and regions in order to take advantage of lower costs, better resources, faster transportation, and bigger markets.[4] The connection between trade and FDI is thus intensified and, for countries in which production is located, opportunities for trade based on comparative advantage can increase.

Both trade and FDI are well recognized today as facilitators of growth and development. They affect development separately and directly as well as indirectly through their interrelationship. Capital, technology, management expertise, training for the local work force, and access to wider markets are some of the benefits that FDI can bring to host countries. These benefits can complement the resources and capabilities of the host country, thereby increasing its export competitiveness (UNCTAD 2002c, chapter 6). Export competitiveness is a key element in the promotion of economic development, in that it can result in (a) increased foreign exchange earnings, which can be used to import the products, services, and technologies necessary for increasing productivity and living standards; (b) diversification away from primary commodity exports toward higher

---

3. Generally, data are as of 2002, although the date differs for some countries and data are unavailable for others.

4. This situation is also referred to as *fragmentation*. See Arndt and Kierzkowski (2001) for a discussion of this topic.

technology exports; (c) better realization of economies of scale through larger and more diverse markets; (d) exposure to higher standards; and (e) easier access to information (UNCTAD 1999, p. 18; 2002c, pp. xx–xxi).

There are, of course, situations in which these potential benefits are not realized in the host country. MNCs may concentrate solely on a host country's static comparative advantages and never develop the dynamic ones. They may fail to build links to the domestic business community. They may not bring high-level technologies or training to the local labor force. They may depart suddenly if conditions in the host country are perceived to have changed so that they no longer meet the MNC's criteria for operating there.[5]

Still, the relationship between global FDI flows and the growth of world GDP can be characterized as a stable and positive one.[6] The overall conclusion of recent studies is that FDI contributes positively to both income growth and factor productivity in host countries, although the precise magnitude of the contribution is difficult to determine.[7] Growth is affected by an increase in total factor productivity or an increase in efficiency in the use of resources in the host country.[8] These increases occur through "the linkages between FDI and foreign trade flows, the spillovers and other externalities vis-à-vis the host country's business sector, and the direct impact on structural factors in the host economy" (OECD 2002, p. 68). Some of these studies found that FDI "crowds out" domestic investment, but others found the opposite to be true. Some even found that "crowding out" could have an overall beneficial effect if scarce domestic funds are released as a result.[9]

---

5. See UNCTAD (2002c, pp. 152–53) for a further discussion of these and other possible negative consequences of FDI.

6. During 1971–2000, the correlation between the FDI and GDP growth rates was 0.3. Similarly, a simple regression of FDI inflows against GDP during the same period is as follows:

FDI inflows = $-190.9 + 0.0251$ (GDP). $R^2 = 0.75$, adjusted $R^2 = 0.55$, and the t-value of GDP coefficients = 6.0 (UNCTAD 2002c, p. 22).

7. "Recent studies" refers to 16 recent empirical studies that examined the effect of FDI on growth of income and productivity and that are reviewed and discussed in OECD (2002, chapter 3). This literature review focuses primarily on four questions: "1) Does FDI significantly affect the rate of growth of income or productivity? 2) Does FDI 'crowd out' or 'crowd in' domestic investment? 3) Do technology and knowledge spillovers take place in the domestic economy?, and 4) Are there any necessary preconditions (e.g., human capital, technological, or financial market development) for these positive effects to materialise?" (OECD 2002, p. 66). The studies covered, the specific questions addressed, the estimation techniques, and the major findings are presented in table III.1 on pages 70–74 of the OECD's report.

8. See Urata (2001) for more on this point.

9. For more on "crowding out," see UNCTAD (2003b, p. 105).

Attracting and reaping the benefits of FDI requires a certain level of development in education, technology, infrastructure, and financial markets. More specifically, macroeconomic stability, institutional predictability, fiscal discipline, efficient and equitable tax systems, prudent public sector debt management, strong domestic financial systems, developed capital markets, transparency, openness to foreign trade, and an educated work force are desirable for this purpose. Creating this enabling environment, in many cases, requires policy changes on the part of national governments (OECD 2002, pp. 27–32).

The links between trade and FDI and their combined effect on growth and development make it necessary for policies in these two areas to support each other in terms of objectives and efficient implementation. Ignoring this need for mutually supportive policies can lead to weakening of the developmental contribution of each area, whereas acting on it can lead to synergies that can further promote growth and development (UNCTAD 1996, p. 73). The importance of this coordination increases as the international production system becomes more integrated.

Many policies for the promotion of trade and, particularly, for the promotion of FDI are developed and implemented at the national level.[10] For some countries, particularly less industrialized countries, a national approach can be difficult because of the lack of knowledge and skills in making policy related to foreign investment and in negotiating and implementing treaties and agreements (OECD 2002, p. 35). In such cases, a regional or multilateral approach can often work better.

Before suggesting a regional approach for the promotion of trade and FDI in East Asia, in the next two sections we assess the region's regional and multilateral profile in these two areas. Examining certain indicators will help determine the region's degree of openness to, and integration with, the global economy.

OPENNESS IN TRADE AND FDI

Both trade and FDI have been significantly liberalized in what the World Bank refers to as the "third wave of integration (or globalization)" (World Bank 2002, p. 326). This "third wave" began in the 1980s and

---

10. Export-processing zones (EPZs) constitute one example of consistent trade and FDI policies at the national level. EPZs include "free-trade zones, duty-free zones, free-investment zones, [and] offshore zones." Activities performed in EPZs include "bonded warehousing, export processing, assembling, border or port trade, and financial services. However, despite these variations, export-oriented manufacturing has been the main focus of most zones" (UNCTAD 2002c, p. 214).

Table 3.1 Openness and Global Integration Indicators

Country or region	Trade				Capital flows			
	Trade in goods[a] % of GDP		Simple mean tariff[b] All products (%)		Gross private capital flows[d] % of GDP		Gross FDI[e] % of GDP	
	1990	2001	1988[c]	2001[c]	1990	2001	1990	2001
Cambodia	22.4	91.7	n.a.	n.a.	3.2	6.2	1.7	3.3
Indonesia	41.5	60.1	22.0	8.4	4.1	6.5	1.0	3.2
Lao PDR	30.5	50.4	n.a.	9.4	3.7	1.4	0.7	1.4
Malaysia	133.4	184.0	17.0	9.2	10.3	6.6	5.3	5.7
Philippines	47.7	88.9	28.0	7.0	4.4	42.0	1.2	2.7
Singapore	309.5	277.6	0.5	0.0	54.6	60.2	20.7	22.0
Thailand	65.7	110.9	38.5	17.0	13.5	9.1	3.0	3.5
Vietnam	79.7	93.6	12.7	15.0	n.a.	7.6	n.a.	4.0
China	32.5	44.0	41.2	15.3	2.5	10.4	1.2	4.9
Hong Kong, China	223.5	242.8	0.0	0.0	n.a.	97.0	n.a.	28.8
Japan	17.1	18.2	6.0	5.1	5.4	12.3	1.7	1.1
Korea	53.4	69.1	18.8	8.7	5.6	11.4	0.7	1.5
Canada	43.7	70.1	8.6	4.5	8.1	21.5	2.7	9.6
Mexico	32.1	54.2	13.4	16.2	9.2	7.9	1.0	4.6
United States	15.8	19.0	5.6	4.0	5.7	11.7	2.8	3.1
East Asia and Pacific	47.0	61.0	n.a.	n.a	5.0	11.1	1.7	4.6
Europe (EMU or EU)[f]	44.9	56.3	3.7	3.9	14.1	49.3	2.9	14.8

n.a. Not applicable.

Note: EMU = European Monetary Union; EU = European Union.

a. Sum of merchandise exports and imports divided by the value of GDP, all in current U.S. dollars.

b. Simple mean tariff is the unweighted average of the effectively applied rates for all products subject to tariffs.

c. Actual year varies by country between 1988 and 1994 for year 1988 and between 1997 and 2001 for year 2001.

d. Sum of absolute values of direct, portfolio, and other investment inflows and outflows recorded in the balance of payments financial account, excluding changes in assets and liabilities of monetary authorities and general government.

e. Sum of absolute values of inflows and outflows of FDI recorded in the balance of payments financial account. This indicator differs from the standard measure of FDI, which captures only inward investment.

f. Source provides the data in this table only for the EMU (not the EU), except for tariff data, which is for the EU.

Source: World Bank (2003, table 6.1, pp. 310–12, and table 6.6, pp. 326–28).

has progressed since then by virtue of transportation and communications technology, declining tariffs, and lower barriers to FDI. East Asia has ridden the crest of this wave, as shown by the indicators in table 3.1.

Trade expansion is an indication of the level of openness of an economy, as measured by the ratio of total trade (imports and exports) to GDP.

As a region, East Asia and the Pacific has a considerably higher trade-to-GDP ratio (61 percent in 2001) than do the European Monetary Union (EMU) and the North American Free Trade Agreement (NAFTA).[11] There is a significant difference in the level of this ratio among the developing East Asian economies, with Singapore and Hong Kong, China, at the high end, reflecting their roles as entrepôts, and China at the low end, reflecting the slower opening of its economy.

Another indicator of openness in trade is import tariffs, which have been reduced significantly over the past decade, largely because of regional and global trade arrangements.[12] In the early 1990s, the import tariffs of East Asian economies—with the notable exceptions of Hong Kong (China), Japan, and Singapore—were much higher than those of the European Union and those applicable under NAFTA. The higher tariffs reflect the region's developing-country status, as well as the earlier trade liberalization of the European Union and the NAFTA countries.[13] By 2001, however, average tariffs in East Asia had declined sharply, particularly in the ASEAN-4 countries (Indonesia, Malaysia, the Philippines, and Thailand), partly because of progress under AFTA and the Bogor Declaration of the Asia-Pacific Economic Cooperation (APEC).[14] As a result of China's preparations for WTO accession, its average tariff dropped from 41.2 percent in 1992 to 15.3 percent in 2001 for all products (primary and manufactured).

The level of private capital flows into a country indicates the strength of its investment climate and reflects the degree of liberalization of its

---

11. The World Bank (2003) provides this ratio for the EMU, rather than the European Union. Note that in table 3.1, ratios are shown separately for Canada, Mexico, and the United States.

12. Import tariffs may be imposed to obtain fiscal revenues as well as to protect certain domestic industries from foreign competition. Nontariff barriers, such as quotas, prohibitions, and licensing schemes, are also used for protection, but they are not included here because of the difficulty of combining them into an aggregate indicator.

13. Although tariffs were reduced significantly after the completion of the Uruguay round in 1993, average import-weighted tariffs fell to about 2.6 percent for high-income countries but only to 13.3 percent for developing countries (World Bank 2001, p. 316).

In table 3.1, Mexico's tariff appears to have risen over the past decade, but, in fact, this rise occurred fairly recently. Mexico raised most of its most-favored-nation import tariffs by 3 to 10 percentage points in 1999 to generate additional revenue for the government, and these surcharges were retained for 2000. These increases, however, did not apply to countries that had signed free trade agreements with Mexico (USTR 2000, p. 284).

Although NAFTA was not signed until 1994 and the European Union was not officially established until 1995, the participating countries had been making efforts toward liberalizing trade long before then (particularly in the case of the European Union).

14. AFTA allows the newer ASEAN members a longer period of time than older members to reduce their tariffs.

financial markets. Table 3.1 shows that in 2001 the ratio of private capital flows to GDP for East Asia and the Pacific was 11.1 percent, which is nearly the same as that of the United States but well below that of the EMU (49.3 percent). The ratio is skewed by the very high ratios of Hong Kong (China) and Singapore, which have well-developed financial markets. The ratios for most other countries in the region, however, are very low, reflecting their less developed financial markets and the prolonged effect of the 1997–98 financial crisis.

The most important capital flows for developing countries, including East Asia, are FDI flows. As financial openness has led to a doubling of FDI relative to GDP globally over the past two decades, the East Asia and Pacific region has been the beneficiary of the largest growth, with its FDI:GDP ratio more than doubling between 1990 and 2001 (World Bank 2003, p. 309). In 2001 and 2002, the Asia-Pacific region led all regions in the number of policy changes designed to create a more favorable investment climate for FDI, making it one of the fastest-liberalizing host regions in the world (UNCTAD 2002c, p. 7; 2003b, p. 40).

East Asia's liberalized trade and FDI were instrumental in the region's growth in the 1980s and early 1990s. During that time, East Asia had opened up to other types of private capital flows (non-FDI), which eventually led to the 1997–98 crisis, because countries in the region were ill prepared to cope with the volatility of these types of flows. The crisis brought to an abrupt end the earlier burst of super growth, discouraged foreign investment, and caused countries in the region to become wary of such investment. Yet these countries still recognize the importance to economic growth of remaining open to trade and FDI.

PATTERNS OF TRADE AND FDI: GLOBAL AND INTRAREGIONAL

East Asia has a history of openness and integration that continue today.[15] However, the data and discussion in the preceding section do not reveal the intraregional and global mix of trade and FDI in the region. This mix can be determined through an examination of trade and investment patterns over the past decade or so.

Trading Patterns

East Asia has experienced tremendous growth in trade over the past two decades, with imports increasing more than fivefold and exports more

---

15. For a review of this historical legacy, see chapter 1 in Sakakibara and Yamakawa (2003a).

than sixfold between 1980 and 2001, reaching US$1.393 billion and US$1.527 billion, respectively. Since 1990, both imports and exports have more than doubled. The growth in imports and exports for both ASEAN and ASEAN+3 (the ASEAN countries plus China, the Republic of Korea, and Japan) mirrors that of the region in both periods.[16]

We will use two measures to analyze East Asia's trade. The first measure is trade share, which indicates the magnitude of trade of one country with another, is easy to calculate, and is commonly used in general discussions of trading affiliations but has a number of shortcomings (discussed later). The second measure is the trade intensity index (TII), which is a more complex measure in terms of its calculation as well as the information it provides. It gives a clearer, more accurate picture of the trading patterns of countries and regions than does the trade share measure. Using these two measures, we will look at current trading patterns and how they have evolved over the past two decades.

Trade Shares

The snapshot of East Asia's trade shares in table 3.2 reveals both the global and the intraregional nature of the region's trade. Reflecting their global aspect, all ASEAN countries reported more than 10 percent of their trade (imports, exports, or both) to be with the European Union and the United States in 2001. Even the smallest nations conduct a significant amount of trade with these two extraregional partners; for example, 64 percent of Cambodia's exports were to the United States and 25 percent were to the European Union. Nearly all East Asian countries also have significant trade with one or more regional partners, with Japan being a major partner for most, followed by Singapore, China, and a few other larger regional countries.

The regional and global trading patterns of East Asian countries have shifted over time, as revealed in table 3.3, which displays the trade shares of selected economies in 1980, 1990, and 2001.

Japan was ASEAN's primary trading partner in both imports and exports in the 1980s. However, this trade relationship weakened between 1990 and 2001, with the share of imports from Japan dropping by 6 percentage points between 1990 and 2001 and the share of exports dropping by 16 percentage points between 1980 and 2001. ASEAN's imports were, of course, negatively affected by the East Asian crisis; however, the post-crisis rate of decline in the dollar value of imports from Japan was greater than the rate of decline in ASEAN's total imports. Although the dollar

---

16. The data source is the International Monetary Fund's Direction of Trade Statistics. The data include the ASEAN+3 countries plus Hong Kong (China) and Taiwan (China).

Table 3.2 Import and Export Shares, 2001 (percent)

Country or regional group	BRU		CAM		CHN		HK		IDN		JPN		KOR		LAO		MYS		MYN		PHL		SGP		TWN		THA		VNM	
	IMP	EXP	IMP	EXP	IMP	EXP	IMP	EXP	IMP	EXP	IMP	EXP	IMP	EXP	IMP	EXP	IMP	EXP	IMP	EXP	IMP	EXP	IMP	EXP	IMP	EXP	IMP	EXP	IMP	EXP
Japan	4.6	46.5	1.4	1.0	17.6	16.9	11.3	5.9	18.2	20.9	—	—	18.9	11.0	1.8	1.4	19.2	13.3	7.6	3.3	20.6	15.7	13.0	7.5	24.1	10.4	22.4	15.3	11.8	17.4
Korea	1.4	12.4	3.4	0.1	9.6	4.7	4.5	1.8	9.3	6.3	4.9	6.3	—	—	1.0	0.0	4.0	3.4	9.5	1.7	6.6	3.2	3.1	3.7	6.3	2.7	3.4	1.9	11.5	2.6
China	1.4	4.1	6.0	1.3	—	—	43.4	36.9	8.0	5.4	16.6	7.7	9.4	12.1	8.3	1.7	5.2	4.3	20.4	4.4	3.2	2.5	5.8	4.3	5.5	3.9	6.0	4.4	12.0	6.8
Hong Kong	4.2	0.0	8.0	0.4	3.9	17.5	—	—	2.4	2.1	0.4	5.8	0.9	6.3	1.4	0.0	2.6	4.6	2.6	0.9	4.3	4.9	2.2	8.6	1.7	21.9	1.3	5.1	3.6	1.8
Taiwan	1.0	0.0	5.4	0.4	11.2	1.9	6.9	2.4	4.2	3.5	4.1	6.0	3.0	3.9	0.4	0.9	5.7	3.7	7.0	0.9	5.4	6.6	4.0	5.0	—	—	4.2	2.9	11.4	2.8
Brunei	—	—	—	—	0.1	0.0	0.0	0.0	0.0	0.0	0.5	0.0	0.3	0.0	—	—	0.0	0.3	0.0	0.0	0.0	0.0	0.1	0.3	0.0	0.0	0.6	0.1	0.0	0.0
Cambodia	—	—	—	—	0.0	0.1	0.0	0.1	0.0	0.0	0.0	0.0	0.0	0.1	—	—	0.0	0.1	—	—	0.0	0.0	0.0	0.3	0.0	0.1	0.0	0.7	0.2	0.7
Indonesia	2.0	0.8	0.7	0.1	1.6	1.1	0.7	0.4	—	—	4.3	1.6	3.2	2.2	0.1	0.2	3.0	1.8	2.6	0.8	2.6	0.4	6.3	2.7	2.4	1.2	2.2	2.1	2.2	1.8
Lao PDR	—	—	—	—	0.0	0.0	0.0	0.0	0.0	0.0	0.0	0.0	0.0	0.0	—	—	0.0	0.0	—	—	0.0	0.0	0.0	0.0	0.0	0.0	0.1	0.6	0.7	0.6
Malaysia	22.7	0.2	1.3	0.8	2.5	1.2	2.5	0.9	4.4	3.1	3.7	2.7	2.9	1.8	3.0	0.0	—	—	8.1	2.6	3.1	3.5	16.2	16.9	3.9	2.5	5.0	4.2	3.1	2.1
Myanmar	0.0	0.0	—	—	0.1	0.2	0.1	0.1	0.4	1.1	0.1	0.3	0.0	0.2	—	—	0.1	0.2	0.3	0.1	0.0	0.0	0.1	0.3	0.3	0.1	1.8	0.5	0.4	1.9
Philippines	0.3	0.0	0.2	0.3	0.8	0.6	1.0	1.0	0.4	1.1	1.8	2.0	1.3	1.7	—	—	2.5	1.5	—	—	—	—	2.1	2.5	3.0	1.7	1.8	1.8	0.4	1.8
Singapore	34.1	5.0	27.4	2.2	2.1	2.2	4.6	2.0	9.7	10.9	1.5	3.6	2.1	2.7	4.0	0.0	12.6	16.9	17.4	3.7	6.1	7.2	—	—	3.1	3.3	4.6	8.1	14.0	5.7
Thailand	3.1	10.6	34.6	0.6	1.9	0.9	1.7	1.0	3.9	1.9	3.0	2.9	1.1	1.2	62.2	19.2	4.0	3.8	—	—	3.0	4.2	4.2	4.2	2.0	1.7	—	—	5.3	2.2
Vietnam	0.2	0.0	7.6	1.9	0.4	0.7	0.1	0.3	0.8	0.6	0.7	0.4	0.3	1.2	11.8	25.1	0.4	0.5	—	—	0.9	0.2	0.7	1.7	0.4	1.4	0.5	1.2	—	—
ASEAN	62.4	16.5	71.8	5.9	9.5	6.9	10.8	5.8	19.3	17.8	15.6	13.5	11.3	11.0	78.5	44.5	22.6	25.1	43.2	33.7	15.8	15.5	29.7	29.0	14.9	12.2	16.2	19.3	25.9	15.1
ASEAN+3	69.8	79.4	82.6	8.3	36.7	28.5	70.0	50.4	54.8	50.4	37.1	27.4	39.6	34.1	89.5	47.6	51.0	46.1	80.7	43.1	46.2	37.0	51.6	44.5	50.8	29.1	48.0	40.9	61.1	41.9
APEC	85.8	98.1	97.5	74.2	71.0	72.8	85.5	78.8	75.0	76.4	69.3	74.7	67.3	70.6	93.5	50.2	78.6	78.6	92.0	63.2	77.9	78.7	76.2	76.5	75.0	77.1	67.8	71.9	82.5	62.8
EU	12.6	1.5	1.9	24.8	14.7	15.4	9.7	14.5	11.5	13.8	12.8	16.0	10.6	13.1	4.3	25.6	12.9	13.6	3.0	14.4	9.3	19.3	11.1	13.0	11.7	14.7	12.2	16.1	10.5	26.8
CER	2.0	6.9	0.1	0.1	2.5	1.5	1.0	1.3	5.4	3.2	4.7	2.2	4.4	1.6	1.2	0.2	2.6	2.7	1.1	0.4	3.0	0.8	2.1	2.9	3.2	1.3	2.6	2.4	2.7	8.2
U.S.	8.6	11.6	1.2	64.2	10.8	20.4	6.7	22.3	7.1	15.3	18.3	30.4	15.9	20.9	0.6	0.9	16.0	20.2	0.5	16.4	16.9	28.0	15.5	15.0	17.0	22.5	11.6	20.3	3.1	7.6

— Not available.

Note: APEC = Asia-Pacific Economic Cooperation; ASEAN = Association of Southeast Asian Nations; ASEAN+3 = ASEAN countries plus China, the Republic of Korea, and Japan; BRU = Brunei; CAM = Cambodia; CER = Closer Economic Relations trade agreement countries; CHN = China; EU = European Union; HK = Hong Kong, China; IDN = Indonesia; JPN = Japan; KOR = Korea; LAO = Lao People's Democratic Republic; MYN = Myanmar; MYS = Malaysia; PHL = Philippines; SGP = Singapore; THA = Thailand; TWN = Taiwan, China; U.S. = United States; VNM = Vietnam. Table reads as trade share of a country in the top row with a partner country in the left-hand column; e.g., starting top left, Brunei's exports to and imports from Japan as a percentage of Brunei's total trade. Singapore does not report its trade with Indonesia to the IMF; therefore, Singapore's trade with Indonesia is estimated using Indonesia's data.

Source: Authors' calculations using data from IMF (2002).

Table 3.3 Trade Shares, Selected Economies and Selected Years (percent)

Trade partner	ASEAN Imports 1980	1990	2001	ASEAN Exports 1980	1990	2001
Japan	21.1	23.0	17.0	29.2	18.9	13.2
Korea	1.6	3.1	4.8	1.5	3.3	3.6
China	2.6	2.9	6.1	1.0	1.8	4.4
ASEAN	17.8	16.3	23.8	18.2	19.6	23.2
ASEAN+3	43.1	45.3	51.7	49.9	43.7	44.5
APEC	63.4	71.2	75.8	72.7	73.6	75.8
CER	3.5	3.1	2.7	2.8	2.1	2.8
EU	13.8	15.4	11.4	12.6	15.7	14.9
U.S.	14.5	14.4	13.3	16.1	19.4	18.0

Trade partner	Japan Imports 1980	1990	2001	Japan Exports 1980	1990	2001
Japan	—	—	—	—	—	—
Korea	2.2	5.0	4.9	4.1	6.1	6.3
China	3.1	5.1	16.6	3.9	2.1	7.7
ASEAN	17.5	12.7	15.6	10.4	11.6	13.5
ASEAN+3	22.7	22.9	37.1	18.4	19.8	27.4
APEC	51.1	61.3	69.3	53.0	67.6	74.7
CER	5.6	6.0	4.7	3.1	2.8	2.2
EU	6.5	16.1	12.8	15.2	20.4	16.0
U.S.	17.4	22.5	18.3	24.5	31.7	30.4

Trade partner	China Imports 1980	1990	2001	China Exports 1980	1990	2001
Japan	26.5	14.1	17.6	22.2	14.3	16.9
Korea	—	0.4	9.6	—	0.7	4.7
China	—	—	—	—	—	—
ASEAN	3.4	5.8	9.5	6.6	6.4	6.9
ASEAN+3	29.9	20.2	36.7	28.8	21.4	28.5
APEC	64.4	64.8	71.0	60.7	73.1	72.8
CER	6.3	2.7	2.5	1.4	0.8	1.5
EU	15.8	16.7	14.7	13.7	9.6	15.4
U.S.	19.6	12.1	10.8	5.4	8.2	20.4

Trade partner	Korea Imports 1980	1990	2001	Korea Exports 1980	1990	2001
Japan	26.3	26.6	18.9	19.2	19.4	11.0
Korea	—	—	—	—	—	—
China	0.1	—	9.4	0.0	—	12.1
ASEAN	6.7	7.3	11.3	6.6	7.8	11.0
ASEAN+3	33.0	33.9	39.6	25.7	27.3	34.1
APEC	61.5	66.8	67.3	60.9	70.3	70.6
CER	3.4	4.4	4.4	1.5	1.7	1.6
EU	7.6	13.0	10.6	16.7	15.4	13.1
U.S.	21.9	22.1	15.9	26.4	29.9	20.9

Note: See table 3.2 note for description of acronyms. Table reads as trade share of a country/region in the top row with a partner in the left-hand column.

Source: Authors' calculation using IMF *Direction of Trade Statistics Yearbook* (various years).

value of exports to Japan more than doubled over the past two decades, this increase did not keep pace with the growth rate of ASEAN's total exports, which rose nearly sixfold over that time. By contrast, intra-ASEAN trade shares appreciated quite considerably between 1980 and 2001 and ASEAN's trade shares with China and the Republic of Korea also showed marked improvement.[17]

The proportion of Japan's trade with the United States and the European Union, although still prominent, has declined since 1990, while the proportion of its trade with ASEAN and China has risen. The United States remains Japan's primary trading partner, with imports from that country making up 18 percent of Japan's total imports, and exports from the United States making up 30 percent of Japan's total exports. More remarkable, however, is that the dollar value of Japan's imports from China has risen nearly fivefold since 1990—to US$58 billion in 2001—and now makes up 16.6 percent of Japan's total imports, surpassing the share of imports from the European Union (12.8 percent) and from ASEAN (15.6 percent). Japan's exports to China are only 7.7 percent of its total exports, but this share continues to increase.

As for China's imports, Japan supplies the largest share (17.6 percent in 2001), among ASEAN, Korea, the European Union, and the United States. Since 1990, Japan, Korea, and ASEAN shares of China's imports have increased but EU and U.S. shares have decreased. In exports from China, the U.S. share has risen dramatically since 1980 to reach 20 percent in 2001, surpassing the shares of Japan and the European Union. This outcome is a complete reversal of the share pattern in 1980, when exports from China to the United States made up the smallest share (5 percent), and exports to Japan made up the largest share (22 percent). This situation reflects improved relations between the United States and China over the past 20 years, as well as the fact that U.S. and EU MNCs are moving production to China and exporting from there.

Korea's trade shares have also shifted markedly over the past 20 years, and although Japan retains the position of largest import share partner, the proportion of imports from that country has declined significantly. The shares of imports from the European Union and the United States have also declined since 1990, while those from China and ASEAN have risen significantly. A similar pattern is evident for Korea's export shares;

---

17. The higher share of intra-ASEAN trade relative to the shares of trade with nongroup partners does not necessarily mean that ASEAN is trading more intraregionally than externally. Given the shortcomings of the trade share measure, we will reserve judgment on this until we look at the trade intensity index.

that is, the shares of exports to Japan, the European Union, and the United States have become smaller, and the shares of exports to China and ASEAN have become much larger, so that the shares for each of these five partners approached parity in 2001, except for the U.S. share, which is still somewhat larger.

Intraregional Trade Shares

In table 3.3 we saw a marked increase in intra-ASEAN trade share over the past decade. This consequence of a significant rise in intraregional trade is supported by the two measures shown in table 3.4, which cover a broader spectrum of East Asian countries over a longer period of time. The absolute measure places a group's intraexports in the context of total world exports, reflecting the degree of importance of its intraregional trade in

Table 3.4 Intraregional Trade: Merchandise Exports within Regional Group

Regional group	Absolute measure[a] (% of world exports)					
	1980	1990	1996	1998	2000	2001
APEC	19.1	27.1	33.2	32.1	35.4	33.8
ASEAN	0.7	0.9	1.6	1.3	1.6	1.5
ASEAN+3	3.7	4.6	7.2	5.5	7.0	6.7
All East Asia[c]	4.6	7.8	12.7	10.5	12.6	11.8
EU	24.3	29.5	24.1	22.7	22.2	22.9
NAFTA	5.4	6.8	8.3	9.7	10.6	10.4
	Relative measure[b] (% of group's total exports)					
APEC	57.9	68.3	71.9	69.7	73.1	72.6
ASEAN	18.2	19.6	25.1	21.5	23.6	23.2
ASEAN+3	29.3	27.0	36.7	28.7	33.8	34.0
All East Asia[c]	33.7	40.3	50.2	42.9	47.7	47.7
EU	60.8	65.9	61.4	57.0	62.1	61.3
NAFTA	33.6	41.4	47.6	51.7	55.7	55.5

Note: NAFTA = North American Free Trade Agreement. See table 3.2 note for description of other acronyms. Service exports are excluded. Although data have been calculated back to 1980 on the basis of current group membership, most of the groups came into existence in later years and their membership may have changed over time. Intratrade in earlier years may not have been affected by the same preferences (as set forth in preferential arrangements) as in recent years.

a. Absolute measure is the sum of exports by members of a group to other members of the group as percent of world exports.

b. Relative measure is the sum of exports by members of a group to other members of the group as percent of total exports by the group.

c. All East Asia includes ASEAN plus Japan, Korea, China, Hong Kong (China), and Taiwan (China). Taiwan is not included in 1980 and 1990 data.

Source: For APEC, EU, and NAFTA, World Bank (2003); for all others, authors' calculations using data from IMF (2002) for the years 2000 and 2001 and earlier Direction of Trade Statistics Yearbooks for prior years.

total world trade. The relative measure places a group's intraexports in the context of the group's own total exports, reflecting the degree of importance of its intraregional trade relative to its extraregional trade.[18]

The patterns (both among regions and for each region over time) are similar for both measures. First, since the middle of the past decade, APEC has had the largest intraexport share of both world exports and its own total exports, followed in order by the European Union, all East Asia or the NAFTA signatories, ASEAN+3, and ASEAN.[19] Second, the fluctuations in the importance of each group's intraregional trade in both world trade and its own trade have generally followed the same pattern over the past two decades.

Intraregional trade for East Asian groups and for NAFTA generally increased in importance relative to both world trade and each group's own trade over the past 10 to 20 years. The European Union, however, is exceptional in that it experienced a decline in intraregional trade after 1990, although that trade has remained fairly stable for the past few years. This situation is noteworthy, considering that the European Union is the region that has become the most integrated during that time.[20]

These results, however, do not indicate that a group's trade is biased in favor of group members. Trade share as a measure of trade has certain shortcomings—primarily that the share size of a trading group is a direct reflection of the number of countries in the group and of the trading volume of those countries; that is, shares are larger for large groups of high-volume-trade countries and smaller for small groups of low-volume-trade countries.[21] Furthermore, the larger the group is, the larger a country's share in that group.[22] Thus, in order to assess the level of

---

18. Petri (1993) refers to these as measures of regional interdependence. Frankel (1997, chapter 2) also discusses these measures.

19. For the absolute measure, all East Asia's share is the third largest and the NAFTA signatories' share is the fourth; for the relative measure, the opposite is true, except in 1996.

20. Because data back to 1980 have been calculated on the basis of current group membership, these increases do not reflect the actual addition of members.

21. This situation is reflected clearly in table 3.4. The table shows that APEC, with its 21 members and its large-volume traders—such as Hong Kong (China), Japan, Singapore, and the United States—has a larger share in both world trade and its own trade than do the NAFTA countries, which are only three, or ASEAN, with its mostly small-volume traders.

22. For example, in table 3.2, exports from Hong Kong, China, to ASEAN are only 6 percent of total trade, but exports from Hong Kong, China, to APEC are 79 percent of total trade. This situation does not necessarily mean that Hong Kong, China, trades more intensively with the countries of APEC than with the countries of ASEAN, but rather that there are more and larger trading countries in the APEC group than there are in ASEAN. See Frankel (1997) for a further discussion of this topic.

East Asia's intraregional trade accurately, we need to know not only the magnitude of intraregional trade of the countries in the region but also whether members of the region trade more intensively with one another than they do with those outside the region. A measure that has been developed to adjust for the shortcomings of trade shares and that comes closer to revealing the true nature of intraregional trade is the TII.[23]

Trade Intensity Index

The TII is used to determine the actual intensity of one member's trade with another member of the same group or, in other words, the bias within a group of members to trade with one another.[24] Table 3.5 shows TIIs for merchandise for East Asian countries in 2001.

Most of the countries shown in table 3.5 have indices above 1.0 with 10 or more regional partners, indicating that their trade with these partners is above the normal level of trade, based on their trade with the rest of the world. Only the smaller countries, such as Cambodia, Lao People's Democratic Republic, and Myanmar, have intense relationships with just a few partners. Singapore has an intense trading relationship with the largest number of countries in the region, followed closely by Malaysia, Thailand, and Korea. Compared with previous years, some economies, including China, Taiwan (China), and Vietnam, have a greater number of regional partners with whom the indices are above 1.0.[25]

Our earlier trade share analysis led us to conclude that the trade of East Asian countries with the United States and the European Union is quite significant. This conclusion was supported by the TII in the case of the

---

23. See Drysdale and Garnaut (1993) for more in-depth analysis of trade using other indices, including the complementarity and bias indices.

24. This measurement is made by adjusting the trade shares of a country or group through some measure of that country's or group's importance in world trade. More specifically, it is the "ratio of the share of a country's exports with another country to the share of that other country in world imports. A number greater than one indicates that a country exports to another country at a greater level than the other is importing from the rest of the world, and a more 'intense' bilateral trading relationship" (de Brouwer 2002, pp. 290, 292).

A number of variations of this index include the "double-relative" measure of Petri (1993) and the "corrected concentration ratio" of Frankel (1997). The ratio used here is that presented in Anderson and Norheim (1993), de Brouwer (2002), and Drysdale and Garnaut (1993). Others have used similar versions of the index—for example, Goto and Hamada (1994); Goto and Kawai (2001); and Yamazawa, Hirata, and Yokota (1991). Rajan and Sen (2002) also calculate this ratio for imports.

25. See Sakakibara and Yamakawa (2003b, p. 13) for this index for 1995–97 and 1998–2000. The equation used to calculate the index for the earlier periods is the same as that used in this chapter, but there may be slight differences in raw data used in the calculations among the three periods. The results, however, are largely comparable. [Error correction: In table 4.5 in Sakakibara and Yamakawa (2003b), the indices for Thailand and Taiwan (China) with each other should be reversed.]

Table 3.5 Trade Intensity Index, 2001

Country	Country															Regional group						
	BRU	CAM	CHN	HK	IDN	JPN	KOR	LAO	MYS	MYN	PHL	SGP	THA	TWN	VNM	ASEAN	ASEAN+3	APEC	EU	NAFTA	CER	USA
BRU	—	—	1.1	0.0	1.3	8.5	5.6	—	0.1	0.0	0.0	2.6	11.0	0.0	0.0	3.1	4.7	2.0	0.0	0.5	5.5	0.6
CAM	—	—	0.3	0.1	0.1	0.2	0.0	—	0.7	—	0.7	1.1	0.6	0.2	7.5	1.1	0.5	1.5	0.7	2.6	0.1	3.5
CHN	0.3	3.3	—	5.4	1.7	3.0	2.1	1.7	1.0	4.3	1.3	1.1	0.9	1.1	2.5	1.2	2.1	1.6	0.4	0.9	1.2	1.1
HK	1.3	5.8	9.4	—	0.7	1.1	0.8	0.4	0.7	0.8	2.1	1.0	1.0	1.4	1.1	1.0	2.9	1.7	0.4	0.9	1.0	1.2
IDN	2.1	0.6	1.4	0.7	—	3.8	2.8	0.0	2.7	2.6	2.3	5.6	2.0	2.1	2.3	3.7	3.1	1.6	0.4	0.7	2.6	0.8
JPN	0.6	0.5	1.9	1.7	2.5	—	2.7	0.2	2.2	1.0	4.2	1.8	2.9	3.4	1.6	2.4	2.3	1.6	0.4	1.2	1.7	1.6
KOR	0.5	2.9	3.1	2.0	3.5	2.0	—	0.3	1.5	3.6	3.6	1.4	1.2	2.3	4.4	2.0	2.3	1.5	0.4	0.9	1.3	1.1
LAO	—	—	0.4	0.0	0.4	0.3	0.0	—	0.0	—	—	0.0	19.8	0.6	97.1	8.3	2.8	1.0	0.7	0.1	0.2	0.1
MYS	14.9	3.0	1.1	1.5	2.9	2.4	1.5	0.2	—	5.3	3.1	8.7	3.9	2.2	2.1	5.9	2.9	1.6	0.4	0.8	2.1	1.1
MYN	0.0	—	1.2	0.3	1.3	0.6	0.8	—	2.2	—	0.2	1.9	—	0.6	—	6.3	2.6	1.3	0.4	0.7	0.3	0.9
PHL	0.6	0.5	0.6	1.6	0.7	2.9	1.5	0.0	3.0	0.4	—	3.7	4.3	3.9	0.7	3.2	2.2	1.6	0.5	1.2	0.6	1.5
SGP	15.6	12.8	1.1	2.7	4.4	1.3	1.7	1.8	14.4	7.9	5.2	—	4.3	2.9	6.4	8.3	2.9	1.6	0.4	0.6	2.2	0.8
THA	2.7	31.3	1.1	1.6	3.4	2.8	0.8	55.2	3.6	12.9	3.8	4.2	—	1.7	4.7	4.4	2.5	1.5	0.5	0.6	1.9	1.1
TWN	0.4	6.3	1.0	6.9	1.9	1.9	1.2	0.1	2.1	3.3	3.7	1.7	1.8	—	5.3	2.2	1.7	1.6	0.4	1.0	1.0	1.2
VNM	0.7	32.4	1.8	0.6	3.0	3.2	1.2	50.6	1.8	0.0	4.1	2.9	2.3	1.7	—	3.0	2.5	1.3	0.8	0.3	6.5	0.4

— Not available.

Note: See table 3.2 note for description of acronyms. Table reads as trade intensity of a country in the left-hand column with a country in the top row. Singapore does not report its trade with Indonesia to the IMF; therefore, Singapore's trade with Indonesia is estimated using Indonesia's data. For calculation of index, see endnotes.

Source: Authors' calculations using data from IMF (2002).

Table 3.6 Top Five Trading Partners for East Asian Economies Based on the Trade Intensity Index

Country	1995–97	2001
Brunei Darussalam	—	Thailand—11.0 Japan—8.5 Rep. of Korea—5.6 CER countries—5.5
Cambodia	Thailand—17.1 Singapore—5.5 Malaysia—2.7 China—2.0	Vietnam—7.5 United States—3.5 Singapore—1.1
China	Hong Kong—5.9 Japan—2.8 Vietnam—2.8 Lao PDR—2.5	Hong Kong —5.4 Myanmar—4.3 Cambodia—3.3 Japan—3.0
Hong Kong, China	China—10.5 Philippines—1.9 Singapore—1.8 Taiwan (China), Vietnam, and the United States—1.6	China—9.4 Cambodia—5.8 Philippines—2.1 Taiwan, China—1.4
Indonesia	Cambodia —6.1 Japan—3.9 Singapore—3.7 Vietnam—3.7	Singapore—5.6 Japan—3.8 Rep. of Korea—2.8 Malaysia—2.7
Japan	Thailand—3.2 Taiwan, China—3.1 Philippines—2.8 Indonesia—2.7	Philippines—4.2 Taiwan, China—3.4 Thailand—2.9 Rep. of Korea—2.7
Korea, Rep. of	Vietnam—6.2 China—3.3 Indonesia—3.1 Philippines—2.4	Vietnam—4.4 Myanmar—3.6 Philippines—3.6 Indonesia—3.5
Lao PDR	Thailand—14.2 Taiwan, China—1.9 Japan—1.6 China and European Union—1.1	Vietnam—97.1 Thailand—19.8
Malaysia	Singapore—8.1 Cambodia—4.2 Thailand—3.1 Vietnam—2.1	Brunei Darussalam—14.9 Singapore—8.7 Myanmar—5.3 Thailand—3.9
Myanmar	—	Malaysia—2.2 Singapore—1.9 Indonesia—1.3 China—1.2

Table 3.6 continued

	1995–97	2001
Philippines	Thailand—2.8 Japan—2.7 Singapore—2.4 United States—2.3	Thailand—4.3 Taiwan, China—3.9 Singapore—3.7 Malaysia—3.0
Singapore	Cambodia—16.7 Malaysia—12.1 Vietnam—7.2 Thailand—4.2	Brunei Darussalam—15.6 Malaysia—14.4 Cambodia—12.8 Myanmar—7.9
Taiwan, China	Hong Kong, China—4.9 Vietnam—3.1 Philippines—2.4 Thailand—2.0	Hong Kong, China—6.9 Cambodia—6.3 Vietnam—5.3 Philippines—3.7
Thailand	Lao PDR—53.8 Cambodia—16.3 Singapore—5.1 Vietnam—3.1	Lao PDR—55.2 Cambodia—31.3 Myanmar—12.9 Vietnam—4.7
Vietnam	Japan—4.1 Australia—3.8 Philippines—3.4 Indonesia—2.7	Lao PDR—50.6 Cambodia—32.4 CER countries—6.5 Philippines—4.1

— Not available.

Note: CER = Closer Economic Relations trade agreement between Australia and New Zealand. Only trade partners with an index above 1.0 are shown.

Source: Compiled from authors' trade intensity index tables.

United States, but not in the case of the European Union. In fact, 9 of the 15 countries listed in the table (for 2001) have an intensity index above 1.0 with the United States, the same countries as in 1998–2000. The intensity indices with the European Union are all well below 1.0.

Table 3.6 indicates the top four trading partners (those with a TII above 1.0) for each East Asian country for 1995–97 and 2001. In 2001, Japan was among the top four trading partners for only three East Asian countries: Brunei Darussalam, China, and Indonesia. The intensity indices of several of these countries with Japan in 2001 are nearly the same as, or even higher than, they were in 1995–97, but Japan's ranking among each country's partners has dropped, indicating a weakening of each country's trade relationship with Japan relative to its other trading partners.[26] This finding is

---

26. For example, China's TII with Japan in 1995–97 was 2.8 and in 2001 increased to 3.0; whereas Japan ranked second in trade intensity as a partner for China in the earlier period, it ranked fourth in 2001.

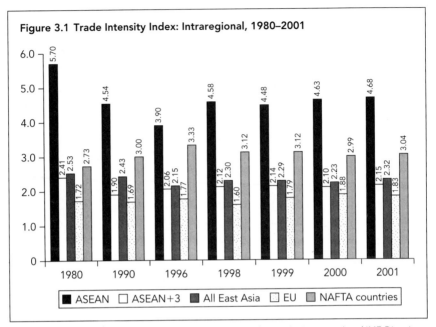

Figure 3.1 Trade Intensity Index: Intraregional, 1980–2001

Legend: ■ ASEAN □ ASEAN+3 ■ All East Asia □ EU ■ NAFTA countries

Sources: Calculated from World Bank *World Development Indicators* (various years) and IMF *Direction of Trade Statistics Yearbook* (various years).

consistent with the findings in our previous trade share analysis.[27] Nevertheless, the indices of East Asian countries with Japan as a partner are, for the most part, above 1.0, except for those of some of the smaller ASEAN members.

For some ASEAN countries, their TII with China as a partner declined between the 1998–2000 period and 2001 (see Sakakibara and Yamakawa 2003b, p. 13, and table 3.5 above). But more significant is that the number of regional countries with an above-normal trading relationship with China (that is, a TII above 1.0) rose from 7 in the earlier period to 10 in 2001. Furthermore, from China's perspective, its TII with its East Asian partners rose in 11 out of 14 cases between these two periods. As China opens up and develops, it broadens its trading sphere to include more regional partners. This pattern will undoubtedly continue with the finalization of the China-ASEAN free trade agreement (FTA).

Figure 3.1 compares TIIs of selected regional groups in Asia, Europe, and North America. Most notable in this figure is that ASEAN has had a

---

27. That analysis (see table 3.3) showed that, between 1990 and 2001, ASEAN's imports from Japan as a share of ASEAN's total imports had declined from 23 percent to 17 percent. For exports, the decline was from 29 percent in 1980 to 19 percent in 1990 to 13 percent in 2001.

much higher intensity index than any of the other groups for all the years shown. Its index of 3.9 to 5.7 was well above that of the European Union (1.7 to 1.9) and of the NAFTA countries (about 3.0), indicating that ASEAN has had a higher degree of intraregional trade than the European Union or the NAFTA countries in 1980 and the 1990s. This finding is the opposite of the findings from our earlier trade share analysis (see table 3.4).

The intensity is much lower for ASEAN+3 (slightly above 2 in most years). This finding could be attributed to China's above-normal external (that is, to the group) trade with Hong Kong, China (with which it has a TII of 5.4), and to Japan's trade with Taiwan, China (with which it has a TII of 3.4). The intensity for all East Asia is higher, which could be because of the inclusion in that group of Hong Kong, China, which trades heavily with China. Both of these groups (ASEAN+3 and all East Asia) have indices greater than that of the European Union, but less than that of the NAFTA group.

ASEAN's TII, however, declined significantly between 1980 and 1996, but in 1998 it returned to its 1990 level. Since 1998, the TIIs of the East Asian groups have remained fairly stable, and in 2001, all three groups recorded the highest TIIs since the mid-1990s. The trade intensity indices of the NAFTA countries and the European Union moved in the opposite direction. That of the NAFTA group rose between 1980 and 1996 but dropped off by 1998, with a further decline in 2000 and no change through 2001. The European Union's index fluctuated somewhat but generally rose between 1980 and 2000, when it reached its highest level of 1.88, dropping off slightly in 2001.[28]

Few clear regional trends emerge in the foregoing discussion, although the discussion does reinforce the argument that East Asia's trade continues to be open and global, with a strong intraregional component. Although the results based on the two different measures—trade share and trade intensity—are not always consistent, some general observations can be made. Despite some decline, the United States remains a major trading partner for most East Asian countries, including Japan. East Asia still conducts a significant (although declining, except for the share of exports from China) share of its trade with the European Union, although the TII reveals no bias.[29] It does not appear from the analysis that East Asia's trade

---

28. Other studies, some covering different timeframes, generally confirm these findings. For example, see Frankel (1997, p. 29) and Goto and Kawai (2001, p. 7). Urata (2002) concurs based on his analysis of the "absolute," "relative," and "double-relative" (calculated differently than the intensity index used in this chapter but still comparable) measures. Schiff and Winters (2003, pp. 32–39) find a similar result for AFTA's trade intensity index in their analysis of 1 year before and 5 years after its implementation.

29. TII is less than 1.0.

is necessarily becoming more intraregional; in fact, there is some indication of the opposite based on trade intensity since 1980. However, there has been a slight rise since 1999. Within the region itself, there are shifts; for example, ASEAN's trade with Japan is weakening, while its trade with China and Korea is rising. Japan is trading slightly less with extraregional partners and more intraregionally, particularly in its imports from China. China is exporting much more to the United States and the European Union but is importing more from within the region.

Trade within the region will almost assuredly continue to change significantly over the next decade, and developing trends will be affected in no small way by further progress in China's economic reforms and liberalization, by developments in Japan's economy as well as in the global economy, and by the direction and extent of regional integration efforts within East Asia. The region has the power to steer these changes in a direction that will be advantageous to its growth and development, but it will take some concerted effort and a well-developed cooperative strategy, not to mention strong commitment on the part of national governments in the region.

Patterns of FDI Flows

FDI plays a critical role in the economic expansion of East Asian economies. The importance of FDI is evidenced by the share of FDI flows in the region's gross fixed capital formation. Over the past decade, this share has been between 7.3 and 14.8 percent for inward FDI and between 3.9 and 9.1 percent for outward FDI.[30] These shares (for inward and outward flows) are comparable to those for the United States and are greater than those for Japan. Since the late 1990s, only the European Union has had larger shares, between 20 and 50 percent.[31]

The rise in FDI inflows to East Asia in the last decade has been remarkable.[32] The value of inflows in the period 1991–96 (an annual average of US$55 billion) increased 2.6 times, to US$144 billion in 2000. Although since then inflows have declined by 35 percent to US$93 billion in 2002, this figure still represents a 69 percent increase since the beginning of the 1990s.[33]

---

30. Includes South, East, and Southeast Asia.

31. The source for data in this section on FDI is UNCTAD (2003b), unless otherwise indicated.

32. East Asia in this context includes the ASEAN+3 countries, Hong Kong (China), and Taiwan (China).

33. These figures refer to inflows in a given year (or average annual for 1991–96) and do not represent accumulated FDI stocks.

Among regional subgroups, ASEAN's inflows declined year on year for the same period (except in 1999), and in 2002 inflows were 31 percent lower than in the 1991–96 period. Inflows to ASEAN+3 were 63 percent higher in 2002 than in the 1991–96 period. The difference in results for these two groups reflects a combination of events, including a sharp increase in flows to China and postcrisis disinvestment in Indonesia, which continued through 2002. The growth in FDI, as in trade, was spurred by significant liberalization in the region during the 1980s and early 1990s, although this growth was reversed for a time by the East Asian financial crisis of 1997–98.

Globally, there was a boom in FDI in 1999–2000, but this growth turned into a general downturn starting in 2001 and continuing through 2002. As mentioned, the East Asian region in general also experienced a decline in flows during the latter 2 years, but it still managed to increase its share of global FDI from about 10 percent in 1999–2000 to more than 14 percent in 2002.[34] The region continues to hold the largest share of FDI inflows among developing regions.

In 2002, China attracted the largest share of inflows in the region, as well as in the developing world, when the value of its inflows reached a high of US$53 billion.[35] Since the early 1990s, when China reported inflows of US$25.5 billion (annual average for 1991–96), its flows have remained above US$40 billion. The country broke a new barrier of US$50 billion in 2002, and there is little reason to believe that the trend will not continue. China has the advantage of a huge domestic market, sustained rapid growth, improved export competitiveness, and its recent accession to the WTO. Also contributing to its flows is the large overseas network of Chinese workers (UNCTAD 2003b, p. 42).

Sources of FDI

A look at the sources of these FDI flows will allow us to assess the flow patterns for East Asia. Figure 3.2 shows the countries and regions that are the primary investors in ASEAN and how their investment levels have

---

34. There were some notable exceptions among individual countries (for example, Brunei Darussalam, China, Lao PDR, Malaysia, and the Philippines).

35. UNCTAD estimates that China's inflows would fall to about US$40 billion in 2002 if round-tripping were taken into account. *Round-tripping* is the investment that comes from locations abroad but is made by investors from China, and it is believed to cause FDI flows to China to be overreported. However, the World Bank estimates that China's round-tripping will decrease in the future as it eliminates preferential treatment for foreign investors over domestic investors (UNCTAD 2003b, pp. 43, 45).

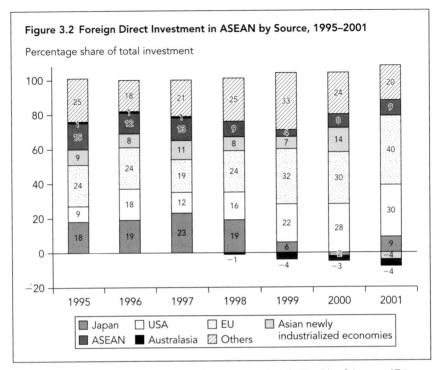

Figure 3.2 Foreign Direct Investment in ASEAN by Source, 1995–2001

Percentage share of total investment

Note: Asian newly industrialized economies are Hong Kong (China), the Republic of Korea, and Taiwan (China). Australasia is Australia and New Zealand. Others include Bermuda, Canada, the Cayman Islands, India, and Pakistan, as well as various Central and South American countries and a few others.

Source: Compiled from ASEAN (2002, tables 3.1.2–3.1.9).

changed from the mid-1990s to 2001. During that time, except in 1997, the largest foreign direct investor in ASEAN was the European Union, which accounted for 19–40 percent of investment.[36] This finding may be at least partly due to the efforts of the Asia-Europe Meeting (ASEM) under its Investment Promotion Action Plan (IPAP).[37] The next largest investor is the United States, with a share of 20–30 percent in the past few years. Although the value of direct investment from the European Union and the United States was down significantly in 2001 from that in 1999

---

36. Not including the category of "Others," which comprises fairly large investments from unspecified countries and unclassified sources, the latter covering the banking sector. Although not specified, this source appears to relate to investment in the banking sector of Thailand in the postcrisis period.

37. ASEM is an informal process of dialogue and cooperation bringing together the 15 EU member states and the European Commission with 10 Asian countries (Brunei Darussalam, China, Indonesia, Japan, Korea, Malaysia, the Philippines, Singapore, Thailand, and Vietnam). IPAP's aim is to contribute to an enhancement of two-way investment flows between Asia and Europe by sharing experience and best practices on investment promotion and policy issues.

(by 41 percent and 37 percent, respectively), disinvestment (primarily in Indonesia and Malaysia) by Australia, Hong Kong (China), Korea, and other unspecified countries in 2001 pushed up the share for the European Union and the United States.

Although all source countries and regions had a net withdrawal of investment from Indonesia in 2000 and 2001, the largest withdrawal was from Japan (US$1.7 billion in 2000 and US$1.1 billion in 2001).[38] Japan was also the individual source having the largest disinvestment in Malaysia in 2001 (US$1.2 billion).[39] Thus, the share of ASEAN's FDI that comes from Japan dropped significantly over this time period—from 23 percent in 1997 to only 9 percent in 2001.

Table 3.7 indicates the major sources of FDI for individual countries in East Asia, but it covers different time periods and types of flows and is drawn from different sources for each country, so comparisons across countries cannot be made. For most of the countries in this table, inward FDI comes from only a few sources—typically about 60–70 percent from only three source countries. The lack of diversification in FDI sources, as well as in destination sectors, which lean heavily toward electrical and electronic products, is a risk factor for East Asian economies.

East Asian countries that appear among the top three sources in this table are Japan and Hong Kong, China, which may not be surprising, but the table also shows that some of the newly industrializing economies (NIEs)—specifically Singapore and Taiwan, China—are among the top three investors in some countries (see Urata 2001, pp. 430–31). From outside the region, the major source of investment, unsurprisingly, is the United States. In figure 3.2, the European Union was shown to be the top investor in ASEAN. The breakdown in table 3.7 shows that this investment comes primarily from only a few European countries—France (in Singapore), the Netherlands (in Malaysia), and the United Kingdom (in Indonesia and Vietnam).[40]

---

38. There were also disinvestments in Indonesia in previous years, beginning in 1997 (during the crisis), when the United States was the only major investor to withdraw. Other source countries withdrew investment beginning in 1998, except the European Union, which began withdrawals in 1999. The United States invested again in 1999, but it disinvested in 2000. All major sources disinvested in 2001.

39. Disinvestment by the group of "other countries not specified" was US$3 billion.

40. The inclusion of the British Virgin Islands and Bermuda among the top three originating countries for China and Hong Kong, China, in table 3.7 is related to the practice of round-tripping and tax haven routing, whereby capital inflows and outflows in the form of FDI move through tax haven economies into and out of Hong Kong, China. The tax haven economies account for large levels of inflows and outflows of FDI related to Hong Kong, China. Although more than half of outward FDI from Hong Kong, China, goes to offshore financial centers (for example, the British Virgin Islands and the Cayman Islands), these funds actually are destined eventually to go elsewhere, including to China.

Table 3.7 Distribution of FDI in Selected Developing Countries

Country and data year	Top three sectors (percent of total)	Top three originating countries (percent of total)
China (1998–2000 accumulated flows)	Manufacturing (46) Real estate management (16) Utilities (6)	Hong Kong, China (41) United States (10) British Virgin Islands (9)
Hong Kong, China (2000 year-end stock)	Investment holding and real estate (60) Wholesale and retail (11) Banking (9)	British Virgin Islands (32) China (31) Bermuda (10)
Indonesia (cumulative 1967 to mid-2000)	Chemical and pharmaceutical (30) Paper (11) Electronics and trading and other services (10)	Japan (16) United Kingdom (9) Singapore (8)
Malaysia (flows 2000–01)	Electrical and electronics (51) Paper, printing, and publishing (9) Nonmetallic mineral products (8)	United States (28) Japan (16) Netherlands (11)
Philippines (flows 2000)	Manufacturing (46) Energy (32) Service export (13)	United States (36) Japan (27) Hong Kong, China (11)
Singapore (2000 inflows)	Electronic products and components (48) Chemicals and chemical products (30) Transportation equipment (5)	United States (40) Japan (16) France (4)
Taiwan (total approved flows 1952–2000)	Electrical and electronics (24) Banking and insurance (15) Services (11)	United States (24) Japan (21) Hong Kong (8)
Thailand (total net inflows 1995–99)	Trade (25) Machinery and transportation (11) Electrical appliances (10)	Japan (27) United States (17) Singapore (13)
Vietnam (flows 2000)	Oil and gas (59) Light industry (18) Heavy industry (9)	United Kingdom (30) India (25) Taiwan, China (15)

Note: Concentrations are not comparable across countries as they are defined differently by national governments.

Source: Compiled from OECD, (2002, p. 56) with additional information from UNCTAD (2001, pp. 24–25).

In table 3.7, Japan ranks first or second as a source of FDI for ASEAN-5 (Indonesia, Malaysia, the Philippines, Singapore, and Thailand) countries, but according to figure 3.2, Japan's share of investment in ASEAN has declined in recent years. Does this mean that Japan is investing less in ASEAN and more in other countries? Although Japan is not included as one of the top three investors in China in table 3.7, Japan's investment in China has been increasing since 1999. Before that, Japan invested far more in ASEAN-4 (Indonesia, Malaysia, the Philippines, and Thailand) than in China, but that investment began to decline sharply in 1997 (UNCTAD 2002c, box III.2., p. 44). By 2002, the share of Japan's outward FDI to China was 8.1 percent, whereas that to ASEAN-4 was lower, at 6.8 percent. The share of outward FDI to the Asian NIEs in that year was the highest of the three destinations, at 9.3 percent.[41] Although FDI outflows from Japan to East Asia rose by 2.8 percent in 2002, this finding reflects primarily increased flows to the Asian NIEs (by 20.3 percent) and to China (by 20.8 percent). Outflows to ASEAN-4 declined by 25.3 percent in 2002. Still, Japan's outward stocks in China (US$12.5 billion) remained below those in ASEAN-4 (US$18.8 billion) and the Asian NIEs (US$24.9 billion) (JETRO 2003, p. 16).

Japanese transnationals began to increase their investment in China in the 1990s. A recent survey conducted by Japan Bank for International Cooperation (JBIC 2003) revealed that the number of Japanese companies having manufacturing bases in China rose from a little over 100 in fiscal year 1993 to about 1,105 in fiscal year 2003.[42] Although the survey showed the number of companies with bases in ASEAN-4 to be even higher (1,157 in fiscal year 2003), it is almost certain that the number in China will surpass the number in ASEAN-4 in another year or so. China has been at the top of the list of promising destinations for manufacturing FDI by Japanese companies over the medium term, as reported in these annual surveys since fiscal year 1996, and in the fiscal year 2003 survey, the location in which the highest proportion of companies (73.9 percent) said they would "strengthen and expand the[ir] overseas business operations" was China (JBIC 2003, p. 4). The specific industries targeted by Japanese investment in China have changed over time. In the mid-1980s, it was the food industry; in the early 1990s, it was the textiles industry; and since the

---

41. Asian NIEs in this case include Singapore in addition to Hong Kong (China), Korea, and Taiwan (China).

42. The survey was conducted in July–September 2003 and covered 932 manufacturing companies that had three or more foreign affiliates, including at least one manufacturing base, as of November 2002. There were 571 valid responses, for an effective response rate of 61.3 percent.

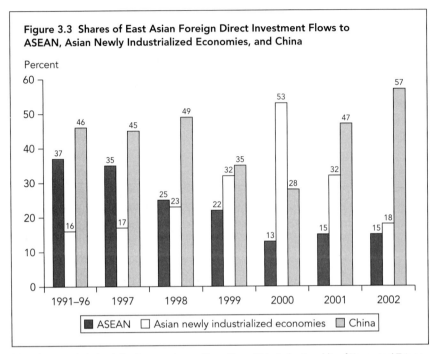

Figure 3.3 Shares of East Asian Foreign Direct Investment Flows to ASEAN, Asian Newly Industrialized Economies, and China

Note: Asian newly industrialized economies are Hong Kong (China), the Republic of Korea, and Taiwan (China).

Source: Compiled from UNCTAD (2003b, annex B.1, pp. 249–52).

end of the 1990s, it has been the chemical, electrical machinery, and transport machinery industries (JETRO 2003, p. 17).

Figure 3.3, which shows the shares of East Asian FDI inflows to ASEAN, the Asian NIEs, and China, gives a fairly clear indication that China is taking shares of FDI from ASEAN. ASEAN countries were able to attract FDI easily in the 1980s because of their relatively high degree of openness in a market comprising fewer recipients than there are today. In the 1990s, competition for FDI increased markedly (ASEAN 2000, p. 6). Figure 3.3 shows that China has received a larger share of East Asian FDI than ASEAN has since the early 1990s, but that the difference between the two was smaller in the early part of that decade. The crisis of 1997–98 had a severe impact on flows to the ASEAN economies but not on flows to China. After China lost share to Hong Kong, China, in 1999 and 2000, its share has increased rapidly, reaching a remarkable 57 percent in 2002.

China's potential to attract large amounts of FDI has caused considerable concern among the ASEAN countries. Its accession to the WTO has made it more attractive to MNCs worldwide, and its lower costs have become a major reason for MNCs in industrial countries to move production there.[43] Malaysia is one country that has lost electronics-related inflows to China.[44] In 2001, Malaysia's inflows dropped to only US$554 million after 2 years of inflows of nearly US$4 billion. This decline has been attributed in part to a loss of flows to China, particularly in electronics production, which in the past has played an important role in Malaysia's economy.[45] In 2002, however, Malaysia was able to make a comeback despite the global downturn in FDI. It received inflows of US$3.2 billion, although this increase came primarily from reinvested earnings while equity continued to decline (UNCTAD 2003b, annex table A.II.1, p. 225).

Although further divergence could occur, it is also possible that China will increase its own outward investment in ASEAN. This possibility is explored later in the discussion of intraregional production networks.

Intraregional FDI

Compared with those of the European Union, Asia's intraregional flows make up a smaller share of total flows. Intra-EU investment increased from 51 percent in 1997 to more than 60 percent in 1999 (UNCTAD 2001, p. 18). In 2001 only 49 percent of the European Union's FDI outflows stayed within the European Union, but that share rose to 66 percent in 2002 (UNCTAD 2003b, p. 70).

By comparison, intra-ASEAN flows are small, at only 7 percent in 1999 and 2000 but rising to 15 percent in 2001 (table 3.8) and to 17 percent in 2002 (UNCTAD 2003b, p. 46).[46] The broader group comprising ASEAN, China, and Hong Kong (China) as host economies and ASEAN, China, Hong Kong (China), Korea, and Taiwan (China) as source economies has a much larger intraregional share, which increased from 37 percent in

---

43. In the JBIC fiscal year 2003 survey, Japanese MNCs were questioned about the anticipated effects of China's WTO entry. Only 10.1 percent responded that China was "progressing" in the protection of intellectual property rights, and only 9 percent saw progress being made on the abolishment of local content and other business requirements. Also, tariff reduction was not seen as proceeding as expected. However, these views do not appear to have dampened their enthusiasm for investing in China (JBIC 2003, p. 18).

44. See Yusuf with others (2003, p. 294) for a list of leading electronics companies that have relocated from Malaysia to China.

45. Malaysia exported 200 billion ringgit (US$52.6 billion) in electronic goods in 2001, almost three-quarters of its total manufacturing exports (B. Low 2002). Another major cause of the decline in Malaysia's inflows was the repayment of intracompany loans, which has been occurring in most of the countries affected by the 1997–98 crisis since 1999. See UNCTAD (2003b, pp. 43–46) for details.

46. The shares of intra-ASEAN flows in table 3.8 differ somewhat from those in figure 3.2. Data in the former are from UNCTAD's FDI/TNC (transnational) database, and data in the latter are from the ASEAN Secretariat's FDI database.

Table 3.8 Intraregional Foreign Direct Investment Flows in Developing Asia, 1999–2001
(millions of US$)

Host economy	ASEAN	China	Hong Kong	Korea	Taiwan	Subtotal of reporting host economy (A)	Total in reporting host economy (B)
					1999		
ASEAN	1,685	78	886	510	347	3,506	25,029
China[a]	3,275	—	16,363	1,275	2,599	23,512	40,318
Hong Kong	759	4,981	—	231	171	6,142	24,581
Total above	5,719	5,059	17,249	2,016	3,117	33,160	89,928
Percentage of A/B						37%	
					2000		
ASEAN	1,259	58	1,045	153	580	3,095	18,625
China[a]	2,838	—	15,500	1,490	2,296	22,124	40,715
Hong Kong	7,703	14,211	—	69	535	22,518	61,940
Total above	11,800	14,269	16,545	1,712	3,411	47,737	121,280
Percentage of A/B						39%	
					2001		
ASEAN	2,334	151	−365	−304	113	1,929	15,211
China[a]	2,970	—	16,717	2,152	2,980	24,819	46,878
Hong Kong	1,930	4,934	—	100	518	7,482	23,776
Total above	7,234	5,085	16,352	1,948	3,611	34,230	85,865
Percentage of A/B						40%	

— Not available.

a. For China, source economy of ASEAN includes only Indonesia, Malaysia, the Philippines, Singapore, and Thailand.

Source: UNCTAD (2003b, table II.1, p. 46).

1999 to 40 percent in 2001. The Asian region has been at the forefront of a movement that began in the 1980s, when MNCs located in developing countries began to increase their outward investment, mostly in other developing countries. South, East, and Southeast Asian firms have accounted for the major portion of these outflows—between 51 and 81 percent of developing-country outflows since 1997 (UNCTAD 2003b, pp. 253–56). This position can be attributed to the export-oriented growth in these countries, which led to the growth of their MNCs; the MNCs then invested intraregionally as well as in industrial countries (UNCTAD 1999, p. 14).

Intraregional flows in the NAFTA area are harder to discern. In the first 7 years of NAFTA (1994–2000), average FDI inflows to Canada were

US$21.4 billion and to Mexico were US$11.7 billion. These amounts were four times and three times, respectively, the average annual amounts the countries received in the 7 years before NAFTA (USTR 2002). It is unclear, however, whether this increase can be attributed to the effects of NAFTA. Mexico has indeed received substantial inflows from the United States since NAFTA, and the country has been integrated into its neighbor's production system, particularly in the automotive industry, which was already deeply integrated in Canada and the United States. However, Canada's share of outward FDI stock from the United States dropped from 17 percent in 1989 to 10 percent in 2000 (Rugman and Brain 2003, p. 3), and since NAFTA, MNCs have closed plants in Canada and have instead exported from the United States to Canada (UNCTAD 2003b, p. 58). Of the total U.S. direct investment outflows in 2001, 25 percent went to Canada and Mexico, with financial services in the latter being a major recipient because of the acquisition of Banamex by Citigroup (UNCTAD 2002c, pp. 40, 82).

Although FDI inflows to East Asia have risen markedly over the past decade, there has been a noticeable shift in flows away from the ASEAN countries to China. The decline in investment in ASEAN is partly due to the effect of the Asian crisis, from which some countries have yet to recover. Recently, however, it has been caused more by the increase in China's attractiveness as a host country—an attractiveness generated largely by its lower wage costs and its highly skilled labor, as well as its increasingly liberalized trade and FDI environment. The region is still highly dependent on investment from the United States and a few European countries, because these countries are home to the largest number of internationally integrated MNCs.

Focusing on the intraregional-extraregional investment scenario should not deflect attention from the internal investment dynamics of the region, particularly where China is concerned. Not only Japan, but also other major regional investors, including Hong Kong (China), Korea, and Taiwan (China), are focusing on China. Table 3.8 shows that between 1999 and 2001 Taiwan, China, reduced its investment in ASEAN by 67 percent while increasing its investment in China by 15 percent. Korea disinvested in ASEAN in 2001 and raised its investment in China by a remarkable 69 percent. And China raised its investment in ASEAN by 94 percent.

Trade and FDI in East Asia: Some Conclusions

Given the strong link between trade and FDI, it might be expected that changes in their patterns would follow a similar trajectory over time. It is true that the factors affecting one often also affect the other (for example, the 1997–98 financial crisis, the prolonged stagnation of Japan's economy, the opening up of China, the downturn in the global—particularly the U.S.—economy beginning in 2000, and changes in the international production system). Although the trade and FDI patterns are broadly consistent, precise similarities are not always evident; however, some general observations can be made concerning both trade and FDI patterns in the region:

- East Asia still does a great deal of trade with, and receives a large amount of direct investment from, the United States and the European Union, albeit from some EU countries more than others.
- Although the United States and certain European countries are still Japan's primary trade and investment partners, there are signs of a shift in both Japan's trade and its FDI from outside to inside the region, and there are shifts within the region as well, such that Japan's shares of trade with and investment in China are beginning to surpass those with ASEAN.
- Although most countries have recovered well from the crisis in terms of trade and FDI, some have not—particularly Indonesia, which is still experiencing disinvestment.
- ASEAN's trade with Japan is declining, while its trade with China and Korea is rising, and ASEAN is receiving less investment from Japan as well.
- The rise of China is having a major effect on the region's trade and FDI patterns as MNCs both inside and outside the region shift operations to that country, often from other countries within the region.

From these observations, we can discern the continuation of the highly liberalized nature of East Asia's trade and direct investment and the importance of maintaining its extraregional relationships. At the same time, intraregional relationships are strengthening as individual countries struggle to find a way to prosper and grow in the shadow of a rising China. In the next section, we will consider a role for regionalism in this dynamic environment.

A ROLE FOR REGIONALISM IN PROMOTING TRADE AND FOREIGN DIRECT INVESTMENT

We have made three observations so far: (a) East Asia's trade and FDI patterns are global and intraregional, (b) the current trend in East Asia is to seek regional solutions for shared issues, and (c) it is welfare enhancing to coordinate trade and FDI policies. Consequently, it is worthwhile to explore possible regional approaches to the promotion of trade and FDI in East Asia. Presented in this section are two such approaches: regional agreements and regional production networks.

Regional Agreements

There are many types of cooperative arrangements designed to promote trade and FDI. These arrangements can be narrow agreements, including only two countries and covering either trade or FDI, or they can be very broad agreements, including more than two countries and covering a wide range of activities. There are also many instances in which investment issues are being included in free trade agreements and regional integration frameworks. The European Union and NAFTA are the primary examples of the latter. Today's FTAs differ from earlier bilateral and regional agreements in that they often include investment provisions. In fact, comprehensive regional agreements that contain both trade and investment provisions are occurring rapidly enough to warrant being called a trend (UNCTAD 2003b, pp. 48, 91).[47]

Both trade and investment agreements have the common goal of liberalizing trade and investment activities and providing nondiscriminatory treatment of participants in the agreement. Investment agreements vary in their provisions as related to performance requirements, breadth of investment promotional measures, inclusion of protection standards, and range of investment issues covered, such as competition, technology transfer, employment, environmental protection, incentives, illicit payments, and conflicting requirements (UNCTAD 2002a, p. 9). Trade agreements focus chiefly on the elimination of tariffs on goods. However, it has been suggested that more recent regional trade agreements may be notable more for their promotion of FDI than for their promotion of trade and, in some cases, promotion of FDI could be the motivation for their formulation (Ethier 1998; Scollay and Gilbert 2001, p. 19).

Table 3.9 lists the primary regional instruments dealing with FDI (adopted between 1980 and 2003) and involving East Asian countries. The number of agreements for East Asia is only 16 out of 160 worldwide that have been formed, but not necessarily adopted, between 1948 and 2003.[48]

---

47. For a thorough discussion of the inclusion of investment provisions in integration agreements, see UNCTAD (2003b) and Schiff and Winters (2003, pp. 101–122).

48. See UNCTAD (2003b, annex table A.I.13) for a complete list of these instruments.

Table 3.9 Main Instruments Involving East Asian Countries and Dealing with Foreign Direct Investment, 1948–2003

Year	Title	Setting	Level
1980	Cooperation Agreement between the European Community and Indonesia, Malaysia, the Philippines, Singapore, and Thailand	ASEAN–European Community	Interregional
1987	Revised Basic Agreement on ASEAN Industrial Joint Ventures	ASEAN	Regional
1987	An Agreement among the Governments of Brunei Darussalam, the Republic of Indonesia, Malaysia, the Republic of the Philippines, the Republic of Singapore, and the Kingdom of Thailand for the Promotion and Protection of Investments	ASEAN	Regional
1994	APEC Non-Binding Investment Principles	APEC	Regional
1995	ASEAN Framework Agreement on Services	ASEAN	Regional
1995	Osaka Action Agenda on Implementation of the Bogor Declaration	APEC	Regional
1996	Protocol to Amend the 1987 Agreement among ASEAN Member Countries for the Promotion and Protection of Investments	ASEAN	Regional
1998	Framework Agreement on the ASEAN Investment Area	ASEAN	Regional
1999	Agreement between the Government of the United States of America and the Government of Japan Concerning Cooperation on Anticompetitive Activities	Japan–US	Bilateral
1999	Short-Term Measures to Enhance ASEAN Investment Climate	ASEAN	Regional
2000	Agreement between New Zealand and Singapore on Closer Economic Partnership	New Zealand–Singapore	Bilateral
2001	Protocol to Amend the Framework Agreement on the ASEAN Investment Area	ASEAN	Regional
2002	Agreement between Japan and the Republic of Singapore for a New-Age Economic Partnership	Japan-Singapore	Bilateral
2002	ASEAN-China Framework Agreement on Comprehensive Economic Cooperation	ASEAN-China	Bilateral
2003	Free Trade Agreement between the Government of the Republic of Chile and the Government of the Republic of Korea	Chile-Korea	Bilateral
2003	Singapore–Australia Free Trade Agreement	Singapore-Australia	Bilateral

Instruments currently under consultation or negotiation (all bilateral except as noted)

ASEAN-India	Japan-Malaysia
ASEAN-Japan	Japan-Mexico
Canada-Singapore	Japan-Thailand
Chile-Japan	Japan-Philippines
China-Japan	Jordan-Singapore
India-Singapore	Mexico-Singapore
Japan-Republic of Korea	Singapore-ASEAN-China (plurilateral)

Note: All agreements are adopted and binding, except those of APEC, which are nonbinding.
Source: UNCTAD (2003b, annex table A.I.13) and other sources.

The relatively small number for East Asia indicates that the region is a newcomer to such arrangements.

Particularly noteworthy are the agreements between New Zealand and Singapore and between Japan and Singapore because of their recognition of the complementarity of trade and FDI. For example, the Japan-Singapore New-Age Economic Partnership Agreement (JSEPA) includes trade-related elements, such as the elimination of tariffs on goods and of nontariff measures inconsistent with WTO measures. It also addresses trade-related issues including rules of origin, customs procedures, paperless trading, and mutual recognition of tests and certifications. However, importantly for promoting investment, it also covers the liberalization of trade in services, the facilitation of investments through promotion and protection, and the movement of people between the two countries.[49] In addition, JSEPA covers issues related to intellectual property, government procurement, and competition, and it enhances economic cooperation in financial services, information and communications technology (ICT), science and technology, human resource development, and other areas. Finally, it includes provisions for the settlement of disputes (Rajan and Sen 2002).

The major drawback to JSEPA is its exclusion of agriculture. Agriculture is excluded partly because Singapore has virtually no agriculture, but also because agriculture is a particularly sensitive area for Japan. The agreement may thus be limited in its versatility as a prototype for other Asian countries where agriculture is of considerable importance. Aside from this exclusion, JSEPA is laudable in its broad coverage of elements important to the promotion of both trade and FDI.

Listed at the bottom of table 3.9 are 14 instruments currently under consultation or in negotiation. Eight of these instruments include Japan as one of the bilateral partners, but ASEAN is also moving ahead rapidly in the formation of comprehensive FTAs with Asian partners. Among its efforts is the prominent ASEAN-China Free Trade Agreement (ACFTA), for which a framework agreement (listed as the ASEAN-China Framework Agreement on Comprehensive Economic Cooperation in table 3.9) was signed in Phnom Penh, Cambodia, in November 2002, designating 2010 as the completion date for the FTA, with an extension to 2015 for the newer ASEAN members. The goal of ACFTA is to promote comprehensive economic cooperation through the elimination of tariff and nontariff barriers on goods, the liberalization of services trade, and the establishment of an open, competitive investment regime. Cooperation

---

49. Services—for example, transportation and communications—are increasingly important today because they link the various segments of production networks worldwide. See Jones and Kierzkowski (2001) for a discussion of this topic.

would be strengthened in the areas of agriculture, ICT, human resource development, investment, and the Mekong River basin development. Cooperation would be extended to include the areas of banking and finance, transportation, telecommunications, industrial cooperation, forestry and fisheries, and energy, among others. Provision for the establishment of a dispute-settlement mechanism is included.

Although some ASEAN members remain wary of China's motives and doubtful of benefits accruing to ASEAN from ACFTA, most in the region see this approach as preferable to adopting a defensive, protectionist stance against the challenge of China. And although China may wish to assume leadership of the region eventually, it can benefit from cooperation with its neighbors, because it needs both a large market for its vast array of goods and resources for its industrial production. ACFTA is indicative of the region's recognition of the importance of cooperation and openness in a broad-based approach to the promotion of trade and investment in the region.

In November 2002, Japan and ASEAN signed a joint declaration to draw up a framework for an FTA to be established within 10 years. The ultimate package is envisioned as broad in coverage, including measures to promote and facilitate trade and investment in financial services, ICT, human resource development, transportation, and other areas. At this time, however, Japan appears to be more actively pursuing bilateral agreements with individual ASEAN countries, including most recently Malaysia, the Philippines, and Thailand.[50]

APEC has contributed to the reduction of tariffs in the region through its Bogor Declaration and promotes free and open investment by encouraging its members to eliminate restrictions through the framework of the WTO Agreement and the APEC Non-Binding Investment Principles. Taking NAFTA as a model, APEC has agreed on a very extensive set of investment principles, but because they are nonbinding and offer no concrete protections, they are viewed as having little effect in promoting intra-APEC investment flows (Schiff and Winters 2003, p. 106). The ASEAN Free Trade Area has succeeded as a regional tariff reduction program and has taken steps to remove nontariff barriers through harmonization of product standards, simplification of customs clearance procedures, and harmonization of sanitary standards.[51] Although known for its

---

50. Formal agreement to enter government-level negotiations on these bilateral FTAs was reached in December 2003. Other countries with which talks are in progress are Chile, China, Korea, and Mexico.

51. See the ASEAN Secretariat Web site, http://www.aseansec.org/4920.htm.

trade measures, AFTA also includes the promotion of FDI among its objectives. The ASEAN Investment Area (AIA) commits its members to grant national treatment to ASEAN investors; to open up their industries; and to promote, protect, and reduce impediments to investment in the region.[52]

There are a number of ways in which trade and investment agreements can be mutually promoting. The reduction in import tariffs has implications for the location of FDI in that it lowers input costs for foreign affiliates, making the host country more attractive for investment. Trade agreements also lead to wider market access. Those agreements that cover a broader range of issues—for example, incentives—can also lower production costs and risks, which would induce more, probably export-oriented, FDI.[53]

The literature on regional trade agreements and their economic effects is extensive, although it does not encompass the implications of investment and services trade because of a lack of data and the limitations of current modeling methodology (Drysdale 2001; Frankel 1997; L. Low 2001; Mistry 2000; Panagariya 1999; Scollay and Gilbert 2001).[54] The general consensus of this literature is that multilateral arrangements (or even better, free trade), are preferable to smaller regional or subregional arrangements. The most extensive recent study on this topic (Scollay and Gilbert 2001 and chapter 4 in this book) concludes that regional trade agreements (both bilateral and plurilaterel) create a "spaghetti bowl" effect and thus reduce the efficiency of regional trade. To avoid the negative effects of this phenomenon, the authors recommend arrangements of larger groupings, on the order of APEC.

Schiff and Winters (2003) examine the effect of regional integration agreements on intrabloc and extrabloc trade for nine blocs, including ASEAN, the European Union, and the NAFTA group, between 1980 and 1996.[55] They conclude that regional integration agreements had a smaller

---

52. The achievements of AIA have included global missions to promote the region, establishment of a database of part and component manufacturers, provision of access to investment and business information on the region, convening of regular forums with business organizations, capacity building through training workshops, and establishment of a working group to develop an FDI dataset (ASEAN 2000, 2001).

53. The degree to which incentives affect investment decisions is uncertain; however, they have been important in the investment strategies of some developing countries, particularly in attracting export-oriented FDI (see UNCTAD 2002c, pp. 204–8).

54. Scollay and Gilbert (2001, pp. 19–20) and Schiff and Winters (2003, p. 102) more recently confirm that a lack of data has limited the number of empirical studies covering the effect of regional integration agreements on investment.

55. Their analysis is based on an earlier study by Soloaga and Winters (2001).

effect on developing countries' trade flows than did the external liberalization that those countries had undertaken at the time (Schiff and Winters 2003, pp. 40–46).

Most studies that cover the mutually promoting benefits of the combined trade-FDI agreements focus on regional integration agreements between industrial countries, such as the members of NAFTA and the European Union. Few focus on agreements between developing countries, such as the members of the Southern Cone Common Market or Mercado Común del Sur (MERCOSUR), AFTA, and AIA. However, a study by Blomström and Kokko (1997) examined industrial and developing-country agreements and found that, theoretically, the capability of a regional integration agreement to attract FDI both internally and externally depends on a number of characteristics, including whether the agreement is between industrial countries, developing countries, or a combination; whether the countries are competitive or complementary; and the degree to which the group is integrated at the outset.[56] Furthermore, there may be a different effect on participating investors than on outside investors depending on how discriminatory the agreement is to outside investors.

The authors' analysis of the South-South arrangement of MERCOSUR, which is similar to ASEAN, suggests that the agreement does increase investment inflows but that they are not likely to be distributed equally among the various members. Also, macroeconomic stability may have been a more important determinant than regional integration.

However, in the case of NAFTA (a North-South arrangement like ASEAN+3), although Blomström and Kokko focus primarily on NAFTA's beneficial effect on inflows to Mexico, they found also a positive effect on inflows to the United States and Canada. Although the increase in FDI inflows to Mexico began with the pre-NAFTA liberalization of Mexico's FDI regulations (from the mid-1980s), the process was enhanced by the implementation of NAFTA. Furthermore, Mexico enjoys a locational advantage in its geographical proximity to its northern neighbors with which trade barriers have been reduced by NAFTA. This advantage, in combination with Mexico's increased market orientation and cheap labor, has attracted investors, particularly from outside the region, not only to the Mexican market but also to the U.S. and Canadian markets. Blomström

---

56. In addition to providing a theoretical discussion of the effects of regional integration agreements on FDI decisions, the study examines three specific cases of North-North integration between developed countries (Canada-U.S. Free Trade Agreement), North-South integration between countries at different levels of development (Mexico within NAFTA), and South-South integration between developing countries (MERCOSUR) integration.

and Kokko point out that "the potential for improved policy credibility and gains from guaranteed access to large northern markets" experienced by Mexico through its membership in NAFTA are general characteristics of North-South agreements (Blomström and Kokko 1997, p. 41).

An example of a South-South bilateral trade agreement (with no investment provision) that has benefited the partners both in trade and in investment is the India–Sri Lanka Free Trade Agreement, which the two countries signed in December 1998. This FTA gave duty-free access to India and Sri Lanka for 4,000 products on a preferential basis. It not only substantially increased the exports of each partner to the other but also stimulated new FDI in a number of product areas, for a total of 37 projects with US$145 million in total investment (UNCTAD 2003b, p. 49).

The automotive industry offers another example of how preferential tariffs under regional trade agreements among developing countries, such as AFTA, have led to an expansion of intra-industry trade and increases in FDI in the member countries (UNCTAD 2002b, p. 65). This result is explained in the next section, in the discussion of regional production networks.

Although not based on an empirical study, UNCTAD's assessment of the possible effects on FDI of selected regional agreements (including AFTA, the AIA agreement, and ACFTA) indicates that these agreements could lead to an increase in all three types of FDI (that is, market-seeking, efficiency-seeking, and resource-seeking investments). In addition, ACFTA could facilitate regional production networks and the division of labor (UNCTAD 2003b, pp. 227–28).

The increase in the number of agreements combining provisions for both trade and FDI indicates broad recognition of the importance of linking trade and FDI in formulating agreements from which economic benefits are expected.[57] It also indicates that policymakers in many countries (both industrial and developing) recognize that MNCs are moving away from the traditional linear internationalization sequence, which begins with exporting before progressing to FDI, to a more integrated approach to establishing an international production network.[58] Furthermore, policies that liberalize trade and investment often precede or accompany

---

57. The coordination of policymaking for trade and FDI is not new. In fact, it has probably occurred more among developing countries than among industrial ones (see UNCTAD 1996, pp. 116–18).

58. An example is Honda's network of operations in motorcycles. Rather than starting its entry into Europe with exports, which was its conventional method, Honda used FDI very early on and integrated its EU operations by taking advantage of the increasingly liberalized framework there (UNCTAD 1996, p. 101).

regional integration arrangements. These policies can lead to increased FDI flows (Balasubramanyam 2002, p. 191).

Although there is no template for regional agreements that guarantee an increase in trade and FDI, it is evident that the selection of partners to the agreement, as well as the structure of the agreement itself, is important in determining whether an agreement will be successful in achieving this outcome. Although larger groupings might be more welfare enhancing, a bilateral approach can be an initial step to a broader multilateral arrangement. In any event, including both industrial and developing countries in the agreement seems advisable, although not absolutely necessary to generate benefits for members. Above all, the more comprehensive the agreement, the better the chance it will lead to the coordination of trade and FDI policies. Finally, forming preferential agreements should be seen as a temporary measure leading eventually to a more multilateral approach.

Regional Production Networks

Establishing regional production networks is another way in which regionalism can play a role in promoting trade and FDI through their links. Regional production networks are broader in concept than regional trade and investment agreements and could be viewed as an extension of those agreements. One of the economic determinants of efficiency-seeking FDI in a host country is "membership of a regional integration agreement conducive to the establishment of regional corporate networks" (UNCTAD 2003b, p. 85).[59] Accepting that the formation of regional agreements is a temporary approach to the promotion of trade and FDI, regional production networks could be the next, or even concurrent, phase for East Asia in its evolution toward the ultimate goal of becoming a fully functioning member of international production networks. This observation is not meant to imply that a regional network should operate outside the international network. Rather, it should operate within and as a part of the international network. Given the multilateral aspect of East Asia's trade and FDI and the changes taking place in international production networking, this operational structure would be essential for the region's continued growth and development.[60]

The European Union and the NAFTA countries play a major role in international production, and they are major providers and recipients of

---

59. Other determinants of this type of FDI are the cost of resources, assets, and other inputs, such as transportation and communications.

60. See Yusuf with others (2003, pp. 271–324) for a thorough discussion of changes occurring in international production networks and their potential effect on East Asian firms.

global FDI. These regions comprise mostly industrial countries, and most large MNCs, which dominate international production networks, are found in industrial countries. In East Asia, there is only one industrial country, plus four NIEs and 10 developing economies. This fact raises the question of the region's firm-level capabilities in the development of production networks. We will later examine some trade and FDI indicators that will help answer this question.

The concept of production networking is not new to East Asia. For decades, Japan played a leading role in the establishment of networks through its "flying geese" model.[61] Japan's lead was followed by the Asian NIEs—Hong Kong (China), Korea, Singapore, and Taiwan (China). Then the ASEAN-4 (Indonesia, Malaysia, the Philippines, and Thailand); China; and, most recently, Vietnam followed suit. All are at different stages of industrial development, and the "flying geese" model is viewed by many to be no longer the predominant growth model for Asia.[62] However, the model helped establish the beginnings of a regional production network through the cross-border activities of MNCs, including trade, FDI, licensing, and subcontracting, and it had the effect of increasing integration in the region.[63]

Japan has the largest share of global outward FDI in East Asia (about 5 percent for both outflows and outward stock in 2001 and 2002). Among developing countries worldwide, South, East, and Southeast Asian firms have accounted for the major portion of FDI outflows (78–81 percent in 2000–02), and these firms invest both in developing countries within the region and in industrial countries around the world. Of this group, the largest share of outward investment is from the NIEs, with Hong Kong, China, having US$18 billion or 52 percent in 2002, followed by Taiwan, China, with US$5 billion or 14 percent and Singapore with US$4 billion or 12 percent. ASEAN-4, however, has only a small share, with Malaysia having the largest portion at US$1.2 billion or 4 percent in 2002. China's share was a remarkable 19 percent in 2001, but it dropped to 8 percent in 2002. Nevertheless, China's 8 percent share still represents a significant increase from its 1 percent share in 2000. Although these small amounts of FDI outflows would not have much effect if they were poured into an economy the size of the United States, the same amount invested in a

---

61. This model was originally conceptualized by Kaname Akamatsu in the 1930s.

62. Yusuf with others (2003, pp. 284–86) points out that although Japanese firms channeled substantial investment flows, technology, and training resources to East Asia, they had a tendency to rely on their own subsidiaries and Japanese suppliers to such an extent that this tendency limited opportunities for local firms to upgrade their competencies.

63. See Ozawa (1999) for a detailed discussion of the "flying geese" paradigm.

country the size of Malaysia or Indonesia could have a significant effect on the local economy.

Given that MNCs are the drivers of international production networks, a look at the number of East Asian MNCs and their share in total foreign assets will give an indication of the region's position in that respect. Also, UNCTAD has developed an index called the transnationality index (TNI), which represents the extent to which host countries and individual firms (with separately calculated indices for each) are involved in international production.[64] Table 3.10 shows these indicators for the largest 50 nonfinancial MNCs from developing countries. It also provides the number of parent corporations based in each economy and the number of foreign affiliates located in each country.

South, East, and Southeast Asia had the greatest number of companies on the top 50 list and the largest share of total foreign assets for at least 1999, 2000, and 2001; the 2001 list shows 33 entries and a 76.4 percent share in total foreign assets. Since 1998, Hong Kong, China, has maintained the same number of firms (11), but the number for Singapore has declined (from 9 to 6). Korea also appears to have lost some firms between 1999 and 2000 (from 9 to 5).[65]

Furthermore, of the 11 newcomers to the top 50 list in 2000, 7 were from East Asia. Three of these were from China, but in 2001 only China National Chemicals remained on the list. Nevertheless, the foreign expansion of Chinese firms has progressed rapidly. China's top 12 MNCs in 2001, which are mostly state-owned enterprises, controlled more than US\$30 billion in foreign assets, had more than 20,000 foreign employees, and reported foreign sales of US\$33 billion. Enterprises that are not state owned, although they are mostly small and medium-size MNCs, are following the same path and have investments in more than 40 countries around the world, including in Asia (UNCTAD 2002c, pp. 61–62).

These data indicate the prominence of East Asia's MNCs among those of developing countries. However, it is possible to see the potential for East Asian firms to become global players by looking at the list of the top

---

64. UNCTAD's TNI for a host country is based on two FDI variables (FDI inflows as a percentage of gross fixed capital formation and FDI inward stock as a percentage of GDP) and two variables related to foreign firms' operations in a host country (value added by foreign affiliates as a percentage of GDP and employment by foreign affiliates as a percentage of total employment). The index for individual firms is calculated as the average of three ratios: foreign assets to total assets, foreign sales to total sales, and foreign employment to total employment. See UNCTAD (2002c) for further details.

65. According to UNCTAD (2002c, p. 102), four Korean companies were dropped from the list in 2000 because of a lack of data. Those companies remained off the list for 2001.

Table 3.10 Home Countries and Regions of the Top 50 Nonfinancial Multinational Corporations from Developing Economies (percent)

Region/country	Average firm-level TNI per country 2000	1999	Share in total foreign assets of top 50 (%) 2001	2000	1999	Number of entries 2001	2000	1999	Latest available year	Parent corporations based in economy[b] (number)	Foreign affiliates located in economy[b] (number)
West Asia	19.3	—	—	0.5	—	—	1	—	—	—	—
Latin America	28.2	48.3	18.5	21.8	22.0	12	12	10	—	—	—
Africa	41.4	46.0	5.1	4.4	5.9	5	4	4	—	—	—
South, East, and Southeast Asia	32.4	39.1	76.4	73.3	72.0	33	33	36	Various	9,934	445,272
Brunei	—	—	—	—	—	—	—	—	2002	—	16
Cambodia	—	—	—	—	—	—	—	—	1997	—	598
China	28.5	—	1.5	3.9	—	1	3	—	2002	350	363,885
Hong Kong	42.0	45.4	37.0	38.9	26.4	11	11	11	2001	948	9,132
India	—	9.6	—	—	0.7	—	—	1	—	—	—
Indonesia	—	—	—	—	—	—	—	—	1995	313	2,241
Korea	23.9	27.8	12.3	13.4	23.2	5	5	9	2002	7,460	12,909
Lao PDR	—	—	—	—	—	—	—	—	1997	—	669
Malaysia	38.1	24.1	5.8	7.2	7.0	4	5	5	1999	—	15,567
Myanmar	—	—	—	—	—	—	—	—	2002	—	6
Philippines	28.1	25.0	0.8	1.1	1.1	1	1	1	1995	—	14,802
Singapore	43.2	58.9	15.4	7.4	11.2	6	6	7	2002	—	14,052
Taiwan	23.1	43.9	3.6	1.4	2.4	5	2	2	2001	606	2,841
Thailand	—	—	—	—	—	—	—	—	1998	—	2,721
Vietnam	—	—	—	—	—	—	—	—	1996	—	1,544
Average/Total[c]/World Total	31.3	34.5	100.0	100.0	100.0	50	50	50	Various	63,834	866,119
From Top 100 List for comparison:									For comparison:		
Australia	—	—	—	—	—	—	—	—	2001	682	2,352
New Zealand	—	—	—	—	—	—	—	—	1998	217	1,106
United States	43.0	—	29.1	27.2	—	—	23	—	2000	3,235	15,712
European Union	67.1	—	54.9	53.0	—	—	49	—	Various	34,291	65,460
Japan	35.9	—	7.3	10.7	—	—	16	—	2002	3,760	3,359

— Not available.

a. Represents number of parent companies/foreign affiliates in the economy shown, as defined by that economy.

b. No entry means data are not available or not reported.

c. Numbers may not sum due to rounding.

Sources: Compiled from UNCTAD (2002c, pp. 108–109; 2003b, pp. 187–88 and 222–23).

100 MNCs worldwide, which includes firms from both industrial and developing countries. In 2000, among a record five firms from developing countries, three East Asian firms made it to this list: Hong Kong's Hutchison Whampoa, Korea's LG Electronics, and Malaysia's Petronas. The latter two appeared for the first time. In 2001, the first two remained on the list, but Petronas was replaced by Singapore's Singtel.

The ranking of the top 100 firms is generally related to the degree of their participation in cross-border mergers and acquisitions, because that is the primary mode of entry for firms investing in industrial countries.[66] The mode of entry for developing countries is primarily greenfield investment—two-thirds of FDI flows to developing countries are greenfield investments—and the share of developing countries in the value of mergers and acquisitions was only 10 percent in early 2000. This situation is gradually changing. In Asia, for example, the share of FDI (inflows) in the form of mergers and acquisitions increased from 8 percent in 1987–89 to 20 percent in 1998–2000 (OECD 2002, p. 50). Furthermore, outward FDI from developing Asia has shifted over the past two years from greenfield investments to mergers and acquisitions (UNCTAD 2002c, pp. 60–61).

Table 3.10 shows a total of 9,934 parent corporations based in South, East, and Southeast Asian countries. (The years vary by country as shown in the table.) These corporations represent 15.6 percent of the total number of parent corporations in the world.[67] Korea alone claims the major portion of these corporations: three-quarters or 7,460, which is more than the number for Japan and the United States combined. Few other countries reported having such enterprises; in addition to the NIEs, only Indonesia did so. It should be noted, however, that data for Singapore and Malaysia were not available for inclusion in this table. Although incomplete, these figures do give some indication of the presence of East Asian parent companies in the world. More remarkable, however, is the number of foreign affiliates in the region: 445,272, which is more than 50 percent of the world total. Even more remarkable is the fact that 82 percent of those affiliates are located in China. This finding further indicates China's

---

66. "The largest 20 companies most actively involved in cross-border mergers and acquisitions accounted for one-fifth of the total value of cross-border merger and acquisition deals during the past 15 years: 1987–2001" (UNCTAD 2002c, p. 89).

67. UNCTAD defines a *parent corporation* as "an enterprise that controls assets of other entities in countries other than its home country, usually by owning a certain equity capital stake," which it states is usually 10 percent. However, it should be noted that each country in table 3.10 reports the number of its parent corporations and foreign affiliates based on its own definition of those entities.

growing dominance in regional FDI and the international production network.

The TNI for host economies in 2000 (at the economy level rather than at the firm level—not included in table 3.10) points to Hong Kong, China, as the most transnational economy in the world, with Singapore sixth and Malaysia tenth. This ranking is based on "the production potential created through inward FDI and the results of this investment" (UNCTAD 2002c, pp. 20–21; 2003b, p. 6).

As for firm-level TNI (table 3.10), developing Asia's average of 32.4 (in 2000) is higher than Latin America's TNI of 28.2 and compares favorably with Japan's TNI of 35.9. Even more remarkable are Singapore's TNI of 43.2 and Hong Kong's TNI of 42, which are equal to that of the United States. Even for Malaysian firms, the average TNI is high at 38.1. In fact, Hong Kong (China) and Singapore have traditionally had the most "transnationalized" companies among developing economies (UNCTAD 2002c, p. 102).

As would be expected, though, the transnationality of firms in developing Asia is below that of firms in industrial countries. The average TNI for the top 100 firms in the world (all but 5 from industrial countries) is 55.7, as compared with 32.4 for firms in developing Asia. Firms in developing economies are smaller and do not have the extensive geographical reach of MNCs in industrial countries, so it is difficult for them to explore markets in industrial countries (UNCTAD 2002c, pp. 109–10). However, it is easier for them to explore markets in their own region, markets to which they are closer geographically and with which they have more familiarity.

Structural shifts in production caused by a number of factors, including changes in technologies, demand patterns, and production organization, are reflected in changing trade patterns (UNCTAD 2002c, p. 143). Table 3.11 shows the trade structure for developing countries and gives an indication of how the East and Southeast Asia region has progressed in export competitiveness over the past 15 years (to 2000). In fact, the region has made the greatest progress among developing regions in the evolution from exporting primary commodities to exporting manufactured goods and services.

A country or region that experiences an increase in market shares over time reveals its dynamic competitiveness and its ability "to keep up with changing technologies and trade patterns" (UNCTAD 2002c, p. 149). UNCTAD's list of economies that have raised their world market shares by at least 0.1 percent (so-called export winners) between 1985 and 2000 reveals that China is at the top of the list of developing countries in all

Table 3.11 Structure of World Trade in Major Product Categories by Region, 1985 and 2000 (percent)

| | Developed countries[a] | | CEE[a] | | Developing countries[a] | | Of which | | | | | | | |
| | | | | | | | East & Southeast Asia[b] | | Latin America & Caribbean | | Middle East & North Africa | | Sub-Saharan Africa | |
Product	1985	2000	1985[c]	2000	1985	2000	1985	2000	1985	2000	1985	2000	1985	2000
Primary products	38.0	40.4	0.8	3.6	61.2	56.0	10.4	9.5	12.5	13.2	21.4	20.9	5.4	4.3
Manufactures based on natural resources	68.7	68.2	1.4	5.2	29.8	26.6	8.4	11.7	7.0	6.5	4.9	3.9	1.7	1.3
Manufactures not based on natural resources	81.9	66.8	0.6	2.4	17.5	30.8	10.8	22.6	2.6	4.6	0.8	1.1	0.4	0.2
Low technology	66.4	49.7	1.2	3.6	32.4	46.6	22.9	33.4	3.2	5.3	1.6	2.7	0.5	0.4
Medium technology	89.2	78.6	0.5	2.6	10.4	18.8	4.7	11.7	2.5	5.0	0.5	0.8	0.3	0.3
High technology	83.2	63.4	0.2	1.3	16.6	35.4	10.9	29.1	2.1	3.6	0.3	0.3	0.3	0.1
Other transactions	71.2	58.4	0.2	1.2	28.6	40.4	5.3	8.6	4.2	4.8	0.9	0.9	4.1	1.9
Total	68.9	63.5	0.8	2.9	30.3	33.6	10.1	18.7	5.8	6.0	6.3	4.0	1.9	1.0

Note: Based on a 3-year average for 1985 (1984–1986) and a 2-year average for 2000 (1999–2000).

a. These three regions add up to 100 percent for each export category.

b. Includes the ASEAN countries plus China, Hong Kong (China), Macau (China), Mongolia, North and South Korea, and Taiwan (China).

c. The share of CEE (Central and Eastern Europe) in exports is understated for 1985 because data are lacking in a number of countries. This also overstates the relative gain in the group's market shares over time.

Source: UNCTAD (2002c, table VI.1, p. 148).

categories of exports, except resource-based manufactures, in which it is third. Hong Kong, China, is on the list in only resource-based manufactures, and Korea, Singapore, and Taiwan, China, are in the top 10 in several categories. Malaysia, the Philippines, and Thailand are also prominent in the list for all sectors (UNCTAD 2002c, pp. 149–50).

Three industrial sectors that have in recent years figured largely in international production networks involving developing countries are clothing, electronics, and automobiles.[68] In the clothing industry, production relocation has taken place largely through subcontracting. In East Asia, the NIEs were the first to be involved in this process. They began with the simple assembly of imported inputs and, after a short time, came to concentrate on skill-intensive activities at home while outsourcing the labor-intensive activities of production to developing East Asian countries with lower wages. End products were then exported back to the home country or to third countries. In essence, there was a movement from "bilateral interregional trade flows to a more fully developed intraregional division of labour incorporating all phases of production and marketing" (UNCTAD 2002b, p. 100). There is reason to believe that this type of regional network will continue in the future, except that the players may change somewhat as competition increases from other East Asian countries and as they strive to upgrade from assembly to full-package manufacturing.

The electronics industry is more globalized than the clothing industry and is driven by MNCs. Japan and the United States have played major roles as investors, whereas East Asian economies have been major host countries because of their low wages, highly skilled labor, good physical infrastructure, and fewer restrictions on exports relative to Japan. Before the early 1990s, Japanese MNCs tended to import components from Japan rather than obtaining them from local suppliers.[69] Finished products would then be exported back to Japan or, in many cases, directly to third markets. This traditional pattern is beginning to change for higher-level electronics, specifically computer products, not only because of tougher competition and the increasing importance of speed in getting products to market, but also because of improvements in production capability in local economies (UNCTAD 2002b, pp. 103–4).

Although this change bodes well for the future of regional production networks, it does not diminish the importance of the global element. In

---

68. A brief summary of these three industries, taken from UNCTAD (2002b, annex 3 to chapter 3, pp. 99–111), is presented here. See original for further details.

69. This tendency was in part because of the centralized management structure of the Japanese MNCs, the long time required to establish local supplier relationships, and the MNCs' preference for in-house component design.

fact, this industry has come to be characterized by the emergence of a new pattern of regional production sharing that has given rise to overlapping and competing international production networks. This situation has both positive and negative implications for East Asian economies in that it allows them to act as suppliers in a wide range of production networks, but it also gives buyers a wider selection of suppliers to choose from (UNCTAD 2002b, p. 105).

The automotive sector in East Asia is one in which trade (through regional trade agreements) and FDI links, as well as the global and regional elements, are particularly evident. Investment in this industry from Japan, the European Union, and the United States has been drawn to ASEAN countries by AFTA's lowering of intraregional trade barriers and raising of import tariffs for nonmembers. Indonesia and Malaysia have benefited in particular. In fact, intraregional trade in motor vehicles and their parts has risen significantly in the AFTA countries. Table 3.12 shows the growth rate in imports from member countries to be very high in 1990–99 (18.6 percent for motor vehicles and 20.8 percent for parts). The negative growth for imports from nonmembers is primarily due to the Asian crisis, but it is also caused by efforts by some countries to develop national industries (UNCTAD 2002b, p. 108).

After the mid-1980s, rapid economic growth in the region, plus the yen's appreciation and the formulation of regional trade agreements, helped the automobile industry develop rapidly. Japanese automakers convinced their Japanese suppliers, which they wanted to use for their production networks, to establish plants in ASEAN countries. In these countries there were preferential tariffs for companies that had a minimum level of national equity. This shift benefited the automakers and strengthened the

Table 3.12 Intraregional Imports of the Automobile Industry

Region	$ million	Share in total imports			Growth rate (percent)		Growth rate in extraregional imports	
	1999	1990	1995	1999	1980–89	1990–99	1980–89	1990–99
AFTA								
Motor vehicles	175	1.1	1.0	5.4	9.4	18.6	1.5	−0.7
Parts of motor vehicles	195	1.1	2.9	9.5	17.3	20.8	14.2	−5.6
World								
Motor vehicles	365,672				10.7	6.6		
Parts of motor vehicles	138,406				10.2	6.4		

Note: Data in this table relate to SITC 781, 782, and 783 (motor vehicles), and to SITC 784 (parts of motor vehicles).
Source: Compiled from UNCTAD (2002b, table 3.A5, p. 108).

competitiveness of the auto industry; it also improved the efficiency of the regional division of labor (Romijn, van Assouw, and Mortimore 2000, p. 139). Thus, a regional production network in automobiles can allow, and has already allowed, this industry to develop in the region, whereas on a national level, the industry's development is constrained by the lack of necessary economies of scale. Nevertheless, the region suffers from intraregional fragmentation of markets and excess capacity in the automobile industry. Furthermore, major restructuring and rationalization are needed, as is an increased supply of engineering talent to enable Southeast Asian parts makers to upgrade to being first-tier suppliers.[70]

From the foregoing discussion, we see the potential for East Asian countries to build further and even improve on the regional production network that was initiated by Japan in the post–World War II period and that has evolved through the development of the region's clothing, electronics, and automotive industries. A description of how recent integration efforts are furthering the development of regional production networks in East Asian automotive and electronics industries can be found in UNCTAD (2003b, p. 51).

MNCs in East Asia, although not as numerous or as large as those in industrial countries, demonstrate an increasing level of transnationality and are prominent among MNCs in all developing countries. Chinese enterprises, especially, have great potential to become major investors in the region. Since the mid-1980s, China has significantly expanded its FDI outward stock from only US$131 million in 1985 to US$28 billion in 2001 (UNCTAD 2002c, annex table B.4, pp. 316–17). In 2001, Prime Minister Zhu Rongji proposed that China implement a "going outside" strategy. Although Chinese firms have been attracted to Latin America, North America, and Europe, they have evinced increasing interest in investing within Asia (Lawrence 2002). If ACFTA is successfully implemented, China's share of investment in ASEAN could increase significantly. In fact, a 2003 survey conducted by UNCTAD revealed that 21 percent (6 out of 28) of respondents in the Asia and Pacific region expect China to be among their top three investors in 2003–05, double the number in the 2001–02 survey (UNCTAD 2003b, pp. 51–52).[71] Further regional integration that includes China could bring FDI and trade-related benefits to both China and the countries of ASEAN.

---

70. For further details on the current and prospective environment for the automobile industry in East Asia, see Yusuf with others (2003, pp. 314–24).

71. UNCTAD's worldwide survey of investment promotion agencies on "prospects for global and regional FDI flows" (UNCTAD 2003a).

It is not necessary for a firm to be a large MNC to participate in a regional production network. The segmentation of the production process allows many smaller firms to concentrate on a single component, or a few related components, that may be used by larger firms in a final product, such as the computer chips that are components of a wide variety of products. Regional production sharing can bring benefits over producing the whole product at the national level, as is common in East Asia now (Arndt 2001, p. 26). However, in the interest of the growth and development of firms and national economies, the goal should be for firms to upgrade from parts supply to the next stage of process innovation and design improvement and then on to original brand manufacturing. The path is fraught with difficulties in the form of high costs associated with upgrading to this stage, designing for final markets in distant countries where customer demands are unfamiliar, and becoming a competitive threat to existing clients as upgrading progresses. Therefore, only a few firms have thus far been successful in making this transition (Yusuf with others 2003, pp. 272, 286–91).

Trying to establish regional production networks presents other problems. Large MNCs are able to locate the various stages of production anywhere in the world to take advantage of differences in factor prices and technologies. There is naturally a broader range of choices globally than regionally. Just as it is impossible for one country to have absolute advantage in all products, it is improbable that one region would either. However, East Asia is highly diversified in its level of development, in the capability of its work force, and in its resources. It is possible through regional cooperation to take advantage of that diversification by bringing together the comparative advantages of individual countries so as to maximize the comparative advantage of the entire region.

MNCs will always operate in their own self-interest and choose locations from that perspective. Although it is impossible to control all factors that might impinge on that decision and equally impossible to force enterprises to choose intraregionally as opposed to extraregionally, it is possible through coordinated policymaking, technology sharing, and capacity building to cultivate an environment that appeals to MNCs. This effort would take some sophistication and considerable cooperation, particularly in the area of policymaking, but there are resources within the region, as well as within the international community, that could be drawn on for this purpose.

Certain policies may need to be eliminated or changed so as not to obstruct cross-border production. Standardization of products and customs regulations would be needed to reduce costs and facilitate the flow of goods. As Arndt (2001, p. 32) points out, "This task is clearly more complex than the traditional focus on the removal of trade barriers. The objective is not simply to free up the flow of goods, but to create an integrated regional production arena." Sometimes there must be dramatic structural changes in the economy of the countries involved. Such changes can mean a decline in the importance of manufacturing in a country's GDP or employment (Cheng, Qiu, and Tan 2001, pp. 182–85). Ideally, a well-developed regional production network would not only promote trade and investment intraregionally but also make the region more attractive to partners from outside the region, as has been the case with the European Union and the NAFTA group.

A difficulty in East Asia is that individual countries, although cognizant of the value of regional cooperation, still tend to protect their own sovereignty and carry out policymaking, particularly for FDI, at the national level. A regional approach can be a stage between a national approach and a global one. Arndt (2001, p. 26) states, "The basic idea is to think of the region rather than the nation as the production base and to spread component production around the region in accordance with comparative advantage." This observation does not imply that competition will disappear within the region as production networks develop. In fact, it will increase—not only between firms within a country but also between countries as firms strive to upgrade their positions in the network. One example is the competition engendered by China's growth of FDI inflows at the expense of other regional economies and by the potential of its firms to become leaders in the regional production network.[72] Networks, however, are not static, and the position of firms and countries within them will change over time.

The appeal of regional production networks for East Asia is that they satisfy the desire to deal with issues through regional cooperation and yet are not entirely self-contained, in that there is still latitude for countries outside the region to invest in and trade with countries of the region, and vice versa. The goal is not to keep out extraregional investment or to limit regional countries that are investing externally, nor should such a network be restricted only to imports from and exports to regional economies. A regional production network is rather a way to optimize the comparative

---

72. Competition for markets will also increase. Examples include Japanese automobiles, which are at a competitive advantage in ASEAN but at a disadvantage against European cars in China. Japanese consumer goods are expected to face increased competition in the region from cheap Chinese consumer electronics and from European, North American, and Korean higher-end products (JETRO 2003, p. 29).

advantages of the region as a means of promoting complementarity in production and trade as opposed to all countries focusing on the same goods and services.

This process should be dynamic rather than static. It should be flexible regarding shifts of production within the region, as well as between regions, remaining always open to being a part of the global production network. To act otherwise would show a failure to acknowledge the current reality of globalization and could be self-destructive.

CONCLUDING REMARKS

The recognition of trade and FDI links has become more important in today's global environment, which is characterized by an increasingly integrated international production network. MNCs, which are at the heart of this network, decide where to invest and from where to trade in pursuit of the most efficient organization of their production activities. Technology has facilitated this process through improved transportation and communication at a reduced cost. As a result, MNCs can locate their production activities anywhere in the world.

Contributing to the economic growth and development in East Asia over the past two decades has been a phenomenal rise in trade and FDI activity, which has been attributed in large part to the region's liberalization of these two areas. Our analysis has revealed the continued multilateral nature of the region's trade and FDI and the importance of its extraregional relationships. Thus, a willingness to remain open is essential to the region's continued development and its achievement of prosperity.

At the same time, we see a very high level of intraregional trade and FDI, with some shifts in trading and investment patterns both from outside to inside the region and within the region itself. East Asia is witnessing a shift in investment away from Southeast Asia (ASEAN) to the north in search of lower costs, and there is a foreboding that China will eventually become the primary production center of the region with an absolute advantage in many types of products.

Because of the recognized need to forestall such an eventuality, as well as the desire for a strong regional identity and a lessening of dependency on the West, regional cooperation efforts are gathering momentum in East Asia. One outcome of this cooperation is the heightened interest in forming regional trade agreements.

Policies dealing with trade and particularly with FDI traditionally have been formulated at the national level in East Asia—generally with little coordination. It is increasingly important that the development and implementation of these policies be coordinated and mutually supporting. In light of East Asia's rising interest in pursuing regional solutions and the importance of policy coordination in the promotion of trade and FDI, we have suggested two approaches that combine these two elements: (a) the formation of regional agreements and (b) the creation of regional production networks.

The formation of regional agreements should specifically encompass aspects of both trade and FDI, with an appreciation of their interactive characteristics. Because this type of broad trade-FDI agreement is relatively new, there are few empirical studies of its welfare-enhancing capabilities. Existing studies indicate that the inclusion of both industrial and developing countries in the agreement can lead to potential advantages from improved policy credibility and guaranteed access to larger markets. In fact, a larger grouping of countries is deemed preferable. But many regional economies are embarking on a path leading to the formation of many bilateral agreements with partners both within the region and outside it. ASEAN and China have taken this concept a step further and adopted a comprehensive agreement.

There are those who believe that the proliferation of bilateral and regional FTAs will only complicate the multilateral negotiations of the WTO. Most of these agreements, however, are still under negotiation or consultation. So although it appears that a "spaghetti bowl" is indeed in the making in East Asia, it is conceivable that over the next 10 years or so these disparate negotiations could coalesce into a broader regional agreement if some standardization and consistency are maintained. Working out agreements in smaller groups, or even bilaterally, could be easier and less daunting for the smaller developing countries of East Asia. There are, of course, certain difficulties that would need to be ironed out, not least of which is the agriculture issue, but it is possible that the resolution of a troubling issue by one group can serve as an incentive for resolution to others. At least, the process of negotiating regional agreements should lead to more interaction and cooperation within the region.

A step beyond, and possible extension of, regional agreements is our proposal for a regional production network. Although the regional production network has the appeal of being broader in context, it is a more complex approach, which necessitates setting the stage for production networking by eliminating restrictive policies and creating an enabling environment for cross-border transactions. The goal here is to maximize the comparative advantages of the region as a whole, which would require a shift in focus on the part of East Asian governments from the national to the regional. This approach would require a longer timeframe than would the implementation of regional agreements, but it could be an extension of such agreements, resulting in a broader approach that could involve the entire region rather than only a few countries. It is possible that through these two approaches East Asia could reach the ultimate goal of being a full-fledged participant in the international production network.

REFERENCES

Anderson, Kym, and Hege Norheim. 1993. "History, Geography, and Regional Economic Integration." In Kym Anderson and Richard Blackhurst, eds., *Regional Integration and the Global Trading System*. Hertfordshire, U.K.: Harvester Wheatsheaf.

Arndt, Sven W. 2001. "Production Networks in an Economically Integrated Region." *ASEAN Economic Bulletin* 18(1):24–34.

Arndt, Sven W., and Henryk Kierzkowski, eds. 2001. *Fragmentation: New Production Patterns in the World Economy*. Oxford, U.K.: Oxford University Press.

ASEAN. 2000. *ASEAN Investment Report 2000: Challenges and Development*. Jakarta: ASEAN Secretariat.

———. 2001. *Annual Report 2000–2001*. Jakarta: ASEAN Secretariat.

———. 2002. *Statistics of Foreign Direct Investment in ASEAN: Comprehensive Data Set*. 2002 edition. Jakarta: ASEAN Secretariat.

Balasubramanyam, V. N. 2002. "Foreign Direct Investment in Developing Countries: Determinants and Impact." In *New Horizons for Foreign Direct Investment*. Paris: OECD.

Blomström, Magnus, and Ari Kokko. 1997. "Regional Integration and Foreign Direct Investment: A Conceptual Framework and Three Cases." Policy Research Working Paper 1750. World Bank, Washington, D.C.

Brainard, S. Lael. 1997. "An Empirical Assessment of the Proximity-Concentration Trade-off between Multinational Sales and Trade." *American Economic Review* 87(4):520–44.

Cheng, Leonard, Larry Qiu, and Guofu Tan. 2001. "Foreign Direct Investment and International Fragmentation of Production." In Sven W. Arndt and Henryk Kierzkowski, eds., *Fragmentation: New Production Patterns in the World Economy*. Oxford, U.K.: Oxford University Press.

De Brouwer, Gordon. 2002. "Does a Formal Common-Basket Peg in East Asia Make Economic Sense?" In Gordon de Brouwer, ed., *Financial Markets and Policies in East Asia*. London: Routledge.

Drysdale, Peter. 2001. "Does Asia Need Regional Trade Arrangements?" Paper presented at the IMF–World Bank Conference on Economic Interdependence: Shaping Asia-Pacific in the 21st Century, Tokyo, March 22–23.

Drysdale, Peter, and Ross Garnaut. 1993. "The Pacific: An Application of a General Theory of Economic Integration." In C. Fred Bergsten and Marcus Noland, eds., *Pacific Dynamism and the International Economic System*. Washington, D.C.: Institute for International Economics.

Ethier, W. J. 1998. "The New Regionalism." *Economic Journal* 108:1149–61.

Feenstra, Robert C., and Gordon H. Hanson. 1996. "Globalization, Outsourcing, and Wage Inequality." *American Economic Review* 86(2):240–45.

Frankel, Jeffrey A. 1997. *Regional Trading Blocs in the World Economic System.* Washington, D.C.: Institute for International Economics.

Fukasaku, Kiichiro, and Fukunari Kimura. 2002. "Globalization and Intra-Firm Trade: Further Evidence." In P. J. Lloyd and Hyun-Hoon Lee, eds., *Frontiers of Research in Intra-industry Trade.* Basingstoke, U.K.: Palgrave.

Goldberg, Linda S., and Michael W. Klein. 1997. "Foreign Direct Investment, Trade, and Real Exchange Rate Linkages in Southeast Asia and Latin America." NBER Working Paper 6344. National Bureau of Economic Research, Cambridge, Mass.

Goto, Junichi, and Koichi Hamada. 1994. "Economic Preconditions for Asian Regional Integration." In Takatoshi Ito and Anne Krueger, eds., *Macroeconomic Linkages: Savings, Exchange Rates, and Capital Flows.* Chicago: University of Chicago Press.

Goto, Junichi, and Masahiro Kawai. 2001. "Macroeconomic Interdependence in East Asia." Paper presented at the International Conference on Economic Interdependence: Shaping Asia-Pacific in the 21st Century, Tokyo, March 22–23.

Hanson, Gordon. 2001. "Should Countries Promote Foreign Direct Investment?" UNCTAD's G-24 Discussion Paper Series 9. United Nations, New York and Geneva.

IMF (International Monetary Fund). 2002. *Direction of Trade Statistics Yearbook.* Washington, D.C.

JBIC (Japan Bank for International Cooperation). 2003. "Survey Report on Overseas Business Operations by Japanese Manufacturing Companies—Results of JBIC FY2003 Survey: Outlook for Japanese Foreign Direct Investment." 15th Annual Survey. English-language edition. Tokyo.

JETRO (Japan External Trade Organization).2003. *2003 JETRO White Paper on International Trade and Foreign Direct Investment (Summary).* Tokyo.

Jones, Ronald W., and Henryk Kierzkowski. 2001. "A Framework for Fragmentation." In Sven W. Arndt and Henryk Kierzkowski, eds., *Fragmentation: New Production Patterns in the World Economy.* Oxford, U.K.: Oxford University Press.

Kleinert, Jörn. 2000. "Growing Trade in Intermediate Goods: Outsourcing, Global Sourcing, or Increasing Importance of MNE Networks?" Kiel Working Paper 1006. Kiel Institute of World Economics, Kiel, Germany.

Lawrence, Susan V. 2002. "China Investment and Trade: China Business Goes Global." *Far Eastern Economic Review* 28 (March):30.

Low, Benjamin. 2002. "Malaysia Losing Electronic Investment to China." *Reuters English News Service,* June 18.

Low, Linda. 2001. "Singapore's RTA Strategy." Paper presented at the Pacific Economic Cooperation Council Trade Policy Forum on Regional Trading Arrangements: Stocktake and Next Steps, Bangkok, June 12–13.

Markusen, J. R., and A. J. Venables. 1998. "Multinational Firms and the New Trade Theory." *Journal of International Economics* 46(2):183–203.

Mistry, Percy S. 2000. "The New Regionalism: Impediment or Spur to Future Multilateralism?" In Bjorn Hettne, Andras Inotai, and Osvaldo Sunkel, eds., *The New Regionalism and the Future of Security and Development.* Vol. 4. London: Macmillan.

OECD (Organisation for Economic Co-operation and Development). 2002. *Foreign Direct Investment for Development: Maximising Benefits, Minimising Costs.* Paris: OECD.

Ozawa, Terutomo. 1999. "Pacific Economic Integration and the 'Flying Geese' Paradigm." In Alan M. Rugman and Gavin Boyd, eds., *Deepening Integration in the Pacific Economies: Corporate Alliances, Contestable Markets, and Free Trade*. Cheltenham, U.K.: Edward Elgar.

Panagariya, Arvind. 1999. *Regionalism in Trade Policy: Essays on Preferential Trading*. Singapore and London: World Scientific.

Petri, Peter A. 1993. "The East Asian Trading Bloc: An Analytical History." In Jeffrey A. Frankel and Miles Kahler, eds., *Regionalism and Rivalry: Japan and the United States in Pacific Asia*. Chicago: University of Chicago Press.

Rajan, Ramkishen S., and Rahul Sen. 2002. "The Japan-Singapore 'New Age' Economic Partnership Agreement: Background, Motivation, and Implications." IPS Working Paper 13. Institute of Policy Studies, Singapore.

Romijn, Henny A., Rikkert van Assouw, and Michael Mortimore. 2000. "TNCs, Industrial Upgrading, and Competitiveness in the Automotive Industry in NAFTA, MERCOSUR, and ASEAN." In *The Competitiveness Challenge: Transnational Corporations and Industrial Restructuring in Developing Countries*. New York and Geneva: UNCTAD.

Rugman, Alan M., and Cecilia Brain. 2003. "Intra-regional Trade and Foreign Direct Investment in North America." Paper presented at the Canada–United States Business Conference, Indiana University, Bloomington, April 11–12.

Sakakibara, Eisuke, and Sharon Yamakawa. 2003a. "Regional Integration in East Asia: Challenges and Opportunities, Part I: History and Institutions." Policy Research Working Paper 3078. World Bank, Washington, D.C. Available on-line at http://econ.worldbank.org/files/27541_wp3078.pdf.

———. 2003b. "Regional Integration in East Asia: Challenges and Opportunities, Part II: Trade, Finance, and Integration." Policy Research Working Paper 3079. World Bank, Washington, D.C. Available on-line at http://econ.worldbank.org/files/ 27543_wp3079.pdf.

Schiff, Maurice, and L. Alan Winters. 2003. *Regional Integration and Development*. Washington, D.C.: World Bank.

Scollay, Robert, and John P. Gilbert. 2001. *New Regional Trading Arrangements in the Asia Pacific?* Washington, D.C.: Institute for International Economics.

Soloaga, Isidro, and L. Alan Winters. 2001. "Regionalism in the Nineties: What Effect on Trade?" Policy Research Working Paper 2156. World Bank, Washington, D.C.

UNCTAD (United Nations Conference on Trade and Development). 1996. *World Investment Report 1996: Investment, Trade, and International Policy Arrangements*. New York and Geneva: United Nations.

———. 1999. *Foreign Direct Investment and Development*. New York and Geneva: United Nations.

———. 2001. *World Investment Report 2001: Promoting Linkages*. New York and Geneva: United Nations.

———. 2002a. "Experiences with Bilateral and Regional Approaches to Multilateral Cooperation in the Area of Long-Term Cross-Border Investment, Particularly Foreign Direct Investment." Advance paper for the Expert Meeting on Experiences with Bilateral and Regional Approaches to Multilateral Cooperation in the Area of Long-Term Cross-Border Investment, Particularly Foreign Direct Investment, Palais des Nations, Geneva, June 12–14.

————. 2002b. *Trade and Development Report 2002.* New York and Geneva: United Nations.

————. 2002c. *World Investment Report 2002: Transnational Corporations and Export Competitiveness.* New York and Geneva: United Nations.

————. 2003a. "Prospects for Global and Regional FDI Flows: UNCTAD's Worldwide Survey of Investment Promotion Agencies." Geneva. Processed.

————. 2003b. *World Investment Report 2003: FDI Policies for Development—National and International Perspectives.* New York and Geneva: United Nations.

Urata, Shujiro. 2001. "Emergence of an FDI-Trade Nexus and Economic Growth in East Asia." In Joseph E. Stiglitz and Shahid Yusuf, eds., *Rethinking the East Asia Miracle.* Washington, D.C.: World Bank and New York: Oxford University Press.

————. 2002. "A Shift from Market-Led to Institution-Led Regional Economic Integration in East Asia." Paper prepared for the Conference on Asian Economic Integration, organized by the Research Institute of Economy, Trade, and Industry, United Nations University, Tokyo, April 22–23.

USTR (U.S. Trade Representative). 2000. "2000 National Trade Estimate Report on Foreign Trade Barriers: Mexico." Available on-line at http://www.ustr.gov/html/2000_contents.html.

————. 2002. "NAFTA at Eight: A Foundation for Economic Growth." May. Available on-line at http://www.ustr.gov/naftareport/nafta8_brochure-eng.pdf.

World Bank. 2002. *World Development Indicators.* Washington, D.C.: World Bank.

————. 2003. *World Development Indicators.* Washington, D.C.: World Bank.

Yamazawa, Ippei, Akira Hirata, and Kazuhiko Yokota. 1991. "Evolving Patterns of Comparative Advantage in the Pacific Economies." In Mohamed Ariff, ed., *The Pacific Economy: Growth and External Stability.* Sydney: Allen and Unwin.

Yusuf, Shahid, with M. Anjum Altaf, Barry Eichengreen, Sudarshan Gooptu, Kaoru Nabeshima, Charles Kenny, Dwight H. Perkins, and Marc Shotten. 2003. *Innovative East Asia: The Future of Growth.* New York: World Bank and Oxford University Press.

CHAPTER 4

NEW REGIONAL TRADING DEVELOPMENTS IN THE ASIA-PACIFIC REGION

John Gilbert, Robert Scollay, and Bijit Bora

S ince 1999, there has been a strong trend within the Asia-Pacific region toward the promotion of regional economic integration through various kinds of preferential trading agreements (PTAs).[1] This situation contrasts with that in the mid-1990s, when the Asia-Pacific Economic Cooperation (APEC), with its nondiscriminatory approach to regional trade liberalization, held center stage as the intended vehicle for economic integration in the region. The arrangements now being proposed range from bilateral agreements among smaller economies of the region to the development of large trading blocs that embrace all or most economies on each side of the Pacific—an East Asian or perhaps Western Pacific trade bloc on the western side of the Pacific and a free trade area of the Americas (FTAA) on the other side.[2] The willingness of the large Northeast Asian economies to consider entering into PTAs is a major point of departure from the past.

These developments raise questions as to whether Asia-Pacific economic integration will continue to be pursued on an Asia-Pacific-wide basis, embracing both sides of the Pacific, or whether the lead role will be taken by separate economic integration processes in East Asia and the Americas.

This chapter seeks to address the implications of these new trends in Asia-Pacific regionalism for the economies of East Asia and for the role that

---

1. In this chapter the term *regional trading agreement* (RTA) has a broader meaning than *preferential trading agreement* (PTA). It includes PTAs such as free trade areas and customs unions, as well as other regional arrangements, such as the Asia-Pacific Economic Cooperation, which are not preferential.

2. East Asia is here taken to comprise the Northeast Asian economies—China, Hong Kong (China), Japan, the Republic of Korea, and Taiwan (China)—and the Southeast Asian economies—members of the Association of Southeast Asian Nations. The Western Pacific takes in these economies, together with Australia and New Zealand.

regionalism may play in their future development. The chapter is organized as follows. The next section briefly reviews the evidence on trade integration in East Asia during the 1990s and summarizes the main developments in Asia-Pacific regionalism during that period. This section is followed by one in which computable general equilibrium (CGE) simulations are used to assess the welfare effects of a selection of the proposed new regional trading agreements (RTAs), including both bilateral agreements and a set of more extensive arrangements that could be described as steps toward an East Asian trading bloc. The results allow us to identify the proposed arrangements that are likely to have the greatest effect and yield the largest welfare gains in the East Asian economies, so that these arrangements can then be analyzed in greater detail. This section also includes discussions on the implications of excluding sensitive sectors, such as agriculture, from such arrangements.

The following section identifies and discusses the changes in production patterns indicated by CGE analysis of the steps toward an East Asian trading bloc, shown in the preceding section to be the RTA developments likely to have the greatest effect on the East Asian economies. These results are reported to highlight both the individual sectors that are likely to face the largest adjustments and the adjustments that will have the most serious implications for the economy as a whole.

The final section considers whether these potential trading agreements are likely to be building blocks or stumbling blocks in moves to achieve free trade in the Asia-Pacific region and a more open international economy. The question is whether these arrangements can be regarded as natural trading blocs, with the favorable properties conventionally associated with such blocs. A gravity model is used to assess how far the arrangements under consideration may be considered natural trading blocs. The results are then compared with the results of the CGE simulations to determine the extent to which support can be found for the proposition that natural trading blocs are more likely to function as building blocks. This section shows that although some of the proposed arrangements may be regarded as natural trading blocs, this perception does not ensure favorable outcomes, in particular the absence or minimization of negative welfare effects on nonmembers.

REGIONAL TRADING ENVIRONMENT

Increasing trade integration has continued to be a feature of Asia-Pacific economic relations through the 1990s and into the current century. Policy reforms in individual economies and the stimulus of APEC have been contributing factors, as were a small number of significant RTAs that operated in the region through most of this period. However, despite the liberalization that has occurred, significant trade barriers remain, suggesting the potential for additional gains from further liberalization. The new round of World Trade Organization (WTO) trade negotiations launched at Doha in November 2001 provides one avenue for further liberalization. Another avenue that many East Asian economies have actively explored over recent years is the establishment of new bilateral and plurilateral PTAs.

Developing Trade Patterns in the Asia-Pacific Region

Table 4.1 summarizes changes in broad trade patterns of the East Asian economies during the 1990s. By the turn of the century, the East Asian economies had achieved an impressive level of intraregional trade. The share of intraregional exports in the total exports of East Asian economies (excluding Brunei Darussalam) ranged from 37 to 56 percent, with the corresponding import shares ranging from 39 to 75 percent.

The Southeast Asian economies exhibited particularly high levels of intraregional trade, with the share of the imports and exports accounted for by other East Asian economies typically exceeding 50 percent and falling below that level only in the case of the exports of Thailand (48 percent), Vietnam (47 percent), and the Philippines (43 percent). Trends in these shares during the 1990s exhibit a degree of variation. In a number of cases, rising shares are observed in the first half of the decade, but these shares declined by the last 3 years of the decade, when the effects of the East Asian economic crisis were being felt. This pattern is observed in both the exports and imports of Brunei Darussalam, Singapore, and Vietnam, as well as in the exports of Thailand, although, except for the exports of Brunei Darussalam, the East Asian share was higher in the last 3 years of the decade than in the first 3. However, there was a steady fall in the East Asian share in the exports of Indonesia and, to a lesser extent, Malaysia, as well as in the imports of Thailand. A steady rise occurred in the East Asian share of both the exports and imports of the Philippines and in the imports of Malaysia.

The share of Southeast Asia itself in the trade of Southeast Asian economies generally grew strongly over the decade, except in the cases of imports and exports of Vietnam and of the exports of Brunei Darussalam and Malaysia. By the last 3 years of the decade, this share ranged from 13 percent for Philippine imports to 26 percent for Malaysian exports. The share of Northeast Asia in the trade of Southeast Asian economies

Table 4.1 Distribution of Imports and Exports of Northeast Asian Economies

Country	Japan 1990–92	Japan 1997–99	Northeast Asia 1990–92	Northeast Asia 1997–99	Southeast Asia 1990–92	Southeast Asia 1997–99	East Asia 1990–92	East Asia 1997–99	CER 1990–92	CER 1997–99	West Pacific 1990–92	West Pacific 1997–99	United States 1990–92	United States 1997–99	NAFTA 1990–92	NAFTA 1997–99	APEC 1990–92	APEC 1997–99	South America 1990–92	South America 1997–99
Brunei Darussalam																				
Imports	10.9	8.1	14.7	15.6	39.1	45.3	53.7	61.0	2.0	2.8	55.7	63.8	17.7	11.9	17.8	13.0	73.5	76.7	0.1	0.0
Exports	56.6	49.8	69.1	68.4	20.6	20.0	89.7	88.5	2.1	1.4	91.8	89.8	1.8	6.3	1.8	6.3	93.7	96.1	0.0	0.0
China																				
Imports	15.7	20.3	50.0	47.2	5.8	8.9	55.7	56.1	2.6	2.4	58.3	58.5	11.8	11.8	14.5	13.3	75.1	75.0	1.9	2.0
Exports	14.1	16.7	61.1	44.1	6.0	6.4	67.1	50.5	0.9	1.4	68.0	52.0	9.1	20.1	10.0	21.6	78.8	74.5	0.5	1.4
Hong Kong, China																				
Imports	16.7	12.7	67.6	65.3	7.9	10.2	75.5	75.5	1.1	1.2	76.7	76.7	7.6	7.5	8.1	8.2	84.9	85.2	0.6	0.6
Exports	5.4	5.6	47.6	43.7	6.8	6.1	54.4	49.8	1.6	1.5	56.0	51.3	23.2	23.0	25.4	24.9	81.6	76.6	0.8	1.4
Indonesia																				
Imports	23.7	18.9	38.6	35.8	9.4	16.0	48.0	51.8	5.8	5.9	53.8	57.7	13.1	10.7	15.0	12.3	69.2	70.6	1.8	1.8
Exports	36.5	21.6	52.5	38.7	11.8	17.0	64.3	55.7	2.2	3.2	66.5	58.9	12.7	14.8	13.6	16.1	80.1	74.9	0.1	0.9
Japan																				
Imports			16.0	20.5	13.5	13.6	29.4	34.2	6.1	4.6	35.5	38.8	22.6	21.0	26.7	24.0	63.6	64.8	2.9	2.4
Exports			19.9	23.1	12.0	13.9	31.9	37.1	2.5	2.3	34.4	39.4	29.7	30.0	32.9	32.6	67.7	72.4	1.2	1.6
Korea, Rep. of																				
Imports	25.5	19.3	31.4	29.0	7.9	9.5	39.3	38.5	4.4	4.8	43.7	43.3	23.3	21.1	25.8	23.1	70.2	68.4	2.2	2.0
Exports	17.1	10.4	28.0	31.1	10.1	13.0	38.1	44.1	1.6	2.0	39.7	46.1	26.3	18.1	29.7	20.4	69.8	67.6	1.5	2.6

Malaysia																				
Imports	25.5	21.9	38.2	37.6	20.0	21.4	58.3	59.0	3.7	2.9	62.0	61.9	16.0	17.1	16.8	17.9	78.9	80.4	1.3	1.0
Exports	14.7	12.1	26.9	26.9	29.6	26.2	56.5	53.1	2.0	2.3	58.6	55.4	17.6	20.1	18.7	21.1	77.2	76.3	0.4	0.7
Philippines																				
Imports	19.8	20.5	37.1	39.3	10.0	13.1	47.1	52.4	3.7	3.1	50.8	55.4	19.2	20.3	20.6	21.1	72.3	76.9	2.1	0.8
Exports	19.1	15.1	29.7	29.3	6.6	13.5	36.3	42.9	1.3	0.8	37.6	43.6	37.6	32.9	39.3	34.0	77.1	77.7	0.2	0.2
Singapore																				
Imports	20.1	16.3	33.0	30.1	21.8	25.9	54.8	56.0	2.0	1.4	56.8	57.4	15.6	16.1	16.2	16.9	73.0	74.4	0.8	0.4
Exports	8.1	7.1	22.6	25.5	25.1	28.4	47.8	53.9	2.8	2.8	50.5	56.6	20.1	18.2	21.1	19.0	71.4	75.5	0.5	0.5
Taiwan, China																				
Imports	31.3	27.0	41.7	40.3	8.5	14.7	50.3	55.0	3.2	3.0	53.5	58.1	22.7	18.8	24.2	19.8	78.4	78.7	2.1	1.5
Exports	11.3	8.9	29.6	34.4	11.0	11.4	40.6	45.8	2.1	1.7	42.7	47.5	30.5	26.1	33.3	29.2	76.3	76.8	0.8	1.2
Thailand																				
Imports	29.5	25.8	43.2	39.1	13.0	14.1	56.2	53.2	2.2	2.3	58.4	55.6	11.0	12.9	12.2	13.9	70.6	69.8	1.6	1.3
Exports	17.5	15.0	26.7	28.5	14.5	19.6	41.1	48.0	1.7	2.0	42.8	50.0	22.1	20.3	23.8	21.8	66.4	70.8	0.3	0.6
Vietnam																				
Imports	6.8	10.7	20.9	44.8	27.6	25.3	48.5	70.0	0.5	1.9	49.0	72.0	0.0	2.9	0.3	3.2	59.7	75.3	0.2	0.3
Exports	24.8	20.3	39.4	30.6	19.0	16.7	58.4	47.3	0.4	6.1	58.9	53.4	0.0	5.1	0.1	6.4	61.2	57.4	0.3	0.4

Note: APEC = Asia-Pacific Economic Cooperation; CER = Closer Economic Relations trade agreement; NAFTA = North American Free Trade Agreement.

Source: IMF (various years).

remained considerably higher, but the trend was less clear cut, with increases over the decade for some Southeast Asian economies being outweighed by falls for others.

The picture for intraregional trade links of Northeast Asian economies was a little more mixed. East Asia accounted for about 50 percent of both imports and exports of China and Taiwan, China, and also of Hong Kong, China (where the figure for imports was 75 percent). However, it accounted for closer to 40 percent of trade in the Republic of Korea (38 percent of imports and 44 percent of exports) and 35 percent of trade in Japan (34 percent of imports and 37 percent of exports). The pattern of rising shares in the first part of the decade followed by falling shares toward the end of the decade is again evident in both the imports and the exports of Japan, as well as in the exports of Korea and Taiwan, China. There was a steady fall, however, in the share of East Asia in the exports of both China and Hong Kong, China, but a steady rise in the East Asian share of imports for Taiwan, China. The East Asian share in the imports of China, Hong Kong, China, and Korea was relatively stable.

A comparison of the 1990–92 and 1997–99 periods shows that the share of Northeast Asia's trade undertaken with Southeast Asia unambiguously increased over the decade, except in the case of exports from Hong Kong, China, despite a drop-off in the second half of the decade in a number of cases. Nevertheless, at the end of the decade Southeast Asia accounted for a much smaller share of Northeast Asian imports and exports (6–14 percent and 9–15 percent, respectively) than they did of the exports and imports of the Southeast Asian economies themselves (14–20 percent and 14–26 percent, respectively). The level of intraregional trade within the Northeast Asian subregion was much higher than the level of intraregional trade within the Southeast Asian economies. Between 20 and 65 percent of the imports and between 23 and 44 percent of the exports of Northeast Asian economies were accounted for by other Northeast Asian economies during 1997–99. Important was an increase in the share of trade being conducted within Northeast Asia in the case of Japanese imports and exports, and also in the case of exports from Korea and Taiwan, China, again despite some drop-off in the second half of the decade. Conversely, the share of Chinese trade accounted for by its Northeast Asian neighbors appears to have steadily fallen over the decade, with the fall in the export share being particularly steep and with gentler falls observed in the case of the imports of Hong Kong, China, and the exports and imports of Korea and Taiwan, China.

Among the region's economic superpowers, Japan accounted for a steadily declining share in both exports and imports of Indonesia, Korea,

Malaysia, Singapore, Taiwan (China), and Thailand, as well as in the exports of the Philippines and imports of Hong Kong (China). The United States at the end of the decade accounted for between 5 and 33 percent of the total exports of individual East Asian economies, but a much smaller share (3 to 21 percent) of total imports. The share of the United States in total exports rose steadily through the decade for China, Indonesia, and Malaysia and fell steadily for Korea and the Philippines. A familiar pattern can be observed in which, throughout the decade, Japan tends to account for a much larger share of the imports than the exports of East Asian economies (except in the cases of Brunei Darussalam, Indonesia, and Vietnam), whereas the opposite is true for the United States, which tends to account for a significantly larger share of exports than of imports (except in the case of China and Indonesia at the beginning of the decade, Korea at the end of the decade, and Brunei Darussalam throughout the decade). The declining share of Chinese exports directed toward East Asia appears to correspond to a rising share directed toward the United States.

TRADE POLICY DEVELOPMENTS

East Asian economies made substantial commitments in the Uruguay Round to reduce their bound tariff rates. As APEC members, they are also committed to the elimination of trade barriers, by 2010 in the case of industrial economies and by 2020 in the case of developing economies, as set out in the Bogor Declaration of 1994. The Pacific Economic Cooperation Council (PECC) has carried out three assessments of progress toward the achievement of APEC's Bogor goals (PECC 1995, 1999; PECC and others 1996). In each case, the review concluded that significant progress was being made toward the Bogor goals, including through the reduction of applied most-favored-nation (MFN) tariffs. It was also noted, though, that progress was uneven both across APEC members and across the range of trade policy measures covered by the APEC agenda. The PECC pointed out that the rate of tariff reduction would have to be accelerated in a number of cases in order to reach the Bogor targets.

The tariff reductions by East Asian economies outlined in the PECC surveys came about partly as a result of reductions in applied tariffs accompanying implementation of Uruguay Round commitments on bound rates and partly as a result of unilateral trade liberalization initiatives undertaken by a number of APEC economies. The PECC commented, "APEC rides on, and mainly reinforces, the liberalization wave sweeping the Asia-Pacific region rather than being the leading force" (PECC and others 1996).

The impression of a significant reduction in trade barriers by East Asian economies is confirmed by the findings of recent WTO *Trade Policy Reviews* (WTO various years), although they also make it clear that some tariffs were in fact increased as part of the response to the East Asian economic crisis of 1997–98. It is also clear from the reviews that some high barriers still exist and that tariff peaks and escalation remain significant, in some cases obscured by nontransparent non–ad valorem tariffs.

Key findings related to tariffs in East Asian economies from recent WTO *Trade Policy Reviews* include the following:

- The simple average of Japan's applied MFN tariffs in 2001 was 6.5 percent, which will decline to 6.3 percent when all Uruguay Round commitments have been implemented. Transparency is enhanced by the fact that 99 percent of tariffs are bound and that applied rates are often equal to bound rates. Transparency is reduced by the use of non–ad valorem tariffs on about 7 percent of tariff lines, mainly in agriculture. Estimated ad valorem equivalents of these tariffs range from 40 to 984 percent. For a number of tariffs, however, no ad valorem tariffs could be calculated because of the absence of any imports, suggesting that the tariffs are prohibitive. Tariff rate quotas apply to about 200 agricultural products (WTO 2001a).
- In 2000, Korea had a simple average applied MFN tariff rate of 13.8 percent, which was down from 14.4 percent in 1996. The average was 7.5 percent for industrial products and about 50 percent for agriculture, for which a number of tariff peaks remain. Escalation remains a feature of the tariff for some products, for which substantial and varied border protection continues to be provided. Tariff reductions on industrial products in 1997 reduced the complexity of the tariff somewhat, with about two-thirds of tariff lines becoming subject to a standard MFN tariff of 8 percent. Prohibitions on sensitive imports from Japan under the Import Diversification Policy were removed in the late 1990s (WTO 2000).
- In Malaysia, both reductions and increases in tariffs occurred in the late 1990s. There were increases in both the number of tariff rates below 10 percent and the number above 30 percent, indicating an increase in the dispersion of tariff rates and the consequent potential for resource misallocation. Following "temporary" increases in some tariffs in 1998 that were imposed as part of the response to the East Asian economic

crisis, the simple average applied MFN tariff rate rose from 8.1 percent in 1997 to 9.2 percent in 2000. Tariff peaks remain in sectors such as automobiles, beverages, textiles, and clothing. Transparency, however, has been increased by the removal of almost all non–ad valorem tariffs, and the average level of protection is lower than indicated by the applied rates because of the widespread use of tariff concessions and the application of preferential rates to imports from Association of Southeast Asian Nations (ASEAN) Free Trade Area (AFTA) members (WTO 2001b).

- In the Philippines, overall protection continued to decline in the mid-1990s, partly because of the implementation of Uruguay Round commitments. Following the East Asian economic crisis, some tariff increases were implemented in 1999 to protect industries such as textiles, clothing, and steel. Residual elements of earlier import-substitution and infant-industry strategies remain in place. Protection has been lowered more rapidly for nonagricultural industries than for agricultural industries, and the balance of protection currently favors agriculture and related processing industries over most other activities, which is a reversal of the situation in 1993 (WTO 1999a).

- In Thailand, the trend in tariffs was also downward in the mid-1990s. The average applied MFN tariff in 1999 was 18 percent with peaks up to 60 percent, compared with an average in 1995 of 23 percent with peaks up to 100 percent. Tariff peaks are generally used to protect domestic producers of agri-food products, clothing, and motor vehicles. Following the East Asian economic crisis, MFN tariffs on some items were increased as a revenue-raising measure, in some cases above bound rates. In the latter cases, imports from WTO members could enter at bound rates if a certificate of origin was produced (WTO 1999b).

- Following the East Asian economic crisis, Indonesia implemented far-reaching tariff cuts, often well beyond its WTO commitments, and removed a wide range of nontariff barriers, as part of an agreed program of economic reform. Most tariffs were reduced to below 10 percent, so that the simple average of applied MFN tariff rates fell from 20 percent in 1994 to 9.5 percent in 1998. Further unilateral tariff reductions were scheduled up to 2003. High tariffs remain in place for alcoholic beverages, motor vehicles, some basic chemicals, and some leather and textile products. Exporters of finished goods to Indonesia also face significant tariff escalation (WTO 1998).

The overall picture is of a region where the trend in tariff rates continues to be downward, despite some increases following the East Asian economic crisis, but where significant tariffs remain in place, indicating continuing scope for further economic gains from trade liberalization.

Asia-Pacific Regionalism in the Mid-1990s

By 1994, there were three PTAs operating in the Asia-Pacific region. The North American Free Trade Agreement (NAFTA), which was by far the largest, entered into force in that year. The AFTA had entered into force earlier, in 1992, and the Australia–New Zealand Closer Economic Relations Agreement (ANZCERTA, usually called the CER Agreement) in 1983.

The center of attention in Asia-Pacific regionalism shifted to APEC following the Bogor Declaration of 1994, in which APEC members committed themselves to achieving free trade and investment in the Asia-Pacific region by 2010 in the case of members from industrial countries and by 2020 for members from developing countries. The modality chosen to pursue this objective was *concerted unilateralism*, which essentially involves voluntary nondiscriminatory liberalization by APEC members.

After considerable initial enthusiasm, some loss of momentum could be observed within APEC by the end of 1998. Experience with the Early Voluntary Sector Liberalization (EVSL) initiative raised questions over the commitment of APEC's two largest member economies to the concerted unilateral approach to liberalization. In addition, members were clearly preparing to divert a large proportion of their trade-negotiating resources to an expected new round of WTO negotiations.

The Trend toward Preferential Liberalization

Since early 1999, a new element in the Asia-Pacific trade environment has been a proliferation of proposals for bilateral and plurilateral trading arrangements in the APEC region. These proposals include ones for new bilateral arrangements within East Asia and between East Asian and Australasian countries. They also include proposals for trans-Pacific arrangements linking Western Pacific (East Asian and Australasian) countries and both NAFTA members and South American APEC members in the Western Pacific. This new emphasis on preferential bilateral arrangements in the APEC region has been strongly endorsed, for example, by the prime minister of Singapore, who refers to the new bilateral and plurilateral proposals as cross-regional free trade areas (CRFTAs).

At the same time, commentators such as Bergsten (2000) have emphasized a new readiness in East Asia to consider the establishment of some form of East Asian economic entity. Although explorations along these lines initially focused primarily on monetary issues, the recent major shift in policy stance by Japan and Korea, which are now actively considering participation in PTAs (including arrangements with each other), removes a longstanding obstacle to the eventual formation of an East Asian trade bloc. Significant political and economic obstacles do, of course, remain. At the ASEAN+3[3] summit in 2000, a study was commissioned on a possible ASEAN+3 free trade area. There has since been a separate proposal for a China-ASEAN free trade area, and a study has reportedly also been commissioned on a Japan-ASEAN free trade area.

On the opposite side of the Pacific, proposals are moving ahead for the establishment of an FTAA, which would in effect establish a preferential trading bloc in the Western Hemisphere. The 2001 Summit of the Americas in Quebec, Canada, strongly endorsed earlier decisions to work toward conclusion of an FTAA agreement by 2005. Simultaneous development of trade blocs on either side of the Pacific would tend to polarize Asia-Pacific trading relations between the two blocs. Such a development would also herald the formal emergence of a tripolar international trading system, with the two new blocs taking their place alongside the long-established European bloc.

These developments raise questions about the future of APEC. In addition to the obvious challenge posed to APEC's nondiscriminatory approach to liberalization, the prospective emergence of a bipolar Pacific runs directly counter to the concept of promoting trans-Pacific economic integration, which had provided an important motivation for the emergence and development of APEC, which, in turn, reflected recognition of the continuing vital importance of trans-Pacific trade flows for most economies on both sides of the Pacific. In other words, APEC was in part promoted precisely to avoid the emergence of a bipolar Pacific and tripolar international trading system—which now appears to be in prospect.

Scollay and Gilbert (2001) briefly reviewed the main features of the trade flows covered by the new preferential proposals in the APEC region and then used CGE simulations to analyze the economic welfare implications of those proposals, along with a range of alternative paths for regional trade liberalization initiatives in the region. The possibilities analyzed were grouped into four main categories:

1. New preferential bilateral and plurilateral arrangements (the CRFTAs)
2. Various possible configurations of an eventual East Asian trade bloc

---

3. ASEAN+3 consists of the members of ASEAN plus China, Japan, and Korea.

3. Achievement of APEC's goals through nondiscriminatory (concerted, unilateral) liberalization
4. Conversion of APEC into a PTA.

Using CGE analysis, the next section explores the welfare implications of a selection of the proposed regional trade liberalization initiatives. This exploration allows conclusions to be drawn as to which arrangements are likely to be most beneficial to the East Asian region, so that the effects of those latter arrangements can be analyzed further.

WELFARE IMPLICATIONS OF SELECTED POTENTIAL REGIONAL TRADE ARRANGEMENTS

The analysis that follows is built around CGE simulation of potential developments in Asia-Pacific regional trading. Using GTAP5, which is the latest database from the Global Trade Analysis Project (GTAP), the simulations update and extend those reported in Scollay and Gilbert (2001) and provide a further breakdown of welfare effects into allocative efficiency effects and terms-of-trade effects, as detailed in the next section.

Not all of the prospective arrangements covered in Scollay and Gilbert (2001) are analyzed here. The earlier study found that many of the proposed bilateral PTAs have relatively minor economic effects, and it would, therefore, not be interesting to repeat an analysis of all of those arrangements. The prospective arrangements are selected on the basis of the following findings in the earlier study:

- Any credible proposal for an East Asian trade bloc will have to be centered on Northeast Asia.
- Although the willingness of Japan and Korea to explore a free trade agreement (FTA) with each other removes a major obstacle to such a development, CGE simulations indicate that the welfare effects for those two countries from such an agreement would be relatively weak or even negative.
- Expanding the proposed arrangement to include other East Asian economies would increase the potential welfare gain for participating economies but would correspondingly increase the negative welfare effects on excluded East Asian economies.
- A full East Asian or Western Pacific FTA would offer enhanced welfare gains for participants and would avoid the negative welfare effects associated with the exclusion of some economies in the region.
- In comparison with an East Asian or Western Pacific trade bloc, APEC offers superior welfare benefits to the region as a whole and to most of

its individual economies. If nondiscriminatory liberalization is not polit-ically feasible, an APEC PTA offers broadly comparable benefits.

- Among the proposed bilateral PTAs, the most significant economic ef-fects are associated with those involving Japan and the United States.
- The large number of proposed trans-Pacific PTAs among the new bilat-eral proposals clearly reflects a desire to preserve the trans-Pacific di-mension in the economic integration of the Asia-Pacific region. The most important trans-Pacific trade flows are those involving the United States, particularly those between the United States and Northeast Asia. The United States, however, initially appeared hesitant to engage in the new trend. In the meantime, a number of East Asian economies have shown interest in establishing PTAs with Canada, Mexico, and other NAFTA partners, as well as with Chile.

On the basis of these considerations, the following regional configurations have been selected for analysis in this study:

- Bilateral PTAs between Japan and Singapore, Singapore and the United States, Canada and Japan, and Korea and Mexico. The first two are in-cluded as the obvious examples of proposed PTAs that are currently un-der negotiation and that involve Japan and the United States. The latter two are chosen as examples of possible PTAs between major East Asian economies and the NAFTA partners of the United States; these choices are not intended to imply that either is among the most likely PTAs to eventuate in practice.
- Steps toward an East Asian trade bloc through a Japan-Korea FTA, a China-Japan-Korea FTA, and an ASEAN+3 FTA.
- The APEC alternative: APEC MFN liberalization and APEC preferen-tial liberalization (APEC PTA).
- The bipolar Pacific–tripolar world possibility.

The ASEAN+3 scenario is simulated in conjunction with implementa-tion of the FTAA. A simulation of the FTAA in isolation is also included.

CGE simulations were conducted of the potential regional trading con-figurations selected. Welfare results are reported first for the various con-figurations modeled as stand-alone arrangements, assuming all other trade policy settings are held constant. A comparison of the results allows con-clusions to be drawn as to which of the arrangements offers the greatest potential benefits to the East Asian region. The CGE technique is then used to explore the implications of excluding agriculture, a very sensitive sector in a number of East Asian economies, from the proposed arrange-ment. This possibility of excluding agriculture has raised concerns and sparked debate in a number of quarters in the region.

Methodology

CGE models are numerical models that are based on general equilibrium theory and are implemented by using a computer program. These models have a number of useful features. They are multisectoral and, in many cases, multiregional, and the behavior of economic agents is modeled explicitly through utility and profit-maximizing assumptions. In addition, these models differ from other multisector tools of analysis in that economy-wide constraints are rigorously enforced. In any economic system, distortions such as trade barriers will often have second-best repercussions far beyond the sector in which they occur. If the distortions are wide ranging, CGE techniques are effective in capturing the relevant feedback and flow-through effects.

The model that we use here is the GTAP model, a publicly available model whose basic structure is documented in Hertel (1997). The model formulation is a standard, multiregion CGE, which assumes perfectly competitive markets and constant returns to scale technology. The major departure of the model from those of standard trade theory is the assumption of product differentiation by national origin, controlled by a set of Armington (1969) substitution elasticities. This modification serves the dual purpose of allowing two-way trade in each product category and avoiding extreme production and trade responses.

All model equations are as in the standard GTAP model and are discussed in detail in Hertel (1997). We close the model by assuming that all factors of production are fully employed, and that all returns to these factors accrue to households in the region in which they are used. Final demand in each region is governed by a single representative household, which allocates regional income across household expenditures, government spending, and savings, using a Cobb-Douglas function.

Because CGE models attempt to capture the features of real world economies, they incorporate data on the structure of production and trade in the economy under consideration. The simulations in this chapter use the prerelease version of the GTAP5 database, a global general equilibrium dataset. The dataset has a base year of 1997. The database has been aggregated to 26 regions and 20 commodities. This database is thus more up to date and more disaggregated by region than the GTAP4 database used in Scollay and Gilbert (2001), which has a base year of 1995.

All of our simulations are run as comparative static experiments from the 1997 base period. In the context of a static model, the sequence of liberalization is irrelevant in terms of the final outcome, but we can consider the implications of the various subregional arrangements to help understand the incentives that may exist at each stage of the liberalization process. In the first set of simulations, each of the RTAs is assumed to be implemented as a traditional FTA. That is, we consider the removal of all import tariffs on a preferential basis between the assumed members, with each member maintaining its own initial extra-RTA tariffs. Although few RTAs have been this clean in reality, the assumption provides a useful bound to the extent of regional liberalization.

Welfare Outcomes for Selected RTA Configurations

The welfare outcomes from the simulations of the various configurations on a stand-alone basis are presented in tables 4.2 to 4.4, in which summaries of estimated welfare effects in U.S. dollar terms and as percentages of gross domestic product (GDP) are juxtaposed to allow ready comparison.

Bilateral PTAs. The outcomes for the sample bilateral proposals reported in table 4.2 show, not surprisingly, that the welfare effects are heavily concentrated in the two participating economies; however, the pattern varies between the different cases. Whereas both Korea and Mexico experience (very small) welfare gains from the Korea-Mexico FTA, in the other three cases one partner loses (Japan in the Japan-Canada and Japan-Singapore FTAs, the United States in the Singapore-U.S. case) while the other partner gains.[4]

In each case, there are widespread though not uniformly negative welfare effects on nonmembers, although these effects are very much smaller than the effects on the two partner economies, except for the United States. These negative effects include both terms-of-trade and allocative efficiency effects, suggesting the presence of trade diversion.

However, when the welfare effects on members as well as nonmembers are expressed as percentages of initial GDP, their significance is generally shown to be negligible. On this basis, the only welfare effects that are significantly different from zero are (a) the positive effects of 0.5 percent of GDP for Canada from a Canada-Japan FTA and (b) the positive effects for Singapore of 0.3 and 0.6 percent from the Japan-Singapore and

---

4. The presence of small welfare losses from the proposed pact with Japan raises the question of why Japan has chosen to seek out preferential arrangements when it has previously been highly supportive of multilateral liberalization. The long-term goals of Japan remain unclear. Statements by officials have indicated that the arrangement with Singapore is seen as a training ground for developing negotiating strategy with other economies. Officials have also openly stated that the choice of Singapore as an initial partner was primarily based on the consideration that the potential for agricultural trade was minimal, a less than encouraging signal of Japan's intentions.

Table 4.2 Welfare Effects (Equivalent Variation Basis) of Bilateral Preferential Trading Agreements

Economy or region	Japan-Canada		Korea-Mexico		Singapore-USA		Singapore-Japan	
	EV (US$ millions)	Percentage of GDP	EV (US$ millions)	Percentage of GDP	EV (US$ millions)	Percentage of GDP	EV (US$ millions)	Percentage of GDP
Australia	−88.8	0.0	−1.5	0.0	−2.1	0.0	−11.5	0.0
New Zealand	−35.8	−0.1	−0.2	0.0	−1.0	0.0	−12.4	0.0
China	−102.9	0.0	−23.3	0.0	−22.1	0.0	−6.3	0.0
Hong Kong, China	6.8	0.0	−7.6	0.0	−20.5	0.0	−12.8	0.0
Japan	−1,171.7	0.0	7.6	0.0	60.2	0.0	−751.1	0.0
Korea, Rep. of	21.4	0.0	175.1	0.0	6.1	0.0	−1.6	0.0
Taiwan, China	25.6	0.0	−3.7	0.0	2.0	0.0	9.2	0.0
Indonesia	−20.9	0.0	−5.0	0.0	−9.9	0.0	−10.4	0.0
Malaysia	7.5	0.0	−6.2	0.0	−13.9	0.0	−7.0	0.0
Philippines	−15.2	0.0	−4.6	0.0	−7.5	0.0	−4.2	0.0
Singapore	14.2	0.0	0.1	0.0	253.9	0.3	481.9	0.6
Thailand	−28.8	0.0	−6.6	0.0	−9.8	0.0	−5.8	0.0
Vietnam	−11.5	−0.1	−3.0	0.0	−4.3	0.0	−6.6	0.0
Canada	3,390.1	0.5	9.5	0.0	4.2	0.0	−11.8	0.0
Mexico	34.7	0.0	117.9	0.0	−2.0	0.0	−3.8	0.0
United States	−1,808.1	0.0	−190.4	0.0	−267.1	0.0	40.5	0.0
Colombia	−18.2	0.0	0.0	0.0	−0.9	0.0	−0.6	0.0
Peru	−16.9	0.0	−0.2	0.0	−0.1	0.0	−0.6	0.0
Venezuela, R.B. de	1.0	0.0	−0.3	0.0	0.1	0.0	−0.8	0.0
Argentina	10.0	0.0	−1.1	0.0	−0.4	0.0	−2.5	0.0
Brazil	−75.0	0.0	−4.2	0.0	−2.8	0.0	−5.7	0.0
Chile	−10.8	0.0	−0.7	0.0	0.2	0.0	−2.2	0.0
Uruguay	2.2	0.0	−0.2	0.0	−0.1	0.0	−0.1	0.0
South America (not elsewhere classified)	−17.3	0.0	−1.3	0.0	0.5	0.0	9.7	0.0
European Union	−92.3	0.0	−1.6	0.0	31.4	0.0	−5.1	0.0
Rest of world	−251.7	0.0	−17.6	0.0	−36.4	0.0	−55.5	0.0
Sum members	2,218.4	0.0	292.9	0.0	−13.2	0.0	−269.2	0.0
Sum nonmembers	−2,470.7	0.0	−262.1	0.0	−29.0	0.0	−107.7	0.0
Sum world	−252.2	0.0	30.9	0.0	−42.2	0.0	−376.9	0.0

Note: EV = equivalent variation.
Source: Authors' simulations.

Table 4.3 Welfare Effects (Equivalent Variation Basis) of Steps to an East Asian Trade Bloc and APEC Liberalization

Economy or region	Japan-Korea		China-Japan-Korea		ASEAN+3		APEC MFN		APEC Preferential	
	EV (US$ millions)	Percentage of GDP	EV (US$ millions)	Percentage of GDP	EV (US$ millions)	Percentage of GDP	EV (US$ millions)	Percentage of GDP	EV (US$ millions)	Percentage of GDP
Australia	−73.9	0.0	−260.8	−0.1	−458.3	−0.1	712.7	0.2	1,353.1	0.3
New Zealand	−16.3	0.0	−65.1	−0.1	−107.2	−0.2	306.1	0.5	657.5	1.0
China	−260.7	0.0	335.3	0.0	−342.4	0.0	1,455.9	0.2	2,104.1	0.2
Hong Kong, China	−10.4	0.0	2,223.3	1.6	2,265.8	1.6	2,662.9	1.9	2,759.0	2.0
Japan	661.2	0.0	4,733.8	0.1	5,886.8	0.1	15,064.7	0.4	15,595.9	0.4
Korea	1,349.2	0.3	3,190.6	0.7	3,237.0	0.7	3,255.1	0.7	4,017.5	0.9
Taiwan, China	−68.2	0.0	−1,298.9	−0.4	−1,937.8	−0.6	1,958.6	0.7	2,529.7	0.8
Indonesia	−47.2	0.0	−265.7	−0.1	793.2	0.4	601.1	0.3	979.4	0.5
Malaysia	−29.0	0.0	−230.9	−0.2	453.5	0.4	215.8	0.2	412.8	0.4
Philippines	−21.0	0.0	−136.4	−0.2	−8.9	0.0	−213.1	−0.3	64.6	0.1
Singapore	−21.3	0.0	−141.1	−0.2	2,107.4	2.5	1,622.9	1.9	1,781.7	2.1
Thailand	−78.6	0.0	−387.4	−0.2	2,523.7	1.6	1,601.0	1.0	2,092.4	1.3
Vietnam	−25.9	−0.1	−130.2	−0.6	685.1	3.1	1,051.4	4.8	724.4	3.3
Canada	−3.3	0.0	−26.7	0.0	−11.9	0.0	920.6	0.1	1,188.4	0.2
Mexico	8.0	0.0	5.4	0.0	3.9	0.0	212.1	0.1	202.0	0.1
United States	−374.7	0.0	−1,268.1	0.0	−2,624.7	0.0	−2,265.1	0.0	3,511.4	0.0
Colombia	−5.4	0.0	−36.9	0.0	−36.1	0.0	329.2	0.3	−194.4	−0.2
Peru	−3.6	0.0	−19.3	0.0	−64.6	−0.1	−70.5	−0.1	71.3	0.1
Venezuela, R.B. de	−5.3	0.0	−11.2	0.0	−8.5	0.0	133.3	0.2	−47.6	−0.1
Argentina	−3.1	0.0	−74.5	0.0	−114.5	0.0	438.4	0.1	−297.3	−0.1
Brazil	−22.6	0.0	−100.4	0.0	−239.0	0.0	1,980.6	0.3	−945.7	−0.1
Chile	−23.4	0.0	−61.1	−0.1	−95.8	−0.1	−16.6	0.0	237.5	0.3
Uruguay	−0.5	0.0	−7.7	0.0	−10.2	−0.1	27.5	0.1	−26.8	−0.1
South America (not elsewhere classified)	−33.6	0.0	−167.5	−0.1	−197.5	−0.2	2,097.4	1.6	−1,205.9	−0.9
European Union	−74.4	0.0	−466.6	0.0	−1,854.7	0.0	7,126.6	0.1	−4,802.1	−0.1
Rest of world	−297.7	0.0	−1,198.1	0.0	−2,112.3	−0.1	3,273.5	0.1	−4,469.3	−0.1
Sum members	2,010.4	0.0	10,483.0	0.2	17,601.3	0.3	29,075.6	0.2	40,282.8	0.2
Sum nonmembers	−1,492.2	0.0	−6,369.1	0.0	−9,869.3	0.0	15,406.5	0.1	−11,989.1	−0.1
Sum world	518.2	0.0	4134.0	0.0	7,732.1	0.0	44,482.1	0.2	28,293.7	0.1

Note: APEC = Asia-Pacific Economic Cooperation; ASEAN+3 = Association of Southeast Asian Nations plus China, the Republic of Korea, and Japan; EV = equivalent variation; MFN = most-favored nation.
Source: Authors' simulations.

Table 4.4 Welfare Effects (Equivalent Variation Basis) of the Free Trade Area of the Americas

Economy or region	FTAA		ASEAN+3 and FTAA		ASEAN+3	
	EV (US$ millions)	Percentage of GDP	EV (US$ millions)	Percentage of GDP	EV (US$ millions)	Percentage of GDP
Australia	−41.4	0.0	−501.1	−0.1	−458.3	−0.1
New Zealand	−63.7	−0.1	−172.4	−0.3	−107.2	−0.2
China	−713.8	−0.1	−1,041.3	−0.1	−342.4	0.0
Hong Kong, China	−50.5	0.0	2,210.1	1.6	2,265.8	1.6
Japan	−832.0	0.0	5,020.3	0.1	5,886.8	0.1
Korea, Rep. of	−560.4	−0.1	2,728.9	0.6	3,237.0	0.7
Taiwan, China	−211.2	−0.1	−2,153.0	−0.7	−1,937.8	−0.6
Indonesia	−108.9	−0.1	692.2	0.3	793.2	0.4
Malaysia	−46.7	0.0	399.7	0.4	453.5	0.4
Philippines	−88.9	−0.1	−91.8	−0.1	−8.9	0.0
Singapore	−56.5	−0.1	2,046.4	2.4	2,107.4	2.5
Thailand	−164.0	−0.1	2,386.1	1.5	2,523.7	1.6
Vietnam	−12.1	−0.1	675.2	3.1	685.1	3.1
Canada	362.9	0.1	341.5	0.1	−11.9	0.0
Mexico	573.0	0.1	575.2	0.1	3.9	0.0
United States	3,600.6	0.0	973.3	0.0	−2,624.7	0.0
Colombia	321.3	0.3	285.7	0.3	−36.1	0.0
Peru	96.5	0.1	36.2	0.1	−64.6	−0.1
Venezuela, R.B. de	451.4	0.5	448.9	0.5	−8.5	0.0
Argentina	1,425.2	0.4	1,325.7	0.4	−114.5	0.0
Brazil	1,473.6	0.2	1,247.3	0.2	−239.0	0.0
Chile	87.9	0.1	−1.5	0.0	−95.8	−0.1
Uruguay	167.4	0.9	159.4	0.8	−10.2	−0.1
South America (not elsewhere classified)	2,138.0	1.6	1,935.0	1.5	−197.5	−0.2
European Union	−3,094.4	0.0	−4,988.5	−0.1	−1854.7	0.0
Rest of world	−884.0	0.0	−3,008.9	−0.1	−2,112.3	−0.1
Sum members	10,697.9	0.1	22,193.2	0.1	17,601.3	0.3
Sum nonmembers	−6,928.3	0.0	−10,664.6	−0.1	−9,869.3	0.0
Sum world	3,769.5	0.0	11,528.6	0.0	7,732.1	0.0

Note: ASEAN+3 = Association of Southeast Asian Nations plus China, the Republic of Korea, and Japan; EV = equivalent variation; FTAA = free trade area of the Americas.
Source: Authors' simulations.

Singapore-U.S. FTAs, respectively. (There are also negative effects, each amounting to 0.1 percent of GDP on New Zealand and Vietnam from a Canada-Japan FTA.) These results are consistent with the finding in Scollay and Gilbert (2001) that, among the many possible bilateral PTA combinations, bilateral FTAs with Japan and the United States are the most likely to offer the prospect of significant welfare gains for other economies in the region.

Steps toward an East Asian trade bloc. Possible steps in the creation of an East Asian trade bloc are discussed in Scollay and Gilbert (2001), where it is argued that Northeast Asia would necessarily form the core of any such arrangement. Thus, a willingness of the Northeast Asian economies to enter into PTAs, including PTAs with each other, is an essential prerequisite for any such development. The proposed Japan-Korea and China-Japan-Korea FTAs can therefore be viewed as essential elements in the construction of an East Asian trade bloc. A link between these three economies and ASEAN, as in the proposed ASEAN+3 FTA, would cover all the market economies of East Asia with the exception of Taiwan, China.

The welfare outcome from the simulations of these developments is summarized in table 4.3. The general pattern is one of positive welfare effects on economies participating in the proposed arrangements, accompanied by widespread negative effects on nonparticipants. This pattern suggests that trade diversion is a significant factor in these negative welfare effects. As in Scollay and Gilbert (2001), the size of the positive welfare effects on members tends to rise as the number of economies covered by the proposed arrangements expands, but the size of the negative effects on nonmembers also increases. However, as progressively more economies of the region are included within the proposed arrangements, these negative welfare effects are increasingly concentrated on economies outside the region. The pattern of increasing welfare gains for participants and welfare losses for nonparticipants is captured in summary form in the rows labeled "Sum members" and "Sum nonmembers" in table 4.3. These increasing losses for nonparticipants occur even though global welfare is also increasing.

A Japan-Korea FTA (table 4.3) produces relatively weak benefits for the two participating economies (0.3 percent of GDP for Korea and close to zero effect for Japan). The widespread negative effects on nonparticipants are negligible when expressed as a percentage of initial GDP, reaching 0.1 percent of GDP only in the case of Vietnam.

Including China in the proposed arrangement significantly improves the welfare outcome for Korea and Japan, to 0.7 percent and 0.1 percent of GDP, respectively. In China's case, however, the welfare gain is negligible, whereas Hong Kong, China, experiences a very significant welfare gain of 1.6 percent of GDP. This pattern of negligible welfare effects on China accompanied by very significant gains for Hong Kong, China, is repeated as the scope of the proposed arrangement is expanded. With the inclusion of China in the FTA, the negative effects on nonmembers start to appear significant, particularly for Taiwan, China, and for the ASEAN economies, which compete directly with China in many markets.

The negative welfare effects on the ASEAN economies are converted into positive effects (except in the case of the Philippines, whose welfare loss is reduced) if the proposal is expanded into an ASEAN+3 FTA, comprising the 10 ASEAN economies plus China, Japan, and Korea. Proportionally to GDP, the ASEAN economies and Korea are the biggest gainers from this arrangement, although for Korea there is only a marginal improvement in the welfare outcome relative to the outcome from the China-Japan-Korea FTA. In comparison with the latter arrangement, Japan enjoys a slightly larger welfare gain, although as a percentage of GDP, the gain is still small. As noted above, the welfare effect on China is negligible, although very slightly inferior to that from the China-Japan-Korea FTA. Hong Kong, China, enjoys virtually identical gains under either arrangement. It is notable that Singapore derives much larger welfare gains from an ASEAN+3 FTA than from either a Japan-Singapore or Singapore-U.S. FTA. Larger welfare losses, however, are suffered by Taiwan, China, and also by Australia and New Zealand. Although the United States and the European Union (EU) also record welfare losses, those losses remain small relative to GDP. Negative welfare effects, mostly of minor magnitude, occur throughout the Western Hemisphere.

Measured in dollar terms, the aggregate combined welfare gains for the members of an ASEAN+3 FTA are 70 percent larger than the gains for the more limited membership of a China-Japan-Korea FTA, and they are also 50 percent larger when expressed as a percentage of the combined GDP of the members of the respective arrangements. Conversely, the welfare losses imposed on nonmembers by the ASEAN+3 FTA are also 50 percent higher than in the case of the China-Japan-Korea FTA. The largest welfare losses are for the European Union and the United States, although those losses are very small relative to the EU and U.S. GDPs.

The results for APEC MFN liberalization (table 4.3) show that this form of RTA offers substantially better welfare gains for the East Asian economies as a whole than even an ASEAN+3 FTA. Measured in dollar terms, the combined welfare gains from APEC MFN liberalization for the 11 East Asian economies in the table are almost double the gains for the same economies under an ASEAN+3 FTA. In comparison with an ASEAN+3 arrangement, APEC MFN liberalization provides substantially higher welfare gains for all the Northeast Asian economies, this time, of course, including Taiwan, China. The improvement in welfare outcomes is especially marked for China and Japan as well as Taiwan, China. The welfare gains, however, are somewhat lower than under an ASEAN+3 FTA for all of the Southeast Asian economies except Vietnam. Nevertheless, there are worthwhile welfare gains under APEC MFN liberalization for all of the East Asian economies except the Philippines. Singapore, again, does much better than in a bilateral arrangement with Japan or the United States, although not as well as in an ASEAN+3 FTA.

A notable feature of the results for APEC MFN liberalization is the positive aggregate welfare effect for non-APEC members, in contrast to all other configurations considered, in which the overall welfare outcome for nonmembers is invariably negative. As a result, the effect on overall global welfare of APEC MFN liberalization is easily the highest of all the configurations shown. In addition to the East Asian economies, there are positive welfare effects for most other APEC members, including Australia, Canada, Mexico, and New Zealand. A potential problem, however, is that there is a welfare loss for the United States, although this loss is very small relative to U.S. GDP. Breaking down this U.S. welfare loss shows that it is entirely due to terms-of-trade effects, which outweigh gains in allocative efficiency.

If APEC liberalizes preferentially, instead of on an MFN basis, welfare losses for the United States and the Philippines are converted into welfare gains, and the welfare outcomes are more favorable (although in some cases only marginally so) for all APEC economies except Vietnam. The combined overall welfare gain for the APEC economies as a group is about 40 percent higher than under APEC MFN liberalization. There is a negative welfare effect, however, on non-APEC economies as a group, in contrast to the positive effect from APEC MFN liberalization, and the effect on overall global welfare is much less favorable. Thus, APEC preferential liberalization is, not surprisingly, likely to have more divisive implications for the global trading system than APEC MFN liberalization. Not all East Asian economies do better under APEC preferential liberalization than under an ASEAN+3 FTA; Singapore and Thailand do better under the latter arrangement.

Finally, the effects of the FTAA, which are shown in table 4.4, are in a sense the mirror image of those for an East Asian trade bloc. A range of positive welfare effects is generated in the Western Hemisphere, with corresponding negative effects on all economies of the Western Pacific. These negative effects are small when expressed as a percentage of GDP, in no case exceeding 0.1 percent. Given that trade blocs on either side of the Pacific produce only relatively small negative welfare effects on economies on the opposite side of the ocean, it is no surprise that the simulation of the FTAA in combination with an ASEAN+3 FTA (table 4.4) produces welfare gains for the members of each group that fall only marginally short of the gains that they register when their respective blocs are analyzed in isolation.

Policy Conclusions

Results for the sample of arrangements simulated here indicate that bilateral PTAs involving East Asian economies are unlikely to have major regionwide welfare effects, although the negative welfare effects on excluded economies may be sufficient to cause irritations in regional trading relationships. Furthermore, the absence of serious negative welfare effects from individual bilateral agreements does not exclude the possibility that a proliferation of such agreements may unnecessarily complicate the regional trading environment for business. These findings are consistent with the conclusions reached in Scollay and Gilbert (2001), where the relevant issues are discussed in greater detail.

Meaningful regionwide economic integration is more likely to occur through PTAs involving larger groups of East Asian economies. Although they differ in details, the results here also broadly support the conclusions reached in Scollay and Gilbert (2001) that preferential agreements among subsets of East Asian economies are likely to be divisive because favorable outcomes for members of such an agreement—for example, the China-Japan-Korea FTA in this study—are achieved at the expense of negative effects on the East Asian economies that are excluded from the agreement.

By contrast, a regionwide PTA, such as the proposed ASEAN+3 FTA, promises improved welfare outcomes for almost all East Asian economies and ensures that these welfare outcomes are almost uniformly positive. Among the preferential arrangements being proposed, the ASEAN+3 FTA thus appeals as the one arrangement likely to be most beneficial to the East Asian economies, both individually and collectively. However, if welfare effects are taken as the criterion, the results here indicate that although the Southeast Asian economies have a strong incentive to consider the ASEAN+3 option, Korea could be expected to be indifferent between this option and a China-Japan-Korea FTA, and China and Japan appear not to have strong incentives to pursue either option.

The results also clearly show that liberalization at the level of APEC continues to offer the East Asian economies significant potential advantages over the various East Asian PTA configurations. In both APEC cases, the combined welfare gains for the East Asian economies as a group are much greater than under the ASEAN+3 FTA scenario. APEC offers much more worthwhile welfare outcomes for China and Japan, the two largest economies in the region. Worthwhile welfare gains are also indicated for the Southeast Asian economies, even though these gains are, in most cases, smaller than those indicated under the ASEAN+3 FTA scenario. APEC preferential liberalization offers somewhat larger welfare gains for East Asia, but APEC MFN liberalization avoids imposing negative welfare effects on non-APEC economies and may therefore be viewed as more supportive of the multilateral trading system. The negative welfare effects on non-APEC economies under APEC preferential liberalization may by viewed as a useful bargaining chip in multilateral negotiations.

It is thus clear that, by the criterion of favorable welfare effects, three scenarios—ASEAN+3 FTA, APEC MFN liberalization, and APEC preferential liberalization—dominate the other scenarios considered here. No one of these scenarios unambiguously dominates the other two in all respects and for all East Asian economies. Nor is it clear at this point which, if any, of these scenarios is likely to eventuate. It is too early to say whether the proposed ASEAN+3 FTA will be realized. Confidence in achieving nondiscriminatory liberalization through the APEC process has clearly waned, at least for the time being, and there is no formal proposal on the table for an APEC-wide preferential trade agreement. The analysis of trade and production effects in the following section will therefore focus on all three of these possible scenarios, thus allowing relevant comparisons to be made as required.

Treatment of Agriculture

In a number of East Asian economies, agriculture is a sensitive sector that might be excluded from regional trading arrangements. In Scollay and Gilbert (2001), simulation results are reported for a Japan-Korea FTA with agriculture both excluded and included. These results show that the exclusion of agriculture unambiguously improves the welfare outcome, not only for Japan and Korea but also for all other economies in the region. The interpretation is that inclusion of a highly uncompetitive sector such as agriculture in a Japan-Korea FTA would increase trade diversion effects, so that—conversely—excluding agriculture improves the welfare outcome. This argument for excluding agriculture is not necessarily taken as conclusive. The counterargument is that accepting the exclusion of agriculture and other sensitive sectors from PTAs as legitimate will help undermine the multilateral trading system by encouraging the countries for which such sectors are sensitive to give priority to preferential liberalization initiatives at the expense of multilateral liberalization.

A survey of a large number of CGE studies of APEC liberalization in Scollay and Gilbert (2000) found that, in such studies, agricultural trade liberalization typically accounts for between 50 and 70 percent of the overall welfare gains projected to result from full APEC trade liberalization. This survey suggests that welfare will be reduced by excluding agriculture from trade agreements among groups that are big enough to include countries with large, internationally competitive agriculture sectors.

Table 4.5 reports results from the present study for simulations both excluding and including agriculture for the ASEAN+3 FTA, APEC MFN liberalization, and APEC preferential liberalization. In all three cases, excluding agriculture from the arrangement unambiguously worsens the welfare for all East Asian economies. The reduction in welfare is in many cases quite large, and in some cases it is very large. For Thailand, for example, the drop in welfare is equal to 1.8 percent of GDP in the case of the ASEAN+3 FTA, 0.9 percent of GDP under APEC MFN liberalization, and 1.2 percent of GDP under APEC preferential liberalization. Exclusion of agriculture reduces the overall combined welfare gains of the East Asian economies by 35 percent in the case of the ASEAN+3 FTA, by 48 percent in the case of APEC MFN liberalization, and by 33 percent in the case of APEC preferential liberalization.

These results are not surprising for APEC in light of the findings reported in Scollay and Gilbert (2000). They also indicate that ASEAN+3 is a sufficiently large and diverse group for the exclusion of agriculture to substantially reduce the prospective overall welfare gains available to the members of the group.

PRODUCTION ADJUSTMENTS

Successful trade liberalization initiatives, particularly far-reaching ones such as the establishment of an East Asian trade area or the achievement of APEC's free trade objectives, change the relative prices facing producers and consumers throughout the region. As a result, there will be movements up and down the supply and demand curves for each sector, as well as shifts in these curves reflecting changes in the relative attractiveness of different products to consumers and in the relative profitability of different lines of production for producers. Reduced trade barriers provide

Table 4.5 Welfare Effects with Agriculture Excluded
(percentage of GDP)

Economy or region	ASEAN+3		APEC most-favored nation		APEC preferential	
	All sectors	Agriculture excluded	All sectors	Agriculture excluded	All sectors	Agriculture excluded
Australia	-0.1	-0.1	0.2	-0.1	0.3	0.0
New Zealand	-0.2	-0.1	0.5	-0.1	1.0	-0.1
China	0.0	-0.3	0.2	-0.1	0.2	0.1
Hong Kong, China	1.6	1.5	1.9	1.7	2.0	1.8
Japan	0.1	0.2	0.4	0.2	0.4	0.3
Korea, Rep. of	0.7	0.5	0.7	0.3	0.9	0.5
Taiwan, China	-0.6	-0.6	0.7	0.6	0.8	0.8
Indonesia	0.4	0.1	0.3	0.2	0.5	0.3
Malaysia	0.4	0.1	0.2	0.1	0.4	0.2
Philippines	0.0	-0.6	-0.3	-0.3	0.1	-0.1
Singapore	2.5	1.7	1.9	1.6	2.1	1.7
Thailand	1.6	-0.2	1.0	0.1	1.3	0.1
Vietnam	3.1	1.3	4.8	2.5	3.3	2.0
Canada	0.0	0.0	0.1	-0.1	0.2	0.0
Mexico	0.0	0.0	0.1	0.0	0.1	0.0
United States	0.0	0.0	0.0	-0.1	0.0	0.0
Colombia	0.0	0.0	0.3	0.1	-0.2	-0.1
Peru	-0.1	0.0	-0.1	0.0	0.1	0.0
Venezuela, R.B. de	0.0	0.0	0.2	0.2	-0.1	0.0
Argentina	0.0	0.0	0.1	0.0	-0.1	0.0
Brazil	0.0	0.0	0.3	0.1	-0.1	0.0
Chile	-0.1	0.0	0.0	-0.2	0.3	-0.1
Uruguay	-0.1	0.0	0.1	0.0	-0.1	-0.1
South America (not elsewhere classified)	-0.2	-0.1	1.6	0.8	-0.9	-0.6
European Union	0.0	0.0	0.1	0.1	-0.1	0.0
Rest of world	-0.1	0.0	0.1	0.1	-0.1	-0.1
Sum members	0.3	0.2	0.2	0.1	0.2	0.1
Sum nonmembers	0.0	0.0	0.1	0.1	-0.1	-0.1
Sum world	0.0	0.0	0.2	0.1	0.1	0.0

Note: APEC = Asia-Pacific Economic Cooperation; ASEAN+3 = Association of Southeast Asian Nations plus China, the Republic of Korea, and Japan.
Source: Authors' simulations.

increased opportunities for producers and consumers to engage in trade to take advantage of price differences between and within economies.

In CGE modeling of trade initiatives, a comparison is made between an initial equilibrium and the new equilibrium that is calculated to prevail after adjustments have been made to consumption, production, and trade in response to the new set of prices brought about by the trade policy change. Changes in production levels are important indicators of the scale of opportunities and challenges faced by each sector in the economy and, consequently, of the adjustment issues each economy is likely to face. This section explores the sectoral changes in production indicated by CGE analysis of the proposed ASEAN+3 FTA, APEC MFN liberalization, and APEC preferential liberalization. These initiatives were identified previously as the ones likely to produce the most favorable outcomes for the East Asian economies.

There are significant differences between these initiatives in the nature of both the market access opportunities and the increased domestic market competition facing the East Asian economies. In the ASEAN+3 FTA, the East Asian economies open their markets to each other, but their markets continue to enjoy the existing levels of protection from the producers of all other economies. APEC preferential liberalization involves a wider market opening, to include access for producers from other APEC members outside East Asia, but protection levels are maintained against producers from outside APEC. Finally, APEC MFN liberalization involves East Asian and other APEC economies all opening their markets to producers in the world on a nondiscriminatory basis (without any reciprocation from non-APEC economies). Therefore, differences in the sectoral effects between the three scenarios should not cause any surprise.

To fully understand the results that follow, one must note that change in trade barriers facing a given sector is only one of the ways in which production in that sector can change in the model. Such change, of course, affects the level of market access in foreign countries or the level of competition faced in the domestic market. Production may also change in a given sector, even though the trade barriers applying to that sector may not alter. This result may occur because changes in trade barriers affecting another sector may change the relative profitability of production in different sectors, thus causing resources to move from one sector to another. Changes in relative profitability may also occur between sectors when barriers are removed from both sectors because of differences in the height of initial barriers or differences in production conditions. For example, in the results reported later, increases in rice production and decreases in wheat production in Korea may be related to changes in relative profitability of rice and wheat production when barriers are removed from both sectors.

Production effects are expressed here in two different ways. The first expresses changes as a percentage of the initial value added in each sector. This form of expression is helpful in identifying the sector that may face the largest challenges or opportunities and that, therefore, may have the greatest incentive to oppose or support a particular trade policy initiative. However, it is also important to take account of the size of the various sectors. A large production change in a tiny sector may have only minor implications for the economy as a whole, whereas a much smaller production change in a large sector may have much greater significance. For example, in the results reported below, very large changes occur in the output of the Indonesian motor vehicle industry, but these changes are shown to be relatively small when expressed as a percentage of total value added in the Indonesian economy in the initial equilibrium. Expressing sectoral production changes as a percentage of total value added in the economy helps assess the significance of the change in each sector for the economy as a whole and, therefore, the size of the adjustment that may be indicated. Changes expressed in this form may, for example, give an indication of employment effects across the sectors.

Table 4.6 shows the percentage of value added accounted for by each sector in each Asian economy in the initial equilibrium, as recorded in the GTAP5 database. Blank cells indicate zero or near-zero production for the sector indicated (strictly speaking, production that is less than 0.05 percent of total value added in the economy). Tables 4.7 to 4.9 then show the percentage change in value added in each sector, as indicated in the simulations of each initiative. Changes in production of between 10 and 25 percent are highlighted in bold italic type, and changes of more than 25 percent are indicated in bold normal type. Finally, in tables 4.10 to 4.12, the same production changes are expressed as a percentage of total value added in each economy in the initial equilibrium. Here the bold italic type indicates large changes of between 0.2 and 0.5 percent of total initial value added in the economy. A change of 0.2 percent of total value added, for example, could result from a 10 percent change in a sector accounting for 2 percent of the economy's value added. Bold italic type is used to highlight very large changes, more than 5 percent of total initial value added in the economy.

Production Effects in Northeast Asia

Among the Northeast Asian economies, some production effects appear consistently across all three scenarios. A large fall in value added occurs in China's motor vehicle industry: by 32 percent in an ASEAN+3 FTA and by 33 percent in both APEC scenarios. In each case, these declines represent

Table 4.6 East Asian Economies' Value Added by Sector at Market Prices
(percentage of total economy value added)

Sector	China	Hong Kong, China	Japan	Korea, Rep. of	Taiwan, China	Indonesia	Malaysia	Philippines	Singapore	Thailand	Vietnam
Rice	2.1	0.0	0.4	1.6	0.5	4.6	4.6	3.8	0.0	1.6	4.3
Wheat and grains	1.9	0.0	0.0	0.1	0.1	1.2	0.0	1.6	0.0	0.1	0.1
Nongrain crops	8.6	0.2	0.8	2.8	1.3	7.6	4.0	8.1	0.4	3.9	4.9
Forestry	1.1	0.0	0.1	0.2	0.0	2.0	2.8	1.7	0.1	2.7	1.1
Fisheries	1.9	0.1	0.2	0.6	0.7	1.9	2.2	4.4	0.1	1.0	1.8
Meat products	5.1	0.6	0.2	0.4	0.8	2.7	1.0	3.4	0.5	1.5	2.3
Dairy products	0.2	0.2	0.2	0.3	0.1	0.0	0.1	0.3	0.1	0.2	0.1
Other food products	3.3	1.6	2.0	1.6	1.2	7.4	1.7	7.7	1.5	4.0	2.8
Mining and quarrying	4.4	2.8	0.1	0.6	0.5	8.8	7.5	0.8	0.5	1.1	6.1
Textiles and apparel	6.6	4.7	1.0	2.8	2.5	2.8	1.4	2.0	1.0	5.8	2.5
Wood products	2.2	1.4	1.9	2.0	2.0	2.8	3.5	1.4	2.6	3.5	0.9
Chemical products	8.8	1.2	3.6	6.6	5.8	4.9	4.8	2.1	6.5	8.1	2.4
Metal products	2.3	0.1	1.5	2.6	2.3	0.9	0.9	0.6	1.0	1.3	0.6
Fabricated metal	1.5	0.7	1.4	1.4	1.6	0.6	1.1	0.2	1.3	1.2	0.1
Automobiles	0.9	0.8	1.8	2.5	0.6	0.5	1.8	0.1	0.5	3.6	0.0
Transportation equipment	0.8	0.3	0.4	0.9	0.7	0.1	0.4	0.1	0.4	0.7	0.1
Electronic equipment	1.9	1.1	3.6	2.2	5.3	2.7	6.4	1.0	7.0	9.4	0.5
Machinery	6.4	2.8	3.2	6.7	3.9	0.5	3.6	0.8	8.0	6.0	0.5
Other manufactures	2.8	0.4	0.7	0.7	0.5	0.5	1.1	0.3	0.7	2.0	0.5
Services	37.3	81.1	76.9	63.6	69.7	47.7	50.9	59.5	67.8	42.2	68.3

Source: Global Trade Analysis Project 5 database.

Table 4.7 Production Effects by Sector for East Asian Economies: ASEAN+3 Free Trade Agreement (percentage change in value added)

Sector	China	Hong Kong, China	Japan	Korea, Rep. of	Taiwan, China	Indonesia	Malaysia	Philippines	Singapore	Thailand	Vietnam
Rice	3.39		-7.23	14.28	-1.00	4.00	7.33	-2.61		24.22	3.06
Wheat and grains	6.89			-78.37	0.24	-1.12		-7.42		3.33	4.97
Nongrain crops	2.09	-0.12	-2.64	-6.13	0.34	0.65	-6.81	6.30		0.11	-1.13
Forestry	-0.87		-0.76	-1.72		0.72	-0.74	-1.13	-3.78	-0.19	12.78
Fisheries	-0.11	-0.69	-1.21	0.97	0.19	-0.20	1.20	-0.23	0.38	2.83	-2.07
Meat products	1.18	-0.31	-6.67	20.53	-1.59	-0.66	2.71	-1.54	-0.01	16.72	-5.11
Dairy products	3.96	11.17	-4.78	9.58	0.72		32.69	15.58	357.7	19.00	-17.62
Other food products	0.60	18.76	-2.91	14.63	-1.24	4.00	15.61	-2.64	39.79	27.48	21.7
Mining and quarrying	-0.79	-0.44	-0.79	-4.44	1.99	-1.24	-0.68	-0.63	-0.17	-1.32	-5.17
Textiles and apparel	3.08	9.07	0.79	16.18	-14.79	-0.01	11.5	9.35	5.00	-6.61	32.40
Wood products	-1.54	1.84	-0.23	1.12	1.25	1.27	1.68	-1.74	1.77	-1.14	-17.57
Chemical products	-1.55	3.59	0.88	1.71	-1.44	-1.64	1.90	-0.57	2.10	-1.56	-11.33
Metal products	-3.20	-2.46	2.15	-3.13	2.10	-5.32	-3.94	0.98	-0.50	-7.39	-23.05
Fabricated metal	-0.51	3.29	0.42	-0.83	2.82	-4.43	-2.13	0.30	8.47	-6.60	-27.18
Automobiles	-31.78	-8.93	3.97	-3.99	2.20	-42.21	-35.83	37.64	-13.28	-30.89	-55.64
Transportation equipment	-0.32	-11.90	3.38	-9.36	7.20	31.46	-3.51	12.74	-9.69	3.54	
Electronic equipment	6.34	-1.29	-0.29	-1.59	1.94	2.69	3.49	8.14	-2.71	3.24	2.04
Machinery	-2.18	6.89	1.32	-5.10	1.95	4.90	-0.83	5.48	-1.34	-0.37	-20.12
Other manufactures	-0.35	11.60	0.82	-0.73	1.34	-11.13	-0.59	-1.64	-3.58	-6.09	-19.03
Services	-0.22	-0.99	-0.07	-0.46	0.14	-0.25	-0.45	-0.78	-1.41	-0.49	-1.31

Note: ASEAN+3 = Association of Southeast Asian Nations plus China, the Republic of Korea, and Japan.
Source: Authors' simulations.

Table 4.8 Production Effects by Sector for East Asian Economies: APEC Most-Favored Nation (percentage change in value added)

Sector	China	Hong Kong, China	Japan	Korea, Rep. of	Taiwan, China	Indonesia	Malaysia	Philippines	Singapore	Thailand	Vietnam
Rice	-1.73		-10.5	11.33	-4.64	0.00	6.23	-2.73		14.77	1.10
Wheat and grains	-6.69			-83.73	-2.19	-0.51		-11.02		8.17	3.03
Nongrain crops	-2.51	0.77	-12.72	-12.11	-3.50	0.08	-12.47	1.50	11.25	-2.20	-2.32
Forestry	-1.09			-5.02		1.08	-1.95	-1.72	-0.50	-1.12	-1.37
Fisheries	-0.64	-0.90	-2.00	0.22	-2.82	-0.43	-0.11	-0.3	0.16	0.40	-2.81
Meat products	2.14	-1.79	-17.4	8.86	1.42	-1.14	-3.3	-3.78	-2.57	1.33	-6.34
Dairy products	1.16	-0.12	-29.81	-8.06	-9.23		2.61	-1.56	6.57	-18.42	-29.93
Other food products	-4.53	1.01	-4.44	11.89	-4.98	0.00	11.51	-2.75	11.87	16.59	-5.25
Mining and quarrying	-0.85	-0.53	1.30	-7.49	-6.72	-0.82	-0.75	0.03	-0.07	-1.09	-4.47
Textiles and apparel	13.67	9.78	-3.39	19.23	23.07	13.67	19.72	40.55	9.91	2.44	52.67
Wood products	-1.48	0.37	-0.57	-0.12	-0.77	1.78	-0.01	-2.92	1.30	-2.12	-18.62
Chemical products	-2.15	1.62	0.79	1.70	5.13	-2.21	4.34	-1.3	0.55	-3.24	-12.4
Metal products	-4.30	-6.37	2.89	-2.21	-2.79	-6.11	-5.2	0.21	-2.59	-6.67	-24.67
Fabricated metal	0.19	1.00	0.57	-1.23	-0.60	-7.60	-5.88	1.10	2.44	-9.68	-26.47
Automobiles	-32.66	-7.79	8.88	0.44	-21.73	-43.08	-36.76	38.54	-8.23	-31.27	
Transportation equipment	2.34	-9.20	5.24	-4.65	18.17	28.12	1.95	22.96	-9.75	-0.97	-49.18
Electronic equipment	11.36	-9.40	0.01	2.79	-1.89	4.15	5.24	13.91	-5.00	6.21	-0.14
Machinery	-2.56	4.00	1.91	-5.08	-0.95	7.92	1.2	13.11	0.11	3.80	-21.95
Other manufactures	2.99	7.89	1.04	0.25	0.69	-7.47	0.65	-0.67	-0.69	1.65	-17.26
Services	0.07	-0.39	0.07	-0.38	-0.68	-0.05	-0.15	-1.02	-0.17	-0.22	-0.37

Note: APEC = Asia-Pacific Economic Cooperation.
Source: Authors' simulations.

150

Table 4.9 Production Effects by Sector for East Asian Economies: APEC Preferential (percentage change in value added)

Sector	China	Hong Kong, China	Japan	Korea, Rep. of	Taiwan, China	Indonesia	Malaysia	Philippines	Singapore	Thailand	Vietnam
Rice	0.66		-8.90	13.84	-0.15	1.23	6.88	-1.19		19.4	1.67
Wheat and grains	-6.12			-82.73	-1.63	-0.38		-10.76		8.57	4.87
Nongrain crops	-1.09	1.36	-10.95	-11.44	-2.59	0.56	-10.55	2.24	12.48	-1.25	-1.84
Forestry	-1.41			-4.20		0.34	-1.66	-2.09	-2.85	-0.91	5.16
Fisheries	-0.08	-0.48	-1.24	0.88	-2.42	-0.29	0.64	-0.08	0.53	1.96	-2.35
Meat products	1.92	-1.85	-14.01	10.80	2.78	-1.15	-1.50	-3.05	-1.18	3.22	-6.57
Dairy products	2.62	0.25	-27.16	-5.74	-6.61		5.55	-0.62	15.31	-11.5	-24.77
Other food products	-1.03	11.08	-2.97	14.46	0.23	1.23	13.57	-1.18	26.02	22.21	7.72
Mining and quarrying	-1.34	-0.66	-0.74	-4.89	-5.92	-1.25	-0.73	-1.73	0.05	-1.66	-5.36
Textiles and apparel	13.48	14.28	-1.51	20.90	26.31	14.24	23.95	45.95	13.81	3.11	49.94
Wood products	-1.94	0.82	-0.51	0.36	-0.95	0.78	0.89	-3.08	1.54	-1.71	-18.41
Chemical products	-2.22	2.35	1.11	1.57	5.40	-2.08	3.61	-0.76	2.37	-2.50	-13.19
Metal products	-4.44	-4.33	2.97	-2.58	-3.22	-6.43	-4.76	-0.41	-0.26	-7.96	-24.63
Fabricated metal	-0.55	2.07	0.64	-0.91	-1.16	-6.25	-4.04	-0.75	4.62	-9.22	-24.95
Automobiles	-32.61	-9.39	9.36	-0.89	-20.01	-42.41	-33.91	44.47	-10.28	-30.69	-52.65
Transportation equipment	-0.21	-11.21	3.34	-9.33	14.75	28.71	1.42	13.90	-7.59	0.23	
Electronic equipment	8.09	-6.27	-0.39	0.82	-4.31	2.88	4.05	11.57	-3.86	4.52	-0.74
Machinery	-2.83	4.69	1.64	-5.08	-1.48	6.79	0.23	9.99	0.35	1.36	-21.51
Other manufactures	0.63	9.61	0.79	0.20	-1.03	-9.74	-0.14	-2.82	-3.31	-1.23	-19.24
Services	-0.11	-0.86	-0.02	-0.47	-0.70	-0.23	-0.54	-1.58	-1.07	-0.66	-1.43

Note: APEC = Asia-Pacific Economic Cooperation.
Source: Authors' simulations.

151

Table 4.10 Production Effects by Sector for East Asian Economies: ASEAN+3 Free Trade Agreement (change as a percentage of initial value added)

Sector	China	Hong Kong, China	Japan	Korea, Rep. of	Taiwan, China	Indonesia	Malaysia	Philippines	Singapore	Thailand	Vietnam
Rice	0.07		-0.03	0.22	0.00	0.18	0.33	-0.10		0.40	0.13
Wheat and grains	0.13		0.00	-0.05	0.00	-0.01		-0.12		0.00	0.01
Nongrain crops	0.18	0.00	-0.02	-0.17	0.00	0.05	-0.27	0.51	0.07	0.00	-0.06
Forestry	-0.01			0.00	0.00	0.01	-0.02	-0.02	0.00	-0.01	0.14
Fisheries	0.00	0.00	0.00	0.01		0.00	0.03	-0.01	0.00	0.03	-0.04
Meat products	0.06	0.00	-0.01	0.08	-0.01	-0.02	0.03	-0.05	0.00	0.25	-0.12
Dairy products	0.01	0.02	-0.01	0.03	0.00		0.03	0.05	0.29	0.04	-0.01
Other food products	0.02	0.29	-0.06	0.23	-0.01	0.29	0.26	-0.20	0.58	1.10	0.61
Mining and quarrying	-0.03	-0.01	0.00	-0.03	0.01	-0.11	-0.05	-0.01	0.00	-0.01	-0.32
Textiles and apparel	0.20	0.42	0.01	0.46	-0.36	0.00	0.17	0.19	0.05	-0.38	0.83
Wood products	-0.03	0.03	0.03	0.02	0.02	0.04	0.06	-0.02	0.05	-0.04	-0.17
Chemical products	-0.14	0.04	0.03	0.11	-0.08	-0.08	0.09	-0.01	0.14	-0.13	-0.27
Metal products	-0.07	0.00	0.03	-0.08	0.05	-0.05	-0.04	0.01	0.00	-0.10	-0.15
Fabricated metal	-0.01	0.02	0.01	-0.01	0.05	-0.03	-0.02	0.00	0.11	-0.08	-0.03
Automobiles	-0.29	-0.07	0.07	-0.10	0.01	-0.23	-0.63	0.05	-0.07	-1.12	
Transportation equipment	0.00	-0.03	0.01	-0.08	0.05	0.03	-0.01	0.01	-0.04	0.03	-0.05
Electronic equipment	0.12	-0.01	-0.01	-0.04	0.10	0.07	0.22	0.08	-0.19	0.30	0.01
Machinery	-0.14	0.19	0.04	-0.34	0.08	0.02	-0.03	0.04	-0.11	-0.02	-0.10
Other manufactures	-0.01	0.04	0.01	-0.01	0.01	-0.05	-0.01	-0.01	-0.02	-0.12	-0.09
Services	-0.08	-0.80	-0.05	-0.29	0.10	-0.12	-0.23	-0.46	-0.96	-0.21	-0.89

Note: ASEAN+3 = Association of Southeast Asian Nations plus China, the Republic of Korea, and Japan.
Source: Authors' simulations.

Table 4.11 Production Effects by Sector for East Asian Economies: APEC Most-Favored Nation
(change as a percentage of initial value added)

Sector	China	Hong Kong, China	Japan	Korea, Rep. of	Taiwan, China	Indonesia	Malaysia	Philippines	Singapore	Thailand	Vietnam
Rice	-0.04		-0.05	0.18	-0.02	0.00	*0.28*	-0.10		*0.24*	0.05
Wheat and grains	-0.13		-0.01	-0.05	0.00	-0.01		-0.17		0.01	0.00
Nongrain crops	*-0.22*	0.00	-0.10	-0.34	-0.05	0.01	*-0.50*	0.12	0.05	-0.09	-0.11
Forestry	-0.01		0.00	-0.01	0.00	0.02	-0.06	-0.03	0.00	-0.03	-0.02
Fisheries	-0.01	0.00	0.00	0.00	-0.02	-0.01	0.00	-0.01	0.00	0.00	-0.05
Meat products	0.11	-0.01	-0.03	0.03	0.01	-0.03	-0.03	-0.13	-0.01	0.02	-0.14
Dairy products	0.00	0.00	-0.05	-0.02	-0.01		0.00	0.00	0.01	-0.04	-0.02
Other food products	-0.15	0.02	-0.09	0.18	-0.06	0.00	0.19	*-0.21*	0.17	*0.66*	-0.15
Mining and quarrying	-0.04	-0.01	0.00	-0.05	-0.04	-0.07	-0.06	0.00	0.00	-0.01	*-0.27*
Textiles and apparel	*0.90*	*0.46*	-0.03	*0.54*	*0.57*	*0.38*	*0.29*	*0.80*	0.10	0.14	*1.34*
Wood products	-0.03	0.01	-0.01	0.00	-0.02	0.05	0.00	-0.04	0.03	-0.07	-0.18
Chemical products	-0.19	0.02	0.03	0.11	*0.30*	-0.11	*0.21*	-0.03	0.04	*-0.26*	*-0.30*
Metal products	-0.10	-0.01	0.04	-0.06	-0.06	-0.05	-0.05	0.00	-0.03	-0.09	-0.16
Fabricated metal	0.00	0.01	0.01	-0.02	-0.01	-0.05	-0.07	0.00	0.03	-0.12	-0.03
Automobiles	*-0.30*	-0.06	0.16	0.01	-0.14	*-0.23*	*-0.64*	0.06	-0.04	*-1.13*	
Transportation equipment	0.02	-0.02	0.02	-0.04	0.12	0.02	0.01	0.02	-0.04	-0.01	-0.04
Electronic equipment	*0.21*	-0.11	0.00	0.06	-0.10	0.11	*0.34*	0.14	*-0.35*	*0.58*	0.00
Machinery	-0.16	0.11	0.06	*-0.34*	-0.04	0.04	0.04	0.11	0.01	*0.23*	-0.10
Other manufactures	0.08	0.03	0.01	0.00	0.00	-0.04	0.01	0.00	0.00	0.03	-0.09
Services	0.03	*-0.32*	0.05	*-0.24*	*-0.47*	-0.02	-0.08	*-0.61*	-0.12	-0.09	*-0.25*

Note: APEC = Asia-Pacific Economic Cooperation.
Source: Authors' simulations.

Table 4.12 Production Effects by Sector for East Asian Economies: APEC Preferential (change as a percentage of initial value added)

Sector	China	Hong Kong, China	Japan	Korea, Rep. of	Taiwan, China	Indonesia	Malaysia	Philippines	Singapore	Thailand	Vietnam
Rice	0.01		-0.04	0.22	0.00	0.06	0.31	-0.05		0.32	0.07
Wheat and grains	-0.11			-0.05	0.00	0.00		-0.17		0.01	0.01
Nongrain crops	-0.09	0.00	-0.09	-0.32	-0.03	0.04	-0.42	0.18	0.05	-0.05	-0.09
Forestry	-0.02			-0.01		0.01	-0.05	-0.04	0.00	-0.02	0.06
Fisheries	0.00	0.00	0.00	0.01	-0.02	-0.01	0.01	0.00	0.00	0.02	-0.04
Meat products	0.10	-0.01	-0.02	0.04	0.02	-0.03	-0.02	-0.10	-0.01	0.05	-0.15
Dairy products	0.00	0.00	-0.05	-0.02	0.00		0.00	0.00	0.01	-0.02	-0.01
Other food products	-0.03	0.17	-0.06	0.22	0.00	0.09	0.22	-0.09	0.38	0.89	0.22
Mining and quarrying	-0.06	-0.02	0.00	-0.03	-0.03	-0.11	-0.05	-0.01	0.00	-0.02	-0.33
Textiles and apparel	0.89	0.67	-0.01	0.59	0.65	0.39	0.35	0.91	0.13	0.18	1.27
Wood products	-0.04	0.01	-0.01	0.01	-0.02	0.02	0.03	-0.04	0.04	-0.06	-0.17
Chemical products	-0.20	0.03	0.04	0.10	0.31	-0.10	0.17	-0.02	0.15	-0.20	-0.32
Metal products	-0.10	-0.01	0.05	-0.07	-0.07	-0.06	-0.05	0.00	0.00	-0.10	-0.16
Fabricated metal	-0.01	0.02	0.01	-0.01	-0.02	-0.04	-0.05	0.00	0.06	-0.11	-0.03
Automobiles	-0.30	-0.08	0.17	-0.02	-0.13	-0.23	-0.59	0.06	-0.05	-1.11	
Transportation equipment	0.00	-0.03	0.01	-0.08	0.10	0.02	0.01	0.01	-0.03	0.00	-0.05
Electronic equipment	0.15	-0.07	-0.01	0.02	-0.23	0.08	0.26	0.12	-0.27	0.43	0.00
Machinery	-0.18	0.13	0.05	-0.34	-0.06	0.03	0.01	0.08	0.03	0.08	-0.10
Other manufactures	0.02	0.03	0.01	0.00	-0.01	-0.05	0.00	-0.01	-0.02	-0.02	-0.10
Services	-0.04	-0.70	-0.02	-0.30	-0.49	-0.11	-0.28	-0.94	-0.73	-0.28	-0.98

Note: APEC = Asia-Pacific Economic Cooperation.
Source: Authors' simulations.

just under 0.3 percent of total value added in the Chinese economy in the initial equilibrium.

In Korea, value added in the textile and apparel sector rises by 16 percent in an ASEAN+3 FTA and by about 20 percent in each of the two APEC scenarios. These rises, respectively, represent just less than and just more than 0.5 percent of total value added in the Korean economy in the initial equilibrium. Value added in the machinery sector falls by an apparently modest 5 percent in each scenario, but this drop is relatively significant in the context of the overall economy, representing 0.3 percent of total value added in the initial equilibrium. Value added in other food products rises sharply, by rather more in the two preferential scenarios (up by just less than 15 percent in each case) than under APEC liberalization (up by 12 percent); this rise equates to about 0.2 percent of value added in the initial equilibrium. There is a moderately large percentage rise in the output of rice, plus a much larger percentage fall in the output of wheat, perhaps reflecting changes in the relative profitability of producing the two crops following liberalization. The output in the larger rice sector is, however, much more significant in relation to the overall economy than the large output fall in the much smaller wheat sector.

Some production effects are much more pronounced in the ASEAN+3 FTA scenario than in the APEC scenarios. For example, value added in the milk products sector in Hong Kong, China, rises by 11 percent in an ASEAN+3 FTA, but there is only minimal effect in the two APEC scenarios, in which competition is faced from more efficient dairy producers in the wider Asia-Pacific region (and also further afield, in the case of APEC MFN liberalization). Value added in the other food products sector in Hong Kong, China, rises significantly under the two preferential scenarios (by 19 percent in the ASEAN+3 FTA and by 11 percent under APEC preferential liberalization) but changes only minimally under APEC MFN liberalization. However, tables 4.10 to 4.12 show that the changes in both the milk products and the other food products sectors are very small relative to the total initial value added in the economy of Hong Kong, China.

There are other sectors in which production is affected much more under the APEC scenarios than in an ASEAN+3 FTA. The leading example is the textile and apparel sector, in which much larger increases in value added in China are registered under the APEC scenarios (a 13 percent increase in each case) than under the ASEAN+3 FTA (a 3 percent increase). Value added in the textile and apparel sector in Hong Kong, China, rises by more in the APEC preferential case (up by 14 percent) than in either the ASEAN+3 FTA or the APEC MFN liberalization case (up by just less than 10 percent in each case). In the case of Taiwan, China, large increases in value added in the textile and apparel sector under the APEC scenarios contrast with a sharp fall of 15 percent under the ASEAN+3 FTA. That outcome is not surprising given that Taiwan, China, is not included in the ASEAN+3 group. The increased value added in the textiles and apparel sector for these economies under APEC liberalization equates to a significant percentage—ranging from 0.46 to 0.90 percent—of total value added in the initial equilibrium.

For China, increases in value added in the electronic equipment sector also become large under the APEC MFN liberalization scenario, and under APEC MFN liberalization, the fall in value added in the nongrain crop sector, although not especially large in percentage terms, rises above 0.2 percent of total initial value added in the economy.

In a number of agricultural sectors in Japan, APEC liberalization also leads to falls in value that appear large or very large in percentage terms, although they appear much less significant when expressed as a percentage of total initial value added. A similar situation applies in the Korean nongrain crop sector. The results for Japan, in fact, are notable because none of the liberalization scenarios produce large changes in the value added in any sector, when measured as a percentage of total initial value added. Expressed in this form, the largest fall in value added in Japan under any of the scenarios is 0.1 percent in the nongrain crop sector under APEC MFN liberalization, whereas the largest rise is 0.17 percent in the motor vehicle sector under APEC preferential liberalization.[5]

For Taiwan, China, APEC liberalization leads to substantial percentage falls in value added in the motor vehicle sector, partly matched by rises in the transportation equipment sector, but these changes appear less significant when expressed as a percentage of total initial value added. On that latter basis, the rise in value added in the chemical sector under both APEC scenarios and the fall in value added in the electronic machinery sector under APEC preferential liberalization are much more significant.

Production Effects in Southeast Asia

In Southeast Asia, there are widespread effects on the motor vehicle sector under all three liberalization scenarios. Very large percentage declines

5. This result suggests that, with the exception of agriculture, trade distortions in the Japanese economy are relatively low. This finding is certainly true with respect to formal barriers (see WTO 2001b), but it is often argued that Japan is heavily protected by nontariff barriers. The GTAP5 database does not capture this issue well, and so our results may be reflecting the fact that our understanding of Japanese protection patterns is limited. Sazanami, Urata, and Kawai (1995) approach this issue from the perspective of unit price differentials in a partial equilibrium model.

in value added in this sector are projected for Indonesia, Malaysia, and Thailand, with a smaller but still large decline in Singapore and a very large rise in value added in the Philippines. When expressed as a percentage of total initial value added, the declines in Malaysia and Thailand (particularly Thailand) continue to appear very large. The decline in Indonesia is also significant, although much less so than might be expected on the basis of the very large decline in value added in the sector itself. The increases in the Philippines and declines in Singapore are of much less significance on an economywide basis. In Indonesia and the Philippines, there are also large percentage increases in value added in the transportation equipment sector, but these increases are also very small relative to total initial value added. In Thailand, however, there are increases in value added in the electronic machinery sector that are small in percentage terms but are shown to be much more significant when expressed as a percentage of total initial value added.

A number of food sources also experience significant effects. In the other food products sector in Malaysia, Singapore, and Thailand, there are very large increases in value added under the ASEAN+3 scenario and smaller, but still significant, increases under the APEC scenarios. All these increases continue to appear of major significance when expressed as a percentage of total initial value added in the respective economies. In Vietnam, interestingly, a large increase in value added in the other food products sector in the ASEAN+3 scenario becomes considerably smaller under APEC preferential liberalization and changes to a small decrease under APEC MFN liberalization.

In Thailand, there are increases in rice output that are very significant under both measures in all three scenarios, whereas in the meat sector, there is a large increase in output under both measures in the ASEAN+3 scenario, but not in the APEC scenarios.

In the Philippines, a significant percentage increase in value added appears in the milk products sector under the ASEAN+3 scenario, but this effect is shown to be very minor when expressed as a percentage of the economy's total initial value added, and it also changes to a small decline in value added under the two APEC scenarios. Similarly, the large percentage decline in value added in the wheat sector indicated under the APEC scenarios (as well as the smaller increase under the ASEAN+3 scenario) also appears much less significant in the economywide context. Conversely, the relatively small percentage increase in value added in the nongrain crop sector in the ASEAN+3 scenario (up 6.3 percent) is of considerable significance when expressed as a percentage of total initial value added (up 0.51 percent). Under the APEC scenarios, the increase in value added in this sector is much smaller.

In Singapore, substantial increases are projected in value added in the nongrain crop sector under all three scenarios, and a very large increase is projected in value added in the milk products sector in the ASEAN+3 FTA. Value added in the milk products sector drops dramatically in the more competitive international environment of APEC liberalization but still remains substantial in the APEC preferential case. Given the small size of these sectors in Singapore, it is not surprising that the increases in these sectors are nevertheless very minor when expressed as a percentage of total initial value added in the economy, except in the case of the milk products sector in the ASEAN+3 scenario, in which the increase remains substantial at 0.23 percent.

As in the case of Northeast Asia, there are widespread significant effects on value added in the textiles and apparel sector, and these effects are greater under the APEC liberalization scenarios than in the ASEAN+3 FTA. The effects on this sector are large across all three liberalization scenarios only in the cases of Malaysia and Vietnam. In Malaysia, there are increases of 11 percent under the ASEAN+3 FTA, 20 percent under APEC MFN liberalization, and 23 percent under APEC preferential liberalization, equating, respectively, to 0.17 percent, 0.28 percent, and 0.35 percent of total initial value added. In Vietnam, the corresponding figures are 32 percent under the ASEAN+3 FTA, 53 percent under APEC MFN liberalization, and 50 percent under APEC preferential liberalization, equating, respectively, to 0.61 percent, 1.34 percent, and 1.27 percent of total initial value added.

In other Southeast Asian economies, the effect on the sector is relatively minor under ASEAN+3 and becomes more significant under the APEC scenarios, particularly APEC preferential liberalization. Thus, under APEC preferential liberalization, increases in value added of 46 percent, 14 percent, and 14 percent are registered, respectively, for the Philippines, Indonesia, and Singapore, with the corresponding increases under APEC MFN liberalization being 41 percent, 14 percent, and 10 percent. Table 4.11 shows that these figures equate to a significant share of total initial value added for the Philippines and Indonesia in particular. In the case of Thailand, a small decrease in the sector's value added under the ASEAN+3 FTA turns into a small increase under the two APEC scenarios.

There are a small number of other manufacturing sectors in which a large effect appears under the APEC scenarios but not under the ASEAN+3 FTA. Value added in the Philippine electronic machinery sector rises by 14 percent under both APEC liberalization scenarios, whereas in the machinery sector there is an increase of 13 percent under APEC MFN liberalization and 10 percent under APEC preferential liberalization. These increases, however, are both small relative to the total initial value added in the economy. On that basis, the declines in output in the Thai chemical sector (0.26 percent under APEC MFN liberalization) and the rise in the Thai machinery sector (0.23 percent under APEC MFN liberalization) appear rather more significant, even though the percentage changes in the value added of the sectors themselves, as indicated in table 4.8, appear relatively minor. Likewise, there are declines in the value added of the Singapore electronic machinery sector that are clearly of considerable significance when measured as a percentage of initial total value added (0.35 percent under APEC MFN liberalization and 0.27 percent under APEC preferential liberalization), despite the percentage declines in value added of the sector itself being relatively small (5 percent and 3.86 percent, respectively).

Finally, the figures for the Vietnam manufacturing sectors are interesting. The very large percentage declines in value added in several of these sectors might suggest that each of the liberalization scenarios would have a devastating effect on the Vietnamese manufacturing sector. When expressed as a percentage of total initial value added in the economy, however, the effects appear to be relatively minor, with only the chemicals sector showing a large decline, which appears under all three scenarios. This result indicates that these manufacturing sectors are still relatively small and suggests the alternative hypothesis that, rather than having a negative implication for Vietnamese manufacturing, liberalization may have a positive effect by inhibiting the development of sectors in which there is currently no comparative advantage, while boosting internationally competitive sectors such as textiles and apparel.

GRAVITY MODELS, CGE SIMULATIONS, AND NATURAL TRADING BLOCS

The prospective emergence of a large trading bloc in East Asia naturally raises questions about the implications of such a development for the global trading system and also for APEC's vision of free and open trade and investment in the wider Asia-Pacific region. Much ink has been spilled on the topic of whether RTAs might constitute building blocks toward the goal of global free trade, or whether they are instead likely to act as stumbling blocks to progress in that direction. (For a detailed discussion of these issues, see Bhagwati and Panagariya 1996.)

An important issue in answering these questions in relation to individual or proposed RTAs is whether and to what extent such agreements have negative effects on the welfare of nonmembers, in particular through trade diversion, and their effects on terms of trade. RTAs that seriously harm nonmembers are obviously more likely to serve as stumbling blocks. Conversely, RTAs that eliminate or minimize harmful effects on nonmembers have a greater probability of serving as building blocks. It is, therefore, not surprising that analytical approaches have been developed that aim to identify categories of RTAs in which harmful effects on members or nonmembers are absent or minimized, as well as ways of configuring RTAs that eliminate or minimize such effects.

An approach that has received attention is based on the concept of *natural trading blocs*, a concept put forward by, for example, Krugman (1991). Krugman suggested that trading blocs composed of economies that are in close geographic proximity can be considered natural trading blocs and are unlikely to result in significant trade diversion effects. This position has been criticized on the grounds that distance primarily affects transportation costs and that these costs are, in principle, no different from any other source of comparative advantage (see Bhagwati and Panagariya 1996, among others).

In this section, we use a method for empirically assessing whether the natural trading bloc hypothesis can provide any reassurance regarding the implications of an East Asian trading bloc for the global and Asia-Pacific trading environment. This approach makes use of a gravity model as well as CGE techniques. A gravity model is first used to assess how far the various RTA configurations identified as steps toward an East Asian trading bloc can be classified as natural trading blocs by using an alternative definition of natural trading bloc than that put forward by Krugman. CGE analysis is then used to assess the degree to which satisfying the criterion for natural trading blocs provides a reliable guide to the degree to which RTAs exhibit favorable welfare effects.

Gravity models require the application of statistical techniques to historical data and are generally applied to ex post analysis of existing RTAs. Frankel (1997) conducted a comprehensive study using this technique. The models can be specified to allow for tests of the propensity for a given group of economies to trade more intensively with each other relative to economies with otherwise similar characteristics. If the group in question already has an RTA in place, the results, taken in conjunction with tests for the general degree of openness of the economies in question, may be interpreted as proxies for the presence or absence of trade creation and trade diversion effects arising from the RTA. Among economies that have no formal RTA in place, the results can also be interpreted as indications of whether an RTA among the economies might be considered a natural trading bloc. According to the hypothesis put forward by Krugman (1991), the welfare effects of such an RTA would be expected to be favorable, with negative welfare effects on nonmembers in particular being absent or minimized.

Welfare effects, however, are not directly observable in gravity models, and it is here that CGE modeling makes its contribution. CGE simulations are used to test whether expected welfare effects are indeed more favorable in those RTAs that conform more strongly to the criterion of a natural trading bloc. In this way, some light can be thrown on the reliability of the hypothesis itself, as well as on the implications of new RTAs in East Asia.

The remainder of this section is organized as follows. In the next subsection, we outline the methods used in our gravity model simulations. A set of basic results is derived before the introduction of a subset of the potential East Asian RTAs into the model. The following section then focuses on results for these new RTA proposals and assesses them for conformity with the criterion of a natural trading bloc. The conclusions drawn from this assessment are then compared and contrasted with the results obtained by analyzing the same proposals in a CGE framework. Tentative conclusions follow in the final subsection.

Gravity Model: Methodology

The basic gravity model approach uses a cross-section of bilateral trade data to attempt to estimate a normal trade pattern and to test for discernible variations from that pattern. If order can be found in the deviations from the pattern, this technique can provide useful information on trade effects of RTAs. Thus, it is necessary to specify and estimate the complete model as the first step in the analysis, even though the discussion will ultimately focus more narrowly on estimates of the specific variables that bear directly on the natural trading bloc properties of the proposed East Asian RTAs.

The gravity model postulates that bilateral trade flows are proportional to the product of the size of the two economies and inversely related to the distance between them. This model is broadly compatible with a wide variety of underlying theoretical models (in particular those emphasizing imperfect competition—see the discussion in Frankel 1997), and it lends itself easily to empirical verification. The basic model estimates the bilateral trade flows as a function of the products of the bilateral GDPs (as a measure of size) and distance (both in log form). Letting i and j index the economies in the model, we have

Eq. 4.1 $\quad \ln(T_{ij}) = \alpha + \beta_1 \ln(GDP_i GDP_j) + \beta_2 \ln(DIST_{ij}) + u_{ij} \qquad \forall \, i < j$

where T_{ij} is the total trade between economies i and j, $DIST_{ij}$ is our distance measure, and u_{ij} is the error term. Most applications expand the basic model to provide further explanatory variables. The model that we use here is of the following well-established form (see Frankel 1997; Freund 2000):

Eq. 4.2 $\quad \ln(T_{ij}) = \alpha + \beta_1 \ln(GDP_i GDP_j) + \beta_2 \ln(DIST_{ij})$
$\qquad\qquad + \beta_3 \ln(PC_i PC_j) + \beta_4 \ln(|PC_i - PC_j|) + \gamma_1 ADJ_{ij}$
$\qquad\qquad + \gamma_2 RTA_{ij} + \gamma_3 OPEN_{ij} + u_{ij} \qquad\qquad \forall \, i < j$

where PC_i is per capita GDP. Note that PC_i enters the equation in two forms: as the product of bilateral per capita GDPs and as the absolute value of the difference. The former can be thought of as capturing the importance of wealth (as opposed to size) as a determinant of trade; the latter can be thought of as capturing the importance of differences between economies. By virtue of the double-logarithmic specification of the estimated function, the parameter estimates on the income and distance variables (β_k) can be interpreted as elasticities. Hence, β_1 represents, for example, the estimated proportional change in T_{ij} induced by a 1 percent change in $GDP_i GDP_j$.

The remaining variables are dummies designed to capture the influence of other factors on trade flows. ADJ_{ij} represents the existence of a common border, and RTA_{ij} represents the existence of an RTA (being one if both countries i and j are members of the RTA in question). $OPEN_{ij}$ is designed to capture the degree of openness of RTA members (being one if country i or country j is a member of the RTA in question) and can be thought of as a way of isolating the effect of the RTA.[6] Note that we use a separate RTA and $OPEN$ dummy for each group under consideration; hence, we can think of RTA and $OPEN$ as vectors of dummy variables representing each of the individual RTAs.

The RTA and $OPEN$ parameters will be the central focus of attention in discussing the natural trading bloc properties of new East Asian RTAs. The RTA parameters are included to indicate the propensity of the

---

6. We consider the effect of the European Union, NAFTA, AFTA, the CER Agreement, MERCOSUR (the Southern Cone Common Market or Mercado Común del Sur), the Andean Pact, and APEC as part of our base scenario. We also consider the degree of integration between China, Japan, Korea, AFTA, the CER Agreement, and other economies in our analysis of new RTA proposals.

economies in the relevant group to trade with each other, relative to otherwise similarly sized and located economies in the model. For economies that have established a formal RTA among themselves, trends in the *RTA* parameter can be interpreted as an indication of the presence or absence of trade creation effects. The use of the *RTA* parameter is not, however, restricted to cases in which a formal RTA exists; it can be estimated for a given group of economies for any year for which the required data are available. The *RTA* parameter should, therefore, perhaps be interpreted more broadly as the indicator of a bloc effect. In cases in which the *RTA* parameter indicates a strong bloc effect despite the absence of any formal agreement, the *RTA* parameter can be interpreted as providing an alternative definition of natural trading bloc to that suggested by Krugman. In other words, the indication of strong and increasing trade integration between economies for which there is no formal RTA in place, with controls for distance and adjacency, may be interpreted as revealing a form of natural trading bloc phenomenon. According to the hypothesis, formal RTAs established among these groups of economies should exhibit favorable welfare effects. This prediction can, in turn, be checked against results of CGE simulations.

The level of trade between a group of economies may be influenced by the general degree of openness of the economies in question, as well as by the existence of a formal RTA or a natural propensity to trade with each other. The *OPEN* parameter is therefore included to control for this openness effect. In cases in which a formal RTA is in place, the *OPEN* parameter also has another use. It can be taken as a broad proxy for the level of protection maintained against nonmembers of the RTA.

Trends in the *OPEN* parameter also provide important evidence about the behavior and effects of existing RTAs. Increases over time in the coefficients on openness may be taken to indicate falling levels of protection against nonmembers, thereby suggesting that perhaps the members of the RTA are reducing their MFN tariffs at the same time as they eliminate barriers between themselves. This effect would, in turn, be expected to be associated with a weakening of trade diversion effects. It would not, however, be legitimate to conclude that in such cases the formation of RTAs has itself promoted the openness. Although such results would not be inconsistent with this hypothesis, the data cannot give us information on causality. We might equally speculate that the success of negotiations under the WTO or the influence of APEC was responsible. As always, we do not observe the counterfactual.

Because the dummy variables cannot be expressed in log form, we interpret the parameter estimates (γ_k) differently. Hence, for example,

$\exp(\gamma_1) - 1$ is the proportional increase (decrease) in trade associated with having a common border. The *RTA* parameters can be interpreted similarly; hence, $\exp(\gamma_2) - 1$ is the proportional increase (decrease) in the propensity to trade of the RTA members, relative to otherwise similarly sized and located economies in the model.

Our trade data come from the Economic Research Service time-series data in the GTAP5 database. The distance data are from the World Distance Tables (Hengeveld 1996) and represent the direct air distance between economies. GDP and per capita GDP data are from the World Bank World Development Indicators database (2000) and are measured in purchasing power parity (PPP) terms. Using data in PPP terms allows us to avoid having arbitrary temporary movements in exchange rates exert undue influence over our results. However, it should be noted that obtaining accurate PPP measures is difficult and could result in an additional source of disturbance in our model. We have a total of 38 economies in the dataset and, hence, 703 potential observations in each annual period, split by agricultural and manufactures trade. (Missing values are dealt with simply by dropping the observation from the regression.) We also have a total of 15 periods, from 1984 to 1998. (We have services trade data for only one year, 1997.)

We run the model using selected annual cross-sections and also using the complete pooled dataset. Using the individual cross-sections gives us a chance to observe changes in the structure of world trade over time. Using the pooled dataset also allows us to better estimate the influence of existing or potential RTAs when there are limited observations in the cross-sections (for example, in the CER Agreement). We apply the model on not only the total merchandise trade, but also the individual agricultural and manufactured trade datasets. Doing so allows us to identify the existence of broad-based sectoral differences in trade patterns.

It is common to estimate a gravity model using the ordinary least squares method, and doing so will produce unbiased and consistent estimates of the model parameters. However, our dataset exhibits evidence of heteroskedastic errors, as is frequently the case with cross-sectional data. In this situation, we can improve the efficiency of our parameter estimates by applying the generalized least squares method. Since the increased error is strongly related to economic size (presumably reflecting measurement errors), we take the approach of weighting each observation by the inverse of the squared bilateral products of GDP. In the pooled dataset with both cross-sectional and time-series elements, we have the additional potential problem of autocorrelation. We deal with this problem through the covariance method, specifying an additional annual dummy variable for all years but the first. This technique can also be interpreted as controlling for the growth and inflation in the world economy (see Bikker 1987).

Basic Results

In our initial gravity model simulations, which are used as a benchmark for subsequent simulations involving the proposed new RTAs in East Asia, *RTA* and *OPEN* parameters are included for seven major existing regional arrangements at different stages of development. Three of these—the European Union, MERCOSUR, and the Andean Pact—are groups composed of economies entirely or largely outside our area of primary interest (the Asia-Pacific region). Of the remaining four groups, three are blocs consisting entirely of a subset of APEC members. These are NAFTA (Canada, Mexico, and the United States); AFTA (in our dataset we identify Indonesia, Malaysia, the Philippines, Singapore, and Thailand); and CER (Australia and New Zealand). The final group is APEC itself.

The inclusion of these arrangements in our modeling is necessary to avoid the distortion that might occur if such potentially influential regional arrangements were ignored as determinants of global trade patterns. The estimated effects of these agreements also provide us with a baseline from which to analyze the effect of the intra-APEC groups that are the focus of this research. In particular, the European Union, as the oldest example of an RTA, provides a convenient baseline by which to evaluate the effects of other arrangements.

The results for both the *RTA* and *OPEN* parameters for these arrangements are of considerable interest in themselves, but they are not directly relevant to the key focus of this chapter, which centers on the potential new RTAs in East Asia. Discussion of these results can be found in the appendix.

The results of our first set of simulations, run on selected annual cross-sections, are also reported in the appendix in tables 4A.1 to 4A.3. For our purposes here, the first point to note is that—as in other studies—the gravity model does a very good job at explaining trade patterns, with adjusted R^2 measures between 0.76 and 0.86 in all of the simulations. Furthermore the basic gravity model variables—*GDP*, *GDPPC* (gross domestic product per capita), and *DIST* (distance)—are all highly significant in most years and take the signs expected. Trade increases with income, but at a decreasing rate (the *GDP* parameter ranges between 0.73 and 0.86). This is consistent with other studies. The same pattern holds with the *GDPPC* parameter (ranging from 0.81 to 1.07). The negative sign on the *DIST* parameter indicates that trade diminishes as distance increases, as we expect (the elasticity estimates are between –0.62 and –0.83). Again, the magnitude of the estimates is consistent with other studies. The difference in *GDPPC* is the only variable that does not seem to have a strong explanatory role in the model. It is significant only in 1986, and, in all cases, it is small. Hence, we find little support for the hypothesis that differences in the absolute value of income are a significant explanatory factor in overall bilateral trade patterns between 1986 and 1998.

The adjacency variable is significant in each year and has the expected positive effect on trade. The estimated effects are quite substantial. Sharing a common border is estimated to increase trade by between 43 and 81 percent, again consistent with the existing literature. The estimated coefficients on all of these variables remain similar in terms of both magnitude and significance when we apply the gravity model on manufactures trade (table 4A.2) and agricultural trade (table 4A.3) separately, although we note that the fit is not as strong in the case of agricultural trade as it is in the case of manufactures trade and total merchandise trade (the adjusted R^2 ranges between 0.52 and 0.63).

Pooled Data and Trade in Services

As indicated in the results and discussion in appendix A, difficulty was encountered in obtaining statistically significant estimates of the degree of trade integration in the Asia-Pacific region by using cross-sectional data. To address this difficulty, we also estimated the model with the dataset pooled across the years 1984–98. By increasing the sample size, this procedure increases the prospect of capturing the effect of arrangements among a smaller subset of our cross-section (for example, NAFTA and the CER Agreement). The results for the total merchandise trade category, as well as for manufactures trade and agricultural trade, are presented in table 4A.4. Also presented in table 4A.4 are the estimates from applying the gravity model to services trade data in 1997.

As the results in table 4A.4 indicate, the pooling technique does help us in the manner intended. Although it makes little difference to our parameter estimates on the basic gravity variables (except that we now obtain a statistically significant but very small effect for the difference in per capita GDP), we are now able to obtain statistically significant results for both NAFTA and the CER Agreement (and for the European Union in the case of agriculture). Discussions of the results for the individual RTAs are also included in appendix A.

In the case of services, despite the limited data, the gravity model again seems to provide a good fit (the adjusted R^2 is 0.72 without openness and

0.89 with).[7] The coefficients on income (both total and per capita) are similar to those estimated on merchandise trade. The coefficient on distance, however, though still negative, is significantly smaller than the coefficient on merchandise trade (–0.07 to –0.19). This finding indicates support for the hypothesis that distance is less important as an explanatory factor in services trade. The results for the effects of individual existing RTAs on services trade are discussed in the appendix.

Gravity Model Results for Potential New Trade Blocs in East Asia: Are They Natural?

Having established our basic results, we introduce into our gravity model the prospective East Asian RTAs that were described earlier in the chapter as potential steps toward an East Asian trading bloc:

- Japan-Korea arrangement
- China-Japan-Korea arrangement
- ASEAN+3 arrangement.

Also introduced for purposes of comparison is a possible Western Pacific FTA, which embraces the two CER economies (Australia and New Zealand) and the ASEAN+3 economies.

We determine the significance of these groupings within our gravity model by using the same dummy variable techniques that we used for existing arrangements and by using the pooled data for merchandise trade and the separate data for agricultural trade and manufactures trade. As noted earlier, the bloc effect that the coefficient on the *RTA* dummy seeks to capture takes the form of a strong and increasing trend toward trade integration among the members of the group, despite the absence of a formal RTA. This finding, in turn, is interpreted as evidence as to whether each group can be considered a natural trading bloc.

We leave the dummies for the existing RTAs in place in the regressions. However, because some of the arrangements listed earlier are closely related to others, we test for each separately rather than at once (and thus avoid problems of collinearity in the regressors). The results are presented in table 4.13 (for convenience, only the coefficients on the two relevant dummies are displayed).

The proposed Japan-Korea bilateral FTA has negative coefficients in all experiments except agriculture (positive but not significant), indicating

---

7. We should note that, because of the way the GTAP database was constructed, the services data are not as clean as the time-series data used in the merchandise trade simulations. Hence, the services results should be interpreted cautiously.

Table 4.13 Estimated Gravity Coefficients for Proposed Regional Trading Agreements: Pooled Data by Sector

Arrangement	Merchandise (1984–98)	Manufactures (1984–98)	Agriculture (1984–98)	Services (1997)
RTA dummy				
Japan-Korea	−0.36	−0.42	0.25	−0.64
	(0.29)	(0.30)	(0.39)	(0.90)
China-Japan-Korea	0.40**	0.40**	0.32•	−0.16
	(0.12)	(0.12)	(0.17)	(0.37)
ASEAN+3	1.15***	1.16***	0.64***	0.85***
	(0.06)	(0.06)	(0.09)	(0.20)
ASEAN+3 and CER economies	1.07***	1.04***	0.95***	0.55***
	(0.05)	(0.05)	(0.08)	(0.17)
OPEN dummy				
Japan-Korea	0.43***	0.43***	0.10•	0.04***
	(0.04)	(0.04)	(0.06)	(0.08)
China-Japan-Korea	0.57***	0.60***	0.07	0.36***
	(0.03)	(0.03)	(0.05)	(0.07)
ASEAN+3	0.49***	0.54***	−0.10•	0.35•
	(0.04)	(0.04)	(0.05)	(0.07)
ASEAN+3 and CER	0.46***	0.50***	−0.18**	0.40
	(0.04)	(0.04)	(0.05)	(0.08)

***Significant at greater than 1 percent level.

**Significant at 1 percent level.

*Significant at 5 percent level.

•Significant at 10 percent level.

Note: ASEAN+3 = Association of Southeast Asian Nations plus China, the Republic of Korea, and Japan; CER = Closer Economic Relations trade agreement; RTA = regional trading agreement. Standard deviations are in parentheses. Each proposed agreement is estimated in isolation, but with existing agreements in place. Coefficients on standard gravity variables are omitted from the table.

Source: Authors' estimations.

that these economies are not strongly integrated. The coefficients on merchandise trade and manufactures trade are weakly significant once the openness dummies are included. Hence, there is little evidence that Japan and Korea form a natural trading bloc, despite their geographical proximity. There may, of course, be many explanations for this result (most obviously the political and economic rivalry between the two nations, as well as the associated bias in trade policy, such as Korea's only recently abandoned Import Sources Diversification Program).

Expanding the Japan-Korea arrangement to include China in a China-Japan-Korea FTA results in a positive estimated coefficient on trade integration between these economies, which is strongly significant in both manufactures trade and overall merchandise trade. Given the lack of integration between Japan and Korea, this finding might suggest that both are natural partners of China and therefore (if we accept the natural trading bloc hypothesis) that a bloc centered on China might be beneficial.

Further expanding the arrangement to include ASEAN, in an ASEAN+3 FTA, results in highly significant positive coefficients (smaller but still positive and significant for agricultural trade, and smaller and more weakly significant for services once the openness dummies are included).

When the two CER economies are added to the group, in the absence of the openness dummies there is a slight decline in the coefficients on manufactures trade and overall trade but an increase in the coefficient on agricultural trade. With the openness dummies included, however, the coefficients on manufactures trade, agricultural trade, and overall trade are consistently larger than in the case of the ASEAN+3 FTA, while retaining their significance.

Thus, the results do lend support to the hypothesis that a potential natural trading bloc exists within East Asia. Furthermore, as the range of economies included in the proposed RTA widens, the coefficients indicating the presence of a natural trading bloc tend to increase—consistently so when the openness dummies are included. Thus, the empirical evidence for a natural trading bloc becomes steadily stronger as we move from a Japan-Korea FTA (where the evidence is, in fact, weak), to a China-Japan-Korea FTA, to an ASEAN+3 FTA, and finally to a Western Pacific FTA.

According to the natural trading bloc hypothesis, we might expect steadily increasing coefficients on the bloc effect dummy to be associated with progressively more favorable welfare effects—and, in particular, with progressively diminishing negative effects on nonmembers. However, the gravity model results can reveal little about the welfare effects of the proposed RTAs. For this purpose, we turn to CGE simulations.

CGE Simulation Results and Sensitivity

Because our method involves comparing the results of gravity model simulations with those of CGE simulations, we need consistent data. Hence, for this purpose, the database has been aggregated to match our gravity sample exactly, with 33 unique regions plus a rest of the world aggregate, and three sectors (agriculture, manufacturing, and services). The dimensions of the model used here thus differ significantly from those used for simulations reported earlier in the chapter, as does the range of economies individually identified. Despite this difference, results are broadly consistent with those of the simulations reported earlier.

Using the GTAP model and the GTAP5 data as described earlier, we have simulated the implementation of each proposed RTA, in isolation, by the complete removal of all tariffs on a preferential basis. The exception is APEC, which we provide as a benchmark. Here, the assumption is of MFN reform. The simulations are all comparatively static and thus emphasize efficiency effects in much the same way as standard models of trade. The estimated welfare effects of each proposal are presented in table 4.14, measured as the equivalent variation in regional income in millions of 1997 U.S. dollars (the estimated monetary equivalent of the change in consumption, evaluated at constant initial prices). Also presented are the estimated approximate standard deviations around the welfare results, obtained using the systematic sensitivity techniques developed by Arndt (1996) and Arndt and Pearson (1998).

The results of CGE simulations are known to be particularly sensitive to the assumed values of the Armington elasticities, and so it is to these values that the computed standard deviations relate. We assume that the lower-level elasticities in the GTAP5 database are the mean values of these parameters, and that there are symmetric triangular distributions around each of these parameters with minima and maxima at mean ± 75 percent. Each sectoral element of the vector is assumed to vary independently. We maintain the assumption that the upper-level Armington parameters are double the lower-level parameters. Because the Armington parameters enter the model as random variables, the model results are also random variables, and it is possible to use numerical integration techniques to obtain approximations of the means and standard deviations. The standard deviations, although only approximations, allow us to observe directly which results are robust when parameter values change and

Table 4.14 Estimated Welfare Effect of Proposed Regional Trading Agreements: Equivalent Variation (1997 US$ million)

Country	Japan-Korea Mean	Standard deviation	China-Japan-Korea Mean	Standard deviation	ASEAN+3 Mean	Standard deviation	ASEAN+3 and CER Mean	Standard deviation	APEC Mean	Standard deviation
Argentina	2.3	(0.3)	-55.1	(3.4)	-74.6	(5.4)	-72.9	(3.2)	1,215.1	(80.2)
Australia	-57.2	(7.1)	-260.8	(27.8)	-493.0	(48.5)	3,940.4	(854.1)	2,797.0	(573.0)
Austria	0.4	(1.6)	12.1	(12.7)	5.0	(23.7)	7.7	(27.8)	-276.3	(125.4)
Belgium	-1.6	(2.3)	-0.3	(19.6)	-54.4	(39.7)	-115.4	(60.8)	-135.2	(38.6)
Brazil	-15.6	(3.5)	-155.9	(27.1)	-227.4	(38.2)	-271.3	(38.6)	2,351.6	(442.3)
Canada	1.0	(0.9)	-50.8	(14.9)	-21.0	(16.2)	-159.1	(31.9)	2,032.9	(1,184.9)
Chile	-13.2	(1.8)	-65.2	(3.5)	-91.0	(5.3)	-114.5	(7.8)	108.2	(92.4)
China	-172.3	(27.6)	249.1	(721.2)	441.0	(651.4)	118.9	(463.1)	1,726.5	(1,800.3)
Colombia	-4.8	(1.0)	-27.2	(6.2)	-27.8	(6.9)	-38.4	(7.4)	747.6	(42.5)
Denmark	-0.4	(0.9)	-1.2	(7.1)	-14.5	(13.7)	-26.0	(19.6)	606.8	(360.0)
Finland	-3.5	(0.6)	-24.7	(3.0)	-62.4	(8.0)	-69.0	(9.3)	29.6	(13.5)
France	5.4	(4.2)	8.2	(48.5)	-86.1	(79.8)	-157.1	(106.5)	1,018.8	(173.3)
Germany	-60.1	(8.4)	-398.6	(76.6)	-803.6	(125.2)	-984.3	(169.7)	1,849.4	(235.2)
Greece	0.5	(0.5)	12.0	(4.2)	19.3	(5.7)	17.4	(11.2)	-273.3	(84.2)
Hong Kong, China	-8.9	(4.1)	2,811.1	(504.7)	3,410.0	(238.5)	3,389.2	(225.2)	6,788.5	(584.9)
India	-2.5	(1.7)	-34.1	(18.5)	-126.5	(34.5)	-227.2	(39.9)	919.7	(155.5)
Indonesia	-54.5	(6.9)	-251.9	(43.5)	621.8	(35.0)	420.6	(33.2)	734.9	(110.5)
Ireland	-14.0	(2.0)	-38.3	(9.8)	-64.3	(18.0)	-68.4	(20.4)	84.8	(53.0)
Italy	-13.4	(4.6)	-96.4	(39.6)	-200.9	(69.6)	-347.9	(92.1)	1,023.0	(117.7)
Japan	1,430.6	(153.9)	5,285.1	(809.9)	8,208.5	(1,080.5)	7,900.8	(1,535.5)	8,819.4	(2,380.8)
Korea, Rep. of	291.8	(102.6)	5,535.2	(1,710.9)	5,700.9	(1,736.8)	5,559.8	(1,742.8)	5,261.9	(1,902.7)
Malaysia	-53.7	(7.1)	-248.1	(37.9)	182.7	(156.1)	72.8	(156.2)	94.2	(222.0)
Mexico	5.0	(1.5)	33.3	(16.7)	62.4	(20.3)	34.9	(28.3)	-1,036.4	(377.2)

(Table continues on the following page.)

Table 4.14 continued

Country	Japan-Korea		China-Japan-Korea		ASEAN+3		ASEAN+3 and CER		APEC	
	Mean	Standard deviation	Mean	Standard deviation	Mean	Standard deviation	Mean	Standard deviation	Mean	Standard deviation
Netherlands	-8.0	(3.3)	-90.7	(29.2)	-188.6	(58.3)	-177.1	(71.6)	447.3	(292.9)
New Zealand	-5.4	(0.9)	-101.3	(16.2)	-141.6	(14.8)	1,484.1	(463.7)	1,301.5	(449.2)
Peru	-0.4	(0.3)	-33.4	(5.4)	-43.2	(6.5)	-53.5	(8.2)	55.6	(78.9)
Philippines	-22.6	(3.7)	-96.5	(16.2)	22.9	(86.6)	-108.4	(74.6)	747.4	(267.1)
Poland	3.8	(1.1)	34.3	(9.7)	35.0	(13.9)	44.0	(15.2)	481.2	(77.3)
Portugal	1.1	(0.5)	17.6	(5.0)	22.0	(6.4)	19.5	(9.0)	276.5	(56.2)
Singapore	-30.4	(10.3)	-135.7	(74.7)	116.2	(167.0)	158.6	(163.6)	-1,183.2	(205.3)
Spain	3.9	(2.4)	19.1	(21.6)	-3.5	(34.1)	-26.5	(45.9)	756.1	(55.5)
Sweden	-5.1	(1.0)	-46.3	(10.8)	-101.4	(18.4)	-121.2	(22.0)	-237.0	(57.5)
Switzerland	-22.9	(3.6)	-76.5	(19.0)	-157.4	(31.1)	-221.3	(47.7)	10.4	(8.9)
Thailand	-49.0	(7.8)	-269.2	(49.9)	1,641.3	(374.3)	1,553.4	(364.9)	1,988.3	(574.9)
Turkey	5.3	(0.7)	37.1	(9.7)	48.7	(12.7)	28.8	(20.0)	-46.1	(115.6)
United Kingdom	-26.2	(8.9)	-40.9	(64.9)	-233.5	(104.8)	-581.9	(208.4)	2,363.8	(525.1)
United States	-381.1	(48.1)	-2,487.6	(287.6)	-4,131.7	(383.4)	-4,758.9	(441.9)	271.6	(1,119.6)
Venezuela	-0.3	(0.2)	-0.6	(3.2)	0.1	(3.5)	-6.0	(4.6)	-20.3	(4.8)
Rest of world	-372.4	(49.4)	-2,731.2	(411.3)	-4,335.9	(564.7)	-5,468.9	(719.6)	1,527.7	(619.2)
Members	1,722.4		13,880.5		20,345.3		24,069.5		30,508.4	
Nonmembers	-1,370.9		-7,644.8		-11,491.7		-13,494.1		14,721.3	
World	351.6		6,235.7		8,853.6		10,575.5		45,229.7	

Note: APEC = Asia-Pacific Economic Cooperation; ASEAN+3 = Association of Southeast Asian Nations plus China, the Republic of Korea, and Japan; CER = Closer Economic Relations trade agreement.

Source: Authors' simulations.

which are not. As a rule, if the mean estimate maintains the same sign within two standard deviations, we can be confident (more than 95 percent) that the sign of the estimated value is correct.

The Japan-Korea simulation alone results in relatively small welfare effects for the participants. The results are robust for Japan, but less so for Korea. Significant welfare losses are estimated to be imposed on nonmembers. Expansion to include China in a China-Japan-Korea FTA substantially increases the total welfare gains available to the members of the arrangement, as well as the gains to the members of the smaller group considered previously. The estimates for China are, however, relatively small and apparently highly sensitive to the parameter assumptions (the results for Hong Kong, China, are larger and robust). The extent of welfare losses to nonmembers also rises, although they fall as a proportion of member welfare gains.

Expanding the arrangement by bringing in ASEAN to form the ASEAN+3 FTA again results in greater gains in mean net welfare for the original members (that is, China, Japan, and Korea). It also results in further welfare gains for the newly included members (although, except for Indonesia and Thailand, the estimated gains to ASEAN members are not very robust). Total member gains rise with this expansion also, as do nonmember losses.

The addition of the two CER economies, Australia and New Zealand, results in a slightly different pattern. The estimated welfare of the two new members rises (by a significant amount and with robust signs), but the estimated welfare of all the preexisting ASEAN+3 members except Singapore declines (albeit only slightly). Total welfare to members again rises, and total welfare to nonmembers again declines. Given that the CER economies are efficient agricultural producers, this result is a little perplexing. Examination of the breakdown (not shown here) reveals that the previous members do gain from bringing in the CER economies in terms of allocative efficiency as a result of expansion of agricultural imports, as we would expect. It is small declines in the terms of trade as a result of losing their preferential access that account for the slight welfare declines (relative to the ASEAN+3 FTA without the CER economies).

The final simulation, of APEC on an MFN basis, provides a benchmark for evaluating the size of the costs and benefits of the new RTA proposals. The estimated total welfare gains to APEC from MFN reform are larger than the gains to APEC from the formation of any other group considered. However, the gains are quite sensitive for some economies (notably Canada, China, Malaysia, and the United States). The choice of

MFN reform under the banner of open regionalism ensures that trade diversion is not a possibility, so that negative welfare effects on nonmembers are largely absent.

Conclusions from Comparing Gravity Model and CGE Results

Our next task is to consider whether the results of gravity model simulations and CGE simulations tell a consistent story in the case of the proposed East Asian RTAs. As well as being of analytical interest, the answer can have a bearing on the degree of confidence we can place in the results from the two approaches and also in the predictions of the natural trading bloc hypothesis.

We focus again on the steps toward an East Asian bloc, together with a Western Pacific FTA. As mentioned earlier, there was little evidence from the gravity approach of strong integration between Japan and Korea, stronger evidence of integration between those two economies and China, stronger evidence still of integration between the three economies and ASEAN, and finally—with the openness dummies included—even stronger evidence of integration between all of the East Asian economies and the two CER economies.

The results of the CGE simulations for the effects on member welfare are broadly consistent with the gravity results. The Japan-Korea simulation alone results in relatively small welfare effects for the participants (at least relative to the size of these economies) and in welfare losses to nonmembers. This finding fits with the gravity model prediction that Japan and Korea are not a natural trading bloc. The addition of China (including Hong Kong, China) to the group results in a very substantial increase in the net welfare of the members, which is composed of increases for both the original members and the new members. Again, this pattern matches with the increase in the degree of intraregional trading bias (relative to the results for a Japan-Korea simulation) that the gravity model approach captures. The pattern is repeated with the addition of ASEAN to form the ASEAN+3 FTA.

When we conduct a CGE simulation of a Western Pacific FTA, which is composed of the ASEAN+3 group plus the two CER economies, there is again correspondence between a further increase in total welfare for members and an increase in intraregional trade bias, as we observe in the gravity model simulations when the openness dummies are included. The results from the gravity model simulations are less clear cut if the openness dummies are not included. For the preexisting ASEAN+3 group, the CGE simulations indicate an increase in welfare derived from allocative efficiency gains, but not in overall welfare, because of the terms-of-trade effects.

Thus, the estimates from the CGE simulations of the effects of these RTAs on the welfare of their members do match quite closely the results of the gravity analysis. As we might expect, stronger bloc effects are associated with larger overall gains for members. The natural trading bloc hypothesis, however, has been used to suggest that natural trading blocs will also be less trade diverting, so that negative welfare effects are absent or at least minimized. Comparing the results from the two models appears to directly contradict this prediction. The bloc effect does become stronger as the range of economies included in an East Asian RTA is expanded, suggesting that the larger blocs are more natural. However, the CGE results indicate that although increasingly natural trading blocs in this sense are associated with larger overall welfare gains for their members, they also impose larger welfare losses on their nonmembers. This finding suggests, in turn, that the extent of trade diversion is also increasing. Moreover, because the pool of nonmember economies is shrinking at each step, greater losses are being imposed on a smaller group of nonmembers.

The results described here can therefore be used to support the notion that a larger East Asian or Western Pacific trading bloc would be in a sense more natural than a new RTA formed from a subset of the East Asian economy. It is not, however, possible to move quickly from that conclusion to an assumption that the larger, more natural trading bloc will be inherently more benign in its implications for the world trading system. Nor is it possible to reject the contrary proposition that such a bloc is more likely to serve as a stumbling block rather than a building block toward a more open international trading system. Those conclusions would require additional arguments. One such argument might be that fear of being negatively affected by an East Asian trading bloc might encourage the members of other large trading blocs in Europe and the Americas to pursue multilateral liberalization more aggressively through the WTO.

We might also speculate that these results support a hypothesis more basic than the natural trading bloc hypothesis—namely, that large blocs are better than small ones (at least for the members involved). The more diverse the group of economies in the RTA, the more likely that one of those economies is an efficient producer of each commodity, and, therefore, the less likely it will be that trade diversion will occur.

The results of the final simulation of APEC MFN liberalization, which we undertake as a benchmark against which to evaluate the potential East Asian RTAs, also support this hypothesis. Compared with the East Asian economies, APEC is a still larger and more diverse group of economies.

As in the simulations reported earlier in the chapter, the estimated total welfare effects on APEC members and nonmembers from APEC MFN liberalization are more favorable than the effects from any of the other arrangements considered, for either the members or the nonmembers of that group. APEC also offers larger overall welfare gains than any of the other alternatives for the East Asian economies as a group (although not necessarily for the individual economies), as well as for the APEC economies as a group.[8] The other distinguishing feature of the APEC MFN results—the favorable overall welfare effect on nonmembers—is due, of course, to its choice of open regionalism, which is understood to embrace a commitment to nondiscriminatory rather than preferential liberalization.

In light of the CGE simulation results for APEC MFN liberalization, it is interesting to note from table 4A.4 that the coefficients on integration for APEC in manufactures, agricultural, and overall trade exceed those shown in table 4.13 for any of the potential East Asian RTAs, again provided that the openness dummies are included.[9] APEC thus appears to be a more natural bloc than any of the East Asian RTAs considered, and one that, unlike the potential East Asian RTAs, does conform to the prediction that liberalization within natural trading blocs allows negative welfare effects on nonmembers to be minimized or avoided altogether. As just noted previously, this distinctive property of APEC is clearly due to the choice of nondiscriminatory rather than preferential liberalization.

Confidence in the ability to achieve APEC MFN liberalization is currently at a low. Nevertheless, the results here, like the results reported earlier, confirm that APEC MFN liberalization offers some advantages over the establishment of a preferential East Asian trading bloc, both for the East Asian economies themselves and for the multilateral trading system. APEC MFN liberalization can clearly be legitimately viewed as a building block toward a more open multilateral trading system. In the meantime, the results here leave open the issue of whether the potential new East Asian RTAs should be regarded as building blocks or stumbling blocks for the achievement of this goal or for the achievement of APEC's trade objectives as an intermediate step. A key issue is the dynamic time-path. Would the welfare costs imposed on nonmembers by these new agreements cause

---

8. These simulations include 9 East Asian economies and 16 APEC economies. This coverage differs from that in the simulations reported earlier in the chapter.

9. If the openness dummies are not included, the APEC coefficients for overall trade and agricultural trade do not exceed those for the Western Pacific FTA, and those for overall trade and manufactures trade are lower than the corresponding coefficients for the ASEAN+3 FTA.

fractures within APEC or the multilateral trading system that would inhibit progress toward achievement of APEC's Bogor goals or a more open multilateral trading system? Or would these welfare costs encourage convergence among the disparate blocs within APEC, which, combined with gradual elimination of barriers to non-APEC members, might lead by a more indirect route to the same ultimate objectives? This question remains an area for future research.

APPENDIX

Tables 4A.1 to 4A.4 of this appendix set out the detailed results for the gravity model simulations discussed in the chapter. The results include coefficients on the *RTA* and *OPEN* dummy variables for seven major existing RTAs that were included in the specification of the model, and this appendix provides some discussion of these results. The rationale for including these RTAs in the model was explained in the chapter.

Bloc Effects

As explained in the chapter, the coefficient on the *RTA* dummy can be taken as an indication of a bloc effect associated with the RTA in question. For years subsequent to the establishment of the RTA, the bloc effect may provide information on the effect of the RTA, with the coefficient being interpreted as a measure of the strength of trade creation effects. For years before the establishment of the RTA, it indicates the propensity of the bloc members to trade with each other relative to other similarly sized and located economies in the model. As noted in the chapter, this finding may be taken as an indication of the extent to which the economies in the bloc constitute a natural trading bloc.

We first discuss the results in tables 4A.1 to 4A.3. Taking the non-APEC-related RTAs first, for the European Union we find no evidence of a significant effect on total merchandise trade in any of the years considered. We find only one marginally significant effect when we separate out manufactures trade (in 1995), and this effect is negative. In agricultural trade, however, we do observe a significant positive effect after 1992 (that is, after the completion of the common market). Agricultural trade between EU members ranges between 57 and 99 percent higher than would otherwise be predicted by the gravity equation. Moreover, the bias is increasing over time. Those results must reflect the pervasive influence of the common agricultural policy and its post-1992 reforms. Introduction of openness variables has no significant effect on the results.

Table 4A.1 Estimated Gravity Equations: Total Merchandise Trade, 1986–98 (at 3-Year Intervals)

Indicator	1986		1989		1992		1995		1998	
(Intercept)	−21.04*** (1.16)	−27.82*** (1.30)	−22.24*** (1.12)	−27.26*** (1.22)	−22.63*** (1.07)	−27.93*** (1.15)	−23.34*** (1.23)	−28.04*** (1.29)	−22.93*** (1.09)	−26.59*** (1.17)
GDP	0.74*** (0.02)	0.84*** (0.03)	0.73*** (0.02)	0.80*** (0.02)	0.73*** (0.02)	0.80*** (0.02)	0.77*** (0.02)	0.83*** (0.02)	0.80*** (0.02)	0.86*** (0.02)
GDP per capita	0.81*** (0.04)	1.01*** (0.04)	0.88*** (0.04)	1.03*** (0.04)	0.91*** (0.03)	1.07*** (0.04)	0.91*** (0.04)	1.06*** (0.04)	0.84*** (0.03)	0.94*** (0.04)
Difference in GDP per capita	0.09** (0.03)	0.08* (0.03)	0.05 (0.03)	0.04 (0.03)	0.04 (0.03)	0.03 (0.03)	−0.01 (0.03)	0.00 (0.03)	0.02 (0.03)	0.02 (0.02)
Distance	−0.76*** (0.06)	−0.62*** (0.06)	−0.72*** (0.06)	−0.62*** (0.06)	−0.77*** (0.05)	−0.69*** (0.05)	−0.78*** (0.06)	−0.71*** (0.06)	−0.83*** (0.05)	−0.79*** (0.05)
Adjacent dummy	0.48* (0.22)	0.61** (0.20)	0.46* (0.21)	0.57** (0.19)	0.52** (0.19)	0.60*** (0.18)	0.48* (0.21)	0.57*** (0.19)	0.36* (0.18)	0.43** (0.16)
EU	0.10 (0.17)	−0.04 (0.15)	0.10 (0.16)	−0.01 (0.14)	0.02 (0.14)	−0.05 (0.13)	−0.20 (0.15)	−0.24. (0.14)	−0.01 (0.13)	−0.07 (0.12)
NAFTA	−1.01 (0.68)	−0.77 (0.62)	−0.98 (0.64)	−0.64 (0.58)	−0.84 (0.59)	−0.48 (0.53)	−0.72 (0.63)	−0.32 (0.57)	−0.54 (0.55)	−0.12 (0.49)
AFTA	1.11*** (0.32)	0.89** (0.29)	1.07*** (0.30)	0.73** (0.28)	0.73** (0.28)	0.36 (0.26)	0.83** (0.30)	0.36 (0.28)	1.03*** (0.26)	0.65** (0.24)
CER	0.42 (0.96)	0.58 (0.88)	0.51 (0.91)	0.70 (0.83)	0.52 (0.84)	0.90 (0.75)	0.47 (0.90)	0.86 (0.81)	0.57 (0.78)	0.82 (0.69)
MERCOSUR	−0.34 (1.09)	−0.24 (1.00)	0.01 (1.03)	−0.03 (0.93)	0.66 (0.94)	0.74 (0.85)	0.98 (1.01)	0.87 (0.91)	1.33 (0.88)	1.30. (0.78)
Andean Pact	0.57 (0.57)	1.22* (0.53)	0.69 (0.54)	1.38** (0.49)	1.81*** (0.49)	2.32*** (0.45)	1.76** (0.54)	2.37*** (0.48)	1.80*** (0.46)	2.44*** (0.42)
APEC	1.01*** (0.11)	1.10*** (0.14)	1.11*** (0.10)	1.12*** (0.13)	1.08*** (0.09)	1.11*** (0.12)	1.13*** (0.10)	1.10*** (0.13)	1.05*** (0.09)	1.12*** (0.11)

Variable					
EU (OPEN dummy)	0.00	−0.07	−0.10	−0.09	0.08
	(0.11)	(0.10)	(0.09)	(0.10)	(0.09)
NAFTA (OPEN dummy)	−1.14***	−0.97***	−0.85***	−0.82***	−0.67***
	(0.13)	(0.12)	(0.11)	(0.11)	(0.10)
AFTA (OPEN dummy)	0.41***	0.48***	0.58***	0.61***	0.61***
	(0.10)	(0.10)	(0.09)	(0.09)	(0.08)
CER (OPEN dummy)	−0.63***	−0.48***	−0.53***	−0.57***	−0.22*
	(0.14)	(0.13)	(0.12)	(0.13)	(0.11)
MERCOSUR (OPEN dummy)	−0.33*	−0.16	−0.21•	0.04	0.03
	(0.14)	(0.13)	(0.12)	(0.13)	(0.11)
Andean Pact (OPEN dummy)	−0.45***	−0.55***	−0.18•	−0.38***	−0.33***
	(0.11)	(0.11)	(0.10)	(0.11)	(0.10)
APEC (OPEN dummy)	0.22*	0.13	0.01	0.10	−0.02
	(0.10)	(0.10)	(0.09)	(0.09)	(0.08)
Observations	696	701	703	703	702
Adjusted R²	0.80	0.82	0.85	0.82	0.86

***Significant at greater than 1 percent level.

**Significant at 1 percent level.

*Significant at 5 percent level.

•Significant at 10 percent level.

Note: AFTA = ASEAN Free Trade Area; APEC = Asia-Pacific Economic Cooperation; ASEAN = Association of Southeast Asian Nations; CER = Closer Economic Relations trade agreement; EU = European Union; GDP = gross domestic product; MERCOSUR = Southern Cone Common Market (Mercado Común del Sur); NAFTA = North American Free Trade Agreement. Standard deviations are in parentheses.

Source: Authors' estimations.

Table 4A.2 Estimated Gravity Equations: Manufactures Trade, 1986–98 (at 3-Year Intervals)

Indicator	1986		1989		1992		1995		1998	
(Intercept)	-28.88*** (1.45)	-21.76*** (1.29)	-27.68*** (1.30)	-22.29*** (1.19)	-28.61*** (1.18)	-22.89*** (1.12)	-28.22*** (1.27)	-23.50*** (1.22)	-27.05*** (1.19)	-23.20*** (1.12)
GDP	0.85*** (0.03)	0.75*** (0.03)	0.80*** (0.03)	0.73*** (0.02)	0.81*** (0.02)	0.74*** (0.02)	0.84*** (0.02)	0.78*** (0.02)	0.87*** (0.02)	0.81*** (0.02)
GDP per capita	1.05*** (0.05)	0.85*** (0.04)	1.06*** (0.05)	0.89*** (0.04)	1.09*** (0.04)	0.92*** (0.04)	1.05*** (0.04)	0.91*** (0.04)	0.95*** (0.04)	0.86*** (0.04)
Difference in GDP per capita	0.08* (0.03)	0.10** (0.04)	0.03 (0.03)	0.04 (0.03)	0.02 (0.03)	0.03 (0.03)	0.00 (0.03)	-0.01 (0.03)	0.01 (0.03)	0.01 (0.03)
Distance	-0.64*** (0.07)	-0.82*** (0.07)	-0.64*** (0.06)	-0.78*** (0.06)	-0.68*** (0.05)	-0.78*** (0.05)	-0.71*** (0.06)	-0.80*** (0.06)	-0.78*** (0.05)	-0.84*** (0.05)
Adjacent dummy	0.60** (0.23)	0.41• (0.24)	0.56** (0.20)	0.41• (0.22)	0.62*** (0.18)	0.51* (0.20)	0.58** (0.19)	0.45* (0.21)	0.46** (0.17)	0.36• (0.18)
EU	-0.04 (0.17)	0.12 (0.18)	-0.05 (0.15)	0.07 (0.17)	-0.05 (0.13)	0.03 (0.15)	-0.27* (0.14)	-0.23 (0.15)	-0.06 (0.12)	-0.01 (0.14)
NAFTA	-0.81 (0.69)	-0.98 (0.75)	-0.70 (0.62)	-0.99 (0.68)	-0.51 (0.54)	-0.88 (0.61)	-0.34 (0.56)	-0.75 (0.63)	-0.13 (0.50)	-0.56 (0.56)
AFTA	1.16*** (0.35)	1.36*** (0.37)	0.54• (0.30)	0.86** (0.32)	0.35 (0.26)	0.75* (0.29)	0.38 (0.27)	0.84** (0.30)	0.66** (0.24)	1.06*** (0.27)
CER	0.70 (0.99)	0.44 (1.07)	0.80 (0.88)	0.46 (0.97)	0.99 (0.77)	0.49 (0.87)	0.93 (0.80)	0.48 (0.90)	0.88 (0.71)	0.57 (0.80)
MERCOSUR	-0.27 (1.11)	-0.51 (1.21)	-0.13 (0.99)	-0.14 (1.09)	0.67 (0.87)	0.50 (0.98)	0.82 (0.89)	0.85 (1.01)	1.30 (0.80)	1.27 (0.90)
Andean Pact	1.46* (0.59)	0.79 (0.63)	1.46*** (0.52)	0.75 (0.57)	2.43*** (0.46)	1.88*** (0.51)	2.46*** (0.48)	1.81*** (0.53)	2.54*** (0.42)	1.86*** (0.48)

APEC	1.00***	1.18***	1.13***	1.20***	1.12***	1.18***	1.13***	1.15***	1.06***
	(0.12)	(0.16)	(0.11)	(0.14)	(0.10)	(0.12)	(0.10)	(0.13)	(0.09)
EU (OPEN dummy)		0.03		−0.09		−0.06		−0.07	
		(0.12)		(0.11)		(0.10)		(0.10)	
NAFTA		−1.19***		−0.96***		−0.87***		−0.85***	
		(0.15)		(0.13)		(0.11)		(0.11)	
(OPEN dummy)		0.31**		0.47***		0.65***		0.60***	
		(0.12)		(0.10)		(0.09)		(0.09)	
AFTA		−0.81***		−0.67***		−0.63***		−0.63***	
		(0.16)		(0.14)		(0.12)		(0.12)	
(OPEN dummy)									
CER (OPEN dummy)									
MERCOSUR		−0.53***		−0.27		−0.28*		−0.09	
		(0.16)		(0.14)		(0.12)		(0.13)	
(OPEN dummy)									
Andean Pact		−0.51***		−0.59***		−0.17		−0.45***	
		(0.13)		(0.12)		(0.10)		(0.11)	
(OPEN dummy)									
APEC									
(OPEN dummy)		0.20•		0.06		0.00		0.05	
		(0.12)		(0.10)		(0.09)		(0.09)	
Observations	690	690	698	698	702	702	701	701	702
Adjusted R^2	0.73	0.77	0.77	0.81	0.81	0.85	0.78	0.83	0.82

(Final column:)

APEC	1.13***
	(0.11)
EU (OPEN dummy)	0.09
	(0.09)
NAFTA	−0.69***
	(0.10)
(OPEN dummy)	0.64***
	(0.08)
AFTA	−0.28*
	(0.11)
MERCOSUR	−0.06
	(0.11)
Andean Pact	−0.39***
	(0.10)
(OPEN dummy)	−0.01
	(0.08)
Observations	702
Adjusted R^2	0.86

***Significant at greater than 1 percent level.

**Significant at 1 percent level.

*Significant at 5 percent level.

•Significant at 10 percent level.

Note: See note to table 4A.1 for acronym definitions. Standard deviations are in parentheses.

Source: Authors' estimations.

Table 4A.3 Estimated Gravity Equations: Agricultural Trade, 1986–98 (at 3-Year Intervals)

Indicator	1986		1989		1992		1995		1998	
(Intercept)	−17.10***	−21.28***	−19.56***	−22.81***	−17.70***	−18.69***	−18.47***	−18.19***	−18.91***	−18.52***
	(1.47)	(1.72)	(1.42)	(1.62)	(1.72)	(1.96)	(1.73)	(1.95)	(1.75)	(1.97)
GDP	0.64***	0.75***	0.66***	0.75***	0.64***	0.71***	0.68***	0.71***	0.70***	0.76***
	(0.03)	(0.03)	(0.03)	(0.03)	(0.03)	(0.04)	(0.03)	(0.04)	(0.03)	(0.04)
GDP per capita	0.45***	0.57***	0.50***	0.59***	0.46***	0.49***	0.44***	0.45***	0.40***	0.39***
	(0.05)	(0.06)	(0.05)	(0.06)	(0.06)	(0.07)	(0.06)	(0.07)	(0.06)	(0.07)
Difference in GDP per capita	0.07	0.08*	0.13**	0.15***	0.07	0.09*	0.11*	0.12**	0.14**	0.13**
	(0.04)	(0.04)	(0.04)	(0.04)	(0.05)	(0.05)	(0.05)	(0.04)	(0.04)	(0.04)
Distance	−0.45***	−0.60***	−0.43***	−0.56***	−0.55***	−0.76***	−0.58***	−0.78***	−0.57***	−0.84***
	(0.08)	(0.08)	(0.07)	(0.08)	(0.08)	(0.09)	(0.08)	(0.08)	(0.08)	(0.08)
Adjacent dummy	0.72**	0.50*	0.67**	0.49*	0.76**	0.38	0.75**	0.42	0.89**	0.44
	(0.27)	(0.26)	(0.26)	(0.25)	(0.30)	(0.29)	(0.28)	(0.27)	(0.28)	(0.27)
EU	0.07	0.05	0.25	0.22	0.45*	0.47*	0.58**	0.59**	0.69**	0.68***
	(0.21)	(0.20)	(0.20)	(0.19)	(0.22)	(0.22)	(0.21)	(0.21)	(0.21)	(0.20)
NAFTA	−0.56	−0.12	−0.58	−0.12	0.15	0.44	0.26	0.47	0.41	0.71
	(0.84)	(0.80)	(0.79)	(0.76)	(0.89)	(0.86)	(0.85)	(0.82)	(0.84)	(0.80)
AFTA	0.85*	0.52	1.08**	0.74*	0.26	0.25	0.19	0.07	0.19	0.17
	(0.39)	(0.38)	(0.38)	(0.36)	(0.45)	(0.44)	(0.43)	(0.42)	(0.43)	(0.41)
CER	1.04	0.76	1.18	0.72	1.29	0.47	1.31	0.71	1.56	0.76
	(1.19)	(1.14)	(1.13)	(1.07)	(1.26)	(1.22)	(1.21)	(1.17)	(1.20)	(1.14)
MERCOSUR	1.01	0.75	1.26	0.95	2.44*	2.07	2.52*	1.88	2.42*	1.86
	(1.34)	(1.29)	(1.27)	(1.21)	(1.42)	(1.37)	(1.35)	(1.32)	(1.35)	(1.29)
Andean Pact	−0.93	−0.62	0.04	0.57	0.38	0.57	0.06	0.16	0.17	0.13
	(0.70)	(0.68)	(0.67)	(0.64)	(0.92)	(0.90)	(0.72)	(0.71)	(0.72)	(0.69)

	(1)	(2)	(3)	(4)	(5)	(6)	(7)	(8)	(9)	(10)
APEC	1.11***	1.05***	1.26***	1.12***	1.12***	1.00***	1.06***	1.02***	0.96***	1.00***
	(0.14)	(0.19)	(0.13)	(0.18)	(0.15)	(0.22)	(0.14)	(0.20)	(0.14)	(0.20)
EU (OPEN dummy)		0.19		0.20		0.17		0.17		0.32*
		(0.15)		(0.14)		(0.16)		(0.16)		(0.15)
NAFTA (OPEN dummy)		−0.60***		−0.72***		−0.33·		−0.08		0.03
		(0.17)		(0.16)		(0.18)		(0.17)		(0.16)
AFTA (OPEN dummy)		0.84***		0.58***		0.06		0.14		0.23
		(0.14)		(0.13)		(0.16)		(0.15)		(0.15)
CER (OPEN dummy)		0.45*		0.50**		0.87***		0.64***		1.08***
		(0.19)		(0.18)		(0.20)		(0.19)		(0.19)
MERCOSUR (OPEN dummy)		0.64***		0.70***		0.91***		1.18***		1.29***
		(0.19)		(0.17)		(0.20)		(0.19)		(0.19)
Andean Pact (OPEN dummy)		0.37*		−0.02		0.58**		0.31·		0.69***
		(0.16)		(0.15)		(0.20)		(0.17)		(0.17)
APEC (OPEN dummy)		0.22		0.44***		0.42**		0.30*		0.18
		(0.14)		(0.13)		(0.16)		(0.15)		(0.14)
Observations	650	650	666	666	628	628	641	641	639	639
Adjusted R²	0.53	0.57	0.58	0.63	0.52	0.56	0.55	0.58	0.56	0.61

***Significant at greater than 1 percent level.

**Significant at 1 percent level.

*Significant at 5 percent level.

·Significant at 10 percent level.

Note: See note to table 4A.1 for acronym definitions. Standard deviations are in parentheses.

Source: Authors' estimations.

For the two South American agreements, we are unable to find any statistically significant results in the case of MERCOSUR. The coefficients are positive and, in some cases, quite large from 1992 onward (the agreement was formed in 1991). For the much older Andean agreement, the estimated intraregional trade bias is substantial and highly statistically significant from 1992 onward. Splitting the data by sector reveals that the integration is very strong for manufactures, but less strong (and not statistically significant) for agriculture.

Turning to the APEC subregional agreements, in the case of NAFTA, we are again unable to find any evidence of a significant trade-creating effect. All of the coefficients on total merchandise and manufactures trade are negative, although there appears to be an increasing trend. Controlling for openness reduces the negative trade bias in cases, but the lack of statistical significance on any of the estimates makes drawing any conclusions difficult. In the case of agriculture, the estimated coefficients are positive and increasing from 1992, when the negotiations were nearing completion; the agreement entered into force 2 years later in 1994. However, the lack of statistical significance again makes it difficult to draw any strong conclusions. Because the lack of significance is at least in part related to the problem of limited observations on intra-NAFTA trade in the cross-sectional data, we return to the question of the effect of NAFTA in our examination of the pooled dataset.

The case of AFTA provides us with some more clear-cut results. From the total merchandise trade estimates, we observe a positive and strongly statistically significant bloc effect. This effect remains positive—and statistically significant in all years except 1992 and 1995—once we take the general openness of these economies into account. (As the high and very strongly significant openness coefficients indicate, the economies of ASEAN are very open to trade relative to other similarly sized economies—although this finding may be inflated somewhat by the unique role played by Singapore.) The estimates of the bias range from 43 percent to a staggering 203 percent (144 percent is the highest estimate when openness is included). The bias was clearly significant before the decision to move forward with an ASEAN free trade area in 1992. From the sectoral gravity equations presented in tables 4A.2 and 4A.3, we observe that most of the intra-ASEAN trade bias is in manufactures trade. Although there does appear to be a slightly significant positive bias in agricultural trade, this bias declines after 1992 and loses statistical significance. Hence, we can conclude that, so far, the propensity of the ASEAN economies to trade intensively with each other has been evident only in manufactures trade.

The CER Agreement has been in place since 1983, before our sample period. However, even within our sample period, we are unable to find any significant evidence of trade-creating effects. Although the estimates are positive and quite large (in particular in agriculture), none are statistically significant. As in the case of NAFTA, this result is a problem of limited observations on intra-CER trade in the cross-sections, which we attempt to deal with by pooling our cross-sectional data.

Our final test is on the significance of an APEC group. We find the coefficients in the merchandise trade equations to be highly statistically significant in all years, as well as being consistent at just over 1 (implying that members of APEC trade with one another roughly 2.7 times as much as otherwise similar economies). Thus, there appears to be a definite APEC effect that is distinct from the effects of RTAs within APEC. The estimates do not appear to be sensitive to the inclusion of an openness parameter. However, we also note that the effect is stable over time, even though APEC was not formally established until 1989 and its trade liberalization objectives were not crystallized until 1994. Hence, though there is evidence of an effective intraregional trade bias among the APEC member economies, it does not appear that APEC's formal implementation has had any effect on that bias or that APEC, since its implementation, has had any effect in increasing the intensity of trade among its members. Essentially the same pattern holds once we separate manufactures and (perhaps surprisingly) agricultural trade: a strong and significant regional bias, but no evidence of any strengthening of trade ties over time.

Pooled Data and Trade in Services

As explained in the chapter, pooling the datasets across the years 1984–98 assists in obtaining statistically significant results. Our results are in table 4A.4. In the case of the NAFTA economies, we obtain a statistically significant negative bias in overall trade and manufactures trade, and a smaller but still negative bias (but insignificant) in agricultural trade. Introducing an openness control lowers the bias and makes it positive (but still insignificant) in the case of agricultural trade.

As for the CER Agreement, we find statistically significant evidence of a regional trade bias in both manufactures and agriculture, as well as overall. The bias is strongest in agricultural trade, and it becomes more positive once we have controlled for openness. Thus, we have evidence to suggest that the CER Agreement has been successful in promoting merchandise trade between Australia and New Zealand.

Table 4A.4 Estimated Gravity Equations: Pooled Data by Sector

Indicator	Merchandise (1984–98)		Manufactures (1984–98)		Agriculture (1984–98)		Services (1997)	
(Intercept)	-21.23*** (0.29)	-26.14*** (0.31)	-21.49*** (0.30)	-26.73*** (0.32)	-17.04*** (0.40)	-18.30*** (0.46)	-22.20*** (0.97)	-27.16*** (0.75)
GDP	0.75*** (0.01)	0.82*** (0.01)	0.76*** (0.01)	0.83*** (0.01)	0.66*** (0.01)	0.73*** (0.01)	0.71*** (0.02)	0.79*** (0.01)
GDP per capita	0.86*** (0.01)	1.01*** (0.01)	0.88*** (0.01)	1.03*** (0.01)	0.45*** (0.01)	0.49*** (0.02)	0.64*** (0.03)	0.76*** (0.03)
Difference in GDP per capita	0.04*** (0.01)	0.04*** (0.01)	0.04*** (0.01)	0.04*** (0.01)	0.08*** (0.01)	0.10*** (0.01)	0.02 (0.03)	-0.02 (0.02)
Distance	-0.77*** (0.01)	-0.68*** (0.01)	-0.81*** (0.02)	-0.69*** (0.02)	-0.51*** (0.02)	-0.69*** (0.02)	-0.19*** (0.05)	-0.07* (0.03)
Adjacent dummy	0.45*** (0.05)	0.56*** (0.05)	0.42*** (0.06)	0.57*** (0.05)	0.73*** (0.07)	0.45*** (0.07)	-0.32* (0.18)	0.02 (0.11)
EU	0.00 (0.04)	-0.08* (0.04)	-0.01 (0.04)	-0.09* (0.04)	0.32*** (0.05)	0.33*** (0.05)	0.36*** (0.13)	0.24** (0.08)
NAFTA	-0.84*** (0.17)	-0.50*** (0.15)	-0.85*** (0.17)	-0.53*** (0.16)	-0.19 (0.22)	0.18 (0.21)	-0.72 (0.53)	-0.55 (0.34)
AFTA	1.00*** (0.08)	0.65*** (0.07)	0.99*** (0.08)	0.63*** (0.08)	0.55*** (0.11)	0.32** (0.10)	1.50*** (0.26)	1.08*** (0.17)
CER	0.52* (0.23)	0.81*** (0.21)	0.50* (0.24)	0.90*** (0.22)	1.20*** (0.31)	0.69* (0.30)	-1.04 (0.76)	-0.45 (0.49)
MERCOSUR	0.39 (0.26)	0.42* (0.24)	0.28 (0.28)	0.41 (0.25)	1.67*** (0.35)	1.25*** (0.34)	-3.50*** (0.86)	-2.51*** (0.54)
Andean Pact	1.18*** (0.14)	1.82*** (0.13)	1.27*** (0.14)	1.93*** (0.13)	-0.41* (0.20)	-0.18 (0.19)	-1.34** (0.45)	-0.61* (0.29)

	(1)	(2)	(3)	(4)	(5)	(6)	(7)	(8)
APEC	1.07***	1.10***	1.09***	1.16***	1.14***	1.04***	0.25**	0.09
	(0.03)	(0.03)	(0.03)	(0.04)	(0.04)	(0.05)	(0.09)	(0.08)
EU (OPEN dummy)		−0.02		0.00		0.18***		0.29***
		(0.03)		(0.03)		(0.04)		(0.06)
NAFTA (OPEN dummy)		−0.89***		−0.91***		−0.32***		−0.36***
		(0.03)		(0.03)		(0.05)		(0.07)
AFTA (OPEN dummy)		0.54***		0.54***		0.45***		1.01***
		(0.03)		(0.03)		(0.04)		(0.06)
CER (OPEN dummy)		−0.50***		−0.62***		0.68***		−0.35***
		(0.03)		(0.04)		(0.05)		(0.08)
MERCOSUR (OPEN dummy)		−0.16***		−0.28***		0.90***		−1.12***
		(0.03)		(0.04)		(0.05)		(0.08)
Andean Pact (OPEN dummy)		−0.41***		−0.43***		0.32***		−0.49***
		(0.03)		(0.03)		(0.04)		(0.06)
APEC (OPEN dummy)		0.11***		0.09***		0.28***		0.08
		(0.02)		(0.03)		(0.04)		(0.06)
Observations	10,506	10,506	10,467	10,467	9,613	9,613	703	703
Adjusted R^2	0.79	0.83	0.78	0.82	0.55	0.58	0.72	0.89

***Significant at greater than 1 percent level.

**Significant at 1 percent level.

*Significant at 5 percent level.

ˆSignificant at 10 percent level.

Note: See note to table 4A.1 for acronym definitions. Standard deviations are in parentheses.

Source: Authors' estimations.

Regarding services, we find a significant positive effect in the case of the European Union (services trade is estimated to be between 27 and 43 percent higher than otherwise similar economies). In MERCOSUR and the Andean Pact, in contrast to the results on merchandise trade, we find a statistically significant and strongly negative services trade bias.

In the case of both NAFTA and the CER Agreement, the estimated coefficients are also negative (perhaps surprising in the case of the CER Agreement, because an explicit arrangement to bring services trade under the agreement was signed in 1988). However, as was the case on merchandise trade results estimated on a single cross-section, the results are statistically insignificant, so we cannot draw any strong conclusions.

For AFTA, we find a strong positive (and highly significant) intraregional service trade bias, again indicating that this group has been particularly successful in promoting intraregional trade. The APEC region as a whole is estimated to have a small positive coefficient on services trade, but this finding loses significance once we control for openness.

Trade-Diverting Effects

The openness variable is needed in our model to control for the general degree of openness of RTA members when estimating the effect of an RTA on trade between members. Observing the level and changes in the degree of openness can give us insights into effects on the level of expected trade of RTA participants with nonmembers. In particular, a decrease in the openness coefficient following the establishment of an RTA may indicate the presence of trade diversion effects. Conversely, increases in the openness coefficient may indicate that protection levels against nonmembers are being reduced, thereby offsetting potential trade diversion effects.

We are interested in both the level of the openness coefficients and any changes in the coefficients over time (in particular if they correspond to postimplementation time periods). Once again, the relevant results are displayed in tables 4A.1 through 4A.3 and in table 4A.4 for the pooled data.

We begin with our extra-APEC control cases. In the European Union, the estimated coefficients on openness are small, vary in sign, and are statistically insignificant; hence, no conclusions can be drawn. In the case of MERCOSUR and the Andean Pact, the estimated openness coefficients are negative but diminishing overall (becoming positive for MERCOSUR in later years but not significant). The coefficients on agricultural trade are generally positive and increasing.

Turning to the APEC subregional groups, we find that, in the case of NAFTA, the openness coefficient is negative but declining over time. The pattern holds when we separate manufactures and agriculture. (The coefficient does become marginally positive in agriculture in 1998, but this result is not significant.) Hence, although the NAFTA economies are not as strongly open to trade as other economies, we cannot find strong evidence of trade-diversion effects. In the services sector (table 4A.4), we again have a negative and significant coefficient (–0.34), but the lack of a time-series element means that we cannot observe whether this coefficient is changing.

The CER Agreement exhibits a similar pattern for total merchandise and manufactures trade. The estimated openness coefficients are negative and significant but diminishing over time. Splitting the data along sectoral lines reveals quite a different pattern in agricultural trade, however. Here, the CER economies are shown to be very open; moreover, their degree of openness is increasing over time. Hence, once again we can find little evidence of strong trade-diversion effects. In the case of services trade, our point estimate for 1997 is negative (–0.35).

The estimated coefficients on openness are positive in all cases for AFTA. Moreover, the estimates increase over time for both manufactures trade and for overall merchandise trade. However, while the coefficients on agricultural trade are estimated to be positive, they are decreasing over time (although they are not statistically significant after 1992). Thus, there is some indication, though inconclusive, of trade diversion in agricultural products occurring in ASEAN, although these economies remain relatively open to agricultural trade.

The simulation results for the APEC group yield no significant negative coefficients on openness. Because APEC has not opted for the preferential approach to regional integration, it is not surprising to find no significant change since 1989 and no clear evidence of a declining trend in the openness coefficients over time. This conclusion applies to the merchandise trade data both as a whole and when separated by agricultural and manufactures trade. The services data indicate that APEC is marginally more open than average, but the result is not statistically significant.

The increasing openness coefficients for the NAFTA, AFTA, and CER groups may be taken as evidence that overall protection levels are declining within each group. This trend is found to apply both in overall merchandise trade and separately in manufacturing and agricultural trade. When the trend continues after the formal establishment of an RTA, it may indicate that the members of the RTA have continued to reduce their external barriers in parallel with the elimination of barriers among themselves. This outcome would be expected to reduce the potential for trade diversion and may be taken as indirect evidence that these RTAs are not hindering progress toward more openness in trade in general.

REFERENCES

Armington, Paul S. 1969. "A Theory of Demand for Products Distinguished by Place of Production." *IMF Staff Papers* 16:159–78.

Arndt, Channing. 1996. "An Introduction to Systematic Sensitivity Analysis via Gaussian Quadrature." Global Trade Analysis Project (GTAP) Technical 2. West Lafayette, Ind.: Center for Global Trade Analysis.

Arndt, Channing, and Ken R. Pearson. 1998. "How to Carry Out Systematic Sensitivity Analysis via Gaussian Quadrature and GEMPACK." Global Trade Analysis Project (GTAP) Technical 3. West Lafayette, Ind.: Center for Global Trade Analysis.

Bergsten, Fred. 2000. "Towards a Tripartite World." *The Economist*, July 15.

Bhagwati, Jagdish, and Arvind Panagariya, eds. 1996. *The Economics of Preferential Trading Agreements*. Washington, D.C.: AEI Press.

Bikker, Jacob. 1987. "An International Trade Flow Model with Substitution: An Extension of the Gravity Model." *Kyklos* 40:315–37.

Frankel, Jeffrey A. 1997. *Regional Trading Blocs in the World Economic System*. Washington, D.C.: Institute for International Economics.

Freund, Caroline. 2000. "Different Paths to Free Trade: The Gains from Regionalism." *Quarterly Journal of Economics* 65:1317–41.

Hengeveld, W. A. B. 1996. "World Distance Tables, 1948–1974." Inter-University Consortium for Political and Social Research Database Reference 6152. Ann Arbor, Mich.: University of Michigan, Institute for Social Research.

Hertel, Thomas. 1997. *Global Trade Analysis: Modeling and Applications*. New York: Cambridge University Press.

IMF (International Monetary Fund). Various years. *Direction of Trade Statistics*. Washington, D.C.

Krugman, Paul. 1991. "Is Bilateralism Bad?" In Elhanan Helpman and Assaf Razin, eds., *International Trade and Trade Policy*. Cambridge, Mass.: MIT Press.

PECC (Pacific Economic Cooperation Council). 1995. *Survey of Impediments to Trade and Investment Liberalization in the APEC Region*. Singapore.

———. 1999. *Assessing APEC Individual Action Plans and Their Contribution to APEC's Goals*. Auckland.

PECC and others. 1996. *Perspectives on the Manila Action Plan for APEC*. Manila.

Sazanami, Yoko, Shujiro Urata, and Hiroki Kawai. 1995. *Measuring the Costs of Protection in Japan*. Washington, D.C.: Institute for International Economics.

Scollay, Robert, and John Gilbert. 2000. "Measuring the Gains from APEC Trade Liberalization: An Overview of CGE Assessments." *World Economy* 23:175–97.

———. 2001. *New Regional Trading Arrangements in the Asia-Pacific?* Washington, D.C.: Institute for International Economics.

WTO (World Trade Organization). 1998. *Trade Policy Review: Indonesia*. Geneva.

———. 1999a. *Trade Policy Review: Philippines*. Geneva.

———. 1999b. *Trade Policy Review: Thailand*. Geneva.

———. 2000. *Trade Policy Review: Korea*. Geneva.

———. 2001a. *Trade Policy Review: Japan*. Geneva.

———. 2001b. *Trade Policy Review: Malaysia*. Geneva.

CHAPTER 5

HARMONIZING COMPETITION POLICIES

Peter Lloyd, Kerrin Vautier, and Paul Crampton

Multilateral organizations such as the Organisation for Economic Co-operation and Development (OECD) and Asia-Pacific Economic Cooperation (APEC) have encouraged cooperation and convergence among national competition policies, and some regional trading agreements (RTAs) have encompassed competition policies. These policies are usually regarded as *deep integration*. *Deep integration* refers to the harmonization of policies that are beyond the border, in contrast to *shallow integration*, which refers to the reduction of traditional border protection measures. Standard examples of deep integration are the harmonization of standards relating to industrial products or to safety, health, or environmental matters; however, any regulatory policies used in common by member countries are candidates for possible harmonization.

This chapter concerns the possibilities of harmonizing law and policies relating to competition in the East Asian region and the benefits of such harmonization. The idea of promoting competition is new to most countries in the region. More than half do not currently have comprehensive national competition laws, but this situation is changing rapidly because a number of countries are drafting or considering them. This context of flux provides a particular opportunity for the harmonization of new laws.

Increasingly, East Asian countries are competing in each other's markets. Intercountry trade in goods and intercountry foreign direct investment (FDI) have increased rapidly as a result of the lowering of barriers to trade in goods, services, and capital. This increased trade and FDI will continue under existing liberalization schedules within the Association of

We acknowledge the generous assistance in the section titled "Outline of the Competition Policies and Laws in East Asia" of Paulina Luczynska of the University of Auckland.

Southeast Asian Nations (ASEAN) and the Uruguay round of World Trade Organization negotiations, and it is likely to receive a boost from the outcome of the present Doha round. The strong trend toward regional trade integration mentioned in chapters 3 and 4 may also add to the momentum. These trends will increase the importance of cross-border aspects of competition policies and laws.

THE ROLE OF COMPETITION POLICY

Competition policy is an imprecise term. In this chapter, we use the term *competition-promoting policies* as a shorthand reference encompassing all government policies that promote competition among producers.

The set of competition-promoting policies is very broad. The literature on contestability of markets emphasizes that competition requires freedom of market entry and exit. At the level of competition across national borders, foreign firms enter markets in other countries by two modes. The first mode is the traditional method of competition by means of producing goods and services in the home country and then exporting them to the foreign country. This mode requires free trade and national treatment of goods and services. The second mode of entry is by establishing an affiliate in the foreign country. This mode requires the right of establishment and national treatment of the affiliate in the entry country so that the affiliate can compete on equal terms with national producers. Thus, the second mode highlights the importance of FDI regulations. Freedom of capital movements is especially important in the case of service industries that require a commercial presence, such as electricity and gas generation and distribution as well as telecommunications. Freedom of labor movement may also be important to those goods and services that require the movement of natural persons such as managers and technical personnel. Privatization, deregulation, and intellectual property are also important for promoting competition. Competition, or antitrust, law is a subset of the competition-promoting policies. In fact, it is the last resort. Whereas other policies remove barriers to or provide incentives for competition, competition or antitrust laws have been put in place to discourage producers who persist in anticompetitive activity. We shall consider all of these competition-promoting policies and laws.

Economists traditionally argue that the primary benefit of competition is that it increases consumer welfare by lowering the prices through lower costs of production and price-cost margins and by increasing the quality and range of goods and services available. Competition does this by promoting the entry into the market of new firms and encouraging more competitive pricing among firms. These gains apply to all markets and all countries. These benefits also accrue to businesses, because many buyers are other businesses rather than final consumers. Promoting competition thereby plays a role in lowering the costs of production in businesses that sell to final consumers and in improving the competitiveness of national exporters in foreign markets. This benefit is particularly important in infrastructure industries that provide other businesses with essential services such as power, water, and transport.

A second benefit relates to the propensity to innovate. There is an old argument that monopoly power increases the rate of innovation on the basis of the incentive effect of monopoly's higher profits. The modern theoretical literature, however, shows that monopoly power has an ambiguous effect on the rate of innovation (see, for example, Tirole 1988, chapter 10). A recent study by Symeonidis (2001), using data from the United Kingdom, showed that introducing restrictive trade practices legislation in that country had no significant effect on the number of innovations. In any case, this argument chiefly supports protection of intellectual property on new processes or products, not maintenance of monopolies in existing product markets. In the countries of East Asia, other than Japan and perhaps the Republic of Korea, new technologies and new products are mostly imported. In this context, the effect of promoting competition on the rate of the diffusion of technologies is more important. Regrettably, there is little empirical research on this aspect of innovation, although the measures adopted in the single market of the European Union (EU) were based on a belief that greater competition would increase the rate of innovation (Emerson and others 1988, chapter 7.2).

In an economy that is carrying out reforms by means of privatization and deregulation, a third benefit from having an explicit competition policy is that such a policy will provide guidance on the nature and timing of privatization and regulation decisions.

The essential principle of competition policy is that of *competitive neutrality*. All businesses should be able to compete on equal terms in the sense that no particular group of enterprises or modes of supply should be favored by government intervention, which distorts competition. This elementary principle has profound implications.

In the case of privatization that involves the sale or leasing of government-owned assets to private sector buyers, competitive neutrality implies that the sale or leasing should be done in a way that is open to all potential buyers or lessors. In most cases, such neutrality can be achieved directly by closed bid tendering with no restrictions on who may participate. The same neutrality principles apply to the allocation of licenses that are limited in number. This situation exists in a large number of industries, such as telecommunications (radio paging, cell telephones, and long-distance and international calls); radio, television, and other broadcasting spectra; and timber stumpage. Government revenue is maximized, and if these property rights are auctioned, the allocations go to the enterprises that operate at the least cost.

Similarly, deregulation should be guided by competition principles. It should promote competition by permitting entry to a deregulated industry for all potential suppliers. Regulations that remain should be targeted at overcoming market failures, and such regulations should be transparent.

HARMONIZATION OF COMPETITION LAW AND POLICIES

Steps to harmonize competition policy across jurisdictions may apply to competition-promoting policies that are broadly defined or to competition law that is defined more narrowly. In this area, the debate about harmonization concerns mainly the harmonization of competition law, because attempts to harmonize competition-promoting policies have been limited to the establishment of broad principles rather than to the harmonization of policies relating to trade, investment liberalization, privatization, or industry regulation or deregulation.

Nature and Benefits of Harmonization

The literature on the harmonization of competition law or policies is sparse. A partial survey of the harmonization of competition law is provided in Waverman, Comanor, and Goto (1997) and Lloyd and Richardson (1999). However, the larger literature on the harmonization of other standards, such as industrial, environmental, or labor standards (see, in particular, Bhagwati and Hudec 1996), helps in establishing some general views relating to harmonization of policies.

The notion of harmonization is vague. "Harmonization can be loosely defined as making the regulatory requirements or government policies of different jurisdictions identical, or at least similar" (Leebron 1996, p. 43). That is, harmonization is convergence of standards or policies. We need to give greater precision to the concept of harmonization.

The notion of harmonization among a group of countries in some policy area is straightforward only when there is one object to be harmonized and this object has a parameter or value that can be located on a single-dimensional continuum. This situation applies, for example, to harmonization of the tariff rate for some tariff item or to the excise tax rate for some excisable commodity.

In the area of competition law, some countries do not have competition laws or do not have laws relating to certain forms of business conduct. In those that do have them, many elements of competition law exist. In fact, there are many more elements of harmonization of competition law than elements of customs procedures or standards. The content of competition laws may be divided into two sets of elements. First are the elements that relate to the laws as a whole. These include the objectives of the laws, the scope of the laws with respect to enterprises or persons covered by the law, the methods of analysis, and the independence of the competition authority. Second are the substantive rules in the law governing specific practices or forms of unilateral and collusive business conduct, mergers and acquisitions, and possibly other elements relating to consumer protection, intellectual property, and subsidies to businesses.

Some elements of competition law can be measured on a line: tests of dominance use market shares or concentration ratios that lie on an interval of the real line (from zero to one), and merger thresholds are expressed in value terms (zero to infinity). But most cannot. A country may have a competition law with respect to some conduct, or it may not. Some authorities apply the *rule of reason*, whereas other authorities prohibit practices considered illegal per se. All such elements can be regarded as binary variables that take on two values: one if the property holds, and zero if it does not.

If the elements of law are binary variables, harmonization takes the form of all countries agreeing to one of the two alternatives. This type of harmonization might be called *qualitative harmonization*, as distinct from the harmonization of, say, tariff rates, which might be called *quantitative harmonization*. Harmonization of competition law is predominantly qualitative harmonization.

Given these complications, we need to refine the definition of harmonization. Harmonization of law will be taken to encompass the development of national law in countries that have none, the selection of a core of standards in all countries, and the convergence of standards for those elements in the core. Harmonization does not necessarily mean uniformity of standards.

Economists do not regard harmonization of any set of standards or policies as an end in itself. Harmonization should be adopted only if it confers net benefits on the countries concerned. Whether it does so will depend in part on the objectives of the policies and in part on the structure of the markets across which policies may be harmonized. In fact, in the general literature on harmonization, two opposing views exist: one favors policy harmonization, and one favors competition among jurisdictions—for example, the literature on tax competition versus that on tax harmonization (see, for example, Genser and Haufler 1996; Sykes 2000). This wider literature shows that there is no general presumption in favor of or against harmonization.

The primary potential benefit from the harmonization of competition laws relates to an increase in the efficiency of markets.[1] This benefit should be interpreted as Pareto-efficiency in the world economy, and it includes improvements in efficiency caused by improvements in the allocation of production among producers and among commodities, as well as improvements in the allocation of aggregate world production among consumers. In the analysis of harmonization of competition law, the main efficiency gains expected will be those resulting from the elimination or reduction of anticompetitive behavior. Harmonization may be desirable across national borders because the markets of nations are connected: many of the domestic competitors are foreign-owned companies, giving rise to concerns in several countries about the conduct of a business located in one country. Differences among the member countries in national competition policies, laws, and law enforcement may give rise to inefficient allocation of resources and consumption in the region, suggesting possible benefits from the harmonization of laws across jurisdictions.

Harmonization of competition standards may also incur costs if the common or minimum standards prohibit business conduct that is welfare improving or allow conduct that is welfare reducing to a country.

One concern is that adopting common standards will reduce the ability of competition authorities to deal with circumstances in one jurisdiction that differ from those of other jurisdictions. Developing countries sometimes argue that they should have a competition policy or law that takes account of their level of development. This argument cannot be sustained. A monopolist or a firm in a dominant position, or enterprises seeking to collude or to merge, all behave in the same essential manner in an industrial or a developing country: they act in pursuit of their own interests. Competition law exists to protect the interests of the less powerful or less

---

1. A second benefit is a reduction in transaction costs—specifically the compliance and enforcement costs associated with doing business across jurisdictions. Any harmonized standards will eliminate the additional costs of doing business across jurisdictions with different policies—that is, the costs of disharmony.

well-informed consumers and producers. Nothing in the level of average per capita incomes or development itself affects qualitatively the analysis of buyer and consumer behavior. Increasingly, the markets for goods and services in an industrial country are part of an integrated world market, as is the case for manufactures and many services such as telecommunication services. Developing countries do, however, have to address the issue of the capacity of their institutions to handle competition law.

To our knowledge, no empirical studies demonstrate the benefits of harmonization of competition laws. Nevertheless, we can make a strong conjecture about the circumstances under which harmonization of standards is likely to yield benefits from improved production and consumption allocations in the world economy. The benefits from harmonization across countries of standards relating to particular forms of business conduct are likely to increase as border barriers to international trade in goods and FDI decrease and, consequently, potential competition across borders increases.

The belief that an active multicountry competition policy would increase the gains from trade liberalization and economic integration more generally was evident in the measures taken by the European Community known as *EC 92*. These measures were expected to lead to a single market. An influential study that was done for the European Commission at the time of the introduction of the EC 92 measures surveyed the empirical literature relating to European Community market integration. The study concluded that "the new competitive pressures brought about by completion of the internal market can be expected to lead to rationalization within European enterprises and thus produce appreciable gains in internal efficiency" (Emerson and others 1988, p. 157).

Issues in Harmonizing Competition Law

Introduction of national policies. Given the preceding definition of harmonization, the most elementary form of harmonization is the development of national competition law in countries that do not at present have such laws. It is not surprising that, under some RTAs, all member countries are required to introduce national competition laws for specified areas of competitive behavior. In negotiating the North American Free Trade Agreement (NAFTA), for example, the United States and Canada insisted on provisions requiring Mexico to introduce a base competition law. Such provisions also exist in the Southern Cone Common Market, or Mercado Común del Sur (MERCOSUR) agreement (see Tavares and Tineo 1998) and in the European Union, where it is part of the *acquis communautaire* that must be adopted by all countries seeking accession. Indeed, the introduction of national competition law is one of the main contributions of RTAs to the development of competition-promoting policies. Similarly, APEC encourages all member economies to apply its agreed competition principles to policy development with a view to enhancing economic efficiency and welfare.

Harmonization of objectives and scope of the law. Competition laws vary considerably in their objectives. In the OECD countries, excluding Japan and Korea, the objectives are strongly oriented toward enhancing consumer welfare or enhancing competition itself. The competition laws of some countries have multiple objectives.

The extent of exemptions varies greatly among countries. In most of the OECD countries, there are few exemptions. The law applies in particular to government-owned enterprises that sell goods or services in markets and to other enterprises subject to direction by the state. Competition law generally covers the natural monopolies and all mergers and acquisitions, subject to a size threshold. By contrast, the Antimonopoly Act of 1947 (Act Concerning Prohibition of Private Monopolization and Maintenance of Fair Trade) of Japan exempts "railway, electricity, gas, or any other business constituting a monopoly by the inherent nature of the said business"; special laws apply to specific industries, cooperatives, recession and rationalization cartels, and resale price maintenance contracts. This list constitutes major exclusions. In Korea, the exemptions are "the acts of an Enterprise or Trade Association conducted in accordance with any Act or any decree to such Act." Cooperatives are also exempted. Korea, therefore, also has a large set of exclusions, though fewer than Japan. These exclusions mean that large segments of the economy selling to both consumers and other businesses are not subject to the competition laws.

Both the objectives of the law and the exemptions will profoundly affect the application of the law in practice. These elements could be standardized or harmonized across countries.

Common or minimum standards for business conduct. There are two aspects of harmonizing competition standards for the substantive rules in the law governing specific practices or forms of business conduct. First, there is the choice of the set of elements of competition law that are to be harmonized. They might be restricted to a small set, a core. Second, there is the choice of standard for each element that is included.

In relation to standards for an element, harmonization can be the adoption of a single common standard or of a minimum standard. In the case of a common standard for some element of competition law, the chosen standard might be one already existing in a member economy, or it might be a model standard.

What is the best choice of standards? Is there a single best choice for every element of competition policy or law? Although principles of economic behavior and analysis are universal, it may be necessary to permit some variation in the best choices among economies to allow for local conditions and differences in legal or regulatory sophistication. To answer these questions, we need to analyze possible cases of cross-country harmonization, using economic models of the industries concerned.

As an example of harmonization of standards relating to collusive behavior of businesses, consider the standards relating to price-fixing cartels. Suppose two countries produce a homogeneous product under constant returns to scale conditions. One country has a lax competition policy permitting a domestic cartel that raises the domestic price, and the other country has a strict policy outlawing cartels.

In this instance, there is a conflict between the interests of producers and consumers within each country (Levinsohn 1996, pp. 345–50). However, both producer interests and consumer interests coincide across countries; what is good for producers in one country is good for producers in the other country, and the same holds for consumers. Essentially, a tolerant competition policy that permits cartelization in one country has effects that spill over into the other country, benefiting its producers and harming its consumers.

The outcome of harmonization depends on whether the harmonization adopts the standards of the lax country or those of the strict country. To assess the change in welfare in each country, one must weight equally the welfare of the producer and consumer groups. If the standards of the strict country are adopted, the country with the lax standards may gain or lose, depending on the size of the producer and consumer effects, whereas the country with the strict standards gains and the world gains. If the standards of the lax country are adopted, the country with the strict policy loses, the country with the lax standards gains if the domestic market is not large, and the world loses.

Hence, the choice of standards clearly matters. The main lesson is that harmonization, in this instance at least, should be toward the standards of the country that has the more pro-competitive policy. This lesson follows the intuition of basic economics. There may, however, be a conflict of interest between the countries, although the world as a whole gains.

Other areas of unilateral and collusive business conduct could be examined in the same way. For example, one variation is to analyze an export cartel. Here there is a clear conflict of interest between the exporting and importing nations.

Agreement is more likely in some areas than in others. In particular, agreement is more likely with respect to practices that jurisdictions tend to prohibit. Hence, harmonization may be feasible in areas of cartel behavior other than price-fixing, such as market allocation, and in collusive bidding and resale price maintenance. The only harmonization agreement reached in the OECD relates to hard-core cartel behavior. For areas where the rule of reason applies, there are added difficulties because harmonization also involves agreeing on the methods of analysis. For example, the laws relating to vertical interfirm arrangements vary greatly among the major OECD countries, and the rule of reason applies widely, making agreement difficult (see Waverman, Comanor, and Goto 1997, part IV).

In the case of mergers, the major concerns are different. One concern is the costs resulting from review of a proposed merger in multiple jurisdictions. This review may cause considerable uncertainty about the outcome, additional costs, and delays in implementing a merger because the merger thresholds and analysis differ considerably among national competition laws. A second concern is that any one country that reviews the merger may block or limit the scope of the merger.

There is a range of harmonization strategies for mergers (see Campbell and Trebilcock 1997). One strategy is review by a centralized supranational authority. Another is adoption of a common standard. The adoption of the most pro-competitive standard by all reviewing jurisdictions will yield a benefit from greater competition, which will normally result in lower prices; however, it may lower welfare if there are economies of scale. In the absence of common standards, national competition authorities may agree to cooperate. In some circumstances, such cooperation may result in the approval in all jurisdictions of a merger that is in the combined interest of the countries concerned. For example, the jurisdictions may agree that the merger will be reviewed only in the jurisdiction in which the major effects occur. Harmonization may also take the weaker form of agreement on procedural issues such as time limits and disclosure requirements, as well as issues such as sharing of information.

Centralized or decentralized harmonization. One general issue of economic analysis that affects the choice of the method of harmonization of competition standards embedded in the substantive rules is whether to seek a centralized or a decentralized solution to the problems of harmonization. Both centralized and decentralized solutions are forms of concerted action, but they differ fundamentally in their approach.

The most centralized solution is establishing a supranational authority that operates among the countries concerned much like the national competition authorities that operate at the national level. This authority would investigate business conduct in whatever countries were involved, consider the interests of all countries, and enforce its law with a single set of standards. It would presumably act to maximize the sum of the welfare of all the nations, rather than the welfare of individual nations. The least centralized solution is the continued reliance on action by national authorities, supplemented by voluntary cooperation among the authorities involved. In between these extremes are several alternatives.

Several factors will determine the costs and benefits of a centralized versus a decentralized solution and the allocation of powers between the levels. These factors include the extent of the powers of national and regional supranational authorities to gather information and investigate private actions, and the extent of their powers to enforce any decision. Such factors may also include the risks of capture of these authorities by private producer interests, which may be greater in one form of action than in others, and the difficulty of agreeing on the objectives of the laws and the methods of analysis of competition cases. A more centralized solution may have advantages of greater uniformity and lower risk of capture, but it may also have disadvantages. These disadvantages include weaker enforcement and greater difficulty in agreeing on objectives and analysis.

In the absence of a world competition authority, a centralized approach is feasible only in RTAs. This choice has been recognized explicitly in the European Union in the debate about the principle of subsidiarity. The adoption of the principle of subsidiarity has led to a mix of decentralized and centralized powers in the area of competition laws as in other laws. Other RTAs, such as NAFTA, the Closer Economic Relations (CER) Agreement between Australia and New Zealand, and MERCOSUR, have adopted a decentralized approach, with some differences among them, as noted later in this chapter.

Competition law enforcement across national borders. The enforcement of national laws when the offending persons reside outside the national jurisdiction has always created difficulties. A number of mechanisms have been developed to enhance national jurisdiction.

One direct mechanism is the extraterritorial application of a country's national laws when the residents of that country are affected by the actions of persons residing in another country. The United States principally has used this method under the *effects doctrine*. The European Union also has applied its competition laws extraterritorially on occasion, but other countries have done so only to a very limited extent. Because this alternative involves a conflict of laws and enforcement powers between nations, other nations have sometimes vigorously opposed such extensions of jurisdiction.

Another proposal for improving enforcement across national boundaries would allow foreign private parties to bring actions in a jurisdiction where an alleged offense has occurred (Mattoo and Subramanian 1997). This mechanism is the reverse of the first mechanism: here, the business whose conduct is challenged resides in the country whose law may be applied, and the affected party resides in the foreign country.

The standard proposal is bilateral cooperation between the authorities of the two jurisdictions whose residents are affected by some form of business conduct such as price-fixing in international markets. A number of countries have formalized their cooperation through bilateral cooperation agreements on competition. These agreements contain provisions for consultation and the exchange of information. More recent agreements contain provisions for negative comity and, in a few cases such as the 1991 United States–European Community agreement, positive comity, which encourages the country in which the business is located to take action in the interests of foreign persons. An alternative mechanism is to include provisions for cooperation in competition law in mutual legal assistance treaties. Most bilateral agreements involve either the United States or the European Union as one party. Bilateral competition cooperation agreements have limitations because they are nonbinding and because the exchange of confidential information is limited. Lloyd and Vautier (1999, chapter 3) survey these agreements. The likelihood of multicountry cooperation is greater in the context of RTAs.

None of these possibilities involve harmonization of standards. Instead they are mechanisms for extending the reach of one nation's laws to involve businesses or parties that reside beyond its borders.

OUTLINE OF THE COMPETITION POLICIES
AND LAWS IN EAST ASIA

This section covers 12 East Asian economies: Brunei Darussalam, China, Hong Kong (China), Indonesia, Japan, Korea, Malaysia, the Philippines, Singapore, Taiwan (China), Thailand, and Vietnam. The Lao People's Democratic Republic and Cambodia are excluded because of the paucity of information relating to these two countries.

These economies represent different forms of market systems: Hong Kong (China) and Singapore have a century-long history of duty-free trade and liberal economic ideals. At the other extreme, China and Vietnam (as well as the Lao People's Democratic Republic and Cambodia) had fully state-regulated markets only one or two decades ago. These specific historical circumstances have an obvious effect on the stages of implementation of competition policy.

Competition Policy Objectives

These economies of the East Asian region generally recognize the importance of promoting competition through pro-competition government policies. However, this recognition is new to most of them, going back only to the adoption in the 1990s of more market-oriented policies. The efforts various international organizations have made to promote the pro-competition approach have also contributed to this recognition.

Most governments do not publish competition policy statements, but information on competition policies in East Asia can be found in the Individual Action Plans (IAPs) submitted by the member economies to the APEC Secretariat each year and on databases held in individual countries.

One aspect of these annual reports is fundamental to the development of competition law: the declared objectives of national competition policies. Competition policy objectives are stated in the selected IAPs of the member economies. Four general groups of economies can be differentiated:[2]

1. Economies whose competition policy follows the objective of efficiency, competition promotion, and consumer welfare: Brunei Darussalam, Hong Kong (China), Malaysia, Singapore, Taiwan (China), and Thailand
2. Economies that regard development of the internal market as a main objective of their competition policy: China and Vietnam
3. Economies which, in assuring the will to promote competition in their markets, emphasize the protection of consumers or of small and medium-size enterprises (SMEs): Indonesia and the Philippines
4. Economies that emphasize fair as well as free competition and have broad objectives related to the balanced development of the national economy: Japan and Korea.

---

2. The economies studied tend to state a number of objectives of their competition policy. The distinction made here is on the basis of the prevailing concern expressed.

The common feature of the economies in the first category is that efficiency in the operation of markets, competition, and consumer benefits are the declared goals of competition policy. However, those economies do not necessarily agree on the methods for achieving these objectives. Brunei Darussalam, Hong Kong (China), and Singapore have not introduced comprehensive competition laws. They claim an efficient and competitive market can be achieved by maintaining a very open economy and by minimizing government involvement in markets (deregulation). In this group, only Thailand has introduced a more comprehensive competition law and associated enforcement regime. Malaysia is still looking tentatively at the need for adoption of such a law and the options.

Economies in the second category do not necessarily reject the objective of broad cooperation among the APEC members and interdependence of markets in the region. However, they emphasize that their main interest in implementing competition policies lies in the development of their own internal market.[3] It is debatable whether this focus on internal matters can be regarded as inconsistent with APEC priorities or whether it is the only logical stage of development for economies that belong to the second group.

Taiwan (China) encourages pro-competitive mergers and provides assistance to industries. In promoting competition policy, Indonesia intends to "take into account the special needs of the SMEs," the well-being of which, along with customer protection, is strictly linked to public welfare (Constitution of 1945). In the Philippines, the statement of the policy to encourage competition notes that the government is constitutionally mandated to protect the Philippines from unfair foreign competition and trade practices, although the specific character of such alleged practices has not been defined.

In the fourth category, section 1 of chapter 1 of Japan's Antimonopoly Act of 1947 declares the following as its purpose:

> This Act . . . aims to promote free and fair competition, to stimulate the creative initiative of entrepreneurs, to encourage business activities of enterprises, to heighten the level of employment and people's real income, and thereby to promote the democratic and wholesome development of the national economy as well as to assure the interests of consumers in general.

---

3. China implements competition policy in order to safeguard the healthy development of the socialist market economy and to transform the planned economic system into a market one. The Vietnamese government follows a similar approach.

In Korea, article 1 of chapter 1 of the Monopoly Regulation and Fair Trade Act declares:

> The purpose of this Act is to encourage fair and free economic competition by prohibiting the abuse of market-dominant positions and the excessive concentration of economic power and by regulating improper concerted acts and unfair business practices, thereby stimulating creative business activities, protecting consumers, and promoting the balanced development of the national economy.

The laws in these two countries have multiple objectives, which include some provision relating to the "wholesome [or balanced] development of the national economy." These statutes are less focused on protecting the interests of the consumers and buyers than are the laws of other OECD countries.

Competition Laws

The variety of perceptions among the 12 economies covered in the study about the importance and place of competition law makes it difficult to assert how many of them actually have a competition law. For the purpose of this chapter, we accept that a form of competition law exists in an economy whenever its legal system addresses behaviors that could be regarded as anticompetitive, such as tie-in sales, price-fixing, or abuse of dominant position in a particular sector. We need to be alert, however, to the crucial difference between those economies that simply have a law on the books and those that can support a claim to have established functional and efficient enforcement mechanisms.

Table 5.1 presents an overview of the status of competition laws. Of the 12 selected economies, 5 have a comprehensive competition or antitrust law. Three of those economies—Indonesia, Taiwan (China), and Thailand—have introduced the law in the past 10 years. But only three of these economies—Japan, Korea, and Taiwan (China)—can claim to have an operational and efficient enforcement mechanism. Thailand's current competition law is relatively new and the practice has not yet developed. The same holds for the Indonesian competition law system. The Philippines has several pieces of legislation for regulating most competition issues and, in that sense, could be included in the foregoing group of economies. However, the Philippines does not have a single central body for enforcing its competition legislation, which would have contributed to the perception of its competition system as being comprehensive. In fact, the issue of enforcement is unclear; no reports are available

Table 5.1 Competition Laws: A Functional Overview

Criterion	Brunei Darussalam	China	Hong Kong, China	Indonesia	Japan	Korea, Rep. of	Malaysia	Philippines	Singapore	Taiwan, China	Thailand	Vietnam
Has introduced a general or comprehensive competition law	No	No	No	Yes	Yes	Yes	No	No	No	Yes	Yes	No
Intends to introduce a general competition law	Uncertain	Yes	No	n.a.	n.a.	n.a.	Uncertain		No	n.a	n.a.	Yes
Has a single enforcement mechanism in place or proposed	No	Yes	No	Yes	Yes	Yes	No	No	No	Yes	Yes	No
Shows evidence of operating the competition law enforcement mechanism	No	Uncertain	No	Uncertain	Yes	Yes	No	Uncertain	No	Yes	Uncertain	No
Has various laws that address competition issues	No	Yes	Yes	n.a.	n.a.	n.a.	No	Yes	No	n.a	n.a.	No

n.a. Not applicable.

referring to enforcement statistics in the APEC competition policy and law database.

Of the remaining six economies, only China and Vietnam expressly indicate an intention to introduce a general competition law in the near future. China's first antitrust law, protecting commercial secrets law, and the implementation regulations of the law for countering unfair competition are said to be in the process of intensive drafting. China has also indicated the governing body that will be responsible for enforcing the forthcoming legislation: the Administration of Industry and Commerce of China, which so far has been handling unfair competition and consumer protection cases (China APEC Individual Action Plan, October 2000). Even though China has no specific antitrust regulation, several regulations in its legal system concern some anticompetitive behavior. For example, the Law of the People's Republic of China for Countering Unfair Competition (1993) prohibits forcing a consumer to buy goods designated by public utility enterprises or enterprises having monopoly status, as well as prohibiting tie-in sales. Vietnam completed a draft Competition Law in early 2001. This draft has chapters dealing with anticompetitive agreements; abuse of dominant position; mergers, consolidation, and acquisition of enterprises; and unfair competition.

Brunei Darussalam has remained silent in its IAPs on the matter of introducing comprehensive competition law. The Malaysian government is in the process of studying the need for such law and its implications. It has established a Working Committee on Competition Policy and Law to explore elements of competition best suited to Malaysia. Following the policy of minimum government intervention, policymakers in Hong Kong, China, claim to use appropriate and pragmatic measures to rectify unfair business practices by means of a sectoral approach to competition issues.[4] In areas in which there is no specific system of regulation, such as mergers and acquisitions or vertical restraints, Hong Kong, China, is satisfied that ad hoc action is sufficient to remedy any abuses of market power.

Table 5.2 summarizes the scope of certain of these laws in relation to forms of business conduct that are prohibited or regulated. Even among the economies that have adopted and enforced competition laws, there are considerable differences in the scope of substantive rules relating to forms of business conduct, in principles of law, in the relative use of per se

---

4. For example, the Broadcasting Authority has the power to regulate competition issues in the broadcasting sector; its counterpart in the telecommunications sector is the Telecommunications Authority (established in June 2000). The Energy Advisory Committee has a subcommittee specializing in matters related to competition in the energy sector.

Table 5.2 Main Conduct Regulated

Country/law	Coverage	Activity targeted	Prohibited unilateral conduct	Prohibited collusive conduct	Mergers and acquisitions requirements
Japan: Act Concerning Prohibition of Private Monopolization and Maintenance of Fair Trade 1947	Comprehensive	Monopolization	Private monopolization: "exclusion or controlling the business activities of other entrepreneurs, thereby causing . . . a substantial restraint of competition"	Private monopolization "by combination or conspiracy with other entrepreneurs causing . . . a substantial restraint of competition" Unfair trade practices (vertical restraints) and unreasonable restraint of trade (horizontal agreements) "by which . . . entrepreneurs mutually restrict or conduct their business activities in such a manner as to fix, maintain, or increase prices, or to limit production, technology, products, facilities, or customers or suppliers, . . . causing . . . a substantial restraint of competition . . . ."	Prior notification Threshold: substantial restraint of competition
Korea, Rep. of: Monopoly Regulation and Fair Trade Act 1980	Corporations engaging in a financial or an insurance business have been excluded from the definition of the dominant market power	Monopolization	Abuse of market-dominant position by unreasonably fixing, maintaining, or altering prices; by unreasonable control of the sale of goods or services; by unreasonable interference with other enterprises; by unreasonable hindering of competition; or by other threats that substantially restrain competition	Business combinations to acquire shares of competitors, to establish interlocking directorates, to create mergers between companies, to carry out takeovers of businesses, to exercise compulsion in business dealings, and to establish new corporations that substantially restrict competition, unless these practices are acknowledged by the Fair Trade Commission	Prior notification Threshold: substantial restriction of competition

Taiwan, China: Fair Trade Law 1991 (revised in 1999, section 9 amended in 2000)	Comprehensive	Specific types of anticompetitive conduct of monopolistic enterprises *Monopolistic enterprise* defined as one that faces no competition or has a dominant position sufficient to enable it to exclude competition in relevant market	Under article 10, directly or indirectly preventing by unfair means of competition by any other enterprises Improperly setting, maintaining, or changing the prices of goods or the remuneration for services Making a trading counterpart give preferential treatment without justification or otherwise abusing market power	According to article 14, "No enterprise shall have any concerted action, unless the concerted action meets the requirements under one of the following circumstances: it is beneficial to the economy as a whole and in the public interest, and the central competent authority has approved such concerted action."	Application for approval, when (a) as a result of the merger the merged enterprise will have one-third of the market share, (b) one of the enterprises in the merger has one-fourth of the market share, or (c) sales for the preceding fiscal year of one of the enterprises in the merger exceeds the threshold amount publicly announced by the central competent authority (article 11) Threshold: size limit, but authorization may be obtained
Indonesia: Law No. 5/1999 on the Prohibition of Monopolistic Practices and Unfair Business Competition (text of law unavailable)	Uncertain	Monopolistic practices; details unavailable	Monopolistic practices Dominant position abuse	Price-fixing Price discrimination Vertical integration Forbidden business agreements, arrangements, and activities	Details unavailable

(Table continues on the following page.)

Table 5.2 continued

Country/law	Coverage	Activity targeted	Prohibited unilateral conduct	Prohibited collusive conduct	Mergers and acquisitions requirements
Thailand: Competition Act 1999 (text not available at the APEC database as of March 29, 2001)	Not applicable to central, provincial, and local government agencies, state-owned enterprises, agricultural operatives established by law, and some other businesses, as prescribed by ministerial regulations. (section 4)	Monopolistic practices; details unavailable	Under section 25, abuse of a dominant position by fixing prices or maintaining unfair price levels; by imposing unfair conditions, directly or indirectly, to limit services, manufactures, and so forth; by ceasing, reducing, or limiting services or imports so that they fall short of market demand; or by interfering with the business operations of others without reasonable cause	Practices leading to monopoly or reducing or limiting competition (section 27) Price-fixing agreements Quantitative limitations Joint agreements to manipulate or control the market Collusion in fixing an agreement or a condition to enable one party to succeed in a bid or auction or allow one party not to compete in a bid or auction Restrictive practices undertaken jointly with overseas operators (section 28)	Prior permission when the merger may result in unfair competition or create a monopoly position (sections 26 and 35)

prohibitions and the rule of reason, and in remedies, as well as, more subtly, in the use of tests and market analysis.

Bollard and Vautier (1998, p. 142) investigated differences among countries in a number of features of competition law, including the scope of substantive rules relating to forms of business conduct, as well as judicial and enforcement characteristics. The authors calculated an index, or convergence scale, for pairs of countries. On this convergence scale, 100 represented an identical pair of competition laws, and zero represented completely different competition regimes. The value of the index for Taiwan (China) and Korea was 53; for Taiwan (China) and Japan, 47; and for Japan and Korea, 54. In comparison, the value for the United States and Canada was 53, and that for Australia and New Zealand was 77.

HARMONIZATION EXPERIENCE IN REGIONAL TRADING AGREEMENTS

Competition policies form part of the regionwide policies of a small minority of the more than 200 RTAs. The first regional agreement related to competition was included in the 1957 Treaty of Rome. This treaty now covers 33 countries.[5] Several other RTAs have incorporated an agreement related to competition; these agreements include the 1990 extension to the Closer Economic Relations Agreement between Australia and New Zealand, the 1991 decision of the forming of the Andean Group (later the Andean Community), the 1992 North American Free Trade Agreement, the 1996 MERCOSUR agreement, the 1996 Canada-Chile Free Trade Agreement, and three recent agreements in Central America. In total, 55 countries are currently involved in at least one of these regional competition agreements. They include a number of developing countries in Central and Latin America and a number of transition economies in Central Europe. Except in the European Union, the development of regional competition-promoting policies was a feature of the 1990s.

We examine here the policies of the European Union, NAFTA, the CER Agreement, MERCOSUR, and the Andean Community. These RTAs are the most important in terms of development of regional law and practice relating to competition.

---

5. These 33 countries are the 15 full members of the European Union, the 3 members of the European Economic Area, the 10 Central and East European countries, and the 5 Mediterranean countries. Of the last 18, 10 are scheduled for admission to the European Union in 2004.

European Union

The European Union has by far the most important RTA in the area of competition-promoting policies (as in many other areas). First, its RTA involves more countries than any other. Second, its regional competition policies are the most comprehensive. In developing these policies, the European Union (and its predecessors, the European Economic Community and the European Community) has pioneered many features of regional rules and cooperation among its members. For example, the European Union established a supranational regional authority (Directorate-General IV, known as DG IV); developed the principle of subsidiarity; and established detailed rules of cooperation and information sharing between the regional and the national competition authorities. Thus, the European Union provides a standard by which to measure the extent of the development of cross-country laws related to competition in other country groups.

Competition policy has been one of the so-called common policies from the outset. In the EU context, *competition policy* means competition law. The European Union has brought about the introduction of national competition laws in its full members. The scope and direction of these policies stem from the adoption in the Treaty of Rome of a goal of economic integration in the form of a common market. The principles of competition-promoting policies were strengthened further in the Maastricht Treaty in 1992, which laid down the general principle of "an open-market economy with free competition."

In relation to competition law, article 81 of the Treaty of Rome controls most investigations and cases that have taken place. It prohibits cartels and other restrictive agreements. Article 82 deals with abuse of dominant positions. (The original articles 85 and 86 were renumbered articles 81 and 82 when the Treaty of Amsterdam came into force on May 1, 1999.)

Article 81 gives particular examples of practices that may restrict competition or abuse a dominant position and that are therefore prohibited. Its list of prohibited practices include those that directly or indirectly fix purchases or selling prices or any other trading conditions; limit or control production, markets, technical development, or investment; and share markets or sources of supply.[6]

---

6. Export cartels organized by EU producers and import cartels in other countries relating to imports from the European Union are outside the scope of article 81 and are therefore permitted; but import cartels by undertakings in the European Union and export cartels among non-EU producers relating to exports to the European Union fall within the scope of article 81.

EU competition law and law enforcement are evolving constantly in response to new market developments and changes in views of competition. For example, on January 1, 2000, new rules for assessing vertical restraints entered into force, and on January 1, 2001, new rules for assessing horizontal cooperation agreements entered into force (see Lücking and Woods 2001).

In relation to harmonizing competition law among its members, the European Union (and formerly the European Economic Community) has evolved a mix of centralized EU-wide law and law administered by national governments. This mixed jurisdiction has been recognized explicitly in the European Union, where the debate about the principle of subsidiarity has posed this choice clearly. The principle of subsidiarity was first laid down explicitly in the Maastricht Treaty, although it has evolved during the whole history of the European Union. It divides between the national governments and the European Union functions that are not the exclusive competence of the European Union. Article 3B of the treaty declares:

> In areas which do not fall within its exclusive competence, the Community shall take action, in accordance with the principle of subsidiarity, only if and insofar as the objectives of the proposed actions cannot be sufficiently achieved by the member States and can therefore, by reason of the scale or effect of the proposed action, be better achieved by the Community.

This principle does not lay down which areas of policy shall be dealt with at the regional level and which at the national level. Rather, it lays down rules that determine the division of responsibilities between these levels. Its main concern is that the objectives of the policies be achieved efficiently. (See CEPR 1993 and Pelkmans 1997, chapters 4 and 12, for further discussion.)

In the context of the choice between centralized or decentralized approaches to competition problems, the EU Merger Regulations are the most explicit attempt to allocate power between the jurisdictions at the levels of the European Union and the national governments under the principle of subsidiarity.[7] The 1990 Merger Regulations stipulate that mergers, acquisitions, and "concentrative" joint ventures should be notified to the European Commission when (a) they are between parties whose

---

7. There are no explicit provisions in the Treaty of Rome related to mergers. The Merger Regulations were added in 1990 as a result of dissatisfaction with the powers related to mergers under old articles 85 and 86 and the increase in mergers during the 1980s, and the regulations were amended in 1997 with effect from March 1, 1998.

combined worldwide annual turnover exceeds 5 billion European currency units (ECU), (b) the turnover throughout the European Union of each of at least two of the undertakings concerned is more than ECU 250 million, and (c) "unless the parties conduct two-thirds or more of their business in one and the same member state." All three conditions have to be met. The conditions mean that the merger powers are not exclusively at the EU level, even when they involve cross-border aspects: "[The second condition] is a clear and precise attempt to base centralization upon the extent of the spillovers between member states" (CEPR 1993, p. 135). The 1998 revised Merger Regulations maintained the thresholds. (The European Commission had proposed that the thresholds be lowered, but the European Council did not approve the proposal.) The 1998 amendments also harmonized the treatment of mergers involving joint ventures and simplified the notification procedures.

The Centre for Economic Policy Research (CEPR 1993, pp. 135–37) evaluated the net gains from centralizing merger controls at the EU level compared with the net gains from coordinating among the national competition authorities. It saw the net gains at each level as a tradeoff between the loss from regulatory capture and gains from the capture of cross-border spillovers. CEPR (1993, pp. 136–37) concluded:

> Merger control is an area in which cooperation to secure the benefits of policy coordination is a particularly unsatisfactory alternative to centralisation, because of the highly discretionary nature of the policy to be implemented and the consequent difficulty for twelve member states in observing whether each is abiding by the terms of a collective agreement. Overall, merger policy is a good illustration of a case where the gains from centralisation are high; but it is also a warning that the central institutions need to be designed in such a way as to ensure that these gains are not dissipated through an increase in rent-seeking and regulatory capture.

In practice, however, the merger thresholds—especially the second threshold—have meant that more than 90 percent of proposed mergers in which one or more parties are located in the European Union escape EU control (Sleuwaegen 1998).

The European Union has led to very substantial convergence of the national competition laws of the member countries. Of the 6 original member states of the European Economic Community in 1957, only the Federal Republic of Germany had comprehensive national competition laws. Although the Treaty of Rome and subsequent treaties do not explicitly require that all member states have competition laws, the member states would find it difficult to operate in the European Union without such laws. All of the current 15 member states have comprehensive competition laws.

This spread of national competition laws among the member states is attributable in large measure to the EU-level competition law in the treaties.

Convergence of competition law means more than the introduction of national competition laws. It also comprises all aspects of those laws across countries: their scope, methods of analysis, and enforcement. That breadth raises the question: Can national laws and EU laws coexist when the national laws have provisions that are different from the comparable provisions of the EU laws?

If conduct is clearly examinable under national laws because it does not affect EU trade or competition, there is no conflict. But if conduct does affect both national trade and EU trade or competition, a conflict may arise. In a key 1969 decision, the European Court of Justice ruled that national authorities could proceed in parallel against practices in question. However, if a conflict arose, the EU law would prevail. Most EU member states have amended their national legislation to bring it into greater conformity with EU law. However, numerous differences persist between the laws of national authorities and EU law.

These differences themselves create pressure for greater convergence. The Directorate-General IV of the European Commission (DG IV 1997, p. 15) has noted that the division of responsibilities between the EU level and the national level will work well only if the national authorities are prepared to apply EU law at the national level. Otherwise, "this would bring with it the danger of forum shopping, with firms seeking out the jurisdiction of the authority they feel will be most favourable to their interests." In its 1997 notice on cooperation between the national competition authorities and the European Commission, the commission called on member states that have not already done so to adopt legislation enabling their competition authority to implement (old) articles 85(1) and 86 of the Treaty of Rome effectively (DG IV 1997).

An issue related to the coexistence of EU and national competition law is cooperation and coordination between the two levels. Coordination procedures have been developed between the European Commission and the competition law authorities of the member states to prevent conduct from being examined at two levels (DG IV 1997).[8] Procedures were developed for sharing of information between the European Commission and the national authorities. Article 20 of EU Council Regulation 17/62 requires both the European Commission and national authorities to keep

---

8. Similar procedures have been developed in the European Economic Area to prevent conduct being examined, in this case, by both the European Commission and the European Free Trade Association's Surveillance Authority. Procedures have also been developed in the courts to demarcate the roles of the courts at the EU and national levels.

the information secret. If conduct or a merger or acquisition falls within the scope of EU law, it is reviewed only at the EU level. The regulations and notices relating both to (old) articles 85 and 86 and to mergers were amended in 1997 to ensure a one-stop shop (DG IV 1997). This process prevents more than one authority from examining such conduct or proposed mergers or acquisitions.

In 1999, the European Commission published a White Paper on modernization of the procedural rules implementing articles 81 and 82 (European Commission 1999). The White Paper proposed reforms that will lead to an increase in the involvement of national competition authorities. The commission also foresaw more private actions through national courts in enforcing EU competition policy (Monti 2000). These reforms are being implemented. They will lead to some measure of decentralization, hence reversing the trend of the first 40 years of the European Economic Community and the European Union. The DG IV (2000, p. 5) justifies these measures on the following grounds:

> The environment in which competition policy finds itself has been largely transformed; the Community has become a market which is strongly integrated, it has also increased in size . . . . In fact national competition authorities, being closer to local markets, are generally in a better position to both detect and suppress the more serious infringements of the Community competition rules.

These reforms represent a significant step back to a more decentralized system (see Rivas 2000). The 2002 introduction of the common currency, the euro, should assist enforcement, too, by making prices more transparent.

Thus, the European Union has brought about a substantial convergence of national competition laws among 15 countries, as well as superimposing common EU competition laws on its member states.

In terms of a broader definition of *competition policy*, the European Union has developed a unique approach to the interaction of industrial policy and competition policy. Control on subsidies is not normally regarded as a part of competition-promoting policies. The sole, but important, exception is the European Union, where *state aids*, as they are called, come within its common competition policy. Article 92 of the Treaty of Rome prohibits any state aids that distort or threaten to distort competition in the region, although the article does allow designated exceptions to this prohibition. These controls have proven to be weak, however, allowing competition in some industries to be substantially distorted by the use of state aids (Buigues, Jacquemin, and Sapir 1995; Pelkmans 1997, chapters 12 and 14). DG IV has complained repeatedly in its annual report on competition policy that state aids are too extensive.

The European Union is profoundly affecting the evolution of competition law throughout Europe. Its rules have been extended to the European Economic Area as well as to the states associated with the European Union in Central and Eastern Europe and the Mediterranean. All of these 18 countries have been obliged to accept the *acquis communautaire* of the European Union, including its competition law. Not all of the features of the competition law currently apply to these countries; for example, they are not subject to the authority of the DG IV.

The 10 Central and Eastern European countries are of particular interest because they are transition economies, like Cambodia, China, the Lao PDR, and Vietnam in East Asia. Competition law in the Central and Eastern European countries is determined by the competition provisions of the agreements they signed with the European Union in 1991. The agreements required that the associated states align their competition laws to the principles of the Treaty of Rome within 3 years. Indeed, this obligation is stricter than that required of the 15 full members. Before the agreements were signed, Romania had no comprehensive national competition law and the other countries had gaps in the coverage of their laws, especially with respect to vertical restraints and mergers, and also had weak enforcement (EBRD 1995). Since the agreements, all the Central and Eastern European countries have developed comprehensive national laws and stronger enforcement. Consequently, the competition laws of the 10 countries have converged with those of the European Union. This process is described in Estrin and Holmes (1998). (Unwillingness to align its relatively lax competition laws with those of the European Union was one of the reasons Switzerland was not willing to participate in the European Economic Area.) The passage of these laws represented a remarkably large and sudden shift in policy and law for countries that had a very high degree of state ownership of enterprises and regulation only a few years ago. Given the lack of development of institutions and laws relating to the operation of markets in transition economies, this example illustrates the advantages for a transition economy of adopting an "off-the-shelf" model of competition law.

NAFTA

A significant degree of convergence has occurred in the competition policies, in the broad sense, of Canada, Mexico, and the United States in recent years. This convergence is primarily reflected in a greater commitment to trade liberalization within the NAFTA area, as well as in the deregulation and privatization initiatives that were spawned in Canada and the United States in the 1980s and in Mexico in the 1990s.

The U.S. experience is especially important because the regulatory reform agenda that the United States began in the late 1970s has helped
launch a global reform movement. The OECD (1999) survey of regulatory
reform in the United States finds that U.S. regulation is based on two
different regulatory styles:

1. The *pro-competition policy stance* of federal regulatory regimes, supported
   by strong competition institutions, has meant that regulators tend to
   prefer policy instruments, such as social regulation and market-driven
   approaches, that are competition neutral over public ownership and
   economic regulations that impede competition. In postwar years, regulation has usually been used to establish conditions for competition
   rather than to replace competition.
2. The *openness and contestability of regulatory processes* weaken information
   monopolies and the powers of special interests, while encouraging
   entrepreneurship, market entry, consumer confidence, and the continual
   search for better regulatory solutions.[9]

Canada moved somewhat in parallel with the United States, albeit
slightly more slowly, to deregulate critical sectors such as telecommunications, transportation, and some parts of the energy sector. To gain entry
into NAFTA and develop a more competitive economy, Mexico has
followed these trends as well. This process has been referred to as "semiconscious parallelism" in which "regulatory principles and procedures
move in the same general direction but at greatly different speeds."[10]

This semiconscious parallelism is at the heart of North American
competition policy convergence. It has had the benefit of allowing the
NAFTA parties to move at their own pace, as required by their local economic, social, and political realities. For example, Canada has lagged
behind the United States in deregulation and privatization, in part because Canada has a longer and deeper history of government intervention, in part because the political shift to the right occurred earlier in the
United States (1981) than in Canada (1983), and in part because the economic pressures to deregulate or privatize flowed directly from U.S.
deregulation and privatization, which allowed U.S. enterprises to become
significantly more competitive than their Canadian rivals in cross-border
markets. Mexico has lagged behind both of its neighbors to the north

---

9. Nevertheless, a small number of U.S. industries, including banking and financial institutions,
securities, futures, insurance, and various parts of the agricultural and national defense sectors,
maintain some degree of competition-limiting regulation or immunity from the antitrust laws.
10. Comment by Joe D'Cruz in Rugman (2001, p. 15).

because it started with a much less developed and more highly regulated economy.

In the narrower area of domestic competition laws, monopolies, and state enterprises, which are the subject of chapter 15 of NAFTA, the achievements of NAFTA have been far more limited. The one particularly noteworthy exception is that, in anticipation of its obligations under chapter 15, Mexico enacted the Federal Economic Competition Law (FECL) in December 1992, shortly after the text of NAFTA was finalized. It was necessary for Mexico to enact the FECL because article 1501 of NAFTA requires each party to "adopt or maintain measures to proscribe anti-competitive business conduct and take appropriate action with respect thereto." Notwithstanding the broad and flexible nature of this language, the FECL succeeded in achieving what many would consider to be an acceptable level of substantive harmonization with Canada's Competition Act and the U.S. antitrust laws, particularly in the areas of the stated objectives of the FECL, hard-core cartel conduct, and—to a lesser extent—merger control.

As between the Canadian and U.S. antitrust laws, no particularly noteworthy areas of statutory convergence have occurred since 1986, when the merger and monopolization provisions of what is now the Competition Act (Canada) were decriminalized and overhauled in a manner that brought them into closer harmony with the U.S. Clayton and Sherman Antitrust Acts.

Except for the previously noted requirement to establish or maintain measures to proscribe anticompetitive business conduct and take appropriate action with respect thereto, NAFTA does not contain any provisions that have led to any meaningful harmonization or even concrete results with respect to competition law. Moreover, at the insistence of the U.S. negotiating team, NAFTA did not address the contentious issue of the interface between antidumping laws and competition laws, other than to establish, in article 1504, the Working Group on Trade and Competition, a group that has not yielded any noteworthy output.

In contrast to those RTAs that are structured to engender deep integration (such as the Treaty of Rome), NAFTA did not create a supranational set of laws or governing institutions. Nor did NAFTA create a common customs tariff or a common currency or harmonize monetary policy between the NAFTA parties. For the most part, NAFTA sought to achieve the more modest objective of creating rules governing trade within North America, while at the same time allowing each country the freedom to pursue its own domestic policy objectives. The market drivers of North American economic integration are sufficiently strong to create pressures for reform within sectors that continue to be fully or partially protected by trade barriers or regulation.

In addition to the foregoing, a significant degree of soft (qualitative) harmonization in the competition laws of Canada, Mexico, and the United States has been achieved. Specifically, there has been a fairly high degree of convergence in the analytical approaches of the Canadian Competition Bureau and U.S. federal antitrust enforcement agencies to the evaluation of mergers, dominant firm behavior, nonprice vertical restraints, hard-core cartel behavior, the intellectual property and competition law inter-face, and immunity or amnesty from prosecution. This convergence is in part attributable to the close relationship between the Canadian Compe-tition Bureau and U.S. federal antitrust enforcement agencies, which work together on many merger and criminal cases. Another factor producing convergence of analysis is the strong influence that U.S. antitrust and legal analysis has in academic and legal circles in Canada. It is noteworthy that certain aspects of the approach that is shared in common by Canada and the United States are reflected in the FECL.[11]

The objectives of the competition laws of Canada, Mexico, and the United States all focus on economic goals and do not include the broader public interest objectives that are found in some competition laws else-where. Nevertheless, there are differences in the objectives of the domes-tic competition laws in North America, the most noteworthy of which may be the fact that Mexico's FECL and Canada's Competition Act appear to be more oriented toward maximizing total surplus, whereas the U.S. antitrust laws are generally considered to be limited to promoting consumer welfare.

With respect to specific restrictive trade practices, although there is a significant degree of core commonality in the approach to anticompeti-tive agreements between competitors,[12] there are important substantive

---

11. For example, article 12 of the FECL sets forth criteria that must be taken into account in defining a relevant market that are similar in many respects to the criteria considered by the courts and enforcement authorities in Canada and the United States. The same is true of the fac-tors identified in article 13 of the FECL, which must be considered in determining whether an economic agent has substantial market power. Nevertheless, significant differences remain with respect to the approach of Mexico's Federal Competition Commission to market definition, market share calculation, and other aspects of the analytical approach that has been embraced in Canada and the United States. (See generally ABA 2001, chapter 10.)

12. This commonality is perhaps best reflected in the area of hard-core cartel conduct. Parties to international price-fixing or market-allocation cartels typically wind up being charged, con-victed, and sentenced in criminal courts in Canada soon after, and sometimes even contempora-neously with, encountering a similar fate in the United States. Although Mexico's FECL adopts a per se illegality approach to this conduct, the Federal Competition Commission's enforcement record to date in this area has been less noteworthy. Significant fines were imposed, however, in 1998 on the Mexican subsidiaries of some of the participants in the lysine cartel.

differences among the competition laws of Canada, Mexico, and the United States. These differences provide a useful example of how convergence proceeds in an RTA that, unlike the European Union, does not adopt a centralized approach.

The basic difference between these laws in relation to anticompetitive agreements among competitors is that U.S. law adopts either a per se or rule of reason approach to such conduct, depending on the type of agreement, whereas Canadian law contemplates a partial rule of reason approach, and Mexican law adopts an approach that is somewhat of a hybrid of the Canadian and U.S. approaches. Specifically, U.S. law applies a per se illegality approach to price-fixing, agreements to restrict output, allocations of markets or customers, certain types of group boycotts, and certain tying arrangements, while applying a rule of reason approach in other cases. When the rule of reason approach is applied, any efficiencies likely to result from the impugned agreement are balanced against the likely anticompetitive effects of the agreement to determine whether, on balance, the restraint is "unreasonable." This balancing of pro-competitive and anticompetitive effects is not considered to be worthwhile with respect to the types of conduct that are subjected to per se illegality, because those types of conduct generally are viewed as being unambiguously harmful and without any redeeming consequences from the perspective of the economy as a whole.

In comparison, while bid-rigging and price maintenance (including vertical price maintenance) are subject to per se illegality treatment under Canada's Competition Act, the basic conspiracy provisions of that legislation require a demonstration that the impugned agreement, if implemented, likely would prevent or lessen competition "unduly." This approach has been characterized as contemplating a partial rule of reason analysis. It requires an assessment of the competitive effects, including a definition of the relevant market, a calculation of the share of the market held by the alleged conspirators, and an evaluation of factors such as the nature of any barriers to entry into the market and the degree of competition provided by nonconspirators or by the parties to the alleged conspiracy (with respect to matters not covered by their agreement).[13] Under Mexico's FECL, anticompetitive agreements can be subjected to per se illegality treatment (absolute monopolistic practices) or partial rule of reason treatment (relative monopolistic practices), depending on the subject matter of the agreement. Broadly speaking, absolute monopolistic practices comprise the same types of horizontal agreements that would be

---

13. *R. v. Nova Scotia Pharmaceutical Society*, [1992] 2 S.C.R. 606, at 650 and 653.

subject to per se illegality in the United States, such as price-fixing, output restriction, market or customer allocation, and bid-rigging. Other anticompetitive agreements are dealt with as relative monopolistic practices and can be subject to fines upon a demonstration that the parties to the agreement have substantial power in the relevant market. This demonstration requires an assessment that is broadly similar to that which is required under the partial rule of reason approach that is followed in Canada.

The domestic competition laws of all three NAFTA parties contain provisions that permit export cartels, including those that adversely affect one or both of the other countries in North America.

With respect to monopolization or abuse of dominant position, once again the laws of Canada and the United States reflect significant substantive differences. Mexico's FECL does not specifically address the subject, although anticompetitive behavior by a dominant firm may run afoul of the FECL's provisions relating to "relative monopolistic practices."[14]

Section 2 of the U.S. Sherman Antitrust Act prohibits monopolization, attempts to monopolize, and conspiracies to monopolize. As with the basic conspiracy provisions of the Sherman Act, proceedings under the monopolization provisions may be brought criminally or civilly, although criminal prosecutions have been virtually nonexistent in recent years.

In contrast, under Canada's Competition Act, abuse of dominance is a matter subject to civil review. Fines and other penal consequences are not imposed. As a practical matter, remedies have been confined to an order to cease engaging in the anticompetitive practice in question. Broadly speaking, this action requires a demonstration that the firm or firms in question have created, increased, or maintained market power in a relevant market by engaging in conduct that is predatory, disciplinary, or exclusionary. As a practical matter, this type of conduct by a firm with market power would also likely violate the Sherman Act in a wide range of cases, notwithstanding the very different wording of that legislation, although the "monopoly power" threshold in the Sherman Act may contemplate a higher intervention threshold than what is required under the Competition Act. However, two important substantive and conceptual differences between the Canadian and U.S. approaches exist: (a) in contrast to the Sherman Act, no order can be made under the Competition

---

14. Among other things, article 10 VII contains a catch-all clause that addresses "any act, in general, that unduly impairs or impedes the competitive process and free access to the production, processing, distribution, and marketing of goods and services." In addition, article 8 prohibits "monopolies . . . as well as practices which . . . lessen, impair, or prevent competition and free access in the production, processing, distribution, and marketing of goods and services."

Act with respect to attempts to gain a dominant or monopolistic position, and (b) joint dominance can be addressed under the Competition Act but not under the Sherman Act.

With respect to mergers, the Canadian and U.S. laws have been very similar since Canada decriminalized mergers in 1986 and adopted a "likely to prevent or lessen competition substantially" test. The test was modeled on section 7 of the U.S. Clayton Antitrust Act, which addresses mergers that may substantially lessen competition or "tend to create a monopoly." In practice, the approach to these laws in the United States and Canada has been very similar, although the intervention threshold in the United States generally is thought to be somewhat lower. In addition, U.S. courts and enforcement authorities have been more prepared to draw adverse inferences from high market shares and concentration levels than their Canadian counterparts, and there is an explicit efficiencies defense in the Canadian statute that has no U.S. equivalent.[15] In comparison, article 16 of Mexico's FECL prohibits mergers whose purpose or effect "is to diminish, impair, or impede competition and free-market access regarding equal, similar, or substantially related goods or services." As with the approach in Canada and the United States, the review of mergers under the FECL has focused primarily on potential anticompetitive horizontal effects (ABA 2001, note 3, p. 26). However, the Federal Competition Commission does not appear to have intervened to prohibit or dissolve many mergers or to seek other remedial relief, such as partial divestiture—a common remedy in Canada and the United States.

With respect to vertical restraints, the United States relies on the general prohibition against contracts, combinations, and conspiracies "in restraint of trade or commerce," which is set forth in section 1 of the Sherman Antitrust Act. The Canada Competition Act and the FECL both contain explicit provisions with respect to price maintenance, tied selling, exclusive dealing, customer or territorial restriction, and refusal

---

15. Given that only one case, which currently is unresolved, has been found to satisfy the requirements of the efficiencies defense in the 15 years since the provision was inserted into the Competition Act, the existence of this defense has not led to any meaningful divergence in the manner in which mergers are reviewed in Canada and the United States. In *Canada (Commissioner of Competition) v. Superior Propane Inc. and ICG Propane* (unreported, Docket A-533-00, April 4, 2001), the Federal Court of Appeal set aside the Competition Tribunal's interpretation of the efficiency exception and remitted the case to the Competition Tribunal for a redetermination. In its instructions to the tribunal, the court stated, "Whatever standard is selected . . . must be more reflective than the total surplus standard of the different objectives of the Competition Act."

to supply. For the most part, these practices do not give rise to a significant level of enforcement activity by the agencies in any of the NAFTA countries.[16]

In summary, under NAFTA, there is a significant degree of conceptual and practical commonality, and there has been a high degree of soft harmonization between Canada and the United States regarding fundamental analytical matters, such as market definition, theories of anticompetitive effects, important assessment criteria (such as ease of entry and the effectiveness of remaining competitors), and methods of analysis applied to specific cross-border cases. This harmonization can be attributed in part to the close working relationship of the enforcement agencies, antitrust practitioners, and expert economists in the two countries, and in part to similarities in the legal and economic training of people involved in this area of work. Harmonization has alleviated the frictions that otherwise might have resulted from the substantive and procedural differences. It remains to be seen whether Mexico will follow the path of its northern neighbors in this regard.

CER Agreement

In relation to the broad definition of competition policies, both Australia and New Zealand have adopted a comprehensive approach to promoting competition. Both countries have privatized and deregulated many industries and have rapidly liberalized trade in goods and FDI. These actions have been taken independently in the two countries, although there has been a considerable demonstration effect running in both directions. The trans-Tasman experience has exhibited important links between trade liberalization, deregulation, overall convergence of Australia's and New Zealand's competition statutes, trans-Tasman competition provisions, and removal of the trans-Tasman antidumping remedy.

CER developments in competition law, including the history of convergence, have been well documented over the past decade or so (see

---

16. The noteworthy exceptions are price maintenance, which is treated as per se illegal and subject to criminal sanctions under Canada's Competition Act, and narrow categories of tied selling and vertical price maintenance, which are treated as per se illegal in the United States. Price discrimination also is subject to per se illegality under the Competition Act and to a substantial lessening of competition. It tends to create a monopoly test in the U.S. Robinson Patman Act, and it is not specifically addressed in Mexico's FECL (see ABA 1994, pp. 148–55). There also are significant substantive differences between the Canadian and U.S. approaches to price discrimination. Finally, there is a broadly common analytical approach taken to predatory pricing in the three NAFTA countries, which explains why enforcement activity in that area has been quite rare in all three jurisdictions.

Lloyd and Vautier 1999, chapter 5 and references therein). Among the conclusions are the following:

- The competition laws of Australia and New Zealand are broadly harmonized. A major revision of the New Zealand Commerce Act in 1986 was based on the prevailing Australian Trade Practices Act. Subsequently, both countries have made further alignment, although some areas of difference remain.
- In 1990, under the CER Agreement, the governments adopted the so-called trans-Tasman competition provisions. These provisions were an extraterritorial extension of their preexisting parent provisions relating to the prohibited use of a powerful market position. For this category of anticompetitive behavior, they establish a trans-Tasman market, but it does not apply to service markets.
- Also in 1990, both governments removed the trans-Tasman antidumping remedy. This action has meant that the pricing of trans-Tasman trade is now governed by competition standards and remedies rather than by traditional trade remedies.
- The objectives of the laws are similar in the two countries, emphasizing the promotion of competition in order to increase the welfare of their citizens.
- Australia and New Zealand have each retained their legislative discretion regarding competition law. Thus, they have opted for a decentralized approach. Although these laws are enforced under separate national jurisdictions, cooperation exists between the enforcement agencies under a bilateral agreement.

In 2001, New Zealand's Commerce Act was amended to strengthen some key provisions by reference to Australian law. Its purpose statement is also being amended to explicitly refer to the long-term benefits to consumers and New Zealanders as a whole. Although adopting Australia's competition law tests of "substantially lessening competition" for business acquisitions and "taking advantage of a substantial degree of power in a market" for unilateral conduct clearly brings New Zealand's statutory language much closer to Australia's, the government has said that the primary driver is strengthening the Commerce Act rather than harmonization for its own sake. Even though a broad-based trans-Tasman competition law was neither the main achievement nor the main objective of the legislative amendments from 1990, Australia and New Zealand are the only two countries in APEC whose competition laws can be said to be closely harmonized.

Through the CER Agreement, Australia and New Zealand, like the European Union, have developed a mechanism to regulate the levels of subsidies on the basis of output. Following the first 5-yearly General Review of CER in 1988, the two countries signed an Agreed Minute on Industry Assistance, in which they agreed not to pay (from July 1, 1990) production bounties or like measures on goods exported to the other country and undertook to try to avoid the adoption of industry-specific measures (bounties, subsidies, and other financial support) that would adversely affect competition within the free trade area. These measures have effectively eliminated trade distortions attributable to subsidies of all forms, a unique achievement among RTAs. Thus, the CER mechanism provides a much stronger control on trade-distorting subsidies than do the controls on state aids in the European Union.

MERCOSUR and the Andean Community

Two RTAs involving developing countries have played a substantial role in the development of national and regional competition policies in their regions. These are the RTAs of MERCOSUR and the Andean Community (De Leon 2001; Tavares 2001; Tavares and Tineo 1998).

By Decision 285, the Andean Community set up an area competition law in 1991. Its substantive provisions related to individual forms of business conduct and the supranational authority both follow closely those of the European Union. Decision 285 prohibits restrictive practices resulting from collusive agreements such as price-fixing, market allocations and tying arrangements, and practices resulting from abuses of dominant position such as refusal to deal, withholding of inputs from competing firms, and discriminatory treatments. Decision 285 does not cover mergers and acquisitions. As with the European Union, these provisions apply when the business conduct affects competition in more than one country of the region, and they take precedence over national laws, but if the practice does not have areawide implications, national law applies.

In contrast, MERCOSUR has adopted a more decentralized approach that is closer to the NAFTA model. In December 1996, the MERCOSUR countries signed the Fortaleza Protocol. This protocol requires that all member countries have a competition law and a competition agency and that the member countries share a common view about the interplay between competition policy and other governmental actions. It seeks to prevent collusive actions or the abuse of a dominant position that reduces competition in the signatory countries' markets. Its list of practices includes price-fixing, reduction or destruction of input and output, market divisions, restrictions of market access, bid-rigging, exclusionary practices, tying arrangements, refusal to deal, resale price maintenance, predatory practices, price discrimination, and exclusive dealings. The protocol does not, however, cover mergers and acquisitions. Investigation is carried out first by the competition authority of each country involved and then by the MERCOSUR Committee of Defense of Competition, which issues a directive. The committee's ruling may, if differences of opinion arise, then be submitted to the MERCOSUR Trade Commission for final adjudication. Enforcement relies entirely on the powers of the national competition authorities.

Although the competition law provisions of these two regional agreements are primarily concerned with the areawide implications of business conduct, MERCOSUR contains a provision for developing common rules at the national level, and Decision 285 was seen as a model for developing the national laws in the Andean Community. At the time that these respective policies were adopted, only one of the five members of the Andean Community (Colombia) and only two of the four members of MERCOSUR (Argentina and Brazil) had national competition laws. In the Andean Community region, Peru and the República Bolivariana de Venezuela introduced national competition laws, and Colombia is preparing legislation, but in the MERCOSUR region, neither Paraguay nor Uruguay has yet introduced a national competition law. Experience with the application of the law in these two RTAs is limited.

PROSPECTS FOR HARMONIZATION OF COMPETITION LAWS IN EAST ASIA

The variation in scope and emphasis of the competition laws among the countries in East Asia raises questions as to whether the countries that do not have national competition laws will introduce such laws and, if they do, whether this would lead to convergence or divergence among the laws.

The first step to harmonizing competition law is accepting that competition is important in a market-oriented economy. In East Asian countries, there is generally a low level of appreciation of the benefits gained from greater competition in an economy. Economic growth has been perceived largely as a process of factor accumulation and increasing total factor productivity. The benefits to consumers of increased competition in markets for goods and services, for a given productive capacity of an economy, need to have a larger weight in policy formation.

Next, the countries need to adopt a broad competition policy, with measures to promote competition in markets for all goods and services.

This policy should include trade liberalization, deregulation, and privatization, all of which promote entry and competition. Competition law should play a supporting role to enforce competitive behavior by all enterprises. A competition policy should guide the nature of deregulation in highly regulated industries and of privatization. Regulatory reform in the East Asian economies has been patchy. Many state monopolies still exist, especially in the transition economies, and some privatized enterprises have dominant market positions with no competition law to restrain their conduct. In the latter case, new regulations may be required.

For all countries that do not have a comprehensive national competition law, the next step is to introduce such a law. There is limited guidance about the particulars of the law for countries seeking to introduce a competition law. No standard or model of national legislation has been developed that is comparable to, for example, the model of prudential regulation developed for the financial sector by the Bank for International Settlements. The United Nations Conference on Trade and Development (UNCTAD 2000) has promulgated a model competition law, and the OECD and World Bank (1999) have provided a framework for the design and implementation of competition law and policy. These models provide a valuable survey of alternatives for the various features of competition law, such as the scope of laws relating to business conduct, but they do not provide a ready-made set of laws. Because there is a very wide variation among countries in terms of all the features of the law, a major problem for any country drafting new legislation is whether to choose a model from another country or to use a composite model.

Considerable guidance for the design of competition law comes from the basic principles developed earlier in this chapter under "The Role of Competition Policy." Further suggestions are contained in the Competition Principles developed by the Pacific Economic Cooperation Council (1999) for APEC. The law should be comprehensive in terms of coverage of business conduct; that is, it should include provisions relating to unilateral and collusive behavior and to mergers and acquisitions. It should be based on the principle of neutrality among all private and state-owned enterprises. The objective of the law should be promoting competition in order to enhance efficiency and the welfare of the consumers of the nation. Exemptions should be limited. National competition law should be enforced by an authority that is an independent agency—that is, one not subject to direction by another government department or ministry or agency—and this authority must receive adequate resources. In the event of a conflict with other national legislation, competition law should generally prevail.

There is a danger that legislation or enforcement methods adopted from a different system may not be suitable to particular local conditions.

The anticompetitive business activities specific to an economy might not be sufficiently clearly addressed. To be effective, a piece of legislation needs to take into account features of the particular economy. It will be interesting to see, for example, whether Thailand and Indonesia, which are both characterized by a large proportion of family-controlled businesses that tend to form intricate pyramids of interdependence, will undertake to assess the influence of these businesses on competition or will tolerate them as traditional methods of business organization.

The developing countries of East Asia have to address many problems that occur in their political and legal systems before new competition laws can be fully enforced. Solutions and resources are needed in the following spheres: a capacity of the enforcement institutions to perform their tasks (this capacity implies an adequate budget as well as a staff with appropriate skills); a developed and implemented system of commercial law; and an unbiased, incorruptible, and independent judiciary.

This institution building should precede or take place at the same time as the preparation of competition legislation. Thus, in some countries, the drafting of national competition legislation will be a part of a broader set of legislative reforms. Some elements of competition law are a part of reforms designed to contain corruption. Much of anticorruption reform centers on activities of the government sector, such as bidding for government contracts and selling productive assets in government-owned enterprises. It is the absence of principles of competition such as open and competitive bidding and of hard, enforceable competition law that has allowed corrupt practices to flourish in these areas.

Cambodia, China, the Lao PDR, and Vietnam are transition economies. Economies in transition from a past system in which many or all enterprises were publicly owned and heavily regulated pose special problems for the introduction of comprehensive competition policies.

Public ownership itself is no obstacle to the application of competition law. Increasingly in the past decade, competition laws in industrial countries have been applied to government enterprises. Exemptions for government enterprises were once widespread in the OECD countries, but most OECD countries have moved in recent years to extend the reach of national competition laws to enterprises owned wholly or substantially by governments.[17] The essential concept of competition in relation to

---

17. This extension includes access regimes for natural monopolies by government-owned enterprises in industries such as telecommunications, electricity generation and distribution, and gas and water distribution. In some industrial countries, some of these services are still provided by government-owned enterprises, but they are subject to the national competition laws, as in most European economies, Australia, Canada, and New Zealand (but not Japan).

government-owned enterprises is *neutrality*—that is, neutrality of market access and treatment between government-owned enterprises and privately owned enterprises. Government should give no advantages to government-owned enterprises. In practice, the major problem is that many state-owned enterprises are less efficient than enterprises that are not state owned in the same industries. For China, empirical studies have verified the efficiency of different types of enterprises in Chinese industries by using stochastic production frontier techniques (for example, Zhang and Zhang 2001) or data envelopment analysis (Hirschberg and Lloyd 2001). These studies have confirmed that the state-owned enterprises are the least efficient enterprises in China, ranking below other Chinese-owned private enterprises as well as foreign-invested enterprises. Many of these state-owned enterprises are also burdened by debt.

In these circumstances, the following reforms, which may include equitization, are particularly important. For enterprises that remain state owned, other measures should be adopted to give managers the incentives to raise the productivity of the enterprises. Measures may also be needed to reduce nonperforming debts of state-owned enterprises. Market reforms and privatization may be accompanied by relaxation of the restrictions on FDI. In this circumstance, competition law should apply to foreign investors. There is no reason to shelter foreign investors from competition from domestic enterprises or other actual or potential foreign investors.

A number of East European precedents exist for the introduction of competition law in transition economies. Since the demise of the former Soviet Union, 10 Eastern European states have become associate members of the European Union and have applied for full membership. These countries have signed agreements that include provisions requiring them to introduce competition laws and, moreover, to align these laws with those of the European Union. Although the process has been difficult, it has guided the transformation of these economies. In particular, it has created a culture of competition and a commitment to competition law that are essential components of successful capitalism.

In the case of the Eastern European states, one of the major difficulties—the choice of national competition policies—was resolved by their having to adopt the EU model of competition law. This model of competition policy is advanced with respect to the comprehensiveness of the policies and their effective enforcement. Yet the success to date shows that it is possible for transition economies to make this policy transition to advanced national competition policies. Indeed, adopting an external model may be easier than developing an internal one.

Harmonization should extend to the areas of soft, or qualitative, harmonization, particularly the objectives of the law and the methods of analysis used when the rule of reason applies. Harmonization is desirable in East Asia because the objectives of competition law vary considerably among the countries with such laws. They should be amended to emphasize the promotion of competition in all markets in order to enhance the welfare of consumers and buyers. Harmonization of the methods of analysis in the region will be more difficult than harmonization of the scope of the law and its objectives because no outstanding example to follow exists in the region, as there does for Mexico in the American hemisphere or for the Eastern European states seeking to join the European Union. The possible role of ASEAN and APEC in these areas is noted below.

Harmonizing competition law in East Asia will be a slow, evolutionary process. In those countries that do not have comprehensive national competition laws, it will require competition advocacy and institution building before or along with the introduction of national competition laws. Competition advocacy and institution building can be assisted by multilateral organizations, in particular the World Bank and APEC, and by development assistance programs of industrial countries, although care will be needed to ensure that this assistance does not lead to divergence among nations receiving advice from different sources.

The Role of ASEAN

Of the 12 economies in East Asia, 7 are members of ASEAN. As discussed previously, among industrial and developing economies, RTAs have played an important part in the introduction and convergence of national competition policies.

Could ASEAN play a leading role in the development of competition policy and law in the Southeast Asian region? Of the 10 current members, 8 do not have comprehensive competition laws. They are the 4 newer members plus Brunei Darussalam, Malaysia, the Philippines, and Singapore. Like the larger East Asian region, ASEAN member economies are a mix of economic systems: 4 of its 12 members are transition economies (Cambodia, the Lao PDR, Myanmar, and Vietnam).

In these circumstances, an active ASEAN program could lead to the introduction of national competition policy and law in the member countries that do not currently have an explicit competition policy and a comprehensive competition law. Competition policy principles could guide industry deregulation and privatization. They could also foster convergence in competition law coverage and standards, including soft harmonization in terms of the objectives of the law, methods of analysis, and enforcement, as the developments in NAFTA and, to a lesser extent, the CER Agreement have demonstrated. The benefits of harmonization increase as the liberalization of trade in goods and services under the ASEAN Free Trade Agreement and the ASEAN Investment Area increases cross-border trade in goods and services. Of course, this increase in liberalization of trade will also increase cross-border competition problems.

ASEAN has not developed a regionwide competition policy or law to date. The 1998 Hanoi Plan of Action, which is the latest statement of ASEAN direction, refers to cooperation to "explore the merits of common competition policy" as a possible area of future integration (ASEAN 1998), but there has been no development under this provision. However, all ASEAN countries have adopted some competition-promoting policies in the past decade through unilateral liberalization of trade, encouragement of FDI, and privatization and deregulation of many industries.

The absence of regional competition law in ASEAN reflects the underdevelopment of competition law among the individual ASEAN countries. Singapore has argued that competition laws are redundant in an economy that is open and contestable with respect to trade in goods and foreign direct investment. Brunei Darussalam and Malaysia have followed the Singapore policy, although Malaysia is not a particularly open economy with respect to either goods trade or FDI. Only Thailand and, since 2000, Indonesia have comprehensive competition laws, but the coverage is not as wide as in OECD countries, and enforcement is less effective.

This underdevelopment of national competition laws does not, however, preclude a regional competition policy or law. The experiences of the European Economic Community and, later, the European Union,[18] as well as the experiences of MERCOSUR and the Andean Community, have shown that it is possible to form competition policies and laws within a region without preexisting national competition laws in all members. Indeed, this sequencing may be a distinct advantage in terms of establishing uniform laws or converging separate national laws.

The ASEAN consensus style of economic policymaking has eschewed common policies outside the areas of border trade liberalization and the associated area of customs harmonization. The ASEAN has no supranational institutions. This style is, however, changing. Since the 1997–98

---

18. At the time of the formation of the European Economic Community, only two (Federal Republic of Germany and the Netherlands) of the original six member countries had national competition laws.

Asian financial crisis, the member countries of ASEAN have on several occasions called for a strengthening of regional cooperation and a progression to regional integration. This change in mood could make it possible to adopt more uniform regionwide competition policy and law. If this change occurs, the models of MERCOSUR and CER, which are based on national laws and national actions with some harmonization among members, are the most likely models. A step in this direction could greatly facilitate the establishment and convergence of national competition laws in all of the countries of the region.

Competition Advocacy: The Role of APEC

All of the 12 East Asian economies described in this chapter are members of APEC. APEC is a consensus-driven intergovernmental cooperation forum. It plays a major role in the development of economic policies among the countries of the region, broadly along the same lines as the OECD does for the industrial countries. Given the early stage of development of competition policy and competition law in East Asia, APEC could play a major advocacy role in this area.

At a meeting in Osaka, Japan, in December 1995, APEC's economic leaders adopted an action plan that covered 15 specific areas, of which competition policy was one. The objective of this policy is as follows:

> APEC economies will enhance the competitive environment in the Asia-Pacific region by introducing or maintaining effective and adequate competition policy and/or laws and associated enforcement policies, ensuring the transparency of the above and promoting cooperation among the APEC economies, thereby maximising, *inter alia*, the efficient operation of markets, competition among producers and consumer benefits. (APEC 1995)

The Committee on Trade and Investment of APEC agreed in 1996 to merge the areas of competition with those of deregulation, which was another of the 15 policy areas named in the Osaka Action Plan.

To make these plans operational, APEC members developed both a Collective Action Plan (CAP) and an Individual Action Plan (IAP) in the area of competition policy. The CAP states that APEC members will gather information, promote dialogue, develop the understanding of competition policy, encourage cooperation among the competition authorities, and consider developing nonbinding principles on competition policy and law in APEC. The IAPs are ongoing and reported by member economies each year. The guidelines for the IAPs require each APEC economy to review its competition policy and laws. The APEC economy must then implement, as appropriate, technical assistance with respect to policy development of the powers and functions of enforcement agencies and with respect to the enforcement of policies and laws in terms of transparency. Finally, it must establish appropriate cooperation arrangements among APEC economies.

The 1999 APEC Leaders' Meeting in Auckland adopted APEC Principles to Enhance Competition and Regulatory Reform (APEC 1999). The emphasis is on principles of competition policy, as distinct from rules or minimum standards. Four core principles are enunciated: comprehensiveness, transparency in policies and processes, accountability, and nondiscrimination. These principles are notable for the broad view of competition policy and the emphasis on strong principles underlying the construction of policies and laws. The principles also include a commitment to review regulations and policies to ensure compliance, technical assistance, and capacity building, and a commitment to develop effective means of cooperation between APEC economy regulatory agencies, including competition authorities.

These APEC principles are nonbinding and are based on the recognition of differences among the economies in their economic circumstances and institutions. Thus, they have no legal force and continue APEC's practice of voluntary implementation of its decisions.

Neither the Osaka Action Plan nor the APEC principles require member economies to develop national competition policies and laws in the manner of NAFTA and some other RTAs. Nor do they attempt to harmonize the features of the law. Overall, the main contributions of the APEC activities have been (a) the development of a form of competition advocacy that is taken seriously by the member economies because APEC is voluntary and cooperative and (b) the development of core principles to underlie policies relating to competition.

CONCLUSIONS

With the growth of cross-border trade and FDI, there are positive net benefits from harmonization in the area of competition law. However, competition law is a particularly difficult area of harmonization because of the many dimensions of the law in terms of anticompetitive business conduct and the application of the law in terms of its objectives, analysis, enforcement, and remedies. Despite the efforts of the OECD, World Bank, UNCTAD, and other multilateral forums, there are no generally agreed standards for competition law to which countries might converge. (The one exception is the OECD agreement on hard-core cartels.)

Harmonization of competition law is not an easy process. The harmonization that has occurred is partial and piecemeal, aside from the exceptional case of the European Union, where common policies have been adopted as an instrument of complete integration. Harmonization seems to have occurred when member nations accept the importance of national competition law, have a culture of enforcing it, and desire closer integration of national economies. Political factors are also important. In the case of Mexico, introducing a national competition law and its convergence to such laws in Canada and the United States was a tradeoff for gaining marketing access for Mexican exports of goods.

In the East Asian region, there is no harmonization of policies other than the adoption of national competition laws by some of the countries. There is, however, a greater appreciation of the role of competition in national economies and across national borders than existed a few years ago, and a greater desire for the integration of the national economies than existed before the Asian financial crisis. This atmosphere has created an environment that is more favorable to the development of national competition law.

It seems likely that harmonization of competition law will progress further in East Asia, but it will be a slow, evolutionary process that is dependent on advocating competition, building institutions, and developing standards and precedents that provide examples of methods of harmonization.

In the next 10 years, the first step should be the adoption in all countries of a stronger commitment to the goal of building a competitive economy that is based on the principle of competitive neutrality in all industries and among all producers. A broad-based approach is called for that includes privatization, deregulation, and (in some cases such as essential services) re-regulation as well as the opening of the economies directly to competition from foreign goods and FDI. All of these strategies will reduce barriers to entry. All countries that do not have a comprehensive national competition law should introduce one within the next 10 years. In writing the legislation, lawmakers should ensure that they follow the general principles developed in this chapter.

Convergence of standards of competition law and the soft harmonization of objectives and analyses of cases will follow only when national laws have been introduced. However, there is an opportunity for establishing common standards and other common features of competition law in the case of ASEAN. Doing so would prevent an initial divergence as each country established its own law, and it would facilitate the prosecution of cases in the region that affect parties in two or more member countries.

The need for this harmonization will increase after the liberalization of trade in goods, services, and capital, which is scheduled to be completed by 2005.

REFERENCES

ABA (American Bar Association). 1994. "Report of the Task Force of the ABA Section of Antitrust Law on the Competition Dimensions of NAFTA." ABA, Section of Antitrust Law, Chicago.

———. 2001. *Competition Laws outside the United States*. ABA, Section of Antitrust Law, Chicago.

APEC (Asia Pacific Economic Cooperation). 1995. "Osaka Action Plan." APEC Secretariat, Singapore.

———. 1999. "APEC Principles to Enhance Competition and Regulatory Reform." APEC Secretariat, Singapore.

ASEAN (Association of Southeast Asian Nations). 1998. "Hanoi Plan of Action." ASEAN Secretariat. Available on-line at http://www.aseansec.org.sg.

Bhagwati, Jagdish N., and Robert E. Hudec, eds. 1996. *Fair Trade and Harmonization: Prerequisites for Free Trade?* Cambridge, Mass.: MIT Press.

Bollard, Alan, and Kerrin M. Vautier. 1998. "The Convergence of Competition Law within APEC and the CER Agreements." In Rong-I Wu and Yun-Peng Chu, eds., *Business, Markets, and Government in the Asia Pacific*. London: Routledge.

Buigues, Pierre, Alexis Jacquemin, and André Sapir. 1995. *European Policies on Competition, Trade, and Industry: Conflict and Complementarities*. Aldershot, U.K.: Edward Elgar.

Campbell, A. Neil, and Michael J. Trebilcock. 1997. "Interjurisdictional Conflict in Merger Review." In Leon Waverman, William S. Comanor, and Akira Goto, eds., *Competition Policy in the Global Economy*. London and New York: Routledge.

CEPR (Centre for Economic Policy Research). 1993. *Making Sense of Subsidiarity: How Much Centralization for Europe?* London: CEPR.

De Leon, Ignacio. 2001. *Latin American Competition Law and Policy*. The Hague: Kluwer.

DG IV (Directorate-General IV of the European Commission). 1997. "European Community Competition Policy 1997." European Commission, Brussels.

———. 2000. "European Competition Policy 2000." European Commission, Brussels.

EBRD (European Bank for Reconstruction and Development). 1995. "Transition Report." EBRD, London.

Emerson, Michael, Michel Aujean, Michel Catinat, Philippe Goybet, Alexis Jacquemin. 1988. *The Economics of 1992: The E. C. Commission's Assessment of the Economic Effects of Completing the Internal Market*. Oxford, U.K.: Oxford University Press.

Estrin, Saul, and Peter Holmes. 1998. *Competition and Economic Integration in Europe*. Cheltenham, U.K.: Edward Elgar.

European Commission. 1999. "White Paper on Modernisation of the Rules Implementing Articles 85 and 86." European Commission, Brussels.

Genser, Bendt, and Andreas Haufler. 1996. "Tax Competition, Tax Coordination, and Tax Harmonization: The Effects of the EMU." *Empirica* 23:59–89.

Hirschberg, Joe, and Peter J. Lloyd. 2001. "Does the Technology of Foreign-Invested Enterprises Spill over to Other Enterprises in China? An Application of Post-DEA Bootstrap Regression Analysis." In Peter J. Lloyd and Xiaoguang Zhang, eds., *Models of the Chinese Economy*. Cheltenham, U.K.: Edward Elgar.

Leebron, David W. 1996. "Lying down with Procrustes: An Analysis of Harmonization Claims." In Jagdish N. Bhagwati and Robert E. Hudec, eds., *Fair Trade and Harmonization: Prerequisites for Free Trade?* Cambridge, Mass.: MIT Press.

Levinsohn, James. 1996. "Competition Policy and International Trade." In Jagdish N. Bhagwati and Robert E. Hudec, eds., *Fair Trade and Harmonization: Prerequisites for Free Trade?* Cambridge, Mass.: MIT Press.

Lloyd, Peter J., and Martin Richardson. 1999. "Harmonizing National Competition Policies When Markets Are Global." In Mordecai E. Kreinen and Michael G. Plummer, eds., *Asia-Pacific Economic Linkages*. Amsterdam: Pergamon.

Lloyd, Peter J., and Kerrin M. Vautier. 1999. *Promoting Competition in Global Markets: A Multi-national Approach*. Cheltenham, U.K.: Edward Elgar.

Lücking, Joachim, and Donncadh Woods. 2001. "Horizontal Cooperation Agreements: New Rules in Force." *Competition Policy Newsletter* 1 (February):8–10.

Mattoo, Aaditya, and Arvind Subramanian. 1997. "Multilateral Rules on Competition Policy: A Possible Way Forward." *Journal of World Trade Law* 31:95–115.

Monti, Mario. 2000. "The Application of Community Law by National Courts." Paper presented at the Conference at the Europäische Rechtsakademie, Trier, Germany, November 27. Available on-line at http://europa.eu.int.

OECD (Organisation of Economic Co-operation and Development). 1999. *Review of Regulatory Reform in the United States*. Paris. Available on-line at http://www.oecd.org.

OECD and the World Bank. 1999. *A Framework for the Design and Implementation of Competition Law and Policy*. Paris and Washington, D.C.

Pacific Economic Cooperation Council (PECC). 1999. "PECC Competition Principles: PECC Principles for Guiding the Development of a Competition-Driven Policy Framework for APEC Economies." Singapore.

Pelkmans, Jacques. 1997. *European Integration: Methods and Economic Analysis*. London: Addison Wesley Longman.

Rivas, José, ed. 2000. *Modernisation and Decentralisation of EC Competition Law*. The Hague: Kluwer.

Rugman, Alan. 2001. "The Impact of Globalization on Canadian Competition Policy." Paper prepared for a conference on Canadian Competition Policy: Preparing for the Future, sponsored by the Richard Ivey School of Business, Industry Canada, and the Competition Bureau, Toronto, June 18–20.

Sleuwaegen, Leon. 1998. "Cross-Border Mergers and EC Competition Policy." *World Economy* 21(8):1077–93.

Sykes, Alan O. 2000. "Regulatory Competition or Regulatory Harmonization? A Silly Question?" *Journal of International Economic Law* 3:257–64.

Symeonidis, George. 2001. "Price Competition, Innovation, and Profitability: Theory and UK Evidence." Centre for Economic Policy Research Discussion Paper 2816. London.

Tavares, José T. 2001. "Competition Policy." In José M. Salazar-Xirinachs and M. Robert, eds., *Towards Free Trade in the Americas*. Washington, D.C.: Brookings Institution Press.

Tavares, José T., and Luis Tineo. 1998. "Harmonization of Competition Policies among MERCOSUR Countries." *Antitrust Bulletin* 43 (Spring):45–70.

Tirole, Jean. 1988. *The Theory of Industrial Organisation*. Cambridge, Mass.: MIT Press.

UNCTAD (United Nations Conference on Trade and Development). 2000. *Model Law on Competition*. Geneva: UNCTAD.

Waverman, Leon, William S. Comanor, and Akira Goto, eds. 1997. *Competition Policy in the Global Economy*. London and New York: Routledge.

Zhang, Xiaoguang, and Siqi Zhang. 2001. "Technical Efficiency in Chinese Industrial Enterprises: The Case of the Iron and Steel Industry." In Peter J. Lloyd and Xiaoguang Zhang, eds., *Models of the Chinese Economy*. Cheltenham, U.K.: Edward Elgar.

CHAPTER 6

THE PUBLIC SECTOR

Carles Boix

The increasing trends toward regional integration, easing of cross-border flows, and erosion of protection for domestic markets, all mentioned in earlier chapters, highlight the emerging importance of public spending on social protection of groups vulnerable to the fluctuations of competitive markets. This chapter examines, in a comparative manner, the size and nature of the public sector in East Asia, with the twin goals of explaining its evolution and making some educated guesses about its future.

East Asian economies have small public sectors, both in absolute terms—that is, in comparison with the rest of the world—and, particularly, in relative terms—that is, given what we should expect for their levels of economic development. Except for Japan, the average East Asian public sector stands at about one-half the size of the standard public sector in member states of the Organisation for Economic Co-operation and Development (OECD). Furthermore, it is about one-third smaller than the average value for countries with similar per capita income levels. The internal analysis of public spending reveals that, whereas public consumption and capital expenditures in East Asia are very similar to the rest of the world, the core programs of the modern welfare state are extremely underdeveloped except in Japan and, in part, the Republic of Korea. Public pension systems, unemployment benefits, sickness-related payments, and public health care remain extremely limited, at least into the late 1990s. As a result, whereas OECD nations on average devote more than 20 percent of their gross domestic product (GDP) to transfers and subsidies, Korea spends about 8 percent of GDP, and Southeast Asian economies spend less than 5 percent.

As revealed later in the statistical analysis, the East Asian welfare state is much smaller relative to the rest of the world than we should expect, given the level of economic development, demographic structure, degree of trade openness, and political institutions of the region. This difference may be due to the weakness of East Asian left-wing parties and union movements—factors that were central in the construction of the European welfare state. It may also be attributable to a substantial degree of pretax income equality, which may have the effect of reducing redistributive tensions and demands. However, it is more likely that the difference is related to a very late democratization and to a particular set of societal preferences about the role of the state in the provision of welfare benefits.

If the evolution of the European public sector is any indication, there is still ample room for expansion of the public sector in East Asia in the next two decades. If European economies are any guide, Northeast Asian countries should witness a considerable increase in the size of their public sectors. Pushed mostly by aging populations, European governments set up generous welfare programs in the 1950s and 1960s that translated into ever-growing levels of public spending from the 1970s onward. In similar fashion, after the wave of democratization in the 1980s and 1990s, new programs in pensions, health care, and unemployment benefits have been set up in countries such as Korea. As in Europe, rapid expansion of older populations in East Asia will automatically ratchet up public spending in the region.

This chapter is organized as follows. The first section describes the evolution of public revenue and public expenditure, both across the world and in East Asia. It then details the internal composition of public spending in several East Asian countries. The next section reviews the existing literature on the causes of growth in the public sector. The following section tests the validity of these theoretical models in accounting for the evolution of the current revenue and final consumption of general government; the total expenditure, size of transfers and subsidies, and total wages of central government; the public debt of central government; and the size of state-owned enterprises. These estimations are made for both a world sample and East Asia in the past decades. The last section uses these estimations to make some projections about the evolution of the public sector in East Asia.

GENERAL EVOLUTION OF THE PUBLIC SECTOR IN THE WORLD AND EAST ASIA

General Evolution of the Public Sector

Three characteristics describe the evolution of the public sector across the world during the past century: first, its steady growth; second, the presence of persistent cross-national differences in its size; and third, a rough

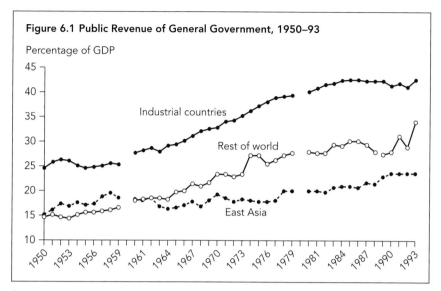

Figure 6.1 Public Revenue of General Government, 1950–93

Percentage of GDP

Source: UN (various years).

stability among nations in the world ranking in terms of public revenue and spending.

During the nineteenth century, excluding times of war, government expenditure remained constant at about 10 percent of GDP. After 1914, however, the size of the public sector started to expand substantially.[1] Figure 6.1 depicts the growth of current revenue of general government as a percentage of GDP in industrial nations, East Asian economies, and the rest of the world from 1950 to 1993. In the early 1950s, total current public revenue averaged 24 percent of GDP in the industrial world.[2] By the mid-1970s, it had risen to 36 percent. By the early 1980s, it had stabilized at about 44 percent. Although the pace of change has been less dramatic, the public sector has also grown in the developing world. Among East Asian economies, current revenues of general government grew by one-third, from about 15 to 20 percent of GDP.[3] The rise of current revenue was sharper in the rest of the world. It averaged 14 percent of GDP in

1. For a first approximation of the fiscally expansive consequences of World Wars I and II, see Peacock and Wiseman (1961).
2. This is an unweighted average for Western Europe, North America, Australia, and New Zealand.
3. The public sector in Japan expanded at a faster pace, which was closer to that of Europe than to that of other East Asian nations: from 20 percent of GDP in the 1960s to more than 30 percent by the late 1970s.

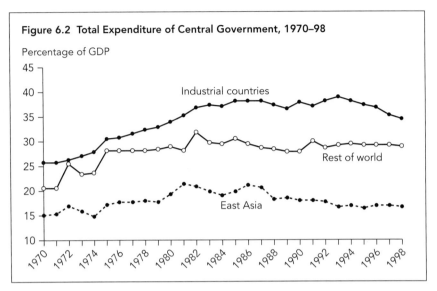

Figure 6.2 Total Expenditure of Central Government, 1970–98

Source: World Bank (1999).

1950, reached 20 percent of GDP by the late 1960s, and then hovered around 27 percent from the late 1970s onward.

Figure 6.2 shows, in turn, the evolution of total expenditure of central government from 1970 until 1999. In the past 5 years in the industrial world, the size of the public sector, which experienced considerable growth until the early 1980s, has stagnated and even undergone a slight decline. In the rest of the world, public spending grew quickly until 1980 and then stagnated for the following two decades, particularly in East Asia.

Despite the steady growth of the public sector, differences across nations have remained substantial. Among industrial economies, public revenue ranged from 31 to 60 percent of GDP—with a standard deviation of 8.9 percent of GDP—in 1985. Cross-national variation has been even sharper in the developing world. In the mid-1980s, it had reached 15 percent of GDP—with public revenue ranging from 6 percent in Sierra Leone to almost 83 percent of GDP in Réunion. By contrast, variation across East Asia is mild compared with other continental areas. In the early 1950s, public revenue ranged from about 10 percent of GDP in Korea and the Philippines to about 22 percent of GDP in Japan, with a standard deviation of 5 percent. In the mid-1980s public revenue went from about 15 percent in the Philippines and Thailand to more than 30 percent in Japan, with the standard deviation remaining at 5 percent.

It is interesting to notice, that, in spite of this growing divergence across nations, there has been a remarkable stability in the relative ranking of nations in terms of the size as a proportion of GDP of their public sector.

Those countries that had a considerable public sector in 1950 continue to have a large public sector today. Similarly, most of those countries with a small state 40 years ago still rank the lowest in terms of the public sector. The levels of public revenue (as a proportion of GDP) in 1950 and in 1990 are highly correlated; the Pearson's correlation is 0.75 (but only 0.37 for OECD nations). Relatively deep structural factors must be playing a strong role in shaping the size of government across countries. Although in the 1960s and 1970s there was a substantial upward drift in the size of the public sector among OECD nations—particularly in Belgium, the Netherlands, and the Scandinavian countries—after the mid-1970s, the public sector expanded again at an extremely uniform (and slower) pace across all nations.

Figures 6.3 and 6.4 display the evolution of the central government's debt and budget balance, respectively, as a percentage of GDP from 1970 to 1998. After experiencing moderate levels of public debt until the early 1980s, East Asian countries witnessed a sharp deterioration in their public finances in the mid-1980s. A very tight fiscal policy from about 1987 to 1996 led to systematic annual surpluses and the reduction of the public debt to pre-1981 levels. This control was sharply at odds with fiscal behavior in the rest of the world, where the budget balance was about 4 to 6 percentage points of GDP lower than in East Asia and where public debt continued to climb until the late 1990s. In 1997–98, however, East Asia experienced a rapid deterioration on the fiscal side: the budget balance

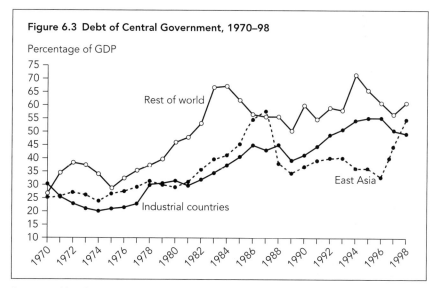

Figure 6.3 Debt of Central Government, 1970–98

Percentage of GDP

Rest of world

Industrial countries

East Asia

Source: World Bank (1999).

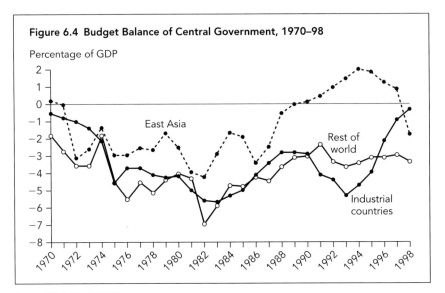

Figure 6.4 Budget Balance of Central Government, 1970–98

Source: World Bank (1999).

plunged to −2 percent of GDP and public debt shot up to almost 60 percent of GDP in 1998.

Internal Distribution of Expenditure

Table 6.1 reports the total expenditure of general and central government, as well as the internal distribution of spending of central government, for the industrial world and for most East Asian countries. The data, which correspond to the period 1993–96, are shown both as a percentage of GDP and as a percentage of the level of spending in the industrial world.

Except for Japan, where public expenditure of general government reaches 37.5 percent of GDP, public expenditure in East Asia fluctuates at about 18 percent of GDP. This percentage is less than half the average in OECD countries. China stands at 13 percent of GDP or about one-third of the level in the industrial world.

Excluding Japan, East Asian countries are substantially centralized. About 85 percent of their public expenditure is controlled by the central government. Accordingly, the data on transfers, wages, and capital expenditure of the central government can be taken as a good approximation of the overall distribution of spending within the public sector. Most East Asian countries devote a very similar proportion of resources to pay their public employees—about 5 percent of GDP. The only exceptions are Korea and Indonesia, with about 2 percent of GDP in wages and salaries,

Table 6.1 Distribution of Public Spending in East Asian Countries, 1993–96

Country	Total public spending		Central government items		General government items	
	General government	Central government	Subsidies and transfers	Wages and salaries	Capital expenditure	Education
As a percentage of GDP						
Industrial world[a]	45	35.3	4.7	4.3	4.8	21.9
China	13.6	8.0	0.7	2.0	—	—
Indonesia	—	15.8	2.4	3.0	0.6	2.5
Japan	37.5	23.7	—	5.0	4.7	8.5
Korea, Rep. of	21.5	17.4	2.2	7.5	3.3	8.3
Malaysia	—	21.4	6.3	1.0	4.0	4.9
Philippines	—	19.3	5.4	3.0	—	3.0
Singapore	16.9	—	4.9	0.5	2.4	2.6
Thailand	—	18.9	5.1	4.3	3.3	1.1
Vietnam	20.3	—	—	2.8	—	—
As percentage of the level of spending in the industrial world						
China	30.2	22.7	16.3	41.7	—	—
Indonesia	—	44.8	51.1	69.8	12.5	11.4
Japan	83.3	67.1	—	116.3	97.9	38.8
Korea, Rep. of	47.8	49.3	46.8	174.4	68.8	37.9
Malaysia	—	60.6	134.0	23.3	83.3	22.4
Philippines	—	54.7	—	114.9	62.5	13.7
Singapore	47.9	—	104.3	11.6	50.0	11.9
Thailand	—	53.5	108.5	100.0	68.8	5.0
Vietnam	45.1	—	—	58.3	—	—

— Not available.

Note: Data are averages for 1993–96, except that data for transfers and subsidies in Japan are for 1990.

a. OECD countries excluding Japan.

Sources: World Bank (1999) and UN (various years).

and China, with a meager 0.7 percent. The level of capital expenditure does not deviate much from that of the industrial world. It is particularly small in Singapore, where interest payments on debt are very low, and much higher in Korea, which was affected by a considerable recession in the mid-1990s. Finally, East Asian countries spend in human capital formation about 3 percent of GDP—a higher amount than in similar middle-income economies—and between two-thirds and one-half of the amount that the industrial world directs to education. Most of the difference between East Asian and OECD countries occurs in secondary and tertiary education, which is much more developed in the OECD countries.

The bulk of the difference between the Asian public sector and the European public sector occurs in the expenditure programs that characterize the welfare state of Western countries—that is, current transfers and subsidies. These two areas together average 4 percent of GDP in East Asia, with a maximum of about 8 percent in Japan and a minimum of less than 1.5 percent in Thailand. The figure for Japan is misleading, because it refers only to central government: the sum of social security and social services expenditure by all levels of government was 19 percent of GDP in Japan in 1997. For the remaining countries, this very low figure simply reflects the general absence of public pension programs and unemployment benefits and the very reduced level of expenditure on public health. Thus, in Korea, for which we have data for the sum of central and local governments, public spending on social security and welfare programs was 2.3 percent of GDP in 1997. The figures are not higher in the remaining cases. As a result, the East Asian average in subsidies and transfers is one-fifth of the size of such subsidies in industrial countries and actually smaller than in Latin America.

Data reported so far have referred to formal budgetary figures. However, several East Asian governments run off-budget programs, which increase the size of their public sectors. These figures are difficult to quantify. In Indonesia, off-budget items, which include reforestation and development funds and pension and housing programs for public employees, fluctuated around 0.5 percent of GDP in the mid-1990s. Another 0.5 percent of GDP derived from educational fees (World Bank 1998). In China, in the 1980s, extrabudgetary funds, comprising surtaxes, levies, and user charges, grew rapidly—from about 2.6 percent of GDP in 1978 to more than 4 percent in 1996 and perhaps 8 to 10 percent in subsequent budgets. Most of these funds are in the hands of local governments (World Bank 2000). The volume of local expenditure and revenue may explain why China performs badly in the estimations reported later.

State-Owned Enterprises

Table 6.2 reports the size of state-owned firms worldwide and in East Asian countries. Size is measured as the value added of public firms as a proportion of total GDP (in the first two columns) and the percentage of gross domestic investment generated by public firms (in the last two columns). Although the data are not comprehensive—there are data for only about 60 countries in the world and for only 3 to 6 in East Asia—it seems to be a reasonable approximation of the weight of the public enterprise sector. East Asian state-owned firms make a contribution to GDP

Table 6.2 Size of State-Owned Enterprises in East Asian Countries, 1970–96

Country or region	Size as percentage of GDP		Size as percentage of gross investment	
	1970–84	1985–90	1985–90	1990–96
China	—	—	29.2	24.9
Indonesia	15.2	14.8	8.9	15.7
Japan	—	—	5.8	6.0
Korea, Rep. of	9.5	10.3	14.3	—
Malaysia	—	17.0	—	25.9
Philippines	1.4	2.3	8.4	9.9
Singapore	—	—	—	—
Thailand	—	5.4	11.5	10.4
Vietnam	—	—	—	—
East Asia	8.7	10.0	13.0	15.5
World	10.9	11.6	19.2	15.5

— Not available.

Sources: Data for size as a percentage of GDP are from Garrett (1998). Data for size as a percentage of gross investment are from World Bank (1999).

similar to that made by such firms in the average country in the world—about 10 percent of GDP and about 15 percent of gross domestic investment. Within East Asia, variation is substantial. Domestic investment by public firms ranges from 6 percent of total investment in Japan to over one-fourth of total investment in China and Malaysia.

THEORETICAL WORK ON THE GROWTH OF THE PUBLIC SECTOR

The growth of the public sector in the last century has spawned a vigorous literature on its causes.[4] Four families of explanations stand out: the impact of economic and social modernization, the redistributive consequence of political conflict, the effects of economic openness, and political institutions.

Economic Development and the Transformation of Social Demands

Demand-side explanations, conceiving the government as a provider of public goods, attribute the growth of the public sector either to social progress and demographic transformations or to different rates of productivity growth in the public and private sectors.

---

4. For extensive reviews, see Holsey and Borcherding (1997) and Lybeck (1988).

In a first attempt to describe the evolution of the public sector, Wagner (1883) stated that public expenditure rises with social progress because the types of goods and services provided by the public sector have a high income elasticity of demand. This explanation treats per capita income as a black box, disregarding how different voters react to the tax burden of more public spending. Therefore, since the 1960s, it has been replaced by a more sophisticated set of models in the past decades.

In general, current models linking the growth of the public sector to the process of economic modernization emphasize two types of causal channels.[5] On the one hand, a modern economy has been claimed to impose new functional requirements on the state, such as setting up a regulatory framework, paying for infrastructure, and generating skilled workers. To fully reap the benefits of technological advances and growing capital flows that are associated with the process of development, policymakers are increasingly pushed to use the state to generate minimum levels of public goods.

On the other hand, the process of modernization has been reported to transform the underlying structure of income flows, as well as the channels through which welfare is provided. Although economic and property arrangements vary substantially in traditional societies, most individuals hold agricultural jobs. In agricultural economies, both the source of income (the exploitation of land) and the volatility of rents (basically linked to weather conditions) are broadly common to most individuals. Although not universal, communal arrangements to share risk—such as common lands or church-distributed benefits—and reliance on extended families for the provision of food, shelter, and care may be fairly extended. These family- and community-based risk-sharing mechanisms substitute for the state.

By contrast, in industrial societies, technological breakthroughs and the expansion of manufacturing and service jobs transform the old economic structure. There are several consequences. First, the distribution of economic risk changes, concentrating in specific segments of the population. More precisely, unemployment spells and work-related accidents, which emerge as the downside of manufacturing-led productivity increases, become important among industrial workers and, particularly, among those most unskilled. In other words, the process of industrialization and the

---

5. Wagner also developed a more general account of the growth of the public sector as a function of the transformation of the traditional society into an industrial economy. In this sense, Wagner's theory can be considered a predecessor of modernization theories. For a discussion, see Lybeck (1988).

formation of a broad class of wage-earners result in stronger pressures for *intragenerational transfers*. In the second place, improvements in material conditions in general and in health technologies in particular prolong life expectancy and eventually lead to a shift in the demographic structure. As the profile of the population matures and the proportion of older cohorts expands, pressure for *intergenerational transfers*, in the form of pensions and health care programs, goes up.[6]

If we look beyond the process of economic modernization and industrialization, the so-called Baumol's cost disease has linked the growth of government to a shift to a postindustrial economic structure. According to Baumol (1967), the combination of similar real wages increments in both the public and the private sectors and a lower productivity growth rate in the public sector (which as a service sector is a relatively labor-intensive industry) compared with the manufacturing sector leads to an increase in the costs of government services in real terms over time. Although Baumol claims only that public employment and public sector costs should grow over time in absolute terms, researchers on the growth of the public sector have often concluded that there should also be an increase in the relative size of the government in the economy.[7]

Redistribution and the Role of Democracy

If economic modernization models explain the growth of the public sector as a result of the new functional needs of industrializing societies, a second set of theories link the expansion of the state to its redistributive consequences. The government is an agency that, in response to social conflict, redistributes income between citizens and social groups. Accordingly, the growth of the public sector is linked to the structure of income distribution across society and to the level of mobilization and organization of the different social and political groups.

Within the sociological profession, Korpi (1989) was among the first to attribute the growth of public spending in the industrial world to the mobilization and strength of the working class. Esping-Andersen (1990) later

---

6. For sociological accounts of the process of economic modernization, see Flora and Alber (1981) and Wilensky (1975). For a recent analysis of the state as an insurer against risk in modern economies, see Moss (2001).

7. For the use of Baumol's model in this direction, see Holsey and Borcherding (1997, pp. 568–69) and the references cited therein. As shown in Boix (2001), this extension of Baumol's work is inaccurate. The higher productivity of manufacturing in the private sector may lead to a higher wage bill in the public sector. But the differential in productivity (which expands the tax base to finance the state) prevents the public sector from automatically taking a bigger share of the economy.

linked the generation and expansion of the welfare state to successive construction of cross-class coalitions of workers with farmers in the period between World Wars I and II, and then with the middle class after World War II. Several political scientists, while acknowledging the influence of these social agents, have made the growth of the welfare state conditional on the level of political institutionalization: only when the working classes were effectively organized into strong unions and left-wing or social democratic parties could they effectively impose their preferences on the policymaking process and secure the expansion of the welfare state.[8]

Taking a formal perspective, Meltzer and Richards (1981) offer a model in which income distribution and the redistributive tensions associated with it predict the final level of public taxes and spending. In their model, higher inequality of market incomes among voters is associated with higher levels of political support for redistributive policies. The basic intuition is that, in an economy with a distribution of income skewed toward the rich, the income of the median voter will be lower than the average income; therefore, the politicians will tax the rich and transfer the revenue to the poorest to win elections.[9] More specifically, the model predicts that the level of the tax rate will depend on the difference between the average income and the income of the median voter. The larger the difference—that is, the more unequal the overall income distribution—the more interested in redistribution the median voter will become and the higher the tax rate will be. Still, the tax rate that the median voter (or the median parliamentarian) approves will stop short of fully equalizing incomes across voters. Since higher taxes and redistribution reduce the incentive to work—and, with that, lower pretax income, from which transfers are financed—the median voter will vote for a tax rate to the point at which his or her net income declines.

The approach of Meltzer and Richards would explain why public expenditure started to increase with the generalization of universal suffrage after World War I. If this approach were right, we should also expect, *ceteris paribus*, lower levels of expenditure in nondemocratic regimes. Similarly, the model allows for a related prediction. As turnout declines among the least wealthy, the public sector should shrink even if the franchise is universal. In other words, in the limit (that is, with all voters abstaining), the size of the public sector in a democracy should be similar to the size of the public sector in an authoritarian system. Finally, it should be equally valid to explain intergenerational (rather than intragenerational)

---

8. For a review and exhaustive test of these hypotheses, see Hicks (1999).
9. For a generalized use of the model, see Persson and Tabellini (2000).

redistribution: as older cohorts grow in size in the population, public expenditure on pensions should rise.

Most studies have found scant support for the strict Meltzer-Richards hypothesis. Perotti (1996) found no significant relationship between inequality and social insurance spending in a sample of 50 rich and poor countries. Rodriguez Caballero (1998) does not find any relationship between welfare spending at the state level in the United States and inequality, and he finds a negative relationship between inequality and social insurance spending for OECD nations. By contrast, more recent studies uphold the hypothesized relationship. Among OECD democracies, Franzese (2002) finds that higher rates of voter participation are associated with higher demands for taxing and spending; this turnout effect is magnified by greater degrees of income inequality. Using 65 countries and about 2,000 country-year observations, Boix (2001) shows that inequality reduces the size of the public sector and that the presence of democratic institutions and higher levels of electoral participation increase the size of the state. Moene and Wallerstein (2001) similarly develop a model in which purely redistributive effects à la Meltzer-Richards, jointly with demands for insurance, fit the data patterns of industrial nations.

The interaction of economic development and democratic institutions. As they stand now, both demand-side models and purely political models are theoretically insufficient. The latter concentrate too much on the effect that an unequal distribution of resources has on the tax rate, to the point of disregarding how economic development alters the underlying structure of preferences in the electorate. As a result, they cannot explain why per capita income is so well correlated with the size of the public sector.

In turn, modernization models, which rely heavily on the idea that politicians respond mechanically to the changing tastes of the median voter, discount the political and institutional arena in which policy is made. That is, they assume politicians to be benevolent planners who, interested in maximizing the national income, automatically use the state to provide for those public goods (such as infrastructure, education, and regulatory agencies) that will let the country reap the benefits of modernization. Yet it cannot be taken for granted that policymakers will always behave as benign planners and pursue the collective welfare over short-term personal gains. Implementation of optimal policies will happen only in the presence of those political or legal institutions that effectively restrain rent-seeking behavior among politicians. Democratic institutions, by easing the task of monitoring policymakers, should lead to a fuller provision of public goods, on average.[10] Similarly, the extent to which politicians will develop pension programs and a public health system will eventually depend on the existence of institutional channels that make politicians responsive to citizens' demands. In short, economic development is a necessary but not sufficient condition for the public sector to grow: the institutional and political mechanisms through which politicians make decisions shape the extent to which the process of modernization affects the size of the state.

To find a way to overcome these deficiencies, in a later section I will test—in addition to the separate effect of economic modernization and democracy—a joint model that integrates both the effect of economic development and the underlying structure of political choice. In this joint model, economic development triggers pressures to enlarge the public sector in two ways. First, the processes of urbanization and industrialization generate incentives for the state to provide certain collective goods such as infrastructure and training. Second, both the emergence of an industrial economy and an aging population shift the underlying distribution of preferences in a way that results in stronger demands for public expenditure. Still, the process of economic development alone is not a sufficient condition for the emergence of a large public sector. Policymakers, who make policy through a political mechanism, choose the public sector that matches the preferences of the median voter. The identity of this voter varies with the electoral franchise in place (as well as with the extent to which voters are mobilized). This variation shapes, in turn, the size of the public sector. Under a democratic regime, politicians respond to the demands of all voters, and the public sector grows parallel to the structural changes generated by the process of development. By contrast, in authoritarian systems, in which all or a substantial part of the electorate is excluded from the decisionmaking process—precisely to avoid the redistributional consequences of democracy—the size of the public sector remains small.

Economic Openness

A third family of models attributes the size of the public sector to the extent to which the domestic economy is integrated in international markets, through trade and financial flows.

---

10. For a discussion of this point in the context of economic growth, see Olson (1993). Przeworski and Limongi (1993) offer a less favorable vision of the monitoring capacity of democracy.

Trade integration and the public sector. In exploring the consequences that the international economy has on the domestic political arena, a growing literature has shown in the past three decades that higher levels of trade systematically lead to a larger public sector across both industrial and developing nations. In a trail-blazing article, Cameron (1978) observed that the best predictor of an increase in the size of the public sector as a share of GDP in the period 1960–75 was the degree of economic openness (as the sum of exports and imports divided by GDP) in 1960 among OECD countries, with a correlation of 0.78. More recently, Rodrik (1998) has corroborated this association for the industrial world and has extended it to explain the level of government consumption in the world sample.

The actual theoretical mechanisms that underlie that statistical relationship are still the object of considerable debate. Broadly speaking, there are two types of theoretical explanations for the correlation between trade openness and the size of the public sector. On the one hand, for a set of scholars such as Cameron (1978), trade openness shapes the structure of the economy in a way that facilitates the formation of organizations and interests that impose high redistributive demands on the state. On the other hand, higher levels of trade integration (coupled with high sectoral concentration in the economy) are seen as leading to growing risks associated with the international business cycle, which in turn put pressure on policymakers to develop publicly financed compensatory programs in favor of the exposed sectors.

In Cameron (1978), small, open economies are characterized by a high degree of industrial concentration—a small number of large firms hold a substantial share of production and employment. As a result of having a small domestic market and fierce competition in exports, export-based countries specialize in a reduced number of sectors, led by companies large enough to contend with the fluctuations in the world market. High levels of industrial concentration facilitate the formation of employers' associations and labor unions. Moreover, the labor force, somewhat less differentiated in occupation and skill and, hence, less fragmented than in larger economies, becomes organized in rather centralized unions. A high degree of unionization and relatively centralized unions then contribute to the expansion of the public sector in two ways. First, they help form strong social democratic and labor parties, which pursue aggressive redistributive agendas that are based on the expansion of the welfare state. Second, they lead to a structure of centralized wage bargaining at the national level. Strongly centralized union movements were particularly able to strike corporatist deals with national governments in the 1960s and 1970s. In those corporatist arrangements, which were usually based on nationwide pacts between the government, unions, and employers, unions offered wage moderation in exchange for expansionary policies geared toward full employment and an expansion of public expenditure in areas such as unemployment benefits, health, or pensions.[11]

Cameron's work was followed by Katzenstein's (1985) analysis of the structure of small, corporatist European countries. Although Katzenstein's work also connects domestic compensation to the level of economic openness, he traces the growth of the public sector to a broader set of incentives than Cameron's. According to Katzenstein, small states are characterized by constraining economies of scale, a small set of economic sectors, and—in particular—considerable dependency on the fluctuations of the world business cycle. As a result, policymakers develop policy instruments that minimize the risks of being small, generally through extensive consultation with all social agents institutionalized in widely cooperative bodies and practices. Unions and employers strike deals to secure wage moderation and flexible procedures to adapt to changes in world demand. States compensate the losers through generous unemployment coverage and public aid to failing industries. The public sector develops full-fledged public programs, in the form of human and physical capital formation, to secure the competitiveness of the country.

Katzenstein's insistence on the risks confronted by small, open economies has been taken up and extended by Rodrik (1998) in a formal setting. According to Rodrik, because more open economies have higher exposure to the risks of turbulent world markets, public expenditure—set by a state conceived as purely a social planner—grows to stabilize aggregate income and deliver social peace and political stability.[12] The model works as follows. First, greater openness increases rather than reduces domestic volatility and risk. Although the world market is less volatile than any domestic economy, particularly of a small country, openness to trade normally implies specialization in production based on the comparative advantage. Accordingly, if all other things remain constant, small, open economies are less diversified than large economies. Second, assuming that an economy cannot purchase insurance from the rest of the world, domestic welfare will vary with fluctuations in domestic

11. In a related idea, in Aukrust (1977), the tradable sector, modeled as an international price-taker, uses public spending to buy the acquiescence of the nontradable sector to low wage increases, thereby ensuring the overall competitiveness (and survival) of the national economy.
12. For a first attempt to point to domestic compensation under a free trade regime as a mechanism to minimize risks, see Bates, Brock, and Tiefenthaler (1991).

production.[13] Third, the three sectors of every economy—a private tradables sector, a private nontradables sector, and the government—feed income streams into a representative household. The government sector is safe from the international economy—that is, its employment and income levels are not correlated with world-driven shocks. Accordingly, if policymakers have as one of their objectives to minimize the risk borne by the household as a result of external shocks, we should expect an expansion of the public sector to correlate with higher levels of trade openness.

Empirical evidence seems to bear out the strength of Rodrik's theoretical standpoint. First, external risk, measured in the form of fluctuations in the terms of trade, is positively associated with income volatility, measured through fluctuations in real GDP: a 10 percent increase in external risk comes with a 1.0–1.6 percent increase in income volatility.[14] Second, trade openness and the volatility related to it correlate with a bigger public sector. For the world sample in the mid-1980s and late 1990s, an increase in trade openness (imports and exports of GDP) of 10 percent is associated with a 2 percent increase in government consumption in GDP. Similarly, the volatility of terms of trade and a high concentration in types of exports (which should increase risk) are correlated with a bigger share of government consumption in GDP.

These findings have been confirmed by further empirical work. Garrett (1998, 2001) has shown that trade openness is associated with higher levels of government consumption and overall spending for world cross-sections in the mid-1980s and the mid-1990s.[15] Similarly, Adserà and Boix (2002), using a panel of data of some 65 developing and industrial nations for the period 1950–90, show that the share of public revenues as a share of GDP is strongly and significantly correlated with trade openness. Controlling for economic development and political institutions, public revenue goes

---

13. Purchasing private insurance is, according to Rodrik (1998), infeasible because of either conflicts between capital market openness and other objectives of governmental policy or incentive and sovereign-risk problems restricting the range and extent of financial instruments available to governments.

14. Using the Summers-Heston database (which includes 147 nations for the period 1950–90 and 4,546 observations), Adserà and Boix (2002) show, too, that the volatility of the business cycle (calculated as the standard deviation of changes in the growth rate in 5-year periods) increases with trade openness. More specifically, for each logged unit of trade openness, the volatility of the business cycle goes up by 0.60 (and it is statistically significant at the 1 percent level). The result is robust when control variables such as per capita income, economic structure, and weight of fuel and primary exports are introduced.

15. Garrett (2001) shows, however, that the relationship breaks down for high-spending countries, at least for the mid-1990s. Higher levels of trade integration have not led to larger public sectors in the past decade.

up from about 23 percent of GDP in a closed economy (if exports and imports equal 10 percent of GDP) to almost 30 percent of GDP (if trade openness equals 50 percent of GDP) and up to almost 35 percent when openness is very high (equal to about 150 percent of GDP).

Factor mobility and the public sector. In contrast to the finding that higher economic openness is associated with greater public spending, for an important strand of the literature, the mobility of factors (or, in more journalistic terms, the progressive globalization of the economy) constrains the ability of governments to tax and spend. The logic of the argument, which is usually applied to capital (mostly because of its reportedly higher mobility relative to labor), is straightforward. Since economic growth depends on investment, and investment, in turn, depends on profits, states and politicians are ultimately constrained by the rational calculations of the holders of capital, who are always in search of the highest rate of return for their assets. To prevent capital from moving to the most profitable countries—and, thus, to prevent decreasing investment rates and economic stagnation—all states are pushed to maximize the rate of return of private investors. To lure these investors, states will outbid each other through low taxes and significant incentives.[16] In short, in a highly internationalized economy, reformism and redistributive policies are severely curtailed by the mobility of factors.

Political Institutions

Finally, institutional models have stressed the effect of bureaucracies (Niskanen 1971), the legislative branch (Shepsle and Weingast 1981), or federalism on the aggregation of preferences and, hence, on the size of the public sector.

Electoral systems. From a theoretical standpoint, the effect of proportional representation on the size of the public sector is unclear. Scholars have contended that, although in plurality systems politicians can target a few marginal districts with very narrowly designed redistributive programs, parties in proportional representation systems need to please a large number of voters across the entire country (Birchfield and Crepaz 1998; Persson and Tabellini 2000; Wilensky 2002). However, provided

---

16. For an analysis of the dependence of the state on capital, see Hirschman (1981) and Przeworski and Wallerstein (1988). The degree of capital mobility varies, depending on the type of capital, and is inversely related to the specificity of assets. The less specific capital is (that is, the more alternative uses it can be put to), the more mobile it is, and the more power or influence capital has over the state. See Alt (1987) and Frieden (1991, pp. 19–22).

that the population is distributed similarly across the country, the policies developed under each institutional framework should be similar for the following reason: cross-national research on governments and on opinions in the industrial democracies has found that whereas majoritarian systems produce governments distant from the preferences of the median voter, proportional systems lead to governments more consistently close to the preferences of the median voter (Huber and Powell 1994; Powell 2000). In other words, whereas under proportional representation policy is always close to the preferences of the median voter, under plurality rule it shows higher variability. Still, over time—that is, on average—policy outcomes should be the same, given similar electorates.

Presidentialism. The downward bias that presidential systems impose on the size of the public sector has been accounted for in at least three ways. Because a system with separation of powers corresponds to a situation in which several players in the political game have veto power over policymaking, and given that recent comparative politics research shows that a higher number of veto players leads to greater stability in policymaking (Boix 1997; Grilli, Masciandaro, and Tabellini 1991; Hallerberg and Basinger 1998, 1999), one may conclude that presidentialism imposes a status quo bias in an otherwise growing public sector. Second, according to Persson and Tabellini (2000), a system of separation of powers, by sharpening the extent of potential conflict among politicians, enables voters to discipline politicians and, therefore, to reduce the level of rents. Finally, since candidates may win the presidency with a plurality of the votes, they do not need to engage in the broad type of spending that takes place in systems of proportional representation.

Federalism. Federalism has also been the object of an extensive debate over its tax effects. Some scholars have stressed its effects as multiplying the number of veto players in the political system and, hence, stabilizing and even depressing expenditure. Other scholars have instead stressed that in a federal system—that is, in an economically integrated yet politically fragmented area—the state's monopoly power is broken by both factor mobility and competition between levels of governments. The capacity of economic agents, and, in particular, capital to move to lightly taxed political subunits leads to a lower tax share across the whole country (Brennan and Buchanan 1980; Przeworski and Wallerstein 1988; Weingast 1995).

Recently Rodden (2000, 2001) has shown that federalism has little independent effect on fiscal outcomes. All else being equal, federations display neither larger nor faster-growing subnational or total deficits than unitary states. However, the internal organization of federal systems—that is, the types of rules that govern the ability of subnational units to borrow and the extent to which the central government may bail them out—matters in a substantial manner. In those countries where lower-level governments are most dependent on intergovernmental transfers and most free of hierarchical borrowing restrictions, subnational politicians have strong incentives to overuse the common pool of public revenue and to run excessive deficits and large public sectors. By contrast, in those federations in which subnational politicians cannot rely on the support of the federation, interstate competition and internal electoral competition discipline politicians. Similarly, subnational units that receive central transfers but are subject to control from the center do not mismanage public funds. At the extreme—that is, with full control from the center—this is simply the case of unitary states.

THE PUBLIC SECTOR IN THE WORLD: AN EMPIRICAL ANALYSIS

Measuring the Size of the Public Sector

To examine the strength of the theories reviewed so far and their applicability to East Asia, I examine the size of both the general government and the central government as a function of the available measures.

For the size of the general government there are two variables:

1. *Current receipts of the general government.* This measure, taken from the *United Nations National Accounts* (UN various years), offers us the best approximation of the size of the public sector, across both programs and levels of government. The data cover approximately 65 countries (about a third are OECD members) from 1950 to 1993, with some variation in the years covered, providing about 2,000 data points.
2. *Final consumption expenditure of the general government as a percentage of GDP.* This measure, taken from the World Bank, covers the period 1960–99 and gives more than 4,600 country-year data points.

I examine the expenditure side of the public sector by focusing on the central government, because data on the expenditure at the general government level are scarce. Naturally, using data at the central government level may lead to biased results for federal systems—such as Argentina, India, and the United States—or purely decentralized ones—such as Sweden, which uses the local sector to provide a substantial part of its social services. Accordingly, the results for the central government have to be checked against the results for the general government. Still, both central and general government data are relatively well correlated. The correlation between current revenue of central government and general government (both as a percentage of GDP) is 0.84 in the sample; the correlation between current revenue of general government and nonmilitary spending of central government is 0.78. Moreover, East Asian countries are relatively centralized—at least 85 percent of all current revenue is collected by the central government. I focus on the following four components of expenditure:

1. Total expenditure of central government as a percentage of GDP
2. Nonmilitary expenditure of central government as a percentage of GDP
3. Transfers and subsidies of central government as a percentage of GDP
4. Wages and salaries of central government as a percentage of GDP.

All these measures are taken from the World Bank's World Development Indicators dataset (World Bank 1999) and run from approximately 1970 to 1999—except nonmilitary expenditure, which runs from 1985 to 1997.

Model and Independent Variables

To determine which variables influence the size of government, I use the following model:

$$\text{Public Sector} = a + b_1(Economy) + b_2(Political\ Institutions)$$
$$+ b_3(Economy*Political\ Institutions) + b_4(Trade) + e_t.$$

Economy includes the set of variables that measure the effects of economic modernization on the size of government:

- The log value of real per capita income, which is a proxy for the shifts in the distribution of preferences associated with economic development, is expected to have a positive effect on the size of the public sector. For the regressions on public revenue, with data starting in 1950, I use constant U.S. dollars of 1985, chain index, expressed in international prices, taken from the Penn World Tables (Heston, Summers, and Aten 2002).[17] For the remaining estimations, I use constant dollars of 1990, taken from the World Bank (1999).
- The average share of the agricultural sector over GDP in 1970–99, taken from the World Bank (1999), is expected to enter negatively in the model.

---

17. Per capita income (chain index) is calculated by first applying the component growth rates between each pair of consecutive years, $t - 1$ and t ($t = 1951$ to 2000), to the current price component shares in year $t - 1$ to obtain the per capita domestic currency growth rate for each year. This growth rate for each year t is then applied backward and forward from 1996 and summed to the constant price net foreign balance to obtain the chain GDP series.

- The percentage of population age 65 years or older, taken from the World Bank (1999), tracks the shift of the median voter to an older age. This should affect the size of government positively.
- Public debt as a percentage of GDP in the previous year is used to control for cyclical pressures and the size of interest payments.

Political Institutions includes these variables:

- The variable *Democratic Regime* indicates whether each country was a competitive democracy in the 5 previous years—and, thus, ranges from 0 (no democracy ever) to 1 (democracy always). To measure the presence of a democratic regime, I follow the index developed by Alvarez and others (1996) for the period 1950–90. I have extended this index for the period 1991–99 (Boix and Rosato 2001). Democratic regimes are defined as those regimes "in which some governmental offices are filled as a consequence of contested elections" (Boix and Rosato 2001, p. 4).[18]
- *Level of Turnout in Democracies* is an interactive term of the variables *Turnout* and *Democratic Regime*. The variable *Turnout* is defined as the proportion of those voting out of all those citizens over the legal voting age and is taken from the International Institute for Democracy and Electoral Assistance (IDEA 1997); it has been calculated for each year on the basis of data from elections that have taken place in the preceding 5 years. Both variables are expected to increase the size of the state.
- The following three variables capture the extent to which different constitutional arrangements distort the representation of the median voter's preferences: (a) a dummy variable for the presence of presidential regimes, (b) a dummy variable coding whether a proportional representation electoral system is used, and (c) a dummy variable that captures the existence of a federal system. The first two variables have been built based on Cox (1997), IDEA (1997), Linz and Valenzuela (1994), Shugart and Carey (1992), and *Keesing's Contemporary Archives* (various years). The variable on federalism follows Downes (2000).

Although the process of modernization generates, on its own, strong pressures to increase the public sector, the size of government can vary, depending, to a large extent, on the political regime in place. Excluding

---

18. I have also regressed the dependent variable on a variable that indicates whether each country was a bureaucracy each year; a variable that indicates whether each country was an autocracy each year; and a variable that indicates whether each country was independent each year. Bureaucracies are those dictatorships that have legislatures. Autocracies are those dictatorships that do not have legislatures and that, therefore, can be thought of as not having any sort of institutionalized rule for operating the government. The presence of autocracies and bureaucracies is also based on the index developed by Alvarez and others (1996).

the provision of public goods, the public sector will remain small in authoritarian regimes. In democratic regimes, governments will meet the demands for transfers fostered by the economic and demographic changes, and the size of the public sector will increase. To capture this prediction, I introduce the interactive term *Economy*Political Institutions*, in which economic development is measured through per capita income and political institutions are measured through two variables: *Democratic Regime* and *Level of Turnout in Democratic Regime*. The expectation is that the interactive term will have a positive effect on the size of government.

Trade may increase the risks associated with the international business cycle and, hence, the political pressures for publicly financed compensatory programs that favor the exposed sectors. The *Trade* variable, which has been found to be a strong predictor of the size of the public sector (see Cameron 1978; Rodrik 1998), is measured in three ways:

1. The log value of the ratio of trade (sum of imports and exports) to GDP, taken from Heston, Summers, and Aten (2002) and World Bank (1999)
2. The ratio of fuel exports to total exports, for 1970–90, taken from World Bank (1999)
3. The proportion of nonfuel primary exports to total exports, for 1970–90, taken from World Bank (1999).

Following Beck and Katz's procedure, I have estimated the pooled cross-sectional time-series model through ordinary least squares, adjusting the standard errors for unequal variation within panels and correcting for autocorrelation.

Empirical Results: The Effect of Development and Democratic Institutions

Tables 6.3 to 6.8 report the effect of the main variables of the model (economic development or modernization, trade openness, political regime, turnout, and interaction of political and economic variables) on the different measures of the size of the public sector:

- Current public revenues for the period 1950–93 in table 6.3
- Public consumption of general government for the period 1960–99 in table 6.4
- Total expenditure of central government in 1970–99 in table 6.5
- Nonmilitary expenditure of central government in 1985–97 in table 6.6
- Subsidies and transfers of central government in table 6.7
- Public wages of central government in table 6.8.

Each table reports three models, each one applied first to the whole sample and then to East Asian countries. The results for the whole sample,

Table 6.3 Public Revenue of General Government as a Percentage of GDP, 1950–93 (coefficients of regressions)

Independent variables	World			East Asia		
	(1)	(2)	(3)	(4)	(5)	(6)
Constant	−24.67	−22.10	16.29***	−6.35	7.44	5.74*
	(8.61)	(8.86)	(3.73)	(11.77)	(12.85)	(2.92)
Per capita income	4.96***	5.43***		2.46^	0.56	
(log)	(1.16)	(1.14)		(1.67)	(1.76)	
Trade openness	3.35***	1.92***	3.03***	1.66**	1.32	4.77***
(log of sum of exports and imports over GDP)	(0.54)	(0.58)	(0.63)	(0.85)	(0.83)	(0.66)
Democratic	−13.64	0.96	0.35	−13.53^	2.36	−0.79
regime	(8.51)	(1.45)	(0.87)	(13.44)	(4.69)	(1.19)
Democratic	1.86*			1.88^		
regime × log of real per capita income	(1.12)			(1.80)		
Level of turnout in		−0.25*			−0.48*	
democratic regimes		(0.13)			(0.25)	
Level of turnout ×		0.03**			0.06**	
log of real per capita income		(0.02)			(0.03)	
Share of			−0.24***			−0.26***
agricultural sector in GDP			(0.04)			(0.04)
Percentage of			1.06***			1.38***
population 65 years or older			(0.25)			(0.14)
North and South	−7.83***	−8.48***	−7.00***			
America	(1.65)	(1.92)	(1.75)			
East Asia	−6.52***	−8.63***	−8.33***			
	(1.66)	(1.83)	(1.80)			
Eastern Europe	−0.06	−0.74	2.97			
	(2.81)	(2.42)	(3.79)			
OECD countries	−1.24	−2.03	−1.10			
	(1.86)	(2.05)	(2.05)			
South Asia	−4.22	−4.19	−4.51*			
	(2.68)	(3.22)	(2.27)			
Sub-Saharan Africa	−1.07	−0.59	−1.34			
	(2.17)	(3.32)	(2.24)			
Number of observations	1,998	1,400	973	183	105	87
R^2	0.4104	0.4781	0.5966	0.4955	0.6369	0.8861
Model chi-square	742.62	662.10	714.72	33.55	39.87	1052.25
Probability > chi-square	0.0000	0.0000	0.0000	0.0000	0.0000	0.0000

*$p < 0.10$. **$p < 0.05$. ***$p < 0.01$.

Note: Estimations were made by ordinary least squares estimation, with panel-corrected standard errors and correction for autocorrelation and for heteroskedastic disturbances between panels. Standard errors are in parentheses. ^ indicates that in a joint test of per capita income, democratic institutions, and the interactive term, the results were statistically significant (probability > chi-square = 0.0000).

Sources: Share of agricultural sector from World Bank (2000). Trade openness from Heston, Summers, and Aten (2002). Coding for democratic regime from Alvarez and others (1996), extended by Boix and Rosato (2001).

Table 6.4 Public Consumption of General Government as a Percentage of GDP, 1960–99
(coefficients of regressions)

Independent variables	World			East Asia		
	(1)	**(2)**	**(3)**	**(4)**	**(5)**	**(6)**
Constant	11.70***	5.34	14.78***	6.32***	7.77***	11.63***
	(2.40)	(3.52)	(1.82)	(2.34)	(2.38)	(2.10)
Per capita income (log)	−0.01	0.29		−0.10	0.23	
	(0.33)	(0.53)		(0.38)	(0.41)	
Trade openness (log of	1.82***	2.55***	1.58***	1.12***	0.22	0.40
sum of exports and	(0.29)	(0.45)	(0.31)	(0.34)	(0.46)	(0.35)
imports over GDP)						
Democratic regime	−6.31**	−0.65	−0.47	0.20	1.60	−0.42
	(2.66)	(0.86)	(0.55)	(3.48)	(1.44)	(0.55)
Democratic regime × log	0.89***			0.01		
of real per capita income	(0.35)			(0.47)		
Level of turnout in		0.01			0.05	
democratic regimes		(0.06)			(0.07)	
Level of turnout × log of		0.00			−0.01	
real per capita income		(0.01)			(0.01)	
Share of agricultural			−0.12***			−0.09***
sector in GDP			(0.02)			(0.03)
Percentage of population			0.02			−0.21*
65 years or older			(0.10)			(0.11)
North and South America	−5.58***	−3.53***	−5.55***			
	(0.82)	(1.06)	(0.99)			
East Asia	−8.52***	−7.67***	−8.02***			
	(0.73)	(0.94)	(0.87)			
Eastern Europe	−5.33***	−3.25***	−5.47***			
	(0.97)	(1.22)	(1.03)			
OECD	−2.92***	−0.73	−0.53			
	(0.97)	(1.27)	(0.83)			
South Asia	−6.55***	−7.31***	−4.90***			
	(1.15)	(1.26)	(1.21)			
Sub-Saharan Africa	−3.42***	−2.78**	−1.78*			
	(0.95)	(1.22)	(1.05)			
Number of observations	4,325	2,623	3,650	333	214	328
R^2	0.1819	0.3100	0.2218	0.2737	0.5525	0.2994
Model chi-square	416.14	441.97	594.27	16.00	14.86	20.70
Probability > chi-square	0.0000	0.0000	0.0000	0.0000	0.0000	0.0000

*$p < 0.10$.   **$p < 0.05$.   ***$p < 0.01$.

Note: Estimations were made by ordinary least squares estimation, with panel-corrected standard errors and correction for autocorrelation and for heteroskedastic disturbances between panels. Standard errors are in parentheses. ^ indicates that in a joint test of per capita income, democratic institutions, and the interactive term, the results were statistically significant (probability > chi-square = 0.0000).

Sources: Share of agricultural sector from World Bank (2000). Trade openness from Heston, Summers, and Aten (2002). Coding for democratic regime from Alvarez and others (1996), extended by Boix and Rosato (2001).

Table 6.5 Total Expenditure of Central Government as a Percentage of GDP, 1970–99 (coefficients of regressions)

Independent variables	World			East Asia		
	(1)	(2)	(3)	(4)	(5)	(6)
Constant	10.65**	9.50	11.99*	10.15*	13.20**	5.00
	(5.09)	(6.68)	(6.13)	(5.96)	(6.48)	(5.45)
Per capita income (log)	0.03	0.26		0.17	0.16	
	(0.74)	(1.10)		(0.87)	(0.94)	
Trade openness (log of sum of exports and imports over GDP)	5.41***	5.56***	4.69***	1.61	0.93	2.67***
	(0.63)	(0.77)	(0.82)	(1.08)	(1.12)	(0.82)
Democratic regime	−13.61**	−1.95	−2.57**	2.68	−2.46	0.05
	(5.89)	(2.32)	(1.28)	(9.69)	(4.34)	(1.18)
Democratic regime × log of real per capita income	1.78**			−0.26		
	(0.77)			(1.24)		
Level of turnout in democratic regimes		−0.05			0.07	
		(0.12)			(0.15)	
Level of turnout × log of real per capita income		0.01			0.00	
		(0.01)			(0.02)	
Share of agricultural sector in GDP			−0.12**			0.03
			(0.05)			(0.06)
Percentage of population 65 years or older			0.82**			0.35
			(0.33)			(0.33)
North and South America	−9.11***	−9.60***	−8.17***			
	(1.58)	(1.95)	(2.86)			
East Asia	−15.78***	−16.54***	−13.46***			
	(1.40)	(1.63)	(2.71)			
Eastern Europe	2.47	−1.18	0.39			
	(1.98)	(1.91)	(1.83)			
OECD	−2.92	−2.93	−2.35			
	(2.11)	(2.41)	(1.57)			
South Asia	−7.27***	−11.51***	−4.91*			
	(2.09)	(2.10)	(2.75)			
Sub-Saharan Africa	−7.05***	−8.94***	−0.95			
	(1.59)	(1.78)	(3.07)			
Number of observations	2,496	1,697	2,125	202	174	228
R^2	0.3249	0.4214	0.4039	0.2607	0.2929	0.3351
Model chi-square	449.37	532.10	759.55	4.32	1.76	25.49
Probability > chi-square	0.0000	0.0000	0.0000	0.3643	0.8819	0.0000

*$p < 0.10$.   **$p < 0.05$.   ***$p < 0.01$.

Note: Estimations were made by ordinary least squares estimation, with panel-corrected standard errors and correction for autocorrelation and for heteroskedastic disturbances between panels. Standard errors are in parentheses. ^ indicates that in a joint test of per capita income, democratic institutions, and the interactive term, the results were statistically significant (probability > chi-square = 0.0000).

Sources: Share of agricultural sector from World Bank (2000). Trade openness from Heston, Summers, and Aten (2002). Coding for democratic regime from Alvarez and others (1996), extended by Boix and Rosato (2001).

Table 6.6 Nonmilitary Expenditure of Central Government as a Percentage of GDP, 1985–97
(coefficients of regressions)

Independent variables	World			East Asia		
	(1)	(2)	(3)	(4)	(5)	(6)
Constant	4.72	10.13	11.99*	10.87	23.29*	−5.33
	(5.94)	(8.01)	(6.13)	(9.48)	(11.77)	(9.32)
Per capita income	−1.07	−0.63		−0.92	−1.36	
(log)	(1.07)	(1.60)		(1.05)	(1.54)	
Trade openness (log of	6.97***	5.59***	4.69***	2.78*	1.14	3.78***
sum of exports and	(1.04)	(1.31)	(0.81)	(1.65)	(1.81)	(1.47)
imports over GDP)						
Democratic regime	−21.01***	−1.45	−2.57**	−13.81	−4.31	1.37
	(7.70)	(3.54)	(1.27)	(10.67)	(4.57)	(1.42)
Democratic regime ×	2.81***			1.94		
log of per capita income	(1.00)			(1.38)		
Level of turnout in		−0.29*			−0.18	
democratic regimes		(0.16)			(0.19)	
Level of turnout × log		0.04**			0.03	
of real per capita income		(0.02)			(0.03)	
Share of agricultural			−0.12**			0.07
sector in GDP			(0.05)			(0.11)
Percentage of			0.82**			0.75
population 65 years			(0.33)			(0.51)
or older						
North and South	−2.90	−5.63*	−8.17***			
America	(2.34)	(3.00)	(2.86)			
East Asia	−11.63***	−13.25***	−13.46***			
	(1.66)	(2.09)	(2.71)			
Eastern Europe	4.60**	1.24	0.39			
	(2.15)	(2.28)	(1.83)			
OECD	4.66**	1.69	−2.35			
	(2.35)	(2.63)	(1.57)			
South Asia	−4.04**	−6.45***	−4.91*			
	(1.92)	(1.83)	(1.75)			
Sub-Saharan Africa	−2.55	−5.16***	−0.95			
	(1.75)	(1.95)	(3.07)			
Number of	1,058	814	975	97	83	103
observations						
R²	0.5539	0.6014	0.5988	0.4740	0.4715	0.4985
Model chi-square	516.52	628.62	740.01	4.52	2.19	14.57
Probability > chi-square	0.0000	0.0000	0.0000	0.3398	0.8224	0.0057

*p < 0.10. **p < 0.05. ***p < 0.01.

Note: Estimations were made by ordinary least squares estimation, with panel-corrected standard errors and correction for autocorrelation and for heteroskedastic disturbances between panels. Standard errors are in parentheses. ^ indicates that in a joint test of per capita income, democratic institutions, and the interactive term, the results were statistically significant (probability > chi-square = 0.0000).

Sources: Share of agricultural sector from World Bank (2000). Trade openness from Heston, Summers, and Aten (2002). Coding for democratic regime from Alvarez and others (1996), extended by Boix and Rosato (2001).

Table 6.7 Subsidies and Transfers of Central Government as a Percentage of GDP, 1970–99
(coefficients of regressions)

Independent variables	World			East Asia		
	(1)	(2)	(3)	(4)	(5)	(6)
Constant	2.64	−0.96	−5.02	3.08	2.61	6.41**
	(2.62)	(4.22)	(6.09)	(3.25)	(2.69)	(3.17)
Per capita income (log)	0.40	1.17		0.53^	0.43^	
	(0.41)	(0.73)		(0.48)	(0.45)	
Trade openness (log of	0.56***	0.55*	1.92***	−0.79	−0.60	−0.94
sum of exports and	(0.26)	(0.33)	(0.61)	(0.50)	(0.50)	(0.47)
imports over GDP)						
Democratic regime	−16.31***	0.08	−0.81	−7.43^	−1.57^	−0.20
	(3.17)	(1.65)	(0.73)	(4.58)	(1.70)	(0.55)
Democratic regime ×	2.34***			0.97*		
log of per capita income	(0.43)			(0.59)		
Level of turnout in		−0.16**			−0.12^	
democratic regimes		(0.08)			(0.07)	
Level of turnout × log of		0.02**			0.02**	
per capita income		(0.01)			(0.01)	
Share of agricultural						
sector in GDP			−0.03			−0.03
			(0.05)			(0.05)
Percentage of population			1.17***			0.54***
65 years or older			(0.37)			(0.21)
North and South America	−4.03***	−5.52***	−1.87			
	(0.80)	(1.09)	(2.81)			
East Asia	−5.66***	−7.51***	−4.00			
	(0.81)	(1.11)	(3.05)			
Eastern Europe	6.18***	2.21	3.16*			
	(1.69)	(1.62)	(1.65)			
OECD	2.90**	1.32	3.08***			
	(1.23)	(1.43)	(1.19)			
South Asia	−1.35	−1.22	−1.00			
	(1.00)	(1.17)	(2.38)			
Sub-Saharan Africa	−4.11***	−4.58***	−1.56			
	(0.75)	(0.91)	(2.91)			
Number of observations	2,248	1,570	1,950	186	171	186
R^2	0.2943	0.3330	0.0835	0.1989	0.2004	0.1890
Model chi-square	954.69	867.40	952.80	44.32	67.31	35.83
Probability > chi-square	0.0000	0.0000	0.0000	0.0000	0.0000	0.0000

*$p < 0.10$.   **$p < 0.05$.   ***$p < 0.01$.

Note: Estimations were made by ordinary least squares estimation, with panel-corrected standard errors and correction for autocorrelation and for heteroskedastic disturbances between panels. Standard errors are in parentheses. ^ indicates that in a joint test of per capita income, democratic institutions, and the interactive term, the results were statistically significant (probability > chi-square = 0.0000).

Sources: Share of agricultural sector from World Bank (2000). Trade openness from Heston, Summers, and Aten (2002). Coding for democratic regime from Alvarez and others (1996), extended by Boix and Rosato (2001).

Table 6.8 Wages and Salaries of Central Government as a Percentage of GDP, 1970–99
(coefficients of regressions)

Independent variables	World			East Asia		
	(1)	(2)	(3)	(4)	(5)	(6)
Constant	7.16	5.62	10.23	0.75	0.34	5.44
	(1.69)	(1.84)	(1.82)	(1.50)	(1.36)	(2.63)
Per capita income (log)	−0.21	−0.17		0.31	0.24	
	(0.23)	(0.26)		(0.26)	(0.25)	
Trade openness (log of	0.93***	1.23***	0.15	0.32	0.51	0.60
sum of exports and	(0.20)	(0.22)	(0.22)	(0.35)	(0.35)	(0.38)
imports over GDP)						
Democratic regime	3.06	−2.06***	0.04	11.12***	1.58	0.77**
	(2.31)	(0.67)	(0.41)	(2.96)	(1.39)	(0.38)
Democratic regime ×	−0.41			−1.39***		
log of per capita income	(0.29)			(0.38)		
Level of turnout in		0.09**			0.12***	
democratic regimes		(0.04)			(0.04)	
Level of turnout × log of		−0.01*			−0.02***	
per capita income		(0.00)			(0.01)	
Share of agricultural sector			−0.04***			−0.04
in GDP			(0.01)			(0.04)
Percentage of population			−0.15**			−0.75***
65 years or older			(0.06)			(0.29)
North and South America	−1.84***	−1.63***	−2.71***			
	(0.49)	(0.50)	(0.63)			
East Asia	−4.99***	−5.19***	−4.88***			
	(0.46)	(0.47)	(0.57)			
Eastern Europe	−3.29***	−2.54***	−2.66***			
	(0.58)	(0.61)	(0.61)			
OECD	−2.78***	−2.66***	−3.06***			
	(0.62)	(0.59)	(0.58)			
South Asia	−5.18***	−5.83***	−3.90***			
	(0.72)	(0.80)	(0.72)			
Sub-Saharan Africa	−2.34***	−2.24***	−1.36**			
	(0.58)	(0.63)	(0.66)			
Number of observations	2,114	1,491	1,837	164	149	164
R^2	0.3684	0.5092	0.3071	0.3164	0.4135	0.3086
Model chi-square	225.41	261.44	128.24	22.91	28.22	14.44
Probability > chi-square	0.0000	0.0000	0.0000	0.0001	0.0000	0.0060

*$p < 0.10$.   **$p < 0.05$.   ***$p < 0.01$.

Note: Estimations were made by ordinary least squares estimation, with panel-corrected standard errors and correction for autocorrelation and for heteroskedastic disturbances between panels. Standard errors are in parentheses. ∧ indicates that in a joint test of per capita income, democratic institutions, and the interactive term, the results were statistically significant (probability > chi-square = 0.0000).

Sources: Share of agricultural sector from World Bank (2000). Trade openness from Heston, Summers, and Aten (2002). Coding for democratic regime from Alvarez and others (1996), extended by Boix and Rosato (2001).

with regional controls, are displayed in the first three columns. The last three columns report the results for the East Asian economies.

The first model (columns 1 and 4) regresses the dependent variable on per capita income, trade openness, democratic regime, and the interaction of regime and income. The second model (columns 2 and 5) substitutes turnout in democratic regimes for political regime (turnout is equated to 0 in authoritarian regimes) and the interaction of electoral participation and per capita income for the previous interaction of regime and income. The third model (columns 3 and 6) explores the mechanisms of development with more detail.

As discussed earlier, economic development or, more generally, modernization is a complex phenomenon that alters the distribution of risk and income across sectors and generations. The third model attempts to unpack the effects of development using more direct measures that capture the change in the underlying distribution of preferences that is caused by the growth of a manufacturing working class (leading to larger intragenerational transfers) and the aging of the population (resulting in an expansion of intergenerational transfers). The model does so by adding two factors: the share of the primary sector in the economy and the proportion of older people in the population. Because observations for those measures are more scarce than per capita income data, the dataset sometimes dwindles to between one-half and two-thirds of the initial sample. Although the results are in line with the model, it is important to bear in mind these data constraints when examining the results. Given that per capita income, the size of the primary sector, and an aging population are strongly correlated—for most years, the size of the primary sector and the proportion of older people in the population explain at least some 85 percent of the variance in the log of per capita income—the level of per capita income was dropped.

Public revenue of general government. Consider first the estimations in column 1 in table 6.3. Both economic development and trade openness, which are strongly significant from a statistical point of view, positively affect the size of government. Democratic regime alone depresses outcome. But this effect has to be viewed in relation to the strong effect of the interactive term of democracy and per capita income. As discussed earlier, the effect of socioeconomic modernization is to a large extent conditional on the political regime and the level of participation.[19]

---

19. The *United Nations National Accounts* (UN various years) do not include data on the size of the public sector in former socialist countries. Using data from the International Monetary Fund (IMF various years), I have run the same regressions in table 6.2, including the total revenues of

The control variables reveal that the public sector in East Asia is smaller than it should be, given its stage of development and the types of political regimes in the region. Public current revenue is about 6.5 percentage points of GDP smaller than in the rest of the world. Column 4, which shows the same calculation restricted to East Asia, confirms this result. The coefficients go in the same direction as in column 1: trade is statistically significant and per capita income, regime, and the interactive term are significant in a joint test. Still, economic development and trade are smaller—by about half of the value in column 1. In other words, economic development and trade openness generate demands on the public sector in East Asia—but they are milder than in the rest of the world.

To interpret the results of columns 1 and 4 in table 6.3, and particularly the effect of the interactive term, I show in figure 6.5 the evolution of current public revenue as a proportion of GDP, as real per capita income rises under both a democratic polity and an authoritarian regime. This illustration is given both for the whole sample (using column 1), with an intercept calculated with the OECD dummy, and for East Asia alone (using column 4). Trade openness has been set equal to the East Asian mean of 85 percent of GDP. The structure of the illustration in figure 6.5 suggests several facts.

In the first place, the level of development has, again, an unconditional effect on the size of the public sector. At low levels of development, the public sector is small. Democratic India, the authoritarian regimes of Sub-Saharan Africa or Central America, or even the limited democracies of nineteenth-century Europe fit into this pattern. The state then grows with per capita income. Regardless of the political regime in place, the size of public revenues increases by about 10 percentage points from very low to medium levels of development, and then another 5–7 percentage points from medium to high levels of development.

In the second place, the nature of the political regime does not affect, on its own, the size of the government. For that to be true, the public sector should always be larger under a democratic system at all income levels. The results show, instead, that democratic regimes in truly developing economies have no incentives to spend more than authoritarian regimes.

general government in Hungary (1981–89), Poland (1984–88), Romania (1972–89), and Yugoslavia (1971–89). No data are available for China, the former German Democratic Republic, the former Soviet Union, or the non-European socialist countries. These regressions, with and without a dummy variable for "planning economies," generate results very similar to the results obtained without any planning systems. The dummy for planning economies indicates that the size of the public sector is about 20–25 percentage points of GDP larger in socialist economies.

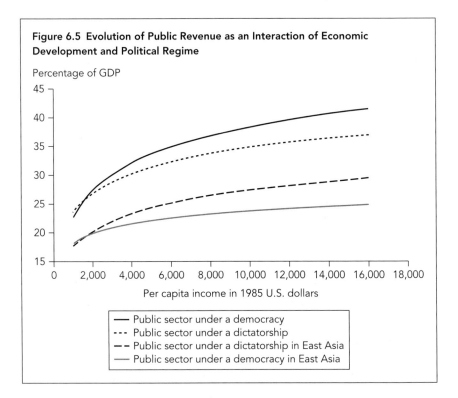

Figure 6.5 Evolution of Public Revenue as an Interaction of Economic Development and Political Regime

At extremely low levels of development, public current revenue is, in fact, somewhat higher in nondemocratic regimes. At a per capita income of US$250 (in 1985 prices), public revenue is about 3 percentage points of GDP lower in democracies than in authoritarian regimes. This result may be due to two factors. First, the demands for transfers associated with development have not affected democratic states. Second, it is likely that authoritarian states are more expensive because of their need to finance their repressive apparatus.[20]

As socioeconomic modernization takes off, democratic institutions lead to larger governments. Larger governments generate a set of demands and needs that democratic politicians need to respond to. Once real per capita income goes over US$1,000, the public sector expands at a faster rate under democratic regimes. With a per capita income of US$6,000, public

---

20. Regressing military spending as a percentage of GDP on per capita income and regime shows that dictatorships spend 2 percentage points of GDP more than democracies (the coefficient is statistically significant at $p < 0.1$).

revenue is about 2 percentage points higher in a democratic country. For a per capita income of US$12,000, public revenue would hypothetically be 4 percentage points higher in a democracy. The historical experience of recent democratic transitions fits these results quite nicely. Consider the paradigmatic case of Spain, where democracy was reestablished in the late 1970s. In 1974, Spain had a per capita income of US$7,291 (in 1985 prices), and its current public revenue amounted to 22.8 percent of GDP. Ten years later, although per capita income had remained stagnant (US$7,330 in 1984), current public revenue had risen to 32.7 percent. Greece and Portugal fit these results as well. In East Asia, a similar phenomenon took place in the Philippines, where current public revenue rose from 14 percent of GDP to 19 percent of GDP after the restoration of democracy in the late 1980s, with no change in per capita income in that period.

Finally, although East Asia follows the same structure as the whole world (again, notice that the illustration for East Asia is based on column 4), the public sector is systematically smaller in that continent in all parameters—by more than 10 percentage points of GDP.

As discussed earlier, who actually votes should matter as much as (or even more than) who is legally entitled to vote. Changes in the level of turnout may shift the position of the median voter and, hence, affect the tax rate. Because individual data on participation are unavailable for all the countries in the sample, this hypothesis can be tested only by using national levels of participation. Nonetheless, holding other things constant, the individual probability of voting has been shown to increase with income; thus, it is plausible to conclude that, as national turnout declines, abstention takes place mostly among the poorest voters.[21] Hence, at lower levels of participation, the difference between median voter income and average income should decline, and if we believe the Meltzer-Richards approach, the size of the public sector should shrink.

Columns 2 and 5 in table 6.3 show the effect of the interactive term of turnout and per capita income.[22] The coefficient is again significant and strongly confirms the theoretical model. In developing countries, participation has no effect. For mid-income nations, however, turnout becomes substantially important. For example, if we apply the model for high levels

---

21. For evidence that, in the absence of mechanisms of political mobilization such as parties or unions, turnout is positively related to income, see Rosenstone and Hansen (1993) and Franklin (1996).

22. The introduction of the variable *Level of Turnout* shrinks the sample by almost 600 observations.

of per capita income, the size of the public sector varies from 37.5 percent of GDP in countries where only two-fifths of the population vote (the cases of the United States and Switzerland) to about 43 percent where everybody votes.[23] Notice also that the effect of turnout is even stronger in East Asia. Naturally, the small size of the sample should make us very cautious about the results.

Although I have not included the results in table 6.3, I have tested the effects of presidentialism, proportional representation, and federalism (see also Boix 2001). Federalism has no effect on the size of the public sector. Still, according to recent work by Rodden (2000, 2001), the public sector is larger in federal systems in which subnational units receive intergovernmental transfers yet oversight by the central government is lax. The public sector is slightly larger in countries governed by proportional representation laws—by about 1.7 percent of GDP.[24] By contrast, presidentialism has a significant negative effect on the size of the public sector. Under presidential systems, public revenues are about 4 percent of GDP lower than under parliamentarian regimes. Although presidentialism significantly depresses participation (by more than 12 percentage points in the sample here), its effect does not wane after we control for turnout. The separation-of-powers structure that comes with presidentialism seems to impose a bias toward the status quo on current policy that slows the growth of government.

Finally, columns 3 and 6 examine the effect of the primary sector and demographic structure on the size of the public sector. The size of the primary sector in the economy has a substantial effect on the evolution of the size of the public sector. A decrease of 1 percentage point of the agricultural sector in the GDP implies an increase of public revenue of 0.25 point of GDP. With all the other variables at their mean levels, public revenues

---

23. For recent evidence on the impact of turnout on the size of transfers using the sample of OECD nations, see Franzese (2002).

24. The coefficient of proportional representation oscillates in size when we exclude specific years or countries. Proportional representation seems to affect the size of government mostly in an indirect way. By reducing barriers to entry and diminishing the incentive to vote strategically, it boosts political participation—a well-known result in the literature on electoral turnout (Franklin 1996)—and, therefore, makes government more responsive to citizens' demands. Controlling for economic development, degree of party competition, and other institutional characteristics (presidentialism and federalism), we find that turnout is about 9 percentage points higher in proportional representation systems than in majoritarian electoral laws in the dataset used here. When turnout is excluded from the regression, proportional representation becomes statistically significant and goes up by 50 percent.

would amount to about 33 percent in a country with no agricultural sector and to about 14 percent in a country with two-thirds of the economy in the primary sector. Modernization, by changing the types of productive activities that most of the population is engaged in and by bolstering an urban working class, accounts for much of the emergence of a significant public sector.

The proportion of older people in the population has, in turn, a strong positive effect on the size of government, thereby confirming the standard literature on the determinants of the welfare state in OECD nations. For each percentage point of older people in the population, the size of the public sector goes up by 1.06 percentage points of GDP. The aging of the median voter has a very similar effect on the size of the public sector in East Asia.[25]

All the models have also been run with a control for the level of public debt as a percentage of GDP. Results are not shown here because the number of observations dwindles to between one-half and one-fourth of the sample in each model. Results are robust when public debt is introduced. Past levels of public debt affect the size of the state significantly and positively: each percentage point of public debt increases public revenue and expenditure by about 0.02 percentage point.

Public consumption of general government. Table 6.4 examines the causes of variation in final public consumption of general government for the period 1960–99. Trade openness substantially affects final consumption—a result that confirms the estimates of Rodrik (1998). Interestingly, economic development has no effect on public consumption alone. But its effect is strong in interaction with democracy. The data in column 3 reveal that a reduction in the weight of agriculture prompts an increase in public consumption. Public consumption turns out to be important in agrarian economies that have a democratic system. This finding may simply reveal that in developing nations redistribution does not take place through transfers but rather through public employment and direct expenditures. Not unexpectedly, the proportion of older people in the population has no effect on public consumption. As we shall see, demographic change is primarily associated with a change in welfare programs based on transfers.

---

25. Adding the proportion of fuel exports to total exports to control for the effect of substantial oil revenues does not change the coefficients in table 6.4. As expected, oil exporters have a larger government, although the effect is small.

Expenditure of central government. Tables 6.5 and 6.6 focus on total expenditure and nonmilitary expenditure of central government, respectively. In table 6.5, column 1 shows that the growth of total expenditure is driven by trade openness, on the one hand, and by the interaction of democracy and development, on the other hand. Development alone has no effect on expenditure, and democracy alone depresses it. East Asia has a much lower level of public spending than the rest of the world—about 16 percent of GDP.

Columns 2 and 3 in table 6.5 confirm what we learned from table 6.3. Turnout in industrial nations boosts the size of the public sector. Similarly, the growth of an industrial sector and an aging population increase total spending. The effect of an older population becomes particularly intense under a democratic system. The fit of the models is poor for the East Asian sample (columns 4 to 6).

The results match our theoretical expectations particularly well for nonmilitary expenditure of central government. As shown in table 6.6, in column 1, trade openness and the interaction of democracy and per capita income have a very strong effect on the size of the state. Under an authoritarian state, nonmilitary spending does not change with economic development. By contrast, with democracy, the level of nonmilitary spending of the central government doubles from about 10 percent of GDP to almost 20 percent of GDP as a country moves from US$1,000 to US$10,000 per capita income. An increase in the level of turnout in industrial countries raises spending considerably (column 2). Agriculture and older population function in the way expected from a theoretical point of view. Finally, in the estimations for East Asia, the sample is extremely small (fewer than 100 observations) and most of the coefficients are not significant. Still, the size and signs of the coefficients are very similar to those obtained for the whole sample.

Subsidies and transfers of central government. As pointed out earlier, most of the difference between East Asia and other regions of the world in the overall size of the public sector occurs in two areas: spending on subsidies and current transfers. Table 6.7 focuses on these expenditures, which constitute the core of the welfare state.

The process of development alone does not change the size of subsidies and transfers (unfortunately, I have no separate data for these two components). Trade openness plays a much smaller role than for total revenues and expenditure—domestic compensation does not seem to take place through the welfare state but rather through public consumption, public employment, and, probably, public capital formation programs.

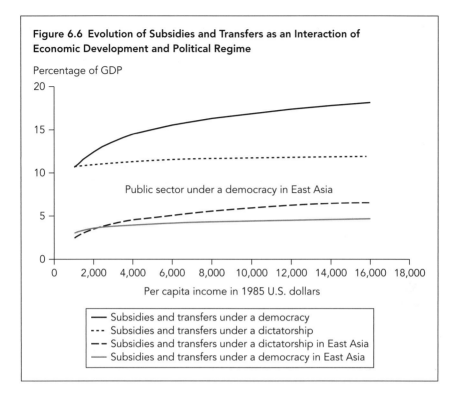

Figure 6.6 Evolution of Subsidies and Transfers as an Interaction of Economic Development and Political Regime

Percentage of GDP

Per capita income in 1985 U.S. dollars

- Subsidies and transfers under a democracy
- - - Subsidies and transfers under a dictatorship
- — Subsidies and transfers under a dictatorship in East Asia
- — Subsidies and transfers under a democracy in East Asia

Figure 6.6 illustrates the evolution of subsidies and transfers of central government as an interaction of development and political regime, both for the whole sample (based on column 1) and for East Asia (based on column 4). Under an authoritarian regime, the size of transfers and subsidies remains unchanged at about 10 percent of GDP. By contrast, under a democratic regime, and once development occurs, the size of the program grows by anywhere from 2 percent to about 18 percent of GDP for high levels of development. It is worth comparing the results in figure 6.6 to the results in figure 6.5. In figure 6.5, the size of the overall public sector grew even under an authoritarian regime—although at a slower pace than under a democratic regime. When we put the two sets of results together, the joint model of development and democracy put forward in the first section of this chapter fits the empirics nicely. The public sector grows as a result of economic modernization—regardless of the political regime in place—through higher expenditure in public goods and investment. But in the area of transfers, such as pensions, universal health care, or unemployment benefits, it does so only after the introduction of democracy. As for East

Asian countries, subsidies and transfers are much smaller at similar levels of development.[26] A shift in political regime gradually increases spending, but less sharply than in the rest of the world. Asian states seem to be insulated from electoral demands for redistributive expenditure in a way that European states are not.

The case of Korea serves as a good example of this statistical result. As reported in OECD (2000), social expenditures in Korea are low. Including spending for labor market policies, they averaged 5 percent of GDP in the late 1990s. This figure reflects the lack of a social safety net until very recently. Unemployment insurance was introduced only in 1995. A health care system was launched in 1977, but it is limited to employees at large companies. The pension system, which covers about 200,000 people, is composed of three occupational pension schemes established for civil servants (1960), military personnel (1963), and private school teachers (1975). In 1988, just after the transition to democracy, the state established a public pension system, the National Pension Scheme; however, its coverage has remained rather limited. To qualify for a reduced old-age pension, a person must have contributed for a minimum period of 10 years. Only 176,000 persons received pensions under the scheme in 1999. All these schemes cover about 6 percent of the labor force. In 1994, pensions accounted for only 6 percent of the income of the elderly in Korea, compared with 90 percent in high-income countries. Instead, family support provided more than two-thirds of the income of the elderly. Another one-quarter of their income came from employment.

In columns 3 and 6, I regress agriculture and the proportion of older people in the population. The latter variable has a very significant effect on transfers and subsidies. For the whole sample, each percentage point of older population increases transfers and subsidies by 1.17 percentage points; thus, the growth in public revenue and nonmilitary expenditure takes place through these sets of programs. For East Asia, the effect is positive but milder: the increase is about half the size of that of the whole sample.

Wages and salaries of central government. Table 6.8 examines the explanatory value of the different models of public sector growth for the expenditure on public employment. The results are instructive when they are compared with those in previous tables. Trade openness has a slight effect on public employment expenditure. The level of development has a

---

26. This finding simply confirms the result of the East Asian dummy (-5.7) in column 1.

negative but statistically insignificant effect. With development, democracies reduce the size of public wages. Again, it is possible that the forms of redistribution that are practiced in agrarian economies are gradually displaced by the new demands for universal welfare state programs. Finally, the level of turnout increases the size of public employment and the proportion of older population deflates it marginally. In the sample of East Asia, democracy boosts the size of public employment, but only in countries with low per capita incomes.

Why Is East Asia Different?

After comparing the results for the whole sample and the East Asia sample, we can draw two main conclusions. From the first section of this chapter, we know, first, that the public sector in East Asia is small. Its size fluctuates between two-thirds and one-half the size of the average OECD public sector. The bulk of the difference lies partly in public consumption, which is one-third smaller in East Asia than in the world average, but it is mostly due to the light weight of subsidies and transfers in the region.

Second, from the statistical results, we can conclude that although the variables that have shaped the size and nature of the public sector in industrial nations and across the globe have also influenced East Asia, they have done so to a lesser degree. In the regressions on public revenue, public consumption, and total expenditure, the coefficients of economic development and trade openness for the East Asian sample were half the size of those for the world sample. For subsidies and transfers, trade openness has no effect in East Asia, and the interaction of democracy and development has a much smaller coefficient than for the whole sample. In short, East Asia seems to be partly insulated from the redistributive pressures that have structured the European welfare state.

Why is East Asia different from the rest of the world? Again, after we control for per capita income and regime, the causes behind the underdevelopment of the Asian public sector are difficult to pinpoint. Four possible explanations stand out:

1. A weak labor movement exists in East Asia, one which has been unable to convert its fiscal demands on the state. Remember that, according to the partisan and strength-of-the-working-class theories reviewed earlier, it was the organizational and mobilization capacities of the working class that explained the growth of the European welfare state. According to data from Garrett (2001), union membership in Western Europe

averaged 40 percent of the labor force in the late 1990s, which is more than double the East Asia average of 17 percent.

2. A lower level of inequality exists in East Asia, which in a strict Meltzer-Richards model might have reduced the redistributive demands of the electorate.

3. The weakness of the East Asian system may be due to the lack of enough time under democracy. Since welfare states build up over time, it is only after many years of democratic governance that public programs are established and grow to maturity.

4. Direct public programs may be the counterpart of a tacit pact between government and business to share the welfare burden, with business providing permanent employment in exchange for a low tax burden. If, as is claimed nowadays, this pact is unraveling, we should observe stronger demands for social protection arising among electors in the future.

Columns 1 and 2 in table 6.9 show the results of regressing nonmilitary expenditure and public expenditure on subsidies and transfers on trade, the democratic regime, the aging population, and the agricultural sector (model 3 in the preceding tables), with and without a control for unionization. Unfortunately, the measure of union membership, taken from Garrett (2001), is available only as a cross-section for the late 1990s. Union membership has a small but not statistically significant effect on the size of the public sector. The dummy for East Asia hardly changes.

Column 4 of table 6.9 tests for the effect of income inequality. To measure inequality, I use the dataset collected by Deininger and Squire (1996). I have used an adjusted Gini coefficient (which varies in a scale from 0 to 100) to control for cross-national variation in the methods used to measure income distribution. This variation is a function of the choice of the recipient unit (individual or household), the use of gross or net income, and the use of expenditure or income. In accordance with the suggestions of Deininger and Squire, the adjusted Gini is equal to the Gini coefficient plus 6.6 points in observations based on expenditure (versus income) and 3 points in observations using net rather than gross income. I have also calculated a 5-year moving average of adjusted Gini coefficients. This procedure has two advantages: it minimizes the volatility in the inequality measures, and it doubles the number of observations (on which the estimation of table 6.5 is based) from 312 to 617 data points (575 in table 6.8).

Income inequality reduces the size of the public sector. For each point of Gini, subsidies and transfers decline by one-fourth of a percentage

Table 6.9 Effect of Unionization and Income Inequality on the Size of Subsidies
and Transfers
(coefficients of regressions)

Independent variables	World		East Asia	
	(1)	(2)	(3)	(4)
Constant	−1.41	−0.73	−6.25***	8.11**
	(5.81)	(5.95)	(1.95)	(3.68)
Trade openness (log of	1.44	1.23	1.14***	0.88**
sum of exports and	(1.28)	(1.33)	(0.39)	(0.39)
imports over GDP)				
Democratic regime	0.16	0.29	−0.93*	−1.03**
	(1.62)	(1.64)	(0.53)	(0.51)
Share of agricultural	−0.18**	−0.19**	0.06	0.02
sector in GDP	(0.09)	(0.09)	(0.04)	(0.03)
Percentage of population	1.18***	1.13***	1.86***	1.47***
65 years or older	(0.18)	(0.20)	(0.11)	(0.14)
Percentage of union		0.02		
members in labor force		(0.03)		
Gini index of income				−0.23***
inequality				(0.05)
East Asia	−5.13**	−4.79*	−3.54***	−4.82***
	(2.32)	(2.41)	(0.54)	(0.67)
Number of observations	65	65	575	575
R^2	0.72	0.73	0.64	0.64
Model chi-square			495.95	546.05
Probability > chi-square			0.0000	0.0000

*$p < 0.10$.   **$p < 0.05$.   ***$p < 0.01$.

Note: For columns 1 and 2, estimations were made by ordinary least squares estimation. For columns 3 and 4, estimations were made by ordinary last squares estimation, with panel-corrected standard errors and correction for autocorrelation and for heteroskedastic disturbances between panels. Standard errors are in parentheses.

Sources: Share of agricultural sector from World Bank (2000). Trade openness from Heston, Summers, and Aten (2002). Coding for democratic regime from Alvarez and others (1996), extended by Boix and Rosato (2001).

point of GDP. Accordingly, the difference between a very equal nation (a Gini of about 30) and a very unequal one (a Gini of about 65) implies a difference of 7.5 percent of GDP.

Finally, to test the cumulative effect of democracy, I have run a cross-sectional regression of the kind in column 2 in table 6.9, substituting total number of years under a democratic regime from 1980 to 1999 for unionization rates. The results, which are not reported here, do not support the thesis that only a prolonged number of years under a democratic regime lead to a large public sector.

Public Deficit of Central Government

Table 6.10 suggests the mechanisms behind the evolution of public deficits. Controlling for the past deficit, we find that growth rates, the level of development, and the size of the public sector have an important

Table 6.10 Budget Balance of Central Government as a Percentage of GDP, 1970–99 (coefficients of regressions)

Independent variables	World	East Asia
Constant	−5.04***	−3.28**
	(1.06)	(1.34)
Public deficit (t − 1)	0.68***	0.86***
	(0.04)	(0.06)
Change in per capita income	0.04*	0.16***
	(0.03)	(0.03)
Per capita income (log)	0.60	0.08
	(0.14)	(0.10)
Trade openness (log)	0.18	0.27
	(0.21)	(0.30)
Democratic regime	−0.28	−0.09
	(0.27)	(0.38)
Total expenditure	−0.04**	0.04
(percentage of GDP) (t − 1)	(0.02)	(0.04)
North and South America	−0.26	
	(0.39)	
East Asia	−0.08	
	(0.32)	
Eastern Europe	0.37	
	(0.38)	
OECD	−1.08**	
	(0.43)	
South Asia	0.11	
	(0.43)	
Sub-Saharan Africa	0.32	
	(0.37)	
Number of observations	2,292	193
R^2	0.5546	0.7969
Model chi-square	1,020.97	490.46
Probability > chi-square	0.0000	0.0000

$*p < 0.10$. $**p < 0.05$. $***p < 0.01$.

Note: Estimations were made by ordinary least squares estimation, with panel-corrected standard errors and correction for autocorrelation and for heteroskedastic disturbances between panels. Standard errors are in parentheses. ^ indicates that in a joint test of per capita income, democratic institutions, and the interactive term, the results were statistically significant (probability > chi-square = 0.0000).

Sources: Share of agricultural sector from World Bank (2000). Trade openness from Heston, Summers, and Aten (2002). Coding for democratic regime from Alvarez and others (1996), extended by Boix and Rosato (2001).

effect on the budget balance. The budget becomes more balanced in booming periods. Industrial nations have better finances. Finally, larger public sectors reduce fiscal solvency slightly. In contrast with the results for the size of the public sector, East Asia does not stand as a different continent in terms of public deficits; the dummy for East Asia is small and statistically not significant. In the separate regression for East Asia, which is displayed in column 2, the effect of the growth rate is much higher than for the entire sample. Each percentage point of growth translates to an increase in the budget balance of about 0.16 percent of GDP (versus 0.04 percent of GDP in column 1). East Asian governments seem to react more rapidly to fluctuations in the business cycle. The effects of per capita income and size of public expenditure disappear, however, for East Asian countries.

State-Owned Enterprises

Table 6.11 explores the causes of variation in the size of the state-owned firms. More open economies have slightly larger public business sectors. Still, the two central determinants of the economic intervention of states through enterprises are (a) the size of fuel exports and (b) location in the Middle East. In countries that have a high proportion of oil exports, states have stepped in to control the rents of fuel. Strong dirigiste tendencies seem to account for the heavy presence of the state in the economy in the Middle East, even after we control for fuel exports. East Asia has no distinctive traits in this area of economic management.

FORECASTING THE EVOLUTION OF THE EAST ASIAN PUBLIC SECTOR

Using the results just discussed, I conclude this chapter by considering how the public sector in East Asia may develop in the next 10–15 years. To do so, I estimate the evolution of public revenue, public consumption, and the sum of subsidies and transfers on the basis of column 6 in tables 6.3, 6.4, and 6.7, respectively.

Table 6.12 reports the resulting values for 1999 and 2015. Public revenues are reported in panel A. Public consumption is displayed in panel B. Subsidies and transfers are shown in panel C. For the purposes of comparison, the table reports the real figures for either 1999 or the latest available year.

To forecast the evolution of the public sector in 2015, I have considered three scenarios. In the first scenario, which is reported in column 1, trade

Table 6.11 Size of State-Owned Enterprises as a Percentage of GDP, 1970–85 (coefficients of regressions)

Independent variables	World
Constant	−2.70
	(7.82)
Per capita income (log)	0.15
	(0.95)
Trade openness (log)	3.03*
	(1.86)
Democratic regime	−2.46
	(1.72)
Fuel exports as a percentage of total exports	0.14***
	(0.04)
North and South America	−2.14
	(2.63)
East Asia	−3.23
	(3.34)
Middle East	19.14***
	(5.78)
Sub-Saharan Africa	−3.01
	(3.98)
Western Europe	−1.05
	(3.63)
Number of observations	105
R^2	0.577
Model chi-square	51.42
Probability > chi-square	0.0000

$*p < 0.10.$ $**p < 0.05.$ $***p < 0.01.$

Note: Estimations were made by ordinary least squares estimation, with panel-corrected standard errors and correction for autocorrelation and for heteroskedastic disturbances between panels. Standard errors are in parentheses. ^ indicates that in a joint test of per capita income, democratic institutions, and the interactive term, the results were statistically significant (probability > chi-square = 0.0000).

Sources: Share of agricultural sector from World Bank (2000). Trade openness from Heston, Summers, and Aten (2002). Coding for democratic regime from Alvarez and others (1996), extended by Boix and Rosato (2001).

openness remains unchanged, the political regime in place changes according to the probabilities calculated in the literature on democracy and development (Przeworski and others 2000), the proportion of older people in the population is taken from World Bank (1999), and the share of agriculture is extrapolated from its trend in the past two decades. In column 2, the same assumptions apply, except for political regime—here I consider what happens if democracy reigns in all countries. In column 3, the assumptions in column 1 apply, except that trade openness increases by 50 percent.

Table 6.12 Forecasting the East Asian Public Sector (percentage of GDP)

Indicator		No regime change[a]	Regime change to democracy	No regime change with trade increase[b]
A. Public revenue				
High-income countries				
Japan	Observed (1993)	32.9		
	1999	31.3	31.3	31.3
	2015	45.6	45.6	46.4
	Change in predicted value	14.4	14.4	15.1
Korea, Rep. of	Observed (1993)	23.4		
	1999	20.9	20.9	20.9
	2015	28.0	28.0	28.9
	Change in predicted value	7.1	7.1	8.0
Singapore	Observed	—		
	1999	26.6	26.6	26.6
	2015	33.2	33.2	34.1
	Change in predicted value	6.6	6.6	7.5
Medium- to low-income countries				
Indonesia	Observed	—		
	1999	15.3	15.3	15.3
	2015	18.2	18.2	19.8
	Change in predicted value	2.9	2.9	4.5
Malaysia	Observed	—		
	1999	19.5	19.5	19.5
	2015	23.8	23.8	24.7
	Change in predicted value	4.3	4.3	5.2
Philippines	Observed (1993)	21.2		
	1999	14.8	14.8	14.8
	2015	18.9	18.9	19.8
	Change in predicted value	4.2	4.2	5.1
Thailand	Observed (1993)	19.9		
	1999	19.0	19.0	19.0
	2015	23.4	23.4	24.3
	Change in predicted value	4.4	4.4	5.3
Communist countries				
China	Observed	—		
	1999	18.0	18.0	18.0
	2015	23.0	22.2	23.8
	Change in predicted value	5.0	4.2	5.8

(Table continues on the following page.)

Table 6.12 continued

Indicator		No regime change[a]	Regime change to democracy	No regime change with trade increase[b]
	B. Public consumption			
High-income countries				
Japan	Observed (1998)	10.2		
	1999	8.4	8.4	8.4
	2015	6.3	6.3	6.3
	Change in predicted value	−2.2	−2.2	−2.2
Korea	Observed (1999)	10.1		
	1999	10.3		
	2015	9.4	9.4	9.5
	Change in predicted value	−0.8	−0.8	−0.7
Singapore	Observed (1997)	9.7		
	1999	11.3	11.3	11.3
	2015	9.8	10.2	10.3
	Change in predicted value	−1.4	−1.1	−1.0
Medium- to low-income countries				
Indonesia	Observed (1999)	6.5		
	1999	9.7	9.7	9.7
	2015	9.8	9.4	9.9
	Change in predicted value	0.2	−0.3	0.2
Malaysia	Observed (1999)	11.1		
	1999	10.8	10.8	10.8
	2015	10.9	10.9	10.9
	Change in predicted value	0.1	0.1	0.1
Philippines	Observed (1999)	12.9		
	1999	9.7	9.7	9.7
	2015	10.0	10.0	10.1
	Change in predicted value	0.3	0.3	0.4
Thailand	Observed (1999)	11.0		
	1999	10.0	10.0	10.0
	2015	10.0	10.1	10.1
	Change in predicted value	0.0	0.1	0.1
Communist countries				
China	Observed (1999)	12.5		
	1999	9.3	9.3	9.3
	2015	9.5	9.1	9.6
	Change in predicted value	0.2	−0.2	0.3

Indicator		No regime change[a]	Regime change to democracy	No regime change with trade increase[b]
	C. Subsidies and transfers			
High-income countries				
Japan	Observed (1990)	8.5		
	1999	13.1	13.1	13.1
	2015	18.7	18.7	18.5
	Change in predicted value	5.6	5.6	5.4
Korea	Observed (1997)	8.5		
	1999	7.5	7.5	7.5
	2015	10.2	10.2	10.0
	Change in predicted value	2.7	2.7	2.5
Singapore	Observed (1998)	1.4		
	1999	7.6	7.6	7.6
	2015	9.9	10.1	10.0
	Change in predicted value	2.4	2.5	2.4
Medium- to low-income countries				
Indonesia	Observed (1997)	6.5		
	1999	6.5	6.5	6.5
	2015	7.5	7.4	7.4
	Change in predicted value	1.0	0.9	0.9
Malaysia	Observed (1997)	4.6		
	1999	6.0	6.0	6.0
	2015	7.1	7.3	7.1
	Change in predicted value	1.1	1.3	1.1
Philippines	Observed (1997)	3.7		
	1999	5.7	5.7	5.7
	2015	6.8	6.8	6.6
	Change in predicted value	1.1	1.1	0.9
Thailand	Observed (1999)	1.7		
	1999	6.8	6.8	6.8
	2015	8.2	8.2	8.0
	Change in predicted value	1.4	1.4	1.2

(Table continues on the following page.)

Table 6.12 continued

Indicator		No regime change[a]	Regime change to democracy	No regime change with trade increase[b]
Communist countries				
China	Observed	—		
	1999	7.9	7.9	7.9
	2015	9.4	9.2	9.2
	Change in predicted value	1.5	1.3	1.3

— Not available.

a. Predictions for 2015 are based on unchanged trade openness relative to 1999.

b. Predictions for 2015 are based on unchanged trade openness relative to 1999, except that trade has been increased 50 percent.

Sources: Predictions for 1999 are based on current values taken from World Bank (1999). Predictions for 2015 are based on following assumptions: the political regime in place is estimated according to the probabilities calculated in Przeworski and others (2000); the percentage of elderly population in 2015 is from World Bank (1999); the share of agriculture has been estimated extrapolating from its trend in the past two decades.

The predicted values are generally in line with the observed values in the three columns—except for Singapore and the Philippines for both public revenue and transfers and except for Thailand for subsidies and transfers.

In Singapore, the fitted values overpredict the size of the public sector: 26.6 percent of GDP for public revenue is too high a figure for what is generally known to be a rather small public sector; similarly, the predicted value of 7.6 percent of GDP in subsidies and transfers is five times larger than the observed value for 1998. The result shows that Singapore deviates very sharply from the standard behavior of the public sector both in Europe and in other high-income countries in East Asia.

In the Philippines, the values underpredict the growth of the public sector by about 6 percentage points—that is, they do not capture the rapid growth experienced by the Philippine public sector from 1986, until which time the public sector had stood at 14 percent of GDP, to 1992, when it peaked at 22.3 percent of GDP. It is interesting to notice that the growth of the Philippine public sector has not been driven by the expansion of standard welfare state programs: subsidies and transfers stood at 3.7 percent of GDP in 1997, about 2 percentage points below what the model predicts.

A similar mismatch occurs for Thailand. Although its public revenues are perfectly in line with their predicted value (19.0 versus 19.9 percent of

GDP), the level of transfers and subsidies, at about 1.7 percent in 1999, is four times lower than what the model predicts. As in the Philippines, the state has responded to the process of political and economic modernization with a larger public sector, but it probably has used other means, such as public consumption and public employment, rather than transfers and subsidies.[27]

With such limitations of the model in mind, consider now the projections made in table 6.12 about the evolution of the public sector up to 2015. Total public revenue experiences an upward trend across East Asia, essentially driven by an aging population and the modernization of the economies. Within that rising trend, high-income countries (Japan and Korea) witness stronger spending pressures. Singapore seems to see a similar increase—but, again, the figures are unreliable given the mismatch between the predicted and real values for that city-state. The remaining countries undergo, instead, very moderate pressures to expand the size of their public sectors. A comparison across columns shows that most of the rising pressure comes from changes in the structure of the economies and of the populations. Trade has a positive but overall marginal effect. The effect of democracy is not important. Still, conclusions in this regard must be made with caution because we are not using the models with the interaction effect of democracy and development.

Panel B shows that public consumption hardly changes over time. In fact, it may fall slightly in high-income countries, probably squeezed by financial demands for other types of expenditure. Finally, panel C shows again that subsidies and transfers respond to an aging population and the demands of urban, nonagrarian economies. Notice that in this case trade exerts a moderate downward pressure on welfare state programs. If we observe table 6.7, this finding is a specific East Asian phenomenon, because trade is positively correlated with transfers in the world sample.

CONCLUSIONS

The public sector in East Asia has been and still is much smaller than the public sector in countries elsewhere that have a similar level of economic development and similar structural characteristics, such as demographics and patterns of economic activities. Overall, public revenues in East Asia are lower by 6 to 8 percentage points of GDP. Total public expenditure is smaller by 10 to 12 percentage points of GDP.

---

27. For example, in 1998 public wages represent 6.5 percent of GDP in the Philippines, compared with less than 2 percent of GDP in Korea.

The difference between East Asian countries and the rest of the world is concentrated in subsidies and transfers—that is, the core set of programs of the welfare state and, perhaps, industrial policies (based on subsidization of firms). By contrast, East Asia performs on average in capital expenditure and human capital formation. Although the purpose of this chapter was to explore the components and explanatory variables of the public sector in East Asia, it may well be that this combination of fiscal thriftiness in transfers and good levels of capital formation partly explains the successful economic performance of East Asia in the past decades.

No single variable can account for the lack of development of the East Asian welfare state in the last third of the twentieth century. More precisely, democracy, urbanization, and demographic change lead to larger public sectors in the same way they do in Europe—but with much less intensity. Other factors, such as the level of unionization (which is lower than in comparable cases in terms of development) or income inequality (which is low and should depress redistributive demands), cannot explain the size of transfers in East Asia. It is likely that the primitive welfare state of East Asia is attributable to prolonged periods of authoritarianism rule. As pointed out in the literature (Haggard 1990), East Asian authoritarian regimes have chosen export-led economic strategies that are based on low labor costs and low taxation. These export-led strategies may have had lingering effects in countries even after democratization. The success of the economic model of East Asia may well have deterred the new regimes of the 1990s from increasing the size of the public sector too quickly. Still, if the Korean case is of any relevance, the state in East Asia should grow. After the transition of 1988, Korea has established comprehensive pension and unemployment programs that will drive public expenditure upward.

More generally, the estimations show that the public sector in East Asia is poised for a rise across the board, particularly in public transfers. This expansion should not create economic havoc. If the European scenario offers any lessons, it is that expansion seems to be politically unavoidable and financially bearable: the departing point in East Asia is a modest public sector—an underdeveloped one in comparison with similar countries—which, therefore, has ample room to grow.

Within East Asia, the public sector is likely to grow at different rates. In medium- to high-income countries, there may be rapid convergence with OECD averages: public revenue may well reach 46 percent of GDP in Japan and about 30 percent or more in Korea. In low-income countries, change will be more moderate. The size of the public sector will hover around 20 percent of GDP in Southeast Asian countries. China should also see some growth, from a public sector that represents one-sixth of its economy to one that claims perhaps about one-fourth of total GDP. Estimates are made difficult by the scarcity of the data. Still, if the new literature on federalism is right—and given how rapidly tax claims from local governments have grown in China in the 1990s—the Chinese public sector may experience a big jump in the future.

East Asia experienced a substantial fiscal crisis in the late 1990s. This crisis has thrown into doubt the very prudent approach to balanced budgets and low public debt that reigned in the region before 1997, except during the early 1990s. However, if the statistical results are reliable, East Asian governments have traditionally been very capable of adjusting in a rapid manner to economic shocks: budget imbalances have been strongly related to cycles, and the public debt was reduced very efficiently in the late 1980s.

REFERENCES

Adserà, Alícia, and Carles Boix. 2002. "Trade, Democracy, and the Size of the Public Sector." *International Organization* 56(2):229–62.

Alt, James E. 1987. "Crude Politics." *British Journal of Political Science* 17(2):149–99.

Alvarez, Mike, José Antonio Cheibub, Fernando Limongi, and Adam Przeworski. 1996. "Classifying Political Regimes." *Studies in Comparative International Development* 31:3–36.

Aukrust, Odd. 1977. "Inflation in the Open Economy: A Norwegian Model." In Lawrence Krause and Walter Salant, eds., *Worldwide Inflation*. Washington, D.C.: Brookings.

Bates, Robert H., Philip Brock, and Jill Tiefenthaler. 1991. "Risk and Trade Regimes: Another Exploration." *International Organization* 45:1–18.

Baumol, William J. 1967. "Macroeconomics of Unbalanced Growth: The Anatomy of the Urban Crisis." *American Economic Review* 57(3):415–26.

Birchfield, Vicki, and Markus Crepaz. 1998. "The Impact of Constitutions' Structures and Collective and Competitive Veto Points on Income Inequality in Industrialized Democracies." *European Journal of Political Research* 34(October):175–200.

Boix, Carles. 1997. "Privatizating the Public Business Sector in the Eighties: Economic Performance, Partisan Responses, and Divided Governments." *British Journal of Political Science* 27:473–96.

———. 2001. "Democracy, Development, and the Public Sector." *American Journal of Political Science* 45:1–17.

Boix, Carles, and Sebastian Rosato. 2001. Political Regimes across the World 1800–2000: A Comprehensive Data Base. University of Chicago.

Brennan, Geoffrey, and James M. Buchanan. 1980. *The Power to Tax: Analytical Foundations of a Fiscal Constitution*. Cambridge, U.K.: Cambridge University Press.

Cameron, David R. 1978. "The Expansion of the Public Economy: A Comparative Analysis." *American Political Science Review* 72:1243–61.

Cox, Gary W. 1997. *Making Votes Count: Strategic Coordination in the World's Electoral Systems*. New York: Cambridge University Press.

Deininger, Klaus, and Lyn Squire. 1996. "A New Data Set Measuring Income Inequality." *The World Bank Economic Review* 19(3):565–91.

Downes, Alexander. 2000. "Federalism and Ethnic Conflict." University of Chicago. Processed.

Esping-Andersen, Gösta. 1990. *The Three Worlds of Welfare Capitalism*. Cambridge, U.K.: Polity Press.

Flora, Peter, and Jan Alber. 1981. "Modernization, Democratization, and the Development of Welfare States in Western Europe." In Peter Flora and Arnold J. Heidenheimer, eds., *The Development of Welfare States in Europe and America*. New Brunswick, N.J.: Transaction Books.

Franklin, Mark N. 1996. "Electoral Participation." In Lawrence LeDuc, Richard G. Niemi, and Pippa Norris, eds., *Comparing Democracies: Elections and Voting in Global Perspective*. Thousand Oaks, Calif.: Sage Publications.

Franzese, Robert. 2002. *Macroeconomic Policies of Developed Democracies*. Cambridge, U.K.: Cambridge University Press.

Frieden, Jeffry A. 1991. *Debt, Development, and Democracy: Modern Political Economy and Latin America, 1965–1985*. Princeton, N.J.: Princeton University Press.

Garrett, Geoffrey. 1998. "Governing in the Global Economy: Economic Policy and Market Integration around the World." Yale University. Processed.

———. 2001. "The Distributive Consequences of Globalization." Yale University. Processed.

Grilli, Vittorio, Donato Masciandaro, and Guido Tabellini. 1991. "Political and Monetary Institutions and Public Financial Policies in the Industrial Countries." *Economic Policy* 13:341–92.

Haggard, Stephan. 1990. *Pathways from the Periphery*. Ithaca, N.Y.: Cornell University Press.

Hallerberg, Mark, and Scott Basinger. 1998. "Internationalization and Changes in Tax Policy in OECD Countries: The Importance of Domestic Veto Players." *Comparative Political Studies* 31:321–52.

———. 1999. "Globalization and Tax Reform: An Updated Case for the Importance of Veto Players." *Politische Vierteljahresschrift* 40:618–27.

Heston, Alan, Robert Summers, and Bettina Aten. 2002. *Penn World Table Version 6.1*. Philadelphia: Center for International Comparisons, University of Pennsylvania.

Hicks, Alexander M. 1999. *Social Democracy and Welfare Capitalism: A Century of Income Security Politics*. Ithaca, N.Y.: Cornell University Press.

Hirschman, Albert O. 1981. "Exit, Voice, and the State." In Albert O. Hirschman, ed., *Essays in Trespassing: Economics to Politics and Beyond*. Cambridge, U.K.: Cambridge University Press.

Holsey, Cheryl M., and Thomas E. Borcherding. 1997. "Why Does Government's Share of National Income Grow? An Assessment of the Recent Literature on the U.S. Experience." In Dennis C. Mueller, ed., *Perspectives on Public Choice: A Handbook*. New York: Cambridge University Press.

Huber, John, and G. B. Powell. 1994. "Congruence between Citizens and Policymakers in Two Visions of Liberal Democracy." *World Politics* 46(April):291–326.

IDEA (International Institute for Democracy and Electoral Assistance). 1997. *Voter Turnout from 1945 to 1997: A Global Report on Political Participation*. Stockholm.

IMF (International Monetary Fund). Various years. *Government Finance Statistics Yearbook*. Washington, D.C.

Katzenstein, Peter. 1985. *Small States in World Markets: Industrial Policy in Europe*. Ithaca, N.Y.: Cornell University Press.

Keesing's Contemporary Archives. Various years. [Yearly publication since 1931.] London: Keesing's Limited.

Korpi, Walter. 1989. "Power, Politics, and State Autonomy in the Development of Social Citizenship: Social Rights during Sickness in Eighteen OECD Countries since 1930s." *American Sociological Review* 54:309–28.

Linz, Juan J., and Arturo Valenzuela. 1994. *The Failure of Presidential Democracy. Volume 1: Comparative Perspectives*. Baltimore, Md.: Johns Hopkins University Press.

Lybeck, Johan A. 1988. "Comparing Government Growth Rates: The Non-Institutional vs. the Institutional Approach." In Johan A. Lybeck and Magnus Henkerson, eds., *Explaining the Growth of Government*. Amsterdam: North-Holland.

Meltzer, Allan H., and Scott F. Richards. 1981. "A Rational Theory of the Size of Government." *Journal of Political Economy* 89:914–27.

Moene, Karl Ove, and Michael Wallerstein. 2001. "Inequality, Social Insurance, and Redistribution." *American Political Science Review* 95(December):859–74.

Moss, David. 2001. *When All Else Fails*. Cambridge, Mass.: Harvard University Press.

Niskanen, William A., Jr. 1971. *Bureaucracy and Representative Government*. Chicago: Aldine-Atherton.

OECD (Organisation for Economic Co-operation and Development). 2000. *Economic Survey of Korea*. Paris.

Olson, Mancur. 1993. "Dictatorship, Democracy, and Development." *American Political Science Review* 87:567–76.

Peacock, Alan T., and Jack Wiseman. 1961. *The Growth of Government Expenditures in the United Kingdom*. Princeton, N.J.: Princeton University Press.

Perotti, Roberto. 1996. "Growth, Income Distribution, and Democracy: What the Data Say." *Journal of Economic Growth* 1:149–87.

Persson, Torsten, and Guido Tabellini. 2000. *Political Economics: Explaining Economic Policy*. Cambridge, Mass.: MIT Press.

Powell, G. Bingham. 2000. *Elections as Instruments of Democracy: Majoritarian and Proportional Visions*. New Haven, Conn.: Yale University Press.

Przeworski, Adam, and Fernando Limongi. 1993. "Political Regimes and Economic Growth." *Journal of Economic Perspectives* 7(3):51–69.

Przeworski, Adam, and Michael Wallerstein. 1988. "Structural Dependence of the State on Capital." *American Political Science Review* 82:11–30.

Przeworski, Adam, Mike Alvarez, José Antonio Cheibub, and Fernando Limongi. 2000. *Democracy and Development*. New York: Cambridge University Press.

Rodden, Jonathan. 2000. "Reviving Leviathan: Fiscal Federalism and the Growth of Government." Department of Political Science, Massachusetts Institute of Technology, Cambridge. Processed.

———. 2001. "The Dilemma of Fiscal Federalism: Grants and Fiscal Performance around the World." Department of Political Science, Massachusetts Institute of Technology, Cambridge. Processed.

Rodriguez Caballero, Francisco. 1998. "Essays on the Political Economy of Inequality, Redistribution, and Growth." Department of Economics, Harvard University, Cambridge, Mass. Processed.

Rodrik, Dani. 1998. "Why Do Open Economies Have Bigger Governments?" *Journal of Political Economy* 106(5):997–1032.

Rosenstone, Steven J., and John Mark Hansen. 1993. *Mobilization, Participation, and Democracy in America.* New York: Macmillan.

Shepsle, Kenneth A., and Barry R. Weingast. 1981. "Political Preferences for the Pork Barrel: A Generalization." *American Journal of Political Science* 25(February):96–111.

Shugart, Matthew S., and John M. Carey. 1992. *Presidents and Assemblies: Constitutional Design and Electoral Dynamics.* New York: Cambridge University Press.

UN (United Nations). Various years. *United Nations National Accounts.* New York.

Wagner, Adolph. 1883. *Finanzwissenschaft.* Translated and reprinted as "Three Extracts on Public Finance." In Richard A. Musgrave and Alan T. Peacock, eds., *Classics on the Theory of Public Finance.* London: Macmillan, 1962.

Weingast, Barry. 1995. "The Economic Role of Political Institutions. Market-Preserving Federalism and Economic Development." *Journal of Law, Economics, and Organization* 11(April):1–31.

Wilensky, Harold L. 1975. *The Welfare State and Equality.* Berkeley, Calif.: University of California Press.

———. 2002. *Rich Democracies: Political Economy, Public Policy, and Performance.* Berkeley, Calif.: University of California Press.

World Bank. 1998. *Indonesia Public Expenditure Review.* Report No. 18691-IND. October 7. Washington, D.C.

———. 1999. *World Development Report of 1999.* New York: Oxford University Press.

———. 2000. *China: Managing Public Expenditures for Better Results.* Report No. 20342-CHA. April 25. Washington, D.C.

CHAPTER 7

CORPORATE GOVERNANCE, INDUSTRIAL POLICY, AND THE RULE OF LAW

Dwight H. Perkins

The 1997–98 crisis, the continuing shift from state to market, democratization, the stress on accountability, and the recent focus on competition and competition law have directed attention to the need for corporate reform in East Asia. Indeed, "reform corporate governance" has become the current mantra both within the region and outside it. Crony capitalism is seen as the structural flaw that laid low the four crisis-hit countries and that caused a decade and more of economic stagnation in Japan. Some fear that China's economy could go the way of Japan or even Indonesia if timely steps are not taken to correct major flaws in corporate governance there.

As this chapter will argue, there is real reason for concern about the way Asian corporations are governed, but much of this concern is taken out of the concrete historical and institutional context in which Asia's current system of corporate governance arose. A common approach is to look at corporate governance practices in North America and Western Europe and then compare those practices with the way business is done in Asia. Reformers analyze the strengths and weaknesses of these practices in postindustrial market economies and then attempt to apply the lessons learned to Asia.

The core concern of the literature on corporate finance in the United States and Europe is how to protect owners of companies, particularly

This chapter has benefited from discussions with and the comments of Shahid Yusuf, William Alford, Richard Cooper, Andrei Shleifer, and Jeremy Stein, plus other members of the workshops where this material has been presented. The author is solely responsible for the conclusions reached here.

minority shareholders, from the predations of corporate managers (Shleifer and Vishny 1997). As the current scandals in the United States with respect to stock options make clear, company managers are often in a position to divert a sizable portion of companies' assets into their own pockets. When this happens on a broad enough scale, minority owners will withdraw their funds from the capital markets or at least from those parts of the markets that deal in equities. Equity market development is thus stunted—and weak equity markets, in turn, slow the development of new companies and the expansion of old ones.

The approach to reform, therefore, was to introduce new laws to protect minority shareholders that would be enforced by an independent judiciary. Alternatively, one could substitute an independent government regulatory agency for the courts, an agency governed by rules rather than by the discretionary judgment of the executive branch of government. Regulatory agencies would substitute for or displace the courts in settling disputes and overseeing bankruptcies and mergers. Such a shift in emphasis occurred in the United States at the end of the nineteenth century and continued into the twentieth century. The belief was that regulatory agencies would administer fairer judgments than the courts because the decisions of the courts could too easily be subverted by the inequality of power that existed between the large corporations that for the most part were the source of the violations and the individuals and small companies that were the victims.[1]

This Western literature on corporate finance does contain many lessons of relevance to the reform process in East Asia. But this Western literature also relies on a number of critical assumptions that make it difficult to apply the rules derived from the analysis without first making a number of major adjustments or additions. First, most analysis of the economies of North America and much of Western Europe assumes that government sets the rules that govern markets but that government does not directly interfere with the functioning of those markets on a regular and discretionary basis. The role of government is to make and enforce the rules, not to decide where industrial investments should be made or how they should be financed. Second, as already pointed out, when rules are violated by companies or individuals, it is the legal system or an independent regulatory agency that is called on to redress the situation, not the prime minister or the minister of planning or finance.

These two critical assumptions about the role of the government and the presence of an efficient and independent judiciary or regulatory agency

---

1. This topic is discussed at length and the argument formalized with a model in Glaeser and Shleifer (2001).

are consistently not applicable in most of East and Southeast Asia. As will be discussed at length later, governments in East Asia have frequently taken the lead in promoting particular industries and even particular companies. Nor do most of the countries in East and Southeast Asia have efficient and independent legal systems or regulatory agencies. The legal and regulatory systems—except in Hong Kong (China) and, to a degree, Singapore—are weak and easily manipulated by the executive branch of the government and, in the worst cases, by anyone with money to bribe judges. Activist government industrial policies and weak judiciaries have a direct bearing on how the countries of East Asia must proceed if they are to achieve meaningful reform of corporate governance in the region. Reform is not just or even primarily a question of passing new laws, although some new laws are needed. The real challenge is to create the institutions that will enforce those laws efficiently and fairly. Creating such institutions will require a fundamental rethinking of the role of government in the economies of the countries in the region.

This chapter begins, therefore, with a discussion of how the institutions governing the economies of East and Southeast Asia developed over the past century. That historical experience has generated institutional structures that were a reasonable response to the requirements of the period when they were created but, in many cases, are barriers to progress today. This historical overview, therefore, helps define what many of these countries must do to restructure their industries and systems of economic governance. With the problems thus defined, the chapter then returns to the question of the best ways to correct the structural weaknesses that have become so apparent in recent years.

THE HISTORICAL BACKGROUND

Before World War II, most businesses in East Asia, other than a few large European, Japanese, and U.S. corporations with investments in the region, were family owned and managed. Outside of Japan, stock markets did not exist and minority shareholders of Asian firms, if any, typically had close personal ties to the owner. Contract disputes among Asian-owned firms—mostly overseas Chinese firms in Southeast Asia and Chinese-owned firms in China, Hong Kong (China), and Taiwan (China)—were rarely settled through the courts. There were good reasons for overseas Chinese and the local populations to avoid the courts in colonial Asia. The courts were run mostly by the colonial powers and for the colonial elite. In China, local magistrates also had little interest in creating a fair and efficient court system for resolving local business disputes.

As Ronald Coase has argued, firms will contract with each other in ways that meet their needs without recourse to a legal system as long as contract enforcement costs are negligible. This was the pattern in Asia even though enforcement costs were not negligible. Firms relied on personal ties of trust that were based on family and family-like regional ties and guilds. Breaches of that trust led to ostracism, in effect making it impossible to do business, or, if ostracism proved unworkable, to the threat of physical harm to the wrongdoer or to the wrongdoer's family by privately controlled thugs. The Shanxi bankers of Qing Dynasty China, for example, had bank offices manned by Shanxi people throughout the empire. As protection against malfeasance by bank managers, their families back in Shanxi were, in effect, held as hostages.

In the first decade or two after independence from colonialism, this mode of doing business continued in most of Southeast Asia plus Taiwan (China) and the Republic of Korea. Locally owned firms remained small and family run. Banks, for the most part, confined their lending to short-term letters of credit and other trade-related loans. The risk of lending for longer-term investments was simply too great. Stock markets, where they existed at all, listed the shares of only a handful of mostly foreign-owned firms that had continued on from the colonial era. Locally owned firms relied for capital on retained earnings and the extended family.

By the 1960s and 1970s, however, government leadership in East and Southeast Asia had been transferred, sometimes violently, from the immediate postcolonial generation—most of that generation had little interest in or knowledge about economic development—to individuals who saw government direction as the means of steering their economies on the road to becoming modern industrial states.[2] The inspiration for this activist role, in part at least, was Japan, where the Ministry of International Trade and Industry (MITI) was seen as the architect of Japan's postwar economic boom (Johnson 1983). Alongside the success of the Japanese experience and the perceived success of the far more radical, state-orchestrated interventionist approach of the Soviet Union, there was widespread faith throughout the developing world in the efficacy of government intervention to accelerate economic development, in general, and industrial development, in particular. Except in Hong Kong (China) and, to a lesser degree, Singapore, therefore, activist governments in East Asia began to own or dominate the banking systems and worked closely with these banks and favored local firms to promote industrialization. In

---

2. In some cases, as in Singapore and, to a degree, Taiwan, China, it was the first generation of postcolonial leaders who presided over the shift to an activist industrial policy.

the cases of China and Vietnam, the governments went even further by erasing the private sector and filling the void with government-owned and -directed industrial and commercial enterprises.

The financing of industrial development came increasingly from the banking system and was directed toward projects favored by government policymakers. In the cases of Indonesia, the Republic of Korea, and Taiwan (China), not to mention China and Vietnam, the banks were government owned as well as directed. In Malaysia and Thailand, as in Japan, the banks and nonbank financial institutions were mostly private but were responsive to government direction. Only in Hong Kong, China, could one say that the banks were independent of the government and made their lending decisions largely on the basis of commercial criteria. Although local stock market development commenced in the 1960s and nonbank financial institutions were started or expanded, the role of those institutions in the capital markets of the region remained small relative to the banks and self-financing.[3]

There was considerable variation within Asia and over time in the way activist governments intervened in the economy. At one end of the spectrum were the centrally planned command economies of China, Vietnam, and the Democratic People's Republic of Korea. A planning commission at either the central or the provincial level decided what each enterprise was to produce and what inputs were to be allocated to that enterprise to allow it to meet its output targets. Inputs were allocated administratively and could not be obtained on any legal market. Enterprises, which usually oversaw only a single factory, were really the lowest-level bureaus of a large hierarchy dominated by ministries, with the planning commission at the top. Plant or enterprise managers were more like lower-level government bureaucrats than businesspeople. The role of the financial system, mainly the mono-bank that combined commercial and central bank functions, was to monitor and enforce the plan. Banks had no independent authority to decide whether to lend to an enterprise. If the enterprise was doing what was called for in the plan, it got the financing it needed.

When China and Vietnam began to convert from a centrally planned command system to a market system, they retained many of the structures of the old system. Enterprises, as defined in the old system, became the independent enterprises of the market system. The resulting industrial organization structures, as will be discussed below, were the least concentrated industrial structures in Asia. Clearly these structures had to be changed to make them suitable for competition in a market-based system,

---

3. This situation mimicked the experience of industrial countries (see Stiglitz and Yusuf 2001).

but how and by whom? The mono-bank in China was broken up into a central bank and four large commercial banks, but those four banks continued to lend money the way the mono-bank did under the old system. If a powerful politician thought that they should lend to a particular enterprise, they did so.

The industrial policies of the other economies of East Asia did not go to the extreme of socialist central planning, but the government was heavily involved in industrial decisions nonetheless. The feature that Indonesia, Malaysia, the Republic of Korea, Taiwan (China), and Thailand had in common was the government's role in supporting certain industries over others. Korea and Taiwan, China, were first off the mark with policies in the 1960s that supported manufacturing firms that were successful in promoting exports abroad. Those firms got access to scarce foreign exchange, to bank loans at favorable rates, and to other subsidies such as generous wastage allowances. By the 1970s, both Korea and Taiwan, China, began a major effort to promote what they conceived to be key heavy industries: steel, machinery, and petrochemicals. Individual private (and some public) firms in Korea were designated by the government to carry out the heavy industry plan. These firms received favored access to credit and foreign exchange, sometimes a monopoly over the domestic Korean market, and heavily subsidized infrastructure support. In the case of Taiwan, China, mainly government-owned enterprises carried out the initial phases of the heavy industry drive, because the government believed that the business community in Taiwan, China, lacked the education and experience for the job. In 1974, when the heavy industry drive was just under way in Taiwan, China, only 16 percent of the central figures of the 100 largest business groups had a university education (Hsueh, Hsu, and Perkins 2001, p. 101). Korean industrial policies led to an industrial organization structure dominated by a few large conglomerates or *chaebol*. In Taiwan, China, there was a dual industrial organization structure before the 1990s, in which the state often owned large enterprises while most private enterprises were small. From the 1980s onward, the Korean government saw the problem as one of how to break up the largest chaebol in order to create a level playing field for everyone else. In Taiwan, China, the government reluctantly began to privatize the large state-owned firms.

The situation in Indonesia and Malaysia was similar in some respects and different in others. In both countries in the 1970s and 1980s, the governments began a drive to create heavy industries in the steel, automobile, and petrochemical sectors. In both countries as well, the goal was to have those firms as much as possible in the hands of the *bumiputera*, the indigenous population, rather than in the hands of foreigners or the local

Chinese. Thus, both countries began their heavy industry efforts with state-owned enterprises because private bumiputera with the necessary experience and resources did not then exist. But these state-owned enterprises, unlike those in Taiwan (China) and Korea, were often highly inefficient. Malaysia then privatized these enterprises, but it did so in a way that ensured that bumiputera would end up in control. Because few bumiputera had the financial resources to buy large automobile and telecommunication enterprises, the government used its control of some of the biggest banks to provide them with the necessary financing.

Thailand, in the initial phases of its postwar development effort, sometimes relied on new firms with key ties to the military. Those ties guaranteed the firms support from the military-dominated governments. Later, Thailand turned more to foreign direct investment, particularly from Japan, to fuel its industrial drive. Industrial policy was then geared toward creating a favorable climate for such investment. Singapore and Hong Kong, China, relied heavily on foreign direct investment for industrialization as well, but Singapore also made extensive use of state-owned enterprises in sectors in which foreigners either were not wanted or could not be attracted. Hong Kong, China, came the closest to being an economy with no government intervention to promote particular firms and industries, but even there the government and the big property developers worked closely together to ensure that property prices remained high.

This brief review of the interventionist industrial policies of the various Asian governments is designed to make two simple points. First, in all or almost all of the economies in the region, there were close ties between the larger enterprises and the government. In some cases, those ties involved direct government ownership, whereas in other cases, the ownership was private but key guidance came from the government. Clearly this situation created problems for the government as a neutral arbiter of business conflicts. Often the government was an active supporter of particular enterprises and their management. Few Asian governments saw their role as one of protecting minority shareholders.

Second, the close government-business ties also created industrial organization structures that did not necessarily reflect market forces. This situation presented the governments with a dilemma. When the countries moved toward greater reliance on market forces, they still had to face the question of what to do about those existing structures. Should they let the existing structures continue, or should they try to break up those deemed to be overconcentrated and consolidate those deemed to be too fragmented? And if the decision was to change the structures, who had the responsibility and authority to implement those changes? Was it the enterprise management or the government? And if the government was going to do the job, how could it then say that its objective was to create a true market system in which the government was only the enforcer of the rule of law, not the director of industrial investment decisions?

REFORMING CORPORATE GOVERNANCE

As already indicated, the main body of the corporate finance literature is concerned with agency problems of how to protect investors from the predations of managers. Closely related is the literature's concern with how suppliers of a firm's capital can ensure that they get some return on their investment rather than see the entire return appropriated by these same managers (Shleifer and Vishny 1997), especially in circumstances where financial reporting and auditing standards are low.[4] Absent these assurances, it is difficult to develop capital markets, particularly stock markets, if most of the participants typically are minority shareholders. But as the discussion above indicates, for most of the private firms in East Asia through the 1960s the suppliers of capital and the managers were one and the same. Minority shareholders, if they existed at all, relied for protection of their investment on personal ties to the owner-manager.

This system, however, was changing, and some separation of investors from management was gradually becoming a reality by the 1970s and thereafter. The number of firms listed on the various national stock exchanges and the total value of listed stock owned expanded, starting in Japan. From the 1980s onward, Japanese firms began reducing their dependence on banks (Stulz 2001).[5] Family control in countries such as the Republic of Korea was maintained by cross-shareholding within a group of companies, and Korea is by no means an extreme case, as can be seen from table 7.1.[6] The rapid expansion in the value of the shares listed on the stock exchanges in Hong Kong (China), Malaysia, Taiwan (China), and Thailand is enlarging the role of minority shareholders in the financing of East Asian firms. However, except for a few very large minority shareholders, most

---

4. A survey by McKinsey and Co. (Coombes and Watson 2000) showed that investors were willing to pay a 20 percent premium for a well-governed company in Taiwan, China, but a 27 percent premium for a well-governed firm in Indonesia. This finding reflects the quality of financial information and strictness of accounting practices.

5. This trend is part of a wider phenomenon that is spurred by the development of information and communications technology. The new technology is making it easier for firms and households to tap the securities markets because of the greater ease of unbundling risks, securitization, and trading of financial products on electronic exchanges (see Mishkin and Strahan 1999).

6. It should be noted that most publicly traded firms worldwide are family controlled, including such large firms as Wal-Mart and Ford in the United States (Burkart, Panunzi, and Shleifer 2002).

Table 7.1 Control of Publicly Traded Companies in East Asia, 1996

Cutoff for voting rights of the largest shareholder	Number of corporations in the sample	Share of corporations under ultimate control	Distribution of ultimate control			
			Family	State	Widely held financial institution	Widely held corporation
10 percent cutoff						
Hong Kong, China	330	99.4	64.7	3.7	7.1	23.9
Indonesia	178	99.4	68.6	10.2	3.8	16.8
Japan	1,240	58.0	13.1	1.1	38.5	5.3
Korea, Rep. of	345	85.7	67.9	5.1	3.5	9.2
Malaysia	238	99.0	57.5	18.2	12.1	11.2
Philippines	120	98.4	42.1	3.6	16.8	35.9
Singapore	221	98.6	52.0	23.6	10.8	12.2
Taiwan, China	141	97.1	65.6	3.0	10.4	18.1
Thailand	167	97.9	56.5	7.5	12.8	21.1
20 percent cutoff						
Hong Kong, China	330	93.1	66.7	1.4	5.2	19.8
Indonesia	178	94.9	71.5	8.2	2.0	13.2
Japan	1,240	20.2	9.7	0.8	6.5	3.2
Korea, Rep. of	345	56.8	48.4	1.6	0.7	6.1
Malaysia	238	89.6	67.2	13.4	2.3	6.7
Philippines	120	80.9	44.6	2.1	7.5	26.7
Singapore	221	84.5	55.4	23.5	4.1	11.5
Taiwan, China	141	73.7	48.2	2.8	5.3	17.4
Thailand	167	93.5	61.6	8.0	8.6	15.3

Note: The table reports the aggregate statistics on the distribution of ultimate control among four ownership groups. The ultimate control is studied at two cutoff levels—10 and 20 percent of voting rights—to show differences in the concentration of control in individual firms.
Source: Claessens and others (1999).

Asian minority shareholders had few rights that were effectively protected by law or government regulation through the 1990s. Companies were run by and for the controlling families, for the most part, and other shareholders could only hope that some of the gains in corporate value that were being achieved would be transferred to them (Backman 1999).

In China, the majority shareholder in most listed companies was not a family but the state itself. Minority shareholders in China, for all practical purposes, did not even have the right to select boards of directors or to hire and fire management. That power remained firmly in the hands of the government and the Communist Party. Portfolio investment from North America and Europe flowing into these stock markets in the late 1980s and 1990s did not noticeably change this indifference toward minority shareholder rights.[7] In the few cases in Asia where minority

---

7. By the late 1990s, minority shareholders in both Japan and Korea had begun to voice their concerns, stung in part by the 1997–98 crisis (Schultz 2001).

shareholder rights were observed, as in the shares held by bumiputera individuals in Malaysia, those rights derived from the political power of the bumiputera, not from protections in the law.

Many minority shareholder rights are inherently difficult to enforce even when there is a will on the part of the government or relevant regulatory agencies. Insider trading, for example, is rampant in Asia, as far as one can tell, but even the United States falls far short of complete enforcement in this area. Corporate accounting practices in Asia also leave large amounts of room for maneuver on the part of management at the expense of shareholders. Improving the accounting system of most Asian economies is clearly a high priority throughout the region, but dubious accounting practices are still a problem in the United States, as recent scandals have demonstrated. Still, many firms in Asia continue to operate with two sets of books, only one of which, usually the doctored one, is available for inspection by the public or the tax authorities.

If minority shareholders continue, at the beginning of the twenty-first century, to possess few rights and little is being done to enhance those rights, the same cannot be said of capital being supplied by banks and others in the form of credit. Steps are being taken to better protect the rights of creditors, but there is still a long way to go before an adequate system is in place. The key to reform in this area involves strengthening bankruptcy procedures.

The Asian financial crisis of 1997–98 revealed widespread weaknesses in the operation of bankruptcy laws and procedures in the most affected countries. Banks and other creditors, both foreign and domestic, found that the existing laws often did little to protect them. Nor did the laws provide reliable procedures for the insolvent firms to work their way out of the crisis or to be liquidated ("Southeast Asia Bankruptcy Law" 2000). Unlike the case of minority shareholder rights, however, ongoing efforts have been made to strengthen bankruptcy laws and procedures in the region, beginning in 1998.

Good bankruptcy legislation is designed to improve the efficiency of the economic system by facilitating the exit of failed firms and paying off creditors in the process, while giving firms that are viable over the long run the opportunity to restructure their finances and make other changes that will restore them to economic health. Closing failed firms is important not only to eliminate business units that drain the country's resources; the example of these closures also discourages other firms not yet in trouble from risky behavior.

Good bankruptcy legislation must first be transparent, in the sense that legal rules for dealing with the insolvency of a firm must be clear and sophisticated. Such legislation should also define precise guidelines about "procedure, proof, notification, time and appeals" ("Southeast Asia Bankruptcy Law" 2000). If the legislation meets these criteria (and sometimes it does not because of the inexperience of those drafting the laws), creditors and firms will know how to play the workout game. This knowledge will reduce strategic behavior on the part of stakeholders that delays and distorts the process. Long-delayed workouts will typically lead to a reduction in the value of assets, and one way to avoid this reduction is to keep the procedures as simple as possible. Another way to shorten the process is to set time limits for the completion of various components. Since the financial crisis, such time limits have been introduced in Indonesia, Korea, and Thailand.

Transparency, however, involves more than good laws. The courts must be consistent in applying those laws to various insolvency situations. In this respect, among the Asian economies considered here, Hong Kong (China) and Singapore have the best-developed legal infrastructure, and Malaysia, too, has had a workable system in place for decades (Pistor and Wellons 1998). Indonesia, Korea, and Thailand have changed their insolvency laws substantially since the financial crisis, but in Indonesia (and the Philippines), the inconsistency and outright corruption of the courts seriously undermine the transparency that the new laws are designed to achieve.[8] The nature of the courts and the rule of law in the various East Asian economies are topics that we shall return to at length in the final part of this chapter.

Another problem with the bankruptcy process in Asia is that the courts have little experience with corporate insolvency processes, and acquiring the necessary knowledge is not a simple matter. Particularly if a firm is large and complex, it can be a daunting challenge for judges with little experience in the area to determine the conditions under which the firm is to be allowed to continue in operation and to restructure itself back to financial health. Outright liquidation of the firm is a less complex task, but it still requires specific expertise. In 1999, Thailand established a separate Bankruptcy Court. In 1998, in Indonesia, the bankruptcy law (dating back to 1911) was revised and four additional commercial courts—with 45 specially trained judges—were created to relieve the burden of insolvency cases on the existing courts ("Law Set to Push Indonesian Debtors over the Edge" 1998).[9] Korea has a specialized division within each district

---

8. This discussion of bankruptcy legislation, including the paragraphs that follow, is largely based on the essay of Nam and Oh (2001).

9. Linnan (1999) has examined the early, halting efforts to implement the Indonesian bankruptcy legislation. In its first year of operation, these efforts had yielded few results. The few voluntary debt reorganizations that they prompted involved mainly debt rescheduling and not much in the way of restructuring.

court that is responsible for insolvency proceedings (Nam and Oh 2001, p. 53).

Other East Asian countries are also struggling with the reform of their bankruptcy procedures. China has had bankruptcy legislation on the books since 1986, but it was only after 1997 that the government actually began to liquidate and reorganize a large number of mostly small and medium-size enterprises. State-owned enterprises, in particular, were kept afloat even when they ran losses year after year and clearly were unable to repay their bank loans. When the government did decide to close some firms and to force the merger of others with more successful enterprises, the decisions were not made by the courts, nor were they made with due regard for correct legal process. The executive branch of the government, using both economic and political criteria, made the decisions. Much the same approach to liquidating provincially owned firms was followed in Vietnam in the early 1990s. Given the weakness of the courts and the absence of alternative mechanisms for handling these decisions, the governments had little choice but to intervene, but government ministries were ill equipped to handle the process well.

The Chinese and Vietnamese cases illustrate another critical criterion for judging whether bankruptcy procedures are fair and efficient. When the executive branch of the government controls the workout or liquidation process, it is highly unlikely that the process will be transparent, although it may be quick. Even when the courts are involved, however, there is still the question of whether court orders are enforceable. Malaysia's courts generally have been effective in enforcing insolvency decisions, although not as effective as Singapore's courts. Korea also now has reliable enforcement mechanisms and has even been able to take on the restructuring and liquidation of large conglomerates such as Daewoo and Hyundai, although these giant company workouts involved more than the courts. Thailand, in contrast, had so many insolvency cases in the wake of the financial crisis that the courts were overwhelmed and timely disposal of the cases was undermined. In Indonesia, not surprisingly given the state of the legal system, bankruptcy enforcement has ranged from weak to nonexistent (Backman 1999; Nam and Oh 2001).

Enforcement is really the central issue in most legislation related to corporate governance. If the laws are ignored or cannot be enforced, the legislation has little practical value, at least in the short run. The enforcement of corporate governance legislation in general and of bankruptcy legislation in particular is not just a question of whether the legal institutions are capable of administering an economic system that is based on the rule of law. The system may well be able to handle most routine contract disputes and still be unable to deal with major bankruptcy cases.

A basic problem in the enforcement of bankruptcy legislation derives from the kinds of industrial policies pursued by many of the economies in the region. As noted above, most East Asian economies pursued industrial policies that involved the executive branch of the government targeting particular sectors and even particular firms for development. In seeking to promote a particular industry, the government not only eased access to foreign exchange, if foreign exchange availability was controlled, but also offered other supportive measures, such as favorable tax treatment and tariff protection. Most of all, governments used their power over the banks to direct credit to those firms.

Governments thus entered into implicit contracts to support the large firms that were chosen to implement their industrial development goals.[10] The nature of this support was generally not made explicit through legislation or formal contracts, but it was no less real. With such arrangements, the implied support does not end when the firm gets into trouble. If firms are to proceed with confidence to carry out the government's wishes, they must also be reasonably sure that, after the government helps them launch the targeted industrial ventures, it will come to their assistance if the projects fail. Failure, after all, may result for reasons having little to do with the management skills of the firm itself—the government's basic idea may have been flawed from the start.

A government that wants to shore up a troubled firm can always rely on taxpayer-financed subsidies, but such subsidies can give rise to political problems. It is generally easier to instruct the government-controlled banks to provide bridging financing. Industrial policies, therefore, not only result in weak industrial firms but also saddle the banking system with nonperforming assets. The implication of industrial policy for bankruptcy processes is unavoidable. Whatever creditors may want the courts to do to recover some of the resources the creditors have lent, the executive branch of the government has an obligation to override those decisions for firms that have done the government's bidding.

The experience of the Republic of Korea illustrates the problem.[11] During the heavy industry and chemical industry drive of the 1970s, the Korean government went to great lengths to ensure the successful development of selected industries and firms, including the large-scale diversion of bank credit to those firms (Kim 1997; Stern and others 1995). Many of the industries so promoted were successful, but some were not, and the new Korean government of the early 1980s was forced to wrestle

---

10. On some of the dealings between officials and chaebol, see Kirk (1999).
11. See, for example, Krueger and Yoo (2001).

with the failures. In the majority of cases, the government decided to continue financing the unsuccessful industries while they were being restructured and, often, put under new management. The process was handled not by the courts but by the executive branch of the government.

In the 1980s and the 1990s, Korea began to try to move away from industrial targeting,[12] but past commitments made it difficult for the government to relinquish all responsibility, especially after the 1997–98 financial crisis. Largely because of the crisis, Korea, by then a democracy, elected a president, Kim Dae Jung, who had no personal or political obligations to the existing industrial arrangements and who expressed a strong desire to see the Korean chaebol restructured and dismantled. He also had to find a way to refinance the banks, most of which were in trouble both because of the financial crisis and because of decades of often misconceived government direction. The challenge facing the government with regard to industrial restructuring was how to enforce its plans. The answer, not surprisingly, was to rely on the government's control of the banks, which was greatly enlarged following the virtual takeover of many of the leading banks by the authorities following the crisis (Kirk 1999). The chaebol, most of which were deeply in debt and basically insolvent, had to turn to the banks for refinancing. Refinancing was made available only if the industrial firms were prepared to make major efforts to implement the government's restructuring objectives. Thus, the intention to create a market economy in which all firms competed on a level playing field and to discontinue industrial policies faltered, and policies tended to return to the interventionist industrial regime of the past.

The eventual goal of the Korean government is to end such *dirigisme*, but it remains to be seen whether successor governments will be willing to let the market and the courts handle company workouts in the future. If the government does succeed in removing itself from the center of these decisions, the various new laws on bankruptcy and minority shareholder rights will, with the support of the courts, become meaningful. The issue of whether the government should continue to try to shape the development of the large conglomerates became important in the presidential election at the end of 2002 and has yet to be resolved.

The evolution of Korean industrial policies and their relationship to bankruptcy and other corporate governance issues is not unique in East

---

12. After peaking in the 1970s during the heavy industry and chemical industry drive (as high as 19 percent), the share of preferential loans from deposit money banks to total loans declined. During the latter half of the 1990s, preferential loans accounted for only a small share (2–3 percent) of total loans (Krueger and Yoo 2001).

Asia. Since at least the mid-1980s, Taiwan, China, has been trying to relinquish industrial targeting and move toward market-determined industrial outcomes.[13] Taiwan, China, has had one advantage over Korea in this regard: many of its industrial enterprises were quite small and not subject to micromanagement by government. When the government did pursue targeted industrial policies, it tended, as already noted, to rely mainly on state-owned enterprises supported by favored treatment from the largely state-owned banks. As the government has disengaged from targeted interventionist policies, the role of corporate governance legislation and the courts has taken on greater significance.

Malaysia has been more reluctant to move away from targeted industrial policies, and the aftermath of the financial crisis has been marked by major executive branch efforts to restructure both the banks and some of the government-favored firms, firms that are mainly but not exclusively owned by newly wealthy bumiputera businesspeople. However, for smaller firms and more generally for firms owned by Malaysian-Chinese—most of which do not receive assistance from the government—the bankruptcy laws and the courts are largely in charge of the workout or liquidation processes where needed. In China and Vietnam, as indicated above, the executive branch of the government, at both the national and provincial levels, is in charge.

Rewriting bankruptcy legislation is, thus, only the first step in moving the economies of East and Southeast Asia to a rule- or law-based system of corporate governance. Enforcement of that legislation by suitably empowered entities is the next step. Even where the courts are reasonably effective, the interventionist industrial policies of the past continue to involve the executive branch of the government in deciding these issues. Executive branch decisionmaking is inevitably far more discretionary and less rule based than the rulings of the legal system. Conceivably, these governments could create special regulatory bodies to handle bankruptcies and other disputes related to corporate governance, but these bodies, if they are to be rule based and effective, would really be performing what in essence is a judicial function.

The logic inducing a shift from discretionary economic intervention by the executive branch is reasonably straightforward, but that does not make it easy to translate into practice. There is also a political logic that makes it difficult to pursue these desirable economic objectives. Discretionary interventions in industrial policy not only create opportunities for individual

---

13. For a discussion of these changes in policies, see Hsueh, Hsu, and Perkins (2001). The industrial policies of the pre-1986 period are also discussed at length in Wade (1990).

rent seeking but also pave the way for financing of political campaigns and political organizations. Few countries anywhere have been able to create transparent and legal means for funding political campaigns. Discretionary government power over industry in Asian countries has made raising funds for political purposes extremely easy (Kirk 1999). In most cases, the politicians expect firms to contribute funds to participate in major economic initiatives of the government. Large Korean firms were expected to ante up large sums of unrecorded cash to the politicians if they wanted to be able to bid on projects that the government was interested in. In Indonesia, President Suharto's business friends were able to support his political organization with hundreds of millions—and probably billions— of dollars of funds obtained through political connections from timber concessions and similar sources. In a few situations, as occurred in Malaysia and under the Kuomintang in Taiwan, China, the ruling party owned or controlled firms that received favored treatment in the awarding of government contracts.

Reforming the economic system, therefore, may also require a parallel reform of the political system and the financing of that system. It is simplistic to argue that introducing democratic processes alone will solve the problem. In Korea, Kim Dae Jung was elected democratically, but two of his sons, along with other members of his government, were charged by prosecutors with illegal influence peddling. Indonesia acquired a democratic government after the fall of President Suharto, but payoffs to politicians continued. Democracy, therefore, is not a panacea, but it is hard to imagine a solution that does not involve open democratic elections together with a free press. Also needed is a legal system capable of protecting the rights of those who criticize government wrongdoing.

COMPETITION POLICIES: WHO DETERMINES MERGERS AND ACQUISITIONS?

While the attention of international organizations and foreign investors has been on changes in the management of insolvency, many of the countries in East Asia have been and continue to be equally concerned with the organization of their industrial sectors. As pointed out above, much of East and Southeast Asia at the beginning of the twenty-first century possessed industrial organization structures that were the product of each country's particular history and bore no clear relationship to the needs of the present. Industrial policy since at least the 1970s—in cases such as Korea and Taiwan (China), and earlier, in the case of Japan—has not only targeted particular industries and firms but has also been concerned with how to create firms and industrial organization structures in a wide range of sectors that would be internationally competitive.

In the United States and Europe, competition policy usually involves efforts by the government, working through the legal system and regulatory bodies, to discourage or to negate actions by individual firms aimed at establishing a dominant market position. The most recent well-known examples in the United States are the breakup of AT&T and the government's attempt to limit the monopoly powers of Microsoft (see Fisher 2000). East Asia also has competition policies with objectives similar to those in Europe and North America, but these laws have had little influence in most of the region—including Japan—until very recently. Aspects of competition policy that have mattered most to governments as diverse as China, Korea, and Malaysia focus on how to create internationally competitive firms, not on how to curb domestic market power. In fact, many countries in the region have, for significant periods, given domestic market monopolies to individual firms, to make it possible for them to earn profits while they gradually become competitive on the international scene. Korea is now moving away from that approach, in part because of international pressure and its participation in the World Trade Organization, but many other countries in the region have yet to do so.

For many countries, the model of how to create internationally competitive firms, particularly in large-scale heavy and chemical industries, was provided first by Japan and later by Korea, as the two countries built up internationally recognized conglomerates such as Toyota, Matsushita, and Hitachi and Hyundai, Samsung, and Daewoo. For governments in Malaysia and China, for example, and, to a lesser degree, for several other governments in the region, the prime task was to create similarly successful and internationally recognized national companies along the lines of the Korean chaebol and the Japanese *keiretsu*.

All countries, of course, go through periods of corporate restructuring through mergers and acquisitions or through sales of subsidiaries. In the market economies of Europe and North America, however, this process is largely left to market forces, which now include cross-national forces in what is a rapidly globalizing world. The rules governing mergers and breakups are set by legislatures and are increasingly coordinated internationally and administered by the legal system. The role of the executive branch of the government is largely confined to helping write the rules and to ensuring that the new arrangements do not unduly restrict competition.

In East Asia, by contrast, industrial organization is governed as much by the actions of governments as it is by the efforts of the firms themselves or by the rules and procedures of the legal or regulatory systems. This activist government role in Asia, which came into full flower in the 1960s and 1970s, is still very much a reality. The objectives of industrial organization policies, however, have changed over time.

In the 1970s, the goal of the Korean government was to support the large conglomerates by putting them in charge of implementing the heavy and chemical industry drive. After 1997 and with the election of President Kim Dae Jung, the goal was to restructure the conglomerates by forcing them to sell off subsidiaries unrelated to what the government considered to be their core businesses. From the latter half of the 1990s, the Chinese government has been busy merging enterprises to form business groups (*jituan*). By the end of 2000, there were 6,027 of these groups, of which 2,655 were large enterprise groups accounting for 57 percent of the assets of the industrial sector and 11 percent of urban employment. Although less than two-thirds of these had majority state ownership, the ones that did held 92 percent of the total assets (China, National Bureau of Statistics 2000, 2001). The models that originally inspired these efforts, at least those sponsored by the government, were the conglomerates of Japan and Korea. Since the financial crisis and the difficulties faced by the Korean chaebol, the ultimate goal of enterprise consolidation has begun to be reconsidered, but the mergers and acquisitions continue.

On a more modest scale, Vietnam has also been inspired by the Korean and Japanese models, although Vietnam's efforts have involved more the relabeling of government bureaus than the creation of truly independent large-scale firms. The relabeled government bureaus often continue to behave like government bureaus and not like the independent conglomerate headquarters that the reorganization had hoped to create. Malaysia, since the 1980s, has struggled with how to create large bumiputera business groups that can compete both internationally and with Malaysia's own Chinese-Malaysian companies. Initially, as pointed out previously, this effort took the form of new state-owned enterprises to produce steel, cement, and, most of all, automobiles.[14] Then these state enterprises were sold off, mainly to favored bumiputera entrepreneurs, but the goal remained the same and had the backing of government-supported loans and other subsidies. After the financial crisis, the government also took on itself the task of restructuring and consolidating the banking system.

With all of this industrial restructuring activity, past and ongoing, one might assume that governments and academic economists know a great

---

14. By 2001, the difficulties confronting the domestic state-owned auto companies—Proton and Perwaja—had forced the government to seek a foreign strategic investor.

deal about how various industries should be organized for a given level of per capita income and a given size of a country's economy. If they were so informed, the decision to promote either mergers or breakups of companies would be a straightforward process of comparing the existing structure with one that promoted greater competition at a given level of development, and then taking steps to bring the existing structure in closer alignment with the preferred structure. European and North American government regulators of competition attempt to proceed along these lines. In the United States, for example, the government calculates the change in the level of concentration resulting every time a merger above a certain size occurs. If the resulting level of concentration exceeds a certain level, a model is then used to estimate the likely effect of the merger on the prices of the goods in question.[15] Developing countries could make a similar calculation, although its utility would be limited by the absence of a theory that defines a normative relationship between the structure of industry and the level of per capita income or the size of the developing country's economy. Moreover, there are few studies that have looked at the degree of concentration in various industries in developing countries.

Given the lack of international normative guidelines, the level of industrial concentration in the emerging economies of East Asia is the outcome of a combination of market forces, institutional constraints designed for other purposes, and direct government intervention to try to improve the industrial organization. The models for China, Malaysia, Vietnam, and, to a lesser degree, several other Asian economies, as discussed, have been the Korean chaebol and the Japanese keiretsu—at least until the financial crisis of 1997–98. On closer inspection, however, the character and suitability of these models raise serious questions. Even before the financial crisis, were these models good examples of highly diversified and successful conglomerates? Were the two models in fact similar to each other in more respects than just that the conglomerates in both cases were large and diversified?

In the case of Japan, the original Asian model for highly diversified conglomerates, there is some uncertainty about the conglomerates' organizational coherence over the past one and a half decades. The prewar period *zaibatsu* (Mitsui, Mitsubishi, and Sumitomo) were closely knit conglomerates that were supposedly dismantled by the allied occupation authorities. The conventional view is that, starting in the 1950s, the old relationships were reconstituted in the postwar keiretsu, in which firms belonging to the group have much closer ties with each other than with outside firms. This closeness involves protective cross-shareholding within the group

---

15. I am indebted to Ariel Pakes for this information.

and association with a main bank that is itself a part of the group and provides much of the financing for members. Firms belonging to a keiretsu typically purchased inputs from other members of the group rather than from outsiders, even when the outsiders could have delivered the desired inputs on more favorable terms.

That is the image of the keiretsu, but doubts have been expressed as to whether such groups are, or even were, especially close knit.[16] There were, to be sure, many individual firms using such names as Sumitomo or Hitachi, but the evidence does not appear to support the view that there is substantial cross-shareholding among the firms bearing the same name. Nor have these member firms borrowed unusually heavily from their main banks as compared with their borrowing from banks not in the group. Many of the members of the Mitsui group, for example, do not use the Mitsui Bank or the Mitsui Trust Bank as their main source of credit. Furthermore, borrowing from banks has declined significantly since the 1980s, because firms have found it convenient to raise money on the stock markets (Stulz 2001). Thus, a compelling question arises whether the keiretsu are real business groups at all, as contrasted to firms that share a name or a common history but are, in fact, run as independent entities.

Whatever the case with the keiretsu, there is no question that the Korean chaebol were groups of firms controlled by a single individual or family. These conglomerates were highly diversified in that they operated in a wide variety of industries (Kim 1997). Among the top 30 chaebol before the financial crisis, the average number of industries per group was 19, and among the 5 largest, the average number of industries included was 30. Cross-shareholding within the group was standard and was the mechanism used by the family to retain control. Among the largest 30 chaebol, the lead family's ownership was roughly 15 to 17 percent of the outstanding shares of the group in the early 1980s, falling to 10 to 12 percent by the mid-1990s. Cross-shareholding within the group accounted for 40 to 45 percent of the shares in the early 1980s and a still high 33 to 35 percent in the mid-1990s (Yoo and Lee 1997, pp. 460–63). These groups, however, were prohibited from owning banks, although they did include other financial institutions. Initially, the banks were largely state owned, and even when they were finally privatized, there were specific rules prohibiting purchase by the chaebol. This formal separation based on ownership, however, did not keep the chaebol from establishing close relationships with the state banks, relationships determined not so much by the banks themselves as by the government's directed lending.

---

16. The brief discussion in this paragraph is drawn from Miwa and Ramseyer (2002).

If Japan and Korea have been seen, until recently at least, as the models that other Asian countries strove to emulate, what in fact have those other countries done, and does what has occurred appear to make economic sense? Before attempting to answer these questions, one should have a picture of the degree of industrial concentration elsewhere in East Asia. Concentration, it should be noted, can have two distinct meanings. One is the level of concentration within an industry—the percentage of sales in the industry controlled by the largest four firms, for example. The other is the control exercised by a conglomerate or family over industry as a whole or the economy as a whole, rather than over an industrial sector. Data on the level of concentration by industry are presented in table 7.2.

The table shows that the levels of industrial concentration varied enormously across the Asian countries for which estimates could be found. At one extreme, with a high level of concentration, are Korea, Malaysia, and the Philippines (at the end of the Ferdinand Marcos years, in 1983 but not later). At the other extreme is China, where in only 4 industrial sectors out of a total of 39 did large firms control more than 60 percent of gross output. Moreover, the number of firms in these highly controlled sectors was several times the number of firms (usually four) used in calculating the concentration ratios for other countries. The exception in China was the petroleum and natural gas sector, where the number of firms with 60 percent or more of gross output was less than four. In 1995, after a period of economic liberalization, the Philippines and Taiwan, China, were more concentrated than China but roughly comparable to Japan and the United States several decades ago. Japan and the United States at this time had quite similar levels of industrial concentration despite the widespread belief to the contrary.[17]

The U.S. pattern of concentration is presumably mainly the result of decisions made by individual firms in response to market forces, the working of the legal system, and the government's decision to pursue or not to pursue perceived antitrust violations. In 1963, Japan's level of concentration was presumably a result of individual firm decisions, measures introduced by the occupation government to break up the conglomerates, and policies of MITI. MITI pursued a highly interventionist industrial policy that included a concern that some sectors had too many firms to be internationally competitive.

In both Korea under Park Chung Hee and the Philippines under Ferdinand Marcos, the high degree of concentration reflected the government's use of directed credit and access to key inputs to assist a few large

---

17. This point was made some time ago by Caves and Uekusa (1976).

Table 7.2 Industrial Concentration Ratios

Indicator	China	United States		Japan	Korea, Rep. of[a]	Malaysia[a]	Philippines		Taiwan, China
Year	1988	1963	1972	1963	1974	1990	1983	1995	1976
Share of industry controlled by the largest firms	Top 18–100	Top 4	Top 4	Top 4	Top 5	Top 4	Top 4	Top 4	Top 4
Number of sectors	39	417	183	512	205	22	31	31	131
Concentration ratio									
80–100 percent	7.7	12.2	6	5.6	26.9	18.2	25.8	9.7	10.7
60–80 percent	5.1	9.1	13.7	7.8	17.9	40.9	41.9	16.1	12.2
40–60 percent	12.8	19.6	26.8	27.9	27.3	31.8	16.1	29	24.4
20–40 percent	17.9	39.3	34.9	25.4	21.9	4.5	16.1	35.5	35.2
0–20 percent	56.4	19.8	18.6	33.3	6	4.5	0	9.7	17.5
Total (percent)	100	100	100	100	100	100	100	100	100

Note: The concentration percentages are based on the value of shipments by the top four firms as a percentage of total shipments in each industry for Japan, Korea, the United States, and probably Taiwan, China. The Philippine data refer to the share of output in each industry. The Chinese data are derived by the author from data from the National Bureau of Statistics and refer to the output produced by firms with over 100 million yuan of gross value output, a number that varies by sector from 0 to 293 firms. The number of firms in the most concentrated sectors (with over 60 percent of the output in that sector) ranges from 18 to 100 firms.

a. Adjusted to account for competition from imports.

Sources: Caves and Uekusa (1976, p. 471); De Vito (1995, p. 22); Hill (2003); Hsiao (1982, pp. 46, 48); and Yoo and Lee (1997, p. 443).

conglomerates or families. The Korean government also allowed explicit monopolies over the domestic market for certain heavy industries, although these monopolies were temporary. There is little doubt, therefore, that the industrial organization of Korea and of the Philippines was determined largely by government policy, not by market forces.

China's industrial organization was not a product of market forces either. Industrial enterprises in China, as pointed out earlier, were in part a creation of the pre-1979 Soviet-style command economy with central planning. Enterprises were not really business organizations but simply factory units under the active and direct supervision of central and provincial government industrial bureaus. Once industrial reforms began in 1984, China attempted to turn these enterprises into truly independent business firms, with limited success. The resulting degree of industrial concentration, however, had little, if anything, to do with market forces.

Given these historical patterns, the Chinese decision to create a more concentrated industrial structure and the Korean decision to move in the opposite direction probably should lead to greater efficiency and competitiveness. The decline in concentration in the Philippines following the liberalization of a number of markets (see Hill 2003) further reinforces the view that there was a good reason to move away from historical patterns of high concentration, which were shaped largely by government rather than market forces.

The question remains, who should be making these decisions? In China and Korea, the outcome is being dictated by government industrial policies that may or may not be market conforming. The same is true of Vietnam. The government is also playing a central role in Malaysia, at least in a limited number of key industries. In all of these instances, the government appears to be trying to make industrial merger and acquisition decisions based primarily on economic and technical criteria as opposed to political or rent-seeking criteria. Former Prime Minister Zhu Rongji and many others in the Chinese government are well-trained engineers, and former Prime Minister Mahathir Mohamed in Malaysia, although trained as a medical doctor, spent much time—including long visits to automobile plants in Korea and elsewhere—better acquainting himself with key industrial sector requirements. But government leaders and bureaucrats, however well intentioned, are poor substitutes for senior businesspeople with expertise and motivation, who have spent much of their lives engaged with the issues of technology, scale, and profitability in their particular industries. Such expertise can be brought to bear on the decisions to merge or divest only if those decisions are market determined.

Hong Kong (China) and Singapore have left decisions on industrial concentration almost entirely to the market. Hong Kong, China, however, no longer has much manufacturing since most of the plants controlled by firms there have moved into mainland China. In Singapore, except for the state-owned monopolies such as Singapore Airlines and the publicly controlled banks, the level of concentration in manufacturing is largely determined by which foreign firms choose to locate there. The openness of these two economies also means that industrial concentration ratios have little bearing on the level of competition present.[18]

Taiwan, China, may be the other economy that is closest to having an industrial organization dictated mainly by market forces. The government in Taiwan, China, did reserve certain sectors for state-owned firms, although their share of the public sector has diminished steadily over time as private firms have been permitted to enter more sectors, such as petrochemicals, which had been reserved for the government's China Petroleum Corporation. The industrial organization structure in Taiwan, China, however, is difficult to interpret. Numerous small firms are often embedded in organizations led by larger firms and are not truly independent except in an accounting sense (Hsueh, Hsu, and Perkins 2001, chapter 4). The same, of course, could be said of some small firms in Japan that serve as just-in-time suppliers to large companies. Thus, there is no industrial organization in Asia that can reliably serve as a wholly market-determined model for others to follow.

Concerns regarding the degree to which individual large firms or conglomerates control industry as a whole in a given country (as opposed to controlling sector by sector) relate partly to economic efficiency. They also relate partly to the desired degree of concentration of political power, especially in countries such as Korea. The relevant data for three Asian economies in a comparison with the United States are presented in table 7.3.

Again, it appears that the major companies in Korea, in comparison with those in the other Asian nations, control the largest share of total manufacturing output and assets, although less than is the case for major corporations in the United States. Single families rarely control the bigger U.S. corporations, however, and thus the degree of economic (and political) power is much less concentrated in the hands of a few individuals in

---

18. Concentration ratios are sometimes presented adjusted for the level of import competition, and these ratios probably more accurately reflect the level of competition in these industries. Such data are available for Malaysia and do show that the level of concentration is much lower if competitive imports are taken into account, but such figures for the other countries were not readily available.

Table 7.3 Business Groups' Concentration Ratios: Share of 100 Largest Firms in Total Manufacturing
(percent)

Concentration ratio as a percentage of	Korea, Rep. of (1990)	Japan (1984)	Taiwan, China (1980)	United States (1985)
Shipments	37.7	27.3	21.9	—
Value added	35.1	—	—	33
Fixed assets	40.8	33	25.9	49.1

— Not available.

Sources: Chou (1988, p. 82) and Yoo and Lee (1997, p. 460).

the United States than in Korea.[19] Taiwan, China, in contrast to Korea, has a much lower share of industry controlled by the top 100 firms. Data have not been found for Hong Kong (China), Malaysia, and Singapore, but the mixture of domestically owned firms, a large number of foreign-owned firms, and—in Singapore, at least—a considerable number of state-owned firms, probably means that the control exerted over the entire manufacturing sector by a few family-based groups is less than in Korea. The Philippine manufacturing sector, on the other hand, is perceived as being dominated by a few powerful families, much as in Korea.

The state remains the largest owner of manufacturing in Vietnam, controlling 39 percent of gross industrial output in 2003, although foreign direct investment firms, which control 36 percent, are catching up fast.[20] In China, state-owned firms (including shareholding firms effectively controlled by the state) accounted for 48 percent of gross industrial output (China, National Bureau of Statistics 2001, p. 116). State ownership, particularly in China, however, does not mean that control is concentrated in the hands of a few individuals or families. Different ministries vie with one another, and provincial and lower-level governments control a large share of total manufacturing and compete with one another.

On the grounds of economic efficiency and competitiveness, economists have often concluded that, when firms diversify across many different industrial sectors, the result is a reduction in the value of the firm relative to what the components would have been worth in the absence of diversification—there is what this literature calls a "diversification

---

19. Another issue is how efficient family ownership is compared with other forms of ownership. Contrary to popular perception, Wiwattanakantang (2001), using detailed ownership data on Thai firms, finds that firms owned by a family are as efficient as foreign-owned firms. One reason for this finding is reduced agency cost.

20. These figures are from Vietnam, General Department of Statistics (2003, p. 5). I am indebted to David Dapice for pointing out this source to me.

discount."[21] Capital markets internal to these conglomerates more often transfer funds to shore up their weaker divisions, rather than transfer funds to those divisions with the best prospects for high rates of return. This conclusion, however, is not without its critics. The problem is one of endogeneity. It is often the weaker firms that decide to diversify, so the diversification discount may be much smaller than is commonly supposed. Furthermore, this conclusion is largely based on the experience of the United States, where capital markets are well developed. In countries where capital markets are underdeveloped, it may be that reallocation of capital across industries is more efficient within large diversified firms than it would be when allocated across independent firms through the capital markets (Stein 2002).

The Kim Dae Jung government in Korea shared the view of those who hold that conglomerates are inefficient and tried to correct the perceived problem by forcing the chaebol to reduce their level of diversification and concentrate on their core businesses. Much of the dislike of high levels of market power in the hands of a few families, however, had more to do with politics than economics. If a few families control the destiny of a major segment of manufacturing, they also control the direction of the economy, which people and how many people get hired, and which companies—other than those that are directly controlled—are chosen as suppliers of key inputs. They also have the resources to fund the political campaigns of their supporters and to withhold funding from their detractors. With these levers, they exercise a degree of political power that is widely perceived to be incompatible with democratic government. This political power, in turn, makes it possible for these conglomerates to protect and perpetuate their economic dominance despite the pressure of market forces that might otherwise erode that dominance over time.

In the early years of industrialization, it might have been desirable for governments to shape industrial organization. Governments in the early stages of development often have little choice but to intervene, given that no alternative institutions exist to guide mergers and acquisitions. But after the experience of the past two decades and given the much more complex economies that exist today in East Asia, little reason exists to believe that the executive branches of governments in Asia are well qualified to intervene. Even where governments have a high level of technical expertise in this area—and not many do have that expertise—there are few guidelines to follow from the experience of other developing countries as

---

21. This discussion is based primarily on Stein (2002). For an earlier work on these issues, see Ravenscraft and Scherer (1987).

to what the optimal industrial organization structure should be. In addition, even where government technicians think they know whether to support or break up a large conglomerate, the actual decision is likely to be heavily influenced by political considerations that will undermine economic efficiency.

Line ministries are thus not well qualified to direct the organization of industry, but the process of mergers, acquisitions, and breakups still needs to be governed by rules. Simply leaving matters in this area to the market and existing institutions with no government involvement may mean that existing inefficient structures will be perpetuated. It may also mean that individual companies will succeed in stifling competition by acquiring excessive control over their markets. The remaining choices are to set up a special regulatory agency that has the technical expertise and the power to make these decisions or, as in the United States, to create a group within the government to deal with competition policy. That group would be required to implement its decisions by bringing a case before the judiciary, thus giving the judiciary final authority to decide whether the case has merit. One approach requires a regulatory body that is independent of political manipulation and independent of the companies it regulates, a goal that few industrial countries and even fewer, if any, developing countries have been successful in achieving. The other approach requires an independent and technically competent judicial system. The state of the judiciary in Asia is the main topic of the final part of this chapter.

ESTABLISHING THE RULE OF LAW

In the earlier discussions of corporate and financial sector governance reforms, the role of the judiciary has repeatedly figured as an essential component of any effort by the countries of East Asia to move away from a system based on central government intervention to one based more on market forces and the independent judgments of individual firms. Brief statements have been made as well about whether the judiciary in one country or another in the region was up to this task. This section addresses the capacity of the judicial systems of these countries explicitly and in greater depth.

Assessing the ability of a judicial system to adequately support efficient and equitable corporate and financial sector governance is no easy task.[22]

---

22. A substantial empirical literature summarized and extended by Beck and others (2001) maintains that the efficacy of the legal system determines the effectiveness of the financial system in promoting growth.

Some quantitative data do exist that purport to measure the effectiveness of judicial systems across a wide range of countries. In addition there are in-depth studies of individual countries, but few of these look at these issues in a comparative framework involving several Asian countries. Both of these approaches have their limitations when it comes to measuring judicial capacity in the various countries of East Asia. Ignoring the problem of measurement, however, is not an option. The main message of this chapter is that the economies of East Asia need to rely less on government intervention and more on the market, but that greater reliance on the market will work efficiently only if there are either judicial or regulatory bodies that are strong enough to enforce the rules governing the market or that can be made strong enough within a reasonable time.

To understand why the judicial systems of many of the countries of East Asia are relatively weak, one should first briefly review the history of modern legal systems in the region (see also Glenn 2000). In the countries that were European colonies, the legal systems were transplants from the European home country. Those that were not colonies, notably China and Japan, had traditional legal systems that continued to exist throughout much of the nineteenth century before being gradually displaced by borrowed transplants from Europe, mainly Germany. These German transplants were then again transplanted to Japan's colonies in Korea and Taiwan, China.

The European colonial systems were largely run by and for the European colonists. The business communities of Southeast Asia, most of which were overseas Chinese, rarely went to court to resolve business disputes and often fared badly when they did. Thus, as suggested earlier in this chapter, these overseas Chinese businesses developed their own ways of enforcing contracts outside the judicial system. Much the same was true of the Chinese in China and others who relied on traditional systems of governance. In China, historically, the county magistrate doubled as a judge mainly in criminal cases. Magistrates played little role in providing a supportive framework for commercial transactions. The traditional system was not very supportive of commerce and saw it mainly as a potential source of revenue. Contract disputes that ended up in court were likely to bankrupt both parties to the dispute or to be decided in favor of one on nonjudicial grounds. When in the twentieth century China did begin to adopt European laws, there was no comparable effort to create strong European-style legal systems.

After the colonies in Asia regained their independence at the end of World War II, the people of the region felt little sense of ownership in the transplanted legal systems. The traditional legal systems, which had never functioned well in the commercial sphere in any case, were also in irretrievable decline. Following the takeover of China, the Communist government adopted many of the laws of the Soviet Union, but then, during the Cultural Revolution (1966–76), it dismantled what little existed in the way of a legal system and abolished the legal profession. When the gradual move toward a market system began in 1978, the Chinese legal system had to be re-created from scratch. Hence, much of East Asia entered the postwar era with a very weak legal system, particularly when it came to providing a framework for commercial transactions. Even in Japan, with a transplanted German legal system in place since the end of the nineteenth century, lawyers and judges played only a minor part in commercial affairs.

A few economies of East Asia did evolve stronger commercial legal systems in the latter part of the twentieth century, and it is instructive to analyze why this development occurred where and when it did. It is widely conceded that the most effective legal systems of the region are those of Hong Kong (China) and Singapore. The quantitative indicators presented in table 7.4 support this conclusion, as do numerous qualitative statements by informed observers. Japan also ranks very high on these quantitative indexes, but there is reason to question whether these indicators reflect reality in the sphere of Japanese commercial law as contrasted to criminal law (Ramseyer and Nakazato 1999). We will return to the strengths and limitations of these quantitative indicators subsequently. Here we are concerned mainly with why Hong Kong (China) and Singapore acquired much stronger legal systems than other countries in the region.

Both Hong Kong (China) and Singapore were major commercial centers before they began building legal systems to serve more than the colonial power. In fact, it was not until the 1970s that the government in Hong Kong, China, embarked on a major effort to develop a legal system that gave a wide variety of rights to individuals. In the 1960s, for example, there were only a few hundred lawyers (solicitors, barristers, and judges combined) for a population of 4 million people. It was not until 1969 that the first law school was established at the University of Hong Kong, and even then there were only 50 graduates a year in the 1970s. By the end of the 1980s, however, a second law school had been established and was graduating 150 or so lawyers a year, and simultaneously Hong Kong, China, was importing more lawyers from the United Kingdom and the United States. At the turn of the century, shortly after the territory reverted to China, it had roughly 5,000 lawyers of all types. By the 1990s, prior to reversion, it was the one economy in Asia where the judiciary had nearly equal standing with the executive, and citizens increasingly saw

Table 7.4 Alternative Measures of the Rule of Law

Economy	Legal origin	Rule of law	Tax compliance	Corruption	Political rights	Risk of expropriation	Business regulation
China		3.58	2.51	6.53	1	—	2
Hong Kong, China	United Kingdom	4.93	4.56	8.52	4	8.29	5
Indonesia	France and Spain	2.39	2.53	2.14	1	7.16	2
Japan	Germany	5.39	4.41	8.51	7	9.67	4
Korea, Rep. of	Germany	3.21	3.29	5.3	6	8.31	3
Malaysia	United Kingdom	4.07	4.34	7.38	4	7.95	4
Philippines	France and Spain	1.64	1.83	2.92	6	5.22	3
Singapore	United Kingdom	5.14	5.05	8.21	3	9.3	5
Taiwan, China	Germany	5.11	3.25	6.85	—	9.12	—
Thailand	United Kingdom	3.75	3.41	5.18	5	7.42	3
Vietnam		—	3.25	4.51	1	—	1
Sweden		6.00	3.39	10.00	—	—	—
United States	United Kingdom	6.00	4.47	8.21	7	9.98	4
111-economy average		3.37	3.22	5.74	—	—	—

— Not available.

Note: The figures in the table are the average answer for each country from a questionnaire in which the respondent was asked to rank the economy in one category or another on a scale (for example, a scale of 1 to 10).

Source: These data are from the datasets compiled by LaPorta and others. The 111-economy average was calculated by the author from a reduced 111-economy subsample of the broader datasets. I am indebted to LaPorta and others for making this dataset available to me.

that system as something that protected them as well as the colonial power.[23]

This growing and relatively independent legal system, where the decisions of the courts are enforced, does not mean that most locally owned businesses rely mainly on the courts to settle major business disputes. Most of the smaller ethnic Chinese businesses still rely on informal mechanisms, built on the relationships of the past, to settle their differences. However, larger Chinese firms and the numerous multinational

---

23. This discussion of the legal system in Hong Kong, China, owes much to an interview with Dean Albert H. Y. Chen of the Law School of the University of Hong Kong. Dean Chen bears no responsibility for any errors in my interpretation of his remarks.

corporations that are headquartered in Hong Kong, China, do make extensive use of the legal system in commercial matters.[24]

In Singapore, as well, the presence of many firms with foreign investment has been one source of demand on the legal system. Singaporeans themselves, by the 1950s and 1960s, had also learned that U.K. law could be used to their advantage, even when the opposing party was the colonial government. This discovery helped them gain a sense of ownership over and appreciation of the U.K. law that they had inherited.[25] That said, the legal system in Singapore at the turn to the twenty-first century was not really independent of the executive branch of the government to a degree comparable with that found in the United Kingdom or the United States. The main task of the courts was and is to help implement the policies of the government, not to challenge them. In the economic sphere, this subordination may not matter a great deal because the Singapore government does not, for the most part, use its discretionary powers to promote particular companies. Settlement of business disputes, therefore, does rely heavily on the courts, because in these kinds of matters the courts are seen as impartial. It is also the case that informal nonjudicial methods of settling disputes such as the collection of debt are not widely used, because many of these methods are likely to entangle those who resort to them in Singapore's formidable criminal law system (Kamarul and Tomasic 1999).

While Hong Kong (China) and Singapore clearly have legal systems that are of significance both socially and in their commercial spheres, in what sense is it valid to say that those systems are 82 and 85 percent, respectively, as effective as the U.S. or Swedish systems, as the data in table 7.4 indicate? One possible answer is that these are ordinal, not cardinal, indexes, and thus one cannot speak of one country's system as being a certain percentage below another in effectiveness. But these indexes are frequently used in analyses of economic growth and corporate governance as if they were cardinal indexes. For our purposes in this chapter, it is sufficient to say that the legal systems of Hong Kong (China) and Singapore are fully capable of supporting a market system governed by the rule of law with minimal discretionary government intervention in that system.

The legal systems of Korea, Malaysia, and Taiwan (China) are often ranked below those of Hong Kong (China) and Singapore, although Taiwan (China) actually ranks higher than Hong Kong (China) in table 7.4.

---

24. For a discussion of how the law has been applied in Hong Kong, China, after the territory's return to China, see Chen (1999, pp. 287–320).

25. For a description of how political activists in Singapore used the law and the legal system to further their goals before independence, see Lee (1998).

Qualitative appraisals of the legal systems of Korea and Taiwan (China) suggest that the two systems are broadly rather similar. Both have the same origin: the German system introduced originally by the Japanese colonialists. Law in both economies was subordinate to decisions of the executive branch of government during the decades of authoritarian rule that ended in both places in the latter half of the 1980s. Governments in both economies pursued highly interventionist industrial policies. In the two legal systems, judges were more like civil servants, and that was true in Japan as well. Judges were graduates of undergraduate law schools who had passed an examination before receiving an additional year or two of formal training. They thus were young and inexperienced and lacked stature.[26]

Japan, the model on which the systems of Korea and Taiwan (China) were built, generally produced only 500 people a year to serve as judges, lawyers, and prosecutors, although by the end of the twentieth century this number had been raised first to 750 and then to about 1,000 a year. On a per capita basis, the 500 a year figure was less than half the production of Hong Kong, China, in the 1970s—a figure that did not give Hong Kong, China, enough legal personnel to handle its commercial disputes. As Lincoln (2001, p. 195) noted, "Unless government authorizes a dramatic increase in the number of lawyers and judges, a deluge of lawsuits initiated by private shareholders will clog the system." Current reform efforts are thus under way to increase the number of lawyers produced to 3,000 a year by 2010 and to allow the establishment of law schools by 2004.[27]

The low number of lawyers in Japan, to be sure, is misleading in some respects. Even though only lawyers can practice law through the courts, there are numerous professions and judicial administrative sciences (patent agent, tax agent, and so forth) that assist companies in legal matters. Companies may hire licensed attorneys, but many of them also hire those who studied law at the undergraduate level. Given that there are about 36,000 university graduates per year from law departments (by comparison, 50,000 pass the bar exam in the United States each year), the number of trained law personnel in Japan is not as small as the number of licensed attorneys suggests. These university graduates from law departments, however, cannot go to court. The shortage of personnel who can go to court, therefore, effectively limits the role of the courts in settling business disputes.

---

26. This discussion and the paragraph that follows owe a great deal to exchanges with William Alford of the Harvard Law School, who bears no responsibility for any errors in interpretation.

27. There are no law schools in Japan. Effectively, law departments at the university level are the training grounds for would-be lawyers (from Asahi.com). However, many schools are now considering offering programs by 2004, including the University of Tokyo.

The number of lawyers in Korea was even more restricted than in Japan. Before 1981, only 100 individuals a year were allowed to pass the examination to become lawyers, judges, and prosecutors. That number was subsequently raised to 300 a year, and then to about 800 a year in the 1990s. Still, at the turn of the century, the total number of people in the legal profession, including judges and prosecutors, was less than 7,000, only slightly more than in Hong Kong, China, which had one-eighth of the population that Korea did. As the economy of Korea has become more complex, the business community has begun to complain that the legal system is both too expensive and too often unavailable. A similar complaint is heard in Japan. In Korea, for example, it was not long ago that the trade ministry had no in-house lawyers at a time when it had to deal increasingly with international trade laws and treaties based on technical legal rules and regulations.

The limited number of Korean lawyers might explain why Korea scores so low on the rule-of-law index, except that the situation is little different in that respect from Japan or Taiwan, China, where judges have backgrounds similar to those in Korea and their numbers (on a per capita basis) are similar. Japan's judiciary, of course, has operated in the context of a democratic society since the 1950s, and that was not the case in either Korea or Taiwan, China, until the late 1980s. In the latter two societies, the advent of democracy ended the clear dominance of the executive over the judiciary. In the case of Taiwan, China, one can observe this fact through the change in behavior of the Council of Grand Justices, which before 1987 took few, if any, steps to limit the inappropriate exercise of power by other branches of government. After 1987, the council not only supported private citizens who brought cases against the government based on the government's failure to comply with the laws, but also declared a number of laws unconstitutional (see Cooney 1999).

Taking the legal systems of Japan, Korea, and Taiwan, China, together, one can probably fairly say that they are not yet up to the task of fully overseeing and enforcing the rules of the market in their economies, but the framework for doing so is in place. These economies must still rely on the many informal mechanisms developed over the years to handle contract disputes and the like—informal mechanisms that are increasingly inadequate for these complex modern economies. What is now required is to continue to expand the size of these legal systems and to strengthen the prestige and competence of judges.

At the time of independence in 1957, Malaysia's legal system was comparable to that of Singapore, but the degree of independence of the Malaysian legal system has eroded significantly since the late 1980s.

Before 1985, Malaysia's legal system retained most of its inherited features. The first three prime ministers of Malaysia were trained in the law in the United Kingdom, and the top judges were formidable figures in Malaysian society. The right of appeal to the Privy Council in the United Kingdom was not ended until 1985. It was not unusual for the courts to decide against the government in some cases.[28]

But from the 1980s onward, with the rise to power of Prime Minister Mahathir, the independence of the judiciary was increasingly circumscribed. The tension between the judiciary and the executive arose because of the government's interventionist development policy, which was designed to promote certain industries and companies, notably companies run by bumiputera businessmen or those with close ties to the ruling political party, the United Malay National Organization. When the courts ruled against these government development initiatives in the award of contracts, for example, the government either managed to win on appeal or, when that failed, amended the constitution to achieve its ends. This reduction in the independence of the courts combined with uncompetitive salaries affected the quality of the judiciary. Businesses still turned to lawyers and the law to draw up contracts, but increasingly these contracts were drawn up in a way that would make it possible to avoid the court system. It was not that the courts had become corrupt or biased in favor of certain parties but that court decisions were less reliably rooted in sound legal reasoning. Because the quality of the legal profession otherwise remains high, however, one can still speak of a legal system that functions reasonably well in the commercial sphere. There is no compelling need for the government to intervene to compensate for the weaknesses of this legal system. To the contrary, the government needs to end the practices that are undermining the strength and integrity of that system.

The weakest legal systems in East Asia are those of China, Indonesia, the Philippines, and Vietnam. In the quantitative rule-of-law index in table 7.4, China actually ranks above Korea, but this ranking is difficult to understand. It is probably reasonable to rank the legal systems of Indonesia and the Philippines below the others. It is widely perceived in both countries that judges are frequently influenced by bribes, which turn civil court battles into an exercise in the balance of economic and political power between the contending parties. One survey of Manila lawyers indicated

---

28. This discussion of Malaysia's legal system is based in part on discussions with knowledgeable lawyers and others in Kuala Lumpur and in part on Teik (1999). See also Pistor and Wellons (1998).

that 48 percent of them knew of a judge who had taken a bribe, presumably implying that 52 percent of the lawyers did not know of a corrupt judge.[29] In Indonesia, in contrast, estimates of the number of judges who are corrupt range from 50 to 90 percent, suggesting that most lawyers must know of judges who are corrupt (Backman 1999, p. 33; Bourchier 1999).

The problem is not that Indonesia and the Philippines do not have good laws on the books. With technical assistance from the International Monetary Fund and the Harvard Institute for International Development, for example, Indonesia had written and enacted a long list of new financial laws, many of them more modern and up to date than those in far more industrial countries (Cole and Slade 1996). When the financial crisis hit Indonesia in 1997–98, however, many of these laws made little difference. Prudential regulations designed to improve the banks' portfolios had been put in place in 1991–92, but little effort was made to rein in the overseas borrowing that was to be the immediate cause of the crisis. And in the immediate aftermath of the crisis, close ties between several of the worst-performing banks and the leaders of the government, as well as their family members and business associates, ensured that the actions of regulators were overridden, whatever the law said. If the courts had been willing to intervene, they would have had little power to do so. The situation in 1997–98, to be sure, would have put heavy pressure on any legal system, but Indonesia's legal system did not perform during noncrisis periods either, at least not when the rich and powerful were involved.

China's and Vietnam's legal systems are probably less corrupt than those of Indonesia and the Philippines, but it is unlikely that they perform much better, despite the lower level of outright bribery. China began the process of restoring its legal system in the early 1980s. There are now shelves full of new laws designed to provide a legal framework for foreign investment and for a market economy. In the 1980s and even more so in the 1990s, the judiciary has been increasingly active in settling economic disputes, especially in the most advanced parts of the country, such as Shanghai. Among the larger firms in the major cities, formal contracts with suppliers are the norm, although disputes still rely mainly on informal negotiation for settlement. Still, in a World Bank survey of 1,500 firms in five major cities, 12.2 percent of the disputes were resolved through the courts; the figure for Shanghai was 22 percent (Steinfeld 2004). China's entrance into the World Trade Organization will further reinforce the role of formal legal

---

29. This survey is referred to in World Bank (2000).

proceedings, but an enormous amount of work still has to be done simply to make Chinese laws on the books compatible with what the World Trade Organization requires. The enforcement of those laws will be even more difficult.[30]

The Chinese legal system must first confront the cauldron of conflicting rules and regulations created by the many different authorities that possess the right to introduce rules and regulations. The job of the courts is thus made much more difficult from the start, because the courts are not supposed to interpret the laws but to adjudicate. More important, when the courts do render decisions, enforcement is problematic. Courts do not have primacy over the ministries and other government organs, and large numbers of court rulings are simply ignored.[31] Informally, in addition, high-level officials of the Communist Party can overrule both the courts and government organizations. The situation in Vietnam is similar to that in China, only the role of the judiciary is even less developed and less independent, in part because Vietnam's economy is at an earlier stage of development.

In China, Indonesia, the Philippines, and Vietnam, therefore, the legal systems are clearly not yet up to the task of overseeing and enforcing the rules of a market economy. There is little choice but to rely on the many informal mechanisms that have grown up as a substitute for a law-based system, however inadequate those systems may be. There is also little choice but to continue to rely on discretionary government intervention in the economy where fundamental restructuring is required. The long-term goal—and *long-term* in this case could mean several decades—should be to build the kind of legal systems that will replace government intervention and these informal institutions. That task needs to start now.

This brief review of the legal systems of East and Southeast Asia leads to a number of conclusions. One is that the quantitative indexes purporting to measure the quality of the different legal systems or related variables are flawed, at best.[32] Our review suggests that the rule-of-law index in table 7.4 probably overstates the strength of the legal system in Taiwan, China, relative both to that of Korea and to those of North America and

---

30. For a discussion of the effect of accession to the World Trade Organization on the legal system, see Kong (2002).

31. For a discussion of these issues at greater length, see Lubman (1999) and Clarke (1996).

32. Recognition of the limitation of some of these indexes has led some scholars to try to find less subjective measures of the performance of the legal system by constructing indexes of specific dispute resolution procedures across countries, such as those used in evicting tenants from rental housing or collecting on bounced checks (see Djankov and others 2001).

Europe. The Philippines' judiciary is probably not worse than that of Indonesia. And the strength of China's system is probably overstated relative to both Korea and the Philippines. These problems with the indexes are hardly surprising, given the way they were compiled. Many indexes of this type are compiled by sending out questionnaires to businesspeople, few of whom are in a position to make more than crude comparisons of a handful of countries where they have direct experience. Other indexes are compiled by asking for the opinions of experts, but experts too seldom have experience in more than one or two systems. The number of people who have sufficient knowledge to make informed comparative judgments across more than three or four countries is far smaller than the number who get asked to fill out such forms. Many of these indexes measure little more than popular opinion at any given point in time.

The far more important conclusion is that the legal systems of many of the Asian nations at the turn of the century are clearly unequal to the task of supporting rules that effectively oversee corporate and financial sector governance. The indexes suggest that the quality of most of the East Asian legal systems is above—often well above—the world average. But if so, the only parts of the world with systems capable of supporting a law-based system of economic management are Europe and North America, plus a handful of other countries that have come close to achieving a similar level of legal development. It is not just China, Indonesia, the Philippines, and Vietnam that need to reform their legal systems. With the possible exception of Hong Kong (China) and Singapore, corporate governance reform will have to be accompanied by equally far-reaching judicial reform in all of the other systems, including Japan.

Is it realistic to expect that East Asia can achieve this goal over the next decade or so? On the positive side, the introduction of democracy into both Korea and Taiwan, China, has made it possible to begin to create a judiciary with the power to curb government actions that violate the law, as well as the power to settle commercial disputes that do not involve the government. Democratic politics have yet to exert equivalent pressures in either Indonesia or the Philippines, however.

The increasingly complex nature of their economies has also induced Japan, Korea, and Taiwan, China, to enhance the capabilities of their judicial systems in the commercial arena. The same has been happening in China, although from a much lower starting point. No comparable influence is yet in evidence in Indonesia, the Philippines, or Vietnam.

On the negative side, the persistence of interventionist industrial policies continues to provide a rationale for the executive branch of the government to overrule the judiciary in China, Malaysia, and Vietnam. More important, at least in the cases of China and Vietnam, the Communist Party's decision to retain a monopoly of power and to exercise that power with wide discretion throughout society clearly stands in the way of a legal system capable of rendering and enforcing independent and fair decisions.

Creating legal systems that are competent, strong, and relatively independent of the executive branch of the government is going to take a long time in many of the Asian countries looked at in this study—time that in the worst situations will be measured in generations rather than years or even decades. But in the more industrial economies and polities of the region, that process is well under way. Not only in Hong Kong (China) and Singapore, but also in Japan, Korea, and Taiwan (China) it is already possible to see an economic system that is governed by the rule of law rather than by government fiat or by mainly informal arrangements among private parties.

CONCLUSION

As this chapter has argued, without question the industrial and financial sectors of most of the economies of East and Southeast Asia require restructuring.[33] If financial markets are to continue to develop in the region and to perform their role efficiently, rules must protect investors who are not the owner-managers of the firms. To start with, much better bankruptcy legislation is needed than has existed in much of the region in the past, and the legislation must be enforced efficiently and fairly. This effort will be highly significant for the long-term health of the banking systems in these economies, but it will be only a first step toward protecting the rights of minority shareholders.

The level of concentration of ownership over financial and industrial firms also must change. In some cases, the direction of change should be toward fewer firms through consolidation of existing enterprises; in other cases, the move should be in the opposite direction through the breakup of excessively concentrated conglomerates.

But the central question addressed in this chapter is not what the ideal corporate governance laws or the ideal level of industrial or financial sector concentration should be. The central point of this chapter is that the market—subject to transparent rules enforced fairly and objectively—should make these decisions whenever possible. Although the 1990s

---

33. Such restructuring could be coordinated by the Asian Financial Institute proposed by Eichengreen in chapter 2.

witnessed substantial change in this regard, the approach to industrialization and financial sector development in much of Asia remains to a greater or lesser degree in conflict with this goal. Outside of Hong Kong (China) and, to a degree, Singapore, it is the executive branch of the government that has taken the lead in making many of these decisions and in enforcing them through the government's command over the banks. This circumstance has led both the industrial firms and the banks to rely on the government when they run into trouble, a situation that has created moral hazards, often in extreme forms.

The challenge for most of the countries in the region is to reduce or eliminate this interventionist government role, but that is easier said than done. One cannot move to a true market system unless a set of institutions exists that is capable of independently, efficiently, and fairly enforcing the rules of a market system. The choices are either an independent judiciary or a set of independent regulatory agencies. Independent regulatory agencies have been difficult to establish, even in the most industrial economies, and in Asia they are generally the creatures of the executive branch of government. That branch, particularly in economies with authoritarian political regimes, is generally closely tied to the large firms that it is charged with regulating. Making governments adopt a more arm's-length relationship with big business has been a halting process. Democratization has helped in this regard in Korea and Taiwan, China, but in Japan it had little effect for decades. In the absence of effective and independent regulatory agencies, countries have the option of establishing independent and efficient legal systems.

The problem that East Asian economies face in creating independent and efficient legal systems is that the region started its industrialization and financial sector development effort from a weak legal base. Most of the former colonies in the region inherited a legal system toward which few in the economy felt much sense of ownership. Even in Hong Kong (China) and Singapore, where the colonial legal system did take root, this ownership was not felt until the final two or three decades of the twentieth century. For those economies that were not colonies, and for the overseas Chinese business community, the inherited Chinese legal tradition was a weak foundation on which to build a modern system of commercial law. Instead, a variety of informal institutions were created that performed many of the tasks of a judicial system, but these informal mechanisms have become increasingly inadequate for the complex modern economies that now exist in much of East Asia.

Creating the legal institutions of a modern market economy is a daunting task for any country. For those that are the furthest behind in this regard—such as China, Indonesia, and Vietnam—the effort will certainly take decades. For economies that are further along in developing a modern legal system, notably Japan, Korea, and Taiwan (China), the timeframe can be much shorter. The basic structure is in place in these last three countries, which mainly need an increase in the numbers and in the competence of judicial and legal personnel plus some rewriting of laws.

But even in the countries that have made substantial progress toward a modern system of commercial law, that system will be constantly undermined as long as the government continues to actively intervene in the economy to achieve industrial policy goals. Abandoning interventionist industrial policies will not be easy. It is not just that government officials and politicians are reluctant to give up power anywhere. It is also that interventionist industrial policies meet certain political needs. Few countries have found a legal and inexpensive way of financing political organizations and campaigns, and, as was discussed above, interventionist industrial policies make it extremely easy to generate the funds required. Either firms give to the party organization or they do not get to participate in government-directed economic activities.

Even if the countries of East Asia are willing to abandon a Korean- or Japanese-style industrial policy, much more institution building will be required for the legal system of a market economy to function properly. At some point, the executive branch of government must also be willing to devolve sufficient power to the judiciary to overrule decisions of the government itself. In the economies of East Asia where this has occurred, in all cases except for Hong Kong, China, the true independence of the judiciary was preceded by the introduction of political democracy and competitive elections.

Establishing a complete market economy with supporting legal institutions, therefore, is going to be a slow process in many of the countries of East and Southeast Asia. Countries such as China, Indonesia, and Vietnam will thus have to continue to rely in part on government intervention to accomplish whatever economic restructuring they consider essential. The cost will be restructuring efforts that continue to generate moral hazards even when implemented by competent technocrats. If politics and rent-seeking play a major role in the process, the results will be worse. Over the long run, the goal will be to get beyond this stage of development to a complete market system, in which these decisions are made by private economic actors who reap the rewards of successful restructuring and in which they themselves, not the general public, pay the price for failure. The only way countries such as China, Indonesia, and Vietnam will ever arrive at that point, however, is if they make a concerted and continuing effort now—even if completion of the process takes decades.

Some may interpret these conclusions as implying that the economies of East and Southeast Asia will not be able to continue the rapid development of the past several decades, but no such implication is warranted. Economic development never depends on having all of the institutions of a modern market economy in place at the start. If it did, no economy would ever have developed. The conclusion that is warranted is that the countries of East and Southeast Asia must steadily improve their market-supporting institutions or they will over time face more and more serious difficulties as their economies become increasingly sophisticated and complex.

REFERENCES

Backman, Michael. 1999. *Asian Eclipse: Exposing the Dark Side of Business in Asia*. Singapore: John Wiley and Sons (Asia).

Beck, Thorsten, Asli Demirgüç-Kunt, Ross Levine, and Vojisl Maksimovic. 2001. "Financial Structure and Economic Development: Firm, Industry, and Country Evidence." In Asli Demirgüç-Kunt and Ross Levine, eds., *Financial Structure and Economic Growth: A Cross-Country Comparison of Banks, Markets, and Development*. Cambridge, Mass.: MIT Press.

Bourchier, David. 1999. "Magic Memos, Collusion, and Judges with Attitude: Notes on the Politics of Law in Contemporary Indonesia." In Kanishka Jayasuriya, ed., *Law, Capitalism, and Power in Asia*. London: Routledge.

Burkart, Mike, Fausto Panunzi, and Andrei Shleifer. 2002. "Family Firms." NBER Working Paper 8776. National Bureau of Economic Research, Cambridge, Mass.

Caves, Richard, and Masu Uekusa. 1976. "Industrial Organization." In Hugh Patrick and Henry Rosovsky, eds., *Asia's New Giant: How the Japanese Economy Works*. Washington, D.C.: Brookings Institution.

Chen, Albert H. Y. 1999. "Hong Kong's Legal System in Transition, 1997–99." In Gungwu Wang and John Wong, eds., *Hong Kong and China: The Challenge of Transition*. Singapore: Times Academic Press.

China, National Bureau of Statistics. 2000. *China's Largest Enterprises in 2000*. Beijing: China Statistics Press.

———. 2001. *China Statistical Yearbook, 2001*. Beijing: China Statistics Press.

Chou, Tein-Chen. 1988. "Aggregate Concentration Ratios and Business Groups: A Case Study of Taiwan." *Taiwan Economic Review* 16(1):82.

Claessens, Stijin, Simeon Djankov, Joseph Fan, and Larry Lang. 1999. "Expropriation of Minority Shareholders in East Asia." Working Paper 2088. World Bank, Washington, D.C. Processed.

Clarke, Donald C. 1996. "The Creation of a Legal Structure for Market Institutions in China." In John McMillan and Barry Naughton, eds., *Reforming Asian Socialism: The Growth of Market Institutions*. Ann Arbor: University of Michigan Press.

Cole, David Chamberlin, and Betty F. Slade. 1996. *Building a Modern Financial System: The Indonesian Experience*. Cambridge, U.K.: Cambridge University Press.

Coombes, Paul, and Mark Watson. 2000. "Three Surveys on Corporate Governance." *McKinsey Quarterly* 4:75–77.

Cooney, Sean. 1999. "A Community Changes: Taiwan's Council of Grand Justices and Liberal Democratic Reform." In Kanishka Jayasuriya, ed., *Law, Capitalism, and Power in Asia*. London: Routledge.

De Vito, Giovanni Nicola. 1995. "Market Distortions and Competition: The Particular Case of Malaysia." Discussion Paper 105. United Nations Conference on Trade and Development, Geneva.

Djankov, Simeon, Rafael LaPorta, Florencio Lopez-de-Silanes, and Andrei Shleifer. 2001. "Legal Structure and Judicial Efficiency: The Lex Mundi Project." World Bank, Washington, D.C. Processed.

Fisher, Franklin. 2000. "The IBM and Microsoft Case: What's the Difference?" *American Economic Review* 90(2):18–21.

Glaeser, Edward, and Andrei Shleifer. 2001. "The Rise of the Regulatory State." NBER Working Paper 8650. National Bureau of Economic Research, Cambridge, Mass.

Glenn, H. Patrick. 2000. *Legal Traditions of the World: Sustainable Diversity in Law*. New York: Oxford University Press.

Hill, Hal. 2003. "Industry." In Arthur Baliscan and Hal Hill, eds., *The Philippine Economy: Development, Policy, and Challenges*. Oxford, U.K.: Oxford University Press.

Hsiao, F. S. 1982. "Wo-guo chanye jizhonglu zhi ceding yu fenxin" [The measurement of industry concentration in Taiwan]. *Taipei City Bank Monthly* 13(5):43–56.

Hsueh, Li-Min, Chen-kuo Hsu, and Dwight H. Perkins. 2001. *Industrialization and the State: The Changing Role of the Taiwan Government in the Economy, 1945–1998*. Cambridge, Mass.: Harvard University Press.

Johnson, Chalmers A. 1983. *MITI and the Japanese Miracle: The Growth of Industrial Policy 1925–1975*. Stanford, Calif.: Stanford University Press.

Kamarul, Bahrin, and Roman Tomasic. 1999. "The Rule of Law and Corporate Insolvency in Six Asian Legal Systems." In Kanishka Jayasuriya, ed., *Law, Capitalism, and Power in Asia*. London: Routledge.

Kim, Eun Mee. 1997. *Big Business, Strong State: Collusion and Conflict in South Korean Development, 1960–1990*. New York: State University of New York Press.

Kirk, Donald. 1999. *Korean Crisis: Unraveling of the Miracle in the IMF Era*. New York: St. Martin's Press.

Kong, Qingjiang. 2002. *China and the World Trade Organization: A Legal Perspective*. New Jersey, Singapore, and London: World Scientific.

Krueger, Anne, and Jungho Yoo. 2001. "Chaebol Capitalism and the Currency-Financial Crisis in Korea." Paper prepared for the Korea Conference, National Bureau of Economic Research, Cambridge, Mass., February 9.

LaPorta, Rafael, Florencio Lopez-de-Silanes, Andrei Shleifer, and Robert Vishny. 1998. "Law and Finance." *Journal of Political Economy* 106(6):1133–55.

"Law Set to Push Indonesian Debtors over the Edge." 1998. *Financial Times*, August 20.

Lee, Jong-Wha. 1998. "Capital Goods Imports and Long-Run Growth." *Journal of Development Economics* 48(1):91–110.

Lincoln, Edward J. 2001. *Arthritic Japan: The Slow Pace of Economic Reform*. Washington, D.C.: Brookings Institution Press.

Linnan, David K. 1999. "Insolvency Reform and the Indonesia Financial Crisis." *Bulletin of Indonesian Economic Studies* 35(2):107–37.

Lubman, Stanley. 1999. *Bird in a Cage: Legal Reform in China after Mao*. Palo Alto, Calif.: Stanford University Press.

Mishkin, Frederic S., and Philip E. Strahan. 1999. "What Will Technology Do to Financial Structure?" NBER Working Paper 6892. National Bureau of Economic Research, Cambridge, Mass.

Miwa, Yoshiro, and J. Mark Ramseyer. 2002. "Banks and Economic Growth: Implications from Japanese History." *Journal of Law and Economics* 45(1):127–64.

Nam, Il Chong, and Soogeun Oh. 2001. "Asian Insolvency Regimes from a Comparative Perspective: Problems and Issues for Reform." In *Insolvency Systems in Asia: An Efficiency Perspective*. Paris: Organisation for Economic Co-operation and Development.

Pistor, Katharina, and Phillip A. Wellons. 1998. *The Role of Law and Legal Institutions in Asian Economic Development, 1960–1995*. Hong Kong, China: Oxford University Press.

Ramseyer, J. Mark, and Minoru Nakazato. 1999. *Japanese Law: An Economic Approach*. Chicago and London: University of Chicago Press.

Ravenscraft, David J., and F. M. Scherer. 1987. *Mergers, Sell-offs, and Economic Efficiency*. Washington, D.C.: Brookings Institution Press.

Schultz, Jennifer. 2001. "Day of the Shareholder." *Far Eastern Economic Review*, September 13, pp. 53–55.

Shleifer, Andrei, and Robert W. Vishny. 1997. "A Survey of Corporate Governance." *Journal of Finance* 52(2):737–75.

"Southeast Asia Bankruptcy Law." 2000. *Oxford Analytica*, August 21.

Stein, Jeremy C. 2002. "Information Production and Capital Allocation: Decentralization vs. Hierarchical Firms." *Journal of Finance* 57(5):1891–922.

Steinfeld, Edward S. 2004. "Chinese Enterprise Development and the Challenge of Global Integration." In Shahid Yusuf, M. Anjum Altaf, and Kaoru Nabeshima, eds., *Global Production Networking and Technological Change in East Asia*. New York: Oxford University Press.

Stern, Joseph J., Ji-hong Kim, Dwight H. Perkins, and Jung-ho Yoo. 1995. *Industrialization and the State: The Korean Heavy and Chemical Industry Drive*. Cambridge, Mass.: Harvard University Press.

Stiglitz, Joseph, and Shahid Yusuf, eds. 2001. *Rethinking the East Asian Miracle*. New York: Oxford University Press.

Stulz, Rene. 2001. "Does Financial Structure Matter for Economic Growth? A Corporate Finance Perspective." In Asli Demirgüç-Kunt and Ross Levine, eds., *Financial Structure and Economic Growth: A Cross-Country Comparison of Banks, Markets, and Development*. Cambridge, Mass.: MIT Press.

Teik, Khoo Boo. 1999. "Between Law and Politics: The Malaysian Judiciary since Independence." In Kanishka Jayasuriya, ed., *Law, Capitalism, and Power in Asia*. London: Routledge.

Vietnam, General Department of Statistics. 2003. *Vietnam Business Briefs*, December 5.

Wade, Robert. 1990. *Governing the Market: Economic Theory and the Role of Government in East Asian Industrialization*. Princeton, N.J.: Princeton University Press.

Wiwattanakantang, Yupana. 2001. "Controlling Shareholders and Corporate Value: Evidence from Thailand." *Finance Journal* 9(4):323–62.

World Bank. 2000. "Philippines: Judicial Reform." World Bank, Washington, D.C. Processed.

Yoo, Seong Min, and Sung Soon Lee. 1997. "Evolution of Industrial Organization and Policy Response in Korea, 1945–1995." In Dong-Se Cha, Kwang Suk Kim, and Dwight H. Perkins, eds., *The Korean Economy, 1945–1995: Performance and Vision for the 21st Century*. Seoul: Korea Development Institute.

CHAPTER 8

GOVERNANCE AND THE INTERNET

Richard Rose

It might be profitable to look upon government somewhat less as a problem of power and somewhat more as a problem of steering. Steering is decisively a matter of communication, and information is absolutely essential for communication.
—Karl W. Deutsch (1966, pp. xxvii)

The Internet's rapid rise has produced conflicting visions of its likely effects. Some are Orwellian in depicting the threat that government would control citizens through massive files recording what individuals say in e-mails. Other visions are politically utopian. For example, Stanford economist Lawrence Lau (2000) rejects Schumpeter's (1952) view of major societal changes imposing both costs and benefits, claiming that the Internet makes possible "creation without destruction" because "there are no vested interests to protect; no existing business to be cannibalized." Such an assertion holds true only if one ignores the existing institutions and practices of governance. If the Internet is to change how governments operate, then existing institutions must change or be reorganized to the point of extinction. In some developing countries, there is an additional complication: modern institutions must be created where they do not exist. Although differing in their forecasts, both Internet utopians and dystopians are technological determinists.

This chapter is a revised version of a paper prepared for a World Bank seminar on East Asia's Future Economy at the Kennedy School of Government, Harvard University, and the East Asia Institute of Columbia University. Thanks to Guo Liang, Chinese Academy of Social Sciences; Takeshi Inoguchi, University of Tokyo; Thomas Riehle and Gus Schattenberg, Ipsos-Reid International; and Adrian Shepherd, Oxford Internet Institute, for research assistance. I also would like to thank Shahid Yusuf for the invitation to write about a novel and stimulating topic and for constructive editorial comments. The paper is part of the author's project on Lesson-Drawing, financed by the Future Governance Programme of the British Economic and Research Council (grant L216252017).

Although Internet technology is much the same around the world, governments are not. Thus, the Internet's effect on governance will depend not only on a country's information technology but also on the preexisting governance practices of a state. Where institutions of governance are not yet (or are only imperfectly) bureaucratic, then radical administrative reforms are necessary before Internet technology can be used to good effect. Where governments have not been committed to openness or have practiced censorship, the Internet's capacity to promote free communication poses a political challenge.

Among the countries of East Asia, great variations exist both in access to technology and in governance. Although differences in Internet access between rich and poor countries are often recognized, there is a tendency to ignore differences in political institutions within the region. To understand the role of the Internet in governance, we must first understand how countries have been governing themselves without the Internet. East Asian economies—China, Hong Kong (China), Indonesia, Japan, the Republic of Korea, Malaysia, Myanmar, the Philippines, Singapore, Taiwan (China), Thailand, and Vietnam—constitute a category rather than a homogeneous group. Political differences between the economies resist Lee Kwan Yew's attempt to assume a common set of Asian cultural values on the region.[1]

The role of the Internet in governance can be understood only in terms of the interaction of new technology with well-established governments. Propositions about e-governance based on an ideal type model of government and politics in the United States or Scandinavia cannot be applied without regard to differences in context in China or Indonesia. A major study of attempts to introduce new information technology while ignoring the realities of governmental context concludes, "Failure predominates" (Heeks and Bhatnagar 1999).

Where East Asian governments are already bureaucratized, open, and accountable, the capacity exists to use of the Internet's potential to increase efficiency and speed up and increase the interaction of citizens with government. However, where governments are still struggling to introduce compliance with bureaucratic rules and there is no readiness to open up to public scrutiny what is done within the black box of government, then proposals to introduce the Internet will have an inspection effect, challenging governors to reform existing practices as a condition of good governance and economic development as well as for effective use of the Internet.

---

1. Compare Yew's view with Fukuyama (2001), Zakaraia (1994), and the global barometer surveys at http://www.globalbarometer.org.

NATIONAL DIFFERENCES IN INTERNET USE

Before the use of the Internet can take off, the infrastructure for its use must be present: telephone lines, widely distributed computers, and so forth. Up to a point, technology can compensate for low levels of early investment in infrastructure; for example, cell phones eliminate the need for telephone lines and even offer a limited amount of Internet access. However, the availability of twenty-first century technology is a function of economic development—and economic differences between and within East Asian societies are of long standing (see Sidorenko and Findlay 2001). Before the so-called digital divide, there was the computer divide, the telephone divide, and the electricity divide.

In Asia as in the Western Hemisphere, there are today two types of digital divide. At the national level, there is a divide between economies where the overwhelming majority of citizens have access to the Internet (for example, Japan or Singapore) and economies where very few have access (such as Myanmar and Vietnam). In economies where access is high, whether individuals use the Internet reflects differences in motivation and familiarity (differences that might be found, for example, between young and old citizens).

Technological Requisites and Social Multipliers of Internet Access

Personal computers (PCs) have brought computing power within the reach of hundreds of millions (and potentially billions) of Asians. Yet today, there are great cross-national differences in the availability of PCs. There are 622 PCs per 1,000 persons in Singapore; thus, many Singaporeans have access to a PC at home as well as at work or school. In Hong Kong (China), Japan, Korea, and Taiwan (China), the situation is similar; there is the equivalent of about one PC for every household. Among the bottom six East Asian countries, the number of PCs ranges from 40 per 1,000 persons in Thailand to very few in Indonesia, Myanmar, and Vietnam. Although differences in computer access exist among countries of the European Union (EU), too, the contrast between East Asian countries is far greater.

Whereas a PC can be used to play solitaire, the Internet is a tool for linking people and organizations in a communications network. When the Internet began to take off in the 1990s, access to telephone lines varied greatly between the most and least industrial countries of East Asia. Even after adjusting for purchasing power parities, charges were especially high not only in Indonesia, Thailand, and Vietnam, but also in Japan (UNDP 2001, table A2.4). During the 1990s, the liberalization of telecommunications increased mainline telephone connections. The development of mobile cell phones has led to an explosion in connections, because a cell phone network is less expensive to build and can readily overcome geographical barriers. Today, Taiwan, China, reports that it has more cell phones than people, and leading East Asian economies have more cell phones per 1,000 persons than the United States. In developing Asian economies, cell phone usage is growing rapidly too, and in the poorest economies it exceeds access to landlines (figure 8.1).

Today, the total number of telephone connections exceeds the total population in five East Asian economies: Hong Kong (China), Japan, Korea, Singapore, and Taiwan (China). The ratio of telephones to population is better than 1:2 in Malaysia, about 1:3 in Thailand and China, and better than 1:5 in the Philippines. This level of diffusion means that, even in economies where a telephone is not a fixture within the household,

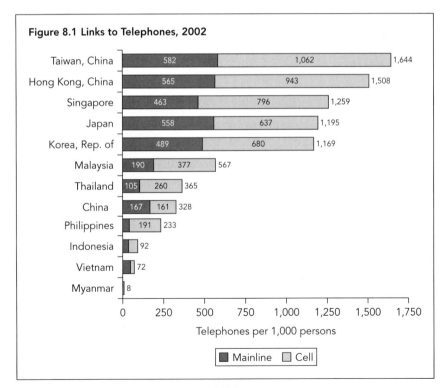

Figure 8.1 Links to Telephones, 2002

Telephones per 1,000 persons

	Mainline	Cell	Total
Taiwan, China	582	1,062	1,644
Hong Kong, China	565	943	1,508
Singapore	463	796	1,259
Japan	558	637	1,195
Korea, Rep. of	489	680	1,169
Malaysia	190	377	567
Thailand	105	260	365
China	167	161	328
Philippines	191		233
Indonesia			92
Vietnam			72
Myanmar			8

■ Mainline □ Cell

Source: International Telecommunications Union (2002).

most people will have a friend with telephone access, and telephones can be found in all but the most remote villages.

Studies of the social uses of technology emphasize, however, that it is misleading to estimate the number of information technology (IT) or Internet users from data about hardware. A computer in a school or library is used by far more people than the business executive's laptop stuffed with confidential data. Social institutions and networks can readily multiply access. In countries of the Organisation for Economic Co-operation and Development (OECD), the median citizen is able to access the Internet in many places—home, work, school, a café, or a friend's house—and the average Internet user regularly signs on from at least two places (Oxford Internet Institute 2003).

In economies at the leading or advancing edge of Internet use, such as Korea and Taiwan (China), people most frequently sign on the Internet at home, and both adults and youths may use a home computer (table 8.1). The global Ipsos-Reid *Face of the Web* (2001, module 8, p. 82) survey

**Table 8.1 Opportunities for Internet Access, 2001
(percentage of population)**

Place of access	Leading-edge economies[a]	Advancing economies[b]	Emergent economies[c]
Home	50	37	19
Someone else's home	46	23	25
Post office or library	47	13	14
Other government building			
Work	38	24	17
School	15	9	10
Internet café or bar	12	7	11
Computer electronic shop	15	8	9
Other fixed location	11	4	9
Mean access points	2.33	1.25	1.14
No Internet access	14	30	33
Never heard of Internet	4	11	17
Total without Internet access	18	41	50

Note: Table shows responses to the following question: "Regardless of whether or not you use the Internet, do you currently have access to the Internet?" Responses were based on a total of 18,713 interviews in 30 countries worldwide.

a. Leading-edge category included 11 economies (such as the Republic of Korea and Sweden) and 6,586 respondents.

b. Advancing category included eight economies (such as France and Taiwan, China) and 4,020 respondents.

c. Emergent category included eight economies (including urban China) and 4,060 respondents.

Source: Ipsos-Reid (2001, p. 8).

calculates that 36 percent of home computers have three or more users, 41 percent have two users, and only 23 percent have just one user.[2] A large portion of the population can access the Internet from public facilities, such as the library or a local post office, which in many countries was historically responsible for providing telephones. The market offers yet another point of access through Internet cafés and kiosks, and so, too, do the homes of friends.

Where Internet use is just now emerging, such as urban China, a population equal in size to that of the United States, household access is not the norm, but urbanites do have a wide variety of access points. Access at work is less important than access through the market or contacts with friends. Even though only a minority of urban Chinese sign on the Internet, they demonstrate a widespread awareness of where the Internet can be accessed: the average Chinese can identify almost as many access points as do residents in countries where the Internet is advancing. In developing countries in East Asia, there appear to be a large number of proxy users—that is, people who could ask a friend or go to a shop, a café, or a kiosk to send an e-mail for them or get them information from the World Wide Web.

The social multiplier effect of the Internet is further heightened through the two-step flow of communication (Katz and Lazarsfeld 1955; Rose 2000). Those who use the Internet as a source of political information are likely to be opinion leaders who talk about politics with other people. This multiplier effect transmits political news to many people who are not Internet users. Moreover, a document received by e-mail can be printed out, photocopied, and passed from hand to hand. In Malaysia, after Deputy Prime Minister Anwar Ibrahim was detained, activists downloaded Internet reports and sold photocopies in the streets and markets of Kuala Lumpur (Wong 2001, p. 385).

Internet Users

The supply of IT resources is a necessary but not sufficient condition for Internet use. To ascertain actual use of the Internet, it is necessary to

---

2. Ipsos-Reid data are drawn from two surveys. Surveys about access to the Internet were conducted in 35 countries in November–December 2000, with a total of 20,701 interviews. In East Asia, nationwide samples were undertaken in Hong Kong (China), Japan, Korea, Singapore, and Taiwan (China); quasi-national samples with some rural coverage were undertaken in Malaysia and the Philippines; and urban-only samples were undertaken in China and Thailand. In December 2000, a second survey in 30 of these 35 countries covered Internet users in the past 30 days. A total of 7,688 interviews were conducted.

collect survey data from individuals. Cross-national comparisons place a
premium on consistency in measurement between economies; therefore,
this chapter cites data on Internet use from the International Telecommunications Union (ITU). The ITU figures tend to underestimate usage
because they are calculated as a percentage of the total population, including children too young to have learned how to sign on and elderly people
too old to bother to learn. Moreover, because Internet usage is expanding
rapidly in Asia, by the time a report is in circulation the percentage of
Internet users will have risen.

East Asian economies are divided between those in which Internet use
is high by OECD standards and those in which it is very low (figure 8.2).
On the one hand, in five economies, two-fifths or more of the population
is already on-line: Hong Kong (China), Japan, Korea, Singapore, and
Taiwan (China). On the other hand, there are half a dozen countries
where fewer than 1 in 10 people is on-line; the median falls between
Malaysia and Thailand. Because up to four-fifths of the population of
China is rural, it falls in the category of countries where Internet use is
low as a percentage of the population.

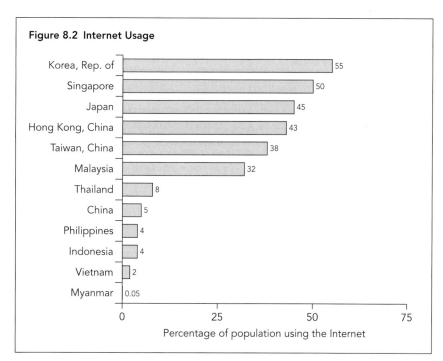

Figure 8.2 Internet Usage

Source: International Telecommunications Union (2003).

Determinants of Internet Use

Many influences of Internet use correlate with each other. For example, a substantial gross domestic product (GDP) per capita is necessary to provide the money for telecommunication infrastructure, and a standard of living above poverty is necessary to have a phone and a PC. Economic determinism is inclined to treat other conditions—such as freedom from media censorship and civil liberties that are associated with using information to hold government accountable—as if they were merely by-products of a society that is modern in social and economic terms. However, political scientists argue that these freedoms are independent of economic conditions, and factor analysis confirms this. A statistical analysis of aggregate influences of Internet uses identifies two factors: the first links technological and economic resources, and the second emphasizes freedom of information and civil rights (table 8.2).

Table 8.2 Contextual Influences on Internet Use

Factor analysis of aggregate data for 12 East Asian nations		
Indicator	Modern resources: Factor 1 (percent)	Freedom of information: Factor 2 (percent)
Variance explained	64.1	30.6
Eigenvalue	4.5	2.1
High integrity		
Tran corruption index	96	97
High technology		
Personal computers	97	13
Main phone lines	93	30
High economic		
GDP per capita purchasing power parity	95	16
Urban population	92	25
Information flow		
Media freedom	12	99
Civil rights	17	98

Multiple regression (dependent variable, percentage of Internet users)				
Indicator	Regression statistics			
	b.	SE	Beta	t
1. Modern resources	195	76.6	87	7.3
2. Freedom of information	77	26.7	35	2.9
Adjusted R-squared 84%				

Sources: Data compiled by international intergovernmental and nongovernmental organizations. The civil rights index from Freedom House has been reversed for consistency in signs.

At the aggregate level, both modern resources and freedom of information are important determinants of Internet use. GDP per capita, urbanization, telephone lines per thousand people, and the Transparency International rating on corruption constitute the principal factors differentiating countries according to their percentage of Internet users. Second in importance is a factor combining freedom of the media and civil rights. In other words, individuals who live in a prosperous society that censors citizens will be less inclined to use the Internet, as will be citizens who live in a free society that is still at a middling level of development (table 8.2). Together, the two factors account for 84 percent of the variance in Internet users among 12 economies of East Asia.

The temporal and causal sequence of development is clear. East Asian economies with a high level of GDP per capita were early in promoting nationwide telecommunication facilities. When PCs came on the market two decades ago, these societies had an educated and prosperous population who could make use of them. Before use of the Internet became widespread, economies high in modern resources had met the preconditions for Internet access. Going on-line therefore augmented established patterns of behavior and communication. By contrast, the preconditions of access are still absent in countries where GDP per capita is low and where there are few telephone lines and computers.

In modern societies, where access is not a problem and a substantial proportion of the population is on-line, Internet use can be conceived of as a matter of digital choice. Individual attributes explain why some people use the Internet and others do not. In societies where half or more of the population is on-line (including five East Asian societies), age is the most important determinant of Internet use (OECD 2003; Oxford Internet Institute 2003).

CONDITIONS FOR INTERNET USE IN GOVERNMENT

A modern state can operate effectively only if accurate information flows freely among its institutions and only if information flows regularly between public officials and governors. The Internet is a means of communicating information accurately, instantly, and over long distances. Therefore, the instrumental question that the Internet raises is, how can public agencies use this new tool to improve the processes of governance? A modern state is also a rule-bound bureaucratic state, because the routines of policy are carried out by low-level public officials applying rules laid down by their political superiors. The

Internet—and the computer even more so—operates according to rule-bound protocols.

The use of the Internet in governance, therefore, requires that government maintain a free and open flow of information within government and between governors and citizens to whom these governors may be accountable. It also requires that public officials carry out the routine delivery of public programs according to rules laid down in public laws. On every continent, the extent to which governments meet both criteria varies, and a government that is not yet, or only imperfectly, bureaucratic and open has yet to meet the conditions for making most effective use of the Internet.

The Internet's Potential for Marginal and Structural Effect on Government

The potential effect of the Internet will vary with the existing context of governance. In some cases, it will make marginal changes in efficiency and information flows, whereas in others, its inspection effect will lead to structural challenges.

Marginal efficiency gains. If a government operates according to impersonal rules, then it is bureaucratically effective. In such circumstances, the Internet has the potential to produce marginal increases in efficiency in internal administration of government and in the delivery of public services to citizens (see OECD 2003 for prescriptions). Following from the role of mainframe computers in enabling government agencies to store and process information, Internet technology can make routine the interaction of public agencies and citizens in filling out tax forms and forms that will entitle the citizens to benefits. E-mails and other Internet facilities can also greatly speed the flow of information within government and with citizens.

But the Internet can hardly transform an already computerized social security system, nor can it easily replace public employees delivering public services on a person-to-person basis, such as primary school teachers and nurses. Moreover, the prior existence of mature bureaucratic organizations institutionalizes many practices, including reliance on "closed" mainframe computer systems, that are path-determined obstacles to using the Internet to create a virtual state (Fountain 2001). Studies of the restricted use at work of the Internet compared with other IT facilities (Oxford Internet Institute 2003) imply that in OECD systems of government the Internet is likely to be a specialized tool with real but marginal advantages in specific settings rather than a general source of innovative transformation.

Multiplying information and increasing its velocity. If a government is already open, the introduction of the Internet will increase the quantity and velocity of political information in circulation. The literature of e-democracy describes how political parties, members of Parliament, civic action groups, and individuals are making some use of the Internet to increase the flow of information between citizens and their elected representatives. Insofar as political parties and activists substitute the Internet for postal services, it has little effect. The ease of communication through the Internet may also multiply the amount of political information. Because there is already plenty of political information in circulation in free societies, this change in medium has marginal effects.

Greater information flows do not increase the time available to governors to process information. Because democratic dialogue is about expressing conflicting opinions about what government ought to do, increasing information inputs to political debate will increase the expression of conflicting views. Political decisionmakers will still need to reconcile competing demands on government, and they may find greater difficulty in doing so because of having more conflicting views fired at them with greater frequency and intensity.

Inspection. If bureaucratic records are not already systematically kept, a proposal to introduce the Internet into governmental processes will have an inspection effect. The systems analysis required for any Internet application will spotlight deficiencies in the management of government records, such as missing data, inaccuracies caused by double-counting or "massaging" of numbers to give an appearance of success, and suppression of information documenting personal favoritism or corruption. Even if paper records are ample, the fact that they have not yet been computerized for digital storage and analysis means that it could require years to make the legacy of paper forms accessible on the Internet. Moreover, if records are kept in a discursive literary format, they are not structured for on-line retrieval.

Political challenge. If a government is not open, the Internet will challenge the regime's commitment to restricting information flows, because it offers a cheap and easy way for organizations and individuals to circulate information that governors have previously kept within narrow circles. If governors censor and limit Web sites within their country, critics and exiles can escalate their challenge by establishing offshore Web sites accessible within that country. Paradoxically, government censorship adds to the value of unofficial and critical information by making it scarce and by encouraging its dissemination through informal networks by word of mouth as well as electronically.

Bureaucratic Processes

The greater the volume of information, the more important it is that the information be structured. The mark of a modern bureaucracy (and a prerequisite for e-governance) is a clear organizational structure—that is, a clear structure of routine information flows within and between organizations. For an organization to use the Internet for anything more than passing verbal messages between individuals, the information itself must be structured so that it can be processed, acted on, disseminated, and retrieved through information technology algorithms.

By definition, a modern state is bureaucratic: officials act according to the rule of law, and they deliver goods and services according to impersonal rules rather than on the basis of favoritism, arbitrary whim, or side payments (Weber 1948, p. 215). Bureaucracies are rule-bound hierarchies in which those at the top of an organization lay down rules that subordinate officials are expected to apply routinely and honestly. Postal charges are an example of bureaucracy in action. Postal clerks do not quote different prices or compete for trade; they charge the rates laid down by national rules. A postal clerk makes no concession in the rates for friends and family. To post a parcel, one must wrap it according to regulations, weigh it, and then apply the rules to determine the charge for its weight, format, and destination. Just as the price of a soft drink from a vending machine is the same for everyone, the rules that govern bureaucracies are impersonal—that is, they are the same for everyone. In fact, Max Weber referred to bureaucracy as offering vending machine justice.

The Internet is rule bound too: a person ordering a book or a cheap air ticket through the World Wide Web is marched through an algorithm that asks the user a series of questions, receives and processes responses according to prespecified formats, and then produces a result. Likewise, bureaucrats administering such routine services as social security benefits march claimants through a rule-based algorithm that asks a series of questions so that they can input the data necessary to calculate the cash benefit to which a claimant is lawfully entitled.

A modern state is a necessary condition for applying IT widely in public administration, because IT depends on impersonal rule-based procedures as well as educated personnel and the money to buy computers. High-tech computer systems will fail in states with low-tech administrators making decisions. In countries where whom you know or what you pay is important in obtaining public services, computer-based administration can, in principle, increase the rule of law. Computer algorithms can be installed in PCs that low-level bureaucrats can be required to use when dealing with claimants, thus greatly reducing the scope for discretion and favoritism. The Internet can be used to transmit the information from local offices to higher-ranking officials, who can use computerized information systems to flag apparent discrepancies between rule-bound behavior and what some low-level officials may be doing. Yet, for the same reason, low-ranking officials can resist the introduction of new technology that will remove the private benefits that they obtain from misapplying the law.

In East Asia, governments vary substantially in the extent to which they are bureaucratic in the modern sense. The degree of variation is illustrated by Transparency International's Corruption Perceptions Index, which combines ratings from multiple sources in order to estimate the extent to which governments follow their own laws.[3] Transparency International's ratings show that some East Asian countries adhere to the rule of law as much as or more than the average EU member state. On a 10-point scale in which 133 economies are rated, Singapore (9.4) and Hong Kong, China (8.0), both rate well above the United States, and Japan is rated near the median EU member state. However, other East Asian states show a degree of evasiveness of rules that is well below the world median. Indonesia and Myanmar are in the bottom tenth of the index, and Vietnam is in the bottom quartile. On the 10-point index, all three countries have scores of 2.4 or less.

Radius of Information

In principle, the Internet offers the opportunity to increase information flows between governors and citizens. The Internet can expedite the flow of information between the central government and field offices and agencies that have been set up according to new public management theories.

---

3. For more information about Transparency International's work, see its Web site at http://www.transparency.org.

In addition, government departments can set up Web sites to inform citizens of their rights and obligations, and they can use the Internet to transact routine activities such as the issue of car or television licenses as well as by post or over the counter. Unlike telephone or airlines charges, the charge for using the Internet is based on time rather than distance. Hence, the Internet is particularly efficient in countries where geography and low income combine to inhibit nationwide communication.

The openness of the Internet can promote political participation and accountability if it is used by civil society organizations such as political parties, the media, and nongovernmental organizations (NGOs) to publicize unofficial criticism of government and to voice demands for action. Writing as chief economist at the World Bank, Joseph Stiglitz (2001, p. 56) has endorsed participatory dialogues as "both helpful to and perhaps even essential for a lasting transformation of societies in low-income and developing countries."

The extent to which the Internet is used to promote openness and accountability depends not only on technology but also on the norms and institutions prevailing within a political system. In most states of the world, including those in continental Europe, public opinion has historically been official opinion; the state determined what information could and could not circulate (Noelle-Neumann 1993). By contrast, Scandinavian governments had a tradition of openness in the flow of information long before the Internet was invented. In Anglo-American countries, there is a tension between demands for freedom of information about government and privacy values that constrain the information that government holds about individuals (Tallo 2004). Before the Internet, Asian governments were much closer to the continental European model of restricting information flows than to the openness of Scandinavia. A few were described by critics as having an "informational black hole," restricting the circulation of information to political and economic insiders (see Haley and Tan 1996).

Today, East Asian governments vary widely in the extent to which they allow civil society organizations to circulate information freely and to hold government accountable through free and fair competitive elections. Freedom House (2003) rates five East Asian political systems as free and open: Japan, Korea, the Philippines, Taiwan (China), and Thailand; four as partly free, Hong Kong (China), Indonesia, Malaysia, and Singapore; and three as not allowing the free circulation of political information: China, Myanmar, and Vietnam (see also Hsieh and Newman 2002).

The ideal preconditions for making efficient use of the Internet are (a) that a government already follows bureaucratic rules and (b) that it is

Table 8.3 Classifying East Asian Systems of Government

	Follows bureaucratic rules	
Accountability	High	Low
High	Japan, Taiwan (China)	Indonesia, Korea (Rep. of), Philippines, Thailand
Low	Hong Kong (China), Singapore	China, Malaysia, Myanmar, Vietnam

Sources: For bureaucratic rules, placement on Transparency International's Corruption Perceptions Index. For accountability, placement on Freedom House's Index of Political Rights and Elections.

open and accountable—but this scenario is only one of four possibilities that arise when governments are classified on those two counts. This classification can be made empirically by using the Transparency International and Freedom House ratings referred to above. Doing so shows that countries distribute into four different categories (table 8.3). Two nations, Japan and Taiwan, China, meet the ideal standards; both are rated as rule-bound bureaucracies and open and accountable. In four countries—Indonesia, Korea, the Philippines, and Thailand—governments are relatively open and accountable, but there are major departures from rule-bound governance. Hong Kong (China) and Singapore are distinctive in showing a high degree of rule-bound bureaucratic governance yet allowing limited accountability and openness. Four East Asian countries—China, Malaysia, Myanmar, and Vietnam—meet neither of the ideal criteria for implementing the Internet, for they are not rule-bound bureaucracies nor are they open and accountable. The substantial contrast in governance within East Asia emphasizes that the uses of the Internet in governance today depend less on the capabilities of Internet technology and more on how governors respond to the opportunities and challenges that the Internet offers.

USES OF THE INTERNET IN GOVERNANCE TODAY

The extent to which government is affected marginally or structurally depends on the extent and composition of its policies. The failure of e-government enthusiasts to understand what government actually does leads to unrealistic claims. For example, routine activities such as writing checks for pensions are readily amenable to efficiency gains through computerization. But writing checks is a very small portion of the total cost of social security administration: the big cost is cashing the checks—and most governments of the world do not have the money to do so for all their elderly citizens.

In the developing economies of East Asia, the range of public services to which the Internet is immediately applicable is very limited. The opportunities the Internet offers for efficiency gains by filing income tax returns on-line are of little relevance in economies where income is low and not legally subject to taxation or where negotiating the minimum tax is the standard operating procedure. Even in industrial Asian economies, the level of public spending—and thus the potential for cost savings—is lower than in EU member states. For example, tax revenue is 41.5 percent of GDP in the median state of the European Union, but only 28.8 percent in Japan and 21.4 percent in Korea. Similarly, public employment in Japan is less than half that in the United States and less than two-fifths that of the median EU member state (OECD 2000).

Web Presence

A United Nations (UN) study of e-governance, which was based on an analysis of the information and facilities that existing government Web sites offer their citizens, has benchmarked the current use of the Internet by governments around the world (UNDPEPA 2003, pp. 10 and following). The UN study has five categories of Web presence, ranging from minimal to seamless. An ideal is represented by a fully integrated capacity for cyberspace access to any combination of public agencies dealing in related ways with a common problem of citizens, such as health services. No government anywhere is ranked as having created seamless on-line access to its services.

Table 8.4 shows the other four categories of Web presence. Among East Asian governments, four—Hong Kong (China), Korea, Singapore, and Taiwan (China)—allow users to conduct a variety of transactions on-line, including calculating or paying taxes and claiming benefits from public agencies. These governments are thus in the highest group worldwide, along with such countries as Finland and the United States. However, since there is no obligation on citizens to use on-line services and many citizens carry on as before, the net cost savings are limited.

Interactive Web sites enable citizens to get answers to frequently asked questions on-line and to download official forms. Moreover, this information is available 24 hours a day, 7 days a week, providing flexibility to citizens and preventing the need for shift work in public offices. The three countries offering interactive Web services differ substantially in the extent to which citizens are on-line. The governments of Malaysia and the

Table 8.4 Web Presence of East Asian Governments

Category of Web presence	Definition	Economies in category
Transactional	Users can pay for services or conduct financial transactions with the government on-line.	Hong Kong (China), Korea, Singapore, Taiwan (China)
Interactive	Users can download official forms, contact agencies, and make appointments and requests.	Japan, Malaysia, Philippines
Information platform	Many government agencies have Web sites with substantial amounts of information, the Web sites are regularly updated, and there are links between Web sites.	China, Indonesia, Thailand, Vietnam
Minimal	Major government agencies have formal Web sites, but the information provided is limited, basic, and not regularly updated.	Myanmar

Source: UNDPEPA (2003).

Philippines are ahead of their citizenry in being oriented to the Internet, whereas the government in Japan has yet to make on-line transactions truly user-friendly.

Four East Asian nations are in the median UN group, which uses the World Wide Web as a platform for providing information to citizens without any interactive features. They are China, Indonesia, Thailand, and Vietnam, and their position is consistent with their lower level of economic development and Internet use. Only one East Asian government, Myanmar, makes a minimal amount of information available on-line.

Establishing an information platform is a precondition for introducing an interactive Web site, and an interactive Web site is a precondition for a transactional Web site. Therefore, it is realistic to regard the current Web presence of governments as temporary rather than fixed evidence of a digital divide. For example, Japan can be expected to increase the transactional element in its e-governance services, and countries with information platforms can be expected to introduce interactive elements. However, the frustrations of national governments trying to upgrade their transactional services to provide a seamless Web facility for citizens caution against assuming that East Asian countries with a well-developed set of services will be able to move further. EU countries have found that there are many "back office" problems in creating links between different computerized databases, some arising from technological difficulties, some from inter-departmental jealousies, and others from data protection laws that prevent the linkage of records held by different government agencies about a single individual (Kubicek, Millard, and Westholm 2003).

Singapore is the paradigm of a government using the Internet to increase the efficiency with which it delivers bureaucratic services to citizens. Its Web site, www.ecitizen.gov.sg, offers electronic assistance about every phase of the life cycle. The site map offers dozens of clickable headings of individual and family interest, starting with children and parenthood, through teenage and youth, courtship and marriage, and the elderly and aging, plus it includes guides to family support and family resources. The site also offers links to agencies dealing with programs about arts and heritage, recreation, sports, defense, safety and security, elections, law, employment, education, health, housing, travel, and transport. In turn, each main section has many subdivisions. As a backup, citizens who have trouble finding what they want on-line are offered help-line telephone numbers.

The Singapore government's Web site is distinctive not only because of its detail but also because of the conditions that make its creation possible. The government is fully bureaucratized; its administration has a very high level of honesty; it is a city-state without barriers from geography or federalism; it regulates many social activities and delivers many services to citizens; and GDP per capita is similar to that of France, Germany, or the United Kingdom rather than that of the median East Asian country. Insofar as Singapore has lessons to offer, they may be to OECD countries on other continents. For example, in 2000, 40 percent of Singapore taxpayers filed their personal income tax return over the Internet, compared with 28 percent of U.S. taxpayers and a far smaller proportion of Europeans.

When a country is far below Singapore's level of bureaucratized governance, an attempt to introduce Internet technology into public administration is likely to be of little use. For example, cash transfers cannot be made to citizens if a government is so poor that it has no income maintenance programs. Even a seemingly straightforward initiative, such as computerizing payments to school teachers in an African country, turned into a disaster when many teachers went months without a salary because the paper-based personnel records on which the system depended for input were inaccurate (Cain 1999, pp. 141 and following).

Bigger problems arise when a dissociation occurs between paper records and informal decisionmaking practices. In such circumstances, a Web site can give a glowing picture of the national economy or falsely precise demographic details, when the reality is different (see, for example, Huang 1996; Rose 2002b). In a country such as China, with bureaucratic controls, *guanxi* relations create differences between what is documented on paper and what happens in practice.

Increased Openness through a Wider Radius of Information

Great variability occurs within as well as across continents in the extent to which governments allow political information to circulate freely and as a right. The UN study of e-governance created an Information Access Index, which combined ratings of the extent to which a government conducted its activities behind an opaque screen and allowed citizens to hold it accountable (figure 8.3). The index correlates highly with an alternative

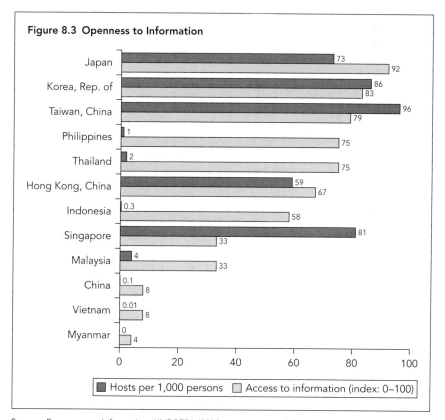

Figure 8.3 Openness to Information

Japan — 73 / 92
Korea, Rep. of — 86 / 83
Taiwan, China — 96 / 79
Philippines — 1 / 75
Thailand — 2 / 75
Hong Kong, China — 59 / 67
Indonesia — 0.3 / 58
Singapore — 81 / 33
Malaysia — 4 / 33
China — 0.1 / 8
Vietnam — 0.01 / 8
Myanmar — 0 / 4

■ Hosts per 1,000 persons □ Access to information (index: 0–100)

Sources: For access to information, UNDPEPA (2003, pp. 27, 62) and, for Hong Kong (China), Myanmar, and Taiwan (China), Freedom House's Media Freedom Index, as reported in Karlekar (2003). For hosts per 1,000 persons, International Telecommunications Union (2003).

measure, the Media Freedom Index, which is compiled by an NGO, Freedom House, on the basis of an assessment of national media laws, political and economic influences on reporting news, harassment of journalists, and confiscation of media facilities.

There are extreme variations in openness between Japan and Myanmar, the countries that are, respectively, most and least open to information (figure 8.3). More than half of all East Asian governments allow information to circulate with few or limited restrictions. Although there is a correlation between political openness and high Internet use, the link is limited. Countries that are above average in political openness include Indonesia, the Philippines, and Thailand, all of which are low in Internet use. In a complementary manner, Malaysia and Singapore are well below the median for political openness but average or well above average in Internet use (see figure 8.2).

In addition to information from the government, the Internet can distribute information about the government without official restrictions. The number of Internet hosts registered in a country is a rough indicator of the quantity of information available electronically in the national language, because sites with a national suffix are less likely to use English than are those registered with an address such as .com, which lacks any geographical reference point.[4] This observation is particularly true of sites with political relevance, such as Web sites of political parties, Web sites of national newspapers, and Web sites operated by civil society institutions and NGOs.

Every East Asian economy except Myanmar has tens of thousands of host sites—more than enough to provide many sources of information to the avid searcher. Japan boasts more than 9 million host sites and Taiwan, China, more than 2 million. When population differences are taken into account, there is almost one Web site for every 10 people in Taiwan, China, and one for every 12 people in Singapore.

Critics of government can use Internet sites to help organize opposition to the government. Criticisms can be expressed more fully and freely on the Internet than in state-controlled broadcasting, and the cost of setting up a Web site is far less than that of printing a newspaper; circulation can be nationwide and instantaneous. Because the barriers to Web entry by NGOs are low, a great diversity of opinions can be found. Whereas the claims of established civil society organizations to representativeness can

---

4. Note that the World Bank (1998, p. 297) assumes that all Internet hosts without a country identification in their electronic address are in the United States, an assumption significantly inflating U.S. preeminence on the Web.

be verified, the representativeness of a floating population of Internet users cannot. Even if Web sites claim to be the "voice of the people," they cannot show evidence of electoral legitimacy. The challenge facing political organizations is not only to appeal to "nerd potatoes" who do not budge from their video display units, but also to mobilize Internet users to take an active part in politics.

A striking example of electoral mobilization was the Korean parliamentary election in 2000, when a civic group posted on its Web site information about the tax evasion and draft-dodging records of 86 candidates. The press had not printed this information. The site received more than 1 million hits on election day, and 58 of the candidates named there were defeated, including some previously favored to win (Cairncross 2001, p. 159).

In Indonesia, Internet access is very limited, but the privatized postal service has established *warpostrom* (electronic mail kiosks) and *wartel* (telecommunication kiosks) at post offices and public places in more than 100 cities and towns throughout the country. After the Asian financial crisis hit in 1997, hundreds of Web sites sprang up to criticize the regime and organize opposition. When President Suharto left office in May 1998, a Jakarta observer described the transfer of power as "the first revolution using the Internet" (quoted in Hill and Sen 2000, p. 119). In the subsequent 1999 election, all contestants, the media, and the National Electoral Commission made extensive use of World Wide Web facilities.

The government of China is distinctive in trying to use the Internet's inspection effect to advance structural changes in governance and the economy while containing Internet-transmitted structural challenges to the monopoly power of the Communist Party (see Hughes and Wacker 2003; Kluver forthcoming). Jiang Zemin, while president of China, said that the Internet is "the engine for the development of the economy and society in the 21st century" (quoted in Sussman 2001, p. 2). To that end, the Chinese government has invested tens of billions of dollars in developing the infrastructure of an Internet-based information society in which there is a steady flow of administrative information between government agencies at the center and between central ministries in Beijing and regional and local officials. The impersonal, rule-bound character of the Internet is seen as reducing the discretionary capacity of low-level officials to exploit those under them and to hide their actions from their hierarchical supervisors. It is also seen as the means of garnering more accurate information about economic activities, information that can be used not only by the central planning system but also by the central tax-collecting authorities. In the words of Zhu Rongji, the former prime minister, in

Chinese e-government, the emphasis is not so much on the *e* but on the *government*, because of the need for a structural "transformation of government in terms of management systems, management values, management patterns, and management methods" (Zhang and Gao 2003).

Concurrently, the Chinese government is seeking to prevent the Internet's use for disseminating political criticism and organizing opposition. To create a "Great Fire Wall" against the spread of unofficial political comment, the government has imposed restrictions on foreign Internet providers, temporarily shut down Internet servers in China, traced individual users to their log-on address, and hacked into Web sites critical of the regime. Possession or distribution of political materials derived from foreign Web sites can be punished with a prison sentence (Wong 2001, p. 382). In effect, the Chinese government is seeking to turn the Internet into an *intranet*—that is, a network delimited by boundaries maintained by the state security service (Dai 2000, pp. 145 and following). However, the amount of government funds and effort devoted to surveillance and control is very small by comparison to public expenditure on giving tens of millions of Chinese access to the Internet.

In seeking to shape the transnational Internet to its domestic political agenda, China faces both technological and social challenges. As Franda (2002, p. 194) notes, "With more than 200,000 different routes around the major nodes of the Internet, attempts by Chinese authorities to program blockages in large numbers of routes would render Internet service almost unusable." Long before the arrival of the Internet, residents of mainland China communicated with diaspora Chinese through a transnational "bamboo" network based on kin, friends, and business partners (Fukuyama 1995, chapter 8; Weidenbaum and Hughes 1996). The Internet gives electronic substance to this network. As Lin (2001, p. 227) says, "No longer is social capital constrained by time or space; cybernetworks open up the possibility of global reaches in social capital. Social ties can now transcend geopolitical boundaries, and exchanges can occur as fast and as willingly as the actors care to participate."

Although the great majority of Chinese-speakers live in China, 95 percent of Chinese-language Web sites are hosted outside the country. Moreover, many in mainland China have electronic contacts outside the country. A cross-national survey found that 30 percent of Chinese Internet users used e-mail to communicate with other countries, compared with about 20 percent of Internet users from Japan, Korea, and Taiwan (China) (Inoguchi 2002, p. 17). A Chinese Academy of Social Sciences study of Internet users (3,159 respondents in five cities) found that 15 percent of time was spent accessing overseas Chinese Web sites, and 9 percent accessing foreign-language Web sites. Most Chinese Web users trust both domestic sites and overseas Chinese Web sites, and about half trust foreign-language Web sites (Guo and Bu 2001, pp. 9, 12).

DYNAMICS OF DEVELOPMENT

So rapidly is the Internet developing in East Asia that any cross-sectional comparison between economies gives an ephemeral picture. The current digital divide is an artifact of economies at different stages in a dynamic process familiar in the diffusion of innovations: some economies are leaders and others are laggards in adoption (Rogers 1995; Rose 2002a). In leading economies, after everyone who wants Internet access has achieved it, the increase in users will level off. By contrast, in lagging countries, there is much greater scope for an increase in users, especially since the expansion of the Internet, like that of a telephone, depends on network effects. Metcalfe's (1996) law—the value of a network rises with the square of the number of participants—implies very rapid diffusion of Internet access after usage takes off, and East Asian countries that are not high in use today—for example, Malaysia and Thailand—have the potential for catching up quickly (Rose 2004).

The supply of Internet facilities is no problem in East Asian societies such as Korea and Singapore. Internet users are already in the majority among people age 15 to 65, and public agencies are already providing a substantial number of transactional and interactive services on-line. The percentage will slowly increase as the oldest generation, disproportionately nonusers, is replaced by young cohorts who are now the heaviest Internet users. But the substantial minority of nonusers includes many people who do not exercise their proxy capability to ask others to use the Internet, because they do not find it useful. In societies where a majority use the Internet today, leveling off in the number of users will occur insofar as the remainder are excluded not by cost or technophobia but by indifference (Oxford Internet Institute 2003).

To increase e-government where Internet use is already high, policymakers must find ways of increasing demand. Governments cannot engage in cut-price marketing of taxes or give loyalty points for using public services. Ways must be found to make e-government services more convenient for citizens. The next structural advance to encourage demand would be creating a one-stop seamless web of public services available by the Internet, thus integrating institutions separated by internal walls within government. The obstacles to creating a seamless web of public services are formidable, involving both organizational barriers within government and popular habits of individuals who continue to rely on the post, telephone, and face-to-face contact, as they did for decades before the Internet was widely available. In industrial countries, e-governance requires limiting investment to the extent that it pays off in better services, lower administrative costs, or both. With technology and organizational capacities now available, efficiency gains are likely to be marginal.

In developing countries, supply is the problem. A significant portion of the population living in places without Internet access is excluded. To secure takeoff in Internet use in these countries, government initiatives can help overcome structural barriers to Internet access. Such initiatives can build on existing public facilities—for example, having the post office provide Internet services for a fee; providing free access through public libraries, and using schools not only to train youths in the use of PCs and the Internet but also to make electronic facilities available after school hours for the whole community. Provided retailers are not overregulated, markets can expand use too. In urban areas, Internet kiosks and cafés can be established. In places where the idea of the Internet is novel, local entrepreneurs can, like village scribes of old, offer to send messages, fill in forms, or locate information on the Internet. Whereas a home PC is used by only a few family members, public access facilities give hundreds of times more people the opportunity to use the Internet in the course of a month.

Insofar as government and market initiatives increase effective demand, developing economies of East Asia will face two challenges to governance. First, there will be an inspection effect when go-ahead, technologically oriented public officials and their advisers try to introduce the Internet into public administration. Second, introducing new technology will reveal the extent of deficiencies in bureaucratic procedures required for structuring, inputting, and retrieving information electronically.

In countries where closed rather than open government has been the norm, the Internet will challenge governors to make more information available about the process of governance. One challenge can be to increase transparency by opening up to Internet scrutiny the process of allocating large and costly public contracts. A similar challenge would be to reduce sloth by allowing citizens who claim entitlements and bureaucratic superiors to exercise electronic surveillance of counter-level bureaucrats. Where governments have been hesitant to be accountable to citizens for their actions, activist civil society groups can use the Internet to publicize their criticisms of governance and to organize meetings.

Differences between systems of East Asian government (table 8.3) and Internet users (figure 8.2) emphasize that the potential effect of the

Internet on governance will be variable within the region. Where Internet usage is high and the government follows bureaucratic rules and is open, the effect is likely to be marginal. It is likely to be limited to increasing the efficiency of an already bureaucratized system and being open to the input of demands for better services from citizens. Where Internet usage is high but the government is not open, then, in addition to efficiency gains, the Internet will improve the quality of information that citizens receive, because it will be more diverse, coming from unofficial as well as official sources. This access can encourage popular challenges to nonaccountable officials. Where the government is not rule bound and Internet usage is low, then the growth in Internet usage will have an inspection effect within the government, calling attention to the inadequacies of its bureaucratic procedures. It will also create channels for citizens to obtain information critical of the government and to mobilize and put pressure on government to reform by introducing more efficient and equitable procedures. Where Internet usage is low and governments are neither open nor rule bound, there is a diffuse challenge of how to break a low-level equilibrium trap that holds back political and economic development.

In a global context, the Internet can be seen as part of the process of liberalization and development promoted through such diverse agencies as the World Trade Organization and the millennium goals of the United Nations (UNDESA 2003). Just as the World Trade Organization treaties emphasize transnational movement of goods and services, so the Internet emphasizes the transnational movement of information of all kinds. Just as the World Bank (1997) emphasizes the need for modern and transparent institutions of governance to promote economic development, so the inspection effect of the Internet spotlights bureaucratic deficiencies and the absence of rule-bound behavior and offers means for governors to undertake bureaucratic modernization within government and for citizens and institutions of civil society to challenge governors to do so.

REFERENCES

Cain, Piers. 1999. "Automatic Personnel Records for Improved Management of Human Resources." In R. Heeks, ed., *Reinventing Government in the Information Age: International Practice in IT-Enabled Public Sector Reform*. London: Routledge.

Cairncross, Frances. 2001. *The Death of Distance 2.0: How the Communications Revolution Will Change Our Lives*. London: Texere.

Dai, Xiudian. 2000. *The Digital Revolution and Governance*. Aldershot, U.K.: Ashgate.

Deutsch, Karl W. 1966. *The Nerves of Government: Models of Political Communication and Control*, 2nd ed. New York: Free Press.

Fountain, Jane. 2001. *Building the Virtual State: Information Technology and Institutional Change*. Washington, D.C.: Brookings Institution.

Franda, Marcus. 2002. *Internet Development and Politics in Five World Regions*. Boulder, Colo.: Lynne Rienner.

Freedom House. 2003. *Freedom in the World 2003*. Available on-line at http://www.freedomhouse.org.

Fukuyama, Francis. 1995. *Trust: The Social Virtues and the Creation of Prosperity*. New York: Free Press.

———. 2001. "Asian Values in the Wake of the Asian Crisis." In Farrukh Iqbal and Jong-Il You, eds., *Democracy, Market Economics and Development*. Washington, D.C.: World Bank, pp. 149–68.

Guo, Liang, and Wei Bu. 2001. *Survey on the Internet Usage and Impact*. Beijing: Centre for Social Development, Chinese Academy of Social Sciences.

Haley, George T., and Chin-Tiong Tan. 1996. "The Black Hole of Southeast Asia: Strategic Decision-Making in an Informational Void." *Management Decision* 34(9):43–55.

Heeks, Richard, and Subhash Bhatnagar. 1999. "Understanding Success and Failure in Information Age Reform." In Richard Heeks, ed., *Reinventing Government in the Information Age: International Practice in IT-Enabled Public Sector Reform*. London: Routledge, pp. 49–75.

Hill, David T., and Krishna Sen. 2000. "The Internet in Indonesia's New Democracy." *Democratization* 7(1):119–36.

Hsieh, John Fuh-Sheng, and David Newman, eds. 2002. *How Asia Votes*. New York: Chatham House.

Huang, Yasheng. 1996. "The Statistical Agency in China's Bureaucratic System." *Communist and Post-Communist Studies* 29(1):59–75.

Hughes, Christopher R., and Gudrun Wacker, eds. 2003. *China and the Internet: Politics of the Digital Leap Forward*. London: Routledge Curzon.

Inoguchi, Takeshi. 2002. "Voice and Accountability: The Media and the Internet in Democratic Development." University of Tokyo, Tokyo. Processed.

International Telecommunications Union. 2002. "Free Statistics Home Page." Available on-line at http://itu.int/ITU-D/ict/statistics.

———. 2003. "Information Technology." Available on-line at http://itu.int/ITU-D/ict/statistics/at_glance/Internet02.pdf.

Ipsos-Reid. 2001. *The Face of the Web: Wave II: 2000–2001*. Module 4, "Social Communications and the Internet"; Module 8, "Internet Use and Access across the Globe"; and Module 9 "Global Internet Attitudinal Segmentation." Vancouver, B.C.

Karlekar, Karin Deutch, ed. 2003. *Freedom of the Press*. Lanham, Md.: Rowman & Littlefield.

Katz, Elihu, and Paul Lazarsfeld. 1955. *Personal Influence*. Glencoe, Ill.: Free Press.

Kluver, Randolph. Forthcoming. "E-Governance in China: Empowering Citizens or Establishing Control." *Journal of Public Policy* 25.

Kubicek, Herbert, Jeremy Millard, and Hilmar Westholm. 2003. "The Long and Winding Road to One-Stop Government." Paper presented at an Oxford Internet Institute and Information, Communication, and Society Conference, Oxford, U.K., September 18.

Lau, Lawrence J. 2000. "Economic Globalization and the Information Technology Revolution." Paper presented at "Economic Globalization: China and Asia," a conference of the National Committee of the Chinese People's Political Consultative Conferences, Beijing, June 15. Available on-line at http://www.stanford.edu/~ljlau.

Lin, Nan. 2001. *Social Capital: A Theory of Social Structure and Action.* New York: Cambridge University Press.

Metcalfe, Robert. 1996. *Packet Communication.* San Jose, Calif.: Peer-to-Peer Communications.

Noelle-Neumann, Elisabeth. 1993. *The Spiral of Silence*, 2nd ed. Chicago: University of Chicago Press.

OECD (Organisation for Economic Co-operation and Development). 2000. *OECD in Figures.* Paris.

———. 2003. *The e-Government Imperative.* Paris.

Oxford Internet Institute. 2003. *Oxford Internet Survey.* Oxford, U.K.: Oxford Internet Institute. Available on-line at http://www.oii.ox.ac.uk/research.

Rogers, Everett. 1995. *Diffusion of Innovations*, 4th ed. New York: Free Press.

Rose, Richard. 2000. "Policy Networks in Globalization: From Local to Cosmopolitan Networking." *NIRA Review* (Tokyo) 7(1):5–9.

———. 2002a. "Digital Divide or Digital Diffusion?" *World Bank Transition Newsletter* 13(4–5):33–35.

———. 2002b. "Economies in Transformation: A Multidimensional Approach to a Cross-Cultural Problem." *East European Constitutional Review* 11(4)–12(1):62–70.

———. 2004. "Some Thoughts on Governance and the Internet in a Space-Time Context." Paper presented at the Oxford Internet Institute Conference on the Internet and Governance in a Global Context, Oxford, U.K., January 8–10.

Schumpeter, Joseph A. 1952. *Capitalism, Socialism, and Democracy*, 4th ed. London: George Allen & Unwin.

Sidorenko, Alexandra, and Christopher Findlay. 2001. "The Digital Divide in East Asia." *Asia-Pacific Economic Literature* 15(2):18–30.

Stiglitz, Joseph. 2001. "Participation and Development." In Joseph Stiglitz and Shahid Yusuf, eds., *Rethinking the East Asian Miracle.* New York: Oxford University Press, pp. 1–54.

Sussman, Leonard R. 2001. "The Internet in Flux." Available on-line at http://www.freedomhouse.org/pfs2001/pfs2000.pdf.

Tallo, Ivar. 2004. "Cross-Cultural Differences in the Regulation of Information Flows." Paper presented at Oxford Internet Institution Conference on the Internet and Governance in a Global Context, Oxford, U.K., January 8–10.

UNDESA (United Nations Department of Economic and Social Affairs). 2003. *E-Government at the Crossroads.* United Nations World Public Sector Report 2003. New York: United Nations.

UNDP (United Nations Development Programme). 2001. *Human Development Report.* New York: Oxford University Press.

UNDPEPA (United Nations Division for Public Economics and Public Administration). 2003. *Benchmarking E-government: A Global Perspective.* New York: United Nations.

Weber, Max. 1948. *From Max Weber*. Edited by Hans H. Gerth and C. Wright Mills. London: Routledge.

Weidenbaum, Murray, and Samuel Hughes. 1996. *Bamboo Network*. New York: Martin Kessler/Basic Books.

Wong, Loong. 2001. "The Internet and Social Change in Asia." *Peace Review* 13(3):381–87.

World Bank. 1997. *The State in a Changing World*. Washington, D.C.

———. 1998. *World Development Indicators*. Washington, D.C.

Zakaraia, Fareed. 1994. "A Conversation with Lee Kuan Yew." *Foreign Affairs* 73(2):109–27.

Zhang, Y., and H. Gao. 2003. "An Analysis of the Macro-Benefits of China's e-Government." *China Economic Times*.

CHAPTER 9

EDUCATION FOR GROWTH: DEEPENING OR WIDENING?

Howard Pack

Only through the intermediation of human capital can policy prescriptions, whether for improved governance, regulation, rule of law, or innovative growth, be implemented successfully. Increased democratization could be expected to generate the types of demands mentioned in previous chapters; the supply response has to rest largely on the system of higher education. This chapter examines the role that education has played in the region in the past and projects its role in the future.

The growth of the economies of East Asia over four decades was propelled by the rapid growth of their industrial sectors. High investment rates permitted rapid capital accumulation, and the economies adopted industrial technologies from more advanced countries and assimilated them fairly successfully. The economic environment for this effort was good macroeconomic policy supplemented by policies that provided strong incentives to become progressively more proficient, thereby encouraging firms to quickly assimilate the new technologies. In most of the economies, the preferred organization of industry was reliance on a relatively small number of very large firms that were capable of reaping economies of scale. Exceptions occurred in Hong Kong (China), the township and village enterprises in China, and Taiwan (China).

The crisis in the late 1990s in some of the economies in East and Southeast Asia precipitated a search for policies to restore the "miracle" growth rates that had prevailed earlier. Many solutions have been suggested, the most popular being those that, if adopted, would generate little political disagreement and not endanger existing economic interests. Serious financial deregulation has been only slowly implemented, although some recent accounts suggest an acceleration (Kirk 2002). Conglomerates such as the *chaebol* in the Republic of Korea have only reluctantly divested themselves of divisions in which they have little competitive advantage, such as Hynix, the semiconductor manufacturer spun off by Hyundai, one of the two largest chaebol. Required reforms in Indonesia and Thailand have been incompletely implemented.

The Internet mania in the countries of the Organisation for Economic Co-operation and Development (OECD) and the accompanying equity bubble, particularly in the United States, offered, for a fleeting moment, an appealing nostrum, partly because the Internet promised a new area for public intervention in fostering the development of information and communications technology (ICT). It was viewed as generating little political friction and posed little immediate threat to vested economic interests. Yet any sober reading of the problems facing these economies and their firms suggests that the contribution of ICT or the Internet to the solution of their difficulties would be minor. Many of the problems have occurred in precisely those firms that are most technologically advanced and that presumably have excellent computer and information skills, such as Daewoo and Hynix in Korea. Some of the troubles of these firms result from substantial cyclical declines in prices in their major products (semiconductors); others represent the expansion of firms into areas in which they had excess capacity (autos), given world and local demand, or in which their competence was limited (resorts). Given the exceptionally high rates of tertiary enrollment in engineering and science (table 9.1), it is not obvious that the problems stem from insufficient supplies of technically competent personnel rather than inadequate management and financial skills.

To understand the potential effects of more ICT skills, one can examine the experience of India, which has enjoyed rapid growth in software exports. Although India is industrially less advanced than much of Asia, one segment of India's economy is arguably much more advanced. Examining the history and impact of India's software sector suggests some of the requirements for generating such a sector and its likely effect on other sectors. Although India's software sector clearly has had limited effects on both upstream and downstream industries, it is unlikely that the major constraint on Asian growth is the generation of greater ICT skills or limited use of the Internet. Although some modicum will be necessary to stay abreast of current developments and to use those that are relevant, ICT skills and Internet use hardly constitute the magic bullet that will restore Asian growth rates to those of the golden decades.

The remainder of this chapter analyzes the education requirements of the Asian countries in terms of derived demand. Although some analysts argue for a process akin to manpower planning, as advocated by many

Table 9.1 University Graduates by Field
(percent)

Economy	Year	Social science	Natural science and engineering
China	1994	22.1	35.0
Hong Kong, China	1994	34.4	41.9
Korea, Rep. of	1997	28.1	38.3
Singapore	1995	24.3	57.9
Asian Mean		27.3	43.3
Germany	1996	26.5	34.7
Ireland	1997	36.4	36.1
Italy	1996	31.5	23.0
Switzerland	1995	22.9	28.0
United Kingdom	1997	33.3	27.7
United States	1995	36.3	18.9
OECD mean		31.2	28.1

Source: UNESCO (1999, table II16).

analysts in the early decades of development thinking, it is more appropriate to consider in detail the problems that now characterize the fast-growing Asian economies or, in terms of the World Bank's influential volume *The East Asian Miracle* (1993), the high-performing Asian economies (HPAEs). The following section sets out some of the major problems that a variety of analyses have identified as obstacles to a renewal of rapid growth, as well as the remedies that have been suggested for these problems. The subsequent section considers the policies necessary to achieve the desired changes, followed by a section on the education requirements implied by the policy changes.

RECENT PROBLEMS OF THE ASIAN ECONOMIES

There is a huge literature analyzing the problems facing the HPAEs since 1997. The following discussion is a distillation of the difficulties that are widely perceived as major impediments to future growth. Although individual authors and institutions may have different emphases, almost all cite a similar set of problems.[1] This chapter reflects mainly Korean

---

1. Among the studies are Furman and Stiglitz (1998), McKinsey Global Institute (1998), OECD (1999), Radelet and Sachs (1998), Stiglitz and Yusuf (2001), and World Bank (1998, 1999, 2000).

experience, but its discussion holds, with necessary qualifications, for most of the HPAEs. It is difficult in one chapter to consider the entire range of development issues that face the economies of East Asia. Nevertheless, in many of the countries, the financial crisis of 1997–98 highlighted similar problems that centered on corporate governance, efficiency of capital markets, and quality and regulation of the financial system. Although total factor productivity (TFP) levels in manufacturing and other sectors were still substantially below international best practice (McKinsey Global Institute 1998), rates of TFP growth had been sufficiently high to permit a narrowing of the gap relative to OECD countries (Pack 2001b). Although an improvement in manufacturing productivity is important, diversification into other sectors and the better functioning of the "software" of the economy, especially of the financial sectors, are critical in all of the economies. Currently, the Asian economies remain heavily concentrated in manufacturing when compared with the OECD countries (table 9.2).

Rapid growth from roughly 1965 to 1997 (resuming in some economies in 1999) was propelled by high investment in physical and human capital. Although there is an extensive debate on the role of TFP growth, no calculation suggests that it accounted for more than one-third of growth. Nevertheless, this achievement is not trivial given the extraordinary growth in the factors deployed by these economies (Pack 2001b). The allocation of capital among sectors was heavily influenced by government policies. There is a lively debate on the benefits, if any, of industrial policies, but no one doubts that widespread government intervention in critical

Table 9.2 East Asian Comparative Indicators, 2000
(percentage of gross domestic product)

Country	Value added in manufacturing	Value added in services
China	34	33
Indonesia	26	37
Korea, Rep. of	31	54
Malaysia	31	40
Thailand	31	49
France	19	72
Italy	22	68
Netherlands	17	70
United Kingdom	19	70

Source: World Bank (2003).

markets was typical of the HPAEs.[2] The slide that began in late 1996, and which accelerated in the second half of 1997, had numerous causes, ranging from the decline in semiconductor prices to the unhedged foreign exchange borrowing by firms and banks whose sales were largely domestic.

Although emphasis on the relative importance of specific characteristics differs among analysts, most observers agree that a number of new departures are necessary. The following are among the most important, and the discussion is designed to illustrate some of the complexities of designing a manpower strategy. The problems are discussed first, and then the proposed remedies and their skill requirements are analyzed.

Improving the Efficiency of Banks

During its period of rapid growth, Korea, like the other HPAEs, benefited from a very high saving and investment rate. Much of the saving was placed in banks that, in turn, followed government guidance on the sectors (and often the firms) to which loans should be offered at concessionary rates (World Bank 1993, chapter 6). The banks' ability to assess business plans and risks was impaired during the three decades of government guidance, with a consequent growth in nonperforming loans.[3] During this period, foreign competition in the banking sector was largely precluded, and banks operated at low levels of efficiency relative to their peers abroad (McKinsey Global Institute 1998). Moreover, the ready availability of funds at low rates encouraged excessive debt-equity ratios (Claessens, Djankov, and Xu 2000; Dollar and Hallward-Dreimeier 2000; World Bank 1998) that increased the fragility of these institutions.

Increasing Quality of Governance and Transparency of Firms

In most corporations, the internal transactions have been difficult to understand, and in many cases, they do not conform to international accounting standards, though reform has begun. The chaebol structure, with its many interlocking directors and branches that cross-subsidize others, generates an internal capital market that is insulated from market forces and may not be conducive to efficiency. In an early period, this structure may have had benefits, because firms could internalize externalities that may have flowed among related production activities. Historically,

---

2. Noland and Pack (2003) provide a review.

3. A plausible argument can be made that, in the early part of this period, guided lending had beneficial effects by limiting the demand for speculative loans (see World Bank 1993, chapter 6).

minority shareholders have not been protected, a situation that may discourage efforts to improve the firms' performance because current management cannot be challenged. It is likely that this structure facilitated the expansion into areas far from the core competence of firms.

Relaxing Inflexible Labor Markets

The East Asian Miracle (World Bank 1993, chapter 4) noted the importance of "shared growth" in the Asian countries, which ensured that most members of the society benefited from rapid growth. Although labor unions were weak, firms avoided layoffs during periods of slow growth, and this practice became embedded in legislation. Although this practice was conducive to harmonious labor relations during a period when most sectors were expanding at very rapid rates, such inflexibility became a liability when the sectoral structure of production had to change more quickly. Some sectors and firms were under pressure to contract, and the relatively inflexible labor agreements made this effort difficult. One requirement for facilitating greater flexibility is relaxation of legislation and custom on firing, combined with introduction of a comprehensive social safety net to protect those unemployed. Creation of such a safety net is still an incomplete undertaking in Korea and other Asian economies.

Decreasing Lack of Competition and Emphasis on Large-Scale Firms

Although Korea was vigorous in pursuing exports, its domestic market for both tradable goods and services was often protected by tariffs and quantitative restrictions on imports. Foreign competition was precluded by the discouragement of foreign direct investment (FDI) in both goods and services. In the nontraded goods sectors, the absence of FDI also limited the pressures on domestic firms. In the effort to build large industrial firms to exploit scale economies in production and marketing, small and medium-size enterprises were starved of funds. The banking system actively discriminated against them at the government's behest, and despite some efforts to establish an official bank that would lend to small and medium-size enterprises, much of Korea's industrial growth was concentrated in the largest firms. The potential innovativeness in smaller firms was forgone, not only in Korea but also in Malaysia, Singapore, and Thailand. In contrast, more size-neutral policies in Taiwan, China— combined with centralized technical support—resulted in many small innovative firms that also exhibited great flexibility in shifting among products within a sector and among sectors.

Adding to the problems facing the Korean economy is a strong preference among workers for employment in large firms or the government, a phenomenon that parallels behavior in Japan.

Improving Efficiency

The manufacturing share of gross domestic product (GDP) in Korea (as well as in Malaysia, Singapore, and Thailand) is high relative to its peers in per capita income. Having catapulted into the ranks of higher-income countries through its extraordinary manufacturing growth, Korea has been reluctant to allow an evolution toward other sectors even though income elasticities of demand in all countries suggest this evolution is normal. The growth of real wages has decreased the competitiveness of many manufacturing sectors in Korea and in many of the more advanced newly industrialized economies in Asia, though not yet in China. Some of the recent dramatic changes in the international organization of manufacturing also suggest the need to reduce reliance on the sector. Although manufacturing based on research and development (R&D) involving advanced technical processes—exemplified by Samsung's production of plasma displays and mobile phones—can provide the basis for continuing some types of manufacturing, simpler products are less likely to be profitable. Such products are less profitable not only because of wage growth but also because of the rise of specialist firms, such as Flextronics, that manufacture to order and enjoy very large economies of scope. New products that do not involve exceptionally complex production processes are increasingly being subcontracted to such firms. Hence, even if a country's firms perform applied R&D, some of the products that are generated are nevertheless likely to be produced by international firms such as Flextronics, with much of the value added accruing abroad.

In the normal evolution of an economy whose income per capita increases, service sectors will grow as a percentage of national income. In Korea, many services are provided relatively inefficiently, according to calculations at the firm level (McKinsey Global Institute 1998). This finding is supported by anecdotal evidence about companies in Malaysia and Thailand. There is a great temptation to search for new manufacturing champions rather than to allow the emergence of new service sectors.[4] At the same time, even large Korean firms exhibit a considerable gap

---

4. Singapore has recently emphasized the biotechnology sector as its future leading sector, signing agreements with major universities in the United States to establish greater competence in its universities.

between their realized TFP levels and the best practice in other OECD countries, especially in the United States, and efforts to reduce this gap are necessary.

POLICIES REQUIRED

In light of the preceding diagnoses, the following discussion suggests some of the necessary changes and considers the implied education requirements. Even by late 2003, more than 6 years after the crisis began, only some of the proposed policies have been put into place. Even where the government has begun to implement the remedies, the extent to which they have been fully carried out is not always clear. Although many of the proposals are based on the Korean experience, the required adjustments are broadly necessary in most of the Asian economies. The precise mix differs across nations, but almost all require similar major modifications in the institutional and policy regime.

Increasing Bank and Financial Market Efficiency

The private sector institutions must add more qualified personnel and improve their practices, and the public sector needs to improve supervision and monitoring of the financial system and to adopt and implement standard accounting practices. These tasks are not simple, as witnessed by the problems that have cropped up in the United States since 2002. Auditing the accounts of financial institutions requires well-trained accountants, auditors, and risk specialists. Insofar as the private financial institutions assume multiple roles (such as lending, underwriting new issues, stock transactions, and other activities), the regulators must have the skills to understand each of the activities and their potential interaction. Despite the large pool of accounting and finance graduates in the United States, regulatory institutions have had considerable difficulty establishing the necessary auditing and risk-control procedures. Korea and other Asian economies presumably have still greater difficulty. The number of university students enrolled in business, accounting, and finance is low; most tertiary students are enrolled in engineering, science, and computer science. The small supply of graduates must be sufficient to staff the private institutions and their regulators. Although one would expect wages of such graduates to increase relative to other fields, the speed of any resultant response in enrollments is unknown. In the meantime, retraining existing staff and hiring those already in the private sector are required.

A detailed example of the skills required is provided in a recent McKinsey and Company (2000) analysis of the changes necessary in Korea if the country is to continue its exceptional growth. The survey reflected McKinsey's considerable experience in advising Korean firms. It notes (p. 63) that "individual Korean banks need to fill four key positions or ensure that managers occupying these positions have the requisite skills: (1) Chief Executive Officer; (2) Chief Financial Officer; (3) Chief Risk Officer; and (4) Chief Distribution Officer." A similar list of executive skills in regulating agencies is supplied. The study argues that the performance in both the private and public sectors of those currently in these positions in Korea is not high, a phenomenon that is partly attributable to the earlier suppression of the financial sector (Noland and Pack 2003).

In principle, greater participation by international accounting firms (assuming that Andersen's interactions with Enron and WorldCom are an exception) could improve the performance of the private sector, but few governments would choose to allow regulation to be carried out solely by these firms. Moreover, the size of the role will inevitably be limited by the language competence of the international firms.

The financial sectors should be opened to foreign competitors, who could transfer international best practice that local firms would eventually emulate. Nevertheless, the foreign firms would inevitably have to compete for the limited pool of technically competent graduates fluent in the local language. This conundrum suggests that a beneficial short-term strategy would be intensive foreign-language training, probably in English, for some recent and prospective graduates who could facilitate the potential role of foreign firms.

Increasing the Quality of Governance and Transparency

Mandatory codes of corporate governance need to be adopted, and accounting for all firms must be made to conform to international best practice. Implementing these plans requires both accountants and lawyers. Despite some perceptions, expressed largely before the Asian crisis, of the negative productivity of lawyers (presumably relative to engineers), it is clear that their skills are necessary. The lack of credibility of income statements and balance sheets, as well as their inaccuracy, impairs the allocative function of the capital market and reduces productivity growth.[5] In the period of rapid growth, this issue may have been secondary insofar as large firms provided their own internal capital market for various subsidiaries

---

5. Obviously the United States is not immune to the same problems.

and may have had some sense of relative risk and return. As firms expanded and required external financing, the poor quality of financial reports became a serious hindrance.

In addition, the absence of mechanisms by which executives could be held accountable for their performance, especially by minority shareholders, may have led to firm decisions that resulted in low private and social returns. Asian firms typically have had much lower rates of return on equity capital (or any other measure of capital) than firms in Western Europe or the United States (Claessens, Djankov, and Xu 2000). The inability to focus management's attention on redressing this result hinders improved performance. Again, a rewritten legal code is important, and more legal training is critical.

Improving Labor Market Flexibility

A recent joint World Bank–OECD analysis of Korean education (Dahlman and Andersson 2000, p. 19) argues that Korea "needs to develop better industrial relations, make worker benefits fully portable, reorient training schemes to meet the demands of a more flexible economy, and ease restrictions on temporary workers." In most of the OECD countries, labor relations are implemented by specialists, who have learned the procedures on the job after a basic university education or who have studied these issues in MBA or industrial relations programs. Pension specialists are mainly graduates of business, statistics, or mathematics programs that allow students to master complex actuarial problems. The design of portable pension systems requires interaction among labor relations specialists, actuaries, and lawyers. Such programs appear to be largely absent from Korean universities, but foreign training, for example, at the School of Industrial Relations at Cornell University, might initially fill the need. However, these programs typically use a U.S. or U.K. institutional framework, and they may neglect important country-specific perceptions and preferences of both employers and employees, which suggests the need for a Korean university to initiate such a program.

Increasing Competition

Until very recently, competition policy was not a major concern in most of the OECD countries. The United States had a fairly aggressive policy, varying from administration to administration, that stemmed from the Clayton and Sherman Antitrust Acts, which were legislated because of populist pressures beginning in the 1890s. In contrast, in both Europe and Japan, official policy sanctioned cartels until relatively recently. Korea's rapid development was characterized by competitive behavior in international markets, with significant protection of the local market. Such protection included tariffs, quotas, de facto legality of cartels, intensive regulation of financial services and infrastructure, and limits on FDI. There has been a significant reduction in protective trade measures, though some sectors, such as autos, continue to receive protection. More liberalization of FDI, especially allowing investment in financial services, is likely to provide more competition and enhance learning of international best practice (McKinsey Global Institute 1998, chapter 3). Korea now has a Fair Trade Commission, but the vigor of enforcement could be increased, as could that of bankruptcy proceedings. Again, the education necessary is in law, economics, and business.

As previously noted, the very high percentage of GDP originating in large-scale firms reflects the Korean government's strategy to rely on the chaebol during the initial attempt at building the economy. The difficulties in obtaining financing and the general discouragement of entrepreneurial effort in small firms may have led to the suppression of Korea's equivalents of Michael Dell and Bill Gates, as well as depressing more conventional entry into markets dominated by the chaebol. It is notable that, except in software, the same firms have been prominent in Korea for 30 or more years. Although most small firms in all countries begin with loans from family and acquaintances, successful ones soon outgrow such financing and need access to either bank loans or venture capital. Yet Korea's banks do not appear to have the skills to evaluate business plans of small firms, and venture capital is still in its infancy.

The required policy changes include improving antitrust legislation, developing an improved enforcement agency, encouraging FDI in banking and venture capital, and improving bank abilities to evaluate smaller loan requirements. To implement this agenda, Korea needs to educate economists, lawyers, business students, and public policy analysts—areas in which current enrollments are low and in which universities are weak relative to their science and engineering programs.

Improving Efficiency

It is always tempting to continue following a successful strategy; however, as many corporations and investors throughout the world have rediscovered in the past few years, there are inflection points in growth rates, and changes in strategy may be necessary. Korea (like other East Asian economies) has used the manufacturing sector to propel its standard of living to high levels. Yet income elasticities of demand within the country suggest that the service sector will expand with a commensurate decline in manufacturing's share of GDP. On the other hand, many policymakers continue to emphasize the need to further "deepen" the manufacturing sector.

Information and communications technology. One magic bullet solution has been proposed in the form of greater ICT investment and competence. Is adopting information technology capacity within firms and the growth of firms' ability to take advantage of the Internet likely to improve the functioning of the nonsoftware sector? There are two distinct issues: (a) the effects of purchasing ICT on the efficiency of firms and (b) the effects of using ICT to tap the Internet. Given that in Asia there are network externalities and that the diffusion of the technology is far from complete, it is still too early to obtain even a preliminary set of insights at this early stage of computer and Internet diffusion within Asia.[6] Yet lessons from the United States are suggestive.

In the United States, the upsurge of investment in ICT had no discernible effect on rates of TFP growth for a very long period. Indeed, in the mid-1980s, many journalists and some academics in the United States were urging the adoption of Japanese-style industrial policies precisely to accelerate the growth rate of TFP, which had declined from about 1.5 percent per year between 1945 and 1973 to less than 0.5 percent per year. Yet this weak productivity performance came in the midst of a surge in ICT investment and the early diffusion of personal computers that began around 1980. In that period, the discussion focused on the need for the United States to improve business management techniques, including adopting Japanese practices such as just-in-time delivery and quality circles. Additional ICT investment was rarely mentioned as a cure for slowing productivity growth.

The acceleration in U.S. TFP growth in the late 1990s may have stemmed from the long-delayed effects of cumulative ICT investment.

---

6. Although many efforts are being made to assess the effect of ICT, it is instructive to note that many early efforts to determine the effect of the Green Revolution in Asian agriculture were riddled with errors because they were made during the early stages, when the adoption of the technology was still in the middle of the typical logistic pattern of diffusion. In addition, the errors typically had a pessimistic bias, whereas current assessments, often based on limited evidence, of the implications of ICT and the Internet appear to have an excessively optimistic outlook.

Despite high levels of investment in ICT and a good higher education system in the United States, U.S. TFP growth was quite low in the period from 1973 to 1995. Asian economies, for reasons considered below, are unlikely to experience a better performance.

Even at the end of a quarter century of high investment in ICT, there is little agreement about its contribution to U.S. economic performance, and there is a large range of estimates of the effect of ICT investment on TFP growth rates. Some analysts such as Gordon (2000) and Oliner and Sichel (2000) found that the quickening of TFP growth rates in the United States since 1995 reflects cyclical performance and argue that the rate of growth of TFP will revert to lower levels, though Gordon (2003) has reversed his view. The earlier analyses contend that almost the entire acceleration has been caused by improvement in the memory chip–producing sector and not in the memory chip–using sectors. If this is indeed the case, as recent research suggests (McKinsey Global Institute 2001), then some of the Asian countries that are major producers of items such as memory chips might experience accelerated TFP growth. However, the effect within Asian economies will be limited if hardware prices fall rapidly, and the benefits of increasing productivity will accrue largely to the purchasing nations of the OECD. In any case, growing (physical) TFP in processors, memory chips, scanners, and pointing devices cannot have a major effect on economywide rates of growth of TFP, because these sectors are still relatively small in the Asian economies. In light of huge losses in 2001 and 2002 at major chip manufacturers in Asia, such as Hynix, Fujitsu, and Toshiba, it has become even clearer that establishing production in this segment of the new economy is no guarantee of accelerated growth.

When one considers the probable effect of growing investments in ICT in Asia, there are some reasons to be skeptical about ICT's short- and intermediate-term effects. The introduction of computers and telecommunication equipment requires a large number of simultaneous organizational changes that depend on considerable worker and management flexibility if the benefits of the new investment are to be realized (Brynjolfsson and Hitt 2000; Milgrom and Roberts 1990). But for many Asian firms such flexibility would constitute a huge departure from existing practice, which has often emphasized achieving long production runs with relatively unchanged routines.[7] Such sweeping changes have been difficult to achieve in the United States, and experiments in plants in other

---

7. The industrial relations literature provides few examples of the emulation in the rest of Asia of Japanese quality circles and other worker-management innovations.

Table 9.3 Changes in Work Practices Required to Assimilate Computer-Based Production Strategies

Principles of the "old" factory	Principles of the "new" factory
• Have designed equipment	• Have flexible computer-based equipment
• Have large inventories	• Have low inventories
• Tie pay to amount produced	• Pay all operators same flat rate
• Keep line running no matter what	• Stop line if not running at speed
• Provide thorough final inspection by quality assurance	• Make operators responsible for quality
• Make raw materials in-house	• Outsource all materials
• Have narrow job functions	• Have flexible job responsibilities
• Separate areas by machine type	• Organize areas in work cells
• Let salaried employees make decisions	• Let all employees contribute ideas
• Have hourly workers carry them out	• Have supervisors fill in on-line
• Allow functional groups to work independently	• Have concurrent engineering
• Have vertical communication flow	• Practice line rationalization
• Have several management layers	• Have few management layers

Source: Brynjolfsson and Hitt (2000).

countries such as Sweden (Volvo) have not always been successful. Is it likely that they can be implemented in Asian economies?

Many criticisms of the primary and secondary school systems note their emphasis on rote education.[8] Workers trained in these traditions may not be very flexible. To obtain a flavor of the extensive changes required, consider a list of changes required in an old-style factory if it is to exploit the possibilities of ICT investment—the absorption of the potential of the Internet would necessitate even more extensive alterations in firm practice.

The changes shown in table 9.3, following Brynjolfsson and Hitt (2000), are enormous. Among the major transformations are vertical disintegration implied in outsourcing, loss of hierarchical management, and greater worker innovation and flexibility.[9] Yet even without the introduction of ICT, Asian firms had some difficulty in rapidly increasing TFP.

---

8. For references and discussion, see Dahlman and Andersson (2000).

9. Bresnahan, Brynjolfsson, and Hitt (1999) make the same point that successful use of information technology requires complementary changes in organization if productivity gains are to be realized. If this observation is true in the United States, where firms are fairly advanced in such practices, the typical Asian firm will have all the more difficulty in realizing productivity gains solely from adopting information technology.

Although a range of estimates suggests TFP growth was 2 to 3 percent in manufacturing in most economies, it was not particularly high considering the massive purchase of new equipment and the borrowing of new technology from abroad through technology contracts and consultants.[10] Given their initial distance from the international best practice frontier in terms of the vintage of equipment—as well as from best management practice—more rapid progress might have been expected.

One possibility is that firms had difficulty absorbing new equipment into their earlier routines. If faster textile looms in a standard industrial activity, weaving, were difficult to absorb, the introduction of greater computerization may not be accompanied by a massive increase in TFP. As late as 1998, TFP levels in a Korean semiconductor firm were only about half those of a peer U.S. firm, despite the presumably widespread use in such a firm of ICT (McKinsey Global Institute 1998). Production technologies are difficult to master even in traditional sectors.[11] Realizing the potential of the Internet, which might include decreasing vertical integration and allowing external suppliers to manage a firm's inventories of parts, would constitute a huge change in routine for firms that have often not fully mastered their major core processes.

Hulten and Srinivasan (1999) provide an interesting piece of evidence on India, suggesting some acceleration of TFP in the late 1980s after a dismal performance for 40 years. Most likely this acceleration was simply the result of better economic policies following economic liberalization. There is no evidence of ICT investment or domestic sales of India's burgeoning software sector contributing to the acceleration, despite the high level of Indian competence in ICT and software.

Given the preceding discussion, what is likely to be the effect of Internet activity as opposed to ICT investment in the Asian economies? In the United States, it is not obvious that the Internet has led to a massive reduction in costs or—its mirror image—growth in TFP. Some firms have used business-to-business (B2B) Web sites to allow less vertical integration—these gains reflecting the greater efficiency of specialist firms that benefit from economies of scope. Yet even in the United States, little systematic evidence of more rapid TFP growth attributable to the Internet is

---

10. For evidence of TFP levels relative to U.S. firms in manufacturing, see McKinsey Global Institute (1998). Often, relative Korean TFP is roughly 50 to 60 percent. Nelson and Pack (1999) and Pack (2001b) discuss the difficulties of obtaining precise measures of TFP growth rates in the Asian countries.

11. For an excellent account of such difficulties in individual firms in a large number of Korean sectors, see Kim (1997).

visible yet, despite widespread access and the existence of a highly educated, computer-literate work force. The large increases in productivity as the United States came out of recession in 2003 may be attributable to ICT or to the growing utilization of workers who were retained during the recession, reflecting firms' memory of the tight labor market of the late 1990s.

The uncertain effect of ICT investment on TFP is magnified when one tries to establish magnitudes for the total effect of the Internet. Consumer welfare has undoubtedly increased because of the convenience of shopping on-line, which also allows lower prices and greater choice. Although case study evidence demonstrates the producer surplus generated by B2B sites, the gains seem to be relatively small.

The absence of measured effects of the Internet does not imply that Asian economies can ignore it: they must keep up-to-date to know what is going to be and what could be valuable to adopt, but there is little compelling evidence of immediate need. However, if Asian economies that are still heavily reliant on manufacturing are to gradually reduce the size of the sector given changing comparative advantage and a shift toward services, they will have to become more Internet conversant. It is not clear that this action requires a major commitment to computer science at the university level. Whereas the design of software, as in the case of India, may be based on high-quality graduates in computer science, many of the skills required for interacting on the Internet are more elementary. Firewall programs can be purchased, and Web site design can be carried out by imaginative high school graduates or technical training institute graduates. Few insurance employees or investment bankers are conversant with elementary programming; they rely on software provided by the relatively small number of computer specialists in their firms, who, in turn, most often put into operation software purchased from external vendors.

Traditional modes of productivity enhancement. Korea and, almost certainly, the other major Asian economies have TFP levels well below those in the OECD countries.[12] The preceding section provides a skeptical view that these differences will be significantly narrowed simply by greater ICT activity. McKinsey Global Institute (1998) and McKinsey and Company (2000) provide a long list of practices that require improvement. Some reflect the requirement to address customer needs:

> Korea is currently designing products based on what designers and engineers believe to be technologically possible—not necessarily based on

---

12. For a detailed analysis, see McKinsey Global Institute (1998), which compares the productivity of similar Korean and OECD firms.

the products' ability to address some unique customer need. . . . Creating more effective products requires that Korean companies install new product design processes that start with market intelligence and increase product design/engineering capabilities, especially the ability to improve the products' aesthetic features in addition to their functional performance. (McKinsey and Company 2000, p. 39)

The same volume documents the low output relative to potential achieved in manufacturing resulting from the lack of modern methods of production planning, as well as from the poor logistics and distribution capacities of existing manufacturing firms. Even discounting the possibility of slight exaggeration in the pursuit of further consulting contracts, such shortfalls from best practice are typical and have been noted by many observers. Such deficiencies account for the lower TFP levels in Korean firms relative to those in the OECD. They are found not only in manufacturing but also in the service sector, though the specifics obviously differ.

Rectifying these deficiencies requires a systematic effort, which ranges from training existing personnel, to hiring new graduates with skills in operations management, to establishing incentive payment systems. Although more engineering and computer science graduates are one (probably small) part of the solution, the greater need lies in increasing the number of graduates with "softer" skills, an issue to which I now turn.

IMPLICATIONS FOR EDUCATION

Higher Education Requirements

The preceding analyses of the requirements for continuing growth in Korea have several important threads. First, many of the problems require "softer" skills than those that have been emphasized in Korea during its spectacular growth. Although part of Korea's achievement has been propelled by large investments in education, these have been concentrated in science and engineering. This specialization reflects the growth in demand in these disciplines and the preference of graduates to work for large, well-known chaebol, which they perceive as offering lower lifetime risk as well as considerable prestige. But it also may reflect the lack of familiarity with other possible specialties, such as labor relations in the private sector or antitrust law in the public sector.

Merely initiating programs in these specialties may not be sufficient to attract students unless there is simultaneously a perception that remunerative jobs will be available. Fashioning a correct signaling mechanism that

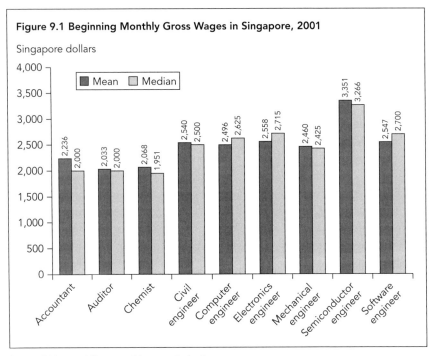

Figure 9.1 Beginning Monthly Gross Wages in Singapore, 2001

Singapore dollars

Source: Web site of Singapore Monetary Authority.

induces students to enroll in such programs but does not lead to over-shooting will be a challenge that requires considerable ingenuity. Singapore has more than twice the per capita income of Korea and presumably has higher levels of TFP. Moreover, Singapore has restruc-tured its economy more toward services than Korea. Thus, it is natural to look to Singapore for guidance about likely wage structures required to elicit the training and effort that are appropriate to a changed production structure. Figure 9.1 shows, however, a quite compressed structure of beginning wages. Differences in initial wages are typically less than 20 per-cent, except for semiconductor engineers. And they are typically lower for the business skills represented, accounting and auditing, than for those in engineering. Perhaps changes in these differentials are all that is required to elicit the necessary supply response. Comparable data for earlier years are not available, so the changes in differentials over time in Singapore cannot be determined. Unfortunately, data on initial wages by occupation are not available in Korea or other Asian economies.[13]

---

13. The International Labour Organisation has a database on average wages by occupation for more than 200 countries (see http://laborsta.ilo.org). The database covers 159 occupations, but it does not contain the occupations of interest.

A growth in enrollments that exceeds actual job possibilities will have adverse consequences on incentives. However, the emigration of educated labor in these softer fields is less likely than in sciences and engineering. One possibility for matching enrollments with jobs is for government agencies to fully fund the training of their future employees, with the proviso that the graduates must work for the agency for a fixed period after graduation. A program such as this has been initiated in Singapore. Under the program, students are fully financed to study at foreign universities, and when they return, they work at their sponsoring agency for at least 5 years.

For many of the more advanced Asian economies, the issue that will crystallize is whether they should spend still larger amounts on university training. This issue is similar to the question of whether they should undertake their own research or license industrial technologies. Those who advocate the generation of domestic technologies argue that, even though undertaking R&D would be more costly in the short run than licensing technology or permitting FDI to bring new technologies, in the long term doing so is the only way to move up the value chain. However, although some firms in Korea and Taiwan, China, have engaged in their own research, they have nevertheless often lagged the world frontier. Although their own efforts have kept them running in place, few of the large Korean firms that have undertaken major research efforts have earned high rates of return on equity, which is one source of recent financial problems (Claessens, Djankov, and Xu 2000). While it is arguable that they would have had still lower rates of return if they had forgone R&D and relied on licensing, this position is not obvious.

In the case of additional, and expensive, university training for a generation of computer scientists, some attempt is necessary to assess the benefits and costs. Indian experience suggests few spillovers to nonsoftware sectors even though several of the firms (for example, Tata Consulting) are themselves spin-offs of major industrial conglomerates (Pack 2001a).

Nonuniversity Skill Requirements

The preceding section addressed so-called higher-level skill requirements in an advanced, newly industrialized country that is still fairly far from the world's best practice. The implications of Korea's economic position for nonuniversity education have not been considered explicitly. Given Korea's disproportionate concentration in manufacturing—and within it concentration in a few sectors such as autos, semiconductors, and electronics—it seems likely that on the margin these sectors will see significant shrinking in their relative size and that other economic activity, particularly in services, will experience concomitant growth. The specific education and skill requirements are not easy to forecast because the nature of these services is rapidly evolving in more advanced economies and existing vectors of skills and education are not necessarily a good guide to future requirements. In such a rapidly changing economic environment, the ability to adjust and productively engage in new sectors and to learn the appropriate technologies will be exceedingly important.

Although growth models and empirical tests of such models view education as either conferring externalities on all economic activity (Lucas 1988) or multiplying the stock of productive factors (Mankiw, Romer, and Weil 1992), a view suggested by Nelson and Phelps (1966) seems more appropriate. They argue that education matters when technical changes are occurring, conferring on the better-educated population a greater facility in dealing with rapid advances. Clearly, those who go on to university education will have a comparative advantage in productively assimilating new technologies and in being able to adapt to new industries. What, then, is the appropriate education for the half of the labor force that will not be university educated?

Although there will undoubtedly be a temptation to "stream" high school graduates or to use apprentice systems, shifting from systems of rote learning to more interactive and problem-solving learning is likely to be much more fruitful. Dahlman and Andersson (2000) suggest a number of modes for improving elementary and high school education, and they ascribe considerable importance to reducing class size to OECD levels. Even though the U.S. literature on class size and performance yields few strong conclusions, one can conjecture that large size is less conducive to interaction among teachers and students. In large classes, it may be possible to teach the process for solving trigonometry problems (and, hence, allow the realization of higher scores on standardized tests), but it is more difficult to impart alternative ways of conceptualizing a problem. Given Korea's achievements in enrollment rates, the quality of education as well as the quantity may constitute an important component for future competitiveness in new sectors. Reducing class size is a nostrum that is often proposed; however, its benefits, at least in the United States, are open to question. But given the exceptionally large size of classes in Korea, it seems likely that nonmarginal changes could have significant benefits.

The National Innovation System

As noted earlier, two issues exist for all of the Asian economies—namely, improving actual practice toward existing best practice and, at least in some areas, trying to push best practice forward. In addition, the allocation of resources among sectors needs improving, something that might flow from improvements in the financial sector and greater flexibility of the labor markets. Given Korea's earlier achievements, it seems likely that Korea will succeed in these goals, although both will require applying considerable political will, accumulating relevant skills, and changing the legal and institutional framework. From a longer-term perspective, Korea's continued success in manufacturing will depend on its ability to develop new technology, both products and processes, rather than simply to be adept at importing and assimilating already-existing technologies. In services, by contrast, the absorption of existing knowledge and practices is of prime importance.

Because Korea's experience has so closely paralleled that of Japan (and not entirely by accident), it is useful to recall that Japan's post–World War II resurgence was based on considerable technological borrowing (Nagaoka 1989; Ozawa 1974) of new equipment designs, pure knowledge transfers through licensing agreements, and other modes. By the early 1970s, Japan was being pressed by lower-wage countries, and it embarked on innovation efforts in manufacturing to provide the next phase of sustained development. Korea faces a similar problem: it cannot rely on low wages as a source of competitive advantage, and it has adopted most of the modern production methods in manufacturing, even if it has yet to achieve the same TFP as the countries in which the technology originates. Korea must, therefore, look to innovation, not only in manufacturing but also in services, given that it can be assumed that Korea will sooner or later reduce the gap between current and best practice in manufacturing even as that sector shrinks. The same is true of such economies as Singapore and Taiwan, China.

In lower-wage countries such as China, Indonesia, Malaysia, and Thailand, opportunities for fruitful use of foreign technologies continue to provide an attractive option for growth, and this section is less relevant. Nonetheless, even in these countries, an initiation of some innovation efforts can provide the necessary accumulation of learning so that future efforts at innovation will be easier. More basic innovation requires a complex of institutions and networks that Nelson (1993) and others—see particularly Hou and Gee (1993) on Taiwan, China, and Kim (1993) on Korea—term the *national innovation system*. This system includes research institutions, universities, and businesses that engage in R&D. Merely setting up components of the system does not work; the critical issue is obtaining fruitful interaction between users and generators of research as well as providing the training necessary to maintain a high level of research productivity. Nevertheless, most of the Asian economies of interest devote relatively low resources to R&D, and, as Dahlman and Andersson (2000) note, even Korea, which now spends more than 2 percent of GDP on research, has relatively low productivity by such conventional measures as patents.

Many paths have been suggested for building up greater research capacity. Some analysts advocate strengthening a few higher education institutions in the larger Asian economies, such as China and Korea, that can then educate PhDs who are themselves at the world frontier. Others argue that this strategy is very expensive in the near term, and it would be better to provide advanced training abroad while local education institutions work with the private sector to generate the knowledge necessary for more immediate applications, ranging from software to manufactured products. There is no single correct answer, though some recent experience from India is suggestive.

Lately, the Indian software sector has achieved extraordinary growth, much of it concentrated in Bangalore. Part of this growth is based on the strength of the Indian Institutes of Technology, along with other less research-oriented institutions. Bangalore has a reputation for technical excellence and an abundant supply of information technology graduates from 3 universities, 14 engineering colleges, and 47 polytechnic schools. Despite this educational base and the abilities of some local firms, a catalytic factor has been the transfer of knowledge and management skills by foreign firms. Of Indian software firms, 48 percent are foreign owned, joint ventures, or owned by Indian nationals with intensive participation by foreigners. Although wholly owned foreign firms make up only a small fraction of software firms in India, they account for a disproportionately large share of the investment made by the software industry. Although revenues in the sector were growing before the influx of foreign firms, they have facilitated software exports, which constitute the largest part of current sales.

Foreign firms, often staffed by Indian expatriates, also invested in India, started new Indian firms, helped raise U.S. venture capital, provided expertise, and convinced venture capital firms to operate in India or to pay greater attention to opportunities in India. In recent years, nonresident Indians have gone a step further in assisting the Indian software industry. Aware of the obstacles some Indian firms face in raising capital for their software start-ups, some of these nonresident Indians actively raised venture capital from U.S. investment firms; others organized conferences in the United States to heighten the awareness of the potential of India's software industry (Kripalani 2000). A group of nonresident Indians in the United States also founded a mentoring group for technology entrepreneurs in India to network with their counterparts in the United States and to learn from their counterparts' experiences (Biers and Dhume 2000). Finally, nonresident Indians have been actively involved in recent lobbying efforts urging the government of India to revamp its telecommunication policies and other regulations that have impeded the growth of the Indian software industry (Kripalani 2000).

This brief account suggests that even a fairly advanced education system and a robust private sector have their greatest effect if they are part of an international network—perhaps of education institutions but also, no less important, of similar firms in other countries. But with some notable exceptions—such as the experience of Taiwan, China, with the Hschinchu Science Park and the Institute for Technological Research and Innovation (see Hou and Gee 1993)—most Asian research institutions have not been well connected to the international innovation system. Educating more researchers without efforts to embed them in productive networks is likely to have low returns.

CONCLUSIONS

The title of this chapter asks whether the appropriate education policy for countries such as Korea is deepening or widening. *Deepening* here is interpreted to mean placing still greater emphasis on science, engineering, and computer-related subjects. *Widening* implies that a new set of skills must be deployed to create more financial analysts, accountants, actuaries, labor relations specialists, antitrust lawyers, and public policy analysts. These attributes are not mutually exclusive. Korea needs more of both. It must continue to educate those who will directly contribute to the ability to help reallocate resources to new sectors as well as to increase the productivity of existing sectors. However, both reallocation and improved productivity will be contingent on policies that will require careful public guidance. Safety nets, improved corporate governance, and bank regulation necessitate activities that are best undertaken by the public sector. Although Korea achieved spectacular growth while ignoring such public activities, future growth is likely to be contingent on them.

The same prescriptions hold for countries such as Malaysia and Thailand, with some modifications in light of a few special characteristics. Indeed, they also hold for China, a much larger country but with many related problems, such as the precarious situation of state-owned enterprises and their burden on the banking sector. Accession to the World Trade Organization will present China with problems that include adjustments required in the agricultural sector and rapid reduction of industrial protection rates. Successfully coping with all of these challenges will require better public policy.

The Asian economies have shown their prowess in developing manufacturing and will continue to do so. Continued development will require coping with some of the legacies of earlier success. Fortunately, all of these problems can be redressed, although a more nuanced policy regime will be required.

REFERENCES

Biers, Dan, and Sadanand Dhume. 2000. "In India, a Bit of California." *Far Eastern Economic Review* 163(44):38–40.

Bresnahan, Timothy F., Erik Brynjolfsson, and Lorin M. Hitt. 1999. "Information Technology, Workplace Organization, and the Demand for Skilled Labor: Firm-Level Evidence." NBER Working Paper 7136. National Bureau of Economic Research, Cambridge, Mass.

Brynjolfsson, Eric, and Loren M. Hitt. 2000. "Beyond Computation: Information Technology, Organizational Transformation, and Business Performance." *Journal of Economic Perspectives* 14(4):23–46.

Claessens, Stijn, Simeon Djankov, and Lixin Colin Xu. 2000. "Corporate Performance in the East Asian Financial Crisis." *World Bank Research Observer* 15:23–46.

Dahlman, Carl, and Tomas Andersson. 2000. *Korea and the Knowledge-Based Economy.* Washington D.C.: World Bank Institute.

Dollar, David, and Mary Hallward-Dreimeier. 2000. "Crisis, Adjustment, and Reform in Thailand's Industrial Firms." *World Bank Research Observer* 15:1–22.

Furman, Jason, and Joseph E. Stiglitz. 1998. "Economic Crises: Evidence and Insights from East Asia." *Brookings Papers on Economic Activity* 30(2):1–114.

Gordon, Robert J. 2000. "Does the 'New Economy' Measure Up to the Great Inventions of the Past?" *Journal of Economic Perspectives* 14(4):49–74.

———. 2003. "Exploding Productivity Growth: Context, Causes, and Implications." *Brookings Papers on Economic Activity* 2:207–79.

Hou, Chi-Ming, and San Gee. 1993. "National Systems Supporting Technical Advance in Industry: The Case of Taiwan." In Richard R. Nelson, ed., *National Innovation Systems: A Comparative Analysis.* New York: Oxford University Press.

Hulten, Charles, and Sylaja Srinivasan. 1999. "Indian Manufacturing Industry: Elephant or Tiger?" University of Maryland, College Park. Processed.

Kim, Linsu. 1993. "National System of Industrial Innovation: Dynamics of Capability Building in Korea." In Richard R. Nelson, ed., *National Innovation Systems: A Comparative Analysis.* New York: Oxford University Press.

———. 1997. *From Imitation to Innovation: Dynamics of Korea's Technological Learning.* Boston: Harvard Business School Press.

Kirk, Don. 2002. "Rescue Winding Down for Korea Banks." *New York Times,* May 23, 2002.

Kripalani, Manjeet. 2000. "A Typhoon of Venture Capital?" *Business Week* (New York), January 31, 2000, p. 28.

Lucas, Robert, Jr. 1988. "On the Mechanics of Economic Development." *Journal of Monetary Economics* 22(1):3–42.

Mankiw, Gregory, David Romer, and David Weil. 1992. "A Contribution to the Empirics of Economic Growth." *Quarterly Journal of Economics* 107(2):407–38.

McKinsey and Company. 2000. *Korea in the Third Millennium.* Seoul.

McKinsey Global Institute. 1998. *Productivity-Led Growth for Korea.* Seoul and Washington, D.C.

———. 2001. *U.S. Productivity Growth—1995–2000.* Washington, D.C.

Milgrom, Paul, and John Roberts. 1990. "The Economics of Modern Manufacturing: Technology, Strategy, and Organization." *American Economic Review* 80(3):511–28.

Nagaoka, Sadao. 1989. "Overview of Japanese Industrial Technology Development." Industry Series Paper 6. World Bank, Washington, D.C.

Nelson, Richard R., ed. 1993. *National Innovation Systems: A Comparative Analysis.* New York: Oxford University Press.

Nelson, Richard R., and Howard Pack. 1999. "The Asian Growth Miracle and Modern Growth Theory." *Economic Journal* 109:416–36.

Nelson, Richard R., and Edmund Phelps. 1966. "Investment in Humans, Technological Diffusion, and Economic Growth." *American Economic Review* 56(1–2):69–75.

Noland, Marcus, and Howard Pack. 2003. *Industrial Policy in an Era of Globalization: Lessons from Asia.* Washington, D.C.: Institute for International Economics.

OECD (Organisation for Economic Co-operation and Development). 1999. *Asia and the Global Crisis: The Industrial Dimension.* Paris.

Oliner, Stephen D., and Daniel E. Sichel. 2000. "The Resurgence of Growth in the Late 1990s: Is Information Technology the Story?" *Journal of Economic Perspectives* 14(4):3–22.

Ozawa, Terutomo. 1974. *Japan's Technological Challenge to the West, 1950–74: Motivation and Accomplishment.* Cambridge, Mass.: MIT Press.

Pack, Howard. 2001a. "The Development Effects of the Indian Software Sector." Department of Business and Public Policy, Wharton School, University of Pennsylvania, Philadelphia. Processed.

———. 2001b. "Technological Change and Growth in East Asia: Macro and Micro Perspectives." In Joseph Stiglitz and Shahid Yusuf, eds., *The Asian Miracle Revisited.* New York: Oxford University Press.

Radelet, Steven, and Jeffrey D. Sachs. 1998. "The East Asian Financial Crisis: Diagnosis, Remedies, Prospects." *Brookings Papers on Economic Activity* 30(1):1–74.

Stiglitz, Joseph, and Shahid Yusuf. 2001. *Rethinking the East Asian Miracle.* New York: Oxford University Press.

UNESCO (United Nations Educational, Scientific, and Cultural Organization). 1999. *Statistical Yearbook.* New York.

World Bank. 1993. *The East Asian Miracle.* New York: Oxford University Press.

———. 1998. *East Asia: The Road to Recovery.* Washington, D.C.

———. 1999. *Korea: Establishing a New and Sustained Foundation for Growth.* Washington, D.C.

———. 2000. *East Asia, Recovery and Beyond.* Washington, D.C.

———. 2003. *World Development Indicators.* Washington, D.C.

CHAPTER 10

VENTURE CAPITAL INDUSTRIES

Martin Kenney, Kyonghee Han, and Shoko Tanaka

I nnovation is an increasingly knowledge-intensive activity, and the link between such activity, small firms with high growth potential, and their funding through venture capital has been vividly established during the recent technological boom. Venture capital has provided financing for some of the most dynamic, innovative firm clusters in the world. During the past two decades, the venture capital investing phenomenon has diffused internationally—there are now 36 national venture capital associations. A short roster of U.S. firms funded by venture capital includes 3Com, Amgen, Cisco, DEC, Federal Express, Genentech, Intel, Oracle, and Sun Microsystems. In Taiwan, China, the world's leading maker of notebook computers, Quanta, and the world's largest motherboard maker, Asustek, received financial support from venture capitalists. In Israel, firms receiving venture capital funding include Amdocs, Checkpoint, and Mercury Online. From this list, it is clear that venture capital has been an important contributor to economic growth. Yet, despite this diffusion, in most nations the venture capital industry itself remains fragile and of limited significance.

This chapter examines the development and current condition of the venture capital industries in 11 East Asian economies. Interest by East Asian nations in venture capital can be traced back to at least 1951, when a director of Nomura Securities visiting New York was quoted by the *Wall Street Journal* ("Japan's Recovery" 1951) as saying that Japan suffered from

Kyonghee Han had primary responsibility for the section on the Republic of Korea, and Shoko Tanaka had primary responsibility for the section on Japan. The authors thank Yili Liu and Tzechien Kao for their assistance in Taiwan, China, as well as the many venture capitalists who willingly provided their views on the development of the industry. Shahid Yusuf and Mir Anjum Altaf provided important comments and suggestions that significantly improved the chapter. Martin Kenney would like to thank the World Bank and the Alfred P. Sloan Foundation for supporting the research reported in this chapter. The authors bear sole responsibility for the opinions and any errors in this manuscript.

a scarcity of venture capital. Fifty years later, nearly every East Asian economy has some venture capital, although a great disparity exists among
these economies in the level of development, practices, and sophistication
of venture capitalists.

Despite the existence of venture capital in East Asia, to date no Asian
venture capital firm has entered the first rank of global venture capital
firms (which includes companies such as Accel Partners, Greylock, Kleiner
Perkins Caufield & Byers, Sequoia Capital, Warburg Pincus, and
Venrock). Leading Asian venture capitalists have attributed this gap to
factors ranging from an endemic lack of experienced management to over-
regulation, problems in educational systems (especially at the postgradu-
ate level), a need for better funding of research, and an unwillingness of
entrepreneurs to cooperate and build firms (Hsu 1999; Tan 2001). These
and other reasons have prevented Asia from creating venture capital firms
that are leaders on the global stage. Neither has Asia, with the exception
of Taiwan, China, given rise to a sufficient number of start-ups providing
the extremely large returns necessary to justify the growth of vibrant, self-
sustaining venture capital industries.

Any national venture capital industry is shaped by its institutional context. The supply-side variables affecting the successful development of a
venture capital industry include the level of economic development, existence of national systems of innovation, levels of entrepreneurship, labor
practices, corporate ownership regulations, educational achievement, and
business cultures. Critical demand-side variables are new firms commercializing new business opportunities capable of justifying high-risk equity
investments. Any economy sufficiently complex to have a viable venture
capital industry is most likely to have forces both encouraging and discouraging the development of venture capital and, hence, the evolution
will be punctuated rather than monotonic. Quite naturally, an institution
such as the venture capital industry, which is so dependent on the national
(and, in some cases, subnational) environment, will experience differing
national evolutionary trajectories.

Our goal is to describe the evolution of the different venture capital
markets in Asia. We begin by describing venture capital as a practice and
then sketch the birth and development of venture capital in the United
States. A history of the evolution of venture capital in Asia follows. To simplify this discussion, we separate the Asian venture capital markets into
four groups: (a) Japan and the Republic of Korea; (b) Hong Kong (China),
Singapore, and Taiwan (China); (c) China; and (d) developing Asia. The
venture capital industries within these four markets share many common

features. We next examine some of the common institutional issues that cut across all the Asian venture capital industries. Then we briefly discuss the situation in Asia after the dot-com collapse. Finally, the conclusion reflects on the development patterns of the venture capital industry in Asia and its future evolution.

HOW DOES VENTURE CAPITAL WORK?

Before answering the question of how venture capital works, we must define *venture capital*. The classic definition is that venture capitalists make equity investments in small firms. This definition is narrow. For example, in Japan, the bulk of "venture capital" disbursements have been through loans to established firms. A strict definition would largely omit Japan and Korea, two of the most important economies in East Asia. So we adopt an expansive definition of venture capital for the case studies, but we use a stricter definition in our discussion of the venture capital practice so as to create an ideal type as a reference point.

In the United States, venture capital as a practice is relatively easy to define, because venture capital and private equity are quite distinct. This distinction does not hold true in most of the world. For example, both the European Venture Capital Association (EVCA) and the *Asian Venture Capital Journal* combine venture capital and private equity investing in all of their statistics. As a professional investment activity, venture capital is an older practice than private equity (although it is possible to argue that today's private equity resembles the traditional role of Wall Street financiers—that is, using capital to organize and reorganize firms and industrial sectors). For much of the world, however, private equity and venture capital are combined both statistically and in the minds of policymakers. In Europe, a large proportion of what the EVCA considers venture capital is, by U.S. standards, private equity.

Classic venture capital investing requires business opportunities that have the potential for annualized capital gains of greater than 30 to 40 percent, because investments in seed or early-stage firms experience failure rates (that is, bankruptcy or negligible growth) of at least 50 percent. Successful investments must compensate for these failures. When such opportunities do not exist, professional venture capital organizations are difficult to sustain. Venture capitalists cannot survive by funding firms that do not appreciate rapidly; thus, investments are not evaluated on the basis of social goals such as reducing unemployment, increasing research and development (R&D), or building a community's technological tax base. The sole relevant criterion is the potential for large capital gains.

In return for investing, venture capitalists demand a significant equity stake in the firm and seats on the board of directors from which they monitor the firm. Each investment is staged, and the entrepreneurs are given milestones to be achieved before they receive another tranche of funds. Experienced venture capitalists provide more than just money, which is a salient difference between venture capitalists and passive investors. Venture capitalists actively monitor, assist, and even intervene in their portfolio firms. A venture capitalist's experience, connections, and ability can contribute to the firm's growth. The objective is to leverage this involvement to increase the recipient firm's probability of success. This involvement extends to ad hoc assistance in a variety of functions, including recruiting key persons; providing advice; and introducing the firm's officers to potential customers, strategic partners, later-stage financiers, investment bankers, and various other contacts (Florida and Kenney 1988a, 1988b; Gompers 1995). These functions are what differentiate venture capitalists from other funding sources.

Investments are liquidated through bankruptcy, merger, or an initial public offering (IPO) of stock. For this reason, venture capitalists are temporary investors and, in most cases, are members of the firm's board of directors only until the investment is liquidated.[1] For the venture capitalist, the firm is a product to be sold, not retained. Nations that erect impediments to any exit paths (including bankruptcy) handicap the development of venture capital. We do not mean to say that such nations will not have entrepreneurship, only that it is less likely that venture capital as an institution will thrive.

Except in Taiwan, China, the predominant institutional format for venture capital is the venture capital firm operating a series of partnerships called *funds* that raise money from investors consisting of wealthy individuals, corporations, pension funds, foundation, endowments, and various other institutional sources. The general or managing partners are the professional venture capitalists, whereas the investors are passive limited partners. The typical fund operates for a set number of years (usually 10) and then is terminated. Normally, each firm manages more than one fund; one fund is usually fully invested, another one is being invested, and a third is in the process of being raised.

---

1. Exceptions do exist. For example, Arthur Rock, the lead venture capitalist in funding Intel, remained on the Intel board of directors for two decades. Donald Valentine, the lead venture capitalist in funding Cisco, continues on the board fully a decade after it went public.

THE ORIGINS OF VENTURE CAPITAL AS AN INSTITUTION

Before World War II, the source of capital for entrepreneurs everywhere was either the government, government-sponsored institutions meant to invest in such ventures, or informal investors (today, termed *angels*).[2] In general, private banks, unless heavily subsidized or compelled by law, have been unwilling to lend money to newly established firms because of the high risk and lack of collateral.[3] After World War II, a set of intermediaries emerged in the United States that specialized in investing in fledgling firms with the potential for rapid growth. From its beginnings on the U.S. East Coast, venture capital gradually expanded and became an increasingly professionalized institution. During this period, the locus of the industry shifted from New York and Boston on the East Coast to Silicon Valley on the West Coast (Florida and Kenney 1988a, 1988b; Gompers 1994). By the mid-1980s, the ideal typical venture capital firm was based in Silicon Valley, invested largely in electronics, and devoted lesser sums to biomedical technologies.[4] Until the present, in addition to Silicon Valley, the two other major concentrations of venture capital have been Boston and New York City. Internationally, other significant concentrations of venture capital include London, Israel, Hong Kong (China), Singapore, Taiwan (China), and Tokyo.

In the United States, the government has played a role in developing venture capital, although, for the most part, this role has been indirect. For example, the U.S. government generally practiced sound monetary and fiscal policies, thus ensuring relatively low inflation with a stable financial environment and currency. Historically, U.S. tax policy has been favorable to capital gains, and there is some evidence that further lowering of capital gains taxes may have had a positive effect on the availability of venture capital. However, Gompers (1994) has shown that the most important government action in the late 1970s was a loosening of federal government regulations, thereby permitting pension fund managers to invest prudent amounts in venture capital funds.

---

2. On angels, see Robinson and van Osnabrugge (2000).

3. Normally, banks charge interest, a practice that, to be successful, requires the repayment of the principal. Banks cannot afford the loss of their capital when their return is only an interest payment.

4. There are, of course, important venture capital firms headquartered in other regions, and there is a diversity of venture capital specialists. For example, there are funds that specialize in retail ventures. Some of the largest venture capital funds, such as Oak Investment Partners and New Enterprise Associates, have partners devoted to retail ventures, although their main focus is information technology. So there is significant diversity and some specialization in the venture capital industry (Gupta and Sapienza 1992).

The U.S. Securities and Exchange Commission had a reputation, whether fully deserved or not, for strictly enforcing disclosure and probity. Investors perceived the NASDAQ (National Association of Securities Dealers Automated Quotation) stock market, which has been the exit strategy of choice for venture capitalists, to be strictly regulated and, in general, characterized by increasing openness, which allayed their limiting fears of fraud and deception. This general macroeconomic environment of apparent transparency and predictability reduced investor risk. Put differently, for investors, risks of fraud and other opportunistic behavior were believed to be minimized.[5]

Another important government policy was heavy and continuous support for university research funding that supported generations of graduate students' education in the sciences and engineering, producing trained personnel and innovations. U.S. universities, particularly the Massachusetts Institute of Technology (MIT), Stanford, and the University of California, Berkeley, played a particularly important role (for MIT, see DiGregorio and Shane 2003; for Stanford and the University of California, Berkeley, see Kenney and Goe forthcoming). In the United Kingdom, the most active region outside of London for venture capital activity is the Cambridge area, where venture capitalists draw on the university's excellent engineering and medical school faculty.[6] In Taiwan, China, the research institutes in the Hsinchu area have provided important support to start-up firms.

The most important direct U.S. government involvement in encouraging the growth of venture capital was the passage of the Small Business Investment Act of 1958, which authorized the formation of small business investment corporations (SBICs). The SBICs funded a wide variety of small firms. For the development of venture capital, the following features of the SBIC programs were significant. First, individuals could form SBICs with private funds as paid-in capital and then could borrow money on up to a 2:1 ratio. Second, there were tax and other benefits, such as income tax features, capital gains tax pass-through, and an allowance of carried interest as compensation. Third, the commercial banks could use the SBIC program as a vehicle to circumvent the Glass-Steagall Act's prohibition on bank ownership of more than 5 percent of industrial firms. The

---

5. The recent stock market scandals, such as the allocation of IPO shares to favored individuals by investment bankers, indicate that, at least to some degree, this transparency was more a perception than a reality.

6. The greater level of entrepreneurship in Cambridge than in Oxford is likely explained by Cambridge's emphasis on engineering and the sciences.

bank SBICs were especially important in the 1960s and 1970s. The final investment format permitted SBICs to raise money in the public market.

The SBIC program experienced serious problems from its inception. A series of government investigations found widespread misappropriation of funds, incompetence, and fraud (Bean 2001). Also, the Small Business Administration was a bureaucratic government agency whose rules and regulations were constantly changing. Despite the corruption and bureaucracy, from the venture capital point of view, something valuable also occurred. The SBICs allowed a number of individuals to leverage their personal capital, and some were so successful that they left the SBIC program and raised institutional money to become formal venture capitalists. The SBIC program accelerated their capital accumulation, and, just as important, government regulations made these new venture capitalists professionalize their investment activity, which had been informal prior to their entering the program.

The historical record also indicates that government action can harm venture capital. The most salient example was in 1973, when the U.S. Congress, in response to widespread corruption in pension funds, changed federal pension fund regulations. In its haste to prohibit pension fund abuses, Congress passed the Employment Retirement Income Security Act, which made pension fund managers criminally liable for losses incurred in high-risk investments. These investments were interpreted to include venture capital funds. As a result, pension managers shunned venture capital, nearly destroying the industry. This trend was reversed only after active lobbying by the newly created National Venture Capital Association (NVCA) (Pincus 2000; Stults 2000). In 1977, a gradual loosening of regulations commenced, which was completed in 1982. The new interpretation of these pension fund guidelines contributed to first a trickle and then, in the 1980s, a flood of new money into venture capital funds.

Israel is the nation that has most successfully adopted the Silicon Valley–style venture capital practice. The Israeli government played a critical role in the industry's emergence (Autler 2000; Avnimelech and Teubal 2002). The government has a relatively good economic record; there is minimal corruption, massive investment in the military (particularly electronics research), and an excellent higher-education system. The active interaction of Israeli entrepreneurs and venture capitalists with Israelis and Jewish individuals in U.S. high-technology industry provided an important conduit for learning and sharing knowledge. This synergy contributed to Israeli success. A well-known U.S. venture capitalist, Fred Adler, began investing in Israeli start-ups in the early 1970s and, in 1985, was involved in forming the first Israeli venture capital fund (Autler 2000,

p. 40). Nonetheless, the true creation of an Israeli venture capital industry waited until the 1990s, when the government funded Yozma, an organization encouraging the growth of venture capital in Israel. Yozma received US$100 million from the Israeli government and invested US$8 million in each of 10 funds on the condition that they each raise another US$12 million from an overseas venture capital firm (Autler 2000, p. 44). Yozma also retained US$20 million to invest itself. These sibling funds were the backbone of a now vibrant community that invested in excess of US$3 billion in Israel in 2000, although in the first three quarters of 2002 the total investment had declined to US$1.011 billion (Israel Venture Association 2004).

In the United States, venture capital emerged through an organic trial-and-error process, and the role of the government was limited and contradictory. In Israel, the government played a vital role in a supportive environment in which private sector venture capital had already emerged. In the United States, the most important role of the government was indirect, differing from the Israeli government's direct role in assisting the growth of venture capital and from India's situation, in which the government has had to be proactive in removing barriers (Dossani and Kenney 2002).

Measuring the importance of venture capital is quite difficult, because in terms of capital investment it is only a minute portion of the total economy. Moreover, the most powerful systemic benefits of venture capital come in the form of Schumpeterian innovations; however, a by-product is often the creative destruction of other industries, something that ordinary growth accounting would consider a loss. Also, it is possible that the firms backed would have come into existence without venture capital funding, because the entrepreneurs might have garnered investment from other sources or simply boot-strapped the firm by reinvesting retained earnings. For these and other reasons, accounting for the economic effect of venture capital is difficult, and any conclusions are provisional.

The anecdotal evidence of the economic importance of venture capital for the U.S. economy is powerful. In 1999, the U.S. venture capital firm Kleiner Perkins Caufield & Byers claimed that the portfolio firms funded since its inception in 1973 had a total market capitalization of US$657 billion, earned revenue of US$93 billion, and employed 252,000 persons (KPCB 2001). Although extrapolation from Kleiner Perkins Caufield & Byers, which is among the most successful venture capital firms in the world, is risky, it is safe to say that the cumulative effect of the now more than 600 venture capital firms in the United States has been substantial, even for an economy as large as that of the United States. In specific regions, especially Silicon Valley and Boston's Route 128, venture capital has been a vital component of what Bahrami and Evans (2000) term the *entire ecosystem* (see also Lee and others 2000).

The U.S. General Accounting Office (GAO 1982, p. 10) studied the effect of the venture capital industry on the U.S. economy. Extrapolating from 72 publicly listed venture capital–funded firms operating in 1979 (there were 1,332 venture capital–funded firms in existence at that time), the GAO concluded that employment would increase by 1989 by between 522,000 and 2.54 million employees, depending on the annualized growth assumption. A recent study commissioned by the NVCA (2001) and conducted by the consulting firm WEFA estimated venture capital–financed firms had been cumulatively responsible for creating 4.3 million jobs and US\$736 billion in annual revenues in 2000. Another indicator of the significance of venture capital investment is its effect on the innovation process. Kortum and Lerner (2000), using a sample of firms and patent filings, found that venture funding accounted for 8 percent of U.S. industrial innovations in the decade that ended in 1992. They believe that this percentage might have increased to as much as 14 percent by 1998. They found that venture capital investment produced more patents, because a dollar of venture capital was 3.1 times more likely to lead to a patent than was a corporate R&D dollar.

In the United Kingdom, a survey by the British Venture Capital Association (BVCA 1999) found that private equity–financed firms grew at an annual compounded rate of 24 percent, or three times faster than firms in the Financial Times Stock Exchange (FTSE) Index 100 and 70 percent faster than those in the FTSE 250. This finding may not be entirely surprising given that private equity–financed firms are expected to grow faster than publicly traded firms. The BVCA estimated that 2 million Britons, or 10 percent of the current private work force, were employed by venture capital–backed firms. This estimate seems inflated, but it provides one possible indicator of how important private equity and venture capital have been to the growth of the U.K. economy.

In the case of Taiwan, China, there has been little study of the benefits of the venture capital industry. One study quantified the benefits of tax collections from venture capital investments from 1990 to 1992, finding that they were 10 or more times greater than the tax dollars expended (Wang 1995). For Israel, there has been no quantification of the benefits of venture capital, but in 2000, high-technology industry accounted for approximately 25 percent of the entire gross domestic product, and from 1991 to 2000, venture capitalists had backed a total of 1,802 firms (Avnimelech and Teubal 2002).

Venture capital (or, in the case of the United Kingdom, private equity) has made a significant contribution to the economies of Israel, Taiwan (China), the United Kingdom, and the United States and appears to be an efficient method for commercializing innovations. Although there has been only limited research on its macroeconomic effects, there is ample evidence that venture capital has had a significant effect in the United States. It certainly has been the key financier of the U.S. "new economy" firms. Also, in the United States, Israel, and Taiwan, China, it has become a part of the national system of innovation for commercializing R&D. Moreover, it has become a central component of the growth of regions such as Silicon Valley and Route 128.

BUILDING A VENTURE CAPITAL INDUSTRY

A successful venture capital industry is not easy to create. Of the 36 economies with a national venture capital association, fewer than 10 have industries of any significance. As an institution, venture capital is quite fragile and requires a number of preconditions for emergence and growth. The most important single factor for explaining the development of a vibrant venture capital industry is availability of investments capable of providing sufficiently large returns to justify the high risk. In other words, there must be a sufficient supply of opportunities capable of supporting a community of venture capitalists. If the number of venture capitalists is insufficient, a downturn in the economy and the failure of a few could lead to the collapse of the industry. In other words, without a sufficient number of deals, it might be possible to establish a venture capital industry, but the industry would not be sustainable.

Context is also important. There should be a relatively transparent and predictable legal system that offers some protection to investors. If foreign investors are to be encouraged, then currency convertibility is important. It is also necessary that a portion of the labor force be well educated and capable of managing start-up firms through the rapid growth process. All of these attributes appear to be in short supply in a number of East Asian countries. Venture capital requires that entrepreneurs be willing to sell significant amounts of equity to the venture capitalists and be prepared to share control.

In economies where many or most of these conditions are missing, it will be difficult to create a vibrant venture capital industry capable of supporting small start-up firms. There may be a financial sector that labels itself as venture capital industry, but it will differ significantly from our ideal type. Moreover, this venture capital industry is unlikely to exhibit the dynamism experienced by the classic venture capital industries in economies such as Israel, Taiwan (China), the United States, and—more recently—India.

THE HISTORY OF VENTURE CAPITAL IN ASIA

Each Asian economy's venture capital industry has a different evolutionary trajectory, and in every case the government had a role in establishing the industry. The cross-national diffusion through institutions could be conceptualized as a convergence process; however, this perspective is problematic. As an institution, venture capital differs substantially in each of these environments because it is shaped by the political, social, and economic institutions within which it is embedded.

Each political economy thus has a venture capital industry that is shaped by the local economy and that differs significantly from the venture capital industry in other economies. For heuristic purposes, the venture capital industries in Asia can be divided into four groups: (a) Japan and Korea; (b) Hong Kong (China), Singapore, and Taiwan (China); (c) China; and (d) developing Asia, which includes Indonesia, Malaysia, the Philippines, Thailand, and Vietnam. The second category can be further subdivided into two categories, which can be termed the *export-oriented* venture capital industries of Singapore and Hong Kong, China (which most closely resemble the industries of New York and London), and the *technology-oriented* industry of Taiwan, China (which most closely resembles the industry of Silicon Valley).[7]

Given the dramatic differences in the stage of development and the size of these economies, it is not surprising that the size of the venture capital industries should also differ. These national differences are substantial, as table 10.1 indicates. Overall, there has been significant growth in China, Hong Kong (China), Korea, Singapore, and Taiwan (China). The industries in Japan and Indonesia have not grown. In 2002 and 2003, Taiwanese venture capitalists have had difficulty raising new funds because the government removed a tax rebate incentive. Although no data are available for 2002, it is likely that only Hong Kong (China) and China experienced significant expansion; 2003 was a difficult year for venture capitalists throughout Asia, except in China.

---

7. For this distinction, see Florida and Kenney (1988a, 1988b).

Table 10.1 National Venture Capital Pools in Asia
(nominal US$ millions)

Year	United States	China	Hong Kong, China	Indonesia	Japan	Korea, Rep. of	Malaysia	Philippines	Singapore	Taiwan, China	Thailand	Vietnam	Total Asia
1991	30,100	—	—	76	15,352	1,547	75	16	868	412	64	10	18,604
1992	30,300	878	—	57	16,028	1,629	147	26	896	470	90	22	20,243
1993	31,600	1,422	—	99	17,750	1,687	160	58	1,013	508	98	131	22,926
1994	35,300	2,384	—	225	17,750	1,902	194	85	1,833	562	117	247	25,299
1995	40,200	3,458	—	245	14,851	2,567	437	123	3,164	696	165	303	26,009
1996	48,900	3,612	8,019	289	11,254	3,224	448	166	3,981	1,336	201	276	32,806
1997	65,100	3,500	9,632	426	7,722	1,857	406	169	4,468	1,913	177	292	30,562
1998	90,900	3,112	14,462	328	12,513	2,995	460	224	5,258	3,598	242	258	43,450
1999	142,900	3,735	21,203	333	21,729	4,986	667	292	7,791	4,447	265	318	65,766
2000	209,800	5,201	24,128	169	21,138	6,020	587	383	9,286	5,852	597	157	73,518
2001	—	6,044	26,019	153	21,515	6,251	811	291	9,754	6,261	580	114	77,793

— Not available.

Note: All Asian statistics combine venture capital and private equity.

Sources: NVCA, National Venture Capital Association Yearbook (various years); AVCJ, Guide to Venture Capital in Asia (various years).

In each economy, the sources of funds vary, and there are some striking differences between the United States and all of the East Asian economies. The first difference is that in the United States a large number of non-profit institutional funding sources, such as university endowments and foundations, have long-term capital appreciation goals and will commit up to 5 percent of their capital to alternative investments. The second difference is that a number of the Asian governments are willing to invest directly in venture capital, whereas the U.S. government does not generally do so,[8] as evidenced in the aggregate statistics on sources of funds committed to venture capital (see table 10.2).

If one compares Asia with the United States, one finds that an important difference is in funding sources. In Asia, industrial corporations are the largest source of funds, whereas in the United States, industrial corporations have committed little to the private venture capital funds. For example, in Taiwan, China, industrial commitments constituted 53 percent of the total commitments to venture capital, an achievement no doubt fueled by a 20 percent tax rebate. Only in Malaysia were industrial commitments below 20 percent. In most of Asia, pension funds were of little significance. In the case of Hong Kong (China), Japan, and perhaps China, the total contribution attributed to pension funds is partially attributable to U.S. pension funds' investing in Asia. In Malaysia, the pension funds are controlled by the government and directed to invest in venture capital. Endowments and foundations were negligible sources of funds in Asia. In contrast, they provided 20 percent of the U.S. total. In all of the Asian economies, the government had some role in providing capital to the venture capital industry, and in Singapore, the government was the second-largest investor. The sources of funds differ among Asian economies and differ from those in the United States.

Japan and Korea

Japan and Korea share somewhat similar insertions into the global economy and, until recently, have had somewhat similar industrial structures.[9] In contrast to Korea, Japan had a much more vibrant small-firm manufacturing sector whose genesis can be traced to the Tokugawa Shogunate (Amsden 1992; Nishiguchi 1994). In Korea, until the 1980s,

---

8. The Small Business Investment Research grants do provide monies for start-up research projects and thus perform a function superficially similar to that of venture capital.

9. For a discussion of Japanese venture capital using roughly the same sources, see Kuemmerle (2001).

Table 10.2 Sources of Venture Capital Commitments in Asia and the United States, 2000 (percent)

Economy	Corporations	Individuals	Banks	Insurance firms	Pension funds	Government	Other
China	41	3	18	18	12	7	1
Hong Kong, China	37	2	11	32	13	5	0
Indonesia	49	3	15	8	7	10	8
Japan	48	2	25	13	9	2	1
Korea, Rep. of	45	2	23	12	6	10	2
Malaysia	13	5	12	9	50	10	1
Philippines	53	11	20	8	0	6	2
Singapore	37	5	16	12	9	20	1
Taiwan, China	58	9	14	10	4	4	1
Thailand	29	2	38	14	13	4	0
Vietnam	47	4	27	6	5	8	3
United States	3	11	22		37	20	7

Sources: For Asian economies, AVCJ (2003). For the United States, NVCA (2001).

the government actively determined the direction of the economy through direct intervention and subsidization. Only in the 1980s did this dirigiste style of economic planning gradually loosen and give way to a market-driven economy. The venture capital industries in both nations, although similar on many dimensions, do differ in the amount and level of government involvement.

Japan was the first nation in Asia to attempt to create a venture capital industry. In 1963, the Japanese government authorized the use of public funds to create firms like the U.S. SBICs, establishing one firm in each of three cities: Tokyo, Nagoya, and Osaka. These firms supported some existing small and medium-size enterprises (SMEs) by providing stable, long-term capital, but they funded few start-ups (Niimi and Okina 1995). Through March 1996, these three firms cumulatively invested 69.2 billion yen[10] in 2,500 companies, of which 78 had had public stock offerings.

The first private venture capital firms were created in the early 1970s. In 1972, Kyoto Enterprise Development (KED), whose express model was American Research and Development, the first U.S. non-family-funded venture capital firm, was established through investments by 43 prominent Kyoto companies. However, KED failed and was liquidated only 4 years later (Ono 1995). At the same time, in Tokyo the Nippon Enterprise Development was formed by a group of 39 firms. In 1973, Nomura Securities and 15 other shareholders established Japan Godo Finance, which was the precursor to the present JAFCO (Japan Associated Finance Company). Also between 1972 and 1974, other important financial institutions, including major banks (such as Sumitomo, Mitsubishi, and Daiichi Kangyo) and major security firms (such as Yamaichi and Nikko), formed venture capital subsidiaries. This first wave ended following the 1973 oil crisis, when the number of investments declined and the industry stagnated. Of the eight firms formed during this period, six still exist.

In the 1980s, a number of new initiatives to create venture capital industries were launched. From 1982 to 1984, the city banks, security firms, and regional banks formed 37 new venture capital subsidiaries. Their goal was not to fund entrepreneurial start-ups, but rather to use "venture investments" to build relationships with small and medium-size firms in an effort to sell them other services. In terms of their investments, the Japanese venture capitalists did not seek capital gains; rather, they

---

10. At an average conversion rate of 150 yen to the U.S. dollar over this period, this amount would be in excess of US$400 million.

wanted to develop long-term banking relationships with their portfolio firms. The normal investment techniques such as due diligence were not overly rigorous, because they lent to established firms, not new firms. In 1982, JAFCO introduced the limited partnership format (Hamada 1999, pp. 38–41). This venture capital boom also subsided because of a recession in 1986 and 1987, and investment activity declined substantially.

Beginning in the mid-1990s, interest in the role of venture capital was renewed because of the Internet boom in the United States. This time, however, the new venture capital boom coincided with heightened concern on the part of Japanese industrial and government leaders about the continuing stagnation of the economy. So to facilitate new business creation and start-ups in knowledge-intensive and high-technology industries, the Japanese government created a variety of new incentives. For example, in 1995 SMEs were made eligible to receive financial as well as informational support. New laws also encouraged the formation of venture capital firms, and another wave of regional banks and corporations established venture capital affiliates. Also, many independent venture capital firms were formed.

The emergence of Softbank as a funder of new firms was a significant change. Softbank was a Japanese software distribution firm owned by Masayoshi Son, who had made early investments in U.S. Internet start-ups including Yahoo!, Geocities, and E*Trade. When those firms went public, Softbank reaped enormous capital gains, which it invested in 292 Japanese Internet start-ups, as well as in other start-ups around the world. By January 2001, Softbank had invested US$8.8 billion in more than 600 start-ups (Softbank Investment 2001). Softbank was not alone; a number of other Japanese firms such as Hikari Tsushin plunged into venture capital by investing in Internet firms. Moreover, traditional venture capital firms switched from providing loans to established firms to investing in equity in start-ups. During this period, it was also easy to undertake public stock offerings, and many firms went public on two new Japanese markets: MOTHERS (Market for High-Growth and Emerging Stocks) and NASDAQ Japan, which were created to ease the listing of SMEs. In the collapse of the Internet bubble in 2001, Japanese venture capitalists such as Softbank experienced enormous losses, and there has been little investment in new firms.

The first Korean experiment in developing venture capital was in the 1970s. In 1974, the Korean government created what it termed a *venture capital firm*, Korean Technology Advancement Corporation (KTAC). KTAC's funding came from government research institutions, and its objective was to be an intermediary financial institution that assisted in the transfer of research results from government-supported research insti-tutes to technically competent SMEs. This effort does indicate the Korean government's awareness of the venture capital industry, but by U.S. stan-dards, KTAC would not be considered a venture capital firm.

The 1980s were a tumultuous time for Korea, as the country moved from dictatorship to democracy. This political sea change was punctuated by a number of changes in government, resulting in shifting policies. The Korean environment was much more complicated than that of the United States because of the pervasive and often distorting government effort to establish the venture capital industry. Korea returned to the idea of creat-ing venture capital in 1981, when the Korea Technology Development Corporation (KTDC) was incorporated under a special law aimed at sup-porting industry R&D projects (KTB 2001).[11] KTDC was meant to fund R&D and its commercialization (Choi 1987, p. 352); therefore, it did not operate like a classic venture capital firm, supporting entrepreneurial teams capable of creating businesses. In 1982, the Korean Development Investment Corporation (KDIC) formed a joint venture between seven Seoul-based short-term financing companies, a number of international development institutions, Westinghouse, and JAFCO (KDIC 1986).[12] KDIC was organized as a limited liability venture capital firm, with the purpose of fostering and strengthening Korean technology-oriented SMEs through equity investment or equity-type investments. In 1984, yet another venture capital firm, Korean Technology Finance Corporation, was established by the Korea Development Bank.[13] Of these, only KDIC emphasized equity investments and was not an arm of a government agency. Put simply, KDIC was the beginning of Korean private venture capital.

In 1986, the government enacted the Small and Medium-Size Enter-prise Start-up Support (SMESS) Act to support the establishment and growth of small enterprises. Also in 1986, the New Technology Enterprise Financial Support (NTEFS) Act was promulgated to support the four ear-lier venture capital organizations (AVCJ 1992). With these two laws, the Korean venture capital firms were divided into two types, each having dif-ferent roles and characteristics. The first four venture capital companies

---

11. In July 1992, KTDC was renamed the Korea Technology and Banking Network Corporation.

12. In 1996, KDIC changed its name to Trigem Ventures after it was acquired by Trigem Com-puter Inc., Korea's largest PC manufacturer. See http://www.tgventures.co.kr.

13. The Korean Technology Finance Corporation was renamed KDB Capital after it merged with the Korea Development Lease Corporation in 1999. At present, KDB Capital is a subsidiary of the Korea Development Bank. See http://www.kdbcapital.co.kr.

were now called *new technology enterprise financial companies* (NTEFC). NTEFCs were permitted to invest their funds with less government oversight; however, they were required to provide consulting services to the government, especially with respect to directing government funds to SMEs.

The firms covered by the SMESS Act were required to invest in start-up and early-stage enterprises that were fewer than 5 years old. This division of labor reflected the interests of the Ministry of Trade and Industry (MTI), which administered the SMESS Act, and the Ministry of Finance (MOF), which administered the NTEFS Act. However, because of this division, SMESS Act venture capital companies under MTI administration were in a disadvantageous position. Han-Seop Kim (2001), who was a director in KTB at that time, said, "SMESS Act venture capital companies were so restricted, because they were at the boundary of the financial industry that traditionally had been under MOF administration." This situation would become further complicated in 1992, when KTDC, the largest NTEFC, was transferred to the control of the Ministry of Science and Technology and changed its name to Korea Technology & Banking (KTB).[14] The predictable result was confusion and overlap.

To increase Korea's technological capabilities, the government rapidly increased the amount of targeted funds, which the NTEFCs helped direct. The result was that the NTEFCs were also able to expand rapidly. However, these targeted funds were in the form of loans because the government was not interested in equity. The SMESS Act venture capital firms were meant to operate like Western venture capital firms. The passage of the SMESS Act sparked the formation of many new venture capital firms, and in 1990 there were 54 such firms. Despite the rapid growth in the number of venture capital firms, most investments were loans. Most damaging were the inexperienced professionals in these firms, whose poor investments and inability to assist their portfolio firms contributed to the failure of the portfolio firms and of the venture capital firms themselves.

The early 1990s were difficult, though a few start-ups that had been financed in the late 1980s showed some signs of success. The venture capital firms that were formed in response to the regulations promulgated in the mid-1980s experienced bankruptcies among their portfolio firms. In response, the venture capital firms tightened their investment criteria. In August 1993, to counteract this investment slowdown, the government loosened regulations and expanded the industries permissible for

---

14. For further discussion, see Kenney, Han, and Tanaka (2002).

investment, extended the age limit for investment-eligible firms from under 5 years old to under 7 years old, and removed the investment ceilings for fund investors. With the 1994 economic recovery and the reduction of regulations, investment once again increased, although it remained subdued until the Internet mania arrived.

During the late 1990s, the Korean government added yet more incentives for the venture capital industry by changing a number of laws to promote innovative small firms. Also, in 1997, the government launched its own venture capital funds and established a program to provide matching funds for venture capital limited partnerships. In August 1997, the government permitted pension funds to invest up to 10 percent of their capital in venture capital partnerships. In May 1998, the restrictions on foreign investment in Korean venture capital partnerships were lifted, and tax benefits for venture capital were increased. Also, measures were adopted to increase tax benefits for venture capital partnerships. Those efforts catalyzed the establishment of a number of limited partnerships. The Korean experience was remarkable because it went from the depths of the Asian financial crisis to the Internet boom and then the collapse of the "new economy" in 3 years.

In both Japan and Korea, the development of a Silicon Valley–type venture capital industry appears elusive. Policymakers have found it difficult to create a policy mix conducive to entrepreneurial activity, and most managers are unwilling to resign to establish smaller firms. The entrepreneurship that was sparked by the Internet boom has been forgotten in the aftermath of the collapse.

Hong Kong (China), Singapore, and Taiwan (China)

Hong Kong (China), Singapore, and Taiwan (China) share many commonalties, including size, strong ties with Western nations, and industrial structures that are based on exports. In each of these economies, the venture capital industry was established in the early 1980s. The most important difference between them is that the venture capital industries in Hong Kong (China) and Singapore have a financial orientation, whereas the industry in Taiwan (China) has a technology orientation. Moreover, the venture capital industries in Hong Kong (China) and Singapore are dominated by large foreign financial firms, whereas the industry in Taiwan (China) is largely indigenous.

Taiwan, China. The inception of the venture capital industry in Taiwan, China, can be traced to government involvement. However, the strategy adopted by top government officials was quite different from that adopted in Korea. In 1983, after officials and businesspeople from Taiwan, China, made a study trip to the United States and Japan, the government passed legislation providing attractive tax incentives to individuals who were willing to invest in professional venture capital firms. The core of the 1983 legislation was a tax rebate of up to 20 percent for individuals who maintained an approved venture capital investment for at least 2 years. To qualify, the investment had to be made by a venture capital fund approved by the Ministry of Finance (Asian Technology Information Program 1998; Taiwan, China, Ministry of Finance 1996, pp. 9–10). In addition to offering the attractive tax rebate, the law also allowed investment abroad. In the vast majority of cases, the investment was in the United States, where a number of expatriates from Taiwan, China, worked in Silicon Valley. In 1991, the statute was revised to allow corporate investors the same 20 percent tax rebate (Liu 2001). This change dramatically increased the amount of capital available for venture capital when corporations rushed to secure the rebate.

The tax rebate was by far the most important incentive, but there were others. The other incentives included making 80 percent of the venture capital firms' investment income tax exempt in the current fiscal year, providing a grace period of one year. Also, those choosing to reinvest the earnings garnered from a venture capital investment were allowed to deduct the venture capital income from their tax return in that year. This provision encouraged the investors to reinvest their earnings, thereby increasing the capital pool.

The first venture capital firm in Taiwan, China, was an Acer subsidiary, Multiventure Investment Inc. That firm was formed in November 1984 and made its first investment in a Silicon Valley start-up that year (Shih 1996, p. 35). However, the firm that received the most attention was formed by the Silicon Valley investment bank Hambrecht and Quist (H&Q). H&Q launched its fund with investments from major industrial groups in Taiwan, China, and from government-controlled banks and agencies (Kaufman 1986; Sussner 2001). H&Q's first investment was in the Taiwan, China, subsidiary of Data Corporation, a Santa Clara manufacturer of disk drive controllers and floppy disks (Kaufman 1986, p. 7D). This fund was the beginning of what would become H&Q Asia Pacific, which now operates throughout Asia. In 1987, the Walden Group—a San Francisco–based venture capital firm that was owned by Asian Americans—established a fund called International Venture Capital Investment Corporation with investments from various private and government entities and citizens of Taiwan, China. This fund evolved into the Walden International Investment Group. Its first two investments were in

Northern California (Besher 1988, p. C9). As significant as the funds were, important also was the fact that the venture capital firms in Taiwan, China, were learning by doing in Silicon Valley.

The 1990s were a period of rapid growth for the venture capital industry in Taiwan, China. In policy terms, the most important change was the revision of the statute that originally provided tax rebates only for individuals so that corporations could also benefit (Liu 2001). Of course, the most significant factor was the success of the high-technology electronics industry in Taiwan, China, which became the world's major producer of many components used in personal computers, the leading center for outsourcing personal computer assembly, and the location of the two largest semiconductor foundries in the world. These industries were the source of many spin-offs. Despite the great difficulties the venture capital industry in Taiwan, China, has experienced, there is little question that it will survive the current downturn.

Hong Kong, China. The first non-Japanese venture capital operation in Asia was a Citicorp Venture Capital subsidiary that was established in Hong Kong, China, in 1972. By the mid-1980s, Citicorp, which was soon to discontinue venture investing and become a private equity firm, had been joined by six other firms, including two U.S. insurance companies. Those early firms drew on the territory's status as the major Asian financial center and formed the roots of its venture capital industry. For large banks and financial institutions, Hong Kong, China, operated as a headquarters for their Asian venture capital and private equity operations, although the preponderance of investments were in other nations.

The government in Hong Kong, China, has generally adopted a laissez-faire attitude toward the economy, and it displayed little interest in venture capital until 1993, when it formed a government-operated US$32 million venture capital fund to invest in SMEs. However, this fund was not very successful. After the Asian financial crisis, the fund received a further appropriation of HK$750 million (US$96 million) in November 1998. Also, because of the lackluster performance of the government-operated funds, the government changed its strategy and appointed four private sector fund managers (Applied Research Fund 2001, p. 1). During the Internet bubble, Hong Kong, China, established an indigenous venture capital industry focused on investing domestically. However, these firms were experiencing difficulty in the continuing downturn and are unlikely to be able to survive on deals in Hong Kong, China.

During the 1990s, Hong Kong, China, functioned as a window to mainland China and, more generally, a convenient Asian headquarters for Western venture capitalists and private equity firms. The venture capital under management in Hong Kong, China, grew rapidly and, by 2000, rivaled that of Japan (see table 10.1). Despite the large amounts of capital, in 2000 only 9 percent was invested in Hong Kong, China, because of a lack of deals. The importance of Hong Kong, China, as the headquarters' location for global venture capitalists seems quite safe, though recently there has been concern that Shanghai might replace it as the de facto "gateway to China."

Singapore. Venture capital emerged later in Singapore than in Hong Kong, China. In 1983, South East Asia Venture Investment Fund, which was administered by Boston's Advent International, was established in Singapore with investment from the International Finance Corporation (Wang 2002). In 1983 and 1984, Singapore Technologies, a former government-owned industrial conglomerate, informally began investing in start-ups. In 1988, the venture capital activities of Singapore Technologies were spun off into a firm called Vertex Management, and it began investing globally, especially in Silicon Valley (Hock 2001).

In the mid-1990s, the government recognized that, because of rising labor costs, manufacturing could no longer be the driver for Singapore's economy. Its response was to launch an initiative to transform Singapore into a knowledge-based entrepreneurial economy. Policymakers believed that venture capital could assist in this transformation. To accomplish it, the government used tax and various other investment incentives to attract venture capital firms from around the world. For that reason, the 1990s were a period of extremely rapid growth for Singapore's venture capital industry, and assets under management increased from US$830 million in 1991 to US$9.286 billion in 2000 (AVCJ 2001, 2002, 2003). As in the case of Hong Kong, China, international venture capital firms such as JAFCO, H&Q Asia Pacific, and 3i established branch offices in Singapore (Wang 2002). Because the growth of Singapore's venture capital industry was in large measure based on attracting foreign venture capital firms, the character of the industry resembles that of the industry in Hong Kong, China. However, in Singapore, the growth was encouraged by massive subsidies, such as capital investments in venture capital funds, and other incentives. The Technopreneurship Fund alone has invested approximately US$1 billion from 1998 to 2003. Singapore's venture capital industry was heavily dependent on these subsidies, the majority of which were made in 1999, and it is almost certain that Singapore has experienced enormous losses during the current downturn.

Singapore's small size is an important limitation on creating a strong venture capital industry, because internally it can generate only a small deal flow. To overcome the lack of deal flow, the country established numerous programs to increase entrepreneurship. Singapore also is enhancing its role as a service center for entrepreneurs in the rest of the Southeast Asian region; however, these nations also have only limited deal flows. Moreover, Singapore-based venture capitalists must compete with the indigenous venture capitalists. Singapore is striving to enhance its role as an offshore service center for venture capital investors in India as well.

The government has fashioned a comprehensive strategy aimed at establishing a venture capital industry that will not require unending subsidies. Despite this effort, success is not guaranteed because of the lack of local deals. Singapore's strategy of becoming a service center for India seems the most precarious because the Indian government will likely also wish to attract the foreign firms. Ultimately, Singapore's location may not be as attractive as that of Hong Kong, China, which is closer to the most important Asian economies. The continued maturation of Singapore as a venture capital center is by no means guaranteed.

China

From the early 1990s onward, China has presented the most enigmatic venture capital investment opportunity.[15] Because of the country's socialist legacy, the Chinese venture capital industry was established only recently. For example, the Chinese Venture Capital Association was inaugurated in 2002. The impetus for the development of the Chinese venture capital industry was government policy. In 1984, the National Research Center of Science and Technology for Development suggested that China establish a venture capital system to promote high technology (White, Gao, and Zhang 2002). However, it was only in the late 1980s that the Chinese government allowed the formation of the first venture capital firm, which was a government-foreign joint venture. It was followed in the early 1990s by a proliferation of venture capital operations backed by state and local government. Because of the lack of experience, not only among the government officials but also among the entrepreneurs, these early efforts failed (Oster 2001).

According to White, Gao, and Zhang (2002), distinct types of venture capital firms operate in China: local government firms, corporate firms, university firms, and foreign firms. Of course, those are ideal types, and in practice there are many relationships and joint ventures between firms in each category. This proliferation of forms and formats can be understood

---

15. This section draws heavily upon White, Gao, and Zhang (2002).

in two ways. First, it can be understood as a large-scale experiment in which there is a search for the format or formats that will be most effective in the Chinese environment. Second, it may be the case that there is not yet a proven methodology for operating a venture capital firm in the Chinese environment. It is safe to conclude that each of these types of venture capital firms has experienced difficulties. The foreign firms invested heavily in Internet start-ups, nearly all of which either have disappeared or do not allow the investors an exit. Moreover, with the recent inability to use NASDAQ as an exit window (because of investor resistance to IPOs), the disastrous performance of the Hong Kong Growth Enterprise Market, and the government's reluctance to open a second board in Shenzhen, there are few exit strategies. The current venture capital activity in China is predicated on a belief that sometime in the future exit vehicles will emerge.

In summary, despite the government's desire to see greater technological development, and notwithstanding its efforts to make the environment favorable to foreign investment in high-technology start-ups, investors continue to be subject to the vagaries of the Chinese legal and political system. The Western venture capitalists that were attracted to the Chinese market continue to experience marginal returns. The only ones to make profits were those that did Internet deals and were able to quickly list their investments on the NASDAQ. At this time, monies from the government (most often the local and provincial governments) appear to make up anywhere from 12 to 80 percent of the total venture capital invested (AVCJ 2001; "Hidden Risks" 2000). The massive investments by the local and provincial governments seem to be failing, but there is no English-language confirmation of this perception. The national government had abstained from venture capital investing until late 1999, when the Chinese Ministry of Foreign Trade and Economic Cooperation announced that it was establishing a venture capital fund ("China Launches New High Tech Venture Capital Fund" 1999). In 2003, venture capital investment in China continues to expand; however, its profitability has yet to be established. For this reason, the eventual role of the Chinese venture capital industry is not yet certain.

Developing Asia

The five nations (Indonesia, Malaysia, the Philippines, Thailand, and Vietnam) of developing Asia have relatively weak venture capital industries, though Malaysia, in particular, continues to strive to strengthen venture capital. Each of them have made various efforts to establish an industry, but they have foundered on serious deficiencies in terms of their institutional structures, levels of technical and managerial proficiency, political and regulatory environments, and financial sophistication. In these countries, the International Finance Corporation and various other international donors have funded foreign venture capital firms, domestic venture capital firms, and partnerships between foreign and domestic firms in an effort to seed the beginnings of a venture capital industry. Also, national governments have made efforts in this direction. For example, in the early 1980s, the Philippine government established 17 bank-related venture capital firms modeled on the U.S. SBIC experience; however, these firms failed (Arana 2001). Despite these efforts, one or more of these impediments have stymied advancement: the institutional environment, the available human capital, or the infrastructure.

The Global Connections

In the past decade, there has been a significant globalization of the venture capital industry. Despite the spread of venture capital globally, the United States and, more particularly, Silicon Valley remain the center of both venture capitalism and the high-technology industry. In terms of business models and economic development, Silicon Valley was the inspiration for Asian policymakers, entrepreneurs, and venture capitalists. This attraction to Silicon Valley is not unique to Asia; other parts of the world have been similarly inspired. But for non-Japanese Asia, the inspiration seems to have been particularly profound. The reasons include Silicon Valley's location on the Pacific Rim, the massive numbers of Asian nationals trained in U.S. universities, and the seemingly inexorable movement of Silicon Valley manufacturing functions to Asia that began in the 1960s (McKendrick, Doner, and Haggard 2000; Saxenian 1999).

Three links between Silicon Valley and Asia have been especially important. The first was the Asian students who remained in the United States and were employed by Silicon Valley firms. They were rapidly assimilated into the Silicon Valley business structure and soon began launching their own start-ups. Not surprisingly, they maintained close relationships with their friends and family in Asia and frequently turned to them for seed money. The second was the Asian students and seasoned managers who returned to their various nations and joined the Asian operations of Silicon Valley firms or established firms that subcontracted with Silicon Valley firms. The third link was the Asians who were trained in their home country and then joined the overseas operations of Silicon Valley firms. Each of these links was a conduit for virtuous circles of learning and information transfer. This interaction created an awareness of what was occurring in Silicon Valley, not only in terms of the technical and managerial skills that blossomed there, but also of the Silicon Valley worldview.

Taiwan, China, is the economy with the most explicit connections to Silicon Valley. These business ties can be traced to the efforts by firms in Taiwan, China, to become subcontractors to the U.S. personal computer industry and then to create semiconductor foundries. Venture capitalists in Taiwan, China, also used ethnic connections and, more important, their connections with manufacturers there as leverage for participating in U.S. deals. For example, these venture capitalists offered to help U.S. fabless semiconductor start-ups arrange production contracts with the silicon foundries in Taiwan, China. They offered more than money, thus creating value added for the start-up firm.

The venture capital industries in Hong Kong (China) and Singapore share many similarities, though Singapore has a greater number of high-tech start-ups. Hong Kong, China, is almost purely what Florida and Kenney (1988a) termed a *finance-based venture capital center*. Table 10.3 indicates that Hong Kong, China, draws in capital from around Asia and the world, and then exports it. One underlying reason is that it operates as a window to China. Singapore also imports capital then re-exports it (see table 10.3). The difference is that the government in Singapore has invested much of its own capital in efforts to build international links. The most important program was the Technopreneurship Investment Fund (TIF), which was established in 1999. TIF has invested US$1 billion in venture capital and in related areas. As of 2001, TIF had announced 45 different investments in venture capital firms headquartered in Canada, France, Germany, India, Israel, Sweden, Taiwan (China), the United Kingdom, and the United States. In addition to diversifying risks, this investment helped Singapore's government to collect information about

Table 10.3 Import and Export of Venture Capital for Various Asian Nations, 2000 (percent)

Economy	Source			Destination		
	Home	Asia	Non-Asia	Home	Asia	Non-Asia
China	56	17	27	81	17	2
Hong Kong, China	9	20	71	13	84	3
Japan	76	20	4	82	7	11
Korea, Rep. of	68	8	24	94	3	3
Singapore	30	31	39	16	67	17
Taiwan, China	82	6	12	78	9	13

Source: AVCJ (2002).

venture capital practices globally. In return for the investment, these firms often agreed to open offices in Singapore. Singapore also boasts one of the most far-reaching venture capital firms, Vertex Management, which has offices abroad and invests globally.

The largest Korean venture capital firms also have operations abroad, and a number of the large U.S. and European private equity firms have operations in Korea, though the latter are almost entirely devoted to private equity buyouts (Kenney, Han, and Tanaka 2002). Except in Malaysia, the venture capital industries in Asian nations are largely importers of capital. The Philippines and Thailand have nationals working in Silicon Valley as engineers, but there are so many barriers to start-ups that these overseas engineers have not contributed to significant activity.

Venture capital in Asia is now globalized. One dimension of this globalization is the Asian venture capital firms that invest in the United States and, especially, Silicon Valley. Of course, Hong Kong, China, as a base for the import and export of capital has always been globalized. Another dimension is the U.S. firms, particularly those operated by Asians and investing throughout Asia. There is also a powerful intra-Asian investment network. For example, a number of the larger Japanese venture capitalists have operations throughout Asia. An even larger network is the firms espousing a "Greater China" strategy. The investment base of this network includes China, Hong Kong (China), Singapore, and Taiwan (China), as well as the Asian expatriates in Silicon Valley. In November 2001, the venture capital associations of Hong Kong (China), Indonesia, Korea, Malaysia, Singapore, and Taiwan (China) formed the Asian Pacific Venture Capital Alliance (APVCA). In the future, APVCA could contribute to a unification of the Asian venture capital industry.

INSTITUTIONAL ISSUES IN ASIAN VENTURE CAPITAL

The most important institutional issue today in Asian venture capital is whether to allow pension funds in Asian nations to allocate certain percentages for investment in alternative asset classes such as venture capital. The experience in the United States suggests that, as an economic policy, allowing pension funds to invest in venture capital could be a great success. In terms of investment returns, the outcome may not be as clear, because there is evidence that excellent returns are concentrated among only the top venture capital firms. Over the past 20 years, the average annualized return for U.S. venture capital firms was 20.3 percent (NVCA 2001). However, returns vary widely. The top quartile of venture capital firms performed very well, but those in the lower quartile performed badly. For example, Barger (n.d.) found that from 1980 to 1995 the return for the lowest quartile was 6.9 percent—that is, nearly 15 percent lower than the annualized return of the top quartile. In nations where self-dealing or other practices might occur, or where either the venture capital industry or the pension managers may not be experienced, investing in venture capital is risky. Any decision to permit pension funds to invest in venture capital should be phased in gradually or a good possibility exists that there will be a glut of capital with a concomitant drop in returns.

Governance of Portfolio Firms and Venture Capitalists

In much of Asia, the development of venture capital has been hindered by the same type of corporate governance practices as those highlighted in chapter 7. These problems exist in terms of managing the entrepreneur and in the operations of the legal system. In the United States, the lead venture capitalists serve on the firm's board of directors. Investment contracts are structured so that the venture capitalists can force a reluctant entrepreneur to take the firm public. A Silicon Valley entrepreneur understands that, should the firm be successful, there will be a change in ownership through either a public offering or a trade sale; thus, control will shift. When receiving venture capital, the entrepreneurs also understand that venture capitalists will replace them if the investors are dissatisfied with the firm's progress. Entrepreneurs also accept that later rounds of financing will further dilute their ownership. In Silicon Valley, entrepreneurs know that their firm is an alienable asset.

In Asia, the relationship between the entrepreneur and the firm is more personal. For example, entrepreneurs see the firm as an expression of themselves and their family and thus are unwilling to part with significant blocks of stock, either to the venture capitalist or in an IPO. This desire of the entrepreneur to retain control prevents the venture capitalist from making a large investment, having a say in the firm's strategic decisions, or securing an easy exit, thus complicating the investment process and disrupting the ability of the venture capitalist to contribute to a firm's growth and secure a sufficiently large capital gain to make an investment sufficiently lucrative. Ta-Lin Hsu (1999), the founder and chair of H&Q Asia Pacific and dean of venture capitalists investing in Asia, summarized the situation in Asia as follows:

> Most [venture capitalists] over the last 14–15 years went to the passive late stage pre-IPO deals. There you gain 5 percent, 11 percent, or 17 percent of a family-controlled company; you have a board seat, but you don't have a lot

to say. You can have a role in helping the company, but you cannot really add a lot of value because the family ultimately controls things. You can't tell the father to fire his son, or change the family business.

Throughout Asia, entrepreneurs see the firm as the fruits of their labor, and their goal is to pass the firm on to their children. In some economies, especially Taiwan, China, this pattern has changed at least to the point that venture capitalists have some voice.

Not only do these cultural features create governance problems, but also in many of the Asian economies the rights of minority shareholders or even outside shareholders are not strongly protected. For venture capitalists, these weak or nonexistent minority rights create a problem. For example, in Japan the Antimonopoly Law complicates the situation for venture capitalists by prohibiting any single investor (including venture capitalists) from owning more than 49 percent of the equity; further, when shareholding is greater than 25 percent, the shareholder is not allowed to be dominant. After Korea enacted laws to encourage venture capital, it implemented other regulations that limited venture capitalists to less than 50 percent of the total equity. This ambivalent policy makes it difficult for investors to replace the firm's managers even when they are incompetent. In Japan and Korea, the legal environment mitigates against Western-style venture capital monitoring. In other nations, the monitoring and control functions are often frustrated by cultural and legal impediments.

The legal position of the investor varies by economy. The issues of equity and the control that it provides are unresolved for Asian venture capitalists. The lack of control means that Asian venture capitalists have less at stake in their portfolio firm and, therefore, have less motivation to monitor and contribute than do U.S. venture capitalists. The only possible exception is in Taiwan, China, where there has been more experience with Silicon Valley and its methods of corporate control. Quite naturally, in environments where equity investments are not so desirable and there is an inability to closely monitor the firm, making low-risk loans is more sensible than offering equity capital.

Stock Markets and Exit Options

In Asia and around the world, there has been a proliferation of new stock markets specializing in the offerings of young, high-risk firms (see table 10.4). The stated goal of these markets is to provide exit opportunities for investors, and, oddly enough, they often place less emphasis on providing markets in which listing firms raise capital to expand the business. In addition to these new markets, it is possible to list on the U.S.

Table 10.4 New NASDAQ-Like Stock Markets in Asia

Economy	Name	Date
Hong Kong, China	GEM	1999
Japan	MOTHERS	1999
Japan	NASDAQ Japan[a]	2000
Korea. Rep. of	KOSDAQ	1996
Malaysia	MESDAQ	1999
Singapore	SESDAQ	1997

Note: GEM = Growth Enterprise Market; KOSDAQ = Korean Securities Dealers Automated Quotation; MESDAQ = Malaysian Exchange of Securities Dealing and Automated Quotation; MOTHERS = Market for High-Growth and Emerging Stocks; NASDAQ = National Association of Securities Dealers Automated Quotation; SESDAQ = Singapore Dealing and Automated Quotation.

a. Now closed.

Source: Authors' compilation.

NASDAQ, which is the preferred exit for most firms in Asia, except those in Japan and Korea.

The idea of forming specialized stock markets for small firms is not new. In 1961, the Tokyo Stock Exchange had already established a second section with looser listing requirements, and in 1962, it established an over-the-counter (OTC) market. By 1999, these markets were deemed inadequate for smaller firms, and two others were established. In 1986, the Korean government created the Korean OTC market in a bid to support firms that were unable to qualify for the Seoul Stock Exchange. After a strong start, the OTC market faltered, and in the early 1990s, a series of bankruptcies shook public confidence, frightening investors and driving down prices. Another difficulty was that firms were unwilling to make IPOs on the OTC market, because the registration process was onerous. The corporate governance issue also discourages the listing of firms, because after the stock is publicly held, management is no longer protected from investors who can control the board of directors. The Japanese Second Section and OTC markets continue to operate, but their regulations are too stringent for most venture capital–financed firms.

As in other parts of the world, many of the new markets that opened in the mid- and late 1990s initially performed admirably. Firms were listed, the investing public drove their stock prices skyward, and volume grew. This exit path encouraged venture capitalists to invest in even more firms, creating what in many nations appeared to be an equity-driven economy. Vibrant high-tech regions sprang up, such as Bit Valley in Shibuya, Tokyo, or the Kangnam region of Seoul. For example, in 1999 and early 2000, KOSDAQ (Korean Securities Dealers Automated Quotation) grew to become the eighth most highly capitalized stock market in the world and surpassed the Seoul Stock Exchange in value. This activity was good for the new-issues market.

Unfortunately, the Internet bubble collapsed in 2000. As a result, Asian markets experienced deep drops. For example, by the end of December 2000, KOSDAQ had lost 80 percent of its value. This fall effectively closed the KOSDAQ as a viable means of raising capital and as an investor exit. Similarly, the SESDAQ (Singapore Dealing and Automated Quotation) lost nearly two-thirds of its value, and NASDAQ Japan closed in August 2002. The Hong Kong Growth Enterprise Market earned the sobriquet of being the "World's Worst Bourse" (Chung 2000) and fell more than 80 percent from its 1999 high (Slater 2002). These bourses were created during the boom, but they soon became vehicles for speculation. Unfortunately, when the bubble burst, and there was a flight to quality, these exchanges were ravaged. In the stock market upturn of 2003, they recovered somewhat but are of little interest to most investors.

The proliferation of stock exchanges, which increased the number of exit possibilities, was not entirely positive. From a systemic perspective, the benefit of the venture capital process is not the enrichment of the entrepreneur and the venture capitalist; rather, it is the creation of new firms that stimulate Schumpeterian economic growth. Many governments viewed these stock markets solely as mechanisms for providing exits for venture capitalists, not as institutions for providing growth capital for real businesses and a viable investment opportunity for investors. As demonstrated by the announced closures of the German Neuer Markt and the NASDAQ Japan, stock exchanges cannot survive if their sole role is to provide investors with an exit path through which they foist low-quality firms on the investing public. Large numbers of failures and the concomitant losses drive even sophisticated investors from the market, thereby destroying liquidity and threatening the viability of the exchange.

The ongoing global stock market malaise plagues nearly every nation. In Asia nearly all of the new "second" markets for smaller firms are moribund. Many stock markets are thinly traded and illiquid. Even in the United States, where the U.S. Securities and Exchange Commission has been considered a comparatively strong regulator, the IPO market has been plagued by insider trading, shady pre-IPO allocations of stock, misleading analysis, and various other ethical lapses and criminal misdeeds. Unfortunately, recent evidence is emerging that individual venture capitalists were receiving stock kickbacks from investment bankers on the very firms they were taking public, thereby receiving benefits that they did not share with their limited partners. Until investor confidence in the fairness and transparency of public markets returns, exiting through public markets will be quite difficult. In nations without equity cultures, restoring confidence will be even more difficult. Thus, regulators around the world must tighten rules, regulations, and enforcement to ensure that the excesses of the late 1990s are not repeated.

Because bad stock exchanges come to be viewed as casinos rather than as arenas for investment, rehabilitation is difficult. Governments must put in place measures ensuring that, when the IPO markets recover, the excesses will be controlled and the markets will become more transparent and less subject to manipulation. KOSDAQ, SESDAQ, and MOTHERS should survive because of the underlying strength of the national economies of Korea, Singapore, and Japan, respectively. However, as exit paths they may be largely discredited. There is little that the government can do to protect discredited exchanges from investor distrust beyond making increased efforts to protect the integrity of their market's operations by giving stock regulators stronger enforcement powers and requiring greater transparency.

After the Crash

Because the stock market difficulties beginning in March 2000 had not yet completely run their course even by 2004, the effect on venture capital is not yet fully known. In the United States, for the first time in stock market history, during the second quarter of 2002, more funds were disinvested and returned to investors than were raised (NVCA 2002). This trend continued through 2003. In 2003, capital overhang (that is, capital that likely would never be invested profitably) had become a global problem. In 2004, a number of the lower-quality venture capital firms were finding it difficult to raise new funds. After 2001 the growth of venture capital funds in Taiwan, China, slowed to less than 5 percent, after 5 years of greater than 30 percent per year growth. Most of the newer venture capital industries are experiencing the venture capital business cycle and a severe shakeout for the first time.

A recovery of the venture capital industry is predicated on a recovery of exit opportunities. What is most remarkable about this downturn is that, for the first time, globally both stock markets and acquisitions as exit opportunities have disappeared. In earlier downturns, if the stock market was unreceptive, it was often possible to arrange a trade-sale for firms with promising technologies. However, in the current crisis—with the exception of perhaps Microsoft, Intel, and Cisco in the United States; TSMC and Quanta in Taiwan, China; and Wipro, TCS, and Infosys in India—few firms are willing and able to increase their allocation to venture capital because of the low returns, and some have refused to meet already agreed-upon cash calls.

Although the situation is at the moment gloomy, it is also a natural process of purging the excesses from the system. Unfortunately, not only were the excesses large in terms of too many dollars chasing too few deals, but they also gave rise to corruption on a pandemic scale. The rehabilitation will lead to a continuing shakeout of venture capitalists and venture capital firms until at least the end of 2003 and likely well into 2004. Those firms and national industries that cannot survive this shakeout will disband, and, most unfortunately, the skills and experience purchased at the cost of so much capital will be lost.

PROSPECTS FOR VENTURE CAPITAL IN EAST ASIA

The venture capital industries in Asia have differing levels of development and quite different institutional characteristics. If one adopts a Silicon Valley definition of *venture capital*, then probably only Taiwan, China, would qualify as having a venture capital industry. In terms of funding high-technology firms, it is clearly the Asian leader. However, if we accept local definitions of venture capital, then we can conclude that a sustainable venture capital industry exists in Hong Kong (China), Japan, Korea, and Singapore. Venture capital in China continues to appear promising, though at this point the industry remains immature. In the remaining Asian economies, the prospects for venture capital are not as strong.

Except, perhaps, in Hong Kong, China, Asian governments have played an important role in both creating the macroeconomic environment and providing support for the emergence of a venture capital industry. Taiwan, China, is a textbook case for the ways in which the government can alter the risk-reward calculation but not eliminate it. The 20 percent tax rebate created a powerful incentive, but it did not eliminate risk. Moreover, the government created relatively simple and transparent rules that aligned the incentives for the fledgling venture capitalists with the government's objectives. In marked contrast, the Korean efforts created a system that encouraged micromanagement by government bureaucrats and aimed at encouraging the venture capitalists to undertake financial activities for purposes other than maximizing their capital gains from equity investments. These rules and regulations led to the development of risk-averse venture capitalists who concentrated on extending loans rather than investing in equity.

More general issues concern every Asian economy. The first is the concern with creating "exits" as the way to encourage venture capital. Nearly every economy has created a new stock market or section with loosened listing requirements. However, nearly all either began with low liquidity or, after the bursting of the Internet bubble, dropped so precipitously that they now suffer from low liquidity. With such low liquidity, these new markets do not actually offer exit paths. This issue will be important in any recovery.

There can be no doubt that the U.S. venture capital model has worked well in the past and has been successfully transferred to certain nations. Whether it is an appropriate model for all nations can be determined only after examination of that nation's initial conditions. Unfortunately, few other models have proven to be strong substitutes for creating an entrepreneurial environment based on high technology. Thus far, there have not been many successful hybrid models—venture capital seems to be a fragile institution that does not hybridize well. The Asian economies that have been most successful in creating a venture capital industry are those with the closest human ties to the United States—namely, Taiwan (China) and Singapore. Also, these nations have largely adopted the U.S. model with specific changes to suit their environment. In each case, the governments developed policies that singled out venture capital as an important aspect of their efforts to mobilize entrepreneurship.

Despite the many obstacles to creating a vibrant venture capital community, during the past two decades the industry has taken root, especially in Hong Kong (China), North Asia, and Singapore. There are also reasons to be guardedly optimistic about the prospects for China. The current downturn is a major test for the industry in all of these economies, and it is likely that many firms will fail. Unfortunately, there may be little governments can and, indeed, should do to protect venture capital from failure. However, the venture capitalists and national venture capitalist communities able to survive without becoming wards of the government may be poised for growth during the next recovery.

REFERENCES

Amsden, Alice H. 1992. *Asia's Next Giant: South Korea and Late Industrialization*. New York: Oxford University Press.

Applied Research Fund. 2001. "Background of the Applied Research Fund in Hong Kong." Government of Hong Kong, China. Processed.

Arana, Vicente. 2001. "Venture Capital Company." Asian Institute of Management, Makati, Philippines. Accessed June 12, 2001 at http://www.aim.edu.ph/homepage/ABS2000/varana.htm.

Asian Technology Information Program. 1998. "Venture Capital in Taiwan." Report ATIP 98.009. Asian Technology Information Program, Albuquerque, N.M.

Autler, Gerald. 2000. "Global Networks in High Technology: The Silicon Valley-Israel Connection." Department of City and Regional Planning, University of California, Berkeley. Processed.

AVCJ (*Asian Venture Capital Journal*). 1992. *The 1992/1993 Guide to Venture Capital in Asia*. Hong Kong, China.

———. 2001. *The 2001 Guide to Venture Capital in Asia*. Hong Kong, China.

———. 2002. *The 2002 Guide to Venture Capital in Asia*. Hong Kong, China.

———. 2003. *The 2003 Guide to Venture Capital in Asia*. Hong Kong, China.

Avnimelech, Gil, and Morris Teubal. 2002. "Venture Capital-Start-Up Co-evolution and the Emergence of Israel's New High-Tech Cluster." Paper presented at 2002 DRUID Summer Conference on Industrial Dynamics of the New and Old Economy—Who Is Embracing Whom? Copenhagen, June 6–8.

Bahrami, Homa, and Stuart Evans. 2000. "Flexible Re-Cycling and High-Technology Entrepreneurship." In Martin Kenney, ed., *Understanding Silicon Valley: The Anatomy of an Innovative Region*. Stanford, Calif.: Stanford University Press.

Barger, Teresa. n.d. "Issues in Private Equity." From an International Finance Corporation PowerPoint presentation, *Private Equity and Investment Funds*. Available on-line at http://www.ifc.org/funds/pdfs/fund-issues.pdf.

Bean, Jonathan J. 2001. *Big Government and Affirmative Action: The Scandalous History of the Small Business Administration*. Lexington, Ky.: University Press of Kentucky.

Besher, Alexander. 1988. "Taiwan, U.S. Firms Team Up on Venture Capital Fund." *San Francisco Chronicle*, June 13, p. C9.

BVCA (British Venture Capital Association). 1999. "The Economic Impact of Venture Capital in the U.K." London.

"China Launches New High Tech Venture Capital Fund." 1999. *ChinaOnline*, October 5.

Choi, Hyungsup. 1987. "Mobilization of Financial Resources for Technology Development." *Technological Forecasting and Social Change* 31:347–58.

Chung, Yulanda. 2000. "World's Worst Bourse?" *AsiaWeek* 26(31) August 11.

Di Gregorio, Dante, and Scott Shane. 2003. "Why Do Some Universities Generate More Start-ups Than Others." *Research Policy* 32(2):209–27.

Dossani, Rafiq, and Martin Kenney. 2002. "Creating an Environment for Venture Capital in India." *World Development* 30(2):227–53.

Florida, Richard, and Martin Kenney. 1988a. "Venture Capital–Financed Innovation and Technological Change in the U.S." *Research Policy* 17(3):119–37.

———. 1988b. "Venture Capital, High Technology and Regional Development." *Regional Studies* 22(1):33–48.

GAO (U.S. General Accounting Office). 1982. "Government-Industry Cooperation Can Enhance the Venture Capital Process." GAO/AFMD-82-35, August 12.

Gompers, Paul. 1994. "The Rise and Fall of Venture Capital." *Business and Economic History* 23(2):1–26.

———. 1995. "Optimal Investment, Monitoring, and the Staging of Venture Capital." *Journal of Finance* 50:1461–89.

Gupta, Anil, and Harry Sapienza. 1992. "Determinants of Venture Capital Firms' Preferences for Industry Diversity and Geographic Scope of Their Investments." *Journal of Business Venturing* 7:347–62.

Hamada, Yasuyuki. 1999. *Nihon no Bencha Kyapitaru*. Tokyo: Nihon Keizai Shimbun.

"Hidden Risks in China's Venture Capital Investment." 2000. *UltraChina.com*, June 2.

Hock, Chua Joo. 2001. Telephone interview of senior vice president, Vertex Management Inc., by Martin Kenney, Redwood City, Calif., March 29.

Hsu, Ta-Lin. 1999. Interview with Ta-Lin Hsu. *Asian Venture Capital Journal* (December):26.

Israel Venture Association. 2004. "Venture Capital Fund Participated." Available on-line at http://www.ivc-online.com/.

"Japan's Recovery Seen Dependent on Inflow of Venture Capital." 1951. *Wall Street Journal*, November 16, p. 16.

Kaufman, Steve. 1986. "H&Q's Open Door Policy into Far East Venture Capital." *San Jose Mercury News*, November 17, p. 7D.

KDIC (Korean Development Investment Corporation). 1986. *Annual Report*. Seoul.

Kenney, Martin, and W. R. Goe. Forthcoming. "The Role of Social Embeddedness in Professorial Entrepreneurship: A Comparison of Electrical Engineering and Computer Science at UC Berkeley and Stanford." *Research Policy*.

Kenney, Martin, Kyonghee Han, and Shoko Tanaka. 2002. "Scattering Geese: The Venture Capital Industries of East Asia." Report to the World Bank. Washington, D.C.

Kim, Han-Seop. 2001. Telephone interview of the director, Korea Technology & Banking (KTB) Network Corporation, by Kyonghee Han, May 16.

Kortum, Samuel, and Joshua Lerner. 2000. "Assessing the Contribution of Venture Capital to Innovation." *RAND Journal of Economics* 31(4):674–92.

KPCB (Kleiner Perkins Caufield & Byers). 2001. Accessed on-line in 2001 at http://www.kpcb.com. (Information is no longer available on the Web site.)

KTB (Korean Technology and Banking Network Corporation). 2001. Available on-line at http://www.ktb.co.kr.

Kuemmerle, Walter. 2001. "Comparing Catalysts of Change: Evolution and Institutional Differences in the Venture Capital Industries in the U.S., Japan, and Germany." In Robert A. Burgelman and Henry Chesbrough, eds., *Research on Technological Innovation, Management and Policy* 7:227–61. Greenwich, Conn.: JAI Press.

Lee, Chong-Moon, William Miller, Marguerite Gong Hancock, and Henry Rowen. 2000. "The Silicon Valley Habitat." In Chong-Moon Lee, William Miller, Marguerite Gong Hancock, and Henry Rowen, eds., *The Silicon Valley Edge*. Stanford, Calif.: Stanford University Press.

Liu, Bor-Hong D. 2001. Personal interview of director, Business Department, Development Fund, Executive Yuan, by Martin Kenney, Taipei, May 3.

McKendrick, David, Richard Doner, and Stephan Haggard. 2000. *From Silicon Valley to Singapore: Location and Competitive Advantage in the Hard Disk Drive Industry*. Stanford, Calif.: Stanford University Press.

Niimi, Kazumasa, and Yuri Okina. 1995. "Bencha Bijinesu no Seicho o Habamumono ha Nanika." *Japan Research Review* (May). Available on-line at http://www.jri.co.jp/jrr/1995/199505/.

Nishiguchi, Toshihiro. 1994. *Strategic Industrial Sourcing: The Japanese Advantage*. New York: Oxford University Press.

NVCA (National Venture Capital Association). 2001. *National Venture Capital Association Yearbook*. Fort Myers, Va.

———. 2002. *National Venture Capital Association Yearbook*. Fort Myers, Va.

Ono, Masato. 1995. "Venture Capital in Japan: Current Overview." Available on-line at http://www.asahi-net.or.jp/~sh3m-on/vcommune/JAVC/JVCs.htm.

Oster, Shai. 2001. "Nothing Ventured." *AsiaWeek.com*, July 27–August 3.

Pincus, Lionel. 2000. Telephone interview of president and founder, Warburg Pincus, by Martin Kenney, New York, February 7.

Robinson, Robert J., and Mark van Osnabrugge. 2000. *Angel Investing: Matching Start-up Funds with Start-up Companies*. San Francisco: Jossey-Bass.

Saxenian, AnnaLee. 1999. *Silicon Valley's New Immigrant Entrepreneurs*. San Francisco: Public Policy Institute of California.

Shih, Stan. 1996. *Me-too Is Not My Style*. Taipei: Acer Foundation.

Slater, Dan. 2002. "David Webb on Why the GEM Is Failing Hong Kong." *FinanceAsia.com*, July 16. Available on-line at http://www.financeasia.com/articles/4A1088FD-8F94-11D6-81E30090277E174B.cfm.

Softbank Investment. 2001. "Kaisha Gaiyo." Available on-line at http://www.sbinvestment.co.jp.

Stults, Walter B. 2000. Telephone interview of former executive vice president of the National Association of Small Business Investment Companies by Martin Kenney, February 17.

Sussner, Heiner. 2001. Telephone interview of senior managing director, H&Q Asia Pacific, by Martin Kenney, San Francisco, March 30.

Taiwan, China, Ministry of Finance. 1996. "The Venture Capital Industry in the Republic of China." Taipei. Processed.

Tan, Lip-bu. 2001. Presentation by chairman and founder, Walden International, at the 2001 Asian Venture Forum—U.S., Palo Alto, California, May 21–23.

Wang, Clement. 2002. "Differences in the Governance Structure of Venture Capital: The Singaporean Venture Capital Industry." Paper presented at the European Union–United Nations University International Conference on Financial Systems, Corporate Investment in Innovation and Venture Capital, Brussels, November 7–8.

Wang, Lee-Rong. 1995. "Taiwan's Venture Capital: Policies and Impacts." *Journal of Industry Studies* 2(1):83–94.

White, Steven, Jian Gao, and Wei Zhang. 2002. "China's Venture Capital Industry: Institutional Trajectories and System Structure." Paper presented at the European Union–United Nations University International Conference on Financial Systems, Corporate Investment in Innovation and Venture Capital, Brussels, November 7–8.

INDEX

ABOUT THE EDITORS

Shahid Yusuf is a research manager in the Development Economics Research Group at the World Bank. He holds a PhD in economics from Harvard University. Dr. Yusuf is the team leader for the World Bank–Japan project on East Asia's Future Economy. He was the director of the *World Development Report 1999/2000: Entering the 21st Century*. Prior to that, he has served the World Bank in several other capacities.

Dr. Yusuf has written extensively on development issues, with a special focus on East Asia. His publications include *China's Rural Development*, with Dwight Perkins (Johns Hopkins University Press 1984); *The Dynamics of Urban Growth in Three Chinese Cities*, with Weiping Wu (Oxford University Press 1997); *Rethinking the East Asian Miracle*, edited with Joseph Stiglitz (Oxford University Press 2001); *Can East Asia Compete? Innovation for Global Markets*, with Simon Evenett (Oxford University Press 2002); and *Innovative East Asia: The Future of Growth*, for which he was the lead author (Oxford University Press 2003). He has also published widely in various academic journals.

M. Anjum Altaf is a senior economist in the Urban Development Sector Unit of the East Asia and Pacific Region at the World Bank. He holds a PhD in engineering–economic systems and an MA in economics, both from Stanford University, and an MS in electrical and computer engineering from Oregon State University. Prior to joining the Bank, Dr. Altaf was a visiting associate professor and Fulbright Scholar at the University of North Carolina at Chapel Hill (1991–93) and an associate professor at the Applied Economics Research Centre, University of Karachi (1985–91). He has worked in the private sector and is presently a visiting fellow at the Sustainable Development Policy Institute in Islamabad, Pakistan.

Dr. Altaf's research on poverty, migration, and infrastructure policy and on behavioral, environmental, and urban economics has been published in various academic journals. He was a member of the team that prepared the *World Development Report 1999/2000: Entering the 21st Century* and is one of the authors of *Innovative East Asia: The Future of Growth* (Oxford University Press 2003).

Kaoru Nabeshima is an economist in the Development Economics Research Group at the World Bank. He holds a PhD in economics from the University of California, Davis. He is a team member for the World Bank–Japan project on East Asia's Future Economy and is one of the authors of *Innovative East Asia: The Future of Growth* (Oxford University Press 2003). His research interest lies in the economic development of East Asia, especially in the innovation capabilities of firms.

NOTES

NOTES